Samuel Johnson

Johnson's Chief Lives of the Poets

Samuel Johnson

Johnson's Chief Lives of the Poets

ISBN/EAN: 9783744670487

Printed in Europe, USA, Canada, Australia, Japan

Cover: Foto ©ninafisch / pixelio.de

More available books at **www.hansebooks.com**

JOHNSON'S CHIEF
LIVES OF THE POETS

Being those of

MILTON	ADDISON
DRYDEN	POPE
SWIFT	GRAY

AND

MACAULAY'S LIFE OF JOHNSON

SECOND EDITION

With a Preface and Notes

BY

MATTHEW ARNOLD

To which are Appended

MACAULAY'S AND CARLYLE'S ESSAYS ON
BOSWELL'S LIFE OF JOHNSON

NEW YORK
HENRY HOLT AND COMPANY
1889.

PUBLISHERS' NOTES.

The Appendix has been included in consequence of a lately-expressed opinion, that " If a young person were to ask from what portions of English Literature he could gain most benefit in a single sitting, nothing could be more safely recommended than Macaulay's Essay on Boswell's Life of Johnson, and Carlyle's rejoinder to it."

TO THE SECOND EDITION.

After the first edition was published, Mr. Arnold wrote some notes for the use of Students, which are given on pages 431–437. He also made some slight changes in the preface, which have been substantially incorporated in this volume.

CONTENTS.

JOHNSON'S CHIEF LIVES.

By Matthew Arnold.

Da mihi, Domine, scire quod sciendum est—" Grant that the knowledge I get may be the knowledge which is worth having !"—the spirit of that prayer ought to rule our education. How little it does rule it, every discerning man will acknowledge. Life is short and our faculties of attention and of recollection are limited ; in education we proceed as if our life were endless, and our powers of attention and recollection inexhaustible. We have not time or strength to deal with half of the matters which are thrown upon our minds, and they prove a useless load to us. When some one talked to Themistocles of an art of memory, he answered, " Teach me rather to forget !" The sarcasm well criticises the fatal want of proportion between what we put into our minds and their real needs and powers.

From the time when first I was led to think about education, this want of proportion is what has most struck me. It is the great obstacle to progress, yet it is by no means remarked and contended against as it should be. It hardly begins to present itself until we pass beyond the strict elements of education—beyond the acquisition, I mean, of reading, of writing, and of calculating, so far as the operations of common life require. But the moment we pass beyond these, it begins to appear. Languages, grammar, literature, history, geography, mathematics, the knowledge of Nature—what of these is to be taught, how much, and how ? There is no clear, well-grounded consent. The same with religion. Religion is surely to be taught, but what of it is to be taught, and how ? A clear, well-grounded consent is again wanting. And taught in such fashion as things are now, how often must a candid and sensible man, if he could be offered an art of memory to secure all that he has learned of them, as to a very great deal of it be inclined to say with Themistocles, " Teach me rather to forget !"

In England the common notion seems to be that education is advanced in two ways principally : by forever adding fresh matters of instruction, and by preventing uniformity. I should be inclined to prescribe just the opposite course ; to prescribe a severe limitation of the number of matters taught, a severe uniformity in the line of study followed. Wide ranging and the multiplication of matters to be investigated belong to private study, to the development of special aptitudes in the individual learner.

and to the demands which they raise in him. But separate from all this should be kept the broad plain lines of study for almost universal use. I say *almost* universal, because they must of necessity vary a little with the varying conditions of men. Whatever the pupil finds set out for him upon these lines, he should learn ; therefore it ought not to be too much in quantity. The essential thing is that it should be well chosen. If once we can get it well chosen, the more uniformly it can be kept to, the better. The teacher will be more at home ; and besides, when we have got what is good and suitable, there is small hope of gain, and great certainty of risk, in departing from it.

No such lines are laid out, and perhaps no one could be trusted to lay them out authoritatively. But to amuse one's self with laying them out in fancy is a good exercise for one's thoughts. One may lay them out for this or that description of pupil, in this or that branch of study. The wider the interest of the branch of study taken, and the more extensive the class of pupils concerned, the better for our purpose. Suppose we take the department of letters. It is interesting to lay out in one's mind the ideal line of study to be followed by all who have to learn Latin and Greek. But it is still more interesting to lay out the ideal line of study to be followed by all who are concerned with that body of literature which exists in English, because this class is so much more numerous among us. The thing would be, one imagines, to begin with a very brief intro-ductory sketch of our subject ; then to fix a certain series of works to serve as what the French, taking an expression from the builder's busi-ness, call *points de repère*—points which stand as so many natural centres, and by returning to which we can always find our way again, if we are embarrassed ; finally, to mark out a number of illustrative and represen-tative works connecting themselves with each of these *points de repère*. In the introductory sketch we are among generalities, in the group of illustrative works we are among details ; generalities and details have, both of them, their perils for the learner. It is evident that, for purposes of education, the most important parts by far in our scheme are what we call the *points de repère*. To get these rightly chosen and thoroughly known is the great matter. For my part, in thinking of this or that line of study which human minds follow, I feel always prompted to seek, first and foremost, the leading *points de repère* in it.

In editing, for the use of the young, the group of chapters which are now commonly distinguished as those of the Babylonian Isaiah, I drew attention to their remarkable fitness for serving as a point of this kind to the student of universal history. But a work which by many is regarded. as simply and solely a document of religion, there is difficulty, perhaps, in employing for historical and literary purposes. With works of a secular character one is on safer ground. And for years past, whenever I have had occasion to use Johnson's " Lives of the Poets," the thought has

struck me how admirable a *point de repère*, or fixed centre of the sort described above, these lives might be made to furnish for the student of
English literature. If we could but take, I have said to myself, the most
important of the lives in Johnson's volumes, and leave out all the rest,
what a text-book we should have! The volumes at present are a work to
stand in a library, " a work which no gentleman's library should be without." But we want to get from them a text-book, to be in the hands of
every one who desires even so much as a general acquaintance with English literature—and so much acquaintance as this who does not desire?
The work as Johnson published it is not fitted to serve as such a text-
book ; it is too extensive and contains the lives of many poets quite insignificant. Johnson supplied lives of all whom the booksellers proposed to
include in their collection of British poets ; he did not choose the poets
himself, although he added two or three to those chosen by the booksellers.
Whatever Johnson did in the department of literary biography and criticism possesses interest and deserves our attention. But in his " Lives
of the Poets" there are six of pre-eminent interest ; because they are the
lives of men who, while the rest in the collection are of inferior rank,
stand out as names of the first class in English literature—Milton, Dryden, Swift, Addison, Pope, Gray. These six writers differ among themselves, of course, in power and importance, and every one can see that,
if we were following certain modes of literary classification, Milton would
have to be placed on a solitary eminence far above any of them. But if,
without seeking a close view of individual differences, we form a large
and liberal first class among English writers, all these six personages—
Milton, Dryden, Swift, Addison, Pope, Gray—must, I think, be placed
in it. Their lives cover a space of more than a century and a half, from
1608, the year of Milton's birth, down to 1771, the date of the death of
Gray. Through this space of more than a century and a half the six lives
conduct us. We follow the course of what Warburton well calls " the
most agreeable subject in the world, which is literary history," and follow
it in the lives of men of letters of the first class. And the writer of their
lives is himself, too, a man of letters of the first class. Malone calls
Johnson " the brightest ornament of the eighteenth century." He is
justly to be called, at any rate, a man of letters of the first class, and the
greatest power in English letters during the eighteenth century. And in
his " Lives of the Poets," in this mature and most characteristic work, not
finished until 1781, and " which I wrote," as he himself tells us, " in my
usual way, dilatorily and hastily, unwilling to work and working with
vigor and haste," we have Johnson mellowed by years, Johnson in his
ripeness and plenitude treating the subject which he loved best and knew
best. Much of it he could treat with the knowledge and sure tact of a
contemporary ; even from Milton and Dryden he was scarcely further
separated than our generation is from Burns and Scott. Having all these

recommendations, his "Lives of the Poets" do indeed truly stand for what Boswell calls them, "the work which of all Dr. Johnson's writings will perhaps be read most generally and with most pleasure." And in the lives of the six chief personages of the work, the lives of Milton Dryden, Swift, Addison, Pope, and Gray, we have its very kernel and quintessence. True, Johnson is not at his best in all of these six lives equally ; one might have wished, in particular, for a better life of Gray from him   Still these six lives contain very much of his best work ; and it is not amiss, perhaps, to have specimens of a great man's less excellent work by the side of his best. By their subjects, at any rate, the six lives are of pre-eminent interest. In these we have Johnson's series of critical biographies relieved of whatever is less significant, retaining nothing which is not highly significant, brought within easy and convenient compass, and admirably fitted to serve as a *point de repère*, a fixed and thoroughly known centre of departure and return, to the student of English literature.

I know of no such first-rate piece of literature, for supplying in this way the wants of the literary student, existing at all in any other language : or existing in our own language, for any period except the period which Johnson's six lives cover. A student cannot read them without gaining from them, consciously or unconsciously, an insight into the history of English literature and life. He would find great benefit, let me add, from reading in connection with each biography something of the author with whom it deals ; the first two books, say, of "Paradise Lost," in connection with the life of Milton ; "Absalom and Achitophel," and the "Dedication of the Æneid," in connection with the life of Dryden ; in connection with Swift's life, the "Battle of the Books ;" with Addison's, the "Coverley Papers ;" with Pope's, the imitations of the "Satires" and "Epistles" of Horace. The "Elegy in a Country Churchyard" everybody knows, and will have it present to his mind when he reads the life of Gray. But of the other works which I have mentioned how little can this be said ; to how many of us are Pope, and Addison, and Dryden, and Swift, and even Milton himself, mere names, about whose date and history and supposed characteristics of style we may have learned by rote something from a hand-book, but of the real men and of the power of their works we know nothing ! From Johnson's biographies the student will get a sense of what the real men were, and with this sense fresh in his mind he will find the occasion propitious for acquiring also, in the way pointed out, a sense of the power of their works.

This will seem to most people a very unambitious discipline. But the fault of most of the disciplines proposed in education is that they are by far too ambitious. Our improvers of education are almost always for proceeding by way of augmentation and complication ; reduction and simplification, I say, is what is rather required. We give the learner too

much to do, and we are over-zealous to tell him what he ought to think.
Johnson himself has admirably marked the real line of our education
through letters. He says in his life of Pope : "Judgment is forced
upon us by experience. He that reads many books must compare one
opinion or one style with another ; and, when he compares, must necessarily distinguish, reject, and prefer." Nothing could be better. The
aim and end of education through letters is to get this experience. Our
being told by another what its results will properly be found to be, is not,
even if we are told aright, at all the same thing as getting the experience
for ourselves. The discipline, therefore, which puts us in the way of
getting it cannot be called an inconsiderable or inefficacious one. We
should take care not to imperil its acquisition by refusing to trust to it in
its simplicity, by being eager to add, set right, and annotate. It is much
to secure the reading, by young English people, of the lives of the six
chief poets of our nation between the years 1650 and 1750, related by our
foremost man of letters of the eighteenth century. It is much to secure
their reading, under the stimulus of Johnson's interesting recital and
forcible judgments, famous specimens of the authors whose lives are,
before them. Do not let us insist on also reviewing in detail and sup-
plementing Johnson's work for them, on telling them what they ought
really and definitely to think about the six authors and about the exact
place of each in English literature. Perhaps our pupils are not ripe for
it ; perhaps, too, we have not Johnson's interest and Johnson's force ; we
are not the power in letters for our century which he was for his. We
may be pedantic, obscure, dull, every thing that bores, rather than every
thing that stimulates ; and so Johnson and his lives will repel, and
will not be received, because we insist on being received along with
them.

And again, as we bar a learner's approach to Homer and Virgil by our
chevaux-de-frise of elaborate grammar, so we are apt to stop his way to a
piece of English literature by imbedding it in a mass of notes and additional
matter. Mr. Croker's edition of Boswell's "Life of Johnson" is a good
example of the labor and ingenuity which may be spent upon a masterpiece, with the result, after all, really of rather encumbering than illus-
trating it. All knowledge may be in itself good, but this kind of editing
seems to proceed upon the notion that we have only one book to read in
the course of our life, or else that we have eternity to read in. What can
it matter to our generation whether it was Molly Aston or Miss Boothby
whose preference for Lord Lyttelton made Johnson jealous, and produced
in his "Life of Lyttelton" a certain tone of disparagement ? With the
young reader, at all events, our great endeavor should be to bring him
face to face with masterpieces, and to hold him there, not distracting or
rebutting him with needless excursions or trifling details.

I should like to think that a number of young people might be brought to know an important period of our literary and intellectual history, through means of the lives of six of its leading and representative authors, told by a great man. I should like to think that they would go on, under the stimulus of the lives, to acquaint themselves with some leading and representative work of each author. In the six lives they would at least have secured, I think, a most valuable *point de repère* in the history of our English life and literature, a point from which afterward to find their way; whether they might desire to ascend upward to our anterior literature, or to come downward to the literature of yesterday and of the present.

The six lives cover a period of literary and intellectual movement in which we are all profoundly interested. It is the passage of our nation to prose and reason ; the passage to a type of thought and expression, modern, European, and which on the whole is ours at the present day, from a type antiquated, peculiar, and which is ours no longer. The period begins with a prose like this of Milton : '' They who to states and governors of the commonwealth direct their speech, high court of Parliament ! or, wanting such access in a private condition, write that which they foresee may advance the public good ; I suppose them, if at the beginning of no mean endeavor, not a little altered and moved inwardly in their minds.'' It ends with a prose like this of Smollett : '' My spirit began to accommodate itself to my beggarly fate, and I became so mean as to go down toward Wapping, with an intention to inquire for an old school-fellow, who, I understood, had got the command of a small coasting-vessel then in the river, and implore his assistance.'' These are extreme instances ; but they give us no unfaithful notion of the change in our prose between the reigns of Charles I. and of George III. Johnson has recorded his own impression of the extent of the change and of its salutariness. Boswell gave him a book to read, written in 1702 by the English chaplain of a regiment stationed in Scotland. · '' It is sad stuff, sir,'' said Johnson, after reading it ; '' miserably written, as books in general then were. There is now an elegance of style universally diffused. No man now writes so ill as Martin's ' Account of the Hebrides ' is written. A man could not write so ill if he should try. Set a merchant's clerk now to write, and he'll do better.''

It seems as if a simple and natural prose were a thing which we might expect to come easy to communities of men, and to come early to them ; but we know from experience that it is not so. Poetry and the poetic form of expression naturally precede prose. We see this in ancient Greece. We see prose forming itself there gradually and with labor ; we see it passing through more than one stage before it attains to thorough propriety and lucidity, long after forms of consummate accuracy have already been reached and used in poetry. It is a people's growth in practical life and its native turn for developing this life and for making progress in it which awaken the desire for a good prose—a prose plain, direct, intelligible, serviceable. A dead language, the Latin, for a long time furnished the nations of Europe with an instrument of the kind superior to any which they had yet discovered in their own tongue. But nations such as England and France, called to a great historic life, and with powerful interests and gifts either social or practical, were sure to feel the need of having a sound prose of their own, and to bring such a prose forth. They brought it forth in the seventeenth century ; France first, afterward England.

The Restoration marks the real moment of birth of our modern English prose. Men of lucid and direct mental habit there were, such as Chillingworth, in whom before the Restoration the desire and the commencements of a modern prose show themselves. There were men like Barrow, weighty and powerful, whose mental habit the old prose suited, who continued its forms and locutions after the Restoration. But the hour was come for the new prose, and it grew and prevailed. In Johnson's time its victory had long been assured, and the old style seemed barbarous. Johnson himself wrote a prose decidedly modern. The reproach conveyed in the phrase '' Juhnsonian English '' must not mislead us. It is aimed at his words, not at his structure. In Johnson's prose the words are often pompous and long, but the structure is always plain and modern. The prose writers of the eighteenth century have indeed their mannerisms and phrases which are no longer ours. Johnson says of Milton's blame of the universities for permitting young men designed for orders in the Church to act in plays : '' This is sufficiently peevish in a man, who, when he mentions his exile from college, relates, with great luxuriance, the compensation which the pleasures of the theatre afford him. Plays were therefore only criminal when they were acted by academics.'' We should nowadays not say *peevish* here, nor *luxuriance* nor *academics*. Yet the style is ours by its organism, if not by its phrasing. It is by its organism —an organism opposed to length and involvement, and enabling us to be clear, plain, and short—that English style after the Restoration breaks with the style of the times preceding it, finds the true law of prose, and becomes modern ; becomes, in spite of superficial differences, the style of our own day.

Burnet has pointed out how we are under obligations in this matter to Charles II., whom Johnson described as '' the last King of England who was a man of parts.'' A king of England by no means fulfils his whole duty by being a man of parts, or by loving and encouraging art, science, and literature. Yet the artist and the student of the natural sciences will always feel a kindness toward the two Charleses for their interest in art and science ; and modern letters, too, have their debt to Charles II., although it may be quite true that that prince, as Burnet says, '' had little or no literature.'' '' The king had little or no literature, but,'' continues Burnet, "true and good sense, and had got a right notion of style ; for he was in France at the time when they were much set on reforming their language. It soon appeared that he had a true taste. So this helped to raise the value of these men" (Tillotson and others), "when the king approved of the style their discourses generally ran in, which was clear, plain, and short."

It is the victory of this prose style, "clear, plain, and short," over what Burnet calls "the old style, long and heavy," which is the distinguished achievement, in the history of English letters, of the century following the Restoration. From the first it proceeded rapidly and was never checked. Burnet says of the Chancellor Finch, Earl of Nottingham : " He was long much admired for his eloquence, but it was labored and affected, and he saw it much despised before he died." A like revolution of taste brought about a general condemnation of our old prose style, imperfectly disengaged from the style of poetry. By Johnson's time the new style, the style of prose, was altogether paramount in its own proper domain, and in its pride of victorious strength had invaded also the domain of poetry.

That invasion is now visited by us with a condemnation not less strong and general than the condemnation which the eighteenth century passed upon the unwieldy prose of its predecessors. But let us be careful to do justice while we condemn. A thing good in its own place may be bad out of it. Prose requ'res a different style from poetry. Poetry, no doubt, is more excellent in itself than prose. In poetry man finds the highest and most beautiful expression of that which is in him. We had far better poetry than the poetry of the eighteenth century before that century arrived, we have had better since it departed. Like the Greeks, and unlike the French, we can point to an age of poetry anterior to our age of prose, eclipsing our age of prose in glory, and fixing the future character and conditions of our literature. We do well to place our pride in the Elizabethan age and Shakespeare, as the Greeks place theirs in Homer. We did well to return in the present century to the poetry of that older age for illumination and inspiration, and to put aside in a great measure the poetry and poets intervening between Milton and Wordsworth. Milton, in whom our great poetic age expired, was the last of the immortals. Of the five poets whose lives follow his in our present volume, three—Dryden, Addison, and Swift—are eminent prose-writers as well as poets ; two of the three — Swift and Addison — far more distinguished as prose-writers than as poets. The glory of English literature is in poetry, and in poetry the strength of the eighteenth century does not lie.

Nevertheless, the eighteenth century accomplished for us an immense literary progress, and its very shortcomings in poetry were an instrument to that progress, and served it. The example of Germany may show us what a nation loses from having no prose style. The practical genius of

our people could not but urge irresistibly to the production of a real prose
style, because for the purposes of modern life the old English prose, the
prose of Milton and Taylor, is cumbersome, unavailable, impossible. A
style of regularity, uniformity, precision, balance, was wanted. These are
the qualities of a serviceable prose style. Poetry has a different *logic*, as
Coleridge said, from prose ; poetical style follows another law of evolution
than the style of prose. But there is no doubt that a style of regularity, uniformity, precision, balance, will acquire a yet stronger hold upon the mind
of a nation, if it is adopted in poetry as well as in prose, and so comes to
govern both. This is what happened in France. To the practical,
modern, and social genius of the French, a true prose was indispensable.
They produced one of conspicuous excellence, supremely powerful and
influential in the last century, the first to come, and standing at first
alone, a modern prose. French prose is marked in the highest degree
by the qualities of regularity, uniformity, precision, balance. With
little opposition from any deep-seated and imperious poetic instincts, the
French made their poetry conform to the law which was moulding their
prose. French poetry became marked with the qualities of regularity,
uniformity, precision, balance. This may have been bad for French
poetry, but it was good for French prose. It heightened the perfection
with which those qualities, the true qualities of prose, were impressed
upon it. When England, at the Restoration, desired a modern prose, and
began to create it, our writers turned naturally to French literature, which
had just accomplished the very process which engaged them. The king's
acuteness and taste, as we have seen, helped. Indeed, to the admission
of French influence of all kinds, Charles II.'s character and that of his
court were but too favorable. But the influence of the French writers
was, at that moment, on the whole, fortunate, and seconded what was a
vital and necessary effort in our literature. Our literature required a
prose which conformed to the true law of prose ; and, that it might acquire
this the more surely, it compelled poetry, as in France, to conform itself
to the law of prose likewise. The classic verse of French poetry was the
Alexandrine, a measure favorable to the qualities of regularity, uniformity,
precision, balance. Gradually a measure favorable to those very same
qualities—the ten-syllable couplet—established itself as the classic verse
of England, until in the eighteenth century it had become the ruling form
of our poetry. Poetry, or rather the use of verse, entered in a remarkable
degree, during that century, into the whole of the daily life of the civilized
classes ; and the poetry of the century was a perpetual school of the qualities requisite for a good prose, the qualities of regularity, uniformity,
precision, balance. This may have been of no great service to English
poetry, although to say that it has been of no service at all, to say that the
eighteenth century has in no respect changed the conditions for English

poetical style, or that it has changed them for the worse, would be untrue. But it was undeniably of signal service to that which was the great want and work of the hour, English prose.

Do not let us, therefore, hastily despise Johnson and his century for their defective poetry and criticism of poetry. True, Johnson is capable of saying, " Surely no man could have fancied that he read ' Lycidas ' with pleasure had he not known the author !'' True, he is capable of maintaining that " the description of the temple in Congreve's ' Mourning Bride ' was the finest poetical passage he had ever read—he recollected none in Shakespeare equal to it." But we are to conceive of Johnson and of his century as having a special task committed to them, the establishment of English prose ; and as capable of being warped and narrowed in their judgments of poetry by this exclusive task. Such is the common course and law of progress ; one thing is done at a time, and the other things are sacrificed to it. We must be thankful for the thing done, if it is valuable, and we must put up with the temporary sacrifice of other things to this one. The other things will have their turn sooner or later. Above all, a nation with profound poetical instincts, like the English nation, may be trusted to work itself right again in poetry after periods of mistaken poetical practice. Even in the midst of an age of such practice, and with his style frequently showing the bad influence of it, Gray was saved, we may say, and remains a poet whose work has high and pure worth, simply by his knowing the Greeks thoroughly, more thoroughly than any English poet had known them since Milton. Milton was a survivor from the great age of poetry ; Dryden, Addison, Pope, and Swift were mighty workers for the age of prose. Gray, a poet in the midst of the age of prose, a poet, moreover, of by no means the highest force, and of scanty productiveness, nevertheless claims a place among the six chief personages of Johnson's lives, because it was impossible for an English poet, even in that age, who knew the great Greek masters intimately, not to respond to their good influence, and to be rescued from the false poetical practice of his contemporaries. Of such avail to a nation are deep poetical instincts even in an age of prose. How much more may they be trusted to assert themselves after the age of prose has ended, and to remedy any poetical mischief done by it ! And meanwhile the work of the hour, the necessary and appointed work, has been done, and we have got our prose.

Let us always bear in mind, therefore, that the century so well represented by Dryden, Addison, Pope, and Swift, and of which the literary history is so powerfully written by Johnson in his lives, is a century of prose —a century of which the great work in literature was the formation of English prose. Johnson was himself a laborer in this great and needful work, and was ruled by its influences. His blame of genuine poets like Milton and Gray, his over-praise of artificial poets like Pope, are to be taken as the utterances of a man who worked for an age of prose, who was ruled by

Its influences, and could not but be ruled by them. Of poetry he speaks as a man whose sense for that with which he is dealing is in some degree imperfect.

Yet even on poetry Johnson's utterances are valuable, because they are the utterances of a great and original man. That, indeed, he was ; and to be conducted by such a man through an important century cannot but do us good, even though our guide may in some places be less competent than in others. Johnson was the man of an age of prose. Furthermore, Johnson was a strong force of conservatism and concentration, in an epoch which by its natural tendencies seemed to be moving towards expansion and freedom. But he was a great man, and great men are always instructive. The more we study him, the higher will be our esteem for the power of his mind, the width of his interests, the largeness of his knowledge, the freshness, fearlessness, and strength of his judgments. The higher, too, will be our esteem for his character. His well-known lines on Levett's death, beautiful and touching lines, are still more beautiful and touching because they recall a whole history of Johnson's goodness, tenderness, and charity. Human dignity, on the other hand, he maintained, we all know how well, through the whole long and arduous struggle of his life, from his undergraduate days at Oxford, down to the *Jam moriturus* of his closing hour. His faults and strangenesses are on the surface, and catch every eye. But on the whole we have in him a fine and admirable type, worthy to be kept in view for ever, of '' the ancient and inbred integrity, piety, good-nature, and good-humor of the English people.''

It was right that a Life of Johnson himself should stand as an introduction to the present volume, and I long ago conceived the wish that it should be the Life contributed by Lord Macaulay to the '' Encyclopædia Britannica.'' That Life is a work which shows Macaulay at his very best ; a work written when his style was matured and when his resources were in all their fulness. The subject, too, was one which he knew thoroughly, and for which he felt cordial sympathy ; indeed by his mental habit Macaulay himself belonged, in many respects, to the eighteenth century rather than to our own. But the permission to use in this manner a choice work of Lord Macaulay's was no light favor to ask. However, in my zeal for the present volume, I boldly asked it, and by the proprietors of the '' Encyclopædia Britannica,'' the Messrs. Black, it has been kindly and generously accorded. I cannot sufficiently express my sense of obligation to them for their consent, and to Mr. Trevelyan for his acquiescence in it. They have enabled me to fill a long-cherished desire, to tell the story of a whole important age of English literature in one compendious volume—itself, at the same time, a piece of English literature of the very first class. Such a work the reader has in his hands in the present volume ; its editor may well be fearful of injuring it by a single superfluous line, a single unacceptable word,

SAMUEL JOHNSON.

BY LORD MACAULAY.

SAMUEL JOHNSON,* one of the most eminent English writers of the eighteenth century, was the son of Michael Johnson, who was, at the beginning of that century, a magistrate of
Lichfield, and a bookseller of great note in the midland counties. Michael's abilities and attainments seem to have been
considerable. He was so well acquainted with the contents of
the volumes which he exposed to sale, that the country rectors
of Staffordshire and Worcestershire thought him an oracle on
points of learning. Between him and the clergy, indeed, there
was a strong religious and political sympathy. He was a zealous churchman, and, though he had qualified himself for muni-
cipal office by taking the oaths to the sovereigns in possession,
was to the last a Jacobite in heart. At his house, a house
which is still pointed out to every traveller who visits Lichfield, Samuel was born on the 18th of September, 1709. In the
child the physical, intellectual, and moral peculiarities which
afterwards distinguished the man were plainly discernible ;
great muscular strength accompanied by much awkwardness
and many infirmities ; great quickness of parts, with a morbid
propensity to sloth and procrastination ; a kind and generous
heart, with a gloomy and irritable temper. He had inherited
from his ancestors a scrofulous taint, which it was beyond the
power of medicine to remove. His parents were weak enough
to believe that the royal touch was a specific for this malady.
In his third year he was taken up to London, inspected by the
court surgeon, prayed over by the court chaplains, and stroked
and presented with a piece of gold by Queen Anne. One of
his earliest recollections was that of a stately lady in a diamond
stomacher and a long black hood. Her hand was applied in
vain. The boy's features, which were originally noble and not
irregular, were distorted by his malady. His cheeks were
deeply scarred. He lost for a time the sight of one eye, and
he saw but very imperfectly with the other. But the force of
his mind overcame every impediment. Indolent as he was, he
acquired knowledge with such ease and rapidity, that at every
school to which he was sent he was soon the best scholar.
From sixteen to eighteen he resided at home, and was left to

* This essay was contributed to the *Encyclopædia Britannica*.

his own devices. He learned much at this time, though his studies were without guidance and without plan. He ransacked his father's shelves, dipped into a multitude of books, read what was interesting, and passed over what was dull. An ordinary lad would have acquired little or no useful knowledge in such a way ; but much that was dull to ordinary lads was interesting to Samuel. He read little Greek ; for his proficiency in that language was not such that he could take much pleasure in the masters of Attic poetry and eloquence. But he had left school a good Latinist, and he soon acquired, in the large and miscellaneous library of which he now had the command, an extensive knowledge of Latin literatu.e. That Augustan delicacy of taste, which is the boast of the great public schools of England, he never possessed. But he was early familiar with some classical writers, who were quite unknown to the best scholars in the sixth form at Eton. He was peculiarly attracted by the works of the great restorers of learning. Once, while searching for some apples, he found a huge folio volume of Petrarch's works. The name excited his curiosity, and he eagerly devoured hundreds of pages. Indeed, the diction and versification of his own Latin compositions show that he had paid at least as much attention to modern copies from the antique as to the original models.

While he was thus irregularly educating himself, his family was sinking into hopeless poverty. Old Michael Johnson was much better qualified to pore upon books, and to talk about them, than to trade in them. His business declined : his debts increased : it was with difficulty that the daily expenses of his household were defrayed. It was out of his power to support his son at either university ; but a wealthy neighbor offered assistance ; and, in reliance on promises which proved to be of very little value, Samuel was entered at Pembroke College, Oxford. When the young scholar presented himself to the rulers of that society, they were amazed not more by his ungainly figure and eccentric manners, than by the quantity of extensive and curious information which he had picked up during many months of desultory, but not unprofitable study. On the first day of his residence he surprised his teachers by quoting " Macrobius ;" and one of the most learned among them declared that he had never known a freshman of equal attainments.

At Oxford, Johnson resided during about three years. He was poor, even to raggedness ; and his appearance excited a mirth and pity which were equally intolerable to his haughty spirit. He was driven from the quadrangle of Christ Church

by the sneering looks which the members of that aristocratical
society cast at the holes in his shoes. Some charitable person
placed a new pair at his door ; but he spurned them away in a
fury. Distress made him, not servile, but reckless and ungovernable. No opulent gentleman commoner, panting for one-
and-twenty, could have treated the academical authorities with
more gross disrespect. The needy scholar was generally to be
seen under the gate of Pembroke, a gate now adorned with his
effigy, haranguing a circle of lads, over whom, in spite of his
tattered gown and dirty linen, his wit and audacity gave him an
undisputed ascendency. In every mutiny against the discipline of the college he was the ringleader. Much was par-
doned, however, to a youth so highly distinguished by abilities
and acquirements. He had early made himself known by
turning Pope's " Messiah" into Latin verse. The style and
rhythm, indeed, were not exactly Virgilian ; but the translation
found many admirers, and was read with pleasure by Pope himself.

The time drew near at which Johnson would, in the ordinary course of things, have become a Bachelor of Arts ; but he
was at the end of his resources. Those promises of support
on which he had relied had not been kept. His family could
do nothing for him. His debts to Oxford tradesmen were
small indeed, yet larger than he could pay. In the autumn of
1731, he was under the necessity of quitting the university
without a degree. In the following winter his father died.
The old man left but a pittance ; and of that pittance almost
the whole was appropriated to the support of his widow. The
property to which Samuel succeeded amounted to no more
than twenty pounds.

His life, during the thirty years which followed, was one
hard struggle with poverty. The misery of that struggle
needed no aggravation, but was aggravated by the sufferings of
an unsound body and an unsound mind. Before the young
man left the university, his hereditary malady had broken forth
in a singularly cruel form. He had become an incurable hypochondriac. He said long after that he had been mad all his
life, or at least not perfectly sane ; and, in truth, eccentricities
less strange than his have often been thought grounds sufficient
for absolving felons and for setting aside wills. His grimaces,
his gestures, his mutterings, sometimes diverted and sometimes
terrified people who did not know him. At a dinner-table he
would, in a fit of absence, stoop down and twitch off a lady's
shoe. He would amaze a drawing-room by suddenly ejaculat-
ing a clause of the Lord's Prayer. He would conceive an un-

intelligible aversion to a particular alley, and perform a great
circuit rather than see the hateful place. He would set his
heart on touching every post in the streets through which he
walked. If by any chance he missed a post, he would go back
a hundred yards and repair the omission. Under the influence
of his disease, his senses became morbidly torpid, and his imagination morbidly active. At one time he would stand poring
on the town clock without being able to tell the hour. At another he would distinctly hear his mother, who was many miles
off, calling him by his name. But this was not the worst. A
deep melancholy took possession of him, and gave a dark tinge
to all his views of human nature and of human destiny. Such
wretchedness as he endured has driven many men to shoot
themselves or drown themselves. But he was under no temptation to commit suicide. He was sick of life, but he was
afraid of death ; and he shuddered at every sight or sound
which reminded him of the inevitable hour. In religion he
found but little comfort during his long and frequent fits of
dejection ; for his religion partook of his own character. The
light from heaven shone on him indeed, but not in a direct
line, or with its own pure splendor. The rays had to struggle
through a disturbing medium ; they reached him refracted,
dulled and discolored by the thick gloom which had settled on
his soul ; and, though they might be sufficiently clear to guide
him, were too dim to cheer him.

   With such infirmities of body and of mind, this celebrated man
was left, at two-and-twenty, to fight his way through the world.
He remained during about five years in the midland counties.
At Lichfield, his birthplace and his early home, he had inherited some friends and acquired others. He was kindly
noticed by Henry Hervey, a gay officer of noble family, who
happened to be quartered there. Gilbert Walmesley, registrar
of the ecclesiastical court of the diocese, a man of distinguished parts, learning, and knowledge of the world, did himself honor by patronizing the young adventurer, whose repulsive person, unpolished manners, and squalid garb, moved
many of the petty aristocracy of the neighborhood to laughter
or to disgust. At Lichfield, however, Johnson could find no
way of earning a livelihood. He became usher of a grammar
school in Leicestershire ; he resided as a humble companion in
the house of a country gentleman ; but a life of dependence was
insupportable to his haughty spirit. He repaired to Birmingham, and there earned a few guineas by literary drudgery. In
that town he printed a translation, little noticed at the time,
and long forgotten, of a Latin book about Abyssinia. He then

put forth proposals for publishing by subscription the poems of Politian, with notes containing a history of modern Latin verse ; but subscriptions did not come in, and the volume never appeared.

While leading this vagrant and miserable life, Johnson fell in love. The object of his passion was Mrs. Elizabeth Porter, a widow who had children as old as himself. To ordinary spectators, the lady appeared to be a short, fat, coarse woman, painted half an inch thick, dressed in gaudy colors, and fond of exhibiting provincial airs and graces which were not exactly those of the Queensberrys and Lepels. To Johnson, however, whose passions were strong, whose eyesight was too weak to distinguish ceruse from natural bloom, and who had seldom or never been in the same room with a woman of real fashion, his Titty, as he called her, was the most beautiful, graceful, and accomplished of her sex. That his admiration was unfeigned cannot be doubted ; for she was as poor as himself. She accepted, with a readiness which did her little honor, the addresses of a suitor who might have been her son. The marriage, however, in spite of occasional wranglings, proved happier than might have been expected. The lover continued to be under the illusions of the wedding-day till the lady died in her sixty-fourth year. On her monument he placed an inscription extolling the charms of her person and of her manners ; and when, long after her decease, he had occasion to mention her, he exclaimed, with a tenderness half ludicrous, half pathetic, "Pretty creature !"

His marriage made it necessary for him to exert himself more strenuously than he had hitherto done. He took a house in the neighborhood of his native town, and advertised for pupils. But eighteen months passed away, and only three pupils came to his academy. Indeed, his appearance was so strange, and his temper so violent, that his school-room must have resembled an ogre's den. Nor was the tawdry painted grandmother whom he called his Titty well qualified to make provision for the comfort of young gentlemen. David Garrick, who was one of the pupils, used, many years later, to throw the best company of London into convulsions of laughter by mimicking the endearments of this extraordinary pair.

At length Johnson, in the twenty-eighth year of his age, determined to seek his fortune in the capital as a literary adventurer. He set out with a few guineas, three acts of the tragedy of "Irene" in manuscript, and two or three letters of introduction from his friend Walmesley.

Never since literature became a calling in England had it

been a less gainful calling than at the time when Johnson took up his residence in London. In the preceding generation a writer of eminent merit was sure to be munificently rewarded by the government. The least that he could expect was a pension or a sinecure place ; and if he showed any aptitude for politics, he might hope to be a member of parliament, a lord of the treasury, an ambassador, a secretary of state. It would be easy, on the other hand, to name several writers of the nineteenth century, of whom the least successful has received forty thousand pounds from the booksellers. But Johnson entered on his vocation in the most dreary part of the dreary interval which separated two ages of prosperity. Literature had ceased to flourish under the patronage of the great, and had not begun to flourish under the patronage of the public. One man of letters, indeed, Pope, had acquired by his pen what was then considered as a handsome fortune, and lived on a footing of equality with nobles and ministers of state. But this was a solitary exception. Even an author whose reputation was established, and whose works were popular, such an author as Thomson, whose " Seasons" were in every library, such an author as Fielding, whose " Pasquin" had had a greater run than any drama since " The Beggar's Opera," was sometimes glad to obtain, by pawning his best coat, the means of dining on tripe at a cookshop underground, where he could wipe his hands, after his greasy meal, on the back of a Newfoundland dog. It is easy, therefore, to imagine what humiliations and privations must have awaited the novice who had still to earn a name. One of the publishers to whom Johnson applied for employment measured with a scornful eye that athletic though uncouth frame, and exclaimed, " You had better get a porter's knot, and carry trunks." Nor was the advice bad, for a porter was likely to be as plentifully fed and as comfortably lodged as a poet.

Some time appears to have elapsed before Johnson was able to form any literary connection from which he could expect more than bread for the day which was passing over him. He never forgot the generosity with which Hervey, who was now residing in London, relieved his wants during this time of trial. " Harry Hervey," said the old philosopher many years later, " was a vicious man ; but he was very kind to me. If you call a dog Hervey, I shall love him." At Hervey's table Johnson sometimes enjoyed feasts which were made more agreeable by contrast. But in general he dined, and thought that he dined well, on sixpenny worth of meat and a pennyworth of bread at an alehouse near Drury Lane.

The effect of the privations and sufferings which he endured at this time was discernible to the last in his temper and
his deportment. His manners had never been courtly. They
now became almost savage. Being frequently under the necessity of wearing shabby coats and dirty shirts, he became a confirmed sloven. Being often very hungry when he sat down to
his meals, he contracted a habit of eating with ravenous greediness. Even to the end of his life, and even at the tables of
the great, the sight of food affected him as it affects wild beasts
and birds of prey. His taste in cookery, formed in subterra-
nean ordinaries and *Alamode* beefshops, was far from delicate.
Whenever he was so fortunate as to have near him a hare that
had been kept too long, or a meat pie made with rancid butter,
he gorged himself with such violence that his veins swelled
and the moisture broke out on his forehead. The affronts
which his poverty emboldened stupid and low-minded men to
offer to him would have broken a mean spirit into sycophancy,
but made him rude even to ferocity. Unhappily the insolence
which, while it was defensive, was pardonable, and in some
sense respectable, accompanied him into societies where he was
treated with courtesy and kindness. He was repeatedly provoked into striking those who had taken liberties with him.
All the sufferers, however, were wise enough to abstain from
talking about their beatings, except Osborne, the most rapacious and brutal of booksellers, who proclaimed everywhere
that he had been knocked down by the huge fellow whom he
had hired to puff the Harleian Library.

About a year after Johnson had begun to reside in London,
he was fortunate enough to obtain regular employment from
Cave, an enterprising and intelligent bookseller, who was proprietor and editor of the " Gentleman's Magazine." That
journal, just entering on the ninth year of its long existence,
was the only periodical work in the kingdom which then had
what would now be called a large circulation. It was, indeed,
the chief source of parliamentary intelligence. It was not then
safe, even during a recess, to publish an account of the proceedings of either House without some disguise. Cave, however, ventured to entertain his readers with what he called Reports of the Debates of the Senate of Liliput. France was
Blefuscu ; London was Mildendo ; pounds were sprugs ; the
Duke of Newcastle was the Nardac secretary of state ; Lord
Hardwicke was the Hurgo Hickrad ; and William Pulteney was
Wingul Pulnub. To write the speeches was, during several
years, the business of Johnson. He was generally furnished
with notes, meagre indeed and inaccurate, of what had been

said ; but sometimes he had to find arguments and eloquence both for the ministry and for the opposition.   He was himself a Tory, not from rational conviction—for his serious opinion was that one form of government was just as good or as bad as another—but from mere passion, such as inflamed the Capulets against the Montagues, or the Blues of the Roman circus against the Greens.   In his infancy he had heard so much talk about the villanies of the Whigs and the dangers of the Church, that he had become a furious partisan when he could scarcely speak.   Before he was three he had insisted on being taken to hear Sacheverell preach at Lichfield Cathedral, and had listened to the sermon with as much respect, and probably with as much intelligence, as any Staffordshire squire in the congregation.   The work which had been begun in the nursery had been completed by the university.   Oxford, when Johnson resided there, was the most Jacobitical place in England ; and Pembroke was one of the most Jacobitical colleges in Oxford. The prejudices which he brought up to London were scarcely less absurd than those of his own Tom Tempest.   Charles II. and James II. were two of the best kings that ever reigned. Laud, a poor creature who never did, said, or wrote any thing indicating more than the ordinary capacity of an old woman, was a prodigy of parts and learning over whose tomb Art and Genius still continued to weep.   Hampden deserved no more honorable name than that of ''the zealot of rebellion.''   Even the ship money, condemned not less decidedly by Falkland and Clarendon than by the bitterest Roundheads, Johnson would not pronounce to have been an unconstitutional impost. Under a government the mildest that had ever been known in the world, under a government which allowed to the people an unprecedented liberty of speech and action, he fancied that he was a slave ; he assailed the ministry with obloquy which refuted itself, and regretted the lost freedom and happiness of those golden days in which a writer who had taken but one tenth part of the license allowed to him would have been pillo- ried, mangled with the shears, whipped at the cart's tail, and flung into a noisome dungeon to die.   He hated dissenters and stock-jobbers, the excise and the army, septennial parlia- ments, and continental connections.   He long had an aversion to the Scotch, an aversion of which he could not remember the commencement, but which, he owned, had probably originated in his abhorrence of the conduct of the nation during the Great Rebellion.   It is easy to guess in what manner debates on great party questions were likely to be reported by a man whose judgment was so much disordered by party spirit.   A show of

fairness was indeed necessary to the prosperity of the Magazine. But Johnson long afterwards owned that, though he had
saved appearances, he had taken care that the Whig dogs
should not have the best of it ; and, in fact, every passage
which has lived, every passage which bears the marks of his
higher faculties, is put into the mouth of some member of the
opposition.

A few weeks after Johnson had entered on these obscure
labors, he published a work which at once placed him high
among the writers of his age. It is probable that what he had
suffered during his first year in London had often reminded
him of some parts of that noble poem in which Juvenal had
described the misery and degradation of a needy man of letters, lodged among the pigeons' nests in the tottering garrets
which overhung the streets of Rome. Pope's admirable imitations of Horace's Satires and Epistles had recently appeared,
were in every hand, and were by many readers thought superior to the originals. What Pope had done for Horace, Johnson aspired to do for Juvenal. The enterprise was bold and
yet judicious. For between Johnson and Juvenal there was
much in common, much more certainly than between Pope and
Horace.

Johnson's "London" appeared without his name in May,
1738. He received only ten guineas for this stately and vigorous poem ; but the sale was rapid and the success complete.
A second edition was required within a week. Those small
critics who are always desirous to lower established reputation
ran about proclaiming that the anonymous satirist was superior
to Pope in Pope's own peculiar department of literature. It
ought to be remembered, to the honor of Pope, that he joined
heartily in the applause with which the appearance of a rival
genius was welcomed. He made inquiries about the author of
"London." Such a man, he said, could not long be concealed.
The name was soon discovered ; and Pope, with great kindness, exerted himself to obtain an academical degree and the
mastership of a grammar school for the poor young poet. The
attempt failed, and Johnson remained a bookseller's hack.

It does not appear that these two men, the most eminent
writer of the generation which was going out, and the most eminent writer of the generation which was coming in, ever saw
each other. They lived in very different circles, one surrounded
by dukes and earls, the other by starving pamphleteers and in-
dex-makers. Among Johnson's associates at this time may be
mentioned Boyse, who, when his shirts were pledged, scrawled
Latin verses sitting up in bed with his arms through two holes

in his blanket, who composed very respectable sacred poetry
when he was sober, and who was at last run over by a hackney
coach when he was drunk ; Hoole, surnamed the metaphysical
tailor, who, instead of attending to his measures, used to trace
geometrical diagrams on the board where he sat cross-legged ;
and the penitent impostor, George Psalmanazar, who, after
poring all day, in a humble lodging, on the folios of Jewish
rabbis and Christian fathers, indulged himself at night with
literary and theological conversation at an alehouse in the city.
But the most remarkable of the persons with whom at this time
Johnson consorted was Richard Savage, an earl's son, a shoe-
maker's apprentice, who had seen life in all its forms, who had
feasted among blue ribbons in Saint James's Square, and
had lain with fifty pounds weight of irons on his legs, in the
condemned ward of Newgate. This man had, after many
vicissitudes of fortune, sunk at last into abject and hopeless
poverty. His pen had failed him. His patrons had been
taken away by death, or estranged by the riotous profusion
with which he squandered their bounty, and the ungrateful insolence with which he rejected their advice. He now lived by
begging. He dined on venison and champagne whenever he
had been so fortunate as to borrow a guinea. If his questing
had been unsuccessful, he appeased the rage of hunger with
some scraps of broken meat, and lay down to rest under the
Piazza of Covent Garden in warm weather, and, in cold
weather, as near as he could get to the furnace of a glass-house.
Yet, in his misery, he was still an agreeable companion. He
had an inexhaustible store of anecdotes about that gay and
brilliant world from which he was now an outcast. He had
observed the great men of both parties in hours of careless
relaxation, had seen the leaders of opposition without the mask
of patriotism, and had heard the Prime Minister roar with
laughter and tell stories not over decent. During some
months Savage lived in the closest familiarity with Johnson ;
and then the friends parted, not without tears. Johnson
remained in London to drudge for Cave. Savage went to the
West of England, lived there as he had lived everywhere, and,
in 1743, died, penniless and heart-broken, in Bristol jail.
    Soon after his death, while the public curiosity was strongly
excited about his extraordinary character and his not less
extraordinary adventures, a life of him appeared widely different from the catchpenny lives of eminent men which were then
a staple article of manufacture in Grub Street. The style was
indeed deficient in ease and variety ; and the writer was evidently too partial to the Latin element of our language. But

the little work, with all its faults, was a masterpiece. No finer specimen of literary biography existed in any language, living or dead ; and a discerning critic might have confidently predicted that the author was destined to be the founder of a new school of English eloquence.

The Life of Savage was anonymous ; but it was well known in literary circles that Johnson was the writer. During the three years which followed, he produced no important work ; but he was not, and indeed could not be, idle. The fame of his abilities and learning continued to grow. Warburton pronounced him a man of parts and genius ; and the praise of Warburton was then no light thing. Such was Johnson's reputation that, in 1747, several eminent booksellers combined to employ him in the arduous work of preparing a " Dictionary of the English Language," in two folio volumes. The sum which they agreed to pay him was only fifteen hundred guineas ; and out of this sum he had to pay several poor men of letters who assisted him in the humbler parts of his task.

The Prospectus of the Dictionary he addressed to the Earl of Chesterfield. Chesterfield had long been celebrated for the politeness of his manners, the brilliancy of his wit, and the delicacy of his taste. He was acknowledged to be the finest speaker in the House of Lords. He had recently governed Ireland, at a momentous conjuncture, with eminent firmness, wisdom, and humanity ; and he had since become Secretary of State. He received Johnson's homage with the most winning affability, and requited it with a few guineas, bestowed doubtless in a very graceful manner, but was by no means desirous to see all his carpets blackened with the London mud, and his soups and wines thrown to right and left over the gowns of fine ladies and the waistcoats of fine gentlemen, by an absent, awkward scholar, who gave strange starts and uttered strange growls, who dressed like a scarecrow, and ate like a cormorant. During some time, Johnson continued to call on his patron, but, after being repeatedly told by the porter that his lordship was not at home, took the hint, and ceased to present himself at the inhospitable door.

Johnson had flattered himself that he should have completed his Dictionary by the end of 1750, but it was not till 1755 that he at length gave his huge volumes to the world. During the seven years which he passed in the drudgery of penning definitions and marking quotations for transcription, he sought for relaxation in literary labor of a more agreeable kind. In 1749 he published the "Vanity of Human Wishes," an excellent imitation of the Tenth Satire of Juvenal. It is, in truth, not easy to say whether the palm belongs to the ancient or to the modern poet. The couplets in which the fall of Wolsey is described, though lofty and sonorous, are feeble when compared with the wonderful lines which bring before us all Rome in tumult on the day of the fall of Sejanus, the laurels on the doorposts, the white bull stalking towards the Capitol, the statues rolling down from their pedestals, the flatterers of the disgraced minister running to see him dragged with a hook through the streets, and to have a kick at his carcase before it is hurled into the Tiber. It must be owned, too, that in the concluding passage, the Christian moralist has not made the most of his advantages, and has fallen decidedly short of the sublimity of his Pagan model. On the other hand, Juvenal's Hannibal must yield to Johnson's Charles ; and Johnson's vigorous and pathetic enumeration of the miseries of a literary life must be allowed to be superior to Juvenal's lamentation over the fate of Demosthenes and Cicero.

For the copyright of the "Vanity of Human Wishes" Johnson received only fifteen guineas.

A few days after the publication of this poem, his tragedy, begun many years before, was brought on the stage. His pupil, David Garrick, had, in 1741, made his appearance on a humble stage in Goodman's Fields, had at once risen to the first place among actors, and was now, after several years of almost uninterrupted success, manager of Drury Lane Theatre. The relation between him and his old preceptor was of a very singular kind. They repelled each other strongly, and yet attracted each other strongly. Nature had made them of very different clay, and circumstances had fully brought out the natural peculiarities of both. Sudden prosperity had turned Garrick's head. Continued adversity had soured Johnson's temper. Johnson saw with more envy than became so great a man the villa, the plate, the china, the Brussels carpet, which the little mimic had got by repeating, with grimaces and gesticulations, what wiser men had written ; and the exquisitely sensitive vanity of Garrick was galled by the thought that, while all the rest of the world was applauding him, he could obtain from one morose cynic, whose opinion it was impossible to despise, scarcely any compliment not acidulated with scorn. Yet the two Lichfield men had so many early recollections in common, and sympathized with each other on so many points on which they sympathized with nobody else in the vast population of the capital, that, though the master was often provoked by the monkey-like impertinence of the pupil, and the pupil by the bearish rudeness of the master, they remained friends till they were parted by death. Garrick now brought " Irene" out, with alterations sufficient to displease the author, yet not sufficient to make the piece pleasing to the audience. The public, however, listened, with little emotion, but with much civility, to five acts of monotonous declamation. After nine representations the play was withdrawn. It is, indeed, altogether unsuited to the stage, and, even when perused in the closet, will be found hardly worthy of the author. He had not the slightest notion of what blank verse should be. A change in the last syllable of every other line would make the versification of the " Vanity of Human Wishes" closely resemble the versification of " Irene." The poet, however, cleared, by his benefit nights, and by the sale of the copyright of his tragedy, about three hundred pounds, then a great sum in his estimation.

About a year after the representation of " Irene," he began to publish a series of short essays on morals, manners, and literature. This species of composition had been brought into fashion by the success of the " Tatler," and by the still more brilliant success of the " Spectator." A crowd of small writers had vainly attempted to rival Addison. " The Lay Monastery," the " Censor," the " Freethinker," the " Plain Dealer," the " Champion," and other works of the same kind, had had their short day. None of them had obtained a permanent place in our literature ; and they are now to be found only in the libraries of the curious. At length, Johnson undertook the adventure in which so many aspirants had failed. In the thirty-sixth year after the appearance of the last number of the " Spectator" appeared the first number of the " Rambler." From March 1750 to March 1752 this paper continued to come out every Tuesday and Saturday.

From the first the " Rambler" was enthusiastically admired by a few eminent men. Richardson, when only five numbers had appeared, pronounced it equal, if not superior to the " Spectator." Young and Hartley expressed their approbation not less warmly. Bubb Dodington, among whose many faults indifference to the claims of genius and learning cannot be reckoned, solicited the acquaintance of the writer. In consequence probably of the good offices of Dodington, who was then the confidential adviser of Prince Frederic, two of his Royal Highness's gentlemen carried a gracious message to the printing-office, and ordered seven copies for Leicester House. But these overtures seem to have been very coldly received. Johnson had had enough of the patronage of the great to last him all his life, and was not disposed to haunt any other door as he had haunted the door of Chesterfield.

By the public the " Rambler" was at first very coldly received. Though the price of a number was only twopence, the sale did not amount to five hundred. The profits were therefore very small. But as soon as the flying leaves were collected and reprinted, they became popular. The author lived to see thirteen thousand copies spread over England alone. Separate editions were published for the Scotch and Irish markets. A large party pronounced the style perfect, so absolutely perfect that in some essays it would be impossible for the writer himself to alter a single word for the better. Another party, not less numerous, vehemently accused him of having corrupted the purity of the English tongue. The best critics admitted that his diction was too monotonous, too obviously artificial, and now and then turgid even to absurdity. But they did justice to the acuteness of his observations on morals and manners, to the constant precision and frequent brilliancy of his language, to the weighty and magnificent eloquence of many serious passages, and to the solemn yet pleasing humor of some of the lighter papers. On the question of precedence between Addison and Johnson, a question which, seventy years ago, was much disputed, posterity has pronounced a decision from which there is no appeal Sir Roger, his chaplain and his butler, Will Wimble and Will Honeycomb, the Vision of Mirza, the Journal of the Retired Citizen, the Everlasting Club, the Dunmow Flitch, the Loves of Hilpah and Shalum, the Visit to the Exchange, and the Visit to the Abbey, are known to everybody. But many men and women, even of highly cultivated minds, are unacquainted with Squire Bluster and Mrs. Busy, Quisquilius and Venustulus, the Allegory of Wit and Learning, the Chronicle of the Revolutions of a Garret, and the sad fate of Aningait and Ajut.

The last " Rambler" was written in a sad and gloomy hour. Mrs. Johnson had been given over by the physicians. Three days later she died. She left her husband almost brokenhearted. Many people had been surprised to see a man of his genius and learning stooping to every drudgery, and denying himself almost every comfort, for the purpose of supplying a silly, affected old woman with superfluities, which she accepted with but little gratitude. But all his affection had been concentrated on her. He had neither brother nor sister, neither son nor daughter. To him she was beautiful as the Gunnings and witty as Lady Mary. Her opinion of his writings was more important to him than the voice of the pit of Drury Lane

Theatre, or the judgment of the "Monthly Review." The chief support which had sustained him through the most arduous labor of his life was the hope that she would enjoy the fame and the profit which he anticipated from his Dictionary. She was gone ; and in that vast labyrinth of streets, peopled by eight hundred thousand human beings, he was alone. Yet it was necessary for him to set himself, as he expressed it, doggedly to work. After three more laborious years, the Dictionary was at length complete.

It had been generally supposed that this great work would be dedicated to the eloquent and accomplished nobleman to whom the Prospectus had been addressed. He well knew the value of such a compliment ; and therefore, when the day of publication drew near, he exerted himself to soothe, by a show of zealous and at the same time of delicate and judicious kindness, the pride which he had so cruelly wounded. Since the "Ramblers" had ceased to appear, the town had been entertained by a journal called the "World," to which many men of high rank and fashion contributed. In two successive numbers of the "World," the Dictionary was, to use the modern phrase, puffed with wonderful skill. The writings of Johnson were warmly praised. It was proposed that he should be invested with the authority of a dictator, nay, of a pope, over our language, and that his decisions about the meaning and the spelling of words should be received as final. His two folios, it was said, would of course be bought by everybody who could afford to buy them. It was soon known that these papers were written by Chesterfield. But the just resentment of Johnson was not to be so appeased. In a letter written with singular energy and dignity of thought and language, he repelled the tardy advances of his patron. The Dictionary came forth without a dedication. In the preface the author truly declared that he owed nothing to the great, and described the difficulties with which he had been left to struggle so forcibly and pathetically that the ablest and most malevolent of all the enemies of his fame, Horne Tooke, never could read that passage without tears.

The public, on this occasion, did Johnson full justice, and something more than justice. The best lexicographer may well be content if his productions are received by the world with cold esteem. But Johnson's Dictionary was hailed with an enthusiasm such as no similar work has ever excited. It was, indeed, the first dictionary which could be read with pleasure. The definitions show so much acuteness of thought and command of language, and the passages quoted from poets, divines, and philosophers, are so skilfully selected, that a leisure hour may always be very agreeably spent in turning over the pages. The faults of the book resolve themselves, for the most part, into one great fault. Johnson was a wretched etymologist. He knew little or nothing of any Teutonic language except English, which, indeed, as he wrote it, was scarcely a Teutonic language ; and thus he was absolutely at the mercy of Junius and Skinner.

The Dictionary, though it raised Johnson's fame, added nothing to his pecuniary means. The fifteen hundred guineas which the booksellers had agreed to pay him had been advanced and spent before the last sheets issued from the press. It is painful to relate that, twice in the course of the year which followed the publication of this great work, he was arrested and carried to sponging-houses, and that he was twice indebted for his liberty to his excellent friend Richardson. It was still necessary for the man who had been formally saluted by the highest authority as Dictator of the English language to supply his wants by constant toil. He abridged his Dictionary. He proposed to bring out an edition of Shakespeare by subscription ; and many subscribers sent in their names and laid down their money ; but he soon found the task so little to his taste that he turned to more attractive employments. He contributed many papers to a new monthly journal, which was called the " Literary Magazine." Few of these papers have much interest ; but among them was the very best thing that he ever wrote, a masterpiece both of reasoning and of satirical pleasantry, the review of Jenyns's " Inquiry into the Nature and Origin of Evil."

In the spring of 1758, Johnson put forth the first of a series of essays, entitled the " Idler." During two years these essays continued to appear weekly. They were eagerly read, widely circulated, and, indeed, impudently pirated while they were still in the original form, and had a large sale when collected into volumes. The " Idler " may be described as a second part of the " Rambler," somewhat livelier and somewhat weaker than the first part.

While Johnson was busied with his " Idlers," his mother, who had accomplished her ninetieth year, died at Lichfield. It was long since he had seen her ; but he had not failed to contribute largely, out of his small means, to her comfort. In order to defray the charges of her funeral, and to pay some debts which she had left, he wrote a little book in a single week, and sent off the sheets to the press without reading them over. A hundred pounds were paid him for the copyright ; and the purchasers had great cause to be pleased with their bargain ; for the book was "Rasselas."

The success of "Rasselas" was great, though such ladies as Miss Lydia Languish must have been grievously disappointed when they found that the new volume from the circulating library was little more than a dissertation on the author's favorite theme, the Vanity of Human Wishes ; that the Prince of Abyssinia was without a mistress, and the Princess without a lover ; and that the story set the hero and the heroine down exactly where it had taken them up. The style was the subject of much eager controversy. The "Monthly Review" and the "Critical Review" took different sides. Many readers pronounced the writer a pompous pedant, who would never use a word of two syllables where it was possible to use a word of six, and who could not make a waiting-woman relate her adventures without balancing every noun with another noun, and every epithet with another epithet. Another party, not less zealous, cited with delight numerous passages in which weighty meaning was expressed with accuracy and illustrated with splendor. And both the censure and the praise were merited.

About the plan of "Rasselas" little was said by the critics ; and yet the faults of the plan might seem to invite severe criticism. Johnson has frequently blamed Shakespeare for neglecting the proprieties of time and place, and for ascribing to one age or nation the manners and opinions of another. Yet Shakespeare has not sinned in this way more grievously than Johnson. Rasselas and Imlac, Nekayah and Pekuah, are evidently meant to be Abyssinians of the eighteenth century ; for the Europe which Imlac describes is the Europe of the eighteenth century ; and the inmates of the Happy Valley talk familiarly of that law of gravitation which Newton discovered, and which was not fully received even at Cambridge till the eighteenth century. What a real company of Abyssinians would have been may be learned from Bruce's Travels. But Johnson, not content with turning filthy savages, ignorant of their letters, and gorged with raw steaks cut from living cows, into philosophers as eloquent and enlightened as himself or his friend Burke, and into ladies as highly accomplished as Mrs. Lennox or Mrs. Sheridan, transferred the whole domestic system of England to Egypt. Into a land of harems, a land of polygamy, a land where women are married without ever being seen, he introduced the flirtations and jealousies of our ballrooms. In a land where there is boundless liberty of divorce, wedlock is described as the indissoluble compact. "A youth and maiden meeting by chance, or brought together by artifice, exchange glances, reciprocate civilities, go home, and dream of each other. Such," says Rasselas, "is the common process of marriage." Such it may have been, and may still be, in London, but assuredly not at Cairo. A writer who was guilty of such improprieties had little right to blame the poet who made Hector quote Aristotle, and represented Julio Romano as flourishing in the days of the oracle of Delphi.

By such exertions as have been described, Johnson supported himself till the year 1762. In that year a great change in his circumstances took place. He had from a child been an enemy of the reigning dynasty. His Jacobite prejudices had been exhibited with little disguise both in his works and in his conversation. Even in his massy and elaborate Dictionary, he had, with a strange want of taste and judgment, inserted bitter and contumelious reflections on the Whig party. The excise, which was a favorite resource of Whig financiers, he had designated as a hateful tax. He had railed against the commissioners of excise in language so coarse that they had seriously thought of prosecuting him. He had with difficulty been prevented from holding up the Lord Privy Seal by name as an example of the meaning of the word "renegade." A pension he had defined as pay given to a state hireling to betray his country ; a pensioner as a slave of state hired by a stipend to obey a master. It seemed unlikely that the author of these definitions would himself be pensioned. But that was a time of wonders. George the Third had ascended the throne ; and had, in the course of a few months, disgusted many of the old friends and conciliated many of the old enemies of his house. The city was becoming mutinous. Oxford was becoming loyal. Cavendishes and Bentincks were murmuring. Somersets and Wyndhams were hastening to kiss hands. The head of the treasury was now Lord Bute, who was a Tory, and could have no objection to Johnson's Toryism. Bute wished to be thought a patron of men of letters ; and Johnson was one of the most eminent and one of the most needy men of letters in Europe. A pension of three hundred a year was graciously offered, and with very little hesitation accepted.

This event produced a change in Johnson's whole way of life. For the first time since his boyhood he no longer felt the daily goad urging him to the daily toil. He was at liberty, after thirty years of anxiety and drudgery, to indulge his constitutional indolence, to lie in bed till two in the afternoon, and to sit up talking till four in the morning, without fearing either the printer's devil or the sheriff's officer.

One laborious task indeed he had bound himself to perform. He had received large subscriptions for his promised edition of Shakespeare ; he had lived on those subscriptions during some years ; and he could not without disgrace omit to perform his part of the contract. His friends repeatedly exhorted him to make an effort ; and he repeatedly resolved to do so. But, notwithstanding their exhortations and his resolutions, month followed month, year followed year, and nothing was done. He prayed fervently against his idleness ; he determined, as often as he received the sacrament, that he would no longer doze away and trifle away his time ; but the spell under which he lay resisted prayer and sacrament. His private notes at this time are made up of self-reproaches. "My indolence," he wrote on Easter-eve in 1764, "has sunk into grosser sluggishness. A kind of strange oblivion has overspread me, so that I know not what has become of the last year." Easter 1765 came, and found him still in the same state. "My time," he wrote, "has been unprofitably spent, and seems as a dream that has left nothing behind. My memory grows confused, and I know not how the days pass over me." Happily for his honor, the charm which held him captive was at length broken by no gentle or friendly hand. He had been weak enough to pay serious attention to a story about a ghost which haunted a house in Cock Lane, and had actually gone himself, with some of his friends, at one in the morning, to St. John's Church, Clerkenwell, in the hope of receiving a communication from the perturbed spirit. But the spirit, though adjured with all solemnity, remained obstinately silent ; and it soon appeared that a naughty girl of eleven had been amusing herself by making fools of so many philosophers. Churchill, who, confident in his powers, drunk with popularity, and burning with party spirit, was looking for some man of established fame and Tory politics to insult, celebrated the Cock Lane Ghost in three cantos, nicknamed Johnson Pomposo, asked where the book was which had been so long promised and so liberally paid for, and directly accused the great moralist of cheating. This terrible word proved effectual ; and in October, 1765, appeared, after a delay of nine years, the new edition of Shakespeare.

This publication saved Johnson's character for honesty, but added nothing to the fame of his abilities and learning. The preface, though it contains some good passages, is not in his best manner. The most valuable notes are those in which he had an opportunity of showing how attentively he had during many years observed human life and human nature. The best specimen is the note on the character of Polonius. Nothing so

good is to be found even in Wilhelm Meister's admirable ex·
amination of Hamlet. But here praise must end. It would
be difficult to name a more slovenly, a more worthless edition
of any great classic. The reader may turn over play after play
without finding one happy conjectural emendation, or one ingenious and satisfactory explanation of a passage which had
baffled preceding commentators. Johnson had, in his Prospectus, told the world that he was peculiarly fitted for the
task whch he had undertaken, because he had, as a lexicographer, been under the necessity of taking a wider view of the
English language than any of his predecessors. That his
knowledge of our literature was extensive is indisputable. But,
unfortunately, he had altogether neglected that very part of our
literature with which it is especially desirable that an editor of
Shakespeare should be conversant. It is dangerous to assert a
negative. Yet little will be risked by the assertion, that in the
two folio volumes of the English Dictionary there is not a
single passage quoted from any dramatist of the Elizabethan
age except Shakespeare and Ben. Even from Ben the quota-,
tions are few. Johnson might easily, in a few months, have
made himself well acquainted with every old play that was ex·
tant. But it never seems to have occurred to him that this
was a necessary preparation for the work which he had undertaken. He would doubtless have admitted that it would be
the height of absurdity in a man who was not familiar with the
works of Æschylus and Euripides to publish an edition of
Sophocles. Yet he ventured to publish an edition of Shakespeare, without having ever in his life, as far as can be discovered, read a single scene of Massinger, Ford, Decker, Webster,
Marlow, Beaumont, or Fletcher. His detractors were noisy
and scurrilous. Those who most loved and honored him had
little to say in praise of the manner in which he had discharged
the duty of a commentator. He had, however, acquitted himself of a debt which had long lain heavy on his conscience, and
he sank back into the repose from which the sting of satire had
roused him. He long continued to live upon the fame which
he had already won. He was honored by the University of
Oxford with a Doctor's degree, by the Royal Academy with a
professorship, and by the king with an interview, in which his
Majesty most graciously expressed a hope that so excellent a
writer would not cease to write. In the interval, however,
between 1765 and 1775 Johnson published only two or three
political tracts, the longest of which he could have produced in
forty-eight hours, if he had worked as he worked on the " Life
of Savage" and on " Rasselas."

But though his pen was now idle, his tongue was active. The influence exercised by his conversation, directly upon those with whom he lived, and directly on the whole literary world, was altogether without a parallel. His colloquial talents were indeed of the highest order. He had strong sense, quick discernment, wit, humor, immense knowledge of literature and of life, and an infinite store of curious anecdotes. As respected style, he spoke far better than he wrote. Every sentence which dropped from his lips was as correct in structure as the most nicely balanced period of the "Rambler." But in his talk there were no pompous triads, and little more than a fair proportion of words in *osity* and *ation*. All was simplicity, ease, and vigor. He uttered his short, weighty, and pointed sentences with a power of voice and a justness and energy of emphasis of which the effect was rather increased than diminished by the rollings of his huge form, and by the asthmatic gaspings and puffings in which the peals of his eloquence generally ended. Nor did the laziness which made him unwilling to sit down to his desk prevent him from giving instruction or entertainment orally. To discuss questions of taste, of learning, of casuistry, in language so exact and so forcible that it might have been printed without the alteration of a word, was to him no exertion, but a pleasure. He loved, as he said, to fold his legs and have his talk out. He was ready to bestow the overflowings of his full mind on anybody who would start a subject, on a fellow-passenger in a stage coach, or on the person who sat at the same table with him in an eating-house. But his conversation was nowhere so brilliant and striking as when he was surrounded by a few friends, whose abilities and knowledge enabled them, as he once expressed it, to send him back every ball that he threw. Some of these, in 1764, formed themselves into a club, which gradually became a formidable power in the commonwealth of letters. The verdicts pronounced by this conclave on new books were speedily known over all London, and were sufficient to sell off a whole edition in a day, or to condemn the sheets to the service of the trunkmaker and the pastry-cook. Nor shall we think this strange when we consider what great and various talents and acquirements met in the little fraternity. Goldsmith was the representative of poetry and light literature, Reynolds of the arts, Burke of political eloquence and political philosophy. There, too, were Gibbon, the greatest historian, and Jones, the greatest linguist, of the age. Garrick brought to the meetings his inexhaustible pleasantry, his incomparable mimicry, and his consummate knowledge of stage effect. Among the most constant

attendants were two high-born and high-bred gentlemen, closely bound together by friendship, but of widely different characters and habits ; Bennet Langton, distinguished by his skill
in Greek literature, by the orthodoxy of his opinions, and by
the sanctity of his life ; and Topham Beauclerk, renowned for
his amours, his knowledge of the gay world, his fastidious
taste, and his sarcastic wit.   To predominate over such a society was not easy.   Yet even over such a society Johnson predominated.   Burke might indeed have disputed the supremacy
to which others were under the necessity of submitting.
But Burke, though not generally a very patient listener, was
content to take the second part when Johnson was present ;
and the club itself, consisting of so many eminent men, is to
this day popularly designated as Johnson's club.

Among the members of this celebrated body was one to
whom it has owed the greater part of its celebrity, yet who was
regarded with little respect by his brethren, and had not without difficulty obtained a seat among them.   This was James
Boswell, a young Scotch lawyer, heir to an honorable name
and a fair estate.   That he was a coxcomb and a bore, weak,
vain, pushing, curious, garrulous, was obvious to all who
were acquainted with him.   That he could not reason, that he
had no wit, no humor, no eloquence, is apparent from his writings.   And yet his writings are read beyond the Mississippi,
and under the Southern Cross, and are likely to be read as
long as the English exist, either as a living or as a dead language.   Nature had made him a slave and an idolater.   His
mind resembled those creepers which the botanists call para-
sites, and which can subsist only by clinging round the stems
and imbibing the juices of stronger plants.   He must have
fastened himself on somebody.   He might have fastened himself on Wilkes, and have become the fiercest patriot in the Bill
of Rights Society.   He might have fastened himself on Whitefield, and have become the loudest field preacher among the
Calvinistic Methodists.   In a happy hour he fastened himself
on Johnson.   The pair might seem ill matched ; for Johnson
had early been prejudiced against Boswell's country.   To a
man of Johnson's strong understanding and irritable temper
the silly egotism and adulation of Boswell must have been as
teasing as the constant buzz of a fly.   Johnson hated to be
questioned ; and Boswell was eternally catechising him on all
kinds of subjects, and sometimes propounded such questions
as, " What would you do, sir, if you were locked up in a tower
with a baby ?"   Johnson was a water-drinker and Boswell was
a winebibber, and indeed little better than a habitual sot.   It

was impossible that there should be perfect harmony between two such companions. Indeed, the great man was sometimes provoked into fits of passion, in which he said things which the small man, during a few hours, seriously resented. Every quarrel, however, was soon made up. During twenty years the disciple continued to worship the master : the master continued to scold the disciple, to sneer at him, and to love him. The two friends ordinarily resided at a great distance from each other. Boswell practised in the Parliament House of Edinburgh, and could pay only occasional visits to London. During those visits his chief business was to watch Johnson, to discover all Johnson's habits, to turn the conversation to subjects about which Johnson was likely to say something remarkable, and to fill quarto note-books with minutes of what Johnson had said. In this way were gathered the materials out of which was afterwards constructed the most interesting biographical work in the world.

Soon after the club began to exist, Johnson formed a connection less important indeed to his fame, but much more important to his happiness, than his connection with Boswell. Henry Thrale, one of the most opulent brewers in the kingdom, a man of sound and cultivated understanding, rigid principles, and liberal spirit, was married to one of those clever, kind-hearted, engaging, vain, pert, young women, who are perpetually doing or saying what is not exactly right, but who, do or say what they may, are always agreeable. In 1765 the Thrales became acquainted with Johnson, and the acquaintance ripened fast into friendship. They were astonished and delighted by the brilliancy of his conversation. They were flattered by finding that a man so widely celebrated preferred their house to any other in London. Even the peculiarities which seemed to unfit him for civilized society, his gesticulations, his rollings, his puffings, his mutterings, the strange way in which he put on his clothes, the ravenous eagerness with which he devoured his dinner, his fits of melancholy, his fits of anger, his frequent rudeness, his occasional ferocity, increased the interest which his new associates took in him. For these things were the cruel marks left behind by a life which had been one long conflict with disease and with adversity. In a vulgar hack writer such oddities would have excited only disgust. But in a man of genius, learning, and virtue their effect was to add pity to admiration and esteem. Johnson soon had an apartment at the brewery in Southwark, and a still more pleasant apartment at the villa of his friends on Streatham Common. A large part of every year he passed in those abodes, abodes which must have seemed magnificent and luxurious indeed, when compared with the dens in which he had generally been lodged.   But his chief pleasures were derived from what the astronomer of his Abyssinian tale called " the endearing elegance of female friendship."   Mrs. Thrale rallied him, soothed him, coaxed him, and, if she sometimes provoked him by her flippancy, made ample amends by listening to his reproofs with angelic sweetness of temper.   When he was diseased in body and in mind, she was the most tender of nurses.   No comfort that wealth could purchase, no contrivance that womanly ingenuity, set to work by womanly compassion, could devise was wanting to his sick-room.   He requited her kindness by an affection pure as the affection of a father, yet delicately tinged with a gallantry which, though awkward, must have been more flattering than the attentions of a crowd of the fools who gloried in the names, now obsolete, of Buck and Maccaroni. It should seem that a full half of Johnson's life, during about sixteen years, was passed under the roof of the Thrales.   He accompanied the family sometimes to Bath and sometimes to Brighton, once to Wales and once to Paris.   But he had at the same time a house in one of the narrow and gloomy courts on the north of Fleet Street.   In the garrets was his library, a large and miscellaneous collection of books, falling to pieces and begrimed with dust.   On a lower floor he sometimes, but very rarely, regaled a friend with a plain dinner—a veal pie, or a leg of lamb and spinage, and a rice pudding.   Nor was the dwelling uninhabited during his long absences.   It was the home of the most extraordinary assemblage of inmates that ever was brought together.   At the head of the establishment Johnson had placed an old lady named Williams, whose chief recommendations were her blindness and her poverty.   But, in spite of her murmurs and reproaches, he gave an asylum to another lady who was as poor as herself, Mrs. Desmoulins, whose family he had known many years before in Staffordshire. Room was found for the daughter of Mrs. Desmoulins, and for another destitute damsel, who was generally addressed as Miss Carmichael, but whom her generous host called Polly.   An old quack doctor named Levett, who bled and dosed coal-heavers and hackney coachmen, and received for fees crusts of bread, bits of bacon, glasses of gin, and sometimes a little copper, completed this strange menagerie.   All these poor creatures were at constant war with each other, and with Johnson's negro servant Frank.   Sometimes, indeed, they transferred their hostilities from the servant to the master, complained that a better table was not kept for them, and railed or maundered

till their benefac.or was glad to make his escape to Streatham
or to the Mitre Tavern. And yet he, who was generally the
haughtiest and most irritable of mankind, who was but too
prompt to resent any thing which looked like a slight on the
part of a purse-proud bookseller, or of a noble and powerful
patron, bore patiently from mendicants, who, but for his
bounty, must have gone to the workhouse, insults more provoking than those for which he had knocked down Osborne
and bidden defiance to Chesterfield. Year after year Mrs.
Williams and Mrs. Desmoulins, Polly and Levett, continued to
torment him and to live upon him.

The course of life which has been described was interrupted in Johnson's sixty-fourth year by an important event. He
had early read an account of the Hebrides, and had been much
interested by learning that there was so near him a land peopled by a race which was still as rude and simple as in the
middle ages. A wish to become intimately acquainted with a
state of society so utterly unlike all that he had ever seen frequently crossed his mind. But it is not probable that his curiosity would have overcome his habitual sluggishness, and his
love of the smoke, the mud, and the cries of London, had not
Boswell importuned him to attempt the adventure, and offered
to be his squire. At length, in August 1773, Johnson crossed
the Highland line, and plunged courageously into what was
then considered by most Englishmen as a dreary and perilous
wilderness. After wandering about two months through the
Celtic region, sometimes in rude boats which did not protect
him from the rain, and sometimes on small shaggy ponies
which could hardly bear his weight, he returned to his old
haunts with a mind full of new images and new theories. During the following year he employed himself in recording his adventures. About the beginning of 1775 his "Journey to the
Hebrides" was published, and was, during some weeks, the
chief subject of conversation in all circles in which any attention was paid to literature. The book is still read with pleasure. The narrative is entertaining; the speculations, whether
sound or unsound, are always ingenious; and the style, though
too stiff and pompous, is somewhat easier and more graceful
than that of his early writings. His prejudice against the
Scotch had at length become little more than matter of jest;
and whatever remained of the old feeling had been effectually
removed by the kind and respectful hospitality with which he
had been received in every part of Scotland. It was, of
course, not to be expected that an Oxonian Tory should praise
the Presbyterian polity and ritual, or that an eye accustomed to

the hedgerows and parks of England should not be struck by the bareness of Berwickshire and East Lothian. But even in censure Johnson's tone is not unfriendly. The most enlightened Scotchmen, with Lord Mansfield at their head, were well pleased. But some foolish and ignorant Scotchmen were moved to anger by a little unpalatable truth which was mingled with much eulogy, and assailed him whom they chose to consider as the enemy of their country with libels much more dishonorable to their country than any thing that he had ever said or written. They published paragraphs in the newspapers, articles in the magazines, sixpenny pamphlets, five-shilling books. One scribbler abused Johnson for being blear-eyed, another for being a pensioner ; a third informed the world that one of the Doctor's uncles had been convicted of felony in Scotland, and had found that there was in that country one tree capable of supporting the weight of an Englishman. Macpherson, whose Fingal had been proved in the Journey to be an impudent forgery, threatened to take vengeance with a cane. The only effect of this threat was that Johnson reiterated the charge of forgery in the most contemptuous terms, and walked about, during some time, with a cudgel, which, if the impostor had not been too wise to encounter it, would assuredly have descended upon him, to borrow the sublime language of his own epic poem, ''like a hammer on the red son of the furnace.''

Of other assailants Johnson took no notice whatever. He had early resolved never to be drawn into controversy ; and he adhered to his resolution with a steadfastness which is the more extraordinary, because he was, both intellectually and morally, of the stuff of which controversialists are made. In conversation he was a singularly eager, acute, and pertinacious disputant. When at a loss for good reasons he had recourse to sophistry ; and when heated by altercation he made unsparing use of sarcasm and invective. But when he took his pen in hand his whole character seemed to be changed. A hundred bad writers misrepresented him and reviled him ; but not one of the hundred could boast of having been thought by him worthy of a refutation, or even of a retort. The Kenricks, Campbells, MacNicols, and Hendersons, did their best to annoy him, in the hope that he would give them importance by answering them. But the reader will in vain search his works for any allusion to Kenrick or Campbell, to MacNicol or Henderson. One Scotchman, bent on vindicating the fame of Scotch learning, defied him to the combat in a detestable Latin hexameter.

'' Maxime, si tu vis, cupio contendere tecum.''

But Johnson took no notice of the challenge. He had learned, both from his own observation and from literary history, in which he was deeply read, that the place of books in the public estimation is fixed, not by what is written about them, but by what is written in them ; and that an author whose works are likely to live is very unwise if he stoops to wrangle with detractors whose works are certain to die. He always maintained that fame was a shuttlecock, which could be kept up only by being beaten back as well as beaten forward, and which would soon fall if there were only one battledore. No saying was oftener in his mouth than that fine apothegm of Bentley, that no man was ever written down but by himself.

Unhappily, a few months after the appearance of the " Journey to the Hebrides," Johnson did what none of his envious assailants could have done, and to a certain extent succeeded in writing himself down. The disputes between England and her American colonies had reached a point at which no amicable adjustment was possible. Civil war was evidently impending ; and the ministers seem to have thought that the eloquence of Johnson might with advantage be employed to inflame the nation against the opposition here, and against the rebels beyond the Atlantic. He had already written two or three tracts in defence of the foreign and domestic policy of the government ; and those tracts, though hardly worthy of him, were much superior to the crowd of pamphlets which lay on the counters of Almon and Stockdale. But his " Taxation No Tyranny" was a pitiable failure. The very title was a silly phrase, which can have been recommended to his choice by nothing but a jingling alliteration which he ought to have despised. The arguments were such as boys use in debating societies. The pleasantry was as awkward as the gambols of a hippopotamus. Even Boswell was forced to own that, in this unfortunate piece, he could detect no trace of his master's powers. The general opinion was that the strong faculties which had produced the Dictionary and the " Rambler" were beginning to feel the effect of time and of disease, and that the old man would best consult his credit by writing no more.

But this was a great mistake. Johnson had failed, not because his mind was less vigorous than when he wrote " Rasselas" in the evenings of a week, but because he had foolishly chosen, or suffered others to choose for him, a subject such as he would at no time have been competent to treat. He was in no sense a statesman. He never willingly read or thought or talked about affairs of state. He loved biography, literary history, the history of manners ; but political history was positively distasteful to him. The question, at issue between the colonies and the mother country was a question about which he had really nothing to say. He failed, therefore, as the greatest men must fail when they attempt to do that for which they are unfit ; as Burke would have failed if Burke had tried to write comedies like those of Sheridan ; as Reynolds would have failed if Reynolds had tried to paint landscapes like those of Wilson. Happily, Johnson soon had an opportunity of proving most signally that his failure was not to be ascribed to intellectual decay.

On Easter-eve 1777, some persons, deputed by a meeting which consisted of forty of the first booksellers in London, called upon him. Though he had some scruples about doing business at that season, he received his visitors with much civility. They came to inform him that a new edition of the English poets, from Cowley downwards, was in contemplation, and to ask him to furnish short biographical prefaces. He readily undertook the task, a task for which he was pre-eminently qualified. His knowledge of the literary history of England since the Restoration was unrivalled. That knowledge he had derived partly from books, and partly from sources which had long been closed ; from old Grub Street traditions ; from the talk of forgotten poetasters and pamphleteers who had long been lying in parish vaults ; from the recollections of such men as Gilbert Walmesley, who had conversed with the wits of Button ; Cibber, who had mutilated the plays of two generations of dramatists ; Orrery, who had been admitted to the society of Swift ; and Savage, who had rendered services of no very honorable kind to Pope. The biographer therefore sat down to his task with a mind full of matter. He had at first intended to give only a paragraph to every minor poet, and only four or five pages to the greatest name. But the flood of anecdote and criticism overflowed the narrow channel. The work, which was originally meant to consist only of a few sheets, swelled into ten volumes, small volumes, it is true, and not closely printed. The first four appeared in 1779, the remaining six in 1781.

The " Lives of the Poets" are, on the whole, the best of Johnson's works. The narratives are as entertaining as any novel. The remarks on life and on human nature are eminently shrewd and profound. The criticisms are often excellent, and, even when grossly and provokingly unjust, well deserve to be studied. For, however erroneous they may be, they are never silly. They are the judgments of a mind trammelled by prejudice and deficient in sensibility, but vigorous and acute. They therefore generally contain a portion of valuable truth which deserves to be separated from the alloy ; and, at the very worst, they mean something, a praise to which much of what is called criticism in our time has no pretensions.

Savage's Life, Johnson reprinted nearly as it had appeared in 1744. Whoever, after reading that life, will turn to the other lives, will be struck by the difference of style. Since Johnson had been at ease in his circumstances he had written little and had talked much. When, therefore, he, after the lapse of years, resumed his pen, the mannerism which he had contracted while he was in the constant habit of elaborate composition was less perceptible than formerly ; and his diction frequently had a colloquial ease which it had formerly wanted. The improvement may be discerned by a skilful critic in the "Journey to the Hebrides," and in the "Lives of the Poets" is so obvious that it cannot escape the notice of the most careless reader.

Among the Lives the best are perhaps those of Cowley, Dryden, and Pope. The very worst is, beyond all doubt, that of Gray.

This great work at once became popular. There was, indeed, much just and much unjust censure ; but even those who were loudest in blame were attracted by the book in spite of themselves. Malone computed the gains of the publishers at five or six thousand pounds. But the writer was very poorly remunerated. Intending at first to write very short prefaces, he had stipulated for only two hundred guineas. The booksellers, when they saw how far his performance had surpassed his promise, added only another hundred. Indeed Johnson, though he did not despise or affect to despise money, and though his strong sense and long experience ought to have qualified him to protect his own interests, seems to have been singularly unskilful and unlucky in his literary bargains. He was generally reputed the first English writer of his time. Yet several writers of his time sold their copyrights for sums such as he never ventured to ask. To give a single instance, Robertson received four thousand five hundred pounds for the "History of Charles V.," and it is no disrespect to the memory of Robertson to say that the "History of Charles V." is both a less valuable and a less amusing book than the "Lives of the Poets."

Johnson was now in his seventy-second year. The infirmities of age were coming fast upon him. That inevitable event, of which he never thought without horror, was brought near to him ; and his whole life was darkened by the shadow of death.

He had often to pay the cruel price of longevity.   Every year
he lost what could never be replaced.   The strange dependents to whom he had given shelter, and to whom, in spite of
their faults, he was strongly attached by habit, dropped off
one by one ; and, in the silence of his home, he regretted even
the noise of their scolding matches.   The kind and generous
Thrale was no more ; and it would have been well if his wife
had been laid beside him.   But she survived to be the laughing-stock of those who had envied her, and to draw from the
eyes of the old man who had loved her beyond any thing in the
world, tears far more bitter than he would have shed over her
grave.   With some estimable and many agreeable qualities,
she was not made to be independent.   The control of a mind
more steadfast than her own was necessary to her respectability.   While she was restrained by her husband, a man of sense
and firmness indulgent to her taste in trifles, but always the undisputed master of his house, her worst offences had been impertinent jokes, white lies, and short fits of pettishness ending
in sunny good-humor.   But he was gone ; and she was left an
opulent widow of forty, with strong sensibility, volatile fancy,
and slender judgment.   She soon fell in love with a music-mas-
ter from Brescia, in whom nobody but herself could discover any
thing to admire.   Her pride, and perhaps some better feelings,
struggled hard against this degrading passion.   But the struggle irritated her nerves, soured her temper, and at length en-
dangered her health.   Conscious that her choice was one
which Johnson could not approve, she became desirous to
escape from his inspection.   Her manner towards him changed.
She was sometimes cold and sometimes petulant.   She did not
conceal her joy when he left Streatham : she never pressed
him to return ; and if he came unbidden she received him in a
manner which convinced him that he was no longer a welcome
guest.   He took the very intelligible hints which she gave.
He read, for the last time, a chapter of the Greek Testament
in the library which had been formed by himself.   In a solemn
and tender prayer he commended the house and its inmates to
the Divine protection, and, with emotions which choked his
voice and convulsed his powerful frame, left forever that beloved home for the gloomy and desolate house behind Fleet
Street, where the few and evil days which still remained to him
were to run out.   Here, in June 1783, he had a paralytic
stroke, from which, however, he recovered, and which does not
appear to have at all impaired his intellectual faculties.   But
other maladies came thick upon him.   His asthma tormented
him day and night.   Dropsical symptoms made their appear-

ance. While sinking under a complication of diseases, he heard that the woman whose friendship had been the chief happiness of sixteen years of his life, had married an Italian fiddler ; that all London was crying shame upon her ; and that the newspapers and magazines were filled with allusions to the Ephesian matron and the two pictures in Hamlet. He vehemently said that he would try to forget her existence. He never uttered her name. Every memorial of her which met his eye he flung into the fire. She meanwhile fled from the laughter and hisses of her countrymen and countrywomen to a land where she was unknown, hastened across Mont Cenis, and learned, while passing a merry Christmas of concerts and lemonade parties at Milan, that the great man with whose name hers is inseparably associated had ceased to exist.

He had, in spite of much mental and much bodily affliction, clung vehemently to life. The feeling described in that fine but gloomy paper which closes the series of his "Idlers" seemed to grow stronger in him as his last hour drew near. He fancied that he should be able to draw his breath more easily in a southern climate, and would probably have set out for Rome and Naples but for his fear of the expense of the journey. That expense, indeed, he had the means of defraying ; for he had laid up about two thousand pounds, the fruit of labors which had made the fortune of several publishers. But he was unwilling to break in upon this hoard, and he seems to have wished even to keep its existence a secret. Some of his friends hoped that the government might be induced to increase his pension to six hundred pounds a year, but this hope was disappointed, and he resolved to stand one English winter more. That winter was his last. His legs grew weaker ; his breath grew shorter ; the fatal water gathered fast, in spite of incisions which he, courageous against pain, but timid against death, urged his surgeons to make deeper and deeper. Though the tender care which had mitigated his sufferings during months of sickness at Streatham was withdrawn, he was not left desolate. The ablest physicians and surgeons attended him, and refused to accept fees from him. Burke parted from him with deep emotion. Windham sat much in the sick-room, arranged the pillows, and sent his own servant to watch at night by the bed. Frances Burney, whom the old man had cherished with fatherly kindness, stood weeping at the door ; while Langton, whose piety eminently qualified him to be an adviser and comforter at such a time, received the last pressure of his friend's hand within. When at length the moment, dreaded through so many years, came close, the dark cloud passed away from

Johnson's mind.   His temper became unusually patient and gentle ; he ceased to think with terror of death and of that which lies beyond death ; and he spoke much of the mercy of God and of the propitiation of Christ.   In this serene frame of mind he died on the 13th of December, 1784.   He was laid, a week later, in Westminster Abbey, among the eminent men of whom he had been the historian—Cowley and Denham, Dryden and Congreve, Gay, Prior, and Addison.

Since his death the popularity of his works—the " Lives of the Poets," and, perhaps, the " Vanity of Human Wishes" excepted—has greatly diminished.   His Dictionary has been altered by editors till it can scarcely be called his.   An allusion to his " Rambler" or his " Idler" is not readily apprehended in literary circles.   The fame even of " Rasselas" has grown somewhat dim. But though the celebrity of the writings may have declined, the celebrity of the writer, strange to say, is as great as ever. Boswell's book has done for him more than the best of his own books could do.   The memory of other authors is kept alive by their works.   But the memory of Johnson keeps many of his works alive.   The old philosopher is still among us in the brown coat with the metal buttons and the shirt which ought to be at wash, blinking, puffing, rolling his head, drumming with his fingers, tearing his meat like a tiger, and swallowing his tea in oceans.   No human being who has been more than seventy years in the grave is so well known to us.   And it is but just to say that our intimate acquaintance with what he would himself have called the anfractuosities of his intellect and of his temper, serves only to strengthen our conviction that he was both a great and a good man.

THE CHIEF

LIVES OF THE POETS.

BY

DR. SAMUEL JOHNSON.

DR. SAMUEL JOHNSON ON MILTON.

THE life of Milton has been already written in so many forms, and with such minute inquiry, that I might perhaps more properly have contented myself with the addition of a few notes on Mr. Fenton's elegant Abridgment, but that a new narrative was thought necessary to the uniformity of this edition.

JOHN MILTON was by birth a gentleman, descended from the proprietors of Milton, near Thame, in Oxfordshire, one of whom forfeited his estate in the times of York and Lancaster. Which side he took I know not ; his descendant inherited no veneration for the White Rose.

His grandfather, John, was keeper of the forest of Shot-over, a zealous papist, who disinherited his son because he had forsaken the religion of his ancestors.

His father, John, who was the son disinherited, had recourse for his support to the profession of a scrivener. He was a man eminent for his skill in music, many of his compositions being still to be found ; and his reputation in his profession was such that he grew rich, and retired to an estate. He had probably more than common literature, as his son addresses him in one of his most elaborate Latin poems. He married a gentlewoman of the name of Caston, a Welsh family, by whom he had two sons—John, the poet, and Christopher, who studied the law, and adhered, as the law taught him, to the king's party, for which he was a while persecuted ; but having, by his brother's interest, obtained permission to live in quiet, he supported himself so honorably by chamber practice, that, soon after the accession of King James, he was knighted, and made a judge ; but, his constitution being too weak for business, he retired before any disreputable compliances became necessary.

He had likewise a daughter, Anne, whom he married with considerable fortune to Edward Philips, who came from Shrewsbury, and rose in the Crown Office to be secondary : by him she had two sons, John and Edward, who were educated by the poet, and from whom is derived the only authentic account of his domestic manners.

John, the poet, was born in his father's house, at the Spread Eagle, in Bread Street, December 9, 1608, between six and seven in the morning. His father appears to have been very, solicitous about his education ; for he was instructed at first by private tuition, under the care of Thomas Young, who was afterwards chaplain to the English merchants at Hamburg, and of whom we have reason to think well, since his scholar considered him as worthy of an epistolary elegy.

He was then sent to St. Paul's School, under the care of Mr. Gill ; and removed, in the beginning of his sixteenth year, to Christ's College, in Cambridge, where he entered a sizar, February 12, 1624.

He was at this time eminently skilled in the Latin tongue : and he himself, by annexing the dates to his first compositions, a boast of which the learned Politian had given him an example, seems to commend the earliness of his own proficiency to the notice of posterity. But the products of his vernal fertility have been surpassed by many, and particularly by his contemporary Cowley. Of the powers of the mind it is difficult to form an estimate : many have excelled Milton in their first essays, who never rose to works like " Paradise Lost."

At fifteen, a date which he uses till he is sixteen, he translated or versified two Psalms, 114 and 136, which he thought worthy of the public eye ; but they raise no great expectations : they would in any numerous school have obtained praise, but not excited wonder.

Many of his elegies appear to have been written in his eighteenth year, by which it appears that he had then read the Roman authors with very nice discernment. I once heard Mr. Hampton, the translator of Polybius, remark, what I think is true, that Milton was the first Englishman who, after the revival of letters, wrote Latin verses with classic elegance. If any exceptions can be made, they are very few : Haddon and Ascham, the pride of Elizabeth's reign, however they have succeeded in prose, no sooner attempt verse than they provoke derision. If we produced any thing worthy of notice before the elegies of Milton, it was perhaps " Alabaster's Roxana."

Of the exercises which the rules of the University required, some were published by him in his maturer years. They had been undoubtedly applauded, for they were such as few can perform ; yet there is reason to suspect that he was regarded in his college with no great fondness. That he obtained no fellowship is certain ; but the unkindness with which he was treated was not merely negative. I am ashamed to relate, what I fear is true, that Milton was one of the last students in either University that suffered the public indignity of corporal correction.

It was, in the violence of controversial hostility, objected

to him, that he was expelled : this he steadily denies, and it
was apparently not true ; but it seems plain, from his own
verses to Diodati, that he had incurred *rustication*, a temporary dismission into the country, with perhaps the loss of a
term :

> " Me tenet urbs refluâ quam Thamesis alluit undâ,
> Meque nec invitum patria dulcis habet.
> Jam nec arundiferum mihi cura revisere Camum,
> Nec dudum *vetiti* me *laris* angit amor.—
> Nec duri libet usque minas perferre magistri,
> Cæteraque ingenio non subeunda meo.
> Si sit hoc *exilium* patrios adiisse penates,
> Et vacuum curis otia grata sequi,
> Non ego vel *profugi* nomen sortemve recuso,
> Lætus et *exilii* conditione fruor."

I cannot find any meaning but this, which even kindness and
reverence can give the term *vetiti laris*, " a habitation from
which he is excluded ;" or how *exile* can be otherwise interpreted. He declares yet more that he is weary of enduring
*the threats of a rigorous master, and something else, which a
temper like his cannot undergo.* What was more than threat
was probably punishment. This poem, which mentions his
exile, proves likewise that it was not perpetual ; for it concludes with a resolution of returning some time to Cambridge.
And it may be conjectured, from the willingness with which he
has perpetuated the memory of his exile, that its cause was
such as gave him no shame.

He took both the usual degrees ; that of bachelor in 1628,
and that of master in 1632 ; but he left the University with no
kindness for its institution, alienated either by the injudicious
severity of his governors, or his own captious perverseness.
The cause cannot now be known, but the effect appears in his
writings. His scheme of education, inscribed to Hartlib,
supersedes all academical instruction, being intended to comprise the whole time which men usually spend in literature,
from their entrance upon grammar, *till they proceed, as it is
called, masters of arts.* And in his discourse *on the likeliest
way to remove hirelings out of the church*, he ingeniously proposes that " the profits of the lands forfeited by the act for
superstitious uses should be applied to such academies all over
the land, where languages and arts may be taught together ; so
that youth may be at once brought up to a competency of
learning and an honest trade, by which means such of them as
had the gift, being enabled to support themselves (without
tithes) by the latter, may, by the help of the former, become
worthy preachers."

One of his objections to academical education, as it was then conducted, is, that men designed for orders in the church were permitted to act plays, "writhing and unboning their clergy limbs to all the antic and dishonest gestures of Trinculos, buffoons, and bawds, prostituting the shame of that ministry which they had, or were near having, to the eyes of the courtiers and court ladies, their grooms and mademoiselles."

This is sufficiently peevish in a man who, when he mentions his exile from the college, relates, with great luxuriance, the compensation which the pleasures of the theatre afford him. Plays were therefore only criminal when they were acted by academics.

He went to the University with a design of entering into the church, but in time altered his mind ; for he declared that whoever became a clergyman must " subscribe slave, and take an oath withal, which, unless he took with a conscience that could not retch, he must straight perjure himself. He thought it better to prefer a blameless silence before the office of speaking, bought and begun with servitude and forswearing."

These expressions are, I find, applied to the subscription of the Articles ; but it seems more probable that they relate to canonical obedience. I know not any of the Articles which seem to thwart his opinions : but the thoughts of obedience, whether canonical or civil, raised his indignation.

His unwillingness to engage in the ministry, perhaps not yet advanced to a settled resolution of declining it, appears in a letter to one of his friends, who had reproved his suspended and dilatory life, which he seems to have imputed to an insatiable curiosity, and fantastic luxury of various knowledge. To this he writes a cool and plausible answer, in which he endeavors to persuade him that the delay proceeds not from the delights of desultory study, but from the desire of obtaining more fitness for his task ; and that he goes on, *not taking thought of being late, so it gives advantage to be more fit.*

When he left the University, he returned to his father, then residing at Horton, in Buckinghamshire, with whom he lived five years, in which time he is said to have read all the Greek and Latin writers. With what limitations this universality is to be understood, who shall inform us ?

It might be supposed that he who read so much should have done nothing else ; but Milton found time to write the "Mask of Comus," which was presented at Ludlow, then the residence of the Lord President of Wales, in 1634 ; and had the honor of being acted by the Earl of Bridgewater's sons and daughter. The fiction is derived from Homer's Circe ;

but we never can refuse to any modern the liberty of borrowing from Homer :

>   —— a quo ceu fonte perenni
> Vatum Pieriis ora rigantur aquis."

His next production was " Lycidas," an elegy, written in
1637, on the death of Mr. King, the son of Sir John King, secretary for Ireland in the time of Elizabeth, James, and Charles.
King was much a favorite at Cambridge, and many of the
wits joined to do honor to his memory. Milton's acquaintance with the Italian writers may be discovered by a mixture of
longer and shorter verses, according to the rules of Tuscan
poetry, and his malignity to the church by some lines which
are interpreted as threatening its extermination.

He is supposed about this time to have written his
" Arcades ;" for, while he lived at Horton, he used sometimes
to steal from his studies a few days, which he spent at Hare-
field, the house of the Countess Dowager of Derby, where the
" Arcades" made part of a dramatic entertainment.

He began now to grow weary of the country, and had some
purpose of taking chambers in the Inns of Court, when the
death of his mother set him at liberty to travel, for which he
obtained his father's consent, and Sir Henry Wotton's directions ; with the celebrated precept of prudence, *I pensieri
stretti, ed il viso sciolto,* " Thoughts close, and looks loose."

In 1638 he left England, and went first to Paris ; where, by
the favor of Lord Scudamore, he had the opportunity of visiting Grotius, then residing at the French court as ambassador
from Christina of Sweden. From Paris he hasted into Italy,
of which he had with particular diligence studied the language
and literature ; and though he seems to have intended a very
quick perambulation of the country, stayed two months at
Florence ; where he found his way into the academies, and
produced his compositions with such applause as appears to
have exalted him in his own opinion, and confirmed him in the
hope that, " by labor and intense study, which," says he,
" I take to be my portion in this life, joined with a strong propensity of nature," he might " leave something so written to
aftertimes as they should not willingly let it die."

It appears in all his writings that he had the usual concomitant of great abilities, a lofty and steady confidence in himself,
perhaps not without some contempt of others ; for scarcely
any man ever wrote so much, and praised so few. Of his
praise he was very frugal, as he set its value high, and considered his mention of a name as a security against the waste of
time, and a certain preservative from oblivion.

At Florence he could not, indeed, complain that his merit wanted distinction. Carlo Dati presented him with an encomiastic inscription, in the tumid lapidary style ; and Francini wrote him an ode, of which the first stanza is only empty noise ; the rest are perhaps too diffuse on common topics : but the last is natural and beautiful.

From Florence he went to Sienna, and from Sienna to Rome, where he was again received with kindness by the learned and the great. Holstenius, the keeper of the Vatican Library, who had resided three years at Oxford, introduced him to Cardinal Barberini ; and he, at a musical entertainment, waited for him at the door, and led him by the hand into the assembly. Here Selvaggi praised him in a distich, and Salsilli in a tetrastic ; neither of them of much value. The Italians were gainers by this literary commerce ; for the encomiums with which Milton repaid Salsilli, though not secure against a stern grammarian, turn the balance indisputably in Milton's favor.

Of these Italian testimonies, poor as they are, he was proud enough to publish them before his poems ; though he says he cannot be suspected but to have known that they were said *non tam de se, quam supra se.*

At Rome, as at Florence, he stayed only two months—a time indeed sufficient, if he desired only to ramble with an explainer of its antiquities, or to view palaces and count pictures ; but certainly too short for the contemplation of learning, policy, or manners.

From Rome he passed on to Naples, in company of a hermit, a companion from whom little could be expected ; yet to him Milton owed his introduction to Manso, Marquis of Villa, who had been before the patron of Tasso. Manso was enough delighted with his accomplishments to honor him with a sorry distich, in which he commends him for every thing but his religion ; and Milton, in return, addressed him in a Latin poem, which must have raised a high opinion of English elegance and literature.

His purpose was now to have visited Sicily and Greece ; but, hearing of the differences between the king and parliament, he thought it proper to hasten home, rather than pass his life in foreign amusements while his countrymen were contending for their rights. He therefore came back to Rome, though the merchants informed him of plots laid against him by the Jesuits, for the liberty of his conversations on religion. He had sense enough to judge that there was no danger, and therefore kept on his way, and acted as before, neither obtruding nor shunning controversy. He had perhaps given some offence by visiting Galileo, then a prisoner in the Inquisition for philosophical heresy ; and at Naples he was told by Manso that, by his declarations on religious questions, he had excluded himself from some distinctions which he should otherwise have paid him. But such conduct, though it did not please, was yet sufficiently safe ; and Milton stayed two months more at Rome, and went on to Florence without molestation.

From Florence he visited Lucca. He afterwards went to Venice ; and, having sent away a collection of music and other books, travelled to Geneva, which he probably considered as the metropolis of orthodoxy.

Here he reposed as in a congenial element, and became acquainted with John Diodati and Frederick Spanheim, two learned professors of divinity. From Geneva he passed through France ; and came home, after an absence of a year and three months.

At his return he heard of the death of his friend Charles Diodati ; a man whom it is reasonable to suppose of great merit, since he was thought by Milton worthy of a poem, entitled "Epitaphium Damonis," written with the common but childish imitation of pastoral life.

He now hired a lodging at the house of one Russel, a tailor in St. Bride's Churchyard, and undertook the education of John and Edward Philips, his sister's sons. Finding his rooms too little, he took a house and garden in Aldersgate Street, which was not then so much out of the world as it is now ; and chose his dwelling at the upper end of a passage, that he might avoid the noise of the street. Here he received more boys, to be boarded and instructed.

Let not our veneration for Milton forbid us to look with some degree of merriment on great promises and small performance, on the man who hastens home, because his countrymen are contending for their liberty, and, when he reaches the scene of action, vapors away his patriotism in a private boarding-school. This is the period of his life from which all his biographers seem inclined to shrink. They are unwilling that Milton should be degraded to a schoolmaster ; but, since it cannot be denied that he taught boys, one finds out that he taught for nothing, and another that his motive was only zeal for the propagation of learning and virtue ; and all tell what they do not know to be true, only to excuse an act which no wise man will consider as in itself disgraceful. His father was alive ; his allowance was not ample ; and he supplied its deficiencies by an honest and useful employment.

It is told, that in the art of education he performed won·
ders ; and a formidable list is given of the authors, Greek and
Latin, that were read in Aldersgate Street by youths between ten
and fifteen or sixteen years of age. Those who tell or receive
these stories should consider that nobody can be taught faster
than he can learn. The speed of the horseman must be limited by the power of the horse. Every man that has ever undertaken to instruct others can tell what slow advances he has
been able to make, and how much patience it requires to recall
vagrant inattention, to stimulate sluggish indifference, and to
rectify absurd misapprehension.

The purpose of Milton, as it seems, was to teach something
more solid than the common literature of schools, by reading
those authors that treat of physical subjects : such as the
Georgics, and astronomical treatises of the ancients. This
was a scheme of improvement which seems to have busied
many literary projectors of that age. Cowley, who had more
means than Milton of knowing what was wanting to the embellishments of life, formed the same plan of education in his imaginary college.

But the truth is, that the knowledge of external nature, and
the sciences which that knowledge requires or includes, are not
the great or the frequent business of the human mind.
Whether we provide for action or conversation, whether we
wish to be useful or pleasing, the first requisite is the religious
and moral knowledge of right and wrong ; the next is an
acquaintance with the history of mankind, and with those
examples which may be said to embody truth, and prove by
events the reasonableness of opinions. Prudence and justice
are virtues and excellences of all times and of all places ; we
are perpetually moralists, but we are geometricians only by
chance. Our intercourse with intellectual nature is necessary ;
our speculations upon matter are voluntary, and at leisure.
Physiological learning is of such rare emergence, that one may
know another half his life without being able to estimate his
skill in hydrostatics or astronomy ; but his moral and pruden-
tial character immediately appears.

Those authors, therefore, are to be read at schools that
supply most axioms of prudence, most principles of moral
truth, and most materials for conversation ; and those purposes are best served by poets, orators, and historians.

Let me not be censured for this digression as pedantic or
paradoxical ; for, if I have Milton against me, I have Socrates
on my side. It was his labor to turn philosophy from the
study of nature to speculations upon life ; but the innovators

whom I oppose are turning off attention from life to nature. They seem to think that we are placed here to watch the growth of plants, or the motions of the stars : Socrates was rather of opinion that what we had to learn was, how to do good and avoid evil.

"'Οττι τοι ἐν μεγάροισι κακόντ' αγαϑόντε τέτυκται."

Of institutions we may judge by their effects. From this wonder-working academy I do not know that there ever proceeded any man very eminent for knowledge : its only genuine product, I believe, is a small history of poetry, written in Latin by his nephew Philips, of which perhaps none of my readers has ever heard.

That in his school, as in every thing else which he undertook, he labored with great diligence, there is no reason for doubting. One part of his method deserves general imitation. He was careful to instruct his scholars in religion. Every Sunday was spent upon theology ; of which he dictated a short system, gathered from the writers that were then fashionable in the Dutch universities.

He set his pupils an example of hard study and spare diet : only now and then he allowed himself to pass a day of festivity and indulgence with some gay gentlemen of Gray's Inn.

He now began to engage in the controversies of the times, and lent his breath to blow the flames of contention. In 1641 he published a treatise of Reformation, in two books, against the established church ; being willing to help the Puritans, who were, he says, " *inferior to the prelates in learning.*"

Hall, Bishop of Norwich, had published an Humble Remonstrance, in defence of episcopacy ; to which, in 1641, five ministers, of whose names the first letters made the celebrated word *Smectymnuus*, gave their Answer. Of this Answer a Confutation was attempted by the learned Usher ; and to the Confutation Milton published a reply, entitled, " Of Prelatical Episcopacy, and whether it may be deduced from the Apostolical Times, by virtue of those Testimonies which are alleged to that purpose in some late Treatises, one whereof goes under the Name of James, Lord Bishop of Armagh."

I have transcribed this title to show, by his contemptuous mention of Usher, that he had now adopted the puritanical savageness of manners. His next work was, " The Reason of Church Government urged against Prelacy, by Mr. John Milton, 1642." In this book he discovers, not with ostentatious exultation, but with calm confidence, his high opinion of his own powers ; and promises to undertake something, he yet knows not what, that may be of use and honor to his country. "This," says he, "is not to be obtained but by devout prayer to that eternal Spirit that can enrich with all utterance and knowledge, and sends out his seraphim with the hallowed fire of his altar, to touch and purify the lips of whom he pleases. To this must be added, industrious and select reading, steady observation, and insight into all seemly and generous arts and affairs ; till which in some measure be compassed, I refuse not to sustain this expectation." From a promise like this, at once fervid, pious, and rational, might be expected the "Paradise Lost."

He published the same year two more pamphlets, upon the same question. To one of his antagonists, who affirms that he was "vomited out of the University," he answers in general terms. "The fellows of the college wherein I spent some years, at my parting, after I had taken two degrees, as the manner is, signified many times how much better it would content them that I should stay. As for the common approbation or dislike of that place as now it is, that I should esteem or disesteem myself the more for that, too simple is the answerer, if he think to obtain with me. Of small practice were the physician who could not judge, by what she and her sister have of long time vomited, that the worser stuff she strongly keeps in her stomach, but the better she is ever kecking at, and is queasy ; she vomits now out of sickness ; but before it will be well with her she must vomit by strong physic. The University, in the time of her better health, and my younger judgment, I never greatly admired, but now much less."

This is surely the language of a man who thinks that he has been injured. He proceeds to describe the course of his conduct and the train of his thoughts, and, because he has been suspected of incontinence, gives an account of his own purity : "That if I be justly charged," says he, "with this crime, it may come upon me with tenfold shame."

The style of his piece is rough, and such perhaps was that of his antagonist. This roughness he justifies by great examples in a long digression. Sometimes he tries to be humorous : "Lest I should take him for some chaplain in hand, some squire of the body to his prelate, one who serves not at the altar only, but at the court-cupboard, he will bestow on us a pretty model of himself ; and sets me out half a dozen phthisical mottoes, wherever he had them, hopping short in the measure of convulsion fits ; in which labor the agony of his wit having escaped narrowly, instead of well-sized periods, he greets us with a quantity of thumb-ring poesies. And thus ends this section, or rather dissection, of himself." Such is the contro-versial merriment of Milton ; his gloomy seriousness is yet more offensive. Such is his malignity, that hell grows darker at his frown.

His father, after Reading was taken by Essex, came to reside in his house ; and his school increased. At Whitsun-tide, in his thirty-fifth year, he married Mary, the daughter of Mr. Powel, a justice of the peace in Oxfordshire. He brought her to town with him, and expected all the advantages of a conjugal life. The lady, however, seems not much to have delighted in the pleasures of spare diet and hard study ; for, as Philips relates, "having for a month led a philosophic life, after having been used at home to a great house, and much company and joviality, her friends, possibly by her own desire, made earnest suit to have her company the remaining part of the summer ; which was granted, upon a promise of her return at Michaelmas."

Milton was too busy to much miss his wife ; he pursued his studies ; and now and then visited the Lady Margaret Leigh, whom he has mentioned in one of his sonnets. At last Mich-aelmas arrived ; but the lady had no inclination to return to the sullen gloom of her husband's habitation, and therefore very willingly forgot her promise. He sent her a letter, but had no answer ; he sent more, with the same success. It could be alleged that letters miscarry ; he therefore despatched a mes-senger, being by this time too angry to go himself. His mes-senger was sent back with some contempt. The family of the lady were cavaliers.

In a man whose opinion of his own merit was like Mil-ton's, less provocation than this might have raised violent resentment. Milton soon determined to repudiate her for dis-obedience ; and, being one of those who could easily find argu-ments to justify inclination, published (in 1644) " The Doc-trine and Discipline of Divorce ;" which was followed by " The Judgment of Martin Bucer concerning Divorce ;" and the next year, his Tetrachordon, " Expositions upon the four chief Places of Scripture which treat of Marriage."

This innovation was opposed, as might be expected, by the clergy, who, then holding their famous assembly at Westmin-ster, procured that the author should be called before the Lords ; "but that House," says Wood, " whether approving the doctrine, or not favoring his accusers, did soon dismiss him."

There seems not to have been much written against him, nor any thing by any writer of eminence. The antagonist

that appeared is styled by him, *A serving-man turned solicitor.*
Howel, in his Letters, mentions the new doctrine with contempt ; and it was, I suppose, thought more worthy of derision than of confutation. He complains of this neglect in
two sonnets, of which the first is contemptible, and the second
not excellent.

From this time it is observed that he became an enemy
to the Presbyterians, whom he had favored before. He that
changes his party by his humor is not more virtuous than he
that changes it by his interest ; he loves himself rather than
truth.

His wife and her relations now found that Milton was not an
unresisting sufferer of injuries ; and perceiving that he had
begun to put his doctrine in practice, by courting a young
woman of great accomplishments, the daughter of one Doctor
Davis, who was, however, not ready to comply, they resolved to
endeavor a reunion. He went sometimes to the house of
one Blackborough, his relation, in the lane of St. Martin's-
le-Grand, and at one of his usual visits was surprised to see his
wife come from another room, and implore forgiveness on her
knees. He resisted her entreaties for a while ; "but partly,"
says Philips, "his own generous nature, more inclinable to
reconciliation than to perseverance in anger or revenge, and
partly the strong intercession of friends on both sides, soon
brought him to an act of oblivion and a firm league of peace."
It were injurious to omit that Milton afterwards received her
father and her brothers in his own house, when they were distressed, with other royalists.

He published about the same time his "Areopagitica, a
Speech of Mr. John Milton for the Liberty of Unlicensed Printing." The danger of such unbounded liberty, and the danger
of bounding it, have produced a problem in the science of government which human understanding seems hitherto unable to
solve. If nothing may be published but what civil authority
shall have previously approved, power must always be the
standard of truth ; if every dreamer of innovations may propa-
gate his projects, there can be no settlement ; if every mur-
murer at government may diffuse discontent, there can be no
peace ; and if every sceptic in theology may teach his follies,
there can be no religion. The remedy against these evils is to
punish the authors ; for it is yet allowed that every society may
punish, though not prevent, the publication of opinions which
that society shall think pernicious ; but this punishment,
though it may crush the author, promotes the book ; and it
seems not more reasonable to leave the right of printing unre-

strained because writers may be afterwards censured, than it would be to sleep with doors unbolted because by our laws we can hang a thief.

But whatever were his engagements, civil or domestic, poetry was never long out of his thoughts.

About this time (1645) a collection of his Latin and English poems appeared, in which the Allegro and Penseroso, with some others, were first published.

He had taken a larger house in Barbican for the reception of scholars ; but the numerous relations of his wife, to whom he generously granted refuge for a while, occupied his rooms. In time, however, they went away ; "and the house again," says Philips, "now looked like a house of the muses only, though the accession of scholars was not great. Possibly his having proceeded so far in the education of youth may have been the occasion of his adversaries calling him pedagogue and schoolmaster ; whereas it is well known he never set up for a public school, to teach all the young fry of a parish ; but only was willing to impart his learning and knowledge to his relations, and the sons of gentlemen who were his intimate friends, and that neither his writings nor his way of teaching ever savored in the least of pedantry."

Thus laboriously does his nephew extenuate what cannot be denied, and what might be confessed without disgrace. Milton was not a man who could become mean by a mean employment. This, however, his warmest friends seem not to have found ; they therefore shift and palliate. He did not sell literature to all comers at an open shop ; he was a chamber-milliner, and measured his commodities only to his friends.

Philips, evidently impatient of viewing him in this state of degradation, tells us that it was not long continued ; and, to raise his character again, has a mind to invest him with military splendor : "He is much mistaken," he says, "if there was not about this time a design of making him an adjutant-general in Sir William Waller's army. But the new-modelling of the army proved an obstruction to the design." An event cannot be set at a much greater distance than by having been only *designed about some time*, if a man *be not much mistaken*. Milton shall be a pedagogue no longer ; for, if Philips be not much mistaken, somebody at some time designed him for a soldier.

About the time that the army was new-modelled (1645), he removed to a smaller house in Holborn, which opened backward into Lincoln's Inn Fields. He is not known to have published any thing afterwards till the king's death, when, find-

ing his murderers condemned by the Presbyterians, he wrote a
treatise to justify it, and *to compose the minds of the people.*

He made some '' Remarks on the Articles of Peace between
Ormond and the Irish Rebels.'' While he contented himself to
write, he perhaps did only what his conscience dictated ; and
if he did not very vigilantly watch the influence of his own
passions, and the gradual prevalence of opinions, first willingly
admitted, and then habitually indulged ; if objections by being
overlooked were forgotten, and desire superinduced conviction ; he yet shared only the common weakness of mankind,
and might be no less sincere than his opponents. But as faction seldom leaves a man honest, however it might find him,
Milton is suspected of having interpolated the book called
'' Icon Basilike,'' which the Council of State, to whom he was
now made Latin secretary, employed him to censure, by inserting a prayer taken from Sidney's '' Arcadia,'' and imputing it
to the king ; whom he charges, in his '' Iconoclastes,'' with the
use of this prayer, as with a heavy crime, in the indecent language with which prosperity had emboldened the advocates
for rebellion to insult all that is venerable or great : '' Who
would have imagined so little fear in him of the true all-seeing
Deity, as, immediately before his death, to pop into the hands
of the grave bishop that attended him, as a special relic of his
saintly exercises, a prayer stolen word for word from the
mouth of a heathen woman praying to a heathen god ?''

The papers which the king gave to Dr. Juxon on the scaffold the regicides took away, so that they were at least the publishers of this prayer ; and Dr. Birch, who had examined the
question with great care, was inclined to think them the
forgers. The use of it by adaptation was innocent ; and they
who could so noisily censure it, with a little extension of their
malice, could contrive what they wanted to accuse.

King Charles the Second, being now sheltered in Holland,
employed Salmasius, professor of polite learning at Leyden, to
write a defence of his father and of monarchy, and, to excite
his industry, gave him, as was reported, a hundred Jacobuses.
Salmasius was a man of skill in languages, knowledge of
antiquity, and sagacity of emendatory criticism, almost exceeding all hope of human attainment ; and having, by excessive
praises, been confirmed in great confidence of himself, though
he probably had not much considered the principles of society
or the rights of government, undertook the employment without distrust of his own qualifications ; and, as his expedition in
writing was wonderful, in 1649 published '' Defensio Regis.''

To this Milton was required to write a sufficient answer,

which he performed (1651) in such a manner that Hobbes declared himself unable to decide whose language was best or whose arguments were worst. In my opinion, Milton's periods are smoother, neater, and more pointed ; but he delights himself with teasing his adversary as much as with confuting him. He makes a foolish allusion of Salmasius, whose doctrine he considers as servile and unmanly, to the stream of Salmacis, which, whoever entered, left half his virility behind him. Salmasius was a Frenchman, and was unhappily married to a scold. *Tu es Gallus*, says Milton, *et, ut aiunt, nimium gallinaceus.* But his supreme pleasure is to tax his adversary, so renowned for criticisms, with vicious Latin. He opens his book with telling that he has used *persona*, which, according to Milton, signifies only a mask, in a sense not known to the Ro-. mans, by applying it as we apply *person.* But as Nemesis is always on the watch, it is memorable that he has enforced the charge of a solecism by an expression in itself grossly solecistical, when for one of those supposed blunders he says, as Ker, and I think some· one before him, has remarked, *propino te grammatistis tuis* vapulandum. From *vapulo*, which has a passive sense, *vapulandus* can never be derived. No man forgets his original trade ; the rights of nations and of kings sink into questions of grammar if grammarians discuss them.

Milton, when he undertook this answer, was weak of body and dim of sight ; but his will was forward, and what was wanting of health was supplied by zeal. He was rewarded with a thousand pounds, and his book was much read ; for paradox, recommended by spirit and elegance, easily gains attention ; and he, who told every man that he was equal to his king, could hardly want an audience.

That the performance of Salmasius was not dispersed with equal rapidity, or read with equal eagerness, is very credible. He taught only the stale doctrine of authority and the unpleasing duty of submission, and he had been so long not only the monarch but the tyrant of literature, that almost all mankind were delighted to find him defied and insulted by a new name not yet considered as any one's rival. If Christina, as is said, commended the "Defence of the People," her purpose must be to torment Salmasius, who was then at her court ; for neither her civil station nor her natural character could dispose her to favor the doctrine, who was by birth a queen, and by temper despotic.

That Salmasius was, from the appearance of Milton's book, treated with neglect, there is not much proof ; but to a man so long accustomed to admiration, a little praise of his antagonist would be sufficiently offensive, and might incline him to leave Sweden, from which, however, he was dismissed, not with any mark of contempt, but with a train of attendants scarcely less than regal.

He prepared a reply, which, left as it was imperfect, was published by his son in the year of the Restoration. In the beginning, being probably most in pain for his Latinity, he endeavors to defend his use of the word *persona ;* but, if I remember right, he misses a better authority than any that he has found, that of Juvenal in his Fourth Satire :

> "—— Quid agas, cum dira et fœdior omni
> Crimine *persona* est ?"

As Salmasius reproached Milton with losing his eyes in the quarrel, Milton delighted himself with the belief that he had shortened Salmasius's life, and both perhaps with more malignity than reason. Salmasius died at the Spa, September 3, 1653; and, as controvertists are commonly said to be killed by their last dispute, Milton was flattered with the credit of destroying him.

Cromwell had now dismissed the parliament by the authority of which he had destroyed monarchy, and commenced monarch himself, under the title of Protector, but with kingly and more than kingly power. That his authority was lawful, never was pretended ; he himself founded his right only in necessity; but Milton, having now tasted the honey of public employment, would not return to hunger and philosophy ; but, continuing to exercise his office under a manifest usurpation, betrayed to his power that liberty which he had defended. Nothing can be more just than that rebellion should end in slavery ; that he who had justified the murder of his king, for some acts which seemed to him unlawful, should now sell his services and his flatteries to a tyrant, of whom it was evident that he could do nothing lawful.

He had now been blind for some years ; but his vigor of intellect was such that he was not disabled to discharge his office of Latin secretary, or continue his controversies. His mind was too eager to be diverted, and too strong to be subdued.

About this time his first wife died in childbed, having left him three daughters. As he probably did not much love her, he did not long continue the appearance of lamenting her ; but after a short time married Catharine, the daughter of one Captain Woodcock, of Hackney ; a woman doubtless educated in opinions like his own. She died, within a year, of childbirth, or some distemper that followed it, and her husband honored her memory with a poor sonnet.

The first reply to Milton's " Defensio Populi" was published in 1651, called " Apologia pro Rege et Populo Anglicano, contra Johannis Polypragmatici (alias Miltoni) defensionem destructivam Regis et Populi." Of this the author was not known ; but Milton, and his nephew Philips, under whose name he published an answer so much corrected by him that it might be called his own, imputed it to Bramhal ; and, knowing him no friend to regicides, thought themselves at liberty to treat him as if they had known what they only suspected.

Next year appeared " Regii Sanguinis clamor ad Cœlum." Of this the author was Peter du Moulin, who was afterwards prebendary of Canterbury ; but Morus, or More, a French minister, having the care of its publication, was treated as the writer by Milton in his " Defensio Secunda," and overwhelmed by such violence of invective that he began to shrink under the tempest, and gave his persecutors the means of knowing the true author. Du Moulin was now in great danger ; but Milton's pride operated against his malignity ; and both he and his friends were more willing that Du Moulin should escape than that he should be convicted of mistake.

In this second defence he shows that his eloquence is not merely satirical ; the rudeness of his invective is equalled by the grossness of his flattery. " Deserimur, Cromuelle, tu solus superes, ad te summa nostrarum rerum rediit, in te solo consistit, insuperabili tuæ virtuti cedimus cuncti, nemine vel obloquente, nisi quia quales inæqualis ipse honores sibi quærit, aut digniori concessos invidet, aut non intelligit nihil esse in societate hominum magis vel Deo gratum, vel rationi consentaneum, esse in civitate nihil æquius, nihil utilius, quam potiri rerum dignissimum. Eum te agnoscunt omnes, Cromuelle, ea tu civis maximus et gloriosissimus,[1] dux publici consilii, exercitum fortissimorum imperator, pater patriæ gessisti. Sic tu spontanea bonorum omnium et animitus missa voce salutaris."

Cæsar when he assumed the perpetual dictatorship had not more servile or more elegant flattery. A translation may show its servility ; but its elegance is less attainable. Having exposed the unskilfulness or selfishness of the former government, " We were left," says Milton, " to ourselves : the whole national interest fell into your hands, and subsists only in your

---

[1] It may be doubted whether *gloriosissimus* be here used with Milton's boasted purity. *Res gloriosa* is an *illustrious thing ;* but *vir gloriosus* is commonly a *braggart,* as in *miles gloriosus.*

abilities. To your virtue, overpowering and resistless, every man gives way, except some who, without equal qualifications, aspire to equal honors, who envy the distinctions of merit greater than their own, or who have yet to learn that in the coalition of human society nothing is more pleasing to God, or more agreeable to reason, than that the highest mind should have the sovereign power. Such, sir, are you by general confession ; such are the things achieved by you, the greatest and most glorious of our countrymen, the director of our public councils, the leader of unconquered armies, the father of your country ; for by that title does every good man hail you with sincere and voluntary praise.''

Next year, having defended all that wanted defence, he found leisure to defend himself. He undertook his own vindication against More, whom he declares in his title to be justly called the author of the " Regii Sanguinis Clamor.'' In this there is no want of vehemence or eloquence, nor does he forget his wonted wit. '' Morus es ? an Momus ? an uterque idem est ?'' He then remembers that *Morus* is Latin for a mulberry-tree, and hints at the known transformation :

——Poma al a ferebat
Quæ post nigra tulit Morus.

With this piece ended his controversies ; and he from this time gave himself up to his private studies and his civil employment.

As secretary to the Protector he is supposed to have written the " Declaration of the Reasons for a War with Spain.'' His agency was considered as of great importance ; for, when a treaty with Sweden was artfully suspended, the delay was publicly imputed to Mr. Milton's indisposition ; and the Swedish agent was provoked to express his wonder that only one man in England could write Latin, and that man blind.

Being now forty-seven years old, and seeing himself disencumbered from external interruptions, he seems to have recollected his former purposes, and to have resumed three great works which he had planned for his future employment : an epic poem, the history of his country, and a dictionary of the Latin tongue.

To collect a dictionary seems a work of all others least practicable in a state of blindness, because it depends upon perpetual and minute inspection and collation. Nor would Milton probably have begun it after he had lost his eyes ; but, having had it always before him, he continued it, says Philips, " almost to his dying day ; but the papers were so discom-

posed and deficient that they could not be fitted for the press."
The compilers of the Latin dictionary, printed at Cambridge,
had the use of those collections in three folios ; but what was
their fate afterwards is not known.

To compile a history from various authors, when they can
only be consulted by other eyes, is not easy, nor possible, but
with more skilful and attentive help than can be commonly
obtained ; and it was probably the difficulty of consulting and
comparing that stopped Milton's narrative at the Conquest—a
period at which affairs were not yet very intricate nor authors
very numerous.

For the subject of his epic poem, after much deliberation,
long choosing, and beginning late, he fixed upon " Paradise
Lost ;" a design so comprehensive that it could be justified
only by success. He had once designed to celebrate King
Arthur, as he hints in his verses to Mansus ; but " Arthur was
reserved," says Fenton, " to another destiny."

It appears by some sketches of poetical projects left in
manuscript, and to be seen in a library at Cambridge, that he
had digested his thoughts on this subject into one of those wild
dramas which were anciently called Mysteries ; and Philips
had seen what he terms part of a tragedy beginning with the
first ten lines of Satan's address to the sun. These mysteries
consist of allegorical persons ; such as Justice, Mercy, Faith.
Of the tragedy or mystery of " Paradise Lost" there are two
plans :

THE PERSONS.	THE PERSONS.
Michael.	Moses.
Chorus of Angels.	Divine Justice, Wisdom.
Heavenly Love.	Heavenly Love.
Lucifer.	The Evening Star, Hesperus.
Adam, } with the Serpent. Eve, }	Chorus of Angels. Lucifer.
Conscience.	Adam.
Death.	Eve.
Labor.	Conscience.
Sickness, Discontent, Ignorance, with others, } Mutes.	Labor, Sickness, Discontent, Ignorance, Fear, } Mutes.
Faith.	Death, }
Hope.	Faith. Hope. Charity.
Charity.	

PARADISE LOST.

The Persons.

Moses προλογίζει, recounting how he assumed his true
body ; that it corrupts not, because it is with God in the

mount ; declares the like with Enoch and Elijah : besides the purity of the place, that certain pure winds, dews, and clouds preserve it from corruption ; whence exhorts to the sight of God ; tells they cannot see Adam in the state of innocence, by reason of their sin.

Justice,
Mercy,   } debating what should become of man, if he fall.
Wisdom,
Chorus of Angels singing a hymn of the Creation.

ACT II.

Heavenly Love.
Evening Star.
Chorus sing the marriage song, and describe Paradise.

ACT III.

Lucifer contriving Adam's ruin.
Chorus fears for Adam, and relates Lucifer's rebellion and fall

ACT IV.   .

Adam,
Eve,   } fallen.
Conscience cites them to God's examination.
Chorus bewails, and tells the good Adam has lost.

ACT V.

Adam and Eve driven out of Paradise.
— — — presented by an angel with
Labor, Grief, Hatred, Envy, War, Famine, Pesti-
   lence, Sickness, Discontent, Ignorance, Fear, } Mutes.
   Death,
To whom he gives their names. Likewise Winter, Heat,
   Tempest, etc.
Faith,
Hope,   } comfort him and instruct him.
Charity,
   Chorus briefly concludes.

Such was his first design, which could have produced only an allegory, or mystery. The following sketch seems to have attained more maturity :

Adam unparadised.

The angel Gabriel, either descending or entering ; showing, since this globe was created, his frequency as much on earth as in heaven : describes Paradise. Next, the Chorus, showing the reason of his coming to keep his watch in Paradise, after Lucifer's rebellion, by command from God ; and withal expressing his desire to see and know more concerning this excellent new creature, man. The angel Gabriel, as by his name signifying a prince of power, tracing Paradise with a more free office, passes by the station of the Chorus, and, desired by them, relates what he knew of man : as the creation of Eve, with their love and marriage. After this Lucifer appears ; after his overthrow, bemoans himself, seeks revenge on man. The Chorus prepare resistance on his first approach. At last, after discourse of enmity on either side, he departs : whereat the Chorus sings of the battle and victory in heaven against him and his accomplices : as before, after the first act, was sung a hymn of the creation. Here again may appear Lucifer relating and exulting in what he had done to the destruction of man. Man next, and Eve, having by this time been seduced by the Serpent, appears confusedly covered with leaves. Conscience in a shape accuses him ; Justice cites him to a place whither Jehovah called for him. In the mean while the Chorus entertains the stage, and is informed by some angel the manner of the fall. Here the Chorus bewails Adam's fall. Adam then and Eve return ; accuse one another ; but especially Adam lays the blame to his wife ; is stubborn in his offence. Justice appears, reasons with him, convinces him. The Chorus admonisheth Adam, and bids him beware Lucifer's example of impenitence. The angel is sent to banish them out of Paradise ; but before causes to pass before his eyes, in shapes, a mask of all the evils of this life and world. He is humbled, relents, despairs ; at last appears Mercy, comforts him, promises the Messiah ; then calls in Faith, Hope, and Charity ; instructs him ; he repents, gives God the glory, submits to his penalty. The Chorus briefly concludes. Compare this with the former draught.

These are very imperfect rudiments of " Paradise Lost ;" but it is pleasant to see great works in their seminal state, pregnant with latent possibilities of excellence ; nor could there be any more delightful entertainment than to trace their gradual growth and expansion, and to observe how they are sometimes suddenly improved by accidental hints, and sometimes slowly improved by steady meditation.

Invention is almost the only literary labor which blindness cannot obstruct, and therefore he naturally solaced his solitude by the indulgence of his fancy and the melody of his numbers. He had done what he knew to be necessarily previous to poetical excellence ; he had made himse'f acquainted with *seemly arts and affairs ;* his comprehension was extended by various knowledge, and his memory stored with intellectual treasures. He was skilful in many languages, and had by reading and composition attained the full mastery of his own. He would have wanted little help from books, had he retained the power of perusing them.

But while his greater designs were advancing, having now, like many other authors, caught the love of publication, he amused himself as he could, with little productions. He sent to the press (1658) a manuscript of Raleigh, called " The Cabinet Council ;" and next year gratified his malevolence to the clergy by a " Treatise of Civil Power in Ecclesiastical Cases, and the Means of removing Hirelings out of the Church."

Oliver was now dead, Richard was constrained to resign ; the system of extemporary government, which had been held together only by force, naturally fell into fragments when that force was taken away ; and Milton saw himself and his cause in equal danger. But he had still hope of doing something. He wrote letters, which Toland has published, to such men as he thought friends to the new commonwealth ; and even in the year of the Restoration he bated no jot of heart or hope, but was fantastical enough to think that the nation, agitated as it was, might be settled by a pamphlet, called "A ready and easy Way to Establish a Free Commonwealth," which was, however, enough considered to be both seriously and ludicrously answered.

The obstinate enthusiasm of the commonwealthmen was very remarkable. When the king was apparently returning, Harrington, with a few associates as fanatical as himself, used to meet, with all the gravity of political importance, to settle an equal government by rotation ; and Milton, kicking when he could strike no longer, was foolish enough to publish, a few weeks before the Restoration, *Notes* upon a sermon preached by one Griffiths, entitled, "The Fear of God and the King." To these notes an answer was written by L.'Estrange, in a pamphlet petulantly called " No Blind Guides."

But whatever Milton could write, or men of greater activity could do, the king was now about to be restored, with the irresistible approbation of the people. He was therefore no longer secretary, and was consequently obliged to quit the house, which he held by his office ; and, proportioning his sense of danger to his opinion of the importance of his writings, thought it convenient to seek some shelter, and hid himself for a time in Bartholomew Close, by West Smithfield.

I cannot but remark a kind of respect, perhaps unconsciously, paid to this great man by his biographers : every house in which he resided is historically mentioned, as if it were an injury to neglect naming any place that he honored by his pres. ence.

The king, with lenity of which the world has had perhaps no other example, declined to be the judge or avenger of his own or his father's wrongs, and promised to admit into the Act of Oblivion all, except those whom the parliament should except ; and the parliament doomed none to capital punishment but the wretches who had immediately co-operated in the murder of the king. Milton was certainly not one of them ; he had only justified what they had done.

This justification was indeed sufficiently offensive ; and (June 16) an order was issued to seize Milton's " Defence," and Goodwin's " Obstructors of Justice," another book of the same tendency, and burn them by the common hangman. The attorney-general was ordered to prosecute the authors ; but Milton was not seized, nor perhaps very diligently pursued.

Not long after (August 19) the flutter of innumerable bosoms were stilled by an act which the king, that his mercy might want no recommendation of elegance, rather called an Act of Oblivion than of Grace. Goodwin was named, with nineteen more, as incapacitated for any public trust ; but of Milton there was no exception.

Of this tenderness shown to Milton, the curiosity of mankind has not forborne to inquire the reason. Burnet thinks he was forgotten ; but this is another instance which may confirm Dalrymple's observation, who says, that "whenever Burnet's narrations are examined, he appears to be mistaken."

Forgotten he was not, for his prosecution was ordered ; it must be therefore by design that he was included in the general oblivion. He is said to have had friends in the House, such as Marvel, Morrice, and Sir Thomas Clarges ; and undoubtedly a man like him must have had influence. A very particular story of his escape is told by Richardson in his Memoirs, which he received from Pope, as delivered by Betterton, who might have heard it from Davenant. In the war between the king and parliament, Davenant was made prisoner, and condemned to die ; but was spared at the request of Milton. When the turn of success brought Milton into the like danger, Davenant repaid the benefit by appearing in his favor. Here is a reciprocation of generosity and gratitude so pleasing that the tale makes its own way to credit. But if help were wanted, I know not where to find it. The danger of Davenant is certain from his own relation ; but of his escape there is no account. Betterton's narration can be traced no higher, it is not known that he had it from Davenant. We are told that the benefit exchanged was life for.life ; but it seems not certain that Milton's life ever was in danger. Goodwin, who had committed the same kind of crime, escaped with incapacitation ; and, as exclusion from public trust is a punishment which the power of government can commonly inflict without the help of a particular law, it required no great interest to exempt Milton from a censure little more than verbal. Something may be reasonably ascribed to veneration and compassion—to veneration of his abilities and compassion for his distresses—which made it fit to forgive his malice for his learning. He was now poor and blind ; and who would pursue with violence an illustrious enemy depressed by fortune and disarmed by nature ?

The publication of the Act of Oblivion put him in the same condition with his fellow-subjects. He was, however, upon some pretence now not known, in the custody of the sergeant in December ; and when he was released, upon his refusal of the fees demanded, he and the sergeant were called before the House. He was now safe within the shade of oblivion, and knew himself to be as much out of the power of a griping officer as any other man. How the question was determined is not known. Milton would hardly have contended, but that he knew himself to have right on his side.

He then removed to Jewin Street, near Aldersgate Street, and, being blind and by no means wealthy, wanted a domestic companion and attendant ; and therefore, by the recommendation of Dr. Paget, married Elizabeth Minshul, of a gentleman's family in Cheshire, probably without a fortune. All his wives were virgins ; for he has declared that he thought it gross and indelicate to be a second husband : upon what other principles his choice was made cannot now be known ; but marriage afforded not much of his happiness. The first wife left him in disgust, and was brought back only by terror ; the second, indeed, seems to have been more a favorite, but her life was short. The third, as Philips relates, oppressed his children in his lifetime, and cheated them at his death.

Soon after his marriage, according to an obscure story, he was offered the continuance of his employment, and being pressed by his wife to accept it, answered, "You, like other women, want to ride in your coach ; my wish is to live and die an honest man." If he considered the Latin secretary as exercising any of the powers of government, he that had shared authority, either with the parliament or Cromwell, might have forborne to talk very loudly of his honesty ; and if he thought the office purely ministerial, he certainly might have honestly retained it under the king. But this tale has too little evidence to deserve a disquisition ; large offers and sturdy rejections are among the most common topics of falsehood.

He had so much either of prudence or gratitude that he forbore to disturb the new settlement with any of his political or ecclesiastical opinions, and from this time devoted himself to poetry and literature. Of his zeal for learning in all its parts he gave a proof by publishing, the next year (1661), " Accidence commenced Grammar ;" a little book which has nothing remarkable, but that its author, who had been lately defending the supreme powers of his country, and was then writing " Paradise Lost," could descend from his elevation to rescue children from the perplexity of grammatical confusion, and the trouble of lessons unnecessarily repeated.

About this time Elwood, the Quaker, being recommended to him as one who would read Latin to him for the advantage of his conversation, attended him every afternoon except on Sundays. Milton, who, in his letter to Hartlib, had declared that " to read Latin with an English mouth is as ill a hearing as law French," required that Elwood should learn and practise the Italian pronunciation, which, he said, was necessary, if he would talk with foreigners. This seems to have been a task troublesome without use. There is little reason for preferring the Italian pronunciation to our own, except that it is more general ; and to teach it to an Englishman is only to make him a foreigner at home. He who travels, if he speaks Latin, may so soon learn the sounds which every native gives it, that he need make no provision before his journey ; and if strangers visit us, it is their business to practise such conformity to our modes as they expect from us in their own countries. Elwood complied with the directions, and improved himself by his attendance ; for he relates that Milton, having a curious ear, knew by his voice when he read what he did not understand, and would stop him, " and open the most difficult passages."

In a short time he took a house in the Artillery Walk, leading to Bunhill Fields ; the mention of which concludes the register of Milton's removals and habitations. He lived longer in this place than any other.

He was now busied by " Paradise Lost." Whence he drew the original design has been variously conjectured by men who cannot bear to think themselves ignorant of that which, at last, neither diligence nor sagacity can discover. Some find the hint in an Italian tragedy. Voltaire tells a wild and unauthorized story of a farce seen by Milton in Italy, which opened thus : *Let the rainbow be the fiddle-stick of the fiddle of Heaven.* It has been already shown that the first conception was a tragedy or mystery, not of a narrative, but a dramatic work, which he is supposed to have begun to reduce to its present form about the time (1655) when he finished his dispute with the defenders of the king.

He long before had promised to adorn his native country by some great performance, while he had yet, perhaps, no settled design, and was stimulated only by such expectations as naturally arose from the survey of his attainments and the consciousness of his powers. What he should undertake it was difficult to determine. He was "long choosing, and began late."

While he was obliged to divide his time between his private studies and affairs of state, his poetical labor must have been often interrupted ; and perhaps he did little more in that busy time than construct the narrative, adjust the episodes, proportion the parts, accumulate images and sentiments, and treasure in his memory or preserve in writing such hints as books or meditation would supply. Nothing particular is known of his intellectual operations while he was a statesman ; for having every help and accommodation at hand, he had no need of uncommon expedients.

Being driven from all public stations, he is yet too great not to be traced by curiosity to his retirement, where he has been found by Mr. Richardson, the fondest of his admirers, sitting "before his door in a gray coat of coarse cloth, in warm sultry weather, to enjoy the fresh air ; and so, as in his own room, receiving the visits of the people of distinguished parts as well as quality." His visitors of high quality must now be imagined to be few ; but men of parts might reasonably court the conversation of a man so generally illustrious, that foreigners are reported by Wood to have visited the house in Bread Street where he was born.

According to another account, he was seen in a small house, "neatly enough dressed in black clothes, sitting in a room hung with rusty green ; pale but not cadaverous, with chalk-stones in his hands. He said that if it were not for the gout his blindness would be tolerable."

In the intervals of his pain, being made unable to use the common exercises, he used to swing in a chair, and sometimes played upon an organ.

He was now confessedly and visibly employed upon his poem, of which the progress might be noted by those with whom he was familiar ; for he was obliged, when he had composed as many lines as his memory would conveniently retain, to employ some friend in writing them, having, at least for part of the time, no regular attendant. This gave opportunity to observations and reports.

Mr. Philips observes that there was a very remarkable circumstance in the composure of " Paradise Lost," " which I have a particular reason," says he, " to remember ; for whereas I had the perusal of it from the very beginning, for some years, as I went from time to time to visit him, in parcels of ten, twenty, or thirty verses at a time (which, being written by whatever hand came next, might possibly want correction as to the orthography and pointing), having, as the summer came on, not being showed any for a considerable while, and desiring the reason thereof, was answered, that his vein never happily flowed but from the autumnal equinox to the vernal ; and that whatever he attempted at other times was never to his satisfaction, though he courted his fancy never so much ; so that, in all the years he was about this poem, he may be said to have spent half his time therein."

Upon this relation Toland remarks that in his opinion Philips has mistaken the time of the year ; for Milton, in his elegies, declares that with the advance of the spring he feels the increase of his poetical force, *redeunt in carmina vires.* To this it is answered that Philips could hardly mistake time so well marked ; and it may be added that Milton might find different times of the year favorable to different parts of life. Mr. Richardson conceives it impossible that such a work should be suspended for six months, or for one. It may go on faster or slower, but it must go on. By what necessity it must continually go on, or why it might not be laid aside and resumed, it is not easy to discover.

This dependence of the soul upon the seasons, those temporary and periodical ebbs and flows of intellect, may, I suppose, justly be derided as the fumes of vain imagination. *Sapiens dominabitur astris.* The author that thinks himself weather-bound will find, with a little help from hellebore, that he is only idle or exhausted. But while this notion has possession of the head, it produces the inability which it supposes. Our powers owe much of their energy to our hopes ; *possunt quia posse videntur.* When success seems attainable, diligence is enforced ; but when it is admitted that the faculties are suppressed by a cross wind or a cloudy sky, the day is given up without resistance, for who can contend with the course of Nature ?

From such prepossessions Milton seems not to have been free. There prevailed in his time an opinion that the world was in its decay, and that we have, had the misfortune to be produced in the decrepitude of Nature. It was suspected that the whole creation languished, that neither trees nor animals had the height or bulk of their predecessors, and that every thing was daily sinking by gradual diminution. Milton appears to suspect that souls partake of the general degeneracy, and is not without some fear that his book is to be written in *an age too late* for heroic poesy.

Another opinion wanders about the world, and sometimes finds reception among wise men ; an opinion that restrains the operations of the mind to particular regions, and supposes that a luckless mortal may be born in a degree of latitude too high or too low for wisdom or for wit. From this fancy, wild as it is, he had not wholly cleared his head, when he feared lest the *climate* of his country might be *too cold* for flights of imagination.

Into a mind already occupied by such fancies, another not more reasonable might easily find its way. He that could fear lest his genius had fallen upon too old a world, or too chill a climate, might consistently magnify to himself the influence of the seasons, and believe his faculties to be vigorous only half the year.

His submission to the seasons was at least more reasonable than his dread of decaying nature, or a frigid zone, for general causes must operate uniformly in a general abatement of mental power ; if less could be performed by the writer, less likewise would content the judges of his work. Among this lagging race of frosty grovellers he might still have risen into eminence by producing something which they should not willingly let die. However inferior to the heroes who were born in better ages, he might still be great among his contemporaries, with the hope of growing every day greater in the dwindle of posterity. He might still be a giant among the pigmies, the one-eyed monarch of the blind.

Of his artifices of study, or particular hours of composition, we have little account, and there was perhaps little to be told. Richardson, who seems to have been very diligent in his inquiries, but discovers always a wish to find Milton discriminated from other men, relates "that he would sometimes lie awake whole nights, but not a verse could he make ; and on a sudden his poetical faculty would rush upon him with an *impetus* or *æstrum*, and his daughter was immediately called to secure what came. At other times he would dictate perhaps forty lines in a breath, and then reduce them to half the number.''

These bursts of light and involutions of darkness, these transient and involuntary excursions and retrocessions of invention, having some appearance of deviation from the common train of nature, are eagerly caught by the lovers of a wonder. Yet something of this inequality happens to every man in every mode of exertion, manual or mental. The mechanic cannot handle his hammer and his file at all times with equal dexterity ; there are hours, he knows not why, when *his hand is out.* By Mr. Richardson's relation, casually conveyed, much regard cannot be claimed. That in his intellectual hour Milton called for his daughter " to secure what came," may be questioned ; for unluckily it happens to be known that his daughters were never taught to write ; nor would he have been obliged, as is universally confessed, to have employed any casual visitor in disburdening his memory, if his daughter could have performed the office.

The story of reducing his exuberance has been told of other authors, and, though doubtless true of every fertile and copious mind, seems to have been gratuitously transferred to Milton.

What he has told us, and we cannot now know more, is, that he composed much of this poem in the night and morning, I suppose before his mind was disturbed with common business ; and that he poured out with great fluency his unpremeditated verse. Versification, free, like his, from the distresses of rhyme, must, by a work so long, be made prompt and habitual ; and, when his thoughts were once adjusted, the words would come at his command.

At what particular times of his life the parts of his work were written, cannot often be known. The beginning of the third book shows that he had lost his sight ; and the introduction to the seventh that the return of the king had clouded him with discountenance, and that he was offended by the licentious festivity of the Restoration. There are no other internal notes of time. Milton, being now cleared from all effects of his disloyalty, had nothing required from him but the common duty of living in quiet, to be rewarded with the common right of protection ; but this, which, when he skulked from the approach of his king, was perhaps more than he hoped, seems not to have satisfied him ; for no sooner is he safe than he finds himself in danger, " fallen on evil days and evil tongues, and with darkness and with danger compassed round." This darkness, had his eyes been better employed, had undoubtedly deserved compassion ; but to add the mention of danger was ungrateful and unjust. He was fallen indeed on *evil days ;* the time was come in which regicides could no longer boast their wickedness. But of *evil tongues* for Milton to complain required impudence at least equal to his other powers ; Milton, whose warmest advocates must allow that he never spared any asperity of reproach or brutality of insolence.

But the charge itself seems to be false ; for it would be hard to recollect any reproach cast upon him, either serious or ludicrous, through the whole remaining part of his life. He pursued his studies, or his amusements, without persecution, molestation, or insult. Such is the reverence paid to great abilities, however misused : they who contemplated in Milton the scholar and the wit were contented to forget the reviler of his king.

When the plague (1665) raged in London, Milton took refuge at Chalfont, in Bucks ; where Elwood, who had taken the house for him, first saw a complete copy of '' Paradise Lost ;'' and, having perused it, said to him, '' Thou hast said a great deal upon ' Paradise Lost ; ' what hast thou to say upon Paradise found ?''

Next year, when the danger of infection had ceased, he returned to Bunhill Fields, and designed the publication of his poem. A license was necessary, and he could expect no great kindness from a chaplain of the Archbishop of Canterbury. He seems, however, to have been treated with tenderness ; for though objections were made to particular passages, and among them to the simile of the sun eclipsed in the first book, yet the license was granted ; and he sold his copy, April 27, 1667, to Samuel Simmons, for an immediate payment of five pounds, with a stipulation to receive five pounds more when thirteen hundred should be sold of the first edition ; and again, five pounds after the sale of the same number of the second edition ; and another five pounds after the same sale of the third. None of the three editions were to be extended beyond fifteen hundred copies.

The first edition was of ten books, in a small quarto. The titles were varied from year to year ; and an advertisement and the arguments of the books were omitted in some copies, and inserted in others.

The sale gave him in two years a right to his second payment, for which the receipt was signed April 26, 1669. The second edition was not given till 1674 ; it was printed in small octavo ; and the number of books was increased to twelve, by a division of the seventh and twelfth ; and some other small improvements were made. The third edition was published in 1678 ; and the widow, to whom the copy was then to devolve, sold all her claims to Simmons for eight pounds, according to her receipt given December 21, 1680. Simmons had already agreed to transfer the whole right to Brabazon Aylmer, for twenty-five pounds ; and Aylmer sold to Jacob Tonson half, August 17, 1683, and half, March 24, 1690, at a price considerably enlarged. In the history of " Paradise Lost" a deduction thus minute will rather gratify than fatigue.

The slow sale and tardy reputation of this poem have been always mentioned as evidences of neglected merit, and of the uncertainty of literary fame ; and inquiries have been made, and conjectures offered, about the causes of its long obscurity and late reception. But has the case been truly stated ? Have not lamentation and wonder been lavished on an evil that was never felt ?

That in the reigns of Charles and James, the " Paradise Lost" received no public acclamations, is readily confessed. Wit and literature were on the side of the court ; and who that solicited favor or fashion would venture to praise the defender of the regicides ? All that he himself could think his due, from *evil tongues* in *evil days*, was that reverential silence which was generously preserved. But it cannot be inferred that his poem was not read or not, however unwillingly, admired.

The sale, if it be considered, will justify the public. Those who have no power to judge of past times but by their own, should always doubt their conclusions. The call for books was not in Milton's age what it is in the present. To read was not then a general amusement ; neither traders, nor often gentlemen, thought themselves disgraced by ignorance. The women had not then aspired to literature, nor was every house supplied with a closet of knowledge. Those, indeed, who professed learning were not less learned than at any other time ; but of that middle race of students who read for pleasure or accomplishment, and who buy the numerous products of modern typography, the number was then comparatively small. To prove the paucity of readers, it may be sufficient to remark that the nation had been satisfied from 1623 to 1664—that is, forty-one years—with only two editions of the works of Shakespeare, which probably did not together make one thousand copies.

The sale of thirteen hundred copies in two years, in opposition to so much recent enmity, and to a style of versification new to all and disgusting to many, was an uncommon example of the prevalence of genius. The demand did not immediately increase ; for many more readers than were supplied at first the nation did not afford. Only three thousand were sold in eleven years ; for it forced its way without assistance ; its admirers did not dare to publish their opinion ; and the opportunities now given of attracting notice by advertisements were then very few ; the means of proclaiming the publication of new books have been produced by that general literature which now pervades the nation through all its ranks.

But the reputation and price of the copy still advanced, till the Revolution put an end to the secrecy of love, and " Paradise Lost" broke into open view with sufficient security of kind reception.

Fancy can hardly forbear to conjecture with what temper Milton surveyed the silent progress of his work, and marked its reputation stealing its way in a kind of subterraneous current through fear and silence.   I cannot but conceive him calm and confident, little disappointed, not at all dejected, relying on his own merit with steady consciousness, and waiting without impatience the vicissitudes of opinion and the impartiality of a future generation.

In the mean time he continued his studies, and supplied the want of sight by a very odd expedient, of which Philips gives the following account :

Mr. Philips tells us, " that though our author had daily about him one or other to read, some persons of man's estate, who, of their own accord, greedily catched at the opportunity of being his readers, that they might as well reap the benefit of what they read to him as oblige him by the benefit of their reading ; and others of younger years were sent by their parents to the same end ; yet excusing only the daughter by reason of her bodily infirmity and difficult utterance of speech (which, to say truth, I doubt was the principal cause of excusing her) the other two were condemned to the performance of reading, and exactly pronouncing of all the languages of whatever book he should, at one time or other, think fit to peruse—viz., the Hebrew (and, I think, the Syriac), the Greek, the Latin, the Italian, Spanish, and French.   All which sorts of books to be confined to read, without understanding one word, must needs be a trial of patience almost beyond endurance.   Yet it was endured by both for a long time, though the irksomeness of this employment could not be always concealed, but broke out more and more into expressions of uneasiness ; so that at length they were all, even the eldest also, sent out to ' learn some curious and ingenious sorts of manufacture, that are proper for women to learn, particularly embroideries in gold or silver."

In the scene of misery which this mode of intellectual labor sets before our eyes, it is hard to determine whether the daughters or the father are most to be lamented. A language not understood can never be so read as to give pleasure, and very seldom so as to convey meaning. If few men would have had resolution to write books with such embarrassments, few likewise would have wanted ability to find some better expedient.

Three years after his " Paradise Lost" (1667), he published his " History of England," comprising the whole fable of Geoffrey of Monmouth, and continued to the Norman Invasion. Why he should have given the first part, which he seems not to believe, and which is universally rejected, it is difficult to conjecture. The style is harsh ; but it has something of rough vigor, which perhaps may often strike, though it cannot please.

On this history the licenser again fixed his claws, and be fore he would transmit it to the press tore out several parts. Some censures of the Saxon monks were taken away, lest they should be applied to the modern clergy ; and a character of the Long Parliament and Assembly of Divines was excluded ; of which the author gave a copy to the Earl of Anglesey, and which, being afterwards published, has been since inserted in its proper place.

The same year were printed " Paradise Regained " and " Samson Agonistes," a tragedy written in imitation of the ancients, and never designed by the author for the stage. As these poems were published by another bookseller, it has been asked whether Simmons was discouraged from receiving them by the slow sale of the former. Why a writer changed his bookseller a hundred years ago, I am far from hoping to discover. Certainly he who in two years sells thirteen hundred copies of a volume in quarto, bought for two payments of five pounds each, has no reason to repent his purchase.

When Milton showed " Paradise Regained " to Elwood, " This," said he, " is owing to you ; for you put it in my head by the question you put to me at Chalfont, which otherwise I had not thought of."

His last poetical offspring was his favorite. He could not, as Elwood relates, endure to hear " Paradise Lost" preferred to " Paradise Regained." Many causes may vitiate a writer's judgment of his own works. On that which has cost him much labor he sets a high value, because he is unwilling to think that he has been diligent in vain ; what has been produced without toilsome efforts is considered with delight as a proof of vigorous faculties and fertile invention ; and the last work, whatever it be, has necessarily most of the grace of novelty.

Milton, however it happened, had this prejudice, and had it to himself.

To that multiplicity of attainments and extent of comprehension that entitled this great author to our veneration, may be added a kind of humble dignity, which did not disdain the meanest services to literature. The epic poet, the controvertist, the politician, having already descended to accommodate children with a book of rudiments, now, in the last years of his life, composed a book of logic for the initiation of students in philosophy ; and published (1672) *Artis Logicæ plenior Institutio ad Petri Rami Methodum concinnata ;* that is, " A new Scheme of Logic, according to the Method of Ramus." I know not whether, even in this book, he did not intend an act of hostility against the universities ; for Ramus was one of the first oppugners of the old philosophy who disturbed with innovations the quiet of the schools.

His polemical disposition again revived. He had now been safe so long that he forgot his fears, and published a " Treatise of True Religion, Heresy, Schism, Toleration, and the best Means to prevent the Growth of Popery."

But this little tract is modestly written, with respectful mention of the Church of England, and an appeal to the Thirtynine Articles. His principle of toleration is, agreement in the sufficiency of the Scriptures ; and he extends it to all who, whatever their opinions are, profess to derive them from the Sacred Books. The papists appeal to other testimonies, and are therefore, in his opinion, not to be permitted the liberty of either public or private worship ; for though they plead conscience, " we have no warrant," he says, " to regard conscience which is not grounded in Scripture."

Those who are not convinced by his reasons may be perhaps delighted with his wit. The term Roman Catholic is, he says, " one of the Pope's bulls ; it is particular universal, or catholic schismatic."

He has, however, something better. As the best preservative against popery, he recommends the diligent perusal of the Scriptures, a duty from which he warns the busy part of mankind not to think themselves excused.

He now reprinted his juvenile poems, with some additions.

In the last year of his life he sent to the press, seeming to take delight in publication, a collection of " Familiar Epistles in Latin ;" to which, being too few to make a volume, he added some academical exercises, which perhaps he perused with pleasure, as they recalled to his memory the days of youth, but for which nothing but veneration for his name could now procure a reader.

When he had attained his sixty-sixth year, the gout, with which he had been long tormented, prevailed over the enfeebled powers of nature. He died by a quiet and silent expiration, about the 10th of November, 1674, at his house in Bunhill Fields ; and was buried next his father in the chancel of St. Giles, at Cripplegate. His funeral was very splendidly and numerously attended.

Upon his grave there is supposed to have been no memorial ; but in our time a monument has been erected in Westminster Abbey " To the Author of Paradise Lost," by Mr. Benson, who has in the inscription bestowed more words upon himself than upon Milton.

When the inscription for the monument of Philips, in which he was said to be *soli Miltono secundus*, was exhibited to Dr. Sprat, then Dean of Westminster, he refused to admit it ; the name of Milton was, in his opinion, too detestable to be read on the wall of a building dedicated to devotion. Atterbury, who succeeded him, being author of the inscription, permitted its reception. " And such has been the change of public opinion," said Dr. Gregory, from whom I heard this account, " that I have seen erected in the church a statue of that man, whose name I once knew considered as a pollution of its walls."

Milton has the reputation of having been in his youth eminently beautiful, so as to have been called the Lady of his college. His hair, which was of a light brown, parted at the foretop, and hung down upon his shoulders, according to the picture which he has given of Adam. He was, however, not of the heroic stature, but rather below the middle size, according to Mr. Richardson, who mentions him as having narrowly escaped from being short and thick. He was vigorous and active, and delighted in the exercise of the sword, in which he is related to have been eminently skilful. His weapon was, I believe, not the rapier, but the backsword, of which he recommends the use in his book on education.

His eyes are said never to have been bright ; but, if he was a dexterous fencer, they must have been once quick.

His domestic habits, so far as they are known, were those of a severe student. He drank little strong drink of any kind, and fed without excess in quantity, and in his earlier years without delicacy of choice. In his youth he studied late at night ; but afterwards changed his hours, and rested in bed from nine to four in the summer, and five in the winter. The course of his day was best known after he was blind. When he first rose, he heard a chapter in the Hebrew Bible, and then studied till twelve ; then took some exercise for an hour ; then dined, then played on the organ, and sang, or heard another sing ; then studied till six ; then entertained his visitors till eight ; then supped, and, after a pipe of tobacco and a glass of water, went to bed.

So is his life described ; but this even tenor appears attainable only in colleges. He that lives in the world will sometimes have the succession of his practice broken and confused. Visitors, of whom Milton is represented to have had great numbers, will come and stay unseasonably ; business, of which every man has some, must be done when others will do it.

When he did not care to rise early, he had something read to him by his bedside ; perhaps at this time his daughters were employed. He composed much in the morning, and dictated in the day, sitting obliquely in an elbow-chair, with his leg thrown over the arm.

Fortune appears not to have had much of his care. In the civil wars he lent his personal estate to the parliament ; but when, after the contest was decided, he solicited repayment, he met not only with neglect, but sharp rebuke ; and, having tired both himself and his friends, was given up to poverty and hopeless indignation, till he showed how able he was to do greater service. He was then made Latin secretary, with two hundred pounds a year ; and had a thousand pounds for his "Defence of the People." His widow, who, after his death, retired to Namptwich, in Cheshire, and died about 1729, is said to have reported that he lost two thousand pounds by entrusting it to a scrivener ; and that, in the general depredation upon the church, he had grasped an estate of about sixty pounds a year belonging to Westminster Abbey, which, like other sharers of the plunder of rebellion, he was afterwards obliged to return. Two thousand pounds, which he had placed in the Excise Office, were also lost. There is yet no reason to believe that he was ever reduced to indigence. His wants, being few, were competently supplied. He sold his library before his death, and left his family fifteen hundred pounds, on which his widow laid hold, and only gave one hundred to each of his daughters.

His literature was unquestionably great. He read all the languages which are considered either as learned or polite ; Hebrew with its two dialects, Greek, Latin, Italian, French, and Spanish. In Latin his skill was such as places him in the first rank of writers and critics ; and he appears to have culti-

vated Italian with uncommon diligence. The books in which
his daughter, who used to read to him, represented him as most
delighting, after Homer, which he could almost repeat, were
Ovid's Metamorphoses and Euripides. His Euripides is, by
Mr. Cradock's kindness, now in my hands : the margin is
sometimes noted ; but I have found nothing remarkable.

Of the English poets he set most value upon Spenser,
Shakespeare, and Cowley. Spenser was apparently his favorite ; Shakespeare he may easily be supposed to like, with every
other skilful reader ; but I should not have expected that Cowley, whose ideas of excellence were so different from his own,
would have had much of his approbation. His character of
Dryden, who sometimes visited him, was, that he was a good
rhymist, but no poet.

His theological opinions are said to have been first Calvin-
istical ; and afterwards, perhaps when he began to hate the
Presbyterians, to have tended towards Arminianism. In the
mixed questions of theology and government he never thinks
that he can recede far enough from popery or prelacy ; but
what Baudius says of Erasmus seems applicable to him, *magis
habuit quod fugeret, quam quod sequeretur.* He had determined
rather what to condemn than what to approve. He has not
associated himself with any denomination of Protestants : we
know rather what he was not than what he was. He was not
of the Church of Rome ; he was not of the Church of England.

To be of no church is dangerous. Religion, of which the
rewards are distant, and which is animated only by faith and
hope, will glide by degrees out of the mind, unless it be invigorated and reimpressed by external ordinances, by stated calls
to worship, and the salutary influence of example. Milton,
who appears to have had full conviction of the truth of Christianity, and to have regarded the Holy Scriptures with the pro-
foundest veneration, and to have been untainted by any hereti-
cal peculiarity of opinion, and to have lived in a confirmed belief of the immediate and occasional agency of Providence, yet
grew old without any visible worship. In the distribution of
his hours, there was no hour of prayer, either solitary or with
his household ; omitting public prayers, he omitted all.

Of this omission the reason has been sought upon a supposition which ought never to be made, that men live with their
own approbation, and justify their conduct to themselves.
Prayer certainly was not thought superfluous by him, who represents our first parents as praying acceptably in the state of
innocence, and efficaciously after their fall. That he lived

without prayer can hardly be affirmed ; his studies and meditations were an habitual prayer.   The neglect of it in his family was probably a fault for which he condemned himself, and which he intended to correct, but that death, as too often happens, intercepted his reformation.

His political notions were those of an acrimonious and surly republican, for which it is not known that he gave any better reason than that " a popular government was the most frugal ; for the trappings of a monarchy would set up an ordinary commonwealth."   It is surely very shallow policy that supposes money to be the chief good ; and even this, without considering that the support and expense of a court is, for the most part, only a particular kind of traffic, for which money is circulated without any national impoverishment.

Milton's republicanism was, I am afraid, founded in an envious hatred of· greatness, and a sullen desire of independence ; in petulance impatient of control, and pride disdainful of superiority.   He hated monarchs in the state and prelates in the church ; for he hated all whom he was required to obey. It is to be suspected that his predominant desire was to destroy rather than establish, and that he felt not so much the love of liberty as repugnance to authority.

It has been observed that they who most loudly clamor for liberty do not most liberally grant it.   What we know of Milton's character, in domestic relations, is, that he was severe and arbitrary.   His family consisted of women ; and there appears in his books something like a Turkish contempt of females, as subordinate and inferior beings.   That his own daughters might not break the ranks, he suffered them to be depressed by a mean and penurious education.   He thought women made only for obedience, and man only for rebellion.

Of his family some account may be expected.   His sister first married to Mr. Philips, afterwards married to Mr. Agar, a friend of her first husband, who succeeded him in the Crown Office.   She had by her first husband Edward and John, the two nephews whom Milton educated ; and by her second, two daughters.

His brother, Sir Christopher, had two daughters, Mary and Catharine ; and a son, Thomas, who succeeded Agar in the Crown Office, and left a daughter living, in 1749, in Grosvenor Street.

Milton had children only by his first wife : Anne, Mary, and Deborah.   Anne, though deformed, married a master-builder, and died of her first child.   Mary died single.   Deborah married Abraham Clark, a weaver in Spitalfields, and lived seventy-six years, to August 1727. This is the daughter of whom public mention has been made. She could repeat the first lines of Homer, the Metamorphoses, and some of Euripides, by having often read them. Yet here incredulity is ready to make a stand. Many repetitions are necessary to fix in the memory lines not understood ; and why should Milton wish or want to hear them so often ? These lines were at the beginning of the poems. Of a book written in a language not understood, the beginning raises no more attention than the end ; and as those that understand it know commonly the beginning best, its rehearsal will seldom be⁀necessary. It is not likely that Milton required any passage to be so much repeated as that his daughter could learn it ; nor likely that he desired the initial lines to be read at all ; nor that the daughter, weary of the drudgery of pronouncing unideal sounds, would voluntarily commit them to memory.

To this gentlewoman Addison made a present, and promised some establishment, but died soon after. Queen Caroline sent her fifty guineas. She had seven sons and three daughters ; but none of them had any children, except her son Caleb and her daughter Elizabeth. Caleb went to Fort St. George, in the East Indies, and had two sons, of whom nothing is now known. Elizabeth married Thomas Foster, a weaver in Spitalfields ; and had seven children, who all died. She kept a petty grocer's or chandler's shop, first at Holloway, and afterwards in Cock Lane, near Shoreditch Church. She knew little of her grandfather, and that little was not good. She told of his harshness to his daughters, and his refusal to have them taught to write ; and, in opposition to other accounts, represented him as delicate, though temperate, in his diet.

In 1750, April 5, " Comus" was played for her benefit. She had so little acquaintance with diversion or gayety, that she did not know what was intended when a benefit was offered her. The profits of the night were only one hundred and thirty pounds, though Dr. Newton brought a large contribution ; and twenty pounds were given by Tonson, a man who is to be praised as often as he is named. Of this sum, one hundred pounds were placed in the stocks, after some debate between her and her husband in whose name it should be entered ; and the rest augmented their little stock, with which they removed to Islington. This was the greatest benefaction that " Paradise Lost" ever procured the author's descendants ; and to this he who has now attempted to relate his life had the honor of contributing a prologue.

In the examination of Milton's poetical works I shall pay
so much regard to time as to begin with his juvenile productions. For his early pieces he seems to have had a degree of
fondness not very laudable ; what he has once written he
resolves to preserve, and gives to the public an unfinished
poem, which he broke off because he was "nothing satisfied
with what he had done," supposing his readers less nice than
himself. These preludes to his future labors are in Italian,
Latin, and English. Of the Italian I cannot pretend to speak
as a critic ; but I have heard them commended by a man well
qualified to decide their merit. The Latin pieces are lus-
ciously elegant ; but the delight which they afford is rather by
the exquisite imitation of the ancient writers, by the purity of
the diction, and the harmony of the numbers, than by any
power of invention or vigor of sentiment. They are not all
of equal value ; the elegies excel the odes ; and some of the
exercises on Gunpowder Treason might have been spared.

The English poems, though they make no promises of
"Paradise Lost," have this evidence of genius, that they have
a cast original and unborrowed. But their peculiarity is not
excellence ; if they differ from the verses of others, they differ
for the worse ; for they are too often distinguished by repulsive harshness ; the combinations of words are new, but they
are not pleasing ; the rhymes and epithets seem to be laboriously sought and violently applied.

That in the early parts of his life he wrote with much care
appears from his manuscripts, happily preserved at Cambridge, in which many of his smaller works are found as they
were first written, with the subsequent corrections. Such relics show how excellence is acquired ; what we hope ever to do
with ease, we must learn first to do with diligence.

Those who admire the beauties of this great poet sometimes
force their own judgment into false approbation of his little
pieces, and prevail upon themselves to think that admirable
which is only singular. All that short compositions can commonly attain is neatness and elegance. Milton never learned
the art of doing little things with grace ; he overlooked the
milder excellence of suavity and softness ; he was a lion that
had no skill in dangling the kid.

One of the poems on which much praise has been bestowed is "Lycidas," of which the diction is harsh, the
rhymes uncertain, and the numbers unpleasing. What beauty
there is we must therefore seek in the sentiments and images.
It is not to be considered as the effusion of real passion ; for
passion runs not after remote allusions and obscure opinions.

Passion plucks no berries from the myrtle and ivy, nor calls upon Arethuse and Mincius, nor tells of rough satyrs and "fauns with cloven heel." Where there is leisure for fiction there is little grief.

In this poem there is no nature, for there is no truth ; there is no art, for there is nothing new. Its form is that of a pastoral ; easy, vulgar, and therefore disgusting, whatever images it can supply are long ago exhausted ; and its inherent improbability always forces dissatisfaction on the mind. When Cowley tells of Hervey, that they studied together, it is easy to suppose how much he must miss the companion of his labors and the partner of his discoveries ; but what image of tenderness can be excited by these lines ?

> " We drove a-field, and both together heard
> What time the gray fly winds her sultry horn,
> Battening our flocks with the fresh dews of night."

We know that they never drove a-field, and they had no flocks to batten ; and though it be allowed that the representation may be allegorical, the true meaning is so uncertain and remote, that it is never sought, because it cannot be known when it is found.

Among the flocks, and copses, and flowers appear the heathen deities : Jove and Phœbus, Neptune and Æolus, with a long train of mythological imagery, such as a college easily supplies. Nothing can less display knowledge, or less exercise invention, than to tell how a shepherd has lost his companion, and must now feed his flocks alone, without any judge of his skill in piping ; and how one god asks another god what has become of Lycidas, and how neither god can tell. He who thus grieves will excite no sympathy ; he who thus praises will confer no honor.

This poem has yet a grosser fault. With these trifling fictions are mingled the most awful and sacred truths, such as ought never to be polluted with such irreverent combinations. The shepherd likewise is now a feeder of sheep, and afterwards an ecclesiastical pastor, a superintendent of a Christian flock. Such equivocations are always unskilful ; but here they are indecent, and at least approach to impiety, of which, however, I believe the writer not to have been conscious.

Such is the power of reputation justly·acquired, that its blaze drives away the eye from nice examination. Surely no man could have fancied that he read " Lycidas" with pleasure, had he not known the author.

Of the two pieces, " L'Allegro" and " Il Penseroso," I believe opinion is uniform ; every man that reads them reads them with pleasure. The author's design is not, what Theobald has remarked, merely to show how objects derive their colors from the mind, by representing the operation of the same things upon the gay and the melancholy temper, or upon the same man as he is differently disposed ; but rather how, among the successive variety of appearances, every disposition of mind takes hold on those by which it may be gratified.

The cheerful man hears the lark in the morning ; the pensive man hears the nightingale in the evening. The cheerful man sees the cock strut, and hears the horn and hounds echo in the wood ; then walks, not unseen, to observe the glory of the rising sun, or listen to the singing milkmaid, and view the labors of the ploughman and the mower ; then casts his eyes about him over scenes of smiling plenty, and looks up to the distant tower, the residence of some fair inhabitant ; thus he pursues real gayety through a day of labor or of play, and delights himself at night with the fanciful narratives of superstitious ignorance.

The pensive man, at one time, walks unseen to muse at midnight ; and at another hears the sullen curfew. If the weather drives him home, he sits in a room lighted only by glowing embers ; or by a lonely lamp outwatches the north star, to discover the habitation of separate souls, and varies the shades of meditation by contemplating the magnificent or pathetic scenes of tragic and epic poetry. When the morning comes, a morning gloomy with rain and wind, he walks into the dark trackless woods, falls asleep by some murmuring water, and with melancholy enthusiasm expects some dream of prognostication, or some music played by aërial performers.

Both Mirth and Melancholy are solitary, silent inhabitants of the breast, that neither receive nor transmit communication : no mention is therefore made of a philosophical friend or a pleasant companion. The seriousness does not arise from any participation of calamity, nor the gayety from the pleasures of the bottle.

The man of cheerfulness, having exhausted the country, tries what towered cities will afford, and mingles with scenes of splendor, gay assemblies, and nuptial festivities ; but he mingles a mere spectator, as, when the learned comedies of Jonson, or the wild dramas of Shakespeare, are exhibited, he attends the theatre.

The pensive man never loses himself in crowds, but walks the cloister or frequents the cathedral. Milton probably had not yet forsaken the church,

Both his characters delight in music ; but he seems to think that cheerful notes would have obtained from Pluto a complete dismission of Eurydice, of whom solemn sounds only procured a conditional release.

For the old age of Cheerfulness he makes no provision ; but Melancholy he conducts with great dignity to the close of life. His cheerfulness is without levity, and his pensiveness without asperity.

Through these two poems the images are properly selected and nicely distinguished ; but the colors of the diction seem not sufficiently discriminated. I know not whether characters are kept sufficiently apart. No mirth can, indeed, be found in his melancholy ; but I am afraid that I always meet some melancholy in his mirth. They are two noble efforts of imagination.

The greatest of his juvenile performances is the " Mask of Comus," in which may very plainly be discovered the dawn or twilight of " Paradise Lost." Milton appears to have formed very early that system of diction and mode of verse which his maturer judgment approved, and from which he never endeavored nor desired to deviate.

Nor does " Comus" afford only a specimen of his language ; it exhibits likewise his power of description and his vigor of sentiment, employed in the praise and defence of virtue. A work more truly poetical is rarely found ; allusions, images, and descriptive epithets embellish almost every period with lavish decoration. As a series of lines, therefore, it may be considered as worthy of all the admiration with which the votaries have received it.

As a drama it is deficient. The action is not probable. A mask, in those parts where supernatural intervention is admitted, must indeed be given up to all the freaks of imagination ; but, so far as the action is merely human, it ought to be reasonable, which can hardly be said of the conduct of the two brothers ; who, when their sister sinks with fatigue in a pathless wilderness, wander both away together in search of berries too far to find their way back, and leave a helpless lady to all the sadness and danger of solitude. This, however, is a defect overbalanced by its convenience.

What deserves more reprehension is, that the prologue spoken in the wildwood by the attendant Spirit is addressed to the audience ; a mode of communication so contrary to the nature of dramatic representation, that no precedents can support it.

The discourse of the Spirit is too long ; an objection that

may be made to almost all the following speeches ; they have not the sprightliness of a dialogue animated by reciprocal contention, but seem rather declamations deliberately composed, and formally repeated on a moral question. The auditor therefore listens as to a lecture, without passion, without anxiety.

The song of Comus has airiness and jollity ; but, what may recommend Milton's morals as well as his poetry, the invitations to pleasure are so general that they excite no distinct images of corrupt enjoyment, and take no dangerous hold on the fancy !

The following soliloquies of Comus and the Lady are elegant, but tedious. The song must owe much to the voice if it ever can delight. At last the brothers enter with too much tranquillity ; and, when they have feared lest their sister should be in danger, and hoped that she is not in danger, the elder makes a speech in praise of chastity, and the younger finds how fine it is to be a philosopher.

Then descends the Spirit in the form of a shepherd ; and the brother, instead of being in haste to ask his help, praises his singing, and inquires his business in that place. It is remarkable that at this interview the brother is taken with a short fit of rhyming. The Spirit relates that the lady is in the power of Comus ; the brother moralizes again ; and the Spirit makes a long narration, of no use because it is false, and therefore unsuitable to a good being.

In all these parts the language is poetical and the sentiments are generous ; but there is something wanting to allure attention.

The dispute between the Lady and Comus is the most animated and affecting scene of the drama, and wants nothing but a brisker reciprocation of objections and replies to invite attention and detain it.

The songs are vigorous and full of imagery ; but they are harsh in their diction and not very musical in their numbers.

Throughout the whole the figures are too bold, and the language too luxuriant for dialogue. It is a drama in the epic style, inelegantly splendid and tediously instructive.

The Sonnets were written in different parts of Milton's life, upon different occasions. They deserve not any particular criticism ; for of the best it can only be said that they are not bad ; and perhaps only the eighth and the twenty-first are truly entitled to this slender commendation. The fabric of a sonnet, however adapted to the Italian language, has never succeeded in ours, which, having greater variety of termination, requires the rhymes to be often changed.

Those little pieces may be despatched without much anxiety ; a greater work calls for greater care. I am now to examine " Paradise Lost ;" a poem which, considered with respect to design, may claim the first place, and with respect to performance, the second, among the productions of the human mind.

. By the general consent of critics, the first praise of genius is due to the writer of an epic poem, as it requires an assemblage of all the powers which are singly sufficient for other compositions. Poetry is the art of uniting pleasure with truth, by calling imagination to the help of reason. Epic poetry undertakes to teach the most important truths by the most pleasing precepts, and therefore relates some great event in the most affecting manner. History must supply the writer with the rudiments of narration, which he must improve and exalt by a nobler art, must animate by dramatic energy, and diversify by retrospection and anticipation ; morality must teach him the exact bounds and different shades of vice and virtue ; from policy, and the practice of life, he has to learn the discriminations of character and the tendency of the passions, either single or combined ; and physiology must supply him with illustrations and images. To put these materials to poetical use, is required an imagination capable of painting nature and realizing fiction. Nor is he yet a poet till he has attained the whole extension of his language, distinguished all the delicacies of phrase and all the colors of words, and learned to adjust their different sounds to all the varieties of metrical modulation.

Bossu is of opinion that the poet's first work is to find a moral, which his fable is afterwards to illustrate and establish. This seems to have been the process only of Milton ; the moral of other poems is incidental and consequent ; in Milton's only it is essential and intrinsic. His purpose was the most useful and the most arduous ; " to vindicate the ways of God to man ;" to show the reasonableness of religion, and the necessity of obedience to the divine law.

To convey this moral there must be a fable, a narration artfully constructed, so as to excite curiosity and surprise expectation. In this part of his work Milton must be confessed to have equalled every other poet. He has involved in his account of the fall of man the events which preceded and those that were to follow it : he has interwoven the whole system of theology with such propriety, that every part appears to be necessary ; and scarcely any recital is wished shorter for the sake of quickening the progress of the main action.

The subject of an epic poem is naturally an event of great importance. That of Milton is not the destruction of a city, the conduct of a colony, or the foundation of an empire. His subject is the fate of worlds, the revolutions of heaven and of earth ; rebellion against the supreme King, raised by the highest order of created beings ; the overthrow of their host and the punishment of their crime ; the creation of a new race of reasonable creatures, their original happiness and innocence, their forfeiture of immortality, and their restoration to hope and peace.

Great events can be hastened or retarded only by persons of elevated dignity. Before the greatness displayed in Milton's poem all other greatness shrinks away. The weakest of his agents are the highest and noblest of human beings, the original parents of mankind ; with whose actions the elements consented ; on whose rectitude or deviation of will depended the state of terrestrial nature and the condition of all the future inhabitants of the globe.

Of the other agents in the poem, the chief are such as it is irreverence to name on slight occasions. The rest were lower powers ;

> " —— of which the least could wield
> Those elements, and arm him with the force
> Of all their regions ;

powers which only the control of Omnipotence restrains from laying creation waste and filling the vast expanse of space with ruin and confusion. To display the motives and actions of beings thus superior, so far as human reason can examine them, or human imagination represent them, is the task which this mighty poet has undertaken and performed.

In the examination of epic poems much speculation is commonly employed upon the characters. The characters in the "Paradise Lost" which admit of examination are those of angels and of man ; of angels good and evil ; of man in his innocent and sinful state.

Among the angels, the virtue of Raphael is mild and placid, of easy condescension and free communication ; that of Michael is regal and lofty, and, as may seem, attentive to the dignity of his own nature. Abdiel and Gabriel appear occasionally, and act as every incident requires ; the solitary fidelity of Abdiel is very amiably painted.

Of the evil angels the characters are more diversified. To Satan, as Addison observes, such sentiments are given as suit "the most exalted and most depraved being." Milton has been censured by Clarke[1] for the impiety which sometimes breaks from Satan's mouth ; for there are thoughts, as he justly remarks, which no observation of character can justify, because no good man would willingly permit them to pass, however transiently, through his own mind. To make Satan speak as a rebel, without any such expressions as might taint the reader's imagination, was indeed one of the great difficulties in Milton's undertaking ; and I cannot but think that he has extricated himself with great happiness. There is in Satan's speeches little that can give pain to a pious ear. The language of rebellion cannot be the same with that of obedience. The malignity of Satan foams in haughtiness and obstinacy ; but his expressions are commonly general, and not otherwise offensive than as they are wicked.

The other chiefs of the celestial rebellion are very judiciously discriminated in the first and second books ; and the ferocious character of Moloch appears, both in the battle and the council, with exact consistency.

To Adam and to Eve are given, during their innocence, such sentiments as innocence can generate and utter. Their love is pure benevolence and mutual veneration ; their repasts are without luxury, and their diligence without toil. Their addresses to their Maker have little more than the voice of admiration and gratitude. Fruition left them nothing to ask ; and innocence left them nothing to fear.

But with guilt enter distrust and discord, mutual accusation, and stubborn self-defence : they regard each other with alienated minds, and dread their Creator as the avenger of their transgression. At last they seek shelter in his mercy, soften to repentance, and melt in supplication. Both before and after the fall the superiority of Adam is diligently sustained.

Of the *probable* and the *marvellous*, two parts of a vulgar epic poem, which immerge the critic in deep consideration, the " Paradise Lost" requires little to be said. It contains the history of a miracle, of creation and redemption ; it displays the power and the mercy of the Supreme Being : the probable therefore is marvellous, and the marvellous is probable. The substance of the narrative is truth ; and, as truth allows no choice, it is, like necessity, superior to rule. To the accidental or adventitious parts, as to every thing human, some slight exceptions may be made ; but the main fabric is immovably supported.

It is justly remarked by Addison that this poem has, by

[1] Author of the " Essay on Study."

the nature of its subject, the advantage above all others, that it is universally and perpetually interesting. All mankind will, through all ages, bear the same relation to Adam and to Eve, and must partake of that good and evil which extend to themselves.

Of the *machinery*, so called from Θεὸς ἀπὸ μηχανῆς, by which is meant the occasional interposition of supernatural power, another fertile topic of critical remarks, here is no room to speak, because every thing is done under the immediate and visible direction of Heaven ; but the rule is so far observed that no part of the action could have been accomplished by any other means.

Of episodes, I think there are only two contained in Raphael's relation of the war in heaven, and Michael's prophetic account of the changes to happen in this world. Both are closely connected with the great action ; one was necessary to Adam as a warning, the other as a consolation.

To the completeness or integrity of the design, nothing can be objected ; it has distinctly and clearly what Aristotle requires—a beginning, a middle, and an end. There is perhaps no poem, of the same length, from which so little can be taken without apparent mutilation. Here are no funeral games, nor is there any long 'description of a shield. The short digressions at the beginning of the third, seventh, and ninth books might doubtless be spared ; but superfluities so beautiful who would take away ? or who does not wish that the author of the " Iliad" had gratified succeeding ages with a little knowledge of himself ? Perhaps no passages are more frequently or more attentively read than those extrinsic paragraphs ; and, since the end of poetry is pleasure, that cannot be unpoetical with which all are pleased.

The questions, whether the action of the poem be strictly one, whether the poem can be properly termed heroic, and who is the hero, are raised by such readers as draw their principles of judgment rather from books than from reason. Milton, though he entitled " Paradise Lost" only a poem, yet calls it himself heroic song. Dryden petulantly and indecently denies the heroism of Adam, because he was overcome ; but there is no reason why the hero should not be unfortunate, except established practice, since success and virtue do not go necessarily together. Cato is the hero of Lucan ; but Lucan's authority will not be suffered by Quintilian to decide. However, if success be necessary, Adam's deceiver was at last crushed ; Adam was restored to his Maker's favor, and therefore may securely resume his human rank.

After the scheme and fabric of the poem, must be considered its component parts, the sentiments and the diction.

The *sentiments*, as expressive of manners, or appropriated to characters, are, for the greater part, unexceptionably just.

Splendid passages, containing lessons of morality or precepts of prudence, occur seldom. Such is the original formation of this poem, that, as it admits no human manners till the fall, it can give little assistance to human conduct. Its end is to raise the thoughts above sublunary cares or pleasures. Yet the praise of that fortitude, with which Abdiel maintained his singularity of virtue against the scorn of multitudes, may be accommodated to all times ; and Raphael's reproof of Adam's curiosity after the planetary motions, with the answer returned by Adam, may be confidently opposed to any rule of life which any poet has delivered.

The thoughts which are occasionally called forth in the progress are such as could only be produced by an imagination in the highest degree fervid and active, to which materials were supplied by incessant study and unlimited curiosity. The heat of Milton's mind may be said to sublimate his learning, to throw off into his work the spirit of science, unmingled with its grosser parts.

He had considered creation in its whole extent, and his descriptions are therefore learned. He had accustomed his imagination to unrestrained indulgence, and his conceptions therefore were extensive. The characteristic quality of his poem is sublimity. He sometimes descends to the elegant, but his element is the great. He can occasionally invest himself with grace ; but his natural port is gigantic loftiness.[1] He can please when pleasure is required ; but it is his peculiar power to astonish.

He seems to have been well acquainted with his own genius, and to know what it was that nature had bestowed upon him more bountifully than upon others ; the power of displaying the vast, illuminating the splendid, enforcing the awful, darkening the gloomy, and aggravating the dreadful ; he therefore chose a subject on which too much could not be said, on which he might tire his fancy without the censure of extravagance.

The appearances of nature, and the occurrences of life, did not satiate his appetite of greatness. To paint things as they are requires a minute attention, and employs the memory rather than the fancy. Milton's delight was to sport in the

[1] Algarotti terms it *gigantesca sublimità Miltoniana.*

wide regions of possibility ; reality was a scene too narrow for his mind.   He sent his faculties out upon discovery into worlds where only imagination can travel, and delighted to form new modes of existence, and furnish sentiment and action to superior beings, to trace the counsels of hell, or accompany the choirs of heaven.

But he could not be always in other worlds ; he must sometimes revisit earth, and tell of things visible and known.   When he cannot raise wonder by the sublimity of his mind, he gives delight by its fertility.

Whatever be his subject, he never fails to fill the imagination ; but his images and descriptions of the scenes or operations of nature do not seem to be always copied from original form, nor to have the freshness, raciness, and energy of immediate observation.   He saw Nature, as Dryden expresses it, "through the spectacles of books ;" and on most occasions calls learning to his assistance.   The garden of Eden brings to his mind the vale of Enna, where Proserpine was gathering flowers.   Satan makes his way through fighting elements like Argo between the Cyanean rocks ; or Ulysses, between the two Sicilian whirlpools, when he shunned Charybdis on the larboard.   The mythological allusions have been justly censured, as not being always used with notice of their vanity ; but they contribute variety to the narration, and produce an alternate exercise of the memory and the fancy.

His similes are less numerous and more various than those of his predecessors.   But he does not confine himself within the limits of rigorous comparison : his great excellence is amplitude ; and he expands the adventitious image beyond the dimensions which the occasion required.   Thus, comparing the shield of Satan to the orb of the moon, he crowds the imagination with the discovery of the telescope, and all the wonders which the telescope discovers.

Of his moral sentiments it is hardly praise to affirm that they excel those of all other poets ; for this superiority he was indebted to his acquaintance with the sacred writings.   The ancient epic poets, wanting the light of Revelation, were very unskilful teachers of virtue ; their principal characters may be great, but they are not amiable.   The reader may rise from their works with a greater degree of active or passive fortitude, and sometimes of prudence ; but he will be able to carry away few precepts of justice, and none of mercy.

From the Italian writers it appears that the advantages of even Christian knowledge may be possessed in vain.   Ariosto's pravity is generally known; and though the "Deliverance of

Jerusalem" may be considered as a sacred subject, the poet has been very sparing of moral instruction.

In Milton every line breathes sanctity of thought and purity of manners, except when the train of the narration requires the introduction of the rebellious spirits ; and even they are compelled to acknowledge their subjection to God, in such a manner as excites reverence and confirms piety.

Of human beings there are but two ; but those two are the parents of mankind, venerable before their fall for dignity and innocence, and amiable after it for repentance and submission. In the first state their affection is tender without weakness, and their piety sublime without presumption. When they have sinned, they show how discord begins in mutual frailty, and how it ought to cease in mutual forbearance ; how confidence of the divine favor is forfeited by sin, and how hope of pardon may be obtained by penitence and prayer. A state of innocence we can only conceive, if, indeed, in our present misery, it be possible to conceive it ; but the sentiments and worship proper to a fallen and offending being, we have all to learn, as we have all to practise.

The poet, whatever be done, is always great. Our progenitors, in their first state, conversed with angels ; even when folly and sin had degraded them, they had not in their humiliation *the port of mean suitors ;* and they rise again to reverential regard when we find that their prayers were heard.

As human passions did not enter the world before the fall, there is in the " Paradise Lost" little opportunity for the pathetic ; but what little thère is has not been lost. That passion which is peculiar to rational nature, the anguish arising from the consciousness of transgression, and the horrors attending the sense of the Divine displeasure, are very justly described and forcibly impressed. But the passions are moved only on one occasion ; sublimity is the general and prevailing quality of this poem ; sublimity variously modified, sometimes descriptive, sometimes argumentative.

The defects and faults of " Paradise Lost," for faults and defects every work of man must have, it is the business of impartial criticism to discover. As, in displaying the excellence of Milton, I have not made long quotations, because of selecting beauties there had been no end, I shall in the same general manner mention that which seems to deserve censure ; for what Englishman can take delight in transcribing passages which, if they lessen the reputation of Milton, diminish in some degree the honor of our country ?

The generality of my scheme does not admit the frequent

notice of verbal inaccuracies ; which Bentley, perhaps better skilled in grammar than in poetry, has often found, though he sometimes made them, and which he imputed to the obtrusions of a reviser, whom the author's blindness obliged him to employ ; a supposition rash and groundless, if he thought it true ; and vile and pernicious, if, as is said, he in private allowed it to be false.

The plan of " Paradise Lost" has this inconvenience, that it comprises neither human actions nor human manners. The man and woman who act and suffer are in a state which no other man or woman can ever know. The reader finds no transaction in which he can be engaged ; beholds no condition in which he can by any effort of imagination place himself ; he has, therefore, little natural curiosity or sympathy.

We all, indeed, feel the effects of Adam's disobedience ; we all sin like Adam, and like him must all bewail our offences ; we have restless and insidious enemies in the fallen angels ; and in the blessed spirits we have guardians and friends : in the redemption of mankind we hope to be included ; and in the description of heaven and hell we are surely interested, as we are all to reside hereafter either in the regions of horror or of bliss.

But these truths are too important to be new ; they have been taught to our infancy ; they have mingled with our solitary thoughts and familiar conversations, and are habitually interwoven with the whole texture of life. Being therefore not new, they raise no unaccustomed emotion in the mind ; what we knew before we cannot learn ; what is not unexpected cannot surprise.

Of the ideas suggested by these awful scenes, from some we recede with reverence, except when stated hours require their association ; and from others we shrink with horror, or admit them only as salutary inflictions, as counterpoises to our interests and passions. Such images rather obstruct the career of fancy than incite it.

Pleasure and terror are, indeed, the genuine sources of poetry ; but poetical pleasure must be such as human imagination can at least conceive ; and poetical terror such as human strength and fortitude may combat. The good and evil of eternity are too ponderous for the wings of wit ; the mind sinks under them with passive helplessness, content with calm belief and humble adoration.

Known truths, however, may take a different appearance, and be conveyed to the mind by a new train of intermediate images. This Milton has undertaken, and performed with pregnancy and vigor of mind peculiar to himself. Whoever considers the few radical positions which the Scriptures afforded him, will wonder by what energetic operation he expanded them to such extent, and ramified them to so much variety, restrained as he was by religious reverence from licentiousness of fiction.

Here is a full display of the united force of study and genius ; of a great accumulation of materials, with judgment to digest and fancy to combine them : Milton was able to select from nature, or from story, from ancient fable, or from modern science, whatever could illustrate or adorn his thoughts. An accumulation of knowledge impregnated his mind, fermented by study and exalted by imagination.

It has been therefore said, without an indecent hyperbole, by one of his encomiasts, that in reading " Paradise Lost," we read a book of universal knowledge.

But original deficience cannot be supplied. The want of human interest is always felt. " Paradise Lost" is one of the books which the reader admires and lays down, and forgets to take up again. None ever wished it longer than it is. Its perusal is a duty rather than a pleasure. We read Milton for instruction, retire harassed and overburdened, and look elsewhere for recreation ; we desert our master, and seek for companions.

Another inconvenience of Milton's design is, that it requires the description of what cannot be described, the agency of spirits. He saw that immateriality supplied no images, and that he could not show angels acting but by instruments of action : he therefore invested them with form and matter. This, being necessary, was therefore defensible ; and he should have secured the consistency of his system by keeping immateriality out of sight, and enticing his reader to drop it from his thoughts. But he has unhappily perplexed his poetry with his philosophy. His infernal and celestial powers are sometimes pure spirit, and sometimes animated body. When Satan walks with his lance upon the *burning marl*, he has a body ; when, in his passage between hell and the new world, he is in danger of sinking in the vacuity, and is supported by a gust of rising vapors, he has a body ; when he animates the toad, he seems to be mere spirit, that can penetrate matter at pleasure ; when he *starts up in his own shape*, he has at least a determined form ; and when he is brought before Gabriel, he has *a spear and a shield*, which he had the power of hiding in the toad, though the arms of the contending angels are evidently material.

The vulgar inhabitants of Pandemonium, being *incorpo-real spirits*, are *at large, though without number*, in a limited space : yet in the battle, when they were overwhelmed by mountains, their armor hurt them, *crushed in upon their substance, now grown gross by sinning.* This likewise happened to the uncorrupted angels, who were overthrown the *sooner for their arms, for unarmed they might easily as spirits have evaded by contraction or remove.* Even as spirits they are hardly spiritual ; for *contraction* and *remove* are images of matter ; but if they could have escaped without their armor, they might have escaped from it, and left only the empty cover to be battered. Uriel, when he rides on a sunbeam, is material ; Satan is material when he is afraid of the prowess of Adam.

The confusion of spirit and matter which pervades the whole narration of the war of Heaven fills it with incongruity ; and the book in which it is related is, I believe, the favorite of children, and gradually neglected as knowledge is increased.

After the operation of immaterial agents which cannot be explained, may be considered that of allegorical persons which have no real existence. To exalt causes into agents, to invest abstract ideas with form, and animate them with activity, has always been the right of poetry. But such airy beings are, for the most part, suffered only to do their natural office, and retire. Thus Fame tells a tale, and Victory hovers over a general or perches on a standard ; but Fame and Victory can do no more. To give them any real employment, or ascribe to them any material agency, is to make them allegorical no longer, but to shock the mind by ascribing effects to non-entity. In the "Prometheus" of Æschylus we see Violence and Strength, and in the "Alcestis" of Euripides we see Death, brought upon the stage, all as active persons of the drama ; but no precedents can justify absurdity.

Milton's allegory of Sin and Death is undoubtedly faulty. Sin is indeed the mother of Death, and may be allowed to be the portress of hell ; but when they stop the journey of Satan, a journey described as real, and when Death offers him battle, the allegory is broken. That Sin and Death should have shown the way to hell, might have been allowed ; but they cannot facilitate the passage by building a bridge, because the difficulty of Satan's passage is described as real and sensible, and the bridge ought to be only figurative. The hell assigned to the rebellious spirits is described as not less local than the residence of man. It is placed in some distant part of space, separated from the regions of harmony and order by a chaotic waste and an unoccupied vacuity ; but Sin and Death worked up a *mole* of *aggravated soil*, cemented with *asphaltus* ; a work too bulky for ideal architects.

This unskilful allegory appears to me one of the greatest faults of the poem ; and to this there was no temptation but the author's opinion of its beauty.

To the conduct of the narrative some objections may be made. Satan is with great expectation brought before Gabriel in Paradise, and is suffered to go away unmolested. The creation of man is represented as the consequence of the vacuity left in heaven by the expulsion of the rebels ; yet Satan mentions it as a report *rife in heaven* before his departure.

To find sentiments for the state of innocence was very difficult ; and something of anticipation, perhaps, is now and then discovered. Adam's discourse of dreams seems not to be the speculation of a new-created being. I know not whether his answer to the angel's reproof for curiosity does not want something of propriety ; it is the speech of a man acquainted with many other men. Some philosophical notions, especially when the philosophy is false, might have been better omitted. The angel, in a comparison, speaks of *timorous deer*, before deer were yet timorous, and before Adam could understand the comparison.

Dryden remarks that Milton has some flats among his elevations. This is only to say that all the parts are not equal. In every work one part must be for the sake of others : a palace must have passages ; a poem must have transitions. It is no more to be required that wit should always be blazing, than that the sun should always stand at noon. In a great work there is a vicissitude of luminous and opaque parts, as there is in the world a succession of day and night. Milton, when he has expatiated in the sky, may be allowed sometimes to revisit earth ; for what other author ever soared so high, or sustained his flight so long ?

Milton, being well versed in the Italian poets, appears to have borrowed often from them ; and, as every man catches something from his companions, his desire of imitating Ariosto's levity has disgraced his work with the "Paradise of Fools ;" a fiction not in itself ill-imagined, but too ludicrous for its place.

His play on words, in which he delights too often ; his equivocations, which Bentley endeavors to defend by the example of the ancients ; his unnecessary and ungraceful use of terms of art, it is not necessary to mention, because they are easily remarked and generally censured ; and at last bear so little proportion to the whole that they scarcely deserve the attention of a critic.

Such are the faults of that wonderful performance, " Paradise Lost ;" which he who can put in balance with its beauties must be considered not as nice but as dull, as less to be censured for want of candor than pitied for want of sensibility.

Of " Paradise Regained " the general judgment seems now to be right, that it is in many parts elegant, and everywhere instructive. It was not to be supposed that the writer of " Paradise Lost" could ever write without great effusions of fancy and exalted precepts of wisdom. The basis of " Paradise Regained " is narrow ; a dialogue without action can never please like an union of the narrative and dramatic powers. Had this poem been written not by Milton, but by some imitator, it would have claimed and received universal praise.

If " Paradise Regained " has been too much depreciated, " Samson Agonistes" has in requital been too much admired. It could only be by long prejudice, and the bigotry of learning, that Milton could prefer the ancient tragedies, with their encumbrance of a chorus, to the exhibitions of the French and English stages ; and it is only by a blind confidence in the reputation of Milton that a drama can be praised in which the intermediate parts have neither cause nor consequence, neither hasten nor retard the catastrophe.

In this tragedy are, however, many particular beauties, many just sentiments and striking lines ; but it wants that power of attracting the attention which a well-connected plan produces.

Milton would not have excelled in dramatic writing ; he knew human nature only in the gross, and had never studied the shades of character, nor the combinations of concurring, or the perplexity of contending, passions. He had read much, and knew what books could teach ; but had mingled little in the world, and was deficient in the knowledge which experience must confer.

Through all his greater works there prevails an uniform peculiarity of *diction*, a mode and cast of expression which bears little resemblance to that of any former writer ; and which is so far removed from common use that an unlearned reader, when he first opens his book, finds himself surprised by a new language.

This novelty has been, by those who can find nothing wrong in Milton, imputed to his laborious endeavors after words suitable to the grandeur of his ideas. *Our language,* says Addison, *sunk under him.* But the truth is, that, both in prose and verse, he had formed his style by a perverse and pedantic principle. He was desirous to use English words with a foreign idiom. This in all his prose is discovered and condemned ; for there judgment operates freely, neither softened by the beauty nor awed by the dignity of his thoughts ; but such is the power of his poetry that his call is obeyed without resistance, the reader feels himself in captivity to a higher and a nobler mind, and criticism sinks in admiration.

Milton's style was not modified by his subject ; what is shown with greater extent in " Paradise Lost " may be found in " Comus." One source of his peculiarity was his familiarity with the Tuscan poets ; the disposition of his words is, I think, frequently Italian ; perhaps sometimes combined with other tongues.

Of him, at least, may be said what Jonson says of Spenser, that *he wrote no language*, but has formed what Butler calls a *Babylonish dialect*, in itself harsh and barbarous, but made by exalted genius and extensive learning the vehicle of so much instruction and so much pleasure, that, like other lovers, we find grace in its deformity.

Whatever be the faults of his diction he cannot want the praise of copiousness and variety : he was master of his language in its full extent ; and has selected the melodious words with such diligence that from his book alone the art of English poetry might be learned.

After his diction something must be said of his *versification*. The *measure*, he says, *is the English heroic verse without rhyme*. Of this mode he had many examples among the Italians, and some in his own country. The Earl of Surrey is said to have translated one of Virgil's books without rhyme ; and, beside our tragedies, a few short poems had appeared in blank verse, particularly one tending to reconcile the nation to Raleigh's wild attempt upon Guiana, and probably written by Raleigh himself. These petty performances cannot be supposed to have much influenced Milton, who more probably took his hint from Trissino's *Italia Liberata ;* and, finding blank verse easier than rhyme, was desirous of persuading himself that it is better.

Rhyme, he says, and says truly, *is no necessary adjunct of true poetry*. But, perhaps, of poetry, as a mental operation, metre or music is no necessary adjunct : it is, however, by the music of metre that poetry has been discriminated in all languages ; and, in languages melodiously constructed with a due proportion of long and short syllables, metre is sufficient. But one language cannot communicate its rules to another ; where metre is scanty and imperfect, some help is necessary.

The music of the English heroic lines strikes the ear so faintly that it is easily lost, unless all the syllables of every line co-operate together ; this co-operation can be only obtained by the preservation of every verse unmingled with another as a distinct system of sounds ; and this distinctness is obtained and preserved by the artifice of rhyme. The variety of pauses, so much boasted by the lovers of blank verse, changes the measures of an English poet to the periods of a declaimer ; and there are only a few skilful and happy readers of Milton who enable their audience to perceive where the lines end or begin. *Blank verse*, said an ingenious critic, *seems to be verse only to the eye.*

Poetry may subsist without rhyme, but English poetry will not often please ; nor can rhyme ever be safely spared but where the subject is able to support itself. Blank verse makes some approach to that which is called the lapidary style ; has neither the easiness of prose nor the melody of numbers, and therefore tires by long continuance. Of the Italian writers without rhyme, whom Milton alleges as precedents, not one is popular ; what reason could urge in its defence has been confuted by the ear.

But, whatever be the advantages of rhyme, I cannot prevail on myself to wish that Milton had been a rhymer ; for I cannot wish his work to be other than it is ; yet, like other heroes, he is to be admired rather than imitated. He that thinks himself capable of astonishing may write blank verse ; but those that hope only to please must condescend to rhyme.

_ The highest praise of genius is original invention. Milton cannot be said to have contrived the structure of an epic poem, and therefore owes reverence to that vigor and amplitude of mind to which all generations must be indebted for the art of poetical narration, for the textures of the fable, the variation of incidents, the interposition of dialogue, and all the stratagems that surprise and enchain attention. But, of all the borrowers from Homer, Milton is perhaps the least indebted. He was naturally a thinker for himself, confident of his own abilities, and disdainful of help or hindrance : he did not refuse admission to the thoughts or images of his predecessors, but he did not seek them. From his contemporaries he neither courted nor received support ; there is in his writings nothing by which the pride of other authors might be gratified, or favor gained, no exchange of praise, nor solicitation of support. His great works were performed under discountenance, and in blindness ; but difficulties vanished at his touch ; he was born for whatever is arduous ; and his work is not the greatest of heroic poems, only because it is not the first.

DR. SAMUEL JOHNSON ON DRYDEN.

Of the great poet, whose life I am about to delineate, the curiosity which his reputation must excite will require a display more ample than can now be given. His contemporaries, however they reverenced his genius, left his life unwritten ; and nothing therefore can be known beyond what casual mention and uncertain tradition have supplied.

John Dryden was born August 9, 1631, at Aldwinkle, near Oundle, the son of Erasmus Dryden, of Titchmersh, who was the third son of Sir Erasmus Dryden, baronet, of Canons Ashby. All these places are in Northamptonshire ; but the original stock of the family was in the county of Huntingdon.

He is reported by his last biographer, Derrick, to have inherited from his father an estate of two hundred a year, and to have been bred, as was said, an anabaptist. For either of these particulars no authority is given. Such a fortune ought to have secured him from that poverty which seems always to have oppressed him ; or, if he had wasted it, to have made him ashamed of publishing his necessities. But though he had many enemies, who undoubtedly examined his life with a scrutiny sufficiently malicious, I do not remember that he is ever charged with waste of his patrimony. He was, indeed, sometimes reproached for his first religion. I am therefore inclined to believe that Derrick's intelligence was partly true and partly erroneous.

From Westminster School, where he was instructed as one of the King's scholars by Dr. Busby, whom he long after continued to reverence, he was, in 1650, elected to one of the Westminster scholarships at Cambridge.

Of his school performances has appeared only a poem on the death of Lord Hastings, composed with great ambition of such conceits as, notwithstanding the reformation begun by Waller and Denham, the example of Cowley still kept in reputation. Lord Hastings died of the small-pox ; and his poet has made of the pustules first rose-buds and then gems : at last exalts them into stars ; and says,

> " No comet need foretell his change drew on,
> Whose corpse might seem a constellation."

At the University he does not appear to have been eager of

poetical distinction, or to have lavished his early wit either on
fictitious subjects or public occasions. He probably considered that he who proposed to be an author ought first to be
a student. He obtained, whatever was the reason, no fellowship in the college. Why he was excluded cannot now be
known, and it is vain to guess : had he thought himself injured, he knew how to complain. In the " Life of Plutarch "
he mentions his education in the college with gratitude ; but in
a prologue at Oxford, he has these lines :

> " Oxford to him a dearer name shall be
> Than his own mother-university ;
> Thebes did his rude, unknowing youth engage ;
> He chooses Athens in his riper age."

It was not till the death of Cromwell, in 1658, that he became a public candidate for fame, by publishing " Heroic
Stanzas on the late Lord Protector ;" which, compared with
the verses of Sprat and Waller, on the same occasion, were
sufficient to raise great expectations of the rising poet.

When the king was restored, Dryden, like the other pane-
gyrists of usurpation, changed his opinion, or his profession,
and published " ASTREA REDUX, a Poem on the happy Restoration and Return of his most sacred Majesty King Charles
the Second."

The reproach of inconstancy was, on this occasion, shared
with such numbers that it produced neither hatred nor disgrace ! if he changed, he changed with the nation. It was,
however, not totally forgotten when his reputation raised him
enemies.

The same year he praised the new king in a second poem
on his restoration. In the " ASTREA " was the line

> " An horrid *stillness* first *invades* the *ear*,
> And in that silence we a tempest fear—"

for which he was persecuted with perpetual ridicule, perhaps
with more than was deserved. *Silence* is indeed mere privation, and, so considered, cannot *invade ;* but privation likewise
certainly is *darkness*, and probably *cold ;* yet poetry has never
been refused the right of ascribing effects or agency to them as
to positive powers. No man scruples to say that *darkness*
hinders him from his work, or that *cold* has killed the plants.
Death is also privation ; yet who has made any difficulty of assigning to Death a dart and the power of striking ?

In settling the order of his works there is some difficulty ;
for, even when they are important enough to be formally
offered to a patron, he does not commonly date his dedica-

tion ; the time of writing and publishing is not always the same ; nor can the first editions be easily found, if even from them could be obtained the necessary information.

The time at which his first play was exhibited is not certainly known, because it was not printed till it was, some years afterwards, altered and revised ; but since the plays are said to be printed in the order in which they were written, from the dates of some those of others may be inferred ; and thus it may be collected, that in 1663, in the thirty-second year of his life, he commenced a writer for the stage ; compelled undoubtedly by necessity, for he appears never to have loved that exercise of his genius, or to have much pleased himself with his own dramas.

Of the stage, when he had once invaded it, he kept possession for many years ; not indeed without the competition of rivals who sometimes prevailed, or the censure of critics, which was often poignant and often just ; but with such a degree of reputation as made him at least secure of being heard, whatever might be the final determination of the public.

His first piece was a comedy called " The Wild Gallant." He began with no happy auguries ; for his performance was so much disapproved that he was compelled to recall it, and change it from its imperfect state to the form in which it now appears, and which is yet sufficiently defective to vindicate the critics.

I wish that there were no necessity of following the progress of his theatrical fame, or tracing the meanders of his mind through the whole series of his dramatic performances ; it will be fit, however, to enumerate them, and to take especial notice of those that are distinguished by any peculiarity, intrinsic or concomitant ; for the composition and fate of eight-and-twenty dramas include too much of a poetical life to be omitted.

In 1664 he published " The Rival Ladies," which he dedicated to the Earl of Orrery, a man of high reputation both as a writer and as a statesman. In this play he made his essay of dramatic rhyme, which he defends, in his dedication, with sufficient certainty of a favorable hearing ; for Orrery was himself a writer of rhyming tragedies.

He then joined with Sir Robert Howard in " The Indian Queen," a tragedy in rhyme. The parts which either of them wrote are not distinguished.

" The Indian Emperor" was published in 1667. It is a tragedy in rhyme, intended for a sequel to Howard's " Indian Queen." Of this connection notice was given to the audience

by printed bills, distributed at the door ; an expedient supposed to be ridiculed in " The Rehearsal," where Bayes tells
how many reams he has printed, to instil into the audience
some conception of his plot.

In this play is the description of Night, which Rymer has
made famous by preferring it to those of all other poets.

The practice of making tragedies in rhyme was introduced
soon after the Restoration, as it seems by the Earl of Orrery, in
compliance with the opinion of Charles the Second, who had
formed his taste by the French theatre ; and Dryden, who
wrote, and made no difficulty of declaring that he wrote only to
please, and who perhaps knew that by his dexterity of versification he was more likely to excel others in rhyme than without it, very readily adopted his master's preference. He
therefore made rhyming tragedies, till, by the prevalence of
manifest propriety, he seems to have grown ashamed of making
them any longer.

To this play is prefixed a vehement defence of dramatic
rhyme, in confutation of the preface to " The Duke of
Lerma," in which Sir Robert Howard had censured it.

In 1667 he published " Annus Mirabilis, the Year of Wonders," which may be esteemed one of his most elaborate
works.

It is addressed to Sir Robert Howard by a letter, which is
not properly a dedication ; and, writing to a poet, he has interspersed many critical observations, of which some are common,
and some perhaps ventured without much consideration. He
began, even now, to exercise the domination of conscious genius, by recommending his own performance : " I am satisfied
that as the Prince and General" [Rupert and Monk] " are in-
comparably the best subjects I ever had, so what I have written
on them is much better than what I have performed on any
other. As I have endeavored to adorn my poem with noble
thoughts, so much more to express those thoughts with elocution."

It is written in quatrains, or heroic stanzas of four lines ; a
measure which he had learned from the " Gondibert" of Davenant, and which he then thought the most majestic that the
English language affords. Of this stanza he mentions the encumbrances, increased as they were by the exactness which the
age required. It was, throughout his life, very much his custom to recommend his works by representation of the difficulties that he had encountered, without appearing to have sufficiently considered that where there is no difficulty there is no
praise,

There seems to be, in the conduct of Sir Robert Howard
and Dryden towards each other, something that is not now
easily to be explained. Dryden, in his dedication to the Earl
of Orrery, had defended dramatic rhyme ; and Howard, in a
preface to a collection of plays, had censured his opinion.
Dryden vindicated himself in his "Dialogue on Dramatic
Poetry :" Howard, in his preface to "The Duke of Lerma,"
animadverted on the vindication ; and Dryden, in a preface to
"The Indian Emperor," replied to the animadversions with
great asperity, and almost with contumely. The dedication to
this play is dated the year in which the "Annus Mirabilis"
was published. Here appears a strange inconsistency ; but
Langbaine affords some help, by relating that the answer to
Howard was not published in the first edition of the play, but
was added when it was afterwards reprinted ; and as "The
Duke of Lerma" did not appear till 1668, the same year in
which the dialogue was published, there was time enough for
enmity to grow up between authors, who, writing both for the
theatre, were naturally rivals.

He was now so much distinguished that in 1668 he succeeded Sir William Davenant as poet-laureate. The salary of
the laureate had been raised in favor of Jonson, by Charles
the First, from a hundred marks to one hundred pounds a
year, and a tierce of wine : a revenue in those days not inadequate to the conveniences of life.

The same year he published his essay on Dramatic Poetry,
an elegant and instructive dialogue, in which we are told, by
Prior, that the principal character is meant to represent the
Duke of Dorset. This work seems to have given Addison a
model for his Dialogues upon Medals.

"Secret Love, or the Maiden Queen" (1668) is a tragi-
comedy. In the preface he discusses a curious question,
whether a poet can judge well of his own productions ? and
determines very justly that, of the plan and disposition, and
all that can be reduced to principles of science, the author may
depend upon his own opinion ; but that, in those parts where
fancy predominates, self-love may easily deceive. He might
have observed that what is good only because it pleases cannot be pronounced good till it has been found to please.

"Sir Martin Mar-all" (1668) is a comedy, published without preface or dedication, and at first without the name of the
author. Langbaine charges it, like most of the rest, with
plagiarism ; and observes that the song is translated from Voi-
ture, allowing, however, that both the sense and measure are
exactly observed.

" The Tempest" (1670) is an alteration of Shakespeare's play, made by Dryden in conjunction with Davenant ; " whom," says he, " I found of so quick a fancy that nothing was proposed to him in which he could not suddenly produce a thought extremely pleasant and surprising ; and those first thoughts of his, contrary to the Latin proverb, were not always the least happy ; and as his fancy was quick, so likewise were the products of it remote and new. He borrowed not of any other ; and his imaginations were such as could not easily enter into any other man."

The effect produced by the conjunction of these two powerful minds was, that to Shakespeare's monster, Caliban, is added a sister-monster, Sycorax ; and a woman, who, in the original play, had never seen a man, is in this brought acquainted with a man that had never seen a woman.

About this time, in 1673, Dryden seems to have had his quiet much disturbed by the success of "The Empress of Morocco," a tragedy written in rhyme by Elkanah Settle; which was so much applauded as to make him think his supremacy of reputation in some danger. Settle had not only been prosperous on the stage, but, in the confidence of success, had published his play, with sculptures and a preface of defiance. Here was one offence added to another ; and, for the last blast of inflammation, it was acted at Whitehall by the court ladies.

Dryden could not now repress those emotions which he called indignation, and others jealousy ; but wrote upon the play and the dedication such criticism as malignant impatience could pour out in haste.

Of Settle he gives this character : " He's an animal of a most deplored understanding, without reading and conversation. His being is in a twilight of sense, and some glimmering of thought which he never can fashion into wit or English. His style is boisterous and rough hewn, his rhyme incorrigibly lewd, and his numbers perpetually harsh and ill-sounding. The little talent which he has is fancy. He sometimes labors with a thought ; but with the pudder he makes to bring it into the world, 'tis commonly still-born ; so that for want of learning and elocution, he will never be able to express any thing either naturally or justly."

This is not very decent ; yet this is one of the pages in which criticism prevails over brutal fury. He proceeds : " He has a heavy hand at fools, and a great felicity in writing nonsense for them. Fools they will be in spite of him. His king, his two empresses, his villain, and his sub-villain, nay, his hero,

have all a certain natural cast of the father—their folly was
born and bred in them, and something of the Elkanah will be
visible."

This is Dryden's general declamation ; I will not withhold
from the reader a particular remark. Having gone through
the first act, he says, " to conclude this act with the most rumbling piece of nonsense spoken yet :

> " ' To flattering lightning our feign'd smiles conform,
> Which, back'd with thunder, do but gild a storm.'

Conform a smile to lightning, make a *smile* imitate *lightning*, and
flattering lightning : lightning sure is a threatening thing.
And this lightning must *gild a storm.* Now, if I must conform
my smiles to lightning, then my smiles must gild a storm too :
to *gild* with *smiles* is a new invention of gilding. And gild a
storm by being *backed with thunder.* Thunder is part of the
storm ; so one part of the storm must help to *gild* another
part, and help by *backing ;* as if a man would gild a thing the
better for being backed, or having a load upon his back. So
that here is *gilding* by *conforming, smiling, lightning, backing,*
and *thundering.* The whole is as if I should say thus : I will
make my counterfeit smiles look like a flattering stone-horse,
which, being backed with a trooper, does but gild the battle. I
am mistaken if nonsense is not here pretty thick sown. Sure
the poet writ these two lines aboard some smack in a storm,
and, being sea-sick, spewed up a good lump of clotted nonsense at once."

Here is perhaps a sufficient specimen ; but as the pamphlet,
though Dryden's, has never been thought worthy of republica-
tion, and is not easily to be found, it may gratify curiosity to
quote it more largely :

> " ' —Whene'er she bleeds,
> He no severer a damnation needs,
> Than dares pronounce the sentence of her death,
> Than the infection that attends that breath.'

That attends that breath. The poet is at *breath* again ; *breath*
can never 'scape him ; and here he brings in a *breath* that must
be *infectious* with *pronouncing* a sentence ; and this sentence is
not to be pronounced till the condemned party *bleeds ;* that is,
she must be executed first, and sentenced after ; and the *pronouncing* of this *sentence* will be infectious ; that is, others will
catch the disease of that sentence, and this infecting of others
will torment a man's self. The whole is thus : *when she bleeds,
thou needest no greater hell or torment to thyself than infecting of
others by pronouncing a sentence upon her.* What hodge-podge

does he make here ! Never was Dutch grout such clogging, thick, indigestible stuff. But this is but a taste to stay the stomach ; we shall have a more plentiful mess presently.

" Now to dish up the poet's broth, that I promised :

" ' For when we're dead, and our freed souls enlarg'd,
Of nature's grosser burden we're discharg'd ;
Then, gentle as a happy lover's sigh,
Like wand'ring meteors through the air we'll fly,
And in our airy walk, as subtle guests,
We'll steal into our cruel fathers' breasts,
There read their souls, and track each passion's sphere,
See how Revenge moves there, Ambition here ;
And in their orbs view the dark characters
Of sieges, ruins, murders, blood, and wars.
We'll blot out all those hideous draughts, and write
Pure and white forms ; then with a radiant light
Their breasts encircle, till their passions be
Gentle as Nature in its infancy ;
Till, soften'd by our charms, their furies cease,
And their revenge resolves into a peace.
Thus by our death their quarrel ends,
Whom living we made foes, dead we'll make friends.'

If this be not a very liberal mess, I will refer myself to the stomach of any moderate guest. And a rare mess it is, far excelling any Westminster white-broth. It is a kind of giblet porridge, made of the giblets of a couple of young geese, stodged full of *meteors, orbs, spheres, track, hideous draughts, dark characters, white forms,* and *radiant lights,* designed not only to please appetite, and indulge luxury ; but it is also physical, being an approved medicine to purge choler ; for it is propounded, by Morena, as a recipe to cure their fathers of their choleric humors ; and, were it written in characters as barbarous as the words, might very well pass for a doctor's bill. To conclude ; it is porridge, 'tis a recipe, 'tis a pig with a pudding in the belly, 'tis I know not what : for, certainly, never any one that pretended to write sense had the impudence before to put such stuff as this into the mouths of those that were to speak it before an audience, whom he did not take to be all fools ; and after that to print it too, and expose it to the examination of the world. But let us see what we can make of this stuff :

" ' For when we're dead, and our freed souls enlarg'd—'

Here he tells us what it is to be *dead ;* it is to have *our freed souls set free.* Now, if to have a soul set free is to be dead, then to have a *freed soul* set free is to have a dead man die.

" ' Then, gentle as a happy lover's sigh—'

They two like one *sigh*, and that one *sigh* like two wandering meteors,

" ' —shall fly through the air—'

that is, they shall mount above like falling stars, or else they shall skip like two Jacks with lanthorns, or Will with a whisp, and Madge with a candle."

" *And in the airy walk steal into their cruel fathers' breasts, like subtle guests.* So, that their *fathers' breasts* must be in an *airy walk,* an airy *walk* of a *flier. And there they will read their souls, and track the spheres of their passions.* That is, these walking fliers, Jack with a lanthorn, etc., will put on his spectacles, and fall a *reading souls ;* and put on his pumps, and fall a *tracking of spheres :* so that he will read and run, walk and fly, at the same time ! Oh ! nimble Jack ! *Then he will see how revenge here, how ambition there*—The birds will hop about. *And then view the dark characters of sieges, ruins, murders, blood, and wars, in their orbs : track the characters* to their forms ! Oh ! rare sport for Jack ! Never was place so full of game as these breasts ! You cannot stir, but flush a sphere, start a character, or unkennel an orb !"

Settle's is said to have been the first play embellished with sculptures ; those ornaments seem to have given poor Dryden great disturbance. He tries, however, to ease his pain by venting his malice in a parody.

" The poet has not only been so imprudent to expose all this stuff, but so arrogant to defend it with an epistle ;. like a saucy booth-keeper, that, when he had put a cheat upon the people, would wrangle and fight with any that would not like it, or would offer to discover it ; for which arrogance our poet receives this correction ; and, to jerk him a little the sharper, I will not transpose his verse, but by the help of his own words transnonsense sense, that, by my stuff, people may judge the better what his is :

" Great Boy, thy tragedy and sculptures done,
From press and plates, in fleets do homeward run ;
And, in ridiculous and humble pride,
Their course in ballad-singers' baskets guide,
Whose greasy twigs do all new beauties take,
From the gay shows thy dainty sculptures make.
Thy lines a mess of rhyming nonsense yield,
A senseless tale, with flattering fustian fill'd.
No grain of sense does in one line appear,
Thy words big bulks of boisterous bombast bear.
With noise they move, and from players' mouths rebound,
When their tongues dance to thy words' empty sound,
By thee inspir'd the rumbling verses roll,
As if that rhyme and bombast lent a soul ;

And with that soul they seem taught duty too ;
To huffing words does humble nonsense bow,
As if it would thy worthless worth enhance,
To th' lowest rank of fops thy praise advance,
To whom, by instinct, all thy stuff is dear :
Their loud claps echo to the theatre.
From breaths of fools thy commendation spreads,
Fame sings thy praise with mouths of logger-heads.
With noise and laughing each thy fustian greets,
'Tis clapt by choirs of empty-headed cits,
Who have their tribute sent, and homage given,
As men in whispers send loud noise to heaven.

" Thus I have daubed him with his own puddle : and now we are come from aboard his dancing, masking, rebounding, breathing fleet ; and, as if we had landed at Gotham, we meet nothing but fools and nonsense."

Such was the criticism to which the genius of Dryden could be reduced, between rage and terror ; rage with little provocation, and terror with little danger. To see the highest mind thus levelled with the meanest, may produce some solace to the consciousness of weakness, and some mortification to the pride of wisdom. But let it be remembered that minds are not levelled in their powers but when they are first levelled in their desires. Dryden and Settle had both placed their happiness in the claps of multitudes.

" An Evening's Love, or the Mock Astrologer," a comedy (1671), is dedicated to the illustrious Duke of Newcastle, whom he courts by adding to his praises those of his lady, not only as a lover but a partner of his studies. It is unpleasing to think how many names, once celebrated, are since forgotten. Of Newcastle's works nothing is now known but his Treatise on Horsemanship.

The preface seems very elaborately written, and contains many just remarks on the fathers of the English drama. Shakespeare's plots, he says, are in the hundred novels of Cinthio ; those of Beaumont and Fletcher in Spanish stories ; Jonson only made them for himself. His criticisms upon tragedy, comedy, and farce are judicious and profound. He endeavors to defend the immorality of some of his comedies by the example of former writers ; which is only to say that he was not the first nor perhaps the greatest offender. Against those that accused him of plagiarism he alleges a favorable expression of the king : " He only desired that they who accuse me of thefts would steal him plays like mine ;" and then relates how much labor he spends in fitting for the English stage what he borrows from others.

" Tyrannic Love, or the Virgin Martyr" (1672), was another

tragedy in rhyme, conspicuous for many passages of strength and elegance, and many of empty noise and ridiculous turbulence. The rants of Maximin have been always the sport of criticism ; and were at length, if his own confession may be trusted, the shame of the writer.

Of this play he has taken care to let the reader know that it was contrived and written in seven weeks. Want of time was often his excuse, or perhaps shortness of time was his private boast in the form of an apology.

It was written before " The Conquest of Granada," but published after it. The design is to recommend piety. " I considered that pleasure was not the only end of poesy ; and that even the instructions of morality were not so wholly the business of a poet, as that the precepts and examples of piety were to be omitted ; for to leave that employment altogether to the clergy were to forget that religion was first taught in verse, which the laziness or dulness of succeeding priesthood turned afterwards into prose." Thus foolishly could Dryden write, rather than not show his malice to the parsons.

The two parts of " The Conquest of Granada" (1672) are written with a seeming determination to glut the public with dramatic wonders, to exhibit in its highest elevation a theatrical meteor of incredible love and impossible valor, and to leave no room for a wilder flight to the extravagance of posterity. All the rays of romantic heat, whether amorous or warlike, glow in Almanzor by a kind of concentration. He is above all laws ; he is exempt from all restraints ; he ranges the world at will, and governs wherever he appears. He fights without inquiring the cause, and loves in spite of the obligations of justice, of rejection by his mistress, and of prohibition from the dead. Yet the scenes are, for the most part, delightful ; they exhibit a kind of illustrious depravity and majestic madness, such as, if it is sometimes despised, is often reverenced, and in which the ridiculous is mingled with the astonishing.

In the epilogue to the second part of " The Conquest of Granada," Dryden indulges his favorite pleasure of discrediting his predecessors ; and this epilogue he has defended by a long postscript. He had promised a second dialogue, in which he should more fully treat of the virtues and faults of the English poets, who have written in the dramatic, epic, or lyric way. This promise was never formally performed ; but, with respect to the dramatic writers, he has given us in his prefaces, and in this postscript, something equivalent ; but his purpose being to

exalt himself by the comparison, he shows faults distinctly, and
only praises excellence in general terms.

A play thus written, in professed defiance of probability,
naturally drew upon itself the vultures of the theatre. One of
the critics that attacked it was Martin Clifford, to whom Sprat
addressed the Life of Cowley, with such veneration of his critical powers as might naturally excite great expectations of instruction from his remarks. But let honest credulity beware
of receiving characters from contemporary writers. Clifford's
remarks, by the favor of Dr. Percy, were at last obtained ;
and, that no man may ever want them more, I will extract
enough to satisfy all reasonable desire.

In the first letter his observation is only general : " You do
live," says he, " in as much ignorance and darkness as you did
in the womb ; your writings are like a Jack-of-all-trades' shop ;
they have a variety, but nothing of value ; and if thou art not
the dullest plant-animal that ever the earth produced, all that I
have conversed with are strangely mistaken in thee."

In the second he tells him that Almanzor is not more
copied from Achilles than from ancient Pistol. "But I am,"
says he, "strangely mistaken if I have not seen this very
Almanzor of yours in some disguise about this town, and passing under another name. Pr'ythee tell me true, was not this
huffcap once the Indian Emperor? and at another time did he
not call himself Maximin ? Was not Lyndaraxa once called
Almeria ? I mean, under Montezuma, the Indian Emperor.
I protest and vow they are either the same, or so alike that I
cannot, for my heart, distinguish one from the other. You are
therefore a strange unconscionable thief ; thou art not content
to steal from others, but dost rob thy poor wretched self too."

Now was Settle's time to take his revenge. He wrote a
vindication of his own lines ; and, if he is forced to yield any
thing, makes his reprisals upon his enemy. To say that his
answer is equal to the censure is no high commendation. To
expose Dryden's method of analyzing his expressions, he tries
the same experiment upon the same description of the ships in
" The Indian Emperor," of which, however, he does not deny
the excellence ; but intends to show, that by studied miscon-
struction every thing may be equally represented as ridiculous.
After so much of Dryden's elegant animadversions, justice
requires that something of Settle's should be exhibited. The
following observations are therefore extracted from a quarto
pamphlet of ninety-five pages :

> " ' Fate after him below with pain did move,
>   And victory could scarce keep pace above.'

These two lines, if he can show me any sense or thought in, or any thing but bombast and noise, he shall make me believe every word in his observations on ' Morocco ' sense.
'' In the ' Empress of Morocco ' were these lines :

> '' ' I'll travel then to some remoter sphere,
> Till I find out new worlds, and crown you there.'

On which Dryden made this remark :
'' I believe our learned author takes a sphere for country ; the sphere of Morocco ; as if Morocco were the globe of earth and water ; but a globe is no sphere neither, by his leave,'' etc.
'' So *sphere* must not be sense, unless it relates to a circular motion about a globe, in which sense the astronomers use it. I would desire him to expound those lines in ' Granada ' :

> '' ' I'll to the turrets of the palace go,
> And add new fire to those that fight below.
> Thence, hero-like, with torches by my side,
> (Far be the omen tho') my love I'll guide.
> No, like his better fortune I'll appear,
> With open arms, loose veil, and flowing hair,
> Just flying forward from my rolling sphere.'

I wonder, if he be so strict, how he dares make so bold with the *sphere* himself, and to be so critical in other men's writings. Fortune is fancied standing on a globe, not on a *sphere*, as he told us in the first act.
'' Because ' Elkanah's similes are the most unlike things to what they are compared in the world,' I'll venture to start a simile in his ' Annus Mirabilis : ' he gives this poetical description of the ship called the London :

> '' ' The goodly London in her gallant trim,
> The phœnix-daughter of the vanquisht old,
> Like a rich bride does on the ocean swim,
> And on her shadow rides in floating gold.
> Her flag aloft spread ruffling in the wind,
> And sanguine streamers seem'd the flood to fire :
> The weaver, charm'd with what his loom design'd,
> Goes on to sea, and knows not to retire.
> With roomy decks her guns of mighty strength,
> Whose low-laid mouths each mountain billow laves,
> Deep in her draught, and warlike in her length,
> She seems a sea-wasp flying in the waves.'

What a wonderful pother is here, to make all these poetical beautifications of a ship ; that is, a *phœnix* in the first stanza, and but a *wasp* in the last : nay, to make his humble comparison of a *wasp* more ridiculous, he does not say it flies upon the waves as nimbly as a wasp, or the like, but it seemed a *wasp*

But our author at the writing of this was not in his altitudes, to compare ships to floating palaces : a comparison to the purpose was a perfection he did not arrive to till the *Indian Emperor's* days.   But perhaps his similitude has more in it than we imagine ; this ship had a great many guns in her, and they, put all together, made the sting in the wasp's tail ; for this is all the reason I can guess why it seemed a *wasp*.   But because we will allow him all we can to help out, let it be a *phœnix seawasp*, and the rarity of such an animal may do much towards heightening the fancy.

"It had been much more to his purpose, if he had designed to render the senseless play little, to have searched for some such pedantry as this :

> " 'Two ifs scarce make one possibility.
> If justice will take all, and nothing give,
> Justice, methinks, is not distributive,
> To die or kill you is the alternative.
> Rather than take your life, I will not live.'

"Observe how prettily our author chops logic in heroic verse.   Three such fustian canting words as *distributive*, *alternative*, and *two ifs*, no man but himself would have come within the noise of.   But he's a man of general learning, and all comes into his play.

" 'Twould have done well too if he could have met with the rant or two, worth the observation : such as,

> " ' Move swiftly, Sun, and fly a lover's pace,
> Leave months and weeks behind thee in thy race.'

" But surely the sun, whether he flies a lover's or not a lover's pace, leaves weeks and months, nay, years too, behind him in his race.

" Poor Robin, or any other of the philo-mathematics, would have given him satisfaction in the point.

> " ' If I could kill thee now. thy fate's so low,
> That I must stoop ere I can give the blow.
> But mine is fixed so far above thy crown,
> That all thy men,
> Piled on thy back, can never pull it down.'

" Now where that is, Almanzor's fate is fixed, I cannot guess : but, wherever it is, I believe Almanzor, and think that all Abdalla's subjects, piled upon one another, might not pull down his fate so well as without piling ; besides, I think Abdalla so wise a man, that if Almanzor had told him piling his men upon his back might do the feat, he would scarcely bear such a weight, for the pleasure of the exploit ; but it is a huff, and let Abdalla do it if he dare.

> " ' The people like a headlong torrent go,
> And every dam they break or overflow.
> But, unoppos'd, they either lose their force,
> Or wind in volumes to their former course.'

A very pretty allusion, contrary to all sense or reason. Torrents, I take it, let them wind never so much, can never return to their former course, unless he can suppose that fountains can go upwards, which is impossible ; nay more, in the foregoing page he tells us so too ; a trick of a very unfaithful memory.

> " ' But can no more than fountains upward flow.'

Which of a *torrent*, which signifies a rapid stream, is much more impossible. Besides, if he goes to quibble and say that it is impossible by art water may be made return, and the same water run twice in one and the same channel, then he quite confutes what he says ; for it is by being opposed that it runs into its former course ; for all engines that make water so return do it by compulsion and opposition. Or, if he means a headlong torrent for a tide, which would be ridiculous, yet they do not wind in volumes, but come fore-right back (if their upright lies straight to their former course), and that by opposition of the sea-water, that drives them back again.

" And for fancy, when he lights of any thing like it, 'tis a wonder if it be not borrowed. As here, for example of, I find this fanciful thought in his ' Ann. Mirab ' :

> " ' Old father Thames rais'd up his reverend head :
> But fear'd the fate of Simois would return ;
> Deep in his ooze he sought his sedgy bed ;
> And shrunk his waters back into his urn.'

This is stolen from Cowley's ' Davideis,' p. 9 :

> " ' Swift Jordan started, and straight backward fled,
> Hiding amongst thick reeds his aged head.
> And when the Spaniards their assault begin,
> At once beat those without and those within.'

" This Almanzor speaks of himself ; and sure for one man to conquer an army within the city, and another without the city, at once, is something difficult : but this flight is pardonable to some we meet with in ' Granada : ' Osmin, speaking of Almanzor,

> " ' Who, like a tempest that outrides the wind,
> Made a just battle ere the bodies join'd.'

Pray, what does this honorable person mean by a *tempest that outrides the wind!* a tempest that outrides itself? To suppose a tempest without wind is as bad as supposing a man to walk without feet ; for if he supposes the tempest to be something distinct from the wind, yet, as being the effect of wind only, to come before the cause, is a little preposterous ; so that if he takes it one way, or if he takes it the other, those two *ifs* will scarcely make one *possibility.*" Enough of Settle.

" Marriage a-la-mode" (1673) is a comedy dedicated to the Earl of Rochester ; whom he acknowledges not only as the defender of his poetry, but the promoter of his fortune. Langbaine places this play in 1673. The Earl of Rochester, therefore, was the famous Wilmot, whom yet tradition always represents as an enemy to Dryden, and who is mentioned by him with some disrespect in the preface to " Juvenal."

" The Assignation, or Love in a Nunnery," a comedy (1673), was driven off the stage, *against the opinion,* as the author says, *of the best judges.* It is dedicated in a very elegant address to Sir Charles Sedley ; in which he finds an opportunity for his usual complaint of hard treatment and unreasonable censure.

" Amboyna" (1673) is a tissue of mingled dialogue in verse and prose, and was perhaps written in less time than " The Virgin Martyr ;" though the author thought not fit, either ostentatiously or mournfully, to tell how little labor it cost him, or at how short a warning he produced it. It was a temporary performance, written in the time of the Dutch war, to inflame the nation against their enemies ; to whom he hopes, as he declares in his epilogue, to make his poetry not less destructive than that by which Tyrtæus of old animated the Spartans. This play was written in the second Dutch war in 1673.

" Troilus and Cressida" (1679) is a play altered from Shakespeare ; but so altered that, even in Langbaine's opinion, " the last scene in the third act is a masterpiece." It is introduced by a discourse on " The Grounds of Criticism in Tragedy," to which I suspect that Rymer's book had given occasion.

" The Spanish Friar" (1681) is a tragi-comedy, eminent for the happy coincidence and coalition of the two plots. As it was written against the papists, it would naturally at that time have friends and enemies ; and partly by the popularity which it obtained at first, and partly by the real power both of the serious and risible part, it continued long a favorite of the public.

It was Dryden's opinion, at least for some time, and he maintains it in the dedication of this play, that the drama required an alternation of comic and tragic scenes ; and that it is necessary to mitigate by alleviations of merriment the pressure of ponderous events, and the fatigue of toilsome passions. " Whoever," says he, " cannot perform both parts is but half a writer for the stage."

" The Duke of Guise," a tragedy (1683), written in conjunction with Lee, as " Œdipus" had been before, seems to deserve notice only for the offence which it gave to the remnant of the Covenanters, and in general to the enemies of the court, who attacked him with great violence, and were answered by him ; though at last he seems to withdraw from the conflict by transferring the greater part of the blame or merit to his partner. It happened that a contract had been made between them, by which they were to join in writing a play : and " he happened," says Dryden, " to claim the promise just upon the finishing of a poem, when I would have been glad of a little respite. *Two*-thirds of it belonged to him ; and to me only the first scene of the play, the whole fourth act, and the first half, or somewhat more, of the fifth."

This was a play written professedly for the party of the Duke of York, whose succession was then opposed. A parallel is intended between the Leaguers of France and the Covenanters of England ; and this intention produced the controversy.

" Albion and Albanius" (1685) is a musical drama or opera, written, like " The Duke of Guise," against the republicans. With what success it was performed I have not found.

" The State of Innocence and Fall of Man" (1675) is termed by him an opera : it is rather a tragedy in heroic rhyme, but of which the personages are such as cannot decently be exhibited on the stage. Some such production was foreseen by Marvell, who writes thus to Milton :

" Or if a work so infinite be spann'd,
Jealous I was lest some less skilful hand
(Such as disquiet always what is well,
And by ill-imitating would excel),
Might hence presume the whole creation's day
To change in scenes, and show it in a play."

It is another of his hasty productions ; for the heat of his imagination raised it in a month.

This composition is addressed to the Princess of Modena, then Duchess of York, in a strain of flattery which disgraces genius, and which it was wonderful that any man that knew the meaning of his own words could use without self-detestation,

It is an attempt to mingle earth and heaven, by praising human excellence in the language of religion.

The preface contains an apology for heroic verse and poetic license ; by which is meant not any liberty taken in contracting or extending words, but the use of bold fictions and ambitious figures.

The reason which he gives for printing what was never acted cannot be overpassed : " I was induced to it in my own defence, many hundred copies of it being dispersed abroad without my knowledge or consent ; and every one gathering new faults, it became at length a libel against me." These copies, as they gathered faults, were apparently manuscript, and he lived in an age very unlike ours, if many hundred copies of fourteen hundred lines were likely to be transcribed. An author has a right to print his own works, and need not seek an apology in falsehood ; but he that could bear to write the dedication felt no pain in writing the preface.

" Aureng Zebe" (1676) is a tragedy founded on the actions of a great prince then reigning, but over nations not likely to employ their critics upon the transactions of the English stage. If he had known and disliked his own character, our trade was not in those times secure from his resentment. His country is at such a distance, that the manners might be safely falsified and the incidents feigned ; for the remoteness of place is remarked, by Racine, to afford the same conveniences to a poet as length of time.

This play is written in rhyme, and has the appearance of being the most elaborate of all the dramas. The personages are imperial ; but the dialogue is often domestic, and therefore susceptible of sentiments accommodated to familiar incidents. The complaint of life is celebrated ; and there are many other passages that may be read with pleasure.

This play is addressed to the Earl of Mulgrave, afterwards Duke of Buckingham, himself, if not a poet, yet a writer of verses and a critic. In this address Dryden gave the first hints of his intention to write an epic poem. He mentions his design in terms so obscure that he seems afraid lest his plan should be purloined, as, he says, happened to him when he told it more plainly in his preface to " Juvenal." " The design," says he, " you know is great, the story English, and neither too near the present times nor too distant from them."

" All for Love, or the World well Lost " (1678), a tragedy founded upon the story of Antony and Cleopatra, he tells us, " is the only play which he wrote for himself :" the rest were given to the people. It is by universal consent accounted the work in which he has admitted the fewest improprieties of style or character ; but it has one fault equal to many, though rather moral than critical, that, by admitting the romantic omnipotence of Love, he has recommended, as laudable and worthy of imitation, that conduct which, through all ages, the good have censured as vicious, and the bad despised as foolish.

Of this play the prologue and the epilogue, though written upon the common topics of malicious and ignorant criticisms, and without any particular relation to the characters or incidents of the drama, are deservedly celebrated for their elegance and sprightliness.

" Limberham, or the Kind Keeper" (1680), is a comedy, which, after the third night, was prohibited as too indecent for the stage. What gave offence was in the printing, as the author says, altered or omitted. Dryden confesses that its indecency was objected to ; but Langbaine, who yet seldom favors him, imputes its expulsion to resentment, because it " so much exposed the keeping part of the town."

" Œdipus" (1679) is a tragedy formed by Dryden and Lee, in conjunction, from the works of Sophocles, Seneca, and Corneille. Dryden planned the scenes, and composed the first and third acts.

" Don Sebastian" (1690) is commonly esteemed either the first or second of his dramatic performances. It is too long to be all acted, and has many characters and many incidents ; and though it is not without sallies of frantic dignity, and more noise than meaning, yet, as it makes approaches to the possibilities of real life, and has some sentiments which leave a strong impression, it continued long to attract attention. Amidst the distresses of princes and the vicissitudes of empire are inserted several scenes which the writer intended for comic ; but which, I suppose, that age did not much commend, and this would not endure. There are, however, passages of excellence universally acknowledged ; the dispute and the reconciliation of Dorax and Sebastian has always been admired.

This play was first acted in 1690, after Dryden had for some years discontinued dramatic poetry.

" Amphytrion" is a comedy derived from Plautus and Molière. The dedication is dated October, 1690. This play seems to have succeeded at its first appearance, and was, I think, long considered as a very diverting entertainment.

" Cleomenes" (1692) is a tragedy only remarkable as it occasioned an incident related in the " Guardian," and allusively mentioned by Dryden in his preface. As he came out from the representation he was accosted thus by some airy stripling :

" Had I been left alone with a young beauty, I would not have spent my time like your Spartan." " That, sir," said Dryden, " perhaps is true ; but give me leave to tell you that you are no hero."

" King Arthur" (1691) is another opera. It was the last work that Dryden performed for King Charles, who did not live to see it exhibited, and it does not seem to have been ever brought upon the stage. In the dedication to the Marquis of Halifax, there is a very elegant character of Charles, and a pleasing account of his later life. When this was first brought upon the stage, news that the Duke of Monmouth had landed was told in the theatre ; upon which the company departed, and " Arthur" was exhibited no more.

His last drama was " Love Triumphant," a tragi-comedy. In his dedication to the Earl of Salisbury he mentions " the lowness of fortune to which he has voluntarily reduced himself, and of which he has no reason to be ashamed."

This play appeared in 1694. It is said to have been unsuccessful. The catastrophe, proceeding merely from a change of mind, is confessed by the author to be defective. Thus he began and ended his dramatic labors with ill success.

From such a number of theatrical pieces, it will be supposed, by most readers, that he must have improved his fortune ; at least that such diligence with such abilities must have set penury at defiance. But in Dryden's time the drama was very far from that universal approbation which it has now obtained. The playhouse was abhorred by the Puritans, and avoided by those who desired the character of seriousness or decency. A grave lawyer would have debased his dignity, and a young trader would have impaired his credit, by appearing in those mansions of dissolute licentiousness. The profits of the theatre, when so many classes of the people were deducted from the audience, were not great ; and the poet had, for a long time, but a single night. The first that had two nights was Southern ; and the first that had three was Rose. There were, however, in those days, arts of improving a poet's profit, which Dryden forbore to practise ; and a play therefore seldom produced him more than a hundred pounds, by the accumulated gain of the third night, the dedication, and the copy.

Almost every piece had a dedication, written with such elegance and luxuriance of praise, as neither haughtiness nor avarice could be imagined able to resist. But he seems to have made flattery too cheap. That praise is worth nothing of which the price is known.

To increase the value of his copies, he often accompanied

his work with a preface of criticism ; a kind of learning then almost new in English language, and which he, who had considered with great accuracy the principles of writing, was able to distribute copiously as occasions arose. By these dissertations the public judgment must have been much improved ; and Swift, who conversed with Dryden, relates that he regretted the success of his own instructions, and found his readers made suddenly too skilful to be easily satisfied.

His prologues had such reputation, that for some time a play was considered as less likely to be well received if some of his verses did not introduce it. The price of a prologue was two guineas, till, being asked to write one for Mr. Southern, he demanded three : " Not," said he, " young man, out of disrespect to you ; but the players have had my goods too cheap."

Though he declares that in his own opinion his genius was not dramatic, he had great confidence in his own fertility ; for he is said to have engaged, by contract, to furnish four plays a year.

It is certain that in one year, 1678, he published " All for Love," " Assignation," two parts of the " Conquest of Granada," " Sir Martin Mar-all," and the " State of Innocence," six complete plays, with a celerity of performance, which, though all Langbaine's charges of plagiarism should be allowed, shows such facility of composition, such readiness of language, and such copiousness of sentiment, as, since the time of Lopez de Vega, perhaps no other author has ever possessed.

He did not enjoy his reputation, however great, nor his profits, however small, without molestation. He had critics to endure and rivals to oppose. The two most distinguished wits of the nobility, the Duke of Buckingham and Earl of Rochester, declared themselves his enemies.

Buckingham characterized him, in 1671, by the name of Bayes in " The Rehearsal ;" a farce which he is said to have written with the assistance of Butler, the author of " Hudibras ;" Martin Clifford, of the Charter House ; and Dr. Sprat, the friend of Cowley, then his chaplain. Dryden and his friends laughed at the length of time and the number of hands employed upon this performance ; in which, though by some artifice of action it yet keeps possession of the stage, it is not possible now to find any thing that might not have been written without so long delay, or a confederacy so numerous.

To adjust the minute events of literary history is tedious and troublesome ; it requires indeed no great force of understanding, but often depends upon inquiries which there is no opportunity of making, or is to be fetched from books and pamphlets not always at hand.

" The Rehearsal" was played in 1671, and yet is repre-sented as ridiculing passages in " The Conquest of Granada" and " Assignation," which were not published till 1678 ; in " Marriage a-la-mode," published in 1673 ; and in " Tyran-nic Love," in 1677. These contradictions show how rashly satire is applied.

It is said that this farce was originally intended against Davenant, who, in the first draught, was characterized by the name of *Bilboa*. Davenant had been a soldier and an adven-turer.

There is one passage in " The Rehearsal " still remaining, which seems to have related originally to Davenant. Bayes hurts his nose, and comes in with brown paper applied to the bruise ; how this affected Dryden does not appear. Dave-nant's nose had suffered such diminution by mishaps among the women that a patch upon that part evidently denoted him.

It is said likewise that Sir Robert Howard was once meant. The design was probably to ridicule the reigning poet, whoever he might be.

Much of the personal satire, to which it might owe its first reception, is now lost or obscured. Bayes probably imitated the dress and mimicked the manner of Dryden : the cant words which are so often in his mouth may be supposed to have been Dryden's habitual phrases or customary exclama-tions. Bayes, when he is to write, is blooded and purged ; this, as Lamotte relates himself to have heard, was the real practice of the poet.

There were other strokes in " The Rehearsal " by which malice was gratified : the debate between Love and Honor, which keeps Prince Volscius in a single boot, is said to have alluded to the misconduct of the Duke of Ormond, who lost Dublin to the rebels while he was toying with a mistress.

The Earl of Rochester, to suppress the reputation of Dry-den, took Settle into his protection, and endeavored to per-suade the public that its approbation had been to that time misplaced. Settle was a while in high reputation ; his " Em-press of Morocco," having first delighted the town, was carried in triumph to Whitehall, and played by the ladies of the court. Now was the poetical meteor at the highest : the next mo-ment began its fall. Rochester withdrew his patronage, seem-ingly resolved, says one of his biographers, " to have a judg-ment contrary to that of the town ;" perhaps being unable to endure any reputation beyond a certain height, even when he had himself contributed to raise it.

Neither critics nor rivals did Dryden much mischief, unless they gained from his own temper the power of vexing him, which his frequent bursts of resentment give reason to suspect. He is always angry at some past or afraid of some future censure ; but he lessens the smart of his wounds by the balm of his own approbation, and endeavors to repel the shafts of criticism by opposing a shield of adamantine confidence.

The perpetual accusation produced against him was that of plagiarism, against which he never attempted any vigorous defence ; for though he was perhaps sometimes injuriously censured, he would, by denying part of the charge, have confessed the rest ; and, as his adversaries had the proof in their own hands, he, who knew that wit had little power against facts, wisely left, in that perplexity which it generally produces, a question which it was his interest to suppress, and which, unless provoked by vindication, few were likely to examine.

Though the life of a writer, from about thirty-five to sixty-three, may be supposed to have been sufficiently busied by the composition of eight-and-twenty pieces for the stage, Dryden found room in the same space for many other undertakings.

But, how much soever he wrote, he was at least once suspected of writing more ; for, in 1679, a paper of verses, called "An Essay on Satire," was shown about in manuscript, by which the Earl of Rochester, the Duchess of Portsmouth, and others were so much provoked, that, as was supposed (for the actors were never discovered), they procured Dryden, whom they suspected as the author, to be waylaid and beaten. This incident is mentioned by the Duke of Buckingham, the true writer, in his " Art of Poetry," where he says of Dryden,

" Though prais'd and beaten for another's rhymes,
His own deserve as great applause sometimes."

His reputation in time was such that his name was thought necessary to the success of every poetical or literary performance, and therefore he was engaged to contribute something, whatever it might be, to many publications. He prefixed the "Life of Polybius" to the translation of Sir Henry Sheers ; and those of Lucian and Plutarch to versions of their works by different hands. Of the English Tacitus he translated the first book ; and, if Gordon be credited, translated it from the French. Such a charge can hardly be mentioned without some degree of indignation ; but it is not, I suppose, so much to be inferred that Dryden wanted the literature necessary to the perusal of Tacitus, as that, considering himself as hidden in a crowd, he had no awe of the public ; and, writing merely for money, was contented to get it by the nearest way.

In 1680, the " Epistles of Ovid " being translated by the poets of the time, among which one was the work of Dryden, and another of Dryden and Lord Mulgrave, it was necessary to introduce them by a preface ; and Dryden, who on such occasions was regularly summoned, prefixed a discourse upon translation, which was then struggling for the liberty that it now enjoys.   Why it should find any difficulty in breaking the shackles of verbal interpretation, which must forever debar it from elegance, it would be difficult to conjecture, were not the power of prejudice every day observed.   The authority of Jonson, Sandys, and Holiday had fixed the judgment of the nation ; and it was not easily believed that a better way could be found than they had taken, though Fanshaw, Denham, Waller, and Cowley had tried to give examples of a different practice.

In 1681 Dryden became yet more conspicuous by uniting politics with poetry in the memorable satire called "Absalom and Achitophel," written against the faction which, by Lord Shaftesbury's incitement, set the Duke of Monmouth at its head.

Of this poem, in which personal satire was applied to the support of public principles, and in which therefore every mind was interested, the reception was eager, and the sale so large that my father, an old bookseller, told me he had not known it equalled but by Sacheverell's Trial.

The reason of this general perusal Addison has attempted to derive from the delight which the mind feels in the investigation of secrets ; and thinks that curiosity to decipher the names procured readers to the poem.   There is no need to inquire why those verses were read, which, to all the attractions of wit, elegance, and harmony, added the co-operation of all the factious passions, and filled every mind with triumph or resentment.

It could not be supposed that all the provocation given by Dryden would be endured without resistance or reply.   Both his person and his party were exposed in their turns to the shafts of satire, which, though neither so well pointed nor perhaps so well aimed, undoubtedly drew blood.

One of these poems is called "Dryden's Satire on his Muse ;" ascribed, though, as Pope says, falsely, to Somers, who was afterwards chancellor.   The poem, whosesoever it was, has much virulence and some sprightliness.   The writer tells all the ill that he can collect both of Dryden and his friends.

The poem of "Absalom and Achitophel" had two answers, now both forgotten ; one called "Azaria and Hushai ;" the other, "Absalom Senior." Of these hostile compositions, Dryden apparently imputes "Absalom Senior" to Settle, by quoting in his verses against him the second line. "Azaria and Hushai" was, as Wood says, imputed to him, though it is somewhat unlikely that he should write twice on the same occasion. This is a difficulty which I cannot remove, for want of a minuter knowledge of poetical transactions.

The same year he published "The Medal," of which the subject is a medal struck on Lord Shaftesbury's escape from a prosecution, by the *ignoramus* of a grand jury of Londoners.

In both poems he maintains the same principles, and saw them both attacked by the same antagonist. Elkanah Settle, who had answered "Absalom," appeared with equal courage in opposition to "The Medal ;" and published an answer called "The Medal Reversed," with so much success in both encounters that he left the palm doubtful, and divided the suffrages of the nation. Such are the revolutions of fame, or such is the prevalence of fashion, that the man whose works have not yet been thought to deserve the care of collecting them, who died forgotten in a hospital, and whose latter years were spent in contriving shows for fairs, and carrying an elegy or epithalamium, of which the beginning and end were occasionally varied, but the intermediate parts were always the same, to every house where there was a funeral or a wedding, might with truth have had inscribed upon his stone,

Here lies the Rival and Antagonist of Dryden.

Settle was, for his rebellion, severely chastised by Dryden, under the name of "Doeg," in the second part of "Absalom and Achitophel ;" and was, perhaps, for his factious audacity, made the city poet, whose annual office was to describe the glories of the Mayor's day. Of these bards he was the last, and seems not much to have deserved even this degree of regard, if it was paid to his political opinions ; for he afterwards wrote a panegyric on the virtues of Judge Jefferies ; and what more could have been done by the meanest zealot for prerogative ?

Of translated fragments or occasional poems, to enumerate the titles or settle the dates would be tedious, with little use. It may be observed that as Dryden's genius was commonly excited by some personal regard, he rarely writes upon a general topic.

Soon after the accession of King James, when the design of reconciling the nation to the Church of Rome became apparent, and the religion of the court gave the only efficacious title to its favors, Dryden declared himself a convert to popery. This at any other time might have passed with little censure. Sir Kenelm Digby embraced popery ; the two Reynolds reciprocally converted one another ; and Chillingworth himself was awhile so entangled in the wilds of controversy as to retire for quiet to an infallible church. If men of argument and study can find such difficulties or such motives as may either unite them to the Church of Rome or detain them in uncertainty, there can be no wonder that a man who perhaps never inquired why he was a Protestant, should by an artful and experienced disputant be made a papist, overborne by the sudden violence of new and unexpected arguments, or deceived by a representation which shows only the doubts on one part and only the evidence on the other.

That conversion will always be suspected that apparently concurs with interest. He that never finds his error till' it hinders his progress towards wealth or honor will not be· thought to love truth only for herself. Yet it may easily happen that information may come at a commodious time ; and as truth and interest are not by any fatal necessity at variance, that one may by accident introduce the other. When opinions are struggling into popularity, the arguments by which they are opposed or defended become more known ; and he that changes his profession would perhaps have changed it before, with the like opportunities of instruction. This was the then state of popery ; every artifice was used to show it in its fairest form ; and it must be owned to be a religion of external appearance sufficiently attractive.

It is natural to hope that a comprehensive is likewise an elevated soul, and that whoever is wise is also honest. I am willing to believe that Dryden, having employed his mind, active as it was, upon different studies, and filled it, capacious as it was, with other materials, came unprovided to the controversy, and wanted rather skill to discover the right than virtue to maintain it. But inquiries into the heart are not for man ; we must now leave him to his Judge.

The priests, having strengthened their cause by so powerful an adherent, were not long before they brought him into action. They engaged him to defend the controversial papers found in the strong-box of Charles II. ; and, what yet was harder, to defend them against Stillingfleet.

With hopes of promoting popery, he was employed to translate Maimbourg's " History of the League ;" which he published with a large introduction. His name is likewise prefixed to the English Life of Francis Xavier ; but I know not that he ever owned himself the translator. Perhaps the use of his name was a pious fraud ; which, however, seems not to have had much effect, for neither of the books, I believe, was ever popular.

The version of Xavier's Life is commended by Brown, in a pamphlet not written to flatter ; and the occasion of it is said to have been, that the queen, when she solicited a son, made vows to him as her tutelary saint.

He was supposed to have undertaken to translate Varillas's " History of Heresies ;" and, when Burnet published remarks upon it, to have written an Answer ; upon which Burnet makes the following observation :

" I have been informed from England that a gentleman, who is famous both for poetry and several other things, had spent three months in translating M. Varillas's History ; but that, as soon as my Reflections appeared, he discontinued his labor, finding the credit of his author was gone. Now, if he thinks it is recovered by his Answer, he will perhaps go on with his translation ; and this may be, for aught I know, as good an entertainment for him as the conversation that he had set on between the hinds and panthers, and all the rest of animals, for whom M. Varillas may serve well enough as an author ; and this history and that poem are such extraordinary things of their kind, that it will be but suitable to see the author of the worst poem become likewise the translator of the worst history that the age has produced. If his grace and his wit improve both proportionably, he will hardly find that he has gained much by the change he has made, from having no religion, to choose one of the worst. It is true he had somewhat to sink from in matter of wit ; but as for his morals, it is scarcely possible for him to grow a worse man than he was. He has lately wreaked his malice on me for spoiling his three months' labor ; but in it he has done me all the honor that any man can receive from him, which is to be railed at by him. If I had ill-nature enough to prompt me to wish a very bad wish for him, it should be that he would go on and finish his translation. By that it will appear whether the English nation, which is the most competent judge in this matter, has, upon the seeing our debate, pronounced in M. Varillas's favor or in mine.   It is true Mr. D. will suffer a little by it ; but, at least, it will serve to keep him in from other extrava-gances ; and if he gains little honor by this work, yet he can-not lose so much by it as he has done by his last employ-ment.''

Having probably felt his own inferiority in theological con-troversy, he was desirous of trying whether, by bringing poetry to aid his arguments, he might become a more efficacious defender of his new profession.   To reason in verse was, in-deed, one of his powers ; but subtilty and harmony united are still feeble when opposed to truth.

Actuated therefore by zeal for Rome, or hope of fame, he published " The Hind and Panther,'' a poem in which the Church of Rome, figured by the " milk-white Hind,'' defends her tenets against the Church of England, represented by the *Panther*, a beast beautiful, but spotted.

A fable which exhibits two beasts talking theology appears at once full of absurdity ; and it was accordingly ridiculed in the " City Mouse and Country Mouse,'' a parody, written by Montague, afterwards Earl of Halifax, and Prior, who then gave the first specimen of his abilities.

The conversion of such a man, at such a time, was not likely to pass uncensured.   Three dialogues were published by the facetious Thomas Brown, of which the two first were called " Reasons of Mr. Bayes's changing his Religion ;'' and the third, " The Reasons of Mr. Hains the Player's Conver-sion and Re-conversion.''   The first was printed in 1688, the second not till 1690, the third in 1691.   The clamor seems to have been long continued, and the subject to have strongly fixed the public attention.

In the two first dialogues Bayes is brought into the com-pany of Crites and Eugenius, with whom he had formerly debated on dramatic poetry.   The two talkers in the third are Mr. Bayes and Mr. Hains.

Brown was a man not deficient in literature nor destitute of fancy ; but he seems to have thought it the pinnacle of excellence to be a merry fellow ; and therefore laid out his powers upon small jests or gross buffoonery ; so that his per-formances have little intrinsic value, and were read only while they were recommended by the novelty of the event that occa-sioned them.

These dialogues are like his other works : what sense or knowledge they contained is disgraced by the garb in which it is exhibited.   One great source of pleasure is to call Dryden *little Bayes*.   Ajax, who happens to be mentioned, is " he that wore as many cowhides upon his shield as would have furnished half the king's army with shoe-leather."

Being asked whether he had seen the "Hind and Panther," Crites answers : "Seen it ! Mr. Bayes, why I can't stir nowhere but it pursues me ; it haunts me worse than a pewter-buttoned sergeant does a decayed cit. Sometimes I meet it in a bandbox, when my laundress brings home my linen ; sometimes, whether I will or no, it lights my pipe at a coffeehouse ; sometimes it surprises me in a trunk-maker's shop ; and sometimes it refreshes my memory for me on the back-side of a Chancery-lane parcel. For your comfort, too, Mr. Bayes, I have not only seen it, as you may perceive, but have read it too, and can quote it as freely upon occasion as a frugal tradesman can quote that noble treatise, ' The Worth of a Penny,' to his extravagant 'prentice, that revels in stewed apples and penny custards."

The whole animation of these compositions arises from a profusion of ludicrous and affected comparisons. " To secure one's chastity !" says Bayes, " little more is necessary than to leave off a correspondence with the other sex, which, to a wise man, is no greater a punishment than it would be to a fanatic person to forbid seeing " The Cheats" and " The Committee ;" or for my Lord Mayor and aldermen to be interdicted the sight of " The London Cuckolds." This is the general strain, and therefore I shall be easily excused the labor of more transcription.

Brown does not wholly forget past transactions : " You began," says Crites to Bayes, " a very different religion, and have not mended the matter in your last choice. It was but reason that your muse, which appeared first in a tyrant's quarrel, should employ her last efforts to justify the usurpation of the Hind."

Next year the nation was summoned to celebrate the birth of the prince. Now was the time for Dryden to rouse his imagination and strain his voice. Happy days were at hand, and he was willing to enjoy and diffuse the anticipated blessings. He published a poem, filled with predictions of greatness and prosperity—predictions of which it is not necessary to tell how they have been verified.

A few months passed after these joyful notes, and every blossom of popish hope was blasted forever by the Revolution. A papist now could be no longer laureate. The revenue, which he had enjoyed with so much pride and praise, was transferred to Shadwell, an old enemy, whom he had formerly stigmatized by the name of *Og*. Dryden could not decently complain that

he was deposed ; but seemed very angry that Shadwell suc
ceeded him, and has therefore celebrated the intruder's inaugu-
ration in a poem exquisitely satirical, called " Mac Flecknoe ;"
of which the " Dunciad," as Pope himself declares, is an imitation, though more extended in its plan and more diversified
in its incidents.

It is related by Prior that Lord Dorset, when as chamber-
lain he was constrained to eject Dryden from his office, gave
him from his own purse an allowance equal to the salary.
This is no romantic or incredible act of generosity ; a hundred
a year is often enough given to claims less cogent by men less
famed for liberality. Yet Dryden always represented himself
as suffering under a public infliction ; and once particularly
demands respect for the patience with which he endured the
loss of his little fortune. His patron might, indeed, enjoin
him to suppress his bounty ; but, if he suffered nothing, he
should not have complained.

During the short reign of King James he had written nothing for the stage, being, in his opinion, more profitably employed in controversy and flattery. Of praise he might, perhaps, have been less lavish without inconvenience, for James
was never said to have much regard for poetry : he was to be
flattered only by adopting his religion.

Times were now changed : Dryden was no longer the
court-poet, and was to look back for support to his former
trade ; and having waited about two years, either considering
himself as discountenanced by the public, or perhaps expecting
a second Revolution, he produced " Don Sebastian" in 1690,
and in the next four years four dramas more.

In 1693 appeared a new version of Juvenal and Persius.
Of Juvenal he translated the first, third, sixth, tenth, and
sixteenth satires ; and of Persius the whole work. On
this occasion he introduced his two sons to the public as
nurselings of the muses. The fourteenth of Juvenal was
the work of John and the seventh of Charles Dryden. He
prefixed a very ample preface, in the form of a dedication to
Lord Dorset ; and there gives an account of the design which
he had once formed to write an epic poem on the actions
either of Arthur or the Black Prince. He considered the epic
as necessarily including some kind of supernatural agency, and
had imagined a new kind of contest between the guardian
angels of kingdoms, of whom he conceived that each might be
represented zealous for his charge, without any intended opposition to the purposes of the Supreme Being, of which all created minds must in part be ignorant.

This is the most reasonable scheme of celestial interposition that ever was formed. The surprises and terrors of enchantments, which have succeeded to the intrigues and oppositions of pagan deities, afford very striking scenes, and open a vast extent to the imagination ; but, as Boileau observes (and Boileau will be seldom found mistaken), with this incurable defect, that, in a contest between Heaven and Hell, we know at the beginning which is to prevail ; for this reason we follow Rinaldo to the enchanted wood with more curiosity than terror.

In the scheme of Dryden there is one great difficulty, which yet he would, perhaps, have had address enough to surmount. In a war justice can be but on one side ; and, to entitle the hero to the protection of angels, he must fight in defence of indubitable right. Yet some of the celestial beings, thus opposed to each other, must have been represented as defending guilt.

That this poem was never written, is reasonably to be lamented. It would doubtless have improved our numbers and enlarged our language, and might perhaps have contributed by pleasing instructions to rectify our opinions and purify our manners.

What he required as the indispensable condition of such an undertaking, a public stipend, was not likely in these times to be obtained. Riches were not become familiar to us : nor had the nation yet learned to be liberal.

This plan he charged Blackmore with stealing ; '' only,'' says he,'' the guardian angels of kingdoms were machines too ponderous for him to manage.

In 1694 he began the most laborious and difficult of all his works, the translation of Virgil, from which he borrowed two months that he might turn Fresnoy's '' Art of Painting'' into English prose. The preface, which he boasts to have written in twelve mornings, exhibits a parallel of poetry and painting, with a miscellaneous collection of critical remarks, such as cost a mind stored like his no labor to produce them.

In 1697 he published his version of the works of Virgil ; and, that no opportunity of profit might be lost, dedicated the '' Pastorals'' to the Lord Clifford, the '' Georgics'' to the Earl of Chesterfield, and the '' Æneid '' to the Earl of Mulgrave. This economy of flattery, at once lavish and discreet, did not pass without observation.

This translation was censured by Milbourne, a clergyman, styled by Pope '' the fairest of critics,'' because he exhibited his own version to be compared with that which he condemned.

His last work was his " Fables," published in consequence,
as is supposed, of a contract now in the hands of Mr. Tonson ;
by which he obliged himself, in consideration of three hundred
pounds, to finish for the press ten thousand verses.

In this volume is comprised the well-known Ode on St.
Cecilia's Day, which, as appeared by a letter communicated
to Dr. Birch, he spent a fortnight in composing and correcting. But what is this to the patience and diligence of Boileau, whose " Equivoque," a poem of only three hundred and
forty-six lines, took from his life eleven months to write it, and
three years to revise it ?

Part of his book of " Fables" is the first " Iliad " in English, intended as a specimen of a version of the whole. Considering into what hands Homer was to fall, the reader cannot
but rejoice that this project went no further.

The time was now at hand which was to put an end to all
his schemes and labors. On the first of May, 1701, having
been some time, as he tells us, a cripple in his limbs, he died,
in Gerard Street, of a mortification in his leg.

There is extant a wild story relating to some vexatious
events that happened at his funeral, which at the end of Congreve's Life, by a writer of I know not what credit, are thus
related, as I find the account transferred to a biographical dictionary :

" Mr. Dryden dying on the Wednesday morning, Dr.
Thomas Sprat, then Bishop of Rochester and Dean of Westminster, sent the next day to the Lady Elizabeth Howard, Mr.
Dryden's widow, that he would make a present of the ground,
which was forty pounds, with all the other abbey fees. The
Lord Halifax likewise sent to the Lady Elizabeth, and Mr.
Charles Dryden, her son, that, if they would give him leave to
bury Mr. Dryden, he would inter him with a gentleman's private funeral, and afterwards bestow five hundred pounds on a
monument in the abbey ; which, as they had no reason to
refuse, they accepted. On the Saturday following the company came ; the corpse was put into a velvet hearse ; and
eighteen mourning coaches, filled with company, attended.
When they were just ready to move, the Lord Jefferies, son of
the Lord Chancellor Jefferies, with some of his rakish companions, coming by, asked whose funeral it was : and being told
Mr. Dryden's, he said, ' What, shall Dryden, the greatest
honor and ornament of the nation, be buried after this private
manner ! No, gentlemen, let all that loved Mr. Dryden, and
honor his memory, alight and join with me in gaining my
lady's consent to let me have the honor of his interment,

which shall be after another manner than this ; and I will bestow a thousand pounds on a monument in the abbey for him.'
The gentlemen in the coaches, not knowing of the Bishop of
Rochester's favor, nor of the Lord Halifax's generous design
(they both having, out of respect to the family, enjoined the
Lady Elizabeth and her son to keep their favor concealed to
the world, and let it pass for their own expense), readily came
out of their coaches, and attended Lord Jefferies up to the
lady's bedside, who was then sick. He repeated the purport
of what he had before said ; but she absolutely refusing, he fell
on his knees, vowing never to rise till his request was granted.
The rest of the company by his desire kneeled also ; and the
lady, being under a sudden surprise, fainted away. As soon
as she recovered her·speech, she cried, *No, no.* ' Enough,
gentlemen,' replied he ; ' my lady is very good, she says, *Go,
go.*' She repeated her former words with all her strength, but
in vain, for her feeble voice was lost in their acclamations of
joy ; and the Lord Jefferies ordered the hearsemen to carry the
corpse to Mr. Russel's, an undertaker in Cheapside, and leave
it there till he should send orders for the embalmment,which, he
added, should be after the royal manner. His directions were
obeyed, the company dispersed, and Lady Elizabeth and her
son remained inconsolable. The next day Mr. Charles Dryden waited on the Lord Halifax and the bishop, to excuse his
mother and himself, by relating the real truth. But neither his
lordship nor the bishop would admit of any plea ; especially
the latter, who had the abbey lighted, the ground opened, the
choir attending, an anthem ready set, and himself waiting for
some time without any corpse to bury. The undertaker, after
three days' expectance of orders for embalmment without receiving any, waited on the Lord Jefferies ; who, pretending ignorance of the matter, turned it off with an ill-natured jest, saying that those who observed the orders of a drunken frolic
deserved no better ; that he remembered nothing at all of it ;
and that he might do what he pleased with the corpse. Upon
this the undertaker waited upon the Lady Elizabeth and her
son, and threatened to bring the corpse home and set it before
the door. They desired a day's respite, which was granted.
Mr. Charles Dryden wrote a handsome letter to the Lord
Jefferies, who returned it with this cool answer : That he knew
nothing of the matter, and would be troubled no more about
it. He then addressed the Lord Halifax and the Bishop of
Rochester, who absolutely refused to do any thing in it. In
this distress Dr. Garth sent for the corpse to the College of
Physicians, and proposed a funeral by subscription, to which

himself set a most noble example.   At last a day, about three
weeks after Mr. Dryden's decease, was appointed for the interment.   Dr. Garth pronounced a fine Latin oration, at the college, over the corpse ; which was attended to the Abbey by a
numerous train of coaches.   When the funeral was over, Mr.
Charles Dryden sent a challenge to the Lord Jefferies, who
refusing to answer it, he sent several others and went often
himself ; but could neither get a letter delivered nor admittance to speak to him, which so incensed him that he
resolved, since his lordship refused to answer him like a gentleman, that he would watch an opportunity to meet and fight
off-hand, though with all the rules of honor ; which his lordship hearing left the town ; and Mr. Charles Dryden could
never have the satisfaction of meeting him, though he sought it
till his death with the utmost application.''

This story I once intended to omit, as it appears with no
great evidence ; nor have I met with any confirmation, but in a
letter of Farquhar ; and he only relates that the funeral of
Dryden was tumultuary and confused.

Supposing the story true, we may remark that the gradual
change of manners, though imperceptible in the process, appears great when different times, and those not very distant,
are compared.   If at this time a young drunken lord should
interrupt the pompous regularity of a magnificent funeral, what
would be the event but that he would be jostled out of the
way and compelled to be quiet ?   If he should thrust himself
into a house, he would be sent roughly away ; and, what is yet
more to the honor of the present time, I believe that those
who had subscribed to the funeral of a man like Dryden
would not, for such an accident, have withdrawn their contributions.

He was buried among the poets in Westminster Abbey,
where, though the Duke of Newcastle had, in a general dedication prefixed by Congreve to his dramatic works, accepted
thanks for his intention of erecting him a monument, he lay
long without distinction, till the Duke of Buckingham gave
him a tablet, inscribed only with the name of DRYDEN.

He married the Lady Elizabeth Howard, daughter to the
Earl of Berks, with circumstances, according to the satire imputed to Lord Somers, not very honorable to either party :
by her he had three sons, Charles, John, and Henry.   Charles
was usher of the palace to Pope Clement XI., and, visiting
England in 1704, was drowned in an attempt to swim across
the Thames at Windsor.

John was author of a comedy called " The Husband his

own Cuckold." He is said to have died at Rome. Henry entered into some religious order. It is some proof of Dryden's sincerity in his second religion that he taught it to his sons. A man conscious of hypocritical profession in himself is not likely to convert others ; and as his sons were qualified, in 1693, to appear among the translators of Juvenal, they must have been taught some religion before their father's change.

Of the person of Dryden I know not any account ; of his mind, the portrait, which has been left by Congreve, who knew him with great familiarity, is such as adds our love of his manners to our admiration of his genius. " He was," we are told, " of a nature exceedingly humane and compassionate, ready to forgive injuries, and capable of a sincere reconciliation with those who had offended him. His friendship, where he professed it, went beyond his profession. He was of a very easy, of very pleasing access, but somewhat slow, and, as it were, diffident in his advances to others ; he had that in nature which abhorred intrusion into any society whatever. He was therefore less known, and consequently his character became more liable to misapprehensions and misrepresentations ; he was very modest, and very easily to be discountenanced in his approaches to his equals or superiors. As his reading had been very extensive, so was he very happy in a memory tenacious of every thing that he had read. He was not more possessed of knowledge than he was communicative of it ; but then his communication was by no means pedantic or imposed upon the conversation, but just such, and went so far, as, by the natural turn of the conversation in which he was engaged, it was necessarily promoted or required. He was extremely ready and gentle in his correction of the errors of any writer who thought fit to consult him, and full as ready and patient to admit the reprehensions of others in respect of his own oversights or mistakes."

To this account of Congreve nothing can be objected but the fondness of friendship ; and to have excited that fondness in such a mind is no small degree of praise. The disposition of Dryden, however, is shown in this character rather as it exhibited itself in cursory conversation than as it operated on the more important parts of life. His placability and his friendship indeed were solid virtues ; but courtesy and good-humor are often found with little real worth. Since Congreve, who knew him well, has told us no more, the rest must be collected as it can from other testimonies, and particularly from those notices which Dryden has very liberally given us of himself.

The modesty which made him so slow to advance, and so easy to be repulsed, was certainly no suspicion of deficient merit, or unconsciousness of his own value ; he appears to have known, in its whole extent, the dignity of his own character, and to have set a very high value on his own powers and performances. He probably did not offer his conversation, because he expected it to be solicited ; and he retired from a cold reception, not submissive but indignant, with such deference of his own greatness as made him unwilling to expose it to neglect or violation.

His modesty was by no means inconsistent with ostentatiousness ; he is diligent enough to remind the world of his merit, and expresses with very little scruple his high opinion of his own powers ; but his self-commendations are read without scorn or indignation ; we allow his claims and love his frankness.

Tradition, however, has not allowed that his confidence in himself exempted him from jealousy of others. He is accused of envy and insidiousness ; and is particularly charged with inciting Creech to translate Horace that he might lose the reputation which Lucretius had given him.

Of this charge we immediately discover that it is merely conjectural ; the purpose was such as no man would confess ; and a crime that admits no proof why should we believe ?

He has been described as magisterially presiding over the younger writers, and assuming the distribution of poetical fame ; but he who excels has a right to teach, and he whose judgment is incontestable may without usurpation examine and decide.

Congreve represents him as ready to advise and instruct ; but there is reason to believe that his communication was rather useful than entertaining. He declares of himself that he was saturnine, and not one of those whose sprightly sayings diverted company ; and one of his censurers makes him say,

> " Nor wine nor love could ever see me gay ;
> To writing bred, I knew not what to say."

There are men whose powers operate only at leisure and in retirement, and whose intellectual vigor deserts them in conversation ; whom merriment confuses, and objection disconcerts ; whose bashfulness restrains their exertion, and suffers them not to speak till the time of speaking is past ; or whose attention to their own character makes them unwilling to utter at hazard what has not been considered and cannot be recalled.

Of Dryden's sluggishness in conversation it is vain to search or to guess the cause. He certainly wanted neither sentiments nor language ; his intellectual treasures were great, though they were locked up from his own use. "His thoughts," when he wrote, "flowed in upon him so fast, that his only care was which to choose and which to reject." Such rapidity of composition naturally promises a flow of talk ; yet we must be content to believe what an enemy says of him, when he likewise says it of himself. But, whatever was his character as a companion, it appears that he lived in familiarity with the highest persons of his time. It is related, by Carte, of the Duke of Ormond, that he used often to pass a night with Dryden and those with whom Dryden consorted : who they were Carte has not told, but certainly the convivial table at which Ormond sat was not surrounded with a plebeian society. He was indeed reproached with boasting of his familiarity with the great ; and Horace will support him in the opinion that to please superiors is not the lowest kind of merit.

The merit of pleasing must, however, be estimated by the means. Favor is not always gained by good actions or laudable qualities. Caresses and preferments are often bestowed on the auxiliaries of vice, the procurers of pleasure, or the flatterers of vanity. Dryden has never been charged with any personal agency unworthy of a good character : he abetted vice and vanity only with his pen. One of his enemies has accused him of lewdness in his conversation ; but if accusation without proof be credited, who shall be innocent ?

His works afford too many examples of dissolute licentiousness and abject adulation ; but they were probably, like his merriment, artificial and constrained ; the effects of study and meditation, and his trade rather than his pleasure.

Of the mind that can trade in corruption, and can deliberately pollute itself with ideal wickedness for the sake of spreading the contagion in society, I wish not to conceal or excuse the depravity. Such degradation of the dignity of genius, such abuse of superlative abilities, cannot be contemplated but with grief and indignation. What consolation can be had Dryden has afforded, by living to repent and to testify his repentance.

Of dramatic immorality he did not want examples among his predecessors, or companions among his contemporaries ; but in the meanness and servility of hyperbolical adulation I know not whether, since the days in which the Roman emperors were deified, he has been ever equalled, except by Afra Behn in an address to Eleanor Gwyn. When once he has under-

taken the task of praise, he no longer retains shame in himself
nor supposes it in his patron. As many odoriferous bodies are
observed to diffuse perfumes from year to year, without sensible diminution of bulk or weight, he appears never to have im-
poverished his mint of flattery by his expenses, however lavish.
He had all the forms of excellence, intellectual and moral, combined in his mind, with endless variation ; and, when he had
scattered on the hero of the day the golden shower of wit and
virtue, he had ready for him, whom he wished to court on the
morrow, new wit and virtue with another stamp.   Of this kind
of meanness he never seems to decline the practice or lament
the necessity : he considers the great as entitled to encomiastic
homage, and brings praise rather as a tribute than a gift, more
delighted with the fertility of his invention than mortified by
the prostitution of his judgment.   It is indeed not certain that
on these occasions his judgment much rebelled against his interest.   There are minds which easily sink into submission,
that look on grandeur with undistinguishing reverence, and discover no defect where there is elevation of rank and affluence
of riches.

   With his praises of others and of himself is always intermingled a strain of discontent and lamentation, a sullen growl
of resentment, or a querulous murmur of distress.   His works
are undervalued, his merit is unrewarded, and '' he has few
thanks to pay his stars that he was born among Englishmen.''
To his critics he is sometimes contemptuous, sometimes resentful, and sometimes submissive.   The writer who thinks his
works formed for duration mistakes his interest when he mentions his enemies.   He degrades his own dignity by showing
that he was affected by their censures, and gives lasting importance to names which, left to themselves, would vanish from
remembrance.   From this principle Dryden did not often depart ; his complaints are for the greater part general ; he seldom pollutes his pages with an adverse name.   He condescended indeed to a controversy with Settle, in which he perhaps may be considered rather as assaulting than repelling ;
and since Settle is sunk into oblivion, his libel remains injurious only to himself.

   Among answers to critics no poetical attacks or alterca-
tions are to be included ; they are like other poems, effusions
of genius, produced as much to obtain praise as to obviate
censure.   These Dryden practised, and in these he excelled.

   Of Collier, Blackmore, and Milbourne he has made mention in the preface of his '' Fables.''   To the censure of Collier, whose remarks may be rather termed admonitions than

criticisms, he makes little reply ; being, at the age of sixty-eight, attentive to better things than the claps of a play-house. He complains of Collier's rudeness, and the '' horse-play of his raillery ;'' and asserts that '' in many places he has perverted by his glosses the meaning'' of what he censures ; but in other things he confesses that he is justly taxed ; and says, with great calmness and candor, ''I have pleaded guilty to all thoughts or expressions of mine that can be truly accused of obscenity, immorality, or profaneness, and retract them. If he be my enemy, let him triumph ; if he be my friend, he will be glad of my repentance.'' Yet as our best dispositions are imperfect, he left standing in the same book a reflection on Collier of great asperity, and indeed of more asperity than wit.

Blackmore he represents as made his enemy by the poem of '' Absalom and Achitophel,'' which '' he thinks a little hard upon his fanatic patrons ;'' and charges him with borrowing the plan of his '' Arthur'' from the Preface to Juvenal, '' though he had,'' says he, '' the baseness not to acknowledge his benefactor, but instead of it to traduce me in a libel.''

The libel in which Blackmore traduced him was a '' Satire upon Wit ;'' in which, having lamented the exuberance of false wit and the deficiency of true, he proposes that all wit should be recoined before it is current, and appoints masters of assay, who shall reject all that is light or debased.

> '' 'Tis true, that when the coarse and worthless dross
> Is purg'd away, there will be mighty loss :
> E'en Congreve, Southern, manly Wycherly,
> When thus refin'd, will grievous sufferers be.
> Into the melting pot when Dryden comes,
> What horrid stench will rise, what noisome fumes !
> How will he shrink, when all his lewd allay,
> And wicked mixture, shall be purg'd away !''

Thus stands the passage in the last edition ; but in the original there was an abatement of the censure, beginning thus :

> '' But what remains will be so pure, 'twill bear
> Th' examination of the most severe.''

Blackmore, finding the censure resented and the civility disregarded, ungenerously omitted the softer part. Such variations discover a writer who consults his passions more than his virtue ; and it may be reasonably supposed that Dryden imputes his enmity to its true cause.

Of Milbourne he wrote only in general terms, such as are always ready at the call of anger, whether just or not : a short extract will be sufficient. " He pretends a quarrel to me, that I have fallen foul upon priesthood ; if I have, I am only to ask pardon of good priests, and am afraid his share of the reparation will come to little. Let him be satisfied that he shall never be able to force himself upon me for an adversary ; I contemn him too much to enter into competition with him.

" As for the rest of those who have written against me they are such scoundrels that they deserve not the least notice to be taken of them. Blackmore and Milbourne are only distinguished from the crowd by being remembered to their infamy."

Dryden indeed discovered, in many of his writings, an affected and absurd malignity to priests and priesthood, which naturally raised him many enemies, and which was sometimes as unseasonably resented as it was exerted. Trapp is angry that he calls the sacrificer in the " Georgics" *the holy butcher :* the translation is not indeed ridiculous ; but Trapp's anger arises from his zeal, not for the author, but the priest ; as if any reproach of the follies of paganism could be extended to the preachers of truth.

Dryden's dislike of the priesthood is imputed by Langbaine, and I think by Brown, to a repulse which he suffered when he solicited ordination ; but he denies, in the preface to his " Fables," that he ever designed to enter into the church ; and such a denial he would not have hazarded if he could have been convicted of falsehood.

Malevolence to the clergy is seldom at a great distance from irreverence of religion, and Dryden affords no exception to this observation. His writings exhibit many passages, which, with all the allowance that can be made for characters and occasions, are such as piety would not have admitted, and such as may vitiate light and unprincipled minds. But there is no reason for supposing that he disbelieved the religion which he disobeyed. He forgot his duty rather than disowned it. His tendency to profaneness is the effect of levity, negligence, and loose conversation, with a desire of accommodating himself to the corruption of the times, by venturing to be wicked as far as he durst. When he professed himself a convert to popery, he did not pretend to have received any new conviction of the fundamental doctrines of Christianity.

The persecution of critics was not the worst of his vexations ; he was much more disturbed by the importunities of want. His complaints of poverty are so frequently repeated, either with the dejection of weakness sinking in helpless misery, or the indignation of merit claiming its tribute from mankind, that it is impossible not to detest the age which could impose on such a man the necessity of such solicitations, or not to despise the man who could submit to such solicitations without necessity.

Whether by the world's neglect or his own imprudence, I am afraid that the greatest part of his life was passed in exigencies. Such outcries were surely never uttered but in severe pain. Of his supplies or his expenses no probable estimate can now be made. Except the salary of the laureate, to which King James added the office of Historiographer, perhaps with some additional emoluments, his whole revenue seems to have been casual ; and it is well known that he seldom lives frugally who lives by chance. Hope is always liberal ; and they that trust her promises make little scruple of revelling to-day on the profits of the morrow.

Of his plays the profit was not great ; and of the produce of his other works very little intelligence can be had. By discoursing with the late amiable Mr. Tonson, I could not find that any memorials of the transactions between his predecessor and Dryden had been preserved, except the following papers :

" I do hereby promise to pay John Dryden, Esq., or order, on the 25th of March, 1699, the sum of two hundred and fifty guineas, in consideration of ten thousand verses, which the said John Dryden, Esq., is to deliver to me Jacob Tonson, when finished, whereof seven thousand five hundred verses, more or less, are already in the said Jacob Tonson's possession. And I do hereby farther promise, and engage myself to make up the said sum of two hundred and fifty guineas three hundred pounds sterling to the said John Dryden, Esq., his executors, administrators, or assigns, at the beginning of the second impression of the said ten thousand verses.

" In witness whereof, I have hereunto set my hand and seal, this 20th day of March, 1698-9.

" JACOB TONSON.

" Sealed and delivered, being
first duly stamped, pursuant
to the acts of parliament for
that purpose, in the presence of
  " BEN. PORTLOCK,
  " WILL. CONGREVE.'

" March 24, 1698.

" Received then of Mr. Jacob Tonson the sum of two hundred sixty-eight pounds fifteen shillings, in pursuance of an agreement for ten thousand verses, to be delivered by me to the said Jacob Tonson, whereof I have already delivered to him about seven thousand five hundred, more or less : he the said Jacob Tonson being obliged to make up the foresaid sum of two hundred sixty-eight pounds fifteen shillings three hundred pounds, at the beginning of the second impression of the foresaid ten thousand verses ;

" I say, received by me,
" JOHN DRYDEN.

" Witness, CHARLES DRYDEN."

Two hundred and fifty guineas, at 1*l*. 1*s*. 6*d*. is 268*l*. 15*s*.

It is manifest, from the dates of this contract, that it relates to the volume of " Fables," which contains about twelve thousand verses, and for which therefore the payment must have been afterwards enlarged.

I have been told of another letter yet remaining, in which he desires Tonson to bring him money to pay for a watch which he had ordered for his son, and which the maker would not leave without the price.

The inevitable consequence of poverty is dependence. Dryden had probably no recourse in his exigencies but to his bookseller. The particular character of Tonson I do not know ; but the general conduct of traders was much less liberal in those times than in our own ; their views were narrower and their manners grosser. To the mercantile ruggedness of that race the delicacy of the poet was sometimes exposed. Lord Bolingbroke, who in his youth had cultivated poetry, related to Dr. King, of Oxford, that one day when he visited Dryden, they heard, as they were conversing, another person entering the house. " This," said Dryden, " is Tonson. You will take care not to depart before he goes away ; for I have not completed the sheet which I promised him ; and if you leave me unprotected, I must suffer all the rudeness to which his resentment can prompt his tongue."

What rewards he obtained for his poems, besides the payment of the bookseller, cannot be known. Mr. Derrick, who consulted some of his relations, was informed that his " Fables" obtained five hundred pounds from the Duchess of Ormond ; a present not unsuitable to the magnificence of that splendid family ; and he quotes Moyle as relating that forty pounds were paid by a musical society for the use of " Alexander's Feast."

In those days the economy of government was yet unsettled, and the payments of the Exchequer were dilatory and uncertain ; of this disorder there is reason to believe that the laureate sometimes felt the effects ; for, in one of his prefaces, he complains of those who, being entrusted with the distribution of the prince's bounty, suffer those that depend upon it to languish in penury.

Of his petty habits or slight amusements, tradition has retained little. Of the only two men whom I have found, to whom he was personally known, one told me that at the house which he frequented, called Will's Coffee-house, the appeal upon any literary dispute was made to him ; and the other related that his arm-chair, which in the winter had a settled and prescriptive place by the fire, was in the summer placed in the balcony, and that he called the two places his winter and his summer seat. This is all the intelligence which his two survivors afforded me.

One of his opinions will do him no honor in the present age, though in his own time, at least in the beginning of it, he was far from having it confined to himself. He put great confidence in the prognostications of judicial astrology. In the Appendix to the Life of Congreve is a narrative of some of his predictions wonderfully fulfilled ; but I know not the writer's means of information or character of veracity. That he had the configurations of the horoscope in his mind, and considered them as influencing the affairs of men, he does not forbear to hint.

> " The utmost malice of the stars is past.
> Now frequent *trines* the happier lights among,
> And *high-rais'd Jove*, from his dark prison freed,
> Those weights took off that on his planet hung,
> Will gloriously the new-laid works succeed."

He has elsewhere shown his attention to the planetary powers ; and in the preface to his " Fables" has endeavored obliquely to justify his superstition by attributing the same to some of the ancients. The letter, added to this narrative, leaves no doubt of his notions or practice.

So slight and so scanty is the knowledge which I have been able to collect concerning the private life and domestic manners of a man whom every English generation must mention with reverence as a critic and a poet.

DRYDEN may be properly considered as the father of English criticism, as the writer who first taught us to determine upon principles the merit of composition. Of our former poets, the greatest dramatist wrote without rules, conducted through life and nature by a genius that rarely misled and rarely deserted him. Of the rest, those who knew the laws of propriety had neglected to teach them.

Two Arts of English Poetry were written in the days of

Elizabeth by Webb and Puttenham, from which something might be learned, and a few hints had been given by Jonson and Cowley ; but Dryden's " Essay on Dramatic Poetry" was the first regular and valuable treatise on the art of writing.

He who, having formed his opinions in the present age of English literature, turns back to peruse this dialogue, will not perhaps find much increase of knowledge, or much novelty of instruction ; but he is to remember that critical principles were then in the hands of a few, who had gathered them partly from the ancients, and partly from the Italians and French. The structure of dramatic poems was then not generally understood. Audiences applauded by instinct ; and poets perhaps often pleased by chance.

A writer who has obtained his full purpose loses himself in his own lustre. Of an opinion which is no longer doubted, the evidence ceases to be examined. Of an art universally practised, the first teacher is forgotten. Learning once made popular is no longer learning ; it has the appearance of something which we have bestowed upon ourselves, as the dew appears to rise from the field which it refreshes.

To judge rightly of an author, we must transport ourselves to his time, and examine what were the wants of his contemporaries, and what were his means of supplying them. That which is easy at one time was difficult at another. Dryden at least imported his science, and gave his country what it wanted before ; or rather, he imported only the materials, and manufactured them by his own skill.

The dialogue on the drama was one of his first essays of criticism, written when he was yet a timorous candidate for reputation, and therefore labored with that diligence which he might allow himself somewhat to remit, when his name gave sanction to his positions, and his awe of the public was abated, partly by custom and partly by success. It will not be easy to find, in all the opulence of our language, a treatise so artfully variegated with successive representations of opposite probabilities, so enlivened with imagery, so brightened with illustrations. His portraits of the English dramatists are wrought with great spirit and diligence. The account of Shakespeare may stand as a perpetual model of encomiastic criticism ; exact without minuteness, and lofty without exaggeration. The praise lavished by Longinus, on the attestation of the heroes of Marathon by Demosthenes, fades away before it. In a few lines is exhibited a character so extensive in its comprehension, and so curious in its limitations, that nothing can be added, diminished, or reformed ; nor can the editors and admirers of Shakespeare, in all their emulation of reverence, boast of much more than of having diffused and paraphrased this epitome of excellence, of having changed Dryden's gold for baser metal of lower value, though of greater bulk.

In this, and in all his other essays on the same subject, the criticism of Dryden is the criticism of a poet ; not a dull collection of theorems, nor a rude detection of faults, which perhaps the censor was not able to have committed ; but a gay and vigorous dissertation, where delight is mingled with instruction, and where the author proves his right of judgment by his power of performance.

The different manner and effect with which critical knowledge may be conveyed, was perhaps never more clearly exemplified than in the performances of Rymer and Dryden. It was said of a dispute between two mathematicians, " malim cum Scaligero errare, quam cum Clavio recte sapere ;" that " it was more eligible to go wrong with one than right with the other." A tendency of the same kind every mind must feel at the perusal of Dryden's prefaces and Rymer's discourses. With Dryden we are wandering in quest of Truth ; whom we find, if we find her at all, dressed in the graces of elegance ; and, if we miss her, the labor of the pursuit rewards itself ; we are led only through fragrance and flowers. Rymer, without taking a nearer, takes a rougher way ; every step is to be made through thorns and brambles ; and Truth, if we meet her, appears repulsive by her mien, and ungraceful by her habit. Dryden's criticism has the majesty of a queen ; Rymer's has the ferocity of a tyrant.

As he had studied with great diligence the art of poetry, and enlarged or rectified his notions by experience perpetually increasing, he had his mind stored with principles and observations ; he poured out his knowledge with little labor ; for of labor, notwithstanding the multiplicity of his productions, there is sufficient reason to suspect that he was not a lover. To write *con amore*, with fondness for the employment, with perpetual touches and retouches, with unwillingness to take leave of his own idea, and an unwearied pursuit of unattainable perfection, was, I think, no part of his character.

His criticism may be considered as general or occasional. In his general precepts, which depend upon the nature of things and the structure of the human mind, he may doubtless be safely recommended to the confidence of the reader ; but his occasional and particular positions were sometimes interested, sometimes negligent, and sometimes capricious. It is not without reason that Trapp, speaking of the praises which he bestows on

Palamon and Arcite, says, " Novimus judicium Drydeni de poe-
mate quodam *Chauceri*, pulchro sane illo, et admodum laudan-
do, nimirum quod non modo vere epicum sit, sed Iliada etiam
atque Æneada æquet, imo superet.   Sed novimus eodem tem-
pore viri illius maximi non semper accuratissimas esse censu-
ras, nec ad severissimam critices normam exactas : illo judice id
plerumque optimum est, quod nunc præ manibus habet, et in
quo nunc occupatur."

He is therefore by no means constant to himself.   His defence and desertion of dramatic rhyme is generally known.
Spence, in his remarks on Pope's " Odyssey," produces what
he thinks an unconquerable quotation from Dryden's preface
to the " Æneid," in favor of translating an epic poem into
blank verse ; but he forgets that when his author attempted
the " Iliad," some years afterwards, he departed from his
own decision, and translated into rhyme.

When he has any objection to obviate or any license to defend, he is not very scrupulous about what he asserts, nor very
cautious, if the present purpose be served, not to entangle himself in his own sophistries.   But, when all arts are exhausted,
like other hunted animals, he sometimes stands at bay ; when
he cannot disown the grossness of one of his plays, he declares
that he knows not any law that prescribes morality to a comic
poet.

His remarks on ancient or modern writers are not always to
be trusted.   His parallel of the versification of Ovid with that
of Claudian has been very justly censured by Sewel.[1]   His
comparison of the first line of Virgil with the first of Statius
is not happier.   Virgil, he says, is soft and gentle, and would
have thought Statius mad, if he had heard him thundering out

    ' Quæ superimposito moles geminata colosso."

Statius perhaps heats himself, as he proceeds, to exaggeration somewhat hyperbolical ; but undoubtedly Virgil would
have been too hasty if he had condemned him to straw for one
sounding line.   Dryden wanted an instance, and the first that
occurred was impressed into the service.

What he wishes to say, he says at hazard ; he cited Gorbuduc, which he had never seen ; gives a false account of Chapman's versification ; and discovers, in the preface to his " Fables," that he translated the first book of the " Iliad" without
knowing what was in the second.

It will be difficult to prove that Dryden ever made any
great advances in literature.   As, having distinguished himself

     [1] Preface to Ovid's " Metamorphoses."

at Westminster under the tuition of Busby, who advanced his scholars to a height of knowledge very rarely attained in grammar-schools, he resided afterwards at Cambridge, it is not to be supposed that his skill in the ancient languages was deficient, compared with that of common students ; but his scholastic acquisitions seem not proportionate to his opportunities and abilities. He could not, like Milton or Cowley, have made his name illustrious merely by his learning. He mentions but few books, and those such as lie in the beaten track of regular study ; from which, if ever he departs, he is in danger of losing himself in unknown regions.

In his dialogue on the drama he pronounces with great confidence that the Latin tragedy of '' Medea'' is not Ovid's because it is not sufficiently interesting and pathetic. He might have determined the question upon surer evidence ; for it is quoted by Quintilian as the work of Seneca ; and the only line which remains of Ovid's play, for one line is left us, is not there to be found. There was therefore no need of the gravity of conjecture, or the discussion of plot or sentiment, to find what was already known upon higher authority than such discussion can ever reach.

His literature, though not always free from ostentation, will be commonly found either obvious, and made his own by the art of dressing it ; or superficial, which by what he gives shows what he wanted ; or erroneous, hastily collected, and negligently scattered.

Yet it cannot be said that his genius is ever unprovided of matter, or that his fancy languishes in penury of ideas. His works abound with knowledge and sparkle with illustrations. There is scarcely any science or faculty that does not supply him with occasional images and lucky similitudes ; every page discovers a mind very widely acquainted both with art and nature, and in full possession of great stores of intellectual wealth. Of him that knows much it is natural to suppose that he has read with diligence ; yet I rather believe that the knowledge of Dryden was gleaned from accidental intelligence and various conversation, by a quick apprehension, a judicious selection, and a happy memory, a keen appetite of knowledge, and a powerful digestion ; by vigilance that permitted nothing to pass without notice, and a habit of reflection that suffered nothing useful to be lost. A mind like Dryden's, always curious, always active, to which every understanding was proud to be associated, and of which every one solicited the regard, by an ambitious display of himself, had a more pleasant, perhaps a nearer way to knowledge than by the silent progress of soli-

tary reading. I do not suppose that he despised books, or intentionally neglected them ; but that he was carried out by the
impetuosity of his genius to more vivid and speedy instruc-
tors ; and that his studies were rather desultory and fortuitous
than constant and systematical.

It must be confessed that he scarcely ever appears to want
book-learning but when he mentions books ; and to him may
be transferred the praise which he gives his master Charles :

> " His conversation, wit, and parts,
> His knowledge in the noblest useful arts,
> Were such dead authors could not give,
> But habitudes of those that live .
> Who, lighting him, did greater lights receive ;
> He drain'd from all, and all they knew,
> His apprehensions quick, his judgment true,
> That the most learn'd with shame confess,
> His knowledge more, his reading only less."

Of all this, however, if the proof be demanded, I will not
undertake to give it ; the atoms of probability, of which my
opinion has been formed, lie scattered over all his works ; and
by him who thinks the question worth his notice, his works
must be perused with very close attention.

Criticism, either didactic or defensive, occupies almost all
his prose, except those pages which he has devoted to his
patrons ; but none of his prefaces were ever thought tedious.
They have not the formality of a settled style, in which the
first half of the sentence betrays the other. The pauses are
never balanced, nor the periods modelled ; every word seems
to drop by chance, though it falls into its proper place.
Nothing is cold or languid ; the whole is airy, animated, and
vigorous ; what is little is gay ; what is great is splendid.
He may be thought to mention himself too frequently ; but,
while he forces himself upon our esteem, we cannot refuse him
to stand high in his own. Every thing is excused by the play
of images and the sprightliness of expression. Though all is
easy, nothing is feeble ; though all seems careless, there is
nothing harsh ; and though since his earlier works more than
a century has passed, they have nothing yet uncouth or
obsolete.

He who writes much will not easily escape a manner—such
a recurrence of particular modes as may be easily noted. Dryden is always *another and the same ;* he does not exhibit a second time the same elegances in the same form, nor appears to
have any art other than that of expressing with clearness what
he thinks with vigor. His style could not easily be imitated,

either seriously or ludicrously ; for, being always equable and always varied, it has no prominent or discriminative characters. The beauty who is totally free from disproportion of parts and features cannot be ridiculed by an overcharged resemblance.

From his prose, however, Dryden derives only his accidental and secondary praise ; the veneration with which his name is pronounced by every cultivator of English literature, is paid to him as he refined the language, improved the sentiments, and tuned the numbers of English poetry.

After about half a century of forced thoughts and rugged metre, some advances towards nature and harmony had been already made by Waller and Denham ; they had shown that long discourses in rhyme grew more pleasing when they were broken into couplets, and that verse consisted not only in the number but the arrangement of syllables.

But though they did much, who can deny that they left much to do ? Their works were not many, nor were their minds of very ample comprehension. More examples of more modes of composition were necessary for the establishment of regularity and the introduction of propriety in word and thought.

Every language of a learned nation necessarily divides itself into diction, scholastic and popular, grave and familiar, elegant and gross ; and from a nice distinction of these different parts arises a great part of the beauty of style. But, if we except a few minds, the favorites of nature, to whom their own original rectitude was in the place of rules, this delicacy of selection was little known to our authors ; our speech lay before them in a heap of confusion ; and every man took for every purpose what chance might offer him.

There was therefore before the time of Dryden no poetical diction, no system of words at once refined from the grossness of domestic use, and free from the harshness of terms appropriated to particular arts. Words too familiar or too remote defeat the purpose of a poet. From those sounds which we hear on small or on coarse occasions, we do not easily receive strong impressions or delightful images ; and words to which we are nearly strangers, whenever they occur, draw that attention on themselves which they should transmit to things.

Those happy combinations of words which distinguished poetry from prose had been rarely attempted : we had few elegances or flowers of speech ; the roses had not yet been plucked from the bramble, or different colors had not been joined to enliven one another.

It may be doubted whether Waller and Denham could have overborne the prejudices which had long prevailed, and which even then were sheltered by the protection of Cowley. The new versification, as it was called, may be considered as owing its establishment to Dryden ; from whose time it is apparent that English poetry has had no tendency to relapse to its former savageness.

The affluence and comprehension of our language is very illustriously displayed in our poetical translations of ancient writers ; a work which the French seem to relinquish in despair, and which we were long unable to perform with dexterity. Ben Jonson thought it necessary to copy Horace almost word by word ; Feltham, his contemporary and adversary, considers it as indispensably requisite in a translation to give line for line. It is said that Sandys, whom Dryden calls the best versifier of the last age, has struggled hard to comprise every book of the English "Metamorphoses" in the same number of verses with the original. Holiday had nothing in view but to show that he understood his author, with so little regard to the grandeur of his diction, or the volubility of his numbers, that his metres can hardly be called verses ; they cannot be read without reluctance, nor will the labor always be rewarded by understanding them. Cowley saw that such copiers were a servile race ; he asserted his liberty, and spread his wings so boldly that he left his authors. It was reserved for Dryden to fix the limits of poetical liberty, and give us just rules and examples of translation.

When languages are formed upon different principles, it is impossible that the same modes of expression should always be elegant in both. While they run on together, the closest translation may be considered as the best ; but when they divaricate, each must take its natural course. Where correspondence cannot be obtained, it is necessary to be content with something equivalent. "Translation, therefore," says Dryden, "is not so loose as paraphrase, nor so close as metaphrase."

All polished languages have different styles ; the concise, the diffuse, the lofty, and the humble. In the proper choice of style consists the resemblance which Dryden principally exacts from the translator. He is to exhibit his author's thoughts in such a dress of diction as the author would have given them had his language been English : rugged magnificence is not to be softened ; hyperbolical ostentation is not to be repressed ; nor sententious affectation to have its point blunt-

ed.   A translator is to be like his author ; it is not his business
to excel him.

The reasonableness of these rules seems sufficient for the
vindication ; and the effects produced by observing them were
so happy that I know not whether they were ever opposed but
by Sir Edward Sherburne, a man whose learning was greater
than his powers of poetry, and who, being better qualified to
give the meaning than the spirit of Seneca, has introduced his
version of three tragedies by a defence of close translation.
The authority of Horace which the new translators cited in
defence of their practice, he has, by a judicious explanation,
taken fairly from them ; but reason wants not Horace to support it.

It seldom happens that all the necessary causes concur to
any great effect : will is wanting to power, or power to will, or
both are impeded by external obstructions.   The exigencies in
which Dryden was condemned to pass his life are reasonably
supposed to have blasted his genius, to have driven out his
works in a state of immaturity, and to have intercepted the
full-blown elegance which longer growth would have supplied.

Poverty, like other rigid powers, is sometimes too hastily
accused.   If the excellence of Dryden's works was lessened by
his indigence, their number was increased ; and I know not
how it will be proved that if he had written less he would have
written better ; or that indeed he would have undergone the
toil of an author, if he had not been solicited by something
more pressing than the love of praise.

But, as is said by his " Sebastian,"

"What had been, is unknown ; what is, appears."

We know that Dryden's several productions were so many successive expedients for his support ; his plays were therefore
often borrowed ; and his poems were almost all occasional.

In an occasional performance no height of excellence can
be expected from any mind, however fertile in itself, and however stored with acquisitions.   He whose work is general and
arbitrary has the choice of his matter, and takes that which his
inclination and his studies have best qualified him to display
and decorate.   He is at liberty to delay his publication till he
has satisfied his friends and himself, till he has reformed his
first thoughts by subsequent examination, and polished away
those faults which the precipitance of ardent composition is
likely to leave behind it.   Virgil is related to have poured out
a great number of lines in the morning, and to have passed the
day in reducing them to fewer.

The occasional poet is circumscribed by the narrowness of his subject. Whatever can happen to man has happened so often that little remains for fancy or invention. We have been all born ; we have most of us been married ; and so many have died before us, that our deaths can supply but few materials for a poet. In the fate of princes the public has an interest ; and what happens to them, of good or evil, the poets have always considered a business for the muse. But after so many inauguratory gratulations, nuptial hymns, and funeral dirges, he must be highly favored by nature, or by fortune, who says any thing not said before. Even war and conquest, however splendid, suggest no new images ; the triumphant chariot of a victorious monarch can be decked only with those ornaments that have graced his predecessors.

Not only matter but time is wanting. The poem must not be delayed till the occasion is forgotten. The lucky moments of animated imagination cannot be attended ; elegances and illustrations cannot be multiplied by gradual accumulation ; the composition must be despatched while conversation is yet busy and admiration fresh ; and haste is to be made, lest some other event should lay hold upon mankind.

Occasional compositions may, however, secure to a writer the praise both of learning and facility ; for they cannot be the effect of long study, and must be furnished immediately from the treasure of the mind.

The death of Cromwell was the first public event which called forth Dryden's poetical powers. His heroic stanzas have beauties and defects ; the thoughts are vigorous, and, though not always proper, show a mind replete with ideas ; the numbers are smooth ; and the diction, if not altogether correct, is elegant and easy.

Davenant was perhaps at this time his favorite author, though "Gondibert" never appears to have been popular, and from Davenant he learned to please his ear with the stanza of four lines alternately rhymed.

Dryden very early formed his versification ; there are in this early production no traces of Donne's or Jonson's ruggedness ; but he did not so soon free his mind from the ambition of forced conceits. In his verses on the Restoration he says of the king's exile,

> "He, toss'd by fate,
> Could taste no sweets of youth's desired age,
> But found his life too true a pilgrimage."

And afterwards, to show how virtue and wisdom are increased by adversity, he makes this remark :

> " Well might the ancient poets then confer
> On Night the honor'd name of *counsellor*,
> Since struck with rays of prosperous fortune blind,
> We light alone in dark afflictions find."

His praise of Monk's dexterity comprises such a cluster of thoughts unallied to one another as will not elsewhere be easily found :

> " 'Twas Monk, whom Providence design'd to loose
> Those real bonds false freedom did impose.
> The blessed saints that watch'd this turning scene
> Did from their stars with joyful wonder lean,
> To see small clues draw vastest weights along,
> Not in their bulk, but in their order strong.
> Thus pencils can by one slight touch restore
> Smiles to that changed face that wept before.
> With ease such fond chimeras we pursue,
> As fancy frames, for fancy to subdue :
> But when ourselves to action we betake,
> It shuns the mint like gold that chemists make.
> How hard was then his task, at once to be
> What in the body natural we see !
> Man's Architect distinctly did ordain
> The charge of muscles, nerves, and of the brain,
> Through viewless conduits spirits to dispense
> The springs of motion from the seat of sense :
> 'Twas not the hasty product of a day
> But the well-ripen'd fruit of wise delay.
> He, like a patient angler, ere he strook,
> Would let them play awhile upon the hook.
> Our healthful food the stomach labors thus,
> At first embracing what it straight doth crush.
> Wise leeches will not vain receipts obtrude,
> While growing pains pronounce the humors crude ;
> Deaf to complaints, they wait upon the ill,
> Till some safe crisis authorize their skill."

He had not yet learned, indeed he never learned well, to forbear the improper use of mythology. After having rewarded the heathen deities for their care,

> " With Alga who the sacred altar strows ?
> To all the sea-gods Charles an offering owes :
> A bull to thee, Portunus, shall be slain ;
> A ram to you, ye Tempests of the Main."

He tells us, in the language of religion,

> " Pray'r storm'd the skies, and ravish'd Charles from thence,
> As heav'n itself is took by violence."

And afterwards mentions one of the most awful passages of Sacred History.

Other conceits there are, too curious to be quite omitted, as,

> " For by example most we sinn'd before,
> And, glass-like, clearness mix'd with frailty bore."

How far he was yet from thinking it necessary to found his sentiments on nature, appears from the extravagance of his fictions and hyperboles :

> " The winds, that never moderation knew,
> Afraid to blow too much, too faintly blew :
> Or, out of breath with joy, could not enlarge
> Their straiten'd lungs.
> It is no longer motion cheats your view ;
> As you meet it, the land approacheth you ;
> The land returns, and in the white it wears
> The marks of penitence and sorrow bears."

I know not whether this fancy, however little be its value, was not borrowed. A French poet read to Malherbe some verses, in which he represents France as moving out of its place to receive the king. " Though this," said Malherbe, " was in my time, I do not remember it."

His poem on the " Coronation" has a more even tenor of thought. Some lines deserve to be quoted :

> " You have already quench'd sedition's brand ;
> And zeal, that burnt it, only warms the land ;
> The jealous sects that durst not trust their cause,
> So far from their own will as to the laws,
> Him for their umpire and their synod take,
> And their appeal alone to Cæsar make."

Here may be found one particle of that old versification, of which, I believe, in all his works, there is not another :

> " Nor is it duty, or our hope alone,
> Creates that joy, but full *fruition.*"

In the verses to the Lord Chancellor Clarendon, two years afterwards, is a conceit so hopeless at the first view that few would have attempted it, and so successfully labored that though at last it gives the reader more perplexity than pleasure, and seems hardly worth the study that it costs, yet it must be valued as a proof of a mind at once subtle and comprehensive :

> " In open prospect nothing bounds our eye,
> Until the earth seems join'd unto the sky :
> So in this hemisphere our utmost view
> Is only bounded by our king and you :
> Our sight is limited where you are join'd,
> And beyond that no farther heaven can find.

So well your virtues do with his agree,
That though your orbs of different greatness be,
Yet both are for each other's use dispos'd,
His to inclose, and yours to be inclos'd.
Nor could another in your room have been,
Except an emptiness had come between."

The comparison of the Chancellor to the Indies leaves all resemblance, too, far behind it :

" And as the Indies were not found before
Those rich perfumes which from the happy shore
The winds upon their balmy wings convey'd,
Whose guilty sweetness first their world betray'd ;
So by your counsels we are brought to view
A new and undiscover'd world in you."

There is another comparison, for there is little else in the poem, of which, though perhaps it cannot be explained into plain prosaic meaning, the mind perceives enough to be delighted, and readily forgives its obscurity for its magnificence :

" How strangely active are the arts of peace,
Whose restless motions less than wars do cease !
Peace is not freed from labor, but from noise ;
And war more force, but not more pains employs.
Such is the mighty swiftness of your mind,
That, like the earth's, it leaves our sense behind :
While you so smoothly turn and roll our sphere,
That rapid motion does but rest appear.
For as in nature's swiftness, with the throng
Of flying orbs while ours is borne along,
All seems at rest to the deluded eye,
Mov'd by the soul of the same harmony :
So, carried on by your unwearied care,
We rest in peace, and yet in motion share."

To this succeed four lines, which perhaps afford Dryden's first attempt at those penetrating remarks on human nature, for which he seems to have been peculiarly formed :

" Let envy then those crimes within you see,
From which the happy never must be free ;
Envy, that does with misery reside,
The joy and the revenge of ruin'd pride."

Into this poem he seems to have collected all his powers ; and after this he did not often bring upon his anvil such stubborn and unmalleable thoughts ; but, as a specimen of his abilities to unite the most unsociable matter, he has concluded with lines of which I think myself not obliged to tell the meaning :

"Yet unimpair'd with labors, or with time,
  Your age but seems to a new youth to climb.
Thus heavenly bodies do our time beget,
And measure change, but share no part of it :
And still it shall without a weight increase,
Like this new year, whose motions never cease.
For since the glorious course you have begun
Is led by Charles, as that is by the Sun,
It must both weightless and immortal prove,
Because the centre of it is above."

In the "Annus Mirabilis" he returned to the quatrain, which from that time he totally quitted, perhaps from experience of its inconvenience, for he complains of its difficulty. This is one of his greatest attempts. He had subjects equal to his abilities, a great naval war and the fire of London. Battles have always been described in heroic poetry ; but a sea-fight and artillery had yet something of novelty. New arts are long in the world before poets describe them ; for they borrow every thing from their predecessors, and commonly derive very little from nature or from life. Boileau was the first French writer that had ever hazarded in verse the mention of modern war or the effects of gunpowder. We, who are less afraid of novelty, had already possession of those dreadful images. Waller had described a sea-fight. Milton had not yet transferred the invention of fire-arms to the rebellious angels.

This poem is written with great diligence, yet does not fully answer the expectation raised by such subjects and such a writer. With the stanza of Davenant he has sometimes his vein of parenthesis and incidental disquisition, and stops his narrative for a wise remark.

The general fault is, that he affords more sentiment than description, and does not so much impress scenes upon the fancy as deduce consequences and make comparisons.

The initial stanzas have rather too much resemblance to the first lines of Waller's poem on the War with Spain : perhaps such a beginning is natural, and could not be avoided without affectation. Both Waller and Dryden might take their hint from the poem on the civil war of Rome, "Orbem jam totum," etc.

Of the king collecting his navy, he says :

"It seems, as every ship their sovereign knows,
  His awful summons they so soon obey :
So hear the scaly herds when Proteus blows,
  And so to pasture follow through the sea."

It would not be hard to believe that Dryden had written the two first lines seriously, and that some wag had added the

two latter in burlesque. Who would expect the lines that immediately follow, which are indeed perhaps indecently hyperbolical, but certainly in a mode totally different ?

> " To see this fleet upon the ocean move
>   Angels drew wide the curtains of the skies :
> And Heaven, as if there wanted lights above,
>   For tapers made two glaring comets rise."

The description of the attempt at Bergen will afford a very
complete specimen of the descriptions in this poem :

> " And now approach'd their fleet from India, fraught
>   With all the riches of the rising sun :
> And precious sand from southern climates brought,
>   The fatal regions where the war begun.

> " Like hunted castors, conscious of their store,
>   Their way-laid wealth to Norway's coast they bring :
> Then first the North's cold bosom spices bore,
>   And Winter brooded on the Eastern Spring.

> " By the rich scent we found our perfum'd prey,
>   Which, flank'd with rocks, did close in covert lie ;
> And round about their murd'ring cannon lay,
>   At once to threaten and invite the eye.

> " Fiercer than cannon, and than rocks more hard,
>   The English undertake th' unequal war.
> Seven ships alone, by which the port is barr'd,
>   Besiege the Indies, and all Denmark dare.

> " These fight like husbands, but like lovers those ;
>   These fain would keep, and those more fain enjoy :
> And to such height their frantic passion grows,
>   That what both love, both hazard to destroy :

> " Amidst whole heaps of spices lights a ball,
>   And now their odors arm'd against them fly :
> Some preciously by shatter'd porcelain fall,
>   And some by aromatic splinters die :

> " And, though by tempests of the prize bereft,
>   In Heaven's inclemency some ease we find ;
> Our foes we vanquish'd by our valor left,
>   And only yielded to the seas and wind."

In this manner is the sublime too often mingled with the
ridiculous. The Dutch seek a shelter for a wealthy fleet : this
surely needed no illustration ; yet they must fly, not like all
the rest of mankind on the same occasion, but " like hunted
castors ;" and they might with strict propriety be hunted, for
we winded them by our noses—their perfumes betrayed them.
The *husband* and the *lover*, though of more dignity than the

castor, are images too domestic to mingle properly with the horrors of war. The two quatrains that follow are worthy of the author.

The account of the different sensations with which the two fleets retired, when the night parted them, is one of the fairest flowers of English poetry :

> " The night comes on, we eager to pursue
>   The combat still, and they asham'd to leave ;
> Till the last streaks of dying day withdrew,
>   And doubtful moonlight did our rage deceive.

> " In th' English fleet each ship resounds with joy,
>   And loud applause of their great leader's fame :
> In fiery dreams the Dutch they still destroy,
>   And, slumbering, smile at the imagin'd flame.

> " Not so the Holland fleet, who, tir'd and done,
>   Stretch'd on their decks, like weary oxen lie ;
> Faint sweats all down their mighty members run
>   (Vast bulks, which little souls but ill supply).

> " In dreams they fearful precipices tread,
>   Or, shipwreck'd, labor to some distant shore :
> Or, in dark churches, walk among the dead ;
>   They wake with horror, and dare sleep no more."

It is a general rule in poetry that all appropriated terms of art should be sunk in general expressions, because poetry is to speak an universal language. This rule is still stronger with regard to arts not liberal or confined to few, and therefore far-removed from common knowledge ; and of this kind, certainly, is technical navigation. Yet Dryden was of opinion that a sea-fight ought to be described in the nautical language ; " and certainly," says he, " as those who in a logical disputation keep to general terms, would hide a fallacy, so those who do it in poetical description would veil their ignorance."

Let us then appeal to experience ; for by experience at last we learn as well what will please as what will profit. In the battle his terms seem to have been blown away ; but he deals them liberally in the dock :

> " So here some pick out bullets from the side,
>   Some drive old oakum thro' each seam and rift :
> Their left hand does the calking-iron guide,
>   The rattling mallet with the right they lift.

> " With boiling pitch another near at hand
>   (From friendly Sweden brought) the seams instops ;
> Which, well laid o'er, the salt-sea waves withstand,
>   And shake them from the rising beak in drops.

" Some the gall'd ropes with dauby marling bind,
    Or sear-cloth masts with strong tarpauling coats :   ·
    To try new shrouds one mounts into the wind,
    And one below their ease or stiffness notes "

I suppose there is not one term which every reader does
not wish away.

His digression to the original and progress of navigation,
with his prospect of the advancement which it shall receive from
the Royal Society, then newly instituted, may be considered as
an example seldom equalled of seasonable excursion and artful
return.

One line, however, leaves me discontented ; he says that
by the help of the philosophers,

" Instructed ships shall sail to quick commerce,
    By which remotest regions are allied."

Which he is constrained to explain in a note, " by a more exact
measure of longitude."   It had better become Dryden's learning and genius to have labored science into poetry, and have
shown, by explaining longitude, that verse did not refuse the
ideas of philosophy.

His description of the fire is painted by resolute meditation, out of a mind better formed to reason than to feel.   The
conflagration of a city, with all its tumults of concomitant distress, is one of the most dreadful spectacles which this world
can offer to human eyes ; yet it seems to raise little emotion in
the breast of the poet ; he watches the flame coolly from street
to street, with now a reflection and now a simile, till at last he
meets the king, for whom he makes a speech, rather tedious in
a time so busy ; and then follows again the progress of the fire.

There are, however, in this part some passages that deserve
attention ; as in the beginning :

" The diligence of trades and noiseful gain,
    And luxury, more late, asleep were laid !
    All was the Night's, and in her silent reign
    No sound the rest of Nature did invade
    In this deep quiet—"

The expression, " All was the Night's," is taken from
Seneca, who remarks on Virgil's line,

" *Omnia noctis erant, placida composta quiete,*"

that he might have concluded better,

" *Omnia noctis erant.*"

The following quatrain is vigorous and animated :

" The ghosts of traitors from the bridge descend
    With bold fanatic spectres to rejoice ;
  About the fire into a dance they bend,
    And sing their sabbath notes with feeble voice."

His prediction of the improvements which shall be made in the new city is elegant and poetical, and with an event which poets cannot always boast, has been happily verified. The poem concludes with a simile that might have better been omitted.

Dryden, when he wrote this poem, seems not yet fully to have formed his versification, or settled his system of propriety.

From this time he addicted himself almost wholly to the stage, " to which," says he, " my genius never much inclined me," merely as the most profitable market for poetry. By writing tragedies in rhyme he continued to improve his diction and his numbers. According to the opinion of Harte, who had studied his works with great attention, he settled his principles of versification in 1676, when he produced the play of " Aurung Zebe ;" and, according to his own account of the short time in which he wrote " Tyrannic Love" and " The State of Innocence," he soon obtained the full effect of diligence, and added facility to exactness.

Rhyme has been so long banished from the theatre, that we know not its effects upon the passions of an audience ; but it has this convenience, that sentences stand more dependent on each other, and striking passages are therefore easily selected and retained. Thus the description of Night in " The Indian Emperor," and the rise and fall of empire in " The Conquest of Granada," are more frequently repeated than any lines in " All for Love" or " Don Sebastian."

To search his plays for vigorous sallies and sententious elegances, or to fix the dates of any little pieces which he wrote by chance or by solicitation, were labor too tedious and minute.

His dramatic labors did not so wholly absorb his thoughts but that he promulgated the laws of translation in a preface to the English Epistles of Ovid ; one of which he translated himself, and another in conjunction with the Earl of Mulgrave.

" Absalom and Achitophel " is a work so well known that a particular criticism is superfluous. If it be considered as a poem political and controversial, it will be found to comprise all the excellences of which the subject is susceptible ; acrimony of censure, elegance of praise, artful delineation of characters, variety and vigor of sentiment, happy turns of language, and pleasing harmony of numbers ; and all these raised to such a height as can scarcely be found in any other English composition.

It is not, however, without faults ; some lines are inelegant or improper, and too many are irreligiously licentious. The original structure of the poem was defective ; allegories drawn to great length will always break ; Charles could not run continually parallel with David.

The subject had likewise another inconvenience ; it admitted little imagery or description ; and a long poem of mere sentiments easily becomes tedious ; though all the parts are forcible, and every line kindles new rapture, the reader, if not relieved by the interposition of something that soothes the fancy, grows weary of admiration and defers the rest.

As an approach to historical truth was necessary, the action and catastrophe were not in the poet's power ; there is therefore an unpleasing disproportion between the beginning and the end. We are alarmed by a faction formed of many sects, various in their principles, but agreeing in their purpose of mischief ; formidable for their numbers, and strong by their supports ; while the king's friends are few and weak. The chiefs on either part are set forth to view ; but, when expectation is at the height, the king makes a speech, and

" Henceforth a series of new times began."

Who can forbear to think of an enchanted castle, with a wide moat and lofty battlements, walls of marble and gates of brass, which vanishes at once into air when the destined knight blows his horn before it ?

In the second part, written by Tate, there is a long insertion, which, for its poignancy of satire, exceeds any part of the former. Personal resentment, though no laudable motive to satire, can add great force to general principles. Self-love is a busy prompter.

" The Medal," written upon the same principles with " Absalom and Achitophel," but upon a narrower plan, gives less pleasure, though it discovers equal abilities in the writer. The superstructure cannot extend beyond the foundation ; a single character or incident cannot furnish as many ideas as a series of events or multiplicity of agents. This poem, therefore, since time has left it to itself, is not much read, nor perhaps generally understood ; yet it abounds with touches both of humorous and serious satire. The picture of a man whose propensions to mischief are such that his best actions are but inability of wickedness, is very skilfully delineated and strongly colored :

"Power was his aim ; but, thrown from that pretence, ⎫
The wretch turn'd loyal in his own defence,   ⎬
And malice reconcil'd him to his prince.   ⎭
Him, in the anguish of his soul, he serv'd ;
Rewarded faster still than he deserv'd :
Behold him now exalted into trust ;
His counsels oft convenient, seldom just ;
E'en in the most sincere advice he gave,
He had a grudging still to be a knave.
The frauds, he learnt in his fanatic years,
Made him uneasy in his lawful gears,
At least as little honest as he could,
And, like white witches, mischievously good.
To this first bias, longingly, he leans :
And rather would be great by wicked means."

The "Threnodia," which, by a term I am afraid neither authorized nor analogical, he calls "Augustalis," is not among his happiest productions. Its first and obvious defect is the irregularity of its metre, to which the ears of that age, however, were accustomed. What is worse, it has neither tenderness nor dignity ; it is neither magnificent nor pathetic. He seems to look round him for images which he cannot find, and what he has he distorts by endeavoring to enlarge them. "He is," he says, "petrified with grief ;" but the marble sometimes relents, and trickles in a joke :

"The sons of art all med'cines tried,
And every noble remedy applied :
With emulation each essay'd
His utmost skill ; *nay, more, they pray'd :*
Was never losing game with better conduct play'd."

He had been a little inclined to merriment before, upon the prayers of a nation for their dying sovereign : nor was he serious enough to keep heathen fables out of his religion :

"With him the innumerable crowd of arm'd prayers
    Knock'd at the gates of Heaven, and knock'd aloud ;
The first well-meaning rude petitioners
    All for his life assail'd the throne,
All would have brib'd the skies by offering up their own.
So great a throng not Heaven itself could bar ;
'Twas almost borne by force as in the giants' war,
The pray'rs, at least, for his reprieve, were heard ;
His death, like Hezekiah's, was deferr'd."

There is throughout the composition a desire of splendor without wealth. In the conclusion he seems too much pleased with the prospect of the new reign to have lamented his old master with much sincerity.

He did not miscarry in this attempt for want of skill either in lyric or elegiac poetry. His poem on the death of Mrs. Kil-ligrew is undoubtedly the noblest ode that our language ever has produced. The first part flows with a torrent of enthusi-asm. *Fervet immensusque ruit.* All the stanzas indeed are not equal. An imperial crown cannot be one continued dia-mond : the gems must be held together by some less valuable matter.

In his first " Ode for Cecilia's Day," which is lost in the splendor of the second, there are passages which would have dignified any other poet. The first stanza is vigorous and ele-gant, though the word *diapason* is too technical, and the rhymes are too remote from one another.

> " From harmony, from heavenly harmony,
>   This universal frame began ;
> When Nature underneath a heap of jarring atoms lay,
>   And could not heave her head,
> The tuneful voice was heard from high,
>   Arise. ye more than dead.
> Then cold and hot, and moist and dry,
>   In order to their stations leap,
>   And music's power obey.
> From harmony, from heavenly harmony,
>   This universal frame began :
>   From harmony to harmony,
> Through all the compass of the notes it ran,
>   The *diapason* closing full in man."

The conclusion is likewise striking ; but it includes an image so awful in itself that it can owe little to poetry : and I could wish the antithesis of music untuning had found some other place.

> " As from the power of sacred lays
>   The spheres began to move,
> And sung the great Creator's praise
>   To all the bless'd above :
> So, when the last and dreadful hour
> This crumbling pageant shall devour
> The trumpet shall be heard on high,
> The dead shall live, the living die,
> And music shall untune the sky."

Of his skill in elegy he has given a specimen in his " Eleo-nora," of which the following lines discover their author :

> " Though all these rare endowments of the mind
> Were in a narrow space of life confin'd,
> The figure was with full perfection crown'd,
> Though not so large an orb. as truly round :
> As when in glory. through the public place,
> The spoils of conquer'd nations were to pass,

> And but one day for triumph was allow'd,
> The consul was constrain'd his pomp to crowd ;
> And so the swift procession hurried on,
> That all, though not distinctly, might be shown :
> So, in the straiten'd bounds of life confin'd,
> She gave but glimpses of her glorious mind ;
> And multitudes of virtues pass'd along,
> Each pressing foremost in the mighty throng,
> Ambitious to be seen, and then make room
> For greater multitudes that were to come.
> Yet unemploy'd no minute slipp'd away ;
> Moments were precious in so short a stay.
> The haste of Heaven to have her was so great,
> That some were single acts, though each complete ;
> And every act stood ready to repeat.''

This piece, however, is not without its faults ; there is so much likeness in the initial comparison that there is no illustration. As a king would be lamented, Eleonora was lamented :

> '' As. when some great and gracious monarch dies
> Soft whispers, first, and mournful murmurs, rise
> Among the sad attendants ; then the sound
> Soon gathers voice, and spreads the news around,
> Through town and country, till the dreadful blast
> Is blown to distant colonies at last,
> Who then, perhaps, were offering vows in vain
> For his long life, and for his happy reign :
> So slowly, by degrees, unwilling Fame
> Did matchless Eleonora's fate proclaim,
> Till public as the loss the news became.''

This is little better than to say in praise of a shrub that it is as green as a tree ; or of a brook, that it waters a garden, as a river waters a country.

Dryden confesses that he did not know the lady whom he celebrates : the praise being therefore inevitably general, fixes no impression upon the reader, nor excites any tendency to love, nor much desire of imitation. Knowledge of the subject is to the poet what durable materials are to the architect.

The '' Religio Laici,'' which borrows its title from the '' Religio Medici'' of Browne, is almost the only work of Dryden which can be considered as a voluntary effusion ; in this, therefore, it might be hoped that the full effulgence of his genius would be found. But unhappily the subject is rather argumentative than poetical ; he intended only a specimen of metrical disputation :

> ' And this unpolish'd rugged verse I chose,
> As fittest for discourse, and nearest prose.''

This, however, is a composition of great excellence in its kind, in which the familiar is very properly diversified with the solemn, and the grave with the humorous ; in which metre has neither weakened the force nor clouded the perspicuity of argument ; nor will it be easy to find another example equally happy of this middle kind of writing, which, though prosaic in some parts, rises to high poetry in others, and neither towers to the skies nor creeps along the ground.

Of the same kind, or not far distant from it, is " The Hind and Panther," the longest of all Dryden's original poems ; an allegory intended to comprise and to decide the controversy between the Romanists and Protestants. The scheme of the work is injudicious and incommodious ; for what can be more absurd than that one beast should counsel another to rest her faith upon a pope and council ? He seems well enough skilled in the usual topics of argument, endeavors to show the necessity of an infallible judge, and reproaches the reformers with want of unity ; but is weak enough to ask, why, since we see without knowing how, we may not have an infallible judge without knowing where ?

The Hind at one time is afraid to drink at the common brook, because she may be worried ; but, walking home with the Panther, talks by the way of the Nicene fathers, and at last declares herself to be of the Catholic Church.

This absurdity was very properly ridiculed in the " City Mouse and Country Mouse" of Montague and Prior ; and in the detection and censure of the incongruity of the fiction chiefly consists the value of their performance, which, whatever reputation it might obtain by the help of temporary passions, seems, to readers almost a century distant, not very forcible or animated.

Pope, whose judgment was perhaps a little bribed by the subject, used to mention this poem as the most correct specimen of Dryden's versification. It was indeed written when he had completely formed his manner, and may be supposed to exhibit, negligence excepted, his deliberate and ultimate scheme of metre.

We may therefore reasonably infer that he did not approve the perpetual uniformity which confines the sense to couplets, since he has broken his lines in the initial paragraph.

> " A milk-white Hind, immortal and unchang'd,
> Fed on the lawns, and in the forest rang'd :
> Without unspotted, innocent within,
> She fear'd no danger, for she knew no sin.
> Yet had she oft been chas'd with horns and hounds,
> And Scythian shafts. and many-winged wounds
> Aim'd at her heart ; was often forc'd to fly,
> And doom'd to death though fated not to die."

These lines are lofty, elegant, and musical, notwithstanding the interruption of the pause, of which the effect is rather increase of pleasure by variety than offence by ruggedness.

To the first part it was his intention, he says, "to give the majestic turn of heroic poesy ;" and perhaps he might have executed his design not unsuccessfully, had not an opportunity of satire, which he cannot forbear, fallen sometimes in his way. The character of a Presbyterian, whose emblem is the wolf, is not very heroically majestic :

> " More haughty than the rest, the wolfish race
> Appear with belly gaunt and famish'd face ;
> Never was so deform'd a beast of grace.
> His ragged tale betwixt his legs he wears,
> Close clapp'd for shame ; but his rough crest he rears,
> And pricks up his predestinating ears."

His general character of the other sorts of beasts that never go to church, though sprightly and keen, has, however, not much of heroic poesy :

> " These are the chief ; to number o'er the rest,
> And stand like Adam naming every beast,
> Were weary work ; nor will the Muse describe
> A slimy-born and sun-begotten tribe,
> Who, far from steeples and their sacred sound,
> In fields their sullen conventicles found.
> These gross, half-animated lumps I leave ;
> Nor can I think what thoughts they can conceive ;
> But, if they think at all, 'tis sure no higher
> Than matter, put in motion, may aspire :
> Souls that can scarce ferment their mass of clay, ⎫
> So drossy, so divisible are they,   ⎬
> As would but serve pure bodies for allay ;   ⎭
> Such souls as shards produce, such beetle things
> As only buzz to Heaven with evening wings ;
> Strike in the dark, offending but by chance :
> Such are the blindfold blows of ignorance.
> They know no being, and but hate a name ;
> To them the Hind and Panther are the same."

One more instance, and that taken from the narrative part, where style was more in his choice, will show how steadily he kept his resolution of heroic dignity :

> " For when the herd, suffic'd, did late repair
> To ferny heaths and to their forest lair,
> She made a mannerly excuse to stay,
> Proffering the Hind to wait her half the way ;
> That, since the sky was clear an hour of talk
> Might help her to beguile the tedious walk.
> With much good-will the motion was embrac'd,
> To chat awhile on their adventures past :

Nor had the grateful Hind so soon forgot
Her friend and fellow-sufferer in the plot.
Yet, wondering how of late she grew estrang'd,
Her forehead cloudy and her count'nance chang'd,
She thought this hour th' occasion would present
To learn her secret cause of discontent,
Which well she hop'd might be with ease redress'd,)
Considering her a well-bred civil beast, }
And more a gentlewoman than the rest.)
After some common talk what rumors ran,
The lady of the spotted muff began.''

    The second and third parts he professes to have reduced to
diction more familiar and more suitable to dispute and conversation ; the difference is not, however, very easily perceived ;
the first has familiar, and the two others have sonorous, lines.
The original incongruity runs through the whole ; the king is
now Cæsar and now the lion ; and the name Pan is given to
the Supreme Being.
    But when this constitutional absurdity is forgiven, the poem
must be confessed to be written with smoothness of metre, a
wide extent of knowledge, and an abundant multiplicity of
images ; the controversy is embellished with pointed sentences,
diversified by illustrations, and enlivened by sallies of invective. Some of the facts to which allusions are made are now
become obscure, and perhaps there may be many satirical passages little understood.
    As it was by its nature a work of defiance, a composition
which would naturally be examined with the utmost acrimony
of criticism, it was probably labored with uncommon attention, and there are, indeed, few negligences in the subordinate
parts. The original impropriety, and the subsequent unpopu-
larity of the subject, added to the ridiculousness of its first elements, has sunk it into neglect ; but it may be usefully studied
as an example of poetical ratiocination, in which the argument
suffers little from the metre.
    In the poem '' On the Birth of the Prince of Wales,'' noth-
ing is very remarkable but the exorbitant adulation and that
insensibility of the precipice on which the king was then standing, which the laureate apparently shared with the rest of the
courtiers. A few months cured him of controversy, dismissed
him from court, and made him again a playwright and translator.
    Of Juvenal there had been a translation by Stapylton, and
another by Holiday ; neither of them is very poetical. Stapyl-
ton is more smooth ; and Holiday's is more esteemed for the
learning of his notes. A new version was proposed to the

poets of that time, and undertaken by them in conjunction. The main design was conducted by Dryden, whose reputation was such that no man was unwilling to serve the muses under him.

The general character of this translation will be given when it is said to preserve the wit, but to want the dignity, of the original. The peculiarity of Juvenal is a mixture of gayety and stateliness, of pointed sentences, and declamatory grandeur. His points have not been neglected ; but his grandeur none of the band seemed to consider as necessary to be imitated, except Creech, who undertook the thirteenth satire. It is therefore, perhaps, possible to give a better representation of that great satirist, even in those parts which Dryden himself has translated, some passages excepted, which will never be excelled.

With Juvenal was published Persius, translated wholly by Dryden. This work, though, like all other productions of Dryden, it may have shining parts, seems to have been written merely for wages, in an uniform mediocrity, without any eager endeavor after excellence or laborious effort of the mind.

There wanders an opinion among the readers of poetry that one of these satires is an exercise of the school. Dryden says that he once translated it at school ; but not that he preserved or published the juvenile performance.

Not long afterwards he undertook perhaps the most arduous work of its kind, a translation of Virgil, for which he had shown how well he was qualified by his version of the Pollio, and two episodes, one of Nisus and Euryalus, the other of Mezentius and Lausus.

In the comparison of Homer and Virgil, the discriminative excellence of Homer is elevation and comprehension of thought, and that of Virgil is grace and splendor of diction. The beauties of Homer are therefore difficult to be lost, and those of Virgil difficult to be retained. The massy trunk of sentiment is safe by its solidity, but the blossoms of elocution easily drop away. The author, having the choice of his own images, selects those which he can best adorn ; the translator must, at all hazards, follow his original, and express thoughts which perhaps he would not have chosen. When to this primary difficulty is added the inconvenience of a language so much inferior in harmony to the Latin, it cannot be expected that they who read the " Georgics" and the " Æneid" should be much delighted with any version.

All these obstacles Dryden saw, and all these he determined to encounter. The expectation of his work was undoubtedly great , the nation considered its honor as interested in the event. One gave him the different editions of his author, another helped him in the subordinate parts. The arguments of the several books were given him by Addison.

The hopes of the public were not disappointed. He produced, says Pope, "the most noble and spirited translation that I know in any language." It certainly excelled whatever had appeared in English, and appears to have satisfied his friends, and for the most part to have silenced his enemies. Milbourne, indeed, a clergyman, attacked it ; but his outrages seem to be the ebullitions of a mind agitated by a stronger resentment than bad poetry can excite, and previously resolved not to be pleased.

His criticism extends only to the *Preface, Pastorals,* and *Georgics ;* and, as he professes to give his antagonist an opportunity of reprisal, he has added his own version of the first and fourth Pastorals, and the first Georgic. The world has forgotten his book ; but since his attempt has given him a place in literary history, I will preserve a specimen of his criticism by inserting his remarks on the invocation before the first Georgic ; and of his poetry, by annexing his own version.

Ver. 1.
" ' What makes a plenteous harvest, when to turn
The fruitful soil, and when to sow the corn.'

It's *unlucky,* they say, *to stumble at the threshold ;* but what has a *plenteous harvest* to do here ? Virgil would not pretend to prescribe rules for *that* which depends not on the *husbandman's* care, but the *disposition of Heaven* altogether. Indeed, the *plenteous crop* depends somewhat on the *good method of tillage ;* and where the *land's* ill-manur'd, the *corn,* without a miracle, can be but *indifferent :* but the *harvest* may be *good,* which is its *properest* epithet, tho' the *husbandman's skill* were never so *indifferent.* The next *sentence* is *too literal,* and *when to plough* had been Virgil's meaning, and intelligible to everybody ; and *when to sow the corn* is a needless *addition.*

Ver. 3.
" ' The care of sheep, of oxen, and of kine,
And when to geld the lambs, and shear the swine,'

would as well have fallen under the *cura boum qui cultus habendo sit pecori,* as Mr. D.'s *deduction* of particulars.

Ver. 5.
" ' The birth and genius of the frugal bee
I sing, Mæcenas, and I sing to thee.'

But where did *experientia* ever signify *birth and genius?* or what ground was there for such a *figure* in this place? How much more manly is Mr. Ogylby's version !

> " ' What makes rich grounds, in what celestial signs
> 'Tis good to plough, and marry elms with vines ;
> What best fits cattle, what with sheep agrees,
> And several arts improving frugal bees ;
> I sing, Mæcenas.'

Which four lines, tho' faulty enough, are yet much more to the purpose than Mr. D.'s six.

Ver. 22.

> " ' From fields and mountains to my song repair,'

for *patrium linquens nemus, saltusque Lycæi*—very well explained !

Ver. 23, 24.

> " ' Inventor Pallas, of the fattening oil,
> Thou founder of the plough, and ploughman's toil.'

Written as if *these* had been *Pallas's invention*. *The ploughman's toil's* impertinent.

Ver. 25.

> " '—— The shroud-like cypress.'

Why *shroud-like?* Is a *cypress*, pulled up by the *roots*, which the *sculpture* in the *last Éclogue* fills Silvanus's hand with, so very like a *shroud?* Or did not Mr. D. think of that kind of *cypress* us'd often for *scarves and hatbands* at funerals formerly, or for *widows' veils*, etc. ? If so, 'twas a *deep. good thought.*

Ver. 26.

> " '——That wear
> The rural honors, and increase the year.'

What's meant by *increasing the year?* Did the *gods* or *goddesses* add more *months*, or *days*, or *hours* to it ? Or how can *arva tueri* signify to *wear rural honors?* Is this to *translate* or *abuse* an *author?* The next *couplet* is borrowed from Ogylby, I suppose, because *less to the purpose* than ordinary.

Ver. 33.

> " ' The patron of the world, and Rome's peculiar guard.'

Idle, and none of Virgil's, no more than the sense of the *precedent couplet ;* so, again, he *interpolates* Virgil with that and *the round circle of the year to guide powerful of blessings, which thou strew'st around ;* a ridiculous *Latinism*, and an *impertinent addition ;* indeed the whole *period* is but one piece of *absurdity* and *nonsense*, as those who lay it with the *original* must find.

Ver. 42, 43.
" ' And Neptune shall resign the fasces of the sea.'

Was he *consul* or *dictator* there ?

" ' And watery virgins for thy bed shall strive.'

Both absurd *interpolations*.

Ver. 47, 48.
" ' Where in the void of heaven a place is free,
   A h, happy D——n, *were* that place *for thee !* '

But where is *that void?* Or, what does our *translator* mean by it ? He knows what Ovid says *God* did to prevent such a *void* in heaven ; perhaps this was then forgotten ; but Virgil talks more sensibly.

Ver. 49.
" ' The scorpion ready to receive thy laws.'

No, he would not then have *gotten out of his way* so fast.

Ver. 56.
" ' Though Proserpine affects her silent seat.'

What made *her* then so *angry* with *Ascalaphus* for preventing her return ? She was now mus'd to *Patience* under the *determinations of Fate*, rather than *fond* of her *residence*.

Ver. 61, 62, 63.
" ' Pity the poet's and the ploughman's cares,
   Interest thy greatness in our mean affairs,
   And use thyself betimes to hear our prayers.'

Which is such a wretched *perversion* of Virgil's *noble thought* as *Vicars* would have blush'd at : but Mr. Ogylby makes us some amends by his better lines :

" ' O wheresoe'er thou art, from thence incline,
   And grant assistance to my bold design ;
   Pity, with me, poor husbandmen's affairs,
   And now, as if translated, hear our prayers.'

This is *sense*, and *to the purpose :* the other, poor *mistaken stuff*.''

Such were the strictures of Milbourne, who found few abettors, and of whom it may be reasonably imagined that many who favored his design were ashamed of his insolence.

When admiration had subsided, the translation was more coolly examined, and found, like all others, to be sometimes erroneous and sometimes licentious. Those who could find faults thought they could avoid them ; and Dr. Brady attempted in blank verse a translation of the " Æneid," which, when dragged into the world, did not live long enough to cry. I have never seen it ; but that such a version there is, or has been, perhaps some old catalogue informed me.

With not much better success Trapp, when his Tragedy and his Prelections had given him reputation, attempted another blank version of the "Æneid ;" to which, notwithstanding the slight regard with which it was treated, he had afterwards perseverance enough to add the " Eclogues" and " Georgics." His book may continue in existence as long as it is the clandestine refuge of school-boys.

Since the English ear has been accustomed to the mellifluence of Pope's numbers, and the diction of poetry has become more splendid, new attempts have been made to translate Virgil ; and all his works have been attempted by men better qualified to contend with Dryden. I will not engage myself in an invidious comparison, by opposing one passage to another ; a work of which there would be no end, and which might be often offensive without use.

It is not by comparing line with line that the merit of great works is to be estimated, but by their general effects and ultimate result. It is easy to note a weak line, and write one more vigorous in its place ; to find a happiness of expression in the original, and transplant it by force into the version ; but what is given to the parts may be subducted from the whole, and the reader may be weary, though the critic may commend. Works of imagination excel by their allurement and delight ; by their power of attracting and detaining the attention. That book is good in vain which the reader throws away He only is the master who keeps the mind in pleasing captivity ; whose pages are perused with eagerness, and in hope of new pleasure are perused again ; and whose conclusion is perceived with an eye of sorrow, such as the traveller casts upon departing day.

By his proportion of this predomination I will consent that Dryden should be tried ; of this which, in opposition to reason, makes Ariosto the darling and the pride of Italy ; of this which, in defiance of criticism, continues Shakespeare the sovereign of the drama.

His last work was his " Fables," in which he gave us the first example of a mode of writing which the Italians call *refaccimento*, a renovation of ancient writers by modernizing their language. Thus the old poem of " Boiardo" has been new-dressed by Domenichi and Berni. The works of Chaucer, upon which this kind of rejuvenescence has been bestowed by Dryden, require little criticism. The tale of the Cock seems

hardly worth revival ; and the story of "Palamon and
Arcite," containing an action unsuitable to the times in which
it is placed, can hardly be suffered to pass without censure of
the hyperbolical commendation which Dryden has given it in
the general Preface, and in a poetical Dedication, a piece
where his original fondness for remote conceits seems to have
revived.

Of the three pieces borrowed from Boccace, "Sigismunda"
may be defended by the celebrity of the story. "Theodore
and Honoria," though it contains not much moral, yet
afforded opportunities of striking description. And "Cy-
mon" was formerly a tale of such reputation that at the revival
of letters it was translated into Latin by one of the Beroalds.

Whatever subjects employed his pen, he was still improving
our measures and embellishing our language.

In this volume are interspersed some short original poems,
which, with his prologues, epilogues, and songs, may be comprised in Congreve's remark, that even those, if he had written
nothing else, would have entitled him to the praise of excellence in his kind.

One composition must, however, be distinguished. The
"Ode for St. Cecilia's Day," perhaps the last effort of his
poetry, has been always considered as exhibiting the highest
flight of fancy, and the exactest nicety of art. This is allowed
to stand without a rival. If indeed there is any excellence beyond it, in some other of Dryden's works that excellence must
be found. Compared with the "Ode on Killigrew," it may be
pronounced perhaps superior on the whole, but without any
single part equal to the first stanza of the other.

It is said to have cost Dryden a fortnight's labor ; but it
does not want its negligences ; some of the lines are without
correspondent rhymes ; a defect which I never detected but
after an acquaintance of many years, and which the enthusiasm
of the writer might hinder him from perceiving.

His last stanza has less emotion than the former ; but it is
not less elegant in the diction. The conclusion is vicious ; the
music of "Timotheus," which *raised a mortal to the skies*, had
only a metaphorical power ; that of "Cecilia," which *drew an
angel down*, had a real effect : the crown, therefore, could not
reasonably be divided.

In a general survey of Dryden's labors, he appears to have
a mind very comprehensive by nature, and much enriched with
acquired knowledge. His compositions are the effects of a
vigorous genius operating upon large materials.

The power that predominated in his intellectual operations

was rather strong reason than quick sensibility. Upon all occasions that were presented he studied rather than felt, and
produced sentiments not such as nature enforces, but meditation supplies. With the simple and elemental passions, as they
spring separate in the mind, he seems not much acquainted ;
and seldom describes them but as they are complicated by the
various relations of society and confused in the tumults and
agitations of life.

What he says of Love may contribute to the explanation of
his character :

> " Love various minds does variously inspire :
> It stirs in gentle bosoms gentle fire,
> Like that of incense on the altar laid ;
> But raging flames tempestuous souls invade :
> A fire which every windy passion blows,
> With pride it mounts, or with revenge it glows."

Dryden's was not one of the *gentle bosoms :* Love, as it subsists in itself, with no tendency but to the person loved, and
wishing only for correspondent kindness ; such Love as shuts
out all other interest, the Love of the Golden Age, was too
soft and subtle to put his faculties in motion. He hardly conceived it but in its turbulent effervescence with some other
desires ; when it was inflamed by rivalry or obstructed by
difficulties ; when it invigorated ambition or exasperated revenge.

He is, therefore, with all his variety of excellence, not often
pathetic ; and had so little sensibility of the power of effusions
purely natural, that he did not esteem them in others : simplicity gave him no pleasure ; and for the first part of his life he
looked on Otway with contempt, though at last, indeed very
late, he confessed that in his play *there* was *Nature, which is
the chief beauty*.

We do not always know our own motives. I am not certain whether it was not rather the difficulty which he found in
exhibiting the genuine operations of the heart, than a servile
submission to an injudicious audience that filled his plays
with false magnificence. It was necessary to fix attention ;
and the mind can be captivated only by recollection or by curiosity ; by reviving natural sentiments, or impressing new appearances of things ; sentences were readier at his call than images :
he could more easily fill the ear with splendid novelty than
awaken those ideas that slumber in the heart.

The favorite exercise of his mind was ratiocination ; and
that argument might not be too soon at an end, he delighted to
talk of liberty and necessity, destiny and contingence ; these he

discusses in the language of the school, with so much pro-
fundity that the terms which he uses are not always understood. It is indeed learning, but learning out of place.
When once he had engaged himself in disputation thoughts
flowed in on either side : he was now no longer at a loss ; he
had always objections and solutions at command ; '' verbaque
provisam rem''—gave him matter for his verse, and he finds
without difficulty verse for his matter.

In comedy, for which he professes himself not naturally
qualified, the mirth which he excites will perhaps not be found
so much to arise from any original humor, or peculiarity of
character nicely distinguished and diligently pursued, as from
incidents and circumstances, artifices and surprises ; from jests
of action rather than of sentiment. What he had of humorous
or passionate, he seems to have had not from nature, but from
other poets ; if not always as a plagiary, at least as an imitator.

Next to argument his delight was in wild and daring sallies
of sentiment, in the irregular and eccentric violence of wit.
He delighted to tread upon the brink of meaning, where night
and darkness begin to mingle ; to approach the precipice of
absurdity, and hover over the abyss of unideal vacancy. This
inclination sometimes produced nonsense, which he knew ; as,

> '' Move swiftly, Sun, and fly a lover's pace,
> Leave weeks and months behind thee in thy race,
>   Amamel flies
> To guard thee from the demons of the air ;
> My flaming sword above them to display,
> All keen, and ground upon the edge of day.''

And sometimes it issued in absurdities, of which perhaps he
was not conscious :

> ''Then we upon our orb's last verge shall go,
> And see the ocean leaning on the sky,
> From thence our rolling neighbors we shall know,
> And cn the lunar world securely pry.''

These lines have no meaning ; but may we not say, in imitation of Cowley on another book,

> '' 'Tis so like sense, 'twill serve the turn as well '' ?

This endeavor after the grand and the new produced many
sentiments either great or bulky, and many images either just
or splendid :

> '' I am as free as Nature first made man,
> Ere the base laws of servitude began,
> When wild in woods the noble savage ran.

" —'Tis but because the living death ne'er knew,
    They fear to prove it as a thing that's new :
    Let me th' experiment before you try,
    I'll show you first how easy 'tis to die.

" —There with a forest of their darts he strove,
    And stood like Capaneus defying Jove,
    With his broad sword the boldest beating down,
    While Fate grew pale lest he should win the town,
    And turn'd the iron leaves of his dark book
    To make new dooms, or mend what it misto: *.

" —I beg no pity for this mouldering clay ;
    For if you give it burial, there it takes
    Possession of your earth :
    If burnt, and scatter'd in the air, the winds
    That strew my dust diffuse my royalty,
    And spread me o'er your clime ; for where one atom
    Of mine shall light, know there Sebastian reigns."

Of these quotations the two first may be allowed to be great, the two latter only tumid.

Of such selection there is no end. I will add only a few more passages : of which the first, though it may not perhaps be quite clear in prose, is not too obscure for poetry, as the meaning that it has is noble :

" No, there is a necessity in fate,
    Why still the brave bold man is fortunate,
    He keeps his object ever full in sight ;
    And that assurance holds him firm and right.
    True, 'tis a narrow way that leads to bliss,
    But right before there is no precipice ;
    Fear makes men look aside, and so their footing miss." }

Of the images which the two following citations afford, the first is elegant, the second magnificent ; whether either be just, let the reader judge :

" What precious drops are these,
    Which silently each other's track pursue,
    Bright as young diamonds in their infant dew !

" —— Resign your castle ——
    —Enter, brave Sir : for, when you speak the word,
    The gates shall open of their own accord ;
    The genius of the place its Lord shall meet,
    And bow its towery forehead at your feet."

These bursts of extravagance Dryden calls the *Delilahs of the Theatre ;* and owns that many noisy lines of " Maximin and Almanzor" call out for vengeance upon him : " but I knew," says he, " that they were bad enough to please, even when I wrote them." There is surely reason to suspect that he pleased himself as well as his audience ; and that these, like the harlots of other men, had his love, though not his approbation.

He had sometimes faults of a less generous and splendid kind. He makes, like almost all other poets, very frequent use of mythology, and sometimes connects religion and fable too closely without distinction.

He descends to display his knowledge with pedantic ostentation ; as when, in translating Virgil, he says, *tack to the larboard*—and *veer starboard ;* and talks in another work of *virtue spooning before the wind.* His vanity now and then betrays his ignorance :

> " They Nature's king through Nature's optics view'd ;
> Revers'd, they view'd him lessen'd to their eyes."

He had heard of reversing a telescope, and unluckily reverses the object.

He is sometimes unexpectedly mean. When he describes the Supreme Being as moved by prayer to stop the fire of London, what is his expression ?

> " A hollow crystal pyramid he takes,
>   In firmamental waters dipp'd above,
> Of this a broad extinguisher he makes,
>   And hoods the flames that to their quarry strove."

When he describes the last day, and the decisive tribunal, he intermingles this image :

> " When rattling bones together fly,
>   From the four quarters of the sky."

It was indeed never in his power to resist the temptation of a jest. In his " Elegy on Cromwell :"

> " No sooner was the Frenchman's cause embrac'd,
>   Than the light Monsieur the grave Don outweigh'd ;
>   His fortune turn'd the scale ——"

He had a vanity, unworthy of his abilities, to show, as may be suspected, the rank of the company with whom he lived, by the use of French words, which had then crept into conversation : such as *fraicheur* for *coolness, fougue* for *turbulence*, and a few more, none of which the language has incorporated or retained. They continue only where they stood first, perpetual warnings to future innovators.

These are his faults of affection ; his faults of negligence are beyond recital. Such is the unevenness of his compositions, that ten lines are seldom found together without something of which the reader is ashamed. Dryden was no rigid judge of his own pages ; he seldom struggled after supreme excellence, but snatched in haste what was within his reach ; and when he could content others, was himself contented. He did not keep present to his mind an idea of pure perfection ; nor compare his works, such as they were, with what they might be made. He knew to whom he should be opposed. He had more music than Waller, more vigor than Denham, and more nature than Cowley ; and from his contemporaries he was in no danger. Standing therefore in the highest place, he had no care to rise by contending with himself, but, while there was no name above his own, was willing to enjoy fame on the easiest terms.

He was no lover of labor. What he thought sufficient he did not stop to make better ; and allowed himself to leave many parts unfinished, in confidence that the good lines would overbalance the bad. What he had once written he dismissed from his thoughts ; and I believe there is no example to be found of any correction or improvement made by him after publication. The hastiness of his productions might be the effect of necessity ; but his subsequent neglect could hardly have any other cause than impatience of study,

What can be said of his versification will be little more than a dilatation of the praise given it by Pope :

> " Waller was smooth ; but Dryden taught to join
> The varying verse, the full-resounding line,
> The long majestic march, and energy divine."

Some improvements had been already made in English numbers ; but the full force of our language was not yet felt ; the verse that was smooth was commonly feeble. If Cowley had sometimes a finished line, he had it by chance. Dryden knew how to choose the flowing and the sonorous words ; to vary the pauses and adjust the accents ; to diversify the cadence, and yet preserve the smoothness of his metre.

Of triplets and Alexandrines, though he did not introduce the use, he established it. The triplet has long subsisted among us. Dryden seems not to have traced it higher than to Chapman's Homer ; but it is to be found in Phaer's Virgil, written in the reign of Mary ; and in Hall's " Satires," published five years before the death of Elizabeth.

The Alexandrine was, I believe, first used by Spenser, for the sake of closing his stanza with a fuller sound. We had a longer measure of fourteen syllables, into which the "Æneid" was translated by Phaer, and other works of the ancients by other writers, of which Chapman's " Iliad " was, I believe, the last.

The two first lines of Phaer's third "Æneid" will exemplify this measure :

> " When Asia's state was overthrown, and Priam's kingdom stout
> All guiltless, by the power of gods above was rooted out."

As these lines had their break, or *cæsura*, always at the eighth syllable, it was thought, in time, commodious to divide them : and quatrains of lines, alternately, consisting of eight and six syllables, make the most soft and pleasing of our lyric measures : as,

> " Relentless time, destroying power,
> Which stone and brass obey ;
> Who giv'st to ev'ry flying hour
> To work some new decay."

In the Alexandrine, when its power was once felt, some poems, as Drayton's " Polyolbion," were wholly written ; and sometimes the measures of twelve and fourteen syllables were interchanged with one another. Cowley was the first that inserted the Alexandrine at pleasure among the heroic lines of ten syllables, and from him Dryden professes to have adopted it.

The triplet and Alexandrine are not universally approved. Swift always censured them, and wrote some lines to ridicule them. In examining their propriety, it is to be considered that the essence of verse is regularity, and its ornament is variety. To write verse is to dispose syllables and sounds harmonically by some known and settled rule ; a rule, however, lax enough to substitute similitude for identity, to admit change without breach of order, and to relieve the ear without disappointing it. Thus a Latin hexameter is formed from dactyls and spondees differently combined ; the English heroic admits of acute or grave syllables variously disposed. The Latin never deviates into seven feet, or exceeds the number of seventeen syllables ; but the English Alexandrine breaks the lawful bounds, and surprises the reader with two syllables more than he expected.

The effect of the triplet is the same ; the ear has been accustomed to expect a new rhyme in every couplet, but is on a sudden surprised with three rhymes together, to which the reader could not accommodate his voice, did he not obtain notice of the change from the braces of the margins. Surely there is something unskilful in the necessity of such mechanical direction.

Considering the metrical art simply as a science, and consequently excluding all casualty, we must allow that triplets and Alexandrines, inserted by caprice, are interruptions of that constancy to which science aspires. And though the variety which they produce may very justly be desired, yet, to make poetry exact, there ought to be some stated mode of admitting them.

But till some such regulation can be formed, I wish them still to be retained in their present state. They are sometimes convenient to the poet. Fenton was of opinion that Dryden was too liberal and Pope too sparing in their use.

The rhymes of Dryden are commonly just, and he valued himself for his readiness in finding them ; but he is sometimes open to objection.

It is the common practice of our poets to end the second line with a weak or grave syllable :

> " Together o'er the Alps methinks we fly,
> Fill'd with ideas of fair Italy."

Dryden sometimes puts the weak rhyme in the first :

> " Laugh, all the powers that favor tyranny,
> And all the standing army of the sky."

Sometimes he concludes a period or paragraph with the first line of a couplet, which, though the French seem to do it without irregularity, always displeases in English poetry.

The Alexandrine, though much his favorite, is not always very diligently fabricated by him. It invariably requires a break at the sixth syllable ; a rule which the modern French poets never violate, but which Dryden sometimes neglected :

> " And with paternal thunder vindicates his throne."

Of Dryden's works it was said by Pope that " he could select from them better specimens of every mode of poetry than any other English writer could supply." Perhaps no nation ever produced a writer that enriched his language with such a variety of models. To him we owe the improvement, perhaps the completion, of our metre, the refinement of our language, and much of the correctness of our sentiments. By him we were taught *sapere et fari*, to think naturally and express forcibly. Though Davies had reasoned in rhyme before him, it may be perhaps maintained that he was the first who joined argument with poetry. He showed us the true bounds of a translator's liberty. What was said of Rome adorned by Augustus may be applied by an easy metaphor to English poetry embellished by Dryden, *lateritiam invenit, marmorcam reliquit.* He found it brick, and he left it marble.

The invocation before the "Georgics" is here inserted from Mr. Milbourne's version, that, according to his own proposal, his verses may be compared with those which he censures :

"What makes the richest tilth, beneath what signs
To plough, and when to match your elms and vines ;
What care with flocks, and what with herds agrees,
And all the management of frugal bees ;
I sing, Mæcenas ! Ye immensely clear,
Vast orbs of light, which guide the rolling year !
Bacchus, and mother Ceres, if by you
We fatt'ning corn for hungry man pursue ;
If, taught by you, we first the cluster prest,
And thin cold streams with sprightly juice refresht ;
Ye fawns, the present numens of the field,
Wood-nymphs and fawns, your kind assistance yield,
Your gifts I sing : and thou, at whose fear'd stroke
From rending earth the fiery courser broke,
Great Neptune, O assist my artful song !
And thou to whom the woods and groves belong,
Whose snowy heifers on her flow'ry plains
In mighty herds the Cæan Isle maintains !
Pan, happy shepherd, if thy cares divine,
E'er to improve thy Mænalus incline,
Leave thy Lycæan wood and native grove,
And with thy lucky smiles our work approve ;
Be Pallas too, sweet oil's inventor, kind ;
And he who first the crooked plough design'd,
Sylvanus, god of all the woods, appear,
Whose hands a new-drawn tender cypress bear !
Ye gods and goddesses, who e'er with love
Would guard our pastures, and our fields improve :
Ye, who new plants from unknown lands supply,
And with condensing clouds obscure the sky,
And drop them softly thence in fruitful showers ;
Assist my enterprise, ye gentle powers !
  And thou, great Cæsar ! though we know not yet
Among what gods thou'lt fix thy lofty seat :
Whether thou'lt be the kind tutelar god
Of thy own Rome, or with thy awful nod
Guide the vast world, while thy great hand shall bear }
The fruits and seasons of the turning year, }
And thy bright brows thy mother's myrtles wear ; }
Whether thou'lt all the boundless ocean sway,
And seamen only to thyself shall pray ;
Thule, the fairest island, kneel to thee,
And, that thou may'st her son by marriage be,
Tethys will for the happy purchase yield
To make a dowry of her wat'ry field :
Whether thou'lt add to heaven a brighter sign,

And o'er the summer months serenely shine ;
Where between Cancer and Erigone,
There yet remains a spacious room for thee ;
Where the hot Scorpion too his arm declines,
And more to thee than half his arch resigns ;
Whate'er thou'lt be ; for sure the realms below
No just pretence to thy command can show :
No such ambition sways thy vast desires,
Though Greece her own Elysian fields admires.
And now, at last, contented Proserpine,
Can all her mother's earnest prayers decline,
Whate'er thou'lt be, O guide our gentle course ;
And with thy smiles our bold attempts enforce ;
With me th' unknowing rustics' wants relieve,
And, though on earth, our sacred vows receive."

Mr. Dryden, having received from Rymer his " Remarks on the Tragedies of the last Age," wrote observations on the blank leaves ; which, having been in the possession of Mr. Garrick, are by his favor communicated to the public, that no particle of Dryden may be lost.

" That we may less wonder why pity and terror are not now the only springs on which our tragedies move, and that Shakespeare may be more excused, Rapin confesses that the French tragedies now all run on the *tendre ;* and gives the reason, because love is the passion which most predominates in our souls, and that therefore the passions represented become insipid, unless they are conformable to the thoughts of the audience. But it is to be concluded that this passion works not now amongst the French so strongly as the other two did amongst the ancients. Amongst us, who have a stronger genius for writing, the operations from the writing are much stronger ; for the raising of Shakespeare's passions is more from the excellency of the words and thoughts than the justness of the occasion ; and if he has been able to pick single occasions, he has never founded the whole reasonably ; yet, by the genius of poetry in writing, he has succeeded.

" Rapin attributes more to the *dictio*, that is, to the words and discourse of a tragedy, than Aristotle has done, who places them in the last rank of beauties ; perhaps only last in order because they are the last product of the design, of the disposition or connection of its parts ; of the characters, of the manners of those characters, and of the thoughts proceeding from those manners. Rapin's words are remarkable : ' 'Tis not the admirable intrigue, the surprising events, and extraordinary incidents that make the beauty of a tragedy : 'tis the discourses, when they are natural and passionate : so are Shakespeare's.'

" The parts of a poem, tragic or heroic, are,

" 1. The fable itself.

" 2. The order or manner of its contrivance, in relation of the parts to the whole.

" 3. The manners or decency of the characters, in speaking or acting what is proper for them, and proper to be shown by the poet.

" 4. The thoughts which express the manners.

" 5. The words which express those thoughts.

" In the last of these, Homer excels Virgil ; Virgil all the other ancient poets ; and Shakespeare all modern poets.

" For the second of these, the order : the meaning is, that a fable ought to have a beginning, middle, and an end, all just and natural ; so that that part, *e.g.*, which is the middle could not naturally be the beginning or end, and so of the rest : all depend on one another, like the links of a curious chain. If terror and pity are only to be raised, certainly this author follows Aristotle's rules, and Sophocles' and Euripides' example ; but joy may be raised too, and that doubly, either by seeing a wicked man punished or a good man at last fortunate ; or perhaps indignation, to see wickedness prosperous and goodness depressed : both these may be profitable to the end of a tragedy, reformation of manners ; but the last improperly, only as it begets pity in the audience ; though Aristotle, I confess, places tragedies of this kind in the second form.

" He who undertakes to answer this excellent critique of Mr. Rymer, in behalf of our English poets against the Greek, ought to do it in this manner : either by yielding to him the greatest part of what he contends for, which consists in this, that the μῦϑος, *i.e.*, the design and conduct of it, is more conducing in the Greeks to those ends of tragedy which Aristotle and he propose, namely, to cause terror and pity ; yet the granting this does not set the Greeks above the English poets.

" But the answerer ought to prove two things : First. That the fable is not the greatest masterpiece of a tragedy, though it be the foundation of it. .

" Secondly. That other ends as suitable to the nature of tragedy may be found in the English, which were not in the Greek.

" Aristotle places the fable first ; not *quoad dignitatem, sed quoad fundamentum :* for a fable never so movingly contrived to those ends of his, pity and terror, will operate nothing on our affections, except the characters, manners, thoughts, and words are suitable.

" So that it remains for Mr. Rymer to prove, that in all

those, or the greatest part of them, we are inferior to Sophocles and Euripides ; and this he has offered at, in some measure ; but, I think, a little partially to the ancients.

" For the fable itself, 'tis in the English more adorned with episodes, and larger than in the Greek poets ; consequently more diverting. For, if the action be but one, and that plain, without any counterturn of design or episode, *i.e.*, underplot, how can it be so pleasing as the English, which have both underplot and a turned design, which keeps the audience in expectation of the catastrophe ? whereas in the Greek poets we see through the whole design at first.

" For the characters, they are neither so many nor so various in Sophocles and Euripides as in Shakespeare and Fletcher : only they are more adapted to those ends of tragedy which Aristotle commends to us, pity and terror.

" The manners flow from the characters, and consequently must partake of their advantages and disadvantages.

" The thoughts and words, which are the fourth and fifth beauties of tragedy, are certainly more noble and more poetical in the English than in the Greek, which must be proved by comparing them somewhat more equitably than Mr. Rymer has done.

" After all, we need not yield that the English way is less conducing to move pity and terror, because they often show virtue oppressed and vice punished : where they do not both, or either, they are not to be defended.

" And if we should grant that the Greeks performed this' better, perhaps it may admit of dispute whether pity and terror are either the prime or at least the only ends of tragedy.

" 'Tis not enough that Aristotle had said so ; for Aristotle drew his models of tragedy from Sophocles and Euripides ; and if he had seen ours might have changed his mind. And chiefly we have to say (what I hinted on pity and terror, in the last paragraph save one), that the punishment of vice and reward of virtue are the most adequate ends of tragedy, because most conducing to good example of life. Now, pity is not so easily raised for a criminal (and the ancient tragedy always represents its chief person such) as it is for an innocent man ; and the suffering of innocence and punishment of the offender is of the nature of English tragedy : contrarily, in the Greek, innocence is unhappy often, and the offender escapes. Then we are not touched with the sufferings of any sort of men so much as of lovers ; and this was almost unknown to the ancients : so that they neither administered poetical justice, of which Mr. Rymer boasts, so well as we ;

neither knew they the best commonplace of pity, which is love.

" He therefore unjustly blames us for not building on what the ancients left us ; for it seems, upon consideration of the premises, that we have wholly finished what they began.

" My judgment on this piece is this : that it is extremely learned, but that the author of it is better read in the Greek than in the English poets ; that all writers ought to study this critique, as the best account I have ever seen of the ancients ; that the model of tragedy he has here given is excellent and extremely correct ; but that it is not the only model of all tragedy, because it is too much circumscribed in plot, characters, etc. ; and, lastly, that we may be taught here justly to admire and imitate the ancients, without giving them the preference with this author, in prejudice to our own country.

" Want of method in this excellent treatise makes the thoughts of the author sometimes obscure.

" His. meaning, that pity and terror are to be moved, is, that they are to be moved as the means conducing to the ends of tragedy, which are pleasure and instruction.

" And these two ends may be thus distinguished. The chief end of the poet is to please ; for his immediate reputation depends on it.

" The great end of the poem is to instruct, which is performed by making pleasure the vehicle of that instruction ; for poesy is an art, and all arts are made to profit.—*Rapin.*

" The pity, which the poet is to labor for, is for the criminal, not for those or him whom he has murdered, or who have been the occasion of the tragedy. The terror is likewise in the punishment of the same criminal, who, if he be represented too great an offender, will not be pitied ; if altogether innocent, his punishment will be unjust.

" Another obscurity is, where he says Sophocles perfected tragedy by introducing the third actor ; that is, he meant three kinds of action : one company singing or speaking ; another playing on the music ; a third dancing.

" To make a true judgment in this competition betwixt the Greek poets and the English, in tragedy :

" Consider, first, how Aristotle has defined a tragedy. Secondly, what he assigns the end of it to be. Thirdly, what he thinks the beauties of it. Fourthly, the means to attain the end proposed.

" Compare the Greek and English tragic poets justly, and without partiality, according to those rules.

" Then, secondly, consider whether Aristotle has made a

just definition of tragedy ; of its parts, of its ends, and of its beauties ; and whether he, having not seen any others but those of Sophocles, Euripides, etc., had or truly could determine what all the excellences of tragedy are, and wherein they consist.

" Next, show in what ancient tragedy was deficient ; for example, in the narrowness of its plots and fewness of persons ; and try whether that be not a fault in the Greek poets ; and whether their excellency was so great, when the variety was visibly so little ; or whether what they did was not very easy to do.

" Then make a judgment on what the English have added to their beauties ; as, for example, not only more plot, but also new passions ; as, namely, that of love, scarcely touched on by the ancients, except in this one example of Phædra, cited by Mr. Rymer ; and in that how short they were of Fletcher !

" Prove also that love, being an heroic passion, is fit for tragedy, which cannot be denied, because of the example alleged of Phædra ; and how far Shakespeare has outdone them in friendship, etc.

" To return to the beginning of this inquiry : consider if pity and terror be enough for tragedy to move ; and I believe, upon a true definition of tragedy, it will be found that its work extends farther, and that it is to reform manners, by a delightful representation of human life in great persons, by way of dialogue. If this be true, then not only pity and terror are to be moved, as the only means to bring us to virtue, but generally love to virtue and hatred to vice, by showing the rewards of one and punishments of the other ; at least, by rendering virtue always amiable, though it be shown unfortunate ; and vice detestable, though it be shown triumphant.

" If, then, the encouragement of virtue and discouragement of vice be the proper ends of poetry in tragedy, pity and terror, though good means, are not the only. For all the passions, in their turns, are to be set in a ferment ; as joy, anger, love, fear are to be used as the poet's commonplaces ; and a general concernment for the principal actors is to be raised by making them appear such in their characters, their words, and actions, as will interest the audience in their fortunes.

" And if, after all, in a larger sense, pity comprehends this concernment for the good, and terror includes detestation for the bad, then let us consider whether the English have not answered this end of tragedy as well as the ancients, or perhaps better.

" And here Mr. Rymer's objections against these plays are

to be impartially weighed, that we may see whether they are of weight enough to turn the balance against our countrymen.

" It is evident those plays which he arraigns have moved both those passions in a high degree upon the stage.

" To give the glory of this away from the poet, and to place it upon the actors, seems unjust.

" One reason is, because whatever actors they have found the event has been the same ; that is, the same passions have been always moved ; which shows that there is something of force and merit in the plays themselves, conducing to the design of raising these two passions : and suppose them ever to have been excellently acted, yet action only adds grace, vigor, and more life upon the stage ; but cannot give it wholly where it is not first. But, secondly, I dare appeal to those who have never seen them acted, if they have not found these two passions moved within them ; and if the general voice will carry it, Mr. Rymer's prejudice will take off his single testimony.

" This, being matter of fact, is reasonably to be established by this appeal ; as, if one man says it is night when the rest of the world conclude it to be day, there needs no farther argument against him that it is so.

" If he urge that the general taste is depraved, his arguments to prove this can at best but evince that our poets took not the best way to raise those passions ; but experience proves against him that those means which they have used have been successful, and have produced them.

" And one reason of that success is, in my opinion, this : that Shakespeare and Fletcher have written to the genius of the age and nation in which they lived ; for though nature, as he objects, is the same in all places, and reason too the same, yet the climate, the age, the disposition of the people to whom a poet writes may be so different that what pleased the Greeks would not satisfy an English audience.

" And if they proceed upon a foundation of truer reason to please the Athenians than Shakespeare and Fletcher to please the English, it only shows that the Athenians were a more judicious people ; but the poet's business is certainly to please the audience.

" Whether our English audience have been pleased hitherto with acorns, as he calls it, or with bread, is the next question ; that is, whether the means which Shakespeare and Fletcher have used, in their plays, to raise those passions before-named, be better applied to the ends by the Greek poets than by them. And perhaps we shall not grant him this wholly : let it be yielded that a writer is not to run down with the stream, or to please the people by their usual methods, but rather to reform their judgments, it still remains to prove that our theatre needs this total reformation.

"The faults which he has found in their design are rather wittily aggravated in many places than reasonably urged ; and as much may be returned on the Greeks by one who were as witty as himself.

"They destroy not, if they are granted, the foundation of the fabric ; only take away from the beauty of the symmetry ; for example, the faults in the character of the King, in ' King and No-king,' are not, as he calls them, such as render him detestable, but only imperfections which accompany human nature, and are for the most part excused by the violence of his love ; so that they destroy not our pity or concernment for him : this answer may be applied to most of his objections of that kind.

"And Rolla committing many murders, when he is answerable but for one, is too severely arraigned by him ; for it adds to our horror and detestation of the criminal ; and poetic justice is not neglected neither ; for we stab him in our minds for every offence which he commits ; and the point, which the poet is to gain on the audience, is not so much in the death of an offender as the raising a horror of his crimes.

"That the criminal should neither be wholly guilty nor wholly innocent, but so participating of both as to move both pity and terror, is certainly a good rule, but not perpetually to be observed ; for that were to make all tragedies too much alike ; which objection he foresaw, but has not fully answered.

"To conclude therefore : if the plays of the ancients are more correctly plotted, ours are more beautifully written. And if we can raise passions as high on worse foundations, it shows our genius in tragedy is greater ; for in all other parts of it the English have manifestly excelled them."

The original of the following letter is preserved in the library at Lambeth, and was kindly imparted to the public by the Reverend Dr. Vyse.

Copy of an original letter from John Dryden, Esq., to his sons in Italy, from a MS. in the Lambeth Library, marked No. 933, p. 56.

(*Superscribed*)

"Al illustrissimo Sigre.
"Carlo Dryden Camariere
"d'Honore A.S.S.

'In Roma.

"Franca per Mantoua.

" DEAR SONS,

" Being now at Sir William Bowyer's in the country, I can-not write at large, because I find myself somewhat indisposed with a cold, and am thick of hearing, rather worse than I was in town. I am glad to find, by your letter of July 26th, your style, that you are both in health ; but wonder you should think me so negligent as to forget to give you an account of the ship in which your parcel is to come. I have written to you two or three letters concerning it, which I have sent by safe hands, as I told you, and doubt not but you have them before this can arrive to you. Being out of town, I have forgotten the ship's name, which your mother will inquire, and put it into her letter, which is joined with mine. But the master's name I remember : he is called Mr. Ralph Thorp ; the ship is bound to Leghorn, consigned to Mr. Peter and Mr. Thomas Ball, merchants. I am of your opinion, that by Tonson's means almost all our letters have miscarried for this last year. But, however, he has missed of his design in the dedication, though he had prepared the book for it ; for in every figure of Æneas he has caused him to be drawn like King William, with a hooked nose. After my return to town I intend to alter a play of Sir Robert Howard's, written long since, and lately put into my hands ; it is called, 'The Conquest of China by the Tartars.' It will cost me six weeks' study, with the probable benefit of a hundred pounds. In the mean time I am writing a song for St. Cecilia's Feast, who, you know, is the patroness of music. This is troublesome, and no way beneficial ; but I could not deny the stewards of the feast, who came in a body to me to desire that kindness, one of them being Mr. Bridgeman, whose parents are your mother's friends. I hope to send you thirty guineas between Michaelmas and Christmas, of which I will give you an account when I come to town. I remember the counsel you give me in your letter ; but dissembling, though lawful in some cases, is not my talent ; yet, for your sake, I will struggle with the plain openness of my nature, and keep in my just resentments against that degenerate order. In the mean time, I flatter not myself with any manner of hopes, but do my duty, and suffer for God's sake ; being assured, before-hand, never to be rewarded, though the times should alter. Towards the latter end of this month, September, Charles will begin to recover his perfect health, according to his nativity, which, casting it myself, I am sure is true, and all things hitherto have happened accordingly to the very time that I predicted them : I hope at the same time to recover more health, according to my age.   Remember me to poor Harry, whose prayers I earnestly desire.   My Virgil succeeds in the world beyond its desert or my expectation.   You know the profits might have been more ; but neither my conscience nor my honor would suffer me to take them; but I never can repent of my constancy, since I am thoroughly persuaded of the justice of the cause for which I suffer.   It has pleased God to raise up many friends to me amongst my enemies, though they who ought to have been my friends are negligent of me.   I am called to dinner, and cannot go on with this letter, which I desire you to excuse ; and am,

"Your most affectionate father,

" JOHN DRYDEN."

DR. SAMUEL JOHNSON ON SWIFT.

An account of Dr. Swift has been already collected, with great diligence and acuteness, by Dr. Hawkesworth, according to a scheme which I laid before him in the intimacy of our friendship. I cannot therefore be expected to say much of a life, concerning which I had long since communicated my thoughts to a man capable of dignifying his narrations with so much elegance of language and force of sentiment.

Jonathan Swift was, according to an account said to be written by himself, the son of Jonathan Swift, an attorney, and was born at Dublin on St. Andrew's Day, 1667. According to his own report, as delivered by Pope to Spence, he was born at Leicester, the son of a clergyman, who was minister of a parish in Herefordshire. During his life the place of his birth was undetermined. He was contented to be called an Irishman by the Irish ; but would occasionally call himself an Englishman. The question may, without much regret, be left in the obscurity in which he delighted to involve it.

Whatever was his birth, his education was Irish. He was sent at the age of six to the school at Kilkenny, and in his fifteenth year (1682) was admitted into the University of Dublin.

In his academical studies he was either not diligent or not happy. It must disappoint every reader's expectation, that, when at the usual time he claimed the bachelorship of arts, he was found by the examiners too conspicuously deficient for regular admission ; and obtained his degree at last by *special favor*—a term used in that university to denote want of merit.

Of this disgrace it may be easily supposed that he was much ashamed, and shame had its proper effect in producing reformation. He resolved from that time to study eight hours a day, and continued his industry for seven years, with what improvement is sufficiently known. This part of his story well deserves to be remembered ; it may afford useful admonition and powerful encouragement to many men whose abilities have been made for a time useless by their passions or pleasures, and who, having lost one part of life in idleness, are tempted to throw away the remainder in despair.

In this course of daily application he continued three years longer at Dublin ; and in this time, if the observation and memory of an old companion may be trusted, he drew the first sketch of his " Tale of a Tub."

When he was about one-and-twenty (1688), being by the death of Godwin Swift, his uncle, who had supported him, left without subsistence, he went to consult his mother, who then lived at Leicester, about the future course of his life, and, by her direction, solicited the advice and patronage of Sir William Temple, who had married one of Mrs. Swift's relations, and whose father, Sir John Temple, master of the rolls in Ireland, had lived in great familiarity of friendship with Godwin Swift, by whom Jonathan had been to that time maintained.

Temple received with sufficient kindness the nephew of his father's friend, with whom he was, when they conversed together, so much pleased, that he detained him two years in his house. Here he became known to King William, who sometimes visited Temple when he was disabled by the gout, and, being attended by Swift in the garden, showed him how to cut asparagus in the Dutch way.

King William's notions were all military ; and he expressed his kindness to Swift by offering to make him a captain of horse.

When Temple removed to Moor Park he took Swift with him ; and when he was consulted by the Earl of Portland about the expedience of complying with a bill then pending for making parliaments triennial, against which King William was strongly prejudiced, after having in vain tried to show the earl that the proposal involved nothing dangerous to royal power, he sent Swift for the same purpose to the king. Swift, who probably was proud of his employment, and went with all the confidence of a young man, found his arguments, and his art of displaying them, made totally ineffectual by the predetermination of the king ; and used to mention this disappointment as his first antidote against vanity.

Before he left Ireland he contracted a disorder, as he thought, by eating too much fruit. The origin of diseases is commonly obscure. Almost every boy eats as much fruit as he can get, without any great inconvenience. The disease of Swift was giddiness with deafness, which attacked him from time to time, began very early, pursued him through life, and at last sent him to the grave deprived of reason.

Being much oppressed at Moor Park by this grievous malady, he was advised to try his native air, and went to Ireland, but, finding no benefit, returned to Sir William, at whose house he continued his studies, and is known to have read, among other books, " Cyprian " and " Irenæus." He thought exercise of great necessity, and used to run half a mile up and down a hill every two hours.

It is easy to imagine that the mode in which his first degree was conferred left him no great fondness for the University of Dublin, and therefore he resolved to become a master of arts at Oxford. In the testimonial which he produced the words of disgrace were omitted ; and he took his master's degree (July 5, 1692) with such reception and regard as fully contented him.

While he lived with Temple he used to pay his mother at Leicester a yearly visit. He travelled on foot, unless some violence of weather drove him into a wagon ; and at night he would go to a penny lodging, where he purchased clean sheets for sixpence. This practice Lord Orrery imputes to his innate love of grossness and vulgarity : some may ascribe it to his desire of surveying human life through all its varieties ; and others, perhaps with equal probability, to a passion which seems to have been deeply fixed in his heart, the love of a shilling.

In time he began to think that his attendance at Moor Park deserved some other recompense than the pleasure, however mingled with improvement, of Temple's conversation, and grew so impatient that (1694) he went away in discontent.

Temple, conscious of having given reason for complaint, is said to have made him deputy master of the rolls in Ireland, which, according to his kinsman's account, was an office which he knew him not able to discharge. Swift therefore resolved to enter into the church, in which he had at first no higher hopes than of the chaplainship to the Factory at Lisbon ; but, being recommended to Lord Capel, he obtained the prebend of Kilroot, in Connor, of about a hundred pounds a year.

But the infirmities of Temple made a companion like Swift so necessary that he invited him back, with a promise to procure him English preferment in exchange for the prebend, which he desired him to resign. With this request Swift quickly complied, having perhaps equally repented their separation, and they lived on together with mutual satisfaction ; and in the four years that passed between his return and Temple's death, it is probable that he wrote the " Tale of a Tub" and the " Battle of the Books."

Swift began early to think, or to hope, that he was a poet, and wrote Pindaric odes to Temple, to the king, and to the Athenian Society, a knot of obscure men who published a periodical pamphlet of answers to questions, sent, or supposed to be sent, by letters. I have been told that Dryden, having perused these verses, said, " Cousin Swift, you will never be a poet ;" and that this denunciation was the motive of Swift's perpetual malevolence to Dryden.

In 1699 Temple died, and left a legacy with his manuscripts to Swift, for whom he had obtained, from King William, a promise of the first prebend that should be vacant at Westminster or Canterbury.

That this promise might not be forgotten, Swift dedicated to the king the posthumous works with which he was intrusted ; but neither the dedication nor tenderness for the man whom he once had treated with confidence and fondness revived in King William the remembrance of his promise. Swift awhile attended the court, but soon found his solicitations hopeless.

He was then invited by the Earl of Berkeley to accompany him into Ireland as a private secretary ; but, after having done the business till their arrival at Dublin, he then found that one Bush had persuaded the earl that a clergyman was not a proper secretary, and had obtained the office for himself. In a man like Swift such circumvention and inconstancy must have excited violent indignation.

But he had yet more to suffer. Lord Berkeley had the disposal of the deanery of Derry, and Swift expected to obtain it ; but, by the secretary's influence, supposed to have been secured by a bribe, it was bestowed on somebody else ; and Swift was dismissed with the livings of Laracor and Rathbeggin, in the diocese of Meath, which together did not equal half the value of the deanery.

At Laracor he increased the parochial duty by reading prayers on Wednesdays and Fridays, and performed all the offices of his profession with great decency and exactness.

Soon after his settlement at Laracor he invited to Ireland the unfortunate Stella, a young woman whose name was Johnson, the daughter of the steward of Sir William Temple, who, in consideration of her father's virtues, left her a thousand pounds. With her came Mrs. Dingley, whose whole fortune was twenty-seven pounds a year for her life. With these ladies he passed his hours of relaxation, and to them he opened his bosom ; but they never resided in the same house, nor did he see either without a witness. They lived at the parsonage when Swift was away, and when he returned removed to a lodging, or to the house of a neighboring clergyman.

Swift was not one of those minds which amaze the world with early pregnancy ; his first work, except his few poetical essays, was the " Dissensions in Athens and Rome," published (1701) in his thirty-fourth year. After its appearance, paying a visit to some bishop, he heard mention made of the new pamphlet that Burnet had written, replete with political knowledge. When he seemed to doubt Burnet's right to the work, he was told by the bishop that he was " a young man ;" and still persisting to doubt, that he was " a very positive young man."

Three years afterwards (1704) was published " The Tale of a Tub :" of this book charity may be persuaded to think that it might be written by a man of a peculiar character without ill intention ; but it is certainly of dangerous example. That Swift was its author, though it be universally believed, was never owned by himself, nor very well proved by any evidence ; but no other claimant can be produced, and he did not deny it when Archbishop Sharpe and the Duchess of Somerset, by showing it to the queen, debarred him from a bishopric.

When this wild work first raised the attention of the public, Sacheverell, meeting Smalridge, tried to flatter him by seeming to think him the author ; but Smalridge answered with indignation, " Not all that you and I have in the world, nor all that ever we shall have, should hire me to write the ' Tale of a Tub.' "

The digressions relating to Wotton and Bentley must be confessed to discover want of knowledge or want of integrity ; he did not understand the two controversies, or he willingly misrepresented them. But wit can stand its ground against truth only a little while. The honors due to learning have been justly distributed by the decision of posterity.

" The Battle of the Books" is so like the " Combat des Livres," which the same question concerning the ancients and moderns had produced in France, that the improbability of such a coincidence of thoughts without communication is not, in my opinion, balanced by the anonymous protestation prefixed, in which all knowledge of the French book is peremptorily disowned.

For some time after, Swift was probably employed in solitary study, gaining the qualifications requisite for future eminence. How often he visited England, and with what diligence he attended his parishes, I know not. It was not till about four years afterwards that he became a professed author ; and then one year (1708) produced " The Sentiments of a Church-of-England Man ;" the ridicule of Astrology under the name of " Bickerstaff ;" the " Argument against abolishing Christianity ;" and the Defence of the " Sacramental Test."

" The Sentiments of a Church-of-England Man" is written with great coolness, moderation, ease, and perspicuity. The " Argument against abolishing Christianity" is a very happy and judicious irony. One passage in it deserves to be selected :

" If Christianity were once abolished, how could the free-thinkers, the strong reasoners, and the men of profound learning be able to find another subject so calculated, in all points, whereon to display their abilities ? What wonderful productions of wit should we be deprived of from those, whose genius, by continual practice, hath been wholly turned upon raillery and invectives against religion, and would therefore never be able to shine, or distinguish themselves, upon any other subject ? We are daily complaining of the great decline of wit among us, and would take away the greatest, perhaps the only, topic we have left. Who would ever have suspected Asgill for a wit, or Toland for a philosopher, if the inexhaustible stock of Christianity had not been at hand to provide them with materials ? What other subject, through all art or nature, could have produced Tindal for a profound author, or furnished him with readers ? It is the wise choice of the subject that alone adorns and distinguishes the writer. For had a hundred such pens as these been employed on the side of religion, they would have immediately sunk into silence and oblivion."

The reasonableness of a Test is not hard to be proved ; but perhaps it must be allowed that the proper test has not been chosen.

The attention paid to the papers published under the name of " Bickerstaff " induced Steele, when he projected " The Tatler," to assume an appellation which had already gained possession of the reader's notice.

In the year following he wrote a " Project for the Advancement of Religion," addressed to Lady Berkeley ; by whose kindness it is not unlikely that he was advanced to his benefices. To this project, which is formed with great purity of intention, and displayed with sprightliness and elegance, it can only be objected, that, like many projects, it is, if not generally impracticable, yet evidently hopeless, as it supposes more zeal, concord, and perseverance than a view of mankind gives reason for expecting.

He wrote likewise this year "A Vindication of Bickerstaff," and an explanation of " An Ancient Prophecy," part written after the facts, and the rest never completed, but well planned to excite amazement.

Soon after began the busy and important part of Swift's life. He was employed (1710) by the Primate of Ireland to solicit the queen for a remission of the first-fruits and twen-tieth parts to the Irish clergy. With this purpose he had recourse to Mr. Harley, to whom he was mentioned as a man neglected and oppressed by the last ministry, because he had refused to co-operate with some of their schemes. What he had refused has never been told ; what he had suffered was, I suppose, the exclusion from a bishopric by the remonstrances of Sharpe, whom he describes as '' the harmless tool of others' hate,'' and whom he represents as afterwards '' suing for pardon.''

Harley's designs and situation were such as made him glad of an auxiliary so well qualified for his service ; he therefore soon admitted him to familiarity, whether ever to confidence some have made a doubt ; but it would have been difficult to excite his zeal without persuading him that he was trusted, and not very easy to delude him by false persuasions.

He was certainly admitted to those meetings in which the first hints and original plan of action are supposed to have been formed ; and was one of the sixteen ministers, or agents of the ministry, who met weekly at each other's houses, and were united by the name of '' Brothers.''

Being not immediately considered as an obdurate Tory, he conversed indiscriminately with all the wits, and was yet the friend of Steele ; who, in '' The Tatler,'' which began in April,'' 1709, confesses the advantage of his conversation, and mentions something contributed by him to his paper. But he was now immerging into political controversy ; for the year 1710 produced '' The Examiner,'' of which Swift wrote thirty-three papers. In argument he may be allowed to have the advantage ; for where a wide system of conduct and the whole of a public character is laid open to inquiry, the accuser, having the choice of facts, must be very unskilful if he does not prevail ; but, with regard to wit, I am afraid none of Swift's papers will be found equal to those by which Addison opposed him.

He wrote in the year 1711 a '' Letter to the October Club,'' a number of Tory gentlemen sent from the country to Parliament, who formed themselves into a club, to the number of about a hundred, and met to animate the zeal and raise the expectations of each other. They thought, with great reason, that the ministers were losing opportunities ; that sufficient use was not made of the ardor of the nation ; they called loudly for more changes and stronger efforts, and demanded the punishment of part and the dismission of the rest of those whom they considered as public robbers.

Their eagerness was not gratified by the queen or by Harley. The queen was probably slow because she was afraid ; and Harley was slow because he was doubtful ; he was a Tory only by necessity or for convenience, and, when he had power in his hands, had no settled purpose for which he should employ it ; forced to gratify to a certain degree the Tories who supported him, but unwilling to make his reconcilement to the Whigs utterly desperate, he corresponded at once with the two expectants of the crown, and kept, as has been observed, the succession undetermined.   Not knowing what to do, he did nothing ; and, with the fate of a double dealer, at last he lost his power, but kept his enemies.

Swift seems to have concurred in opinion with the '' October Club ;'' but it was not in his power to quicken the tardiness of Harley, whom he stimulated as much as he could, but with little effect.   He that knows not whither to go is in no haste to move.   Harley, who was perhaps not quick by nature, became yet more slow by irresolution, and was content to hear that dilatoriness lamented as natural which he applauded in himself as politic.

Without the Tories, however, nothing could be done ; and, as they were not to be gratified, they must be appeased ; and the conduct of the minister, if it could not be vindicated, was to be plausibly excused.

Early in the next year he published a '' Proposal for correcting, improving, and ascertaining the English Tongue,'' in a letter to the Earl of Oxford, written without much knowledge of the general nature of language, and without any accurate inquiry into the history of other tongues.   The certainty and stability which, contrary to all experience, he thinks attainable, he proposes to secure by instituting an academy, the decrees of which every man would have been willing and many would have been proud to disobey, and which, being renewed by successive elections, would in a short time have differed from itself.

Swift now attained the zenith of his political importance, he published (1712) the '' Conduct of the Allies,'' ten days before the Parliament assembled.   The purpose was to persuade the nation to a peace ; and never had any writer more success. The people, who had been amused with bonfires and triumphal processions, and looked with idolatry on the general and his friends, who, as they thought, had made England the arbitress of nations, were confounded between shame and rage when they found that '' mines had been exhausted and millions destroyed'' to secure the Dutch or aggrandize the emperor, without any advantage to ourselves ; that we had been bribing our neighbors to fight their own quarrel ; and that amongst our enemies we might number our allies.

That is now no longer doubted, of which the nation was then first informed, that the war was unnecessarily protracted to fill the pockets of Marlborough ; and that it would have been continued without end if he could have continued his annual plunder. But Swift, I suppose, did not yet know what he has since written, that a commission was drawn, which would have appointed him general for life, had it not become ineffectual by the resolution of Lord Cowper, who refused the seal.

"Whatever is received," say the schools, "is received in proportion to the recipient." The power of a political treatise depends much upon the disposition of the people ; the nation was then combustible, and a spark set it on fire. It is boasted that between November and January, eleven thousand were sold ; a great number at that time, when we were yet not a nation of readers. To its propagation certainly no agency of power or influence was wanting. It furnished arguments for conversation, speeches for debate, and materials for parliamentary resolutions.

Yet, surely, whoever surveys this wonder-working pamphlet with cool perusal, will confess that its efficacy was supplied by the passions of its readers ; that it operates by the mere weight of facts, with very little assistance from the hand that produced them.

This year (1712) he published his "Reflections on the Barrier Treaty," which carries on the design of his "Conduct of the Allies," and shows how little regard in that negotiation had been shown to the interest of England, and how much of the conquered country had been demanded by the Dutch.

This was followed by "Remarks on the Bishop of Sarum's Introduction to his third Volume of the History of the Reformation ;" a pamphlet which Burnet published as an alarm, to warn the nation of the approach of popery. Swift, who seems to have disliked the bishop with something more than political aversion, treats him like one whom he is glad of an opportunity to insult.

Swift, being now the declared favorite and supposed confidant of the Tory ministry, was treated by all that depended on the court with the respect which dependents know how to pay. He soon began to feel part of the misery of greatness : he that could say that he knew him considered himself as having fortune in his power. Commissions, solicitations, remonstrances, crowded about him ; he was expected to do every man's business, to procure employment for one, and to retain it for another. In assisting those who addressed him, he represents himself as sufficiently diligent ; and desires to have others be-

lievc, what he probably believed himself, that by his intcrposi-
tion many Whigs of merit, and among them Addison and Congreve, were continued in their places.   But every man of
known influence has so many petitions which he cannot grant,
that he must necessarily offend more than he gratifies, as the
preference given to one affords all the rest reason for complaint.   '' When I give away a place,'' said Louis XIV.   ''I
make an hundred discontented, and one ungrateful.''

Much has been said of the equality and independence
which he preserved in his conversation with the ministers, of
the frankness of his remonstrances, and the familiarity of his
friendship.   In accounts of this kind a few single incidents are
set against the general tenor of behavior.   No man, however,
can pay a more servile tribute to the great than by suffering
his liberty in their presence to aggrandize him in his own
esteem.   Between different ranks of the community there is
necessarily some distance ; he who is called by his superior to
pass the interval may properly accept the invitation ; but
petulance and obtrusion are rarely produced by magnanimity ;
nor have often any nobler cause than the pride of importance
and the malice of inferiority.   He who knows himself necessary may set, while that necessity lasts, a high value upon himself ; as, in a lower condition, a servant eminently skilful may
be saucy ; but he is saucy only because he is servile.   Swift
appears to have preserved the kindness of the great when they
wanted him no longer ; and therefore it must be allowed that
the childish freedom, to which he seems enough inclined, was
overpowered by his better qualities.

His disinterestedness has been likewise mentioned ; a strain
of heroism, which would have been in his condition romantic
and superfluous.   Ecclesiastical benefices, when they become
vacant, must be given away ; and the friends of power may, if
there be no inherent disqualification, reasonably expect them.
Swift accepted (1713) the deanery of St. Patrick, the best preferment that his friends could venture to give him.   That ministry was in a great degree supported by the clergy, who were
not yet reconciled to the author of the '' Tale of a Tub,'' and
would not without much discontent and indignation have
borne to see him installed in an English cathedral.

He refused, indeed, fifty pounds from Lord Oxford ; but he
accepted afterwards a draft of a thousand upon the Exchequer, which was intercepted by the queen's death, and which
he resigned, as he says himself, '' *multa gemens*, with many a
groan.''

In the midst of his power and his politics he kept a journal of his visits, his walks, his interviews with ministers, and quarrels with his servant, and transmitted it to Mrs. Johnson and Mrs. Dingley, to whom he knew that whatever befell him was interesting, and no accounts could be too minute. Whether these diurnal trifles were properly exposed to eyes which had never received any pleasure from the presence of the dean, may be reasonably doubted : they have, however, some odd attraction ; the reader, finding frequent mention of names which he has been used to consider as important, goes on in hope of information ; and, as there is nothing to fatigue attention, if he is disappointed he can hardly complain. It is easy to perceive, from every page, that though ambition pressed Swift into a life of bustle, the wish for a life of ease was always returning.

He went to take possession of his deanery as soon as he had obtained it ; but he was not suffered to stay in Ireland more than a fortnight before he was recalled to England, that he might reconcile Lord Oxford and Lord Bolingbroke, who began to look on one another with malevolence, which every day increased, and which Bolingbroke appeared to retain in his last years.

Swift contrived an interview, from which they both departed discontented ; he procured a second, which only convinced him that the feud was irreconcilable ; he told them his opinion, that all was lost. This denunciation was contradicted by Oxford ; but Bolingbroke whispered that he was right.

Before this violent dissension had shattered the ministry, Swift had published, in the beginning of the year (1714), " The Public Spirit of the Whigs," in answer to " The Crisis," a pamphlet for which Steele was expelled from the House of Commons. Swift was now so far alienated from Steele as to think him no longer entitled to decency, and therefore treats him sometimes with contempt and sometimes with abhorrence.

In this pamphlet the Scotch were mentioned in terms so provoking to that irritable nation that, resolving " not to be offended with impunity," the Scotch lords, in a body, demanded an audience of the queen, and solicited reparation. A proclamation was issued, in which three hundred pounds were offered for the discovery of the author. From this storm he was, as he relates, " secured by a sleight ;" of what kind, or by whose prudence, is not known ; and such was the increase of his reputation, that the Scottish " nation applied again that he would be their friend."

He was become so formidable to the Whigs, that his familiarity with the ministers was clamored at in Parliament, partic-

ularly by two men, afterwards of great note, Aislabie and Walpole.

But, by the disunion of his great friends, his importance
and designs were now at an end ; and seeing his services at
last useless, he retired about June (1714) into Berkshire, where,
in the house of a friend, he wrote, what was then suppressed,
but has since appeared under the title of " Free Thoughts on
the present State of Affairs."

While he was waiting in this retirement for events which
time or chance might bring to pass, the death of the queen
broke down at once the whole system of Tory politics ; and
nothing remained but to withdraw from the implacability of
triumphant Whiggism, and shelter himself in unenvied obscurity.

The accounts of his reception in Ireland, given by Lord
Orrery and Dr. Delany, are so different that the credit of the
writers, both undoubtedly veracious, cannot be saved, but by
supposing, what I think is true, that they speak of different
times.   When Delany says that he was received with respect,
he means for the first fortnight, when he came to take legal
possession ; and when Lord Orrery tells that he was pelted by
the populace, he is to be understood of the time when, after
the queen's death, he became a settled resident.

The Archbishop of Dublin gave him at first some disturbance in the exercise of his jurisdiction ; but it was soon discovered that, between prudence and integrity, he was seldom in
the wrong ; and that, when he was right, his spirit did not
easily yield to opposition.

Having so lately quitted the tumults of a party and the intrigues of a court, they still kept his thoughts in agitation, as
the sea fluctuates awhile when the storm has ceased. He
therefore filled his hours with some historical attempts relating
to the " Change of the Ministers" and " The Conduct of the
Ministry."   He likewise is said to have written a " History of
the Four last Years of Queen Anne," which he began in her
lifetime, and afterwards labored with great attention, but never
published.   It was after his death in the hands of Lord Orrery
and Dr. King. A book under that title was published, with
Swift's name, by Dr. Lucas ; of which I can only say, that it
seemed by no means to correspond with the notions that I had
formed of it, from a conversation which I once heard between
the Earl of Orrery and old Mr. Lewis.

Swift now, much against his will, commenced Irishman for
life, and was to contrive how he might be best accommodated
in a country where he considered himself as in a state of exile.
It seems that his first recourse was to piety. The thoughts of

death rushed upon him, at this time, with such incessant importunity, that they took possession of his mind, when he first waked, for many years together.

He opened his house by a public table two days a week, and found his entertainments gradually frequented by more and more visitants of learning among the men and of elegance among the women. Mrs. Johnson had left the country, and lived in lodgings not far from the deanery. On his public days she regulated the table, but appeared at it as a mere guest, like other ladies.

On other days he often dined, at a stated price, with Mr. Worral, a clergyman of his cathedral, whose house was recommended by the peculiar neatness and pleasantry of his wife. To this frugal mode of living, he was first disposed by care to pay some debts which he had contracted, and he continued it for the pleasure of accumulating money. His avarice, however, was not suffered to obstruct the claims of his dignity ; he was served in plate, and used to say that he was the poorest gentleman in Ireland that ate upon plate, and the richest that lived without a coach.

How he spent the rest of his time, and how he employed his hours of study, has been inquired with hopeless curiosity. For who can give an account of another's studies ? Swift was not likely to admit any to his privacies, or to impart a minute account of his business or his leisure.

Soon after (1716), in his forty-ninth year, he was privately married to Mrs. Johnson, by Dr. Ashe, Bishop of Clogher, as Dr. Madden told me, in the garden. The marriage made no change in their mode of life ; they lived in different houses, as before ; nor did she ever lodge in the deanery but when Swift was seized with a fit of giddiness. '' It would be difficult,'' says Lord Orrery, '' to prove that they were ever afterwards together without a third person.''

The Dean of St. Patrick's lived in a private manner, known and regarded only by his friends ; till, about the year 1720, he, by a pamphlet, recommended to the Irish the use, and consequently the improvement, of their manufacture. For a man to use the productions of his own labor is surely a natural right, and to like best what he makes himself is a natural passion. But to excite this passion, and enforce this right, appeared so criminal to those who had an interest in the English trade, that the printer was imprisoned ; and, as Hawkesworth justly observes, the attention of the public being by this outrageous resentment turned upon the proposal, the author was by consequence made popular.

In 1723 died Mrs. Van Homrigh, a woman made unhappy by her admiration of wit, and ignominiously distinguished by the name of Vanessa, whose conduct has been already sufficiently discussed, and whose history is too well known to be minutely repeated. She was a young woman fond of literature, whom Decanus, the dean, called Cadenus by transposition of the letters, took pleasure in directing and instructing ; till, from being proud of his praise, she grew fond of his person. Swift was then about forty-seven, at an age when vanity is strongly excited by the amorous attention of a young woman. 'If it be said that Swift should have checked a passion which he never meant to gratify, recourse must be had to that extenuation which he so much despised, " Men are but men ;" perhaps, however, he did not at first know his own mind, and, as he represents himself, was undetermined. For his admission of her courtship, and his indulgence of her hopes after his marriage to Stella, no other honest plea can be found than that he delayed a disagreeable discovery from time to time, dreading the immediate bursts of distress, and watching for a favorable moment. She thought herself neglected, and died of disappointment ; having ordered by her will the poem to be published in which Cadenus had proclaimed her excellence and confessed his love. The effect of the publication upon the dean and Stella is thus related by Delany :

" I have good reason to believe that they both were greatly shocked and distressed (though it may be differently) upon this occasion. The dean made a tour to the south of Ireland, for about two months, at this time, to dissipate his thoughts, and give place to obloquy. And Stella retired (upon the earnest invitation of the owner) to the house of a cheerful, generous, good-natured friend of the dean's, whom she always much loved and honored. There my informer often saw her ; and, I have reason to believe, used his utmost endeavors to relieve, support, and amuse her, in this sad situation.

" One little incident he told me of on that occasion, I think I shall never forget. As her friend was an hospitable, open-hearted man, well-beloved and largely acquainted, it happened one day that some gentlemen dropped into dinner, who were strangers to Stella's situation ; and as the poem of 'Cadenus and Vanessa' was then the general topic of conversation, one of them said, ' Surely that Vanessa must be an extraordinary woman, that could inspire the dean to write so finely upon her.' Mrs. Johnson smiled, and answered, ' That she thought that point not quite so clear ; for it was well known the dean could write finely upon a broomstick.' "

The great acquisition of esteem and influence was made by the "Drapier's Letters" in 1724. One Wood, of Wolverhampton, in Staffordshire, a man enterprising and rapacious, had, as is said, by a present to the Duchess of Munster, obtained a patent empowering him to coin one hundred and eighty thousand pounds of halfpence and farthings for the kingdom of Ireland, in which there was a very inconvenient and embarrassing scarcity of copper coin ; so that it was possible to run in debt upon the credit of a piece of money ; for the cook or keeper of an ale-house could not refuse to supply a man that had silver in his hand, and the buyer would not leave his money without change.

The project was therefore plausible. The scarcity, which was already great, Wood took care to make greater, by agents who gathered up the old halfpence ; and was about to turn his brass into gold, by pouring the treasures of his new mint upon Ireland ; when Swift, finding that the metal was debased to an enormous degree, wrote letters, under the name of M. B. Drapier, to show the folly of receiving, and the mischief that must ensue by giving, gold and silver for coin worth perhaps not a third part of its nominal value.

The nation was alarmed ; the new coin was universally refused ; but the governors of Ireland considered resistance to the king's patent as highly criminal ; and one Whitshed, then Chief Justice, who had tried the printer of the former pamphlet, and sent out the jury nine times, till by clamor and menaces they were frighted into a special verdict, now presented the Drapier, but could not prevail on the grand jury to find the bill.

Lord Carteret and the privy council published a proclamation, offering three hundred pounds for discovering the author of the Fourth Letter. Swift had concealed himself from his printers, and trusted only his butler, who transcribed the paper. The man, immediately after the appearance of the proclamation, strolled from the house, and stayed out all night and part of the next day. There was reason enough to fear that he had betrayed his master for the reward ; but he came home, and the dean ordered him to put off his livery, and leave the house ; "for," said he, "I know that my life is in your power, and I will not bear, out of fear, either your insolence or negligence." The man excused his fault with great submission, and begged that he might be confined in the house while it was in his power to endanger his master ; but the dean resolutely turned him out, without taking farther notice of him, till the term of the information had expired, and then received him again. Soon afterwards he ordered him and the rest of his servants into his presence, without telling his intentions, and bade them take notice that their fellow-servant was no longer Robert the butler ; but that his integrity had made him Mr. Blakeney, verger of St. Patrick's ; an officer whose income was between thirty and forty pounds a year : yet he still continued for some years to serve his old master as his butler.

Swift was known from this time by the appellation of " The Dean." He was honored by the populace as the champion, patron, and instructor of Ireland ; and gained such power as, considered both in its extent and duration, scarcely any man has ever enjoyed without greater wealth or higher station.

He was from this important year the oracle of the traders and the idol of the rabble, and by consequence was feared and courted by all to whom the kindness of the traders or the populace was necessary. The Drapier was a sign ; the Drapier was a health ; and which way soever the eye or the ear was turned, some tokens were found of the nation's gratitude to the Drapier.

The benefit was indeed great ; he had rescued Ireland from a very oppressive and predatory invasion ; and the popularity which he had gained he was diligent to keep, by appearing forward and zealous on every occasion where the public interest was supposed to be involved. Nor did he much scruple to boast his influence ; for when, upon some attempts to regulate the coin, Archbishop Boulter, then one of the justices, accused him of exasperating the people, he exculpated himself by saying, " If I had lifted up my finger, they would have torn you to pieces."

But the pleasure of popularity was soon interrupted by domestic misery. Mrs. Johnson, whose conversation was to him the great softener of the ills of life, began in the year of the Drapier's triumph to decline ; and two years afterwards was so wasted with sickness that her recovery was considered as hopeless.

Swift was then in England, and had been invited by Lord Bolingbroke to pass the winter with him in France, but this call of calamity hastened him to Ireland, where perhaps his presence contributed to restore her to imperfect and tottering health.

He was now so much at ease, that (1727) he returned to England ; where he collected three volumes of Miscellanies in conjunction with Pope, who prefixed a querulous and apologetical Preface.

This important year sent likewise into the world " Gulliver's Travels," a production so new and strange that it filled
the reader with a mingled emotion of merriment and amazement. It was received with such avidity that the price of the
first edition was raised before the second could be made ; it
was read by the high and the low, the learned and illiterate.
Criticism was for a while lost in wonder ; no rules of judgment
were applied to a book written in open defiance of truth and
regularity. But when distinctions came to be made, the part
which gave the least pleasure was that which describes the flying island, and that which gave most disgust must be the history of the Houyhnhnms.

While Swift was enjoying the reputation of his new work,
the news of the king's death arrived ; and he kissed the hands
of the new king and queen three days after their accession.

By the queen, when she was princess, he had been treated
with some distinction, and was well received by her in her
exaltation ; but whether she gave hopes which she never took
care to satisfy, or he formed expectations which she never
meant to raise, the event was, that he always afterwards
thought on her with malevolence, and particularly charged her
with breaking her promise of some medals which she engaged
to send him.

I know not whether she had not, in her turn, some reason
for complaint. A letter was sent her, not so much entreating,
as requiring, her patronage of Mrs. Barber, an ingenious Irish-
woman, who was then begging subscriptions for her poems.
To this letter was subscribed the name of Swift, and it has all
the appearances of his diction and sentiments ; but it was not
written in his hand, and had some little improprieties. When
he was charged with this letter, he laid hold of the inaccuracies, and urged the improbability of the accusation, but never
denied it ; he shuffles between cowardice and veracity, and
talks big when he says nothing.

He seems desirous enough of recommencing courtier, and
endeavored to gain the kindness of Mrs. Howard, remembering what Mrs. Masham had performed in former times ; but
his flatteries were, like those of other wits, unsuccessful ; the
lady either wanted power, or had no ambition of poetical immortality.

He was seized, not long afterwards, by a fit of giddiness, and
again heard of the sickness and danger of Mrs. Johnson. He
then left the house of Pope, as it seems, with very little ceremony, finding " that two sick friends cannot live together ;" and
did not write to him till he found himself at Chester.

He returned to a home of sorrow : poor Stella was sinking into the grave, and, after a languishing decay of about two months, died in her forty-fourth year, on January 28, 1728. How much he wished her life, his papers show ; nor can it be doubted that he dreaded the death of her whom he loved most, aggravated by the consciousness that himself had hastened it.

Beauty and the power of pleasing, the greatest external advantages that woman can desire or possess, were fatal to the unfortunate Stella. The man whom she had the misfortune to love was, as Delany observes, fond of singularity, and desirous to make a mode of happiness for himself, different from the general course of things and order of Providence. From the time of her arrival in Ireland he seems resolved to keep her in his power, and therefore hindered a match sufficiently advantageous, by accumulating unreasonable demands, and prescribing conditions that could not be performed. While she was at her own disposal he did not consider his possession as secure ; resentment, ambition, or caprice might separate them ; he was therefore resolved to make "assurance doubly sure," and to appropriate her by a private marriage, to which he had annexed the expectation of all the pleasures of perfect friendship without the uneasiness of conjugal restraint. But with this state poor Stella was not satisfied ; she never was treated as a wife, and to the world she had the appearance of a mistress. She lived sullenly on, in hope that in time he would own and receive her ; but the time did not come till the change of his manners and deprivation of his mind made her tell him, when he offered to acknowledge her, that "it was too late." She then gave up herself to sorrowful resentment, and died under the tyranny of him by whom she was in the highest degree loved and honored.

What were her claims to this eccentric tenderness, by which the laws of nature were violated to retain her, curiosity will inquire ; but how shall it be gratified ? Swift was a lover ; his testimony may be suspected. Delany and the Irish saw with Swift's eyes, and therefore add little confirmation. That she was virtuous, beautiful, and elegant, in a very high degree, such admiration from such a lover makes it very probable ; but she had not much literature, for she could not spell her own language ; and of her wit, so loudly vaunted, the smart sayings which Swift himself has collected afford no splendid specimen.

The reader of Swift's "Letter to a Lady on her Marriage," may be allowed to doubt whether his opinion of female excellence ought implicitly to be admitted ; for, if his general thoughts on women were such as he exhibits, a very little sense

in a lady would enrapture and a very little virtue would astonish him. Stella's supremacy, therefore, was perhaps only
local·; she was great because her associates were little.

In some Remarks lately published on the Life of
Swift, his marriage is mentioned as fabulous or doubtful ;
but, alas ! poor Stella, as Dr. Madden told me, related her
melancholy story to Dr. Sheridan, when he attended her as a
clergyman to prepare her for death ; and Delany mentions it
not with doubt, but only with regret. Swift never mentioned
her without a sigh. The rest of his life was spent in Ireland,
in a country to which not even power almost despotic, nor flattery almost idolatrous, could reconcile him. He sometimes
wished to visit England, but always found some reason of delay. He tells Pope, in the decline of life, that he hopes once
more to see him ; '' but if not,'' says he, '' we must part, as all
human beings have parted.''

After the death of Stella, his benevolence was contracted
and his severity exasperated ; he drove his acquaintance from
his table, and wondered why he was deserted. But he continued his attention to the public, and wrote, from time to time,
such directions, admonitions, or censures as the exigency of
affairs, in his opinion, made proper ; and nothing fell from his
pen in vain.

In a short poem on the Presbyterians, whom he always
regarded with detestation, he bestowed one stricture upon
Bettesworth, a lawyer eminent for his insolence to the clergy,
which, from very considerable reputation, brought him into
immediate and universal contempt. Bettesworth, enraged at
his disgrace and loss, went to Swift and demanded whether he
was the author of that poem ? '' Mr. Bettesworth,'' answered
he, '' I was in my youth acquainted with great lawyers, who,
knowing my disposition to satire, advised me, that if any scoundrel or blockhead whom I had lampooned should ask, ' Are
you the author of this paper ?' I should tell him that I was not
the author ; and therefore I tell you, Mr. Bettesworth, that I
am not the author of these lines.''

Bettesworth was so little satisfied with this account that he
publicly professed his resolution of a violent and corporal
revenge ; but the inhabitants of St. Patrick's district embodied
themselves in the dean's defence. Bettesworth declared in
Parliament that Swift had deprived him of twelve hundred
pounds a year.

Swift was popular awhile by another mode of beneficence.
He set aside some hundreds to be lent in small sums to the
poor, from five shillings, I think, to five pounds. He took no

interest, and only required that, at repayment, a small fee should be given to the accountant ; but he required that the day of promised payment should be exactly kept. A severe and punctilious temper is ill qualified for transactions with the poor ; the day was often broken, and the loan was not repaid. This might have been easily foreseen ; but for this Swift had made no provision of patience or pity. He ordered his debtors to be sued. A severe creditor has no popular character ; what then was likely to be said of him who employs the catchpoll under the appearance of charity ? The clamor against him was loud, and the resentment of the populace outrageous ; he was therefore forced to drop his scheme, and own the folly of expecting punctuality from the poor.

His asperity continually increasing, condemned him to solitude ; and his resentment of solitude sharpened his asperity. He was not, however, totally deserted ; some men of learninge and some women of elegance often visited him ; and he wrot from time to time either verse or prose : of his verses he will ingly gave copies, and is supposed to have felt no discontent when he saw them printed. His favorite maxim was, " Vive la bagatelle :" he thought trifles a necessary part of life, and perhaps found them necessary to himself. It seems impossible to him to be idle, and his disorders made it difficult or dangerous to be long seriously studious or laboriously diligent. The love of ease is always gaining upon age, and he had one temptation to petty amusements peculiar to himself ; whatever he did he was sure to hear applauded ; and such was his predominance over all that approached, that all their applauses were probably sincere. He that is much flattered soon learns to flatter himself ; we are commonly taught our duty by fear or shame, and how can they act upon the man who hears nothing but his own praises ?

As his years increased, his fits of giddiness and deafness grew more frequent, and his deafness made conversation difficult : they grew likewise more severe, till, in 1736, as he was writing a poem called " The Legion Club," he was seized with a fit so painful and so long continued, that he never after thought it proper to attempt any work of thought or labor.

He was always careful of his money, and was therefore no liberal entertainer ; but was less frugal of his wine than of his meat. When his friends of either sex came to him in expectation of a dinner, his custom was to give every one a shilling, that they might please themselves with their provision. At last his avarice grew too powerful for his kindness ; he would refuse a bottle of wine, and in Ireland no man visits where he cannot drink.

Having thus excluded conversation and desisted from study, he had neither business nor amusement ; for having by some ridiculous resolution or mad vow determined never to wear spectacles, he could make little use of books in his later years ; his ideas, therefore, being neither renovated by discourse nor increased by reading, wore gradually away, and left his mind vacant to the vexations of the hour, till at last his anger was heightened into madness.

He, however, permitted one book to be published, which had been the production of former years, " Polite Conversation," which appeared in 1738. " The Directions for Servants" was printed soon after his death. These two performances show a mind incessantly attentive, and, when it was not employed upon great things, busy with minute occurrences. It is apparent that he must have had the habit of noting whatever he observed ; for such a number of particulars could never have been assembled by the power of recollection.

He grew more violent, and his mental powers declined till (1741) it was found necessary that legal guardians should be appointed of his person and fortune. He now lost distinction. His madness was compounded of rage and fatuity. The last face that he knew was that of Mrs. Whiteway ; and her he ceased to know in a little time. His meat was brought him cut into mouthfuls ; but he would never touch it while the servant stayed, and at last, after it had stood perhaps an hour, would eat it walking ; for he continued his old habit, and was on his feet ten hours a day.

Next year (1742) he had an inflammation in his left eye, which swelled it to the size of an egg, with boils in other parts : he was kept long waking with the pain, and was not easily restrained by five attendants from tearing out his eye.

The tumor at last subsided ; and a short interval of reason ensuing, in which he knew his physician and his family, gave hopes of his recovery ; but in a few days he sunk into a lethargic stupidity, motionless, heedless, and speechless. But it is said that, after a year of total silence, when his housekeeper, on the 30th of November, told him that the usual bonfires and illuminations were preparing to celebrate his birthday, he answered, " It is all folly ; they had better let it alone."

It is remembered that he afterwards spoke now and then, or gave some intimation of a meaning ; but at last sunk into perfect silence, which continued till about the end of October, 1744, when, in his seventy-eighth year, he expired without a struggle.

When Swift is considered as an author, it is just to estimate his powers by their effects. In the reign of Queen Anne he turned the stream of popularity against the Whigs, and must be confessed to have dictated for a time the political opinions of the English nation. In the succeeding reign he delivered Ireland from plunder and oppression ; and showed that wit, confederated with truth, had such force as authority was unable to resist. He said truly of himself, that Ireland "was his debtor." It was from the time when he first began to patronize the Irish that they may date their riches and prosperity. He taught them first to know their own interest, their weight, and their strength, and gave them spirit to assert that equality, with their fellow-subjects, to which they have ever since been making vigorous advances, and to claim those rights which they have at last established. Nor can they be charged with ingratitude to their benefactor ; for they reverenced him as a guardian and obeyed him as a dictator.

In his works he has given very different specimens both of sentiments and expression. His "Tale of a Tub" has little resemblance to his other pieces. It exhibits a vehemence and rapidity of mind, a copiousness of images, and vivacity of diction such as he afterwards never possessed or never exerted. It is of a mode so distinct and peculiar that it must be considered by itself ; what is true of that is not true of any thing else which he has written.

In his other works is found an equable tenor of easy language, which rather trickles than flows. His delight was in simplicity. That he has in his works no metaphor, as has been said, is not true ; but his few metaphors seem to be received rather by necessity than choice. He studied purity ; and though perhaps all his strictures are not exact, yet it is not often that solecisms can be found ; and whoever depends on his authority may generally conclude himself safe. His sentences are never too much dilated or contracted ; and it will not be easy to find any embarrassment in the complication of his clauses, any inconsequence in his connections, or abruptness in his transitions.

His style was well suited to his thoughts, which are never subtilized by nice disquisitions, decorated by sparkling conceits, elevated by ambitious sentences, or variegated by far-sought learning. He pays no court to the passions ; he excites neither surprise nor admiration ; he always understands himself, and his reader always understands him ; the peruser of Swift wants little previous knowledge ; it will be sufficient that he is acquainted with common words and common things ; he is neither required to mount elevations nor to explore profundities ; his passage is always on a level, along solid ground, without asperities, without obstruction.

This easy and safe conveyance of meaning it was Swift's desire to attain, and for having attained he deserves praise. For purposes merely didactic, when something is to be told that was not known before, it is the best mode ; but against that inattention by which known truths are suffered to lie neglected it makes no provision ; it instructs, but does not persuade.

By his political education he was associated with the Whigs ; but he deserted them when they deserted their principles, yet without running into the contrary extreme : he continued throughout his life to retain the disposition which he assigns to the " Church-of-England Man," of thinking commonly with the Whigs of the state and with the Tories of the church.

He was a churchman rationally zealous ; he desired the prosperity and maintained the honor of the clergy ; of the dissenters he did not wish to infringe the toleration, but he opposed their encroachments.

To his duty as dean he was very attentive. He managed the revenues of his church with exact economy ; and it is said by Delany that more money was, under his direction, laid out in repairs than had ever been in the same time since its first erection. Of his choir he was eminently careful, and, though he neither loved nor understood music, took care that all the singers were well qualified, admitting none without the testimony of skilful judges.

In his church he restored the practice of weekly communion, and distributed the sacramental elements in the most solemn and devout manner with his own hand. He came to church every morning, preached commonly in his turn, and attended the evening anthem, that it might not be negligently performed.

He read the service " rather with a strong, nervous voice, than in a graceful manner ; his voice was sharp and high-toned, rather than harmonious."

He entered upon the clerical state with hope to excel in preaching ; but complained that, from the time of his political controversies, " he could only preach pamphlets." This censure of himself, if judgment be made from those sermons which have been printed, was unreasonably severe.

The suspicions of his irreligion proceeded in a great measure from his dread of hypocrisy ; instead of wishing to seem better, he delighted in seeming worse than he was. He went in London to early prayers, lest he should be seen at church : he read prayers to his servants every morning with such dexterous secrecy that Dr. Delany was six months in his house before he knew it. He was not only careful to hide the good which he did, but willingly incurred the suspicion of evil which he did not. He forgot what himself had formerly asserted, that hypocrisy is less mischievous than open impiety. Dr. Delany, with all his zeal for his honor, has justly condemned this part of his character.

The person of Swift had not many recommendations. He had a kind of muddy complexion, which, though he washed himself with oriental scrupulosity, did not look clear. He had a countenance sour and severe, which he seldom softened by any appearance of gayety. He stubbornly resisted any tendency to laughter.

To his domestics he was naturally rough ; and a man of rigorous temper, with that vigilance of minute attention which his works discover, must have been a master that few could bear. That he was disposed to do his servants good on important occasions is no great mitigation ; benefaction can be but rare, and tyrannic peevishness is perpetual. He did not spare the servants of others. Once when he dined alone with the Earl of Orrery, he said of one that waited in the room, " That man has, since we sat to the table, committed fifteen faults." What the faults were, Lord Orrery, from whom I heard the story, had not been attentive enough to discover. My number may perhaps not be exact.

In his economy he practised a peculiar and offensive parsimony, without disguise or apology. The practice of saving being once necessary, became habitual, and grew first ridiculous, and at last detestable. But his avarice, though it might exclude pleasure, was never suffered to encroach upon his virtue. He was frugal by inclination, but liberal by principle ; and if the purpose to which he destined his little accumulations be remembered, with his distribution of occasional charity, it will perhaps appear that he only liked one mode of expense better than another, and saved merely that he might have something to give. He did not grow rich by injuring his successors, but left both Laracor and the deanery more valuable than he found them. With all this talk of his covetousness and generosity, it should be remembered that he was never rich. The revenue of his deanery was not much more than seven hundred a year.

His beneficence was not graced with tenderness or civility ; he relieved without pity and assisted without kindness ; so that those who were fed by him could hardly love him.

He made a rule to himself to give but one piece at a time, and therefore always stored his pocket with coins of different value.

Whatever he did, he seemed willing to do in a manner peculiar to himself, without sufficiently considering that singularity, as it implies a contempt of the general practice, is a kind of defiance which justly provokes the hostility of ridicule ; he, therefore, who indulges peculiar habits is worse than others, if he be not better.

Of his humor, a story told by Pope may afford a specimen.

"Dr. Swift has an odd blunt way that is mistaken by strangers for ill-nature. 'Tis so odd that there's no describing it but by facts. I'll tell you one that first comes into my head. One evening Gay and I went to see him : you know how intimately we were all acquainted. On our coming in, 'Heyday, gentlemen (says the doctor), what's the meaning of this visit ? How came you to leave the great lords that you are so fond of, to come hither to see a poor dean ?'—'Because we would rather see you than any of them.'—'Ay, any one that did not know so well as I do might believe you. But since you are come, I must get some supper for you, I suppose.'—'No, doctor, we have supped already.'—'Supped already ! that's impossible ! why 'tis not eight o'clock yet.—That's very strange ; but if you had not supped, I must have got something for you. Let me see, what should I have had ? A couple of lobsters ; ay, that would have done very well ; two shillings—tarts, a shilling ; but you will drink a glass of wine with me, though you supped so much before your usual time only to spare my pocket ?'—'No, we had rather talk with you than drink with you.'—'But if you had supped with me, as in all reason you ought to have done, you must then have drank with me. A bottle of wine, two shillings—two and two is four, and one is five ; just two and sixpence apiece. There, Pope, there's half-a-crown for you, and there's another for you, sir ; for I won't save any thing by you I am determined.' —This was all said and done with his usual seriousness on such occasions : and in spite of every thing we could say to the contrary, he actually obliged us to take the money."

In the intercourse of familiar life he indulged his disposition to petulance and sarcasm, and thought himself injured if the licentiousness of his raillery, the freedom of his censures, or the petulance of his frolics was resented or repressed.

He predominated over his companions with very high

ascendancy, and probably would bear none over whom he could not predominate. To give him advice was, in the style of his friend Delany, ' to venture to speak to him." This customary superiority soon grew too delicate for truth ; and Swift, with all his penetration, allowed himself to be delighted with low flattery.

On all common occasions he habitually affects a style of arrogance, and dictates rather than persuades. This authoritative and magisterial language he expected to be received as his peculiar mode of jocularity ; but he apparently flattered his own arrogance by an assumed imperiousness, in which he was ironical only to the resentful, and to the submissive sufficiently serious.

He told stories with great felicity, and delighted in doing what he knew himself to do well ; he was therefore captivated by the respectful silence of a steady listener, and told the same tales too often.

He did not, however, claim the right of talking alone, for it was his rule, when he had spoken a minute, to give room by a pause for any other speaker. Of time, on all occasions, he was an exact computer, and knew the minutes required to every common operation.

It may be justly supposed that there was in his conversation what appears so frequently in his letters, an affectation of familiarity with the great, and ambition of momentary equality sought and enjoyed by the neglect of those ceremonies which custom has established as the barriers between one order of society and another. This transgression of regularity was by himself and his admirers termed greatness of soul. But a great mind disdains to hold any thing by courtesy, and therefore never usurps what a lawful claimant may take away. He that encroaches on another's dignity puts himself in his power ; he is either repelled with helpless indignity or endured by clemency and condescension.

Of Swift's general habits of thinking, if his letters can be supposed to afford any evidence, he was not a man to be either loved or envied. He seems to have wasted life in discontent, by the rage of neglected pride and the languishment of unsatisfied desire. He is querulous and fastidious, arrogant and malignant ; he scarcely speaks of himself but with indignant lamentations, or of others but with insolent superiority when he is gay, and with angry contempt when he is gloomy. From the letters that passed between him and Pope it might be inferred that they, with Arbuthnot and Gay, had engrossed all the understanding and virtue of mankind ; that their merits filled the world, or that there was no hope of more. They show the age involved in darkness, and shade the picture with sullen emulation.

When the queen's death drove him into Ireland, he might be allowed to regret for a time the interception of his views, the extinction of his hopes, and his ejection from gay scenes, important employment, and splendid friendships ; but when time had enabled reason to prevail over vexation, the complaints which at first were natural became ridiculous because they were useless. But querulousness was now grown habitual, and he cried out when he probably had ceased to feel. His reiterated wailings persuaded Bolingbroke that he was really willing to quit his deanery for an English parish ; and Bolingbroke procured an exchange, which was rejected ; and Swift still retained the pleasure of complaining.

The greatest difficulty that occurs in analyzing his character is to discover by what depravity of intellect he took delight in evolving ideas from which almost every other mind shrinks with disgust. The ideas of pleasure, even when criminal, may solicit the imagination ; but what has disease, deformity, and filth, upon which the thoughts can be allured to dwell ? Delany is willing to think that Swift's mind was not much tainted with this gross corruption before his long visit to Pope. He does not consider how he degrades his hero by making him at fifty-nine the pupil of turpitude, and liable to the malignant influence of an ascendant mind. But the truth is that Gulliver had described his Yahoos before the visit ; and he that had formed those images had nothing filthy to learn.

I have here given the character of Swift as he exhibits himself to my perception ; but now let another be heard who knew him better. Dr. Delany, after long acquaintance, describes him to Lord Orrery in these terms :

" My Lord, when you consider Swift's singular, peculiar, and most variegated vein of wit, always intended rightly, although not always so rightly directed ; delightful in many instances, and salutary even where it is most offensive ; when you consider his strict truth, his fortitude in resisting oppression and arbitrary power ; his fidelity in friendship ; his sincere love and zeal for religion ; his uprightness in making right resolutions, and his steadiness in adhering to them ; his care of his church, its choir, its economy, and its income ; his attention to all those that preached in his cathedral, in order to their amendment in pronunciation and style ; as also his remarkable attention to the interest of his successors, preferably to his own present emoluments ; his invincible patriotism, even to a country which he did not love ; his very various, well-devised, well-judged, and extensive charities, throughout his life ; and his whole fortune (to say nothing of his wife's), conveyed to the same Christian purposes at his death ; charities, from which he could enjoy no honor, advantage, or satisfaction of any kind in this world : when you consider his ironical and humorous as well as his serious schemes for the promotion of true religion and virtue ; his success in soliciting for the first-fruits and twentieths, to the unspeakable benefit of the established church of Ireland : and his felicity (to rate it no higher) in giving occasion to the building of fifty new churches in London—

" All this considered, the character of his life will appear like that of his writings : they will both bear to be reconsidered and re-examined with the utmost attention, and always discover new beauties and excellences upon every examination.

" They will bear to be considered as the sun in which the brightness will hide the blemishes ; and whenever petulant ignorance, pride, malice, malignity, or envy interposes to cloud or sully his fame, I take upon me to pronounce that the eclipse will not last long.

" To conclude—No man ever deserved better of any country than Swift did of his ; a steady, persevering, inflexible friend ; a wise, a watchful, and a faithful counsellor, under many severe trials and bitter persecutions, to the manifest hazard both of his liberty and fortune.

" He lived a blessing, he died a benefactor, and his name will ever live an honor, to Ireland."

In the poetical works of Dr. Swift there is not much upon which the critic can exercise his powers. They are often humorous, almost always light, and have the qualities which recommend such compositions, easiness and gayety. They are, for the most part, what their author intended. The diction is correct, the numbers are smooth, and the rhymes exact. There seldom occurs a hard-labored expression or a redundant epithet ; all his verses exemplify his own definition of a good style, they consist of " proper words in proper places."

To divide this collection into classes, and show how some pieces are gross and some are trifling, would be to tell the reader what he knows already, and to find faults of which the author could not be ignorant, who certainly wrote often not to his judgment, but his humor.

It was said, in a preface to one of the Irish editions, that Swift had never been known to take a single thought from any writer, ancient or modern. This is not literally true ; but perhaps no writer can easily be found that has borrowed so little, or that in all his excellences and all his defects has so well maintained his claim to be considered as original.

DR. SAMUEL JOHNSON ON ADDISON.

JOSEPH ADDISON was born on the 1st of May, 1672, at Milston, of which his father, Lancelot Addison, was then rector, near Ambrosebury in Wiltshire, and appearing weak and unlikely to live, he was christened the same day. After the usual domestic education, which from the character of his father may be reasonably supposed to have given him strong impressions of piety, he was committed to the care of Mr. Naish, at Ambrosebury, and afterwards of Mr. Taylor, at Salisbury.

Not to name the school or the masters of men illustrious for literature is a kind of historical fraud, by which honest fame is injuriously diminished ; I would therefore trace him through the whole process of his education. In 1683, in the beginning of his twelfth year, his father being made Dean of Lichfield, naturally carried his family to his new residence, and, I believe, placed him for some time, probably not long, under Mr. Shaw, then master of the school at Lichfield, father of the late Dr. Peter Shaw. Of this interval his biographers have given no account, and I know it only from a story of a *barring-out*, told me when I was a boy, by Andrew Corbet, of Shropshire, who had heard it from Mr. Pigot, his uncle.

The practice of barring-out was a savage license practised in many schools at the end of the last century, by which the boys, when the periodical vacation drew near, growing petulant at the approach of liberty, some days before the time of regular recess took possession of the school, of which they barred the doors, and bade their master defiance from the windows. It is not easy to suppose that on such occasions the master would do more than laugh ; yet if tradition may be credited, he often struggled hard to force or surprise the garrison. The master, when Pigot was a school-boy, was barred-out at Lichfield ; and the whole operation, as he said, was planned and conducted by Addison.

To judge better of the probability of this story, I have inquired when he was sent to the Chartreux ; but, as he was not one of those who enjoyed the founder's benefaction, there is no account preserved of his admission. At the school of the Chartreux, to which he was removed either from that of Salisbury or Lichfield, he pursued his juvenile studies under the care of Dr. Ellis, and contracted that intimacy with Sir Rich-

ard Steele which their joint labors have so effectually recorded.

Of this memorable friendship the greater praise must be
given to Steele. It is not hard to love those from whom nothing can be feared ; and Addison never considered Steele as a
rival, but Steele lived, as he confesses, under an habitual subjection to the predominating genius of Addison, whom he always mentioned with reverence and treated with obsequiousness.

Addison, who knew his own dignity, could not always forbear to show it, by playing a little upon his admirer ; but he
was in no danger of retort : his jests were endured without
resistance or resentment.

But the sneer of jocularity was not the worst. Steele,
whose imprudence of generosity, or vanity of profusion, kept
him always incurably necessitous, upon some pressing exi-
gence, in an evil hour, borrowed a hundred pounds of his
friend, probably without much purpose of repayment ; but
Addison, who seems to have had other notions of a hundred
pounds, grew impatient of delay and reclaimed his loan by an
execution. Steele felt with great sensibility the obduracy of his
creditor, but with emotions of sorrow rather than of anger.

In 1687 he was entered into Queen's College, in Oxford,
where, in 1689, the accidental perusal of some Latin verses
gained him the patronage of Dr. Lancaster, afterwards provost
of Queen's College, by whose recommendation he was elected
into Magdalen College as a Demy, a term by which that society
denominates those which are elsewhere called Scholars—young
men who partake of the founder's benefaction, and succeed in
their order to vacant fellowships.

Here he continued to cultivate poetry and criticism, and
grew first eminent by his Latin compositions, which are indeed
entitled to particular praise. He has not confined himself to
the imitation of any ancient author, but has formed his style
from the general language, such as a diligent perusal of the
productions of different ages happened to supply.

His Latin compositions seem to have had much of his fondness, for he collected a second volume of the " Musæ Anglicanæ," perhaps for a convenient receptacle, in which all his
Latin pieces are inserted, and where his poem on the Peace
has the first place. He afterwards presented the collection to
Boileau, who, from that time, " conceived," says Tickell, " an
opinion of the English genius for poetry." Nothing is better
known of Boileau than that he had an injudicious and peevish
contempt of modern Latin and therefore his profession of

regard was probably the effect of his civility rather than approbation.

Three of his Latin poems are upon subjects on which perhaps he would not have ventured to have written in his own
language, "The Battle of the Pigmies and Cranes," "The
Barometer," and "A Bowling-green." When the matter is
low or scanty, a dead language, in which nothing is mean because nothing is familiar, affords great conveniences, and, by
the sonorous magnificence of Roman syllables, the writer conceals penury of thought and want of novelty often from the
reader, and often from himself.

In his twenty-second year he first showed his power of English poetry by some verses addressed to Dryden ; and soon
afterwards published a translation of the greater part of the
Fourth Georgic, upon Bees ; after which, says Dryden, "my
latter swarm is hardly worth the hiving."

About the same time he composed the arguments prefixed
to the several books of Dryden's Virgil ; and produced an
essay on the "Georgics," juvenile, superficial, and uninstruc-
tive, without much either of the scholar's learning or the
critic's penetration.

His next paper of verses contained a character of the
principal English poets, inscribed to Henry Sacheverell, who
was then, if not a poet, a writer of verses, as is shown by his
version of a small part of Virgil's "Georgics," published in
the Miscellanies ; and a Latin encomium on Queen Mary, in
the "Musæ Anglicanæ." These verses exhibit all the fondness of friendship ; but on one side or the other friendship
was afterwards too weak for the malignity of faction.

In this poem is a very confident and discriminative character
of Spenser, whose work he had then never read. So little
sometimes is criticism the effect of judgment. It is necessary
to inform the reader that about this time he was introduced by
Congreve to Montague, then Chancellor of the Exchequer :
Addison was then learning the trade of a courtier, and subjoined Montague as a poetical name to those of Cowley and of
Dryden.

By the influence of Mr. Montague, concurring, according
to Tickell, with his natural modesty, he was diverted from his
original design of entering into holy orders. Montague
alleged the corruption of men who engaged in civil employments without liberal education ; and declared that, though
he was represented as an enemy to the church, he would never
do it any injury but by withholding Addison from it.

Soon after (in 1695) he wrote a poem to King William,

with a rhyming introduction addressed to Lord Somers.   King
William had no regard to elegance or literature ; his study was
only war ; yet by a choice of ministers, whose disposition was
very different from his own, he procured, without intention, a
very liberal patronage to poetry.   Addison was caressed both
by Somers and Montague.

In 1697 appeared his Latin verses on the peace of
Ryswick, which he dedicated to Montague, and which was
afterwards called by Smith '' the best Latin poem since the
'Æneid.' ''   Praise must not be too rigorously examined ; but
the performance cannot be denied to be vigorous and elegant.

Having yet no public employment, he obtained (in 1699) a
pension of three hundred pounds a year, that he might be enabled to travel.   He stayed a year at Blois, probably to learn
the French language ; and then proceeded in his journey to
Italy, which he surveyed with the eyes of a poet.

While he was travelling at leisure, he was far from being
idle ; for he not only collected his observations on the country,
but found time to write his Dialogues on Medals, and four
acts of '' Cato.''   Such at least is the relation of Tickell.
Perhaps he only collected his materials and formed his plan.

Whatever were his other employments in Italy, he there
wrote the letter to Lord Halifax which is justly considered as
the most elegant, if not the most sublime, of his poetical productions.   But in about two years he found it necessary to hasten home ; being, as Swift informs us, distressed by indigence,
and compelled to become the tutor of a travelling squire, because
his pension was not remitted.

At his return he published his Travels, with a dedication to
Lord Somers.   As his stay in foreign countries was short, his
observations are such as might be supplied by a hasty view,
and consist chiefly in comparisons of the present face of the
country with the descriptions left us by the Roman poets, from
whom he made preparatory collections, though he might have
spared the trouble, had he known that such collections had
been made twice before by Italian authors.

The most amusing passage of his book is his account of the
minute republic of San Marino ; of many parts it is not a very
severe censure to say that they might have been written at
home.   His elegance of language, and variegation of prose and
verse, however, gains upon the reader ; and the book, though
awhile neglected, became in time so much the favorite of the
public that before it was reprinted it rose to five times its
price.

When he returned to England (in 1702) with a meanness of

appearance which gave testimony of the difficulties to which he had been reduced, he found his old patrons out of power, and was therefore, for a time, at full leisure for the cultivation of his mind : and a mind so cultivated gives reason to believe that little time was lost.

But he remained not long neglected or useless. The victory at Blenheim (1704) spread triumph and confidence over the nation ; and Lord Godolphin lamenting to Lord Halifax that it had not been celebrated in a manner equal to the subject, desired him to propose it to some better poet. Halifax told him that there was no encouragement for genius ; that worthless men were unprofitably enriched with public money, without any care to find or employ those whose appearance might do honor to their country. To this Godolphin replied that such abuses should in time be rectified ; and that if a man could be found capable of the task then proposed he should not want an ample recompense. Halifax then named Addison, but required that the treasurer should apply to him in his own person. Godolphin sent the message by Mr. Boyle, afterwards Lord Carleton ; and Addison, having undertaken the work, communicated it to the treasurer, while it was yet advanced no further than the simile of the angel, and was immediately rewarded by succeeding Mr. Locke in the place of commissioner of appeals.

In the following year he was at Hanover with Lord Halifax ; and the year after he was made under secretary of state, first to Sir Charles Hedges, and in a few months more to the Earl of Sunderland.

About this time the prevalent taste for Italian operas inclined him to try what would be the effect of a musical drama in our own language. He therefore wrote the opera of " Rosamond," which, when exhibited on the stage, was either hissed or neglected ; but, trusting that the readers would do him more justice, he published it, with an inscription to the Duchess of Marlborough ; a woman without skill, or pretensions to skill, in poetry or literature. His dedication was therefore an instance of servile absurdity, to be exceeded only by Joshua Barnes's dedication of a Greek Anacreon to the duke.

His reputation had been somewhat advanced by " The Tender Husband," a comedy which Steele dedicated to him, with a confession that he owed to him several of the most successful scenes. To this play Addison supplied a prologue.

When the Marquis of Wharton was appointed lord lieutenant of Ireland, Addison attended him as his secretary, and was made keeper of the records in Birmingham's Tower, with a salary of three hundred pounds a year. The office was little more than nominal, and the salary was augmented for his accommodation.

Interest and faction allow little to the operation of particular dispositions or private opinions. Two men of personal characters more opposite than those of Wharton and Addison could not easily be brought together. Wharton was impious, profligate, and shameless, without regard, or appearance of regard, to right and wrong : whatever is contrary to this may be said of Addison ; but as agents of a party they were connected, and how they adjusted their other sentiments we cannot know.

Addison must, however, not be too hastily condemned. It is not necessary to refuse benefits from a bad man, when the acceptance implies no approbation of his crimes ; nor has the subordinate officer any obligation to examine the opinions or conduct of those under whom he acts, except that he may not be made the instrument of wickedness. It is reasonable to suppose that Addison counteracted, as far as he was able, the malignant and blasting influence of the lieutenant ; and that at least by his intervention some good was done and some mischief prevented.

When he was in office he made a law to himself, as Swift has recorded, never to remit his regular fees in civility to his friends ; "for," said he, "I may have a hundred friends ; and if my fee be two guineas, I shall, by relinquishing my right, lose two hundred guineas, and no friend gain more than two : there is therefore no proportion between the good imparted and the evil suffered."

He was in Ireland when Steele, without any communication of his design, began the publication of the "Tatler," but he was not long concealed ; by inserting a remark on Virgil which Addison had given him, he discovered himself. It is indeed not easy for any man to write upon literature or common life, so as not to make himself known to those with whom he familiarly converses, and who are acquainted with his track of study, his favorite topic, his peculiar notions, and his habitual phrases.

If Steele desired to write in secret, he was not lucky ; a single month detected him. His first "Tatler" was published April 22 (1709), and Addison's contribution appeared May 26. Tickell observes that the "Tatler" began and was concluded without his concurrence. This is doubtless literally true ; but the work did not suffer much by his unconsciousness of its commencement or his absence at its cessation ; for he continued his assistance to December 23, and the paper stopped

on January 2. He did not distinguish his pieces by any signa-
ture ; and I know not whether his name was not kept secret till
the papers were collected into volumes.

To the " Tatler," in about two months, succeeded the
" Spectator ;" a series of essays of the same kind, but written
with less levity, upon a more regular plan, and published daily.
Such an undertaking showed the writers not to distrust their
own copiousness of materials or facility of composition, and
their performance justified their confidence. They found,
however, in their progress, many auxiliaries. To attempt a
single paper was no terrifying labor ; many pieces were offered,
and many were received.

Addison had enough of the zeal of party, but Steele had at
that time almost nothing else. The " Spectator," in one of
the first papers, showed the political tenets of its authors ; but
a resolution was soon taken of courting general approbation
by general topics and subjects on which faction had produced
no diversity of sentiments, such as literature, morality, and
familiar life. To this practice they adhered with few devia-
tions. The ardor of Steele once broke out in praise of Marlborough ; and when Dr. Fleetwood prefixed to some sermons
a preface overflowing with Whiggish opinions, that it might be
read by the queen, it was reprinted in the " Spectator."

To teach the minuter decencies and inferior duties, to regulate the practice of daily conversation, to correct those de-
pravities which are rather ridiculous than criminal, and remove
those grievances which, if they produce no lasting calamities,
impress hourly vexation, was first attempted by Casa in his
book of Manners, and Castiglione in his " Courtier ;" two
books yet celebrated in Italy for purity and elegance, and
which, if they are now less read, are neglected only because
they have effected that reformation which their authors intended, and their precepts now are no longer wanted. Their
usefulness to the age in which they were written is sufficiently
attested by the translations which almost all the nations of
Europe were in haste to obtain.

This species of instruction was continued, and perhaps advanced, by the French ; among whom La Bruyère's " Manners
of the Age," though, as Boileau remarked, it is written without connection, certainly deserves praise for liveliness of description and justness of observation.

Before the " Tatler" and " Spectator," if the writers for
the theatre are excepted, England had no masters of common
life. No writers had yet undertaken to reform either the
savageness of neglect or the impertinence of civility ; to show

when to speak or to be silent ; how to refuse or how to comply. We had many books to teach us our more important
duties, and to settle opinions in philosophy or politics ; but an
Arbiter Elegantiarum, a judge of propriety, was yet wanting,
who should survey the track of daily conversation, and free it
from thorns and prickles, which tease the passer, though they
do not wound him.

For this purpose nothing is so proper as the frequent publication of short papers, which we read not as study but amusement. If the subject be slight, the treatise is short. The busy
may find time, and the idle may find patience.

This mode of conveying cheap and easy knowledge began
among us in the civil war, when it was much the interest of
either party to raise and fix the prejudices of the people. At
that time appeared " Mercurius Aulicus," " Mercurius Rus-
ticus," and " Mercurius Civicus." It is said that when any
title grew popular it was stolen by the antagonist, who by this
stratagem conveyed his notions to those who would not have
received him had he not worn the appearance of a friend.
The tumult of those unhappy days left scarcely any man
leisure to treasure up occasional compositions ; and so much
were they neglected that a complete collection is nowhere to
be found.

These Mercuries were succeeded by L'Estrange's " Obser-
vator," and that by Lesley's " Rehearsal," and perhaps by
others ; but hitherto nothing had been conveyed to the people
in this commodious manner but controversy relating to the
church or state, of which they taught many to talk whom
they could not teach to judge.

It has been suggested that the Royal Society was instituted
soon after the Restoration to divert the attention of the people
from public discontent. The " Tatler" and " Spectator" had
the same tendency ; they were published at a time when two
parties, loud, restless, and violent, each with plausible declarations, and each perhaps without any distinct termination of its
views, were agitating the nation : to minds heated with political contest they supplied cooler and more inoffensive reflections ; and it is said by Addison, in a subsequent work, that
they had a perceptible influence upon the conversation of that
time, and taught the frolicsome and the gay to unite merriment
with decency ; an effect which they can never wholly lose,
while they continue to be among the first books by which both
sexes are initiated in the elegances of knowledge.

The " Tatler" and " Spectator" adjusted, like Casa, the
unsettled practice of daily intercourse by propriety and polite-

ness ; and, like La Bruyere, exhibited the *Characters and Manners of the Age.* The personages introduced in these papers were not merely ideal ; they were then known, and conspicuous in various stations. Of the " Tatler" this is told by Steele in his last paper ; and of the " Spectator" by Budgell in the preface to " Theophrastus," a book which Addison has recommended, and which he was suspected to have revised, if he did not write it. Of those portraits, which may be supposed to be sometimes embellished and sometimes aggravated, the originals are now partly known and partly forgotten.

But to say that they united the plans of two or three eminent writers, is to give them but a small part of their due praise ; they superadded literature and criticism, and sometimes towered far above their predecessors, and taught, with great justness of argument and dignity of language, the most important duties and sublime truths.

All these topics were happily varied with elegant fictions and refined allegories, and illuminated with different changes of style and felicities of invention.

It is recorded by Budgell, that of the characters feigned or exhibited in the " Spectator," the favorite of Addison was Sir Roger de Coverley, of whom he had formed a very delicate and discriminate idea, which he would not suffer to be violated ; and, therefore, when Steele had shown him innocently picking up a girl in the Temple, and taking her to a tavern, he drew upon himself so much of his friend's indignation that he was forced to appease him by a promise of forbearing Sir Roger for the time to come.

The reason which induced Cervantes to bring his hero to the grave, *para mi sola nacio'Don Quixote, y yo para él*, made Addison declare, with undue vehemence of expression, that he would kill Sir Roger, being of opinion that they were born for one another, and that any other hand would do him wrong.

It may be doubted whether Addison ever filled up his original delineation. He describes his knight as having his imagination somewhat warped ; but of this perversion he has made very little use. The irregularities in Sir Roger's conduct seem not so much the effects of a mind deviating from the beaten track of life by the perpetual pressure of some overwhelming idea, as of habitual rusticity, and that negligence which solitary grandeur naturally generates.

The variable weather of the mind, the flying vapors of incipient madness, which from time to time cloud reason, with-

out eclipsing it, it requires so much nicety to exhibit, that Addison seems to have been deterred from prosecuting his own
design.

To Sir Roger, who, as a country gentleman, appears to be
a Tory, or, as it is gently expressed, an adherent to the landed
interest, is opposed Sir Andrew Freeport, a new man, a wealthy
merchant, zealous for the moneyed interest, and a Whig.
Of this contrariety of opinions it is probable more conse--
quences were at first intended than could be produced when
the resolution was taken to exclude party from the paper.   Sir
Andrew does but little, and that little seems not to have
pleased Addison, who, when he dismissed him from the club,
changed his opinions.   Steele had made him, in the true spirit
of unfeeling commerce, declare that he "would not build a
hospital for idle people ;" but at last he buys land, settles in
the country, and builds, not a manufactory, but a hospital for
twelve old husbandmen ; for men with whom a merchant has
little acquaintance, and whom he commonly considers with little kindness.

Of essays, thus elegant, thus instructive, and thus commo-
diously distributed, it is natural to suppose the approbation
general, and the sale numerous.   I once heard it observed
that the sale may be calculated by the product of the tax, related in the last number to produce more than twenty pounds
a week, and therefore stated at one and twenty pounds, or three
pounds ten shillings a day : this, at a halfpenny a paper, will
give sixteen hundred and eighty for the daily number.

This sale is not great ; yet this, if Swift be credited, was
likely to grow less ; for he declares that the "Spectator,"
whom he ridicules for his endless mention of the fair sex, had
before his recess wearied his readers.

The next year (1713), in which "Cato" came upon the
stage, was the grand climacteric of Addison's reputation.
Upon the death of Cato, he had, as is said, planned a tragedy
in the time of his travels, and had for several years the first
four acts finished, which were shown to such as were likely to
spread their admiration.   They were seen by Pope, and by
Cibber, who relates that Steele, when he took back the copy,
told him, in the despicable cant of literary modesty, that, whatever spirit his friend had shown in the composition, he doubted
whether he would have courage sufficient to expose it to the
censure of a British audience.

The time, however, was now come when those who
affected to think liberty in danger affected likewise to think
that a stage play might preserve it ; and Addison was impor-

tuned, in the name of the tutelary deities of Britain, to show his courage and his zeal by finishing his design.

To resume his work he seemed perversely and unaccountably unwilling ; and by a request, which perhaps he wished to be denied, desired Mr. Hughes to add a fifth act. Hughes supposed him serious ; and, undertaking the supplement, brought in a few days some scenes for his examination ; but he had in the mean time gone to work himself and produced half an act, which he afterwards completed, but with brevity irregularly disproportionate to the foregoing parts, like a task performed with reluctance and hurried to its conclusion.

It may yet be doubted whether "Cato" was made public by any change of the author's purpose ; for Dennis charged him with raising prejudices in his own favor by false positions of preparatory criticism, and with poisoning the town by contradicting in the "Spectator" the established rule of poetical justice, because his own hero, with all his virtues, was to fall before a tyrant. The fact is certain ; the motives we must guess.

Addison was, I believe, sufficiently disposed to bar all avenues against all danger. When Pope brought him the prologue, which is properly accommodated to the play, there were these words : "Britons, arise ! be worth like this approved ;" meaning nothing more than, Britons, erect and exalt yourselves to the approbation of public virtue. Addison was frighted lest he should be thought a promoter of insurrection, and the line was liquidated to "Britons, attend."

Now "heavily in clouds came on the day, the great, the important day," when Addison was to stand the hazard of the theatre. That there might, however, be left as little hazard as was possible, on the first night, Steele, as himself relates, undertook to pack an audience. This, says Pope, had been tried for the first time in favor of the "Distrest Mother ;" and was now, with more efficacy, practised for "Cato."

The danger was soon over. The whole nation was at that time on fire with faction. The Whigs applauded every line in which liberty was mentioned, as a satire on the Tories ; and the Tories echoed every clap, to show that the satire was unfelt. The story of Bolingbroke is well known. He called Booth to his box, and gave him fifty guineas for defending the cause of liberty so well against a perpetual dictator. The Whigs, says Pope, design a second present, when they can accompany it with as good a sentence.

The play, supported thus by the emulation of factious praise, was acted night after night for a longer time than, I believe, the public had allowed to any drama before ; and the author, as Mrs. Porter long afterwards related, wandered through the whole exhibition behind the scenes with restless and unappeasable solicitude.

When it was printed, notice was given that the Queen would be pleased if it was dedicated to her ; " but, as he had designed that compliment elsewhere, he found himself obliged," says Tickell, " by his duty on the one hand, and his honor on the other, to send it into the world without any dedication."

Human happiness has always its abatements ; the brightest sunshine of success is not without a cloud. No sooner was " Cato" offered to the reader than it was attacked by the acute malignity of Dennis, with all the violence of angry criticism. Dennis, though equally zealous, and probably by his temper more furious, than Addison, for what they called liberty, and though a flatterer of the Whig ministry, could not sit quiet at a successful play ; but was eager to tell friends and enemies that they had misplaced their admirations. The world was too stubborn for instruction ; with the fate of the censurer ot Corneille's Cid, his animadversions showed his anger without effect, and " Cato" continued to be praised.

Pope had now an opportunity of courting the friendship of Addison, by vilifying his old enemy, and could give resentment its full play, without appearing to revenge himself. He therefore published " A Narrative of the Madness of John Dennis ;" a performance which left the objections to the play in their full force, and therefore discovered more desire of vexing the critic than of defending the poet.

Addison, who was no stranger to the world, probably saw the selfishness of Pope's friendship ; and, resolving that he should have the consequences of his officiousness to himself, informed Dennis by Steele that he was sorry for the insult ; and that whenever he should think fit to answer his remarks he would do it in a manner to which nothing could be objected.

The greatest weakness of the play is in the scenes of love, which are said by Pope to have been added to the original plan upon a subsequent review, in compliance with the populai practice of the stage. Such an authority it is hard to reject ; yet the love is so intimately mingled with the whole action that it cannot easily be thought extrinsic and adventitious ; for, if it were taken away, what would be left ? or how were the four acts filled in the first draught ?

At the publication the wits seemed proud to pay their attendance with encomiastic verses. The best are from an unknown hand, which will perhaps lose somewhat of their praise when the author is known to be Jeffreys.

"Cato" had yet other honors. It was censured as a party-play by a scholar of Oxford, and defended in a favorable examination by Dr. Sewel. It was translated by Salvini into Italian, and acted at Florence ; and by the Jesuits of St. Omer's into Latin, and played by their pupils. Of this version a copy was sent to Mr. Addison : it is to be wished that it could be found, for the sake of comparing their version of the soliloquy with that of Bland.

A tragedy was written on the same subject by Des Champs, a French poet, which was translated with a criticism on the English play. But the translator and the critic are now forgotten.

Dennis lived on unanswered, and therefore little read. Addison knew the policy of literature too well to make his enemy important by drawing the attention of the public upon a criticism which, though sometimes intemperate, was often irrefragable.

While "Cato" was upon the stage, another daily paper, called the "Guardian," was published by Steele. To this Addison gave great assistance, whether occasionally or by previous engagement is not known.

The character of the "Guardian" was too narrow and too serious : it might properly enough admit both the duties and decencies of life, but seemed not to include literary speculations, and was in some degree violated by merriment and burlesque. What had the guardian of the lizards to do with clubs of tall or of little men, with nests of ants or with Strada's prolusions ?

Of this paper nothing is necessary to be said, but that it found many contributors, and that it was a continuation of the "Spectator" with the same elegance and the same variety, till some unlucky sparkle from a Tory paper set Steele's politics on fire, and wit at once blazed into faction. He was soon too hot for neutral topics, and quitted the "Guardian" to write the "Englishman."

The papers of Addison are marked in the "Spectator" by one of the letters in the name of Clio, and in the "Guardian" by a hand ; whether it was, as Tickell pretends to think, that he was unwilling to usurp the praise of others, or, as Steele, with far greater likelihood, insinuates, that he could not without discontent impart to others any of his own. I have heard that his avidity did not satisfy itself with the air of renown, but that with great eagerness he laid hold on his proportion of the profits.

Many of these papers were written with powers truly comic, with nice discrimination of characters, and accurate observation of natural or accidental deviation from propriety ; but it was not supposed that he had tried a comedy on the stage till Steele after his death declared him the author of the " Drummer." This, however, Steele did not know to be true by any direct testimony ; for, when Addison put the play into his hands, he only told him it was the work of a " Gentleman in the company ;" and, when it was received, as is confessed, with cold disapprobation, he was probably less willing to claim it. Tickell omitted it in his collection ; but the testimony of Steele, and the total silence of any other claimant, has determined the public to assign it to Addison, and it is now printed with his other poetry. Steele carried the " Drummer" to the play-house, and afterwards to the press, and sold the copy for fifty guineas.

To the opinion of Steele may be added the proof supplied by the play itself, of which the characters are such as Addison would have delineated, and the tendency such as Addison would have promoted. That it should have been ill received would raise wonder, did we not daily see the capricious distribution of theatrical praise.

He was not all this time an indifferent spectator of public affairs. He wrote, as different exigencies required (in 1707), " The present State of the War, and the Necessity of an Augmentation ;" which, however judicious, being written on temporary topics, and exhibiting no peculiar powers, laid hold on no attention, and has naturally sunk by its own weight into neglect. This cannot be said of the few papers entitled " The Whig Examiner," in which is employed all the force of gay malevolence and humorous satire. Of this paper, which just appeared and expired, Swift remarks, with exultation, that " it is now down among the dead men." He might well rejoice at the death of that which he could not have killed. Every reader of every party, since personal malice is past and the papers which once inflamed the nation are read only as effusions of wit, must wish for more of the Whig Examiners ; for on no occasion was the genius of Addison more vigorously exerted, and on none did the superiority of his powers more evidently appear. His " Trial of Count Tariff," written to expose the treaty of commerce with France, lived no longer than the question that produced it.

Not long afterwards an attempt was made to revive the " Spectator," at a time indeed by no means favorable to literature, when the succession of a new family to the throne filled the nation with anxiety, discord, and confusion ; and either the turbulence of the times or the satiety of the readers put a stop to the publication, after an experiment of eighty numbers, which were afterwards collected into an eighth volume, per- haps more valuable than any of those that went before it. Ad- dison produced more than a fourth part, and the other contrib- utors are by no means unworthy of appearing as his associ- ates. The time that had passed during the suspension of the " Spectator," though it had not lessened his power of humor, seems to have increased his disposition to seriousness : the proportion of his religious to his comic papers is greater than in the former series.

The " Spectator," from its re-commencement, was pub- lished only three times a week ; and no discriminative marks were added to the papers. To Addison, Tickell has ascribed twenty-three.

The " Spectator" had many contributors ; and Steele, whose negligence kept him always in a hurry, when it was his turn to furnish a paper, called loudly for the letters, of which Addison, whose materials were more, made little use ; having recourse to sketches and hints, the product of his former studies, which he now reviewed and completed : among these are named by Tickell the Essays on Wit, those on the Pleas- ures of the Imagination, and the Criticism on Milton.

When the House of Hanover took possession of the throne, it was reasonable to expect that the zeal of Addison would be suitably rewarded. Before the arrival of King George, he was made secretary to the regency, and was required by his office to send notice to Hanover that the queen was dead, and that the throne was vacant. To do this would not have been diffi- cult to any man but Addison, who was so overwhelmed with the greatness of the event, and so distracted by choice of ex- pression, that the lords, who could not wait for the niceties of criticism, called Mr. Southwell, a clerk in the House, and ordered him to despatch the message. Southwell readily told what was necessary in the common style of business, and valued himself upon having done what was too hard for Ad- dison.

He was better qualified for the " Freeholder," a paper which he published twice a week, from December 23, 1715, to the middle of the next year. This was undertaken in defence of the established government, sometimes with argument and sometimes with mirth. In argument he had many equals ; but his humor was singular and matchless. Bigotry itself must be delighted with the Tory fox-hunter.

There are, however, some strokes less elegant and less decent ; such as the Pretender's Journal, in which one topic of ridicule is his poverty.   This mode of abuse had been employed by Milton against King Charles II.

> " —— Jacobœi
> Centum, exulantis viscera marsupii regis."

And Oldmixon delights to tell of some alderman of London, that he had more money than the exiled princes ; but that which might be expected from Milton's savageness or Oldmixon's meanness was not suitable to the delicacy of Addison.

Steele thought the humor of the " Freeholder" too nice and gentle for such noisy times ; and is reported to have said that the ministry made use of a lute when they should have called for a trumpet.

This year (1716)[1] he married the Countess Dowager of Warwick, whom he had solicited by a very long and anxious courtship, perhaps with behavior not very unlike that of Sir Roger to his disdainful widow ; and who, I am afraid, diverted herself often by playing with his passion.   He is said to have first known her by becoming tutor to her son.   " He formed," said Tonson, " the design of getting that lady from the time when he was first recommended into the family."   In what part of his life he obtained the recommendation, or how long, and in what manner, he lived in the family, I know not.   His advances at first were certainly timorous, but grew bolder as his reputation and influence increased ; till at last the lady was persuaded to marry him, on terms much like those on which a Turkish princess is espoused, to whom the Sultan is reported to pronounce, " Daughter, I give thee this man for thy slave."   The marriage, if uncontradicted report can be credited, made no addition to his happiness ; it neither found them nor made them equal.   She always remembered her own rank, and thought herself entitled to treat with very little ceremony the tutor of her son.   Rowe's ballad of the " Despairing Shepherd " is said to have been written, either before or after marriage, upon this memorable pair ; and it is certain that Addison has left behind him no encouragement for ambitious love.

The year after (1717) he rose to his highest elevation, being made secretary of state.   For this employment he might justly be supposed qualified by long practice of business, and by his regular ascent through other offices ; but expectation is often disappointed ; it is universally confessed that he was unequal to the duties of his place.   In the House of Commons he could not speak, and therefore was useless to the defence of

[1] August 2.

the government. In the office, says Pope, he could not issue an order without osing his time in quest of fine expressions. What he gained in rank he lost in credit ; and, finding by experience his own inability, was forced to solicit his dismission, with a pension of fifteen hundred pounds a year. His friends palliated this relinquishment, of which both friends and enemies knew the true reason, with an account of declining health and the necessity of recess and quiet.

He now returned to his vocation, and began to plan literary occupations for his future life. He purposed a tragedy on the death of Socrates ; a story of which, as Tickell remarks, the basis is narrow, and to which I know not how love could have been appended. There would, however, have been no want either of virtue in the sentiments or elegance in the language.

He engaged in a nobler work, a defence of the Christian religion, of which part was published after his death ; and he designed to have made a new poetical version of the '' Psalms.''

These pious compositions Pope imputed to a selfish motive, upon the credit, as he owns, of Tonson ; who, having quarrelled with Addison, and not loving him, said, that when he laid down the secretary's office, he intended to take orders and obtain a bishopric ; '' for,'' said he, '' I always thought him a priest in his heart.''

That Pope should have thought this conjecture of Tonson worth remembrance, is a proof, but indeed, so far as I have found, the only proof, that he retained some malignity from their ancient rivalry. Tonson pretended but to guess it ; no other mortal ever suspected it ; and Pope might have reflected that a man who had been secretary of state in the ministry of Sunderland knew a nearer way to a bishopric than by defending religion or translating the '' Psalms.''

It is related that he had once a design to make an English Dictionary, and that he considered Dr. Tillotson as the writer of highest authority. There was formerly sent to me by Mr. Locker, clerk of the Leathersellers' Company, who was eminent for curiosity and literature, a collection of examples collected from Tillotson's works, as Locker said, by Addison. It came too late to be of use, so I inspected it but slightly, and remember it indistinctly. I thought the passages too short.

Addison, however, did not conclude his life in peaceful studies ; but relapsed, when he was near his end, to a political dispute.

It so happened that (1718–19) a controversy was agitated

with great vehemence between those friends of long continuance, Addison and Steele   It may be asked, in the language of
Homer, what power or what cause should set them at variance.
The subject of their dispute was of great importance.   The
Earl of Sunderland proposed an act called "The Peerage
Bill ;" by which the number of peers should be fixed, and the
king restrained from any new creation of nobility, unless when
an old family should be extinct.   To this the lords would naturally agree ; and the king, who was yet little acquainted with
his own prerogative, and, as is now well known, almost indifferent to the possessions of the crown, had been persuaded to
consent.   The only difficulty was found among the Commons,
who were not likely to approve the perpetual exclusion of
themselves and their posterity.   The bill therefore was eagerly
opposed, and among others by Sir Robert Walpole, whose
speech was published.

The lords might think their dignity diminished by improper
advancements, and particularly by the introduction of twelve
new peers at once, to produce a majority of Tories in the last
reign ; an act of authority violent enough, yet certainly legal,
and by no means to be compared with that contempt of
national right with which, some time afterwards, by the instiga-
tion of Whiggism, the Commons, chosen by the people for three
years, chose themselves for seven.   But, whatever might be the
disposition of the Lords, the people had no wish to increase
their power.   The tendency of the bill, as Steele observed in a
letter to the Earl of Oxford, was to introduce an aristocracy ;
for a majority in the House of Lords, so limited, would have
been despotic and irresistible.

To prevent this subversion of the ancient establishment,
Steele, whose pen readily seconded his political passions,
endeavored to alarm the nation by a pamphlet called " The
Plebeian."   To this an answer was published by Addison,
under the title of " The Old Whig," in which it is not discovered that Steele was then known to be the advocate for the
Commons.   Steele replied by a second " Plebeian ;" and,
whether by ignorance or by courtesy, confined himself to his
question, without any personal notice of his opponent.   Nothing hitherto was committed against the laws of friendship or
proprieties of decency ; but controvertists cannot long retain
their kindness for each other.   The " Old Whig" answered
the " Plebeian," and could not forbear some contempt of " little Dicky, whose trade it was to write pamphlets." [1] Dicky,
however, did not lose his settled veneration for his friend ; but
contented himself with quoting some lines of " Cato," which

[1] See note on page 430.

were at once detection and reproof. The bill was laid aside during that session ; and Addison died before the next, in which its commitment was rejected by two hundred and sixty-five to one hundred and seventy-seven.

Every reader surely must regret that these two illustrious friends, after so many years passed in confidence and endearment, in unity of interest, conformity of opinion, and fellowship of study, should finally part in acrimonious opposition. Such a controversy was *Bellum plus quam civile*, as Lucan expresses it. Why could not faction find other advocates ? but among the uncertainties of the human state, we are doomed to number the instability of friendship.

Of this dispute I have little knowledge but from the " Biographia Britannica." The " Old Whig " is not inserted in Addison's works, nor is it mentioned by Tickell in his life ; why it was omitted, the biographers doubtless give the true reason ; the fact was too recent, and those who had been heated in the contention were not yet cool.

The necessity of complying with times and of sparing persons is the great impediment of biography. History may be formed from permanent monuments and records ; but lives can only be written from personal knowledge, which is growing every day less, and in a short time is lost forever. What is known can seldom be immediately told ; and when it might be told, it is no longer known. The delicate features of the mind, the nice discriminations of character, and the minute peculiarities of conduct, are soon obliterated ; and it is surely better that caprice, obstinacy, frolic, and folly, however they might delight in the description, should be silently forgotten than that, by wanton merriment and unseasonable detection, a pang should be given to a widow, a daughter, a brother, or a friend. As the process of these narratives is now bringing me among my contemporaries, I begin to feel myself " walking upon ashes under which the fire is not extinguished," and coming to the time of which it will be proper rather to say " nothing that is false, than all that is true."

The end of this useful life was now approaching. Addison had for some time been oppressed by shortness of breath, which was now aggravated by a dropsy ; and, finding his danger pressing, he prepared to die conformably to his own precepts and professions.

During this lingering decay, he sent, as Pope relates, a message by the Earl of Warwick to Mr. Gay, desiring to see him . Gay, who had not visited him for some time before, obeyed the summons, and found himself received with great kindness. The purpose for which the interview had been solicited was then discovered. Addison told him that he had injured him ; but that, if he recovered, he would recompense him. What the injury was he did not explain ; nor did Gay ever know, but supposed that some preferment designed for him had, by Addison's intervention, been withheld.

Lord Warwick was a young man of very irregular life, and perhaps of loose opinions. Addison, for whom he did not want respect, had very diligently endeavored to reclaim him ; but his arguments and expostulations had no effect. One experiment, however, remained to be tried : when he found his life near its end, he directed the young lord to be called ; and when he desired, with great tenderness, to hear his last injunctions, told him, "I have sent for you, that you may see how a Christian can die." What effect this awful scene had on the earl, I know not : he likewise died himself in a short time.

In Tickell's excellent "Elegy" on his friend are these lines :

> "He taught us how to live ; and, oh ! too high
> The price of knowledge ! taught us how to die,"

in which he alludes, as he told Dr. Young, to this moving interview.

Having given directions to Mr. Tickell for the publication of his works, and dedicated them on his death-bed to his friend Mr. Craggs, he died June 17, 1719, at Holland House, leaving no child but a daughter.

Of his virtue it is a sufficient testimony that the resentment of party has transmitted no charge of any crime. He was not one of those who are praised only after death ; for his merit was so generally acknowledged that Swift, having observed that his election passed without a contest, adds, that, if he proposed himself for king, he would hardly have been refused.

His zeal for his party did not extinguish his kindness for the merit of his opponents ; when he was secretary in Ireland, he refused to intermit his acquaintance with Swift.

Of his habits, or external manners, nothing is so often mentioned as that timorous or sullen taciturnity which his friends called modesty by too mild a name. Steele mentions with great tenderness "that remarkable bashfulness, which is a cloak that hides and muffles merit ;" and tells us, "that his abilities were covered only by modesty, which doubles the beauties which are seen, and gives credit and esteem to all that are concealed." Chesterfield affirms that "Addison was the most timorous and awkward man that he ever saw." And Addison, speaking of his own deficience in conversation, used to say of himself, that, with respect to intellectual "wealth, he could draw bills for a thousand pounds, though he had not a guinea in his pocket."

That he wanted current coin for ready payment, and by that want was often obstructed and distressed ; that he was often oppressed by an improper and ungraceful timidity, every testimony concurs to prove ; but Chesterfield's representation is doubtless hyperbolical. That man cannot be supposed very inexpert in the arts of conversation and practice of life, who, without fortune or alliance, by his usefulness and dexterity, became secretary of state ; and who died at forty-seven, after having not only stood long in the highest rank of wit and literature, but filled one of the most important offices of state.

The time in which he lived had reason to lament his obstinacy of silence ; "for he was," says Steele, "above all men in that talent called humor, and enjoyed it in such perfection that I have often reflected, after a night spent with him apart from all the world, that I had had the pleasure of conversing with an intimate acquaintance of Terence and Catullus, who had all their wit and nature, heightened with humor more exquisite and delightful than any other man ever possessed." This is the fondness of a friend ; let us hear what is told us by a rival. "Addison's conversation," says Pope, "had something in it more charming than I have found in any other man. But this was only when familiar ; before strangers, or, perhaps, a single stranger, he preserved his dignity by a stiff silence."

This modesty was by no means inconsistent with a very high opinion of his own merit. He demanded to be the first name in modern wit ;·and, with Steele to echo him, used to depreciate Dryden, whom Pope and Congreve defended against them. There is no reason to doubt that he suffered too much pain from the prevalence of Pope's poetical reputation ; nor is it without strong reason suspected that, by some disingenuous acts, he endeavored to obstruct it : Pope was not the only man whom he insidiously injured, though the only man of whom he could be afraid.

His own powers were such as might have satisfied him with conscious excellence. Of very extensive learning he has indeed given no proofs. He seems to have had small acquaintance with the sciences, and to have read little except Latin and French ; but of the Latin poets his Dialogues on Medals show that he had perused the works with great diligence and skill. The abundance of his own mind left him little in need of adventitious sentiments ; his wit always could suggest what the occasion demanded. He had read with critical eyes the important volume of human life, and knew the heart of man from the depths of stratagem to the surface of affectation.

What he knew he could easily communicate. " This," says Steele, " was particular in this writer, that, when he had taken his resolution, or made his plan for what he designed to write, he would walk about a room, and dictate it into language with as much freedom and ease as any one could write it down, and attend to the coherence and grammar of what he dictated."

Pope, who can be less suspected of favoring his memory, declares that he wrote very fluently, but was slow and scrupulous in correcting ; that many of his " Spectators" were written very fast, and sent immediately to the press ; and that it seemed to be for his advantage not to have time for much revisal.

" He would alter," says Pope, " any thing to please his friends, before publication ; but would not retouch his pieces afterwards ; and I believe not one word in ' Cato ' to which I made an objection was suffered to stand."

The last line of " Cato" is Pope's, having been originally written,

> " And oh ! 'twas this that ended Cato's life."

Pope might have made more objections to the six concluding lines. In the first couplet the words " from hence" are improper ; and the second line is taken from Dryden's Virgil. Of the next couplet, the first verse, being included in the second, is therefore useless ; and in the third *discord* is made to produce *strife*.

Of the course of Addison's familiar day, before his marriage, Pope has given a detail. He had in the house with him Budgell, and perhaps Philips. His chief companions were Steele, Budgell, Philips, Carey, Davenant, and Colonel Brett. With one or other of these he always breakfasted. He studied all the morning, then dined at a tavern, and went afterwards to Button's.

Button had been a servant in the Countess of Warwick's family, who, under the patronage of Addison, kept a coffee-house on the south side of Russel Street, about two doors from Covent Garden. Here it was that the wits of that time used to assemble. It is said, when Addison had suffered any vexation from the countess, he withdrew the company from Button's house.

From the coffee-house he went again to a tavern, where he often sat late, and drank too much wine. In the bottle discontent seeks for comfort, cowardice for courage, and bashful-ness for confidence.   It is not unlikely that Addison was first seduced to excess by the manumission which he obtained from the servile timidity of his sober hours.   He that feels oppres-sion from the presence of those to whom he knows himself superior will desire to set loose his powers of conversation ; and who that ever asked succors from Bacchus was able to pre-serve himself from being enslaved by his auxiliary ?

Among those friends it was that Addison displayed the elegance of his colloquial accomplishments, which may easily be supposed such as Pope represents them.   The remark of Mandeville, who, when he had passed an evening in his com-pany, declared that he was a parson in a tie-wig, can detract little from his character ; he was always reserved to strangers, and was not incited to uncommon freedom by a character like that of Mandeville.

From any minute knowledge of his familiar manners, the intervention of sixty years has now debarred us.   Steele once promised Congreve and the public a complete description of his character ; but the promises of authors are like the vows of lovers.   Steele thought no more on his design, or thought on it with anxiety that at last disgusted him, and left his friend in the hands of Tickell.

One slight lineament of his character Swift has preserved. It was his practice, when he found any man invincibly wrong, to flatter his opinions by acquiescence, and sink him yet deeper in absurdity.   This artifice of mischief was admired by Stella ; and Swift seems to approve her admiration.

His works will supply some information.   It appears, from his various pictures of the world, that, with all his bashfulness, he had conversed with many distinct classes of men, had sur-veyed their ways with very diligent observation, and marked with great acuteness the effects of different modes of life. He was a man in whose presence nothing reprehensible was out of danger ; quick in discerning whatever was wrong or ridiculous, and not unwilling to expose it.   '' There are,'' says Steele, '' in his writings many oblique strokes upon some of the wittiest men of the age.''   His delight was more to excite mer-riment than detestation ; and he detects follies rather than crimes.

If any judgment be made, from his books, of his moral char-acter, nothing will be found but purity and excellence.   Knowl-edge of mankind, indeed, less extensive than that of Addison will show that to write and to live are very different.   Many who praise virtue do no more than praise it.   Yet it is reasonable to believe that Addison's professions and practice were at no great variance, since, amidst that storm of faction in which most of his life was passed, though his station made him conspicuous and his activity made him formidable, the character given him by his friends was never contradicted by his enemies : of those with whom interest or opinion united him he had not only the esteem, but the kindness ; and of others, whom the violence of opposition drove against him, though he might lose the love, he retained the reverence.

It is justly observed by Tickell that he employed wit on the side of virtue and religion. He not only made the proper use of wit himself, but taught it to others ; and from his time it has been generally subservient to the cause of reason and of truth. He has dissipated the prejudice that had long connected gayety with vice and easiness of manners with laxity of principles. He has restored virtue to its dignity, and taught innocence not to be ashamed. This is an elevation of literary character " above all Greek, above all Roman fame." No greater felicity can genius attain than that of having purified intellectual pleasure, separated mirth from indecency, and wit from licentiousness ; of having taught a succession of writers to bring elegance and gayety to the aid of goodness ; and, if I may use expressions yet more awful, of having " turned many to righteousness."

Addison, in his life, and for some time afterwards, was considered by the greater part of his readers as supremely excelling both in poetry and criticism. Part of his reputation may be properly ascribed to the advancement of his fortune ; when, as Swift observes, he became a statesman, and saw poets waiting at his levee, it was no wonder that praise was accumulated upon him. Much likewise may be more honorably ascribed to his personal character : he who, if he had claimed it, might have obtained the diadem, was not likely to be denied the laurel.

But time quickly puts an end to artificial and accidental fame ; and Addison is to pass through futurity protected only by his genius. Every name which kindness or interest once raised too high is in danger, lest the next age should, by the vengeance of criticism, sink it in the same proportion. A great writer has lately styled him " an indifferent poet and a worse critic."

His poetry is first to be considered ; of which it must be confessed that it has not often those felicities of diction which give lustre to sentiments, or that vigor of sentiment that animates diction ; there is little of ardor, vehemence, or transport ; there is very rarely the awfulness of grandeur, and not very often the splendor of elegance. He thinks justly, but he thinks faintly. This is his general character ; to which, doubtless, many single passages will furnish exceptions.

Yet, if he seldom reaches supreme excellence, he rarely sinks into dulness, and is still more rarely entangled in absurdity. He did not trust his powers enough to be negligent. There is in most of his compositions a calmness and equabil-| ity deliberate and cautious, sometimes with little that delights, but seldom with any thing that offends.

Of this kind seem to be his poems to Dryden, to Somers, and to the King. His "Ode on St. Cecilia" has been imitated by Pope, and has something in it of Dryden's vigor. Of his account of the English poets, he used to speak as a "poor thing ;" but it is not worse than his usual strain. He has said, not very judiciously, in his character of Waller,

> "Thy verse could show ev'n Cromwell's innocence ;
> And compliment the storms that bore him hence.
> Oh ! had thy Muse not come an age too soon,
> But seen great Nassau on the British throne,
> How had his triumph glitter'd in thy page !"

What is this but to say, that he who could compliment Cromwell had been the proper poet for King William ? Addison, however, never printed the piece.

The letter from Italy has been always praised, but has never been praised beyond its merit. It is more correct, with less appearance of labor, and more elegant, with less ambition of ornament, than any other of his poems. There is, however, one broken metaphor, of which notice may properly be taken :

> " Fir'd with that name,
> I bridle in my struggling Muse with pain,
> That longs to launch into a nobler strain."

To *bridle a goddess* is no very delicate idea ; but why must she be *bridled ?* because she *longs to launch ;* an act which was never hindered by a *bridle :* and whither will she *launch ?* into a *nobler strain.* She is in the first line a *horse*, in the second a *boat ;* and the care of the poet 'is to keep his *horse* or his *boat* from *singing*.

The next composition is the far-famed "Campaign," which Dr. Warton has termed a "Gazette in Rhyme," with harshness not often used by the good-nature of his criticism. Before a censure so severe is admitted, let us consider that war is a frequent subject of poetry, and then inquire who has described it with more justness and force. Many of our own writers tried their powers upon this year of victory ; ye. Addison's is confessedly the best performance ; his poem is the work of a man not blinded by the dust of learning ; his images are not borrowed merely from books. The superiority which he confers upon his hero is not personal prowess and "mighty bone," but deliberate intrepidity, a calm command of his passions, and the power of consulting his own mind in the midst of danger. The rejection and contempt of fiction is rational and manly.

It may be observed that the last line is imitated by Pope :

> " Marlb'rough's exploits appear divinely bright—
> Rais'd of themselves their genuine charms they boast,
> And those that paint them truest, praise them most."

This Pope had in his thoughts ; but, not knowing how to use what was not his own, he spoiled the thought when he had borrowed it :

> " The well-sung woes shall soothe my pensive ghost ;
> He best can paint them who shall feel them most."

Martial exploits may be *painted ;* perhaps *woes* may be *painted ;* but they are surely not *painted* by being *well-sung :* it is not easy to paint in song or to sing in colors.

No passage in the "Campaign" has been more often mentioned than the simile of the angel, which is said in the "Tatler" to be "one of the noblest thoughts that ever entered into the heart of man," and therefore worthy of attentive consideration. Let it be first inquired whether it be a simile. A poetical simile is the discovery of likeness between two actions, in their general nature dissimilar, or of causes terminating by different operations in some resemblance of effect. But the mention of another like consequence from a like cause, or of a like performance by a like agency, is not a simile, but an exemplification. It is not a simile to say that the Thames waters fields as the Po waters fields ; or that as Hecla vomits flames in Iceland, so Ætna vomits flames in Sicily. When Horace says of Pindar, that he pours his violence and rapidity of verse as a river swoln with rain rushes from the mountain ; or of himself, that his genius wanders in quest of poetical decorations, as the bee wanders to collect honey ; he, in either case, produces a simile ; the mind is impressed with the resemblance of things generally unlike, as unlike as intellect and body. But if Pindar had been described as writing with the copiousness and grandeur of Homer, or Horace had told that he reviewed and finished his own poetry with the same care as Isocrates polished his orations, instead of similitude, he would have exhibited almost identity ; he would have given the same portraits with different names. In the poem now examined, when the English are represented as gaining a fortified pass, by repetition of attack and perseverance of resolution, their obstinacy of courage and vigor of onset is well illustrated by the sea that breaks, with incessant battery, the dikes of Holland. This is a simile ; but when Addison, having celebrated the beauty of Marlborough's person, tells us that " Achilles thus was formed with every grace," here is no simile, but a mere exemplification. A simile may be compared to lines converging at a point, and is more excellent as the lines approach from greater distance ; an exemplification may be considered as two parallel lines which run on together without approximation, never far separated, and never joined.

Marlborough is so like the angel in the poem, that the action of both is almost the same, and performed by both in the same manner. Marlborough "teaches the battle to rage ;" the angel " directs the storm :" Marlborough is " unmoved in peaceful thought ;" the angel is " calm and serene :" Marlborough stands " unmoved amidst the shock of hosts ;" the angel rides " calm in the whirlwind." The lines on Marlborough are just and noble ; but the simile gives almost the same images a second time.

But perhaps this thought, though hardly a simile, was remote from vulgar conceptions, and required great labor of research or dexterity of application. Of this Dr. Madden, a name which Ireland ought to honor, once gave me his opinion. " If I had set," said he, " ten school-boys to write on the battle of Blenheim, and eight had brought me the angel, I should not have been surprised."

The opera of " Rosamond," though it is seldom mentioned, is one of the first of Addison's compositions. The subject is well chosen, the fiction is pleasing, and the praise of Marlborough, for which the scene gives an opportunity, is, what perhaps every human excellence must be, the product of good-luck, improved by genius. The thoughts are sometimes tender ; the versification is easy and gay. There is doubtless some advantage in the lines, which there is little temptation to load with expletive epithets. The dialogue seems commonly better than the songs. The two comic characters of Sir Trusty and Grideline, though of no great value, are yet such as the poet intended. Sir Trusty's account of the death of Rosamond is, I think, too grossly absurd. The whole drama is airy

and elegant ; engaging in its process, and pleasing in its conclusion.   If Addison had cultivated the lighter parts of poetry,
he would probably have excelled.

The tragedy of " Cato," which, contrary to the rule observed in selecting the works of other poets, has by the weight
of its character forced its way into the late collection, is unquestionably the noblest production of Addison's genius.   Of
a work so much read it is difficult to say any thing new.
About things on which the public thinks long, it commonly
attains to think right, and of " Cato" it has been not unjustly
determined that it is rather a poem in dialogue than a drama,
rather a succession of just sentiments in elegant language than
a representation of natural affections, or of any state probable
or possible in human life.   Nothing here " excites or assuages
emotion ;" here is " no magical power of raising fantastic terror or wild anxiety."   The events are expected without solicitude, and are remembered without joy or sorrow.   Of the
agents we have no care ; we consider not what they are doing
or what they are suffering ; we wish only to know what they
have to say.   Cato is a being above our solicitude ; a man of
whom the gods take care, and whom we leave to their care
with heedless confidence.   To the rest neither gods nor men
can have much attention ; for there is not one amongst them
that strongly attracts either affection or esteem.   But they are
made the vehicles of such sentiments and such expression, that
there is scarcely a scene in the play which the reader does not
wish to impress upon his memory.

When " Cato" was shown to Pope, he advised the author
to print it, without any theatrical exhibition ; supposing that it
would be read more favorably than heard.   Addison declared
himself of the same opinion ; but urged the importunity of his
friends for its appearance on the stage.   The emulation of parties made it successful beyond expectation ; and its success has
introduced or confirmed among us the use of dialogue too declamatory, or of unaffecting elegance and chill philosophy.

The universality of applause, however it might quell the
censure of common mortals, had no other effect than to harden
Dennis in fixed dislike ; but his dislike was not merely capricious.   He found and showed many faults ; he showed them
indeed with anger, but he found them with acuteness, such as
ought to rescue his criticism from oblivion ; though, at last, it
will have no other life than it derives from the work which it
endeavors to oppress.

Why he pays no regard to the opinion of the audience, he
gives his reason by remarking that,

" A deference is to be paid to a general applause, when it appears that the applause is natural and spontaneous ; but that little regard is to be had to it when it is affected and artificial. Of all the tragedies which in his memory have had vast and violent runs, not one has been excellent, few have been tolerable, most have been scandalous. When a poet writes a tragedy, who knows he has judgment, and who feels he has genius, that poet presumes upon his own merit, and scorns to make a cabal. That people come coolly to the representation of such a tragedy, without any violent expectation, or delusive imagination, or invincible prepossession ; that such an audience is liable to receive impressions which the poem shall naturally make on them, and to judge by their own reason and their own judgments, and that reason and judgment are calm and serene, not formed by nature to make proselytes, and to control and lord it over the imaginations of others. But that when an author writes a tragedy, who knows he has neither genius nor judgment, he has recourse to the making a party, and he endeavors to make up in industry what is wanting in talent, and to supply by poetical craft the absence of poetical art ; that such an author is humbly contented to raise men's passions by a plot without doors, since he despairs of doing it by that which he brings upon the stage. That party, and passion, and prepossession are clamorous and tumultuous things, and so much the more clamorous and tumultuous by how much the more erroneous : that they domineer and tyrannize over the imaginations of persons who want judgment, and sometimes too of those who have it ; and, like a fierce and outrageous torrent, bear down all opposition before them."

He then condemns the neglect of poetical justice ; which is always one of his favorite principles.

" It is certainly the duty of every tragic poet, by the exact distribution of poetical justice, to imitate the Divine dispensation, and to inculcate a particular providence. It is true, indeed, upon the stage of the world, the wicked sometimes prosper and the guiltless suffer. But that is permitted by the Governor of the world, to show, from the attribute of his infinite justice, that there is a compensation in futurity, to prove the immortality of the human soul, and the certainty of future rewards and punishments. But the poetical persons in tragedy exist no longer than the reading or the representation ; the whole extent of their enmity is circumscribed by those ; and, therefore, during that reading or representation, according to their merits or demerits, they must be punished or rewarded. If this is not done, there is no impartial distribution of poetical justice, no instructive lecture of a particular providence, and no imitation of the Divine dispensation.   And yet the author of this tragedy does not only run counter to this, in the fate of his principal character, but everywhere, throughout it, makes virtue suffer and vice triumph ; for not only Cato is vanquished by Cæsar, but the treachery and perfidiousness of Syphax prevail over the honest simplicity and the credulity of Juba ; and the sly subtlety and dissimulation of Portius over the generous frankness and open-heartedness of Marcus.''

Whatever pleasure there may be in seeing crimes punished and virtue rewarded, yet, since wickedness often prospers in real life, the poet is certainly at liberty to give it prosperity on the stage.   For if poetry has an imitation of reality, how are its laws broken by exhibiting the world in its true form ?   The stage may sometimes gratify our wishes ; but if it be truly the " *mirror of life,*'' it ought to show us sometimes what we are to expect.

Dennis objects to the characters, that they are not natural or reasonable ; but as heroes and heroines are not beings that are seen every day, it is hard to find upon what principles their conduct shall be tried.   It is, however, not useless to consider what he says of the manner in which Cato receives the account of his son's death.

'' Nor is the grief of Cato, in the fourth act, one jot more in nature than that of his son and Lucia in the third.   Cato receives the news of his son's death not only with dry eyes, but with a sort of satisfaction ; and in the same page sheds tears for the calamity of his country, and does the same thing in the next page upon the bare apprehension of the danger of his friends.   Now, since the love of one's country is the love of one's countrymen, as I have shown upon another occasion, I desire to ask these questions : Of all our countrymen, which do we love most, those whom we know or those whom we know not ?   And of those whom we know, which do we cherish most, our friends or our enemies ?   And of our friends, which are the dearest to us, those who are related to us or those who are not ?   And of all our relations, for which have we most tenderness, for those who are near to us or for those who are remote ?   And of our near relations, which are the nearest, and consequently the dearest to us, our offspring or others ?   Our offspring most certainly ; as Nature, or, in other words, Providence, has wisely contrived for the preservation of mankind. Now, does it not follow from what has been said, that for a man to receive the news of his son's death with dry eyes, and to weep at the same time for the calamities of his country, is a wretched

affectation and a miserable inconsistency ? Is not that, in plain
English, to receive with dry eyes the news of the deaths of
those for whose sake our country is a name so dear to us, and
at the same time to shed tears for those for whose sakes our
country is not a name so dear to us ?''

But this formidable assailant is less resistible when he
attacks the probability of the action and the reasonableness of
the plan. Every critical reader must remark that Addison
has, with a scrupulosity almost unexampled on the English
stage, confined himself in time to a single day, and in place to
rigorous unity. The scene never changes, and the whole
action of the play passes in the great hall of Cato's house at
Utica. Much therefore is done in the hall, for which any
other place would be more fit ; and this impropriety affords
Dennis many hints of merriment and opportunities of triumph.
The passage is long ; but as such disquisitions are not common, and the objections are skilfully formed and vigorously
urged, those who delight in critical controversy will not think
it tedious.

'' Upon the departure of Portius, Sempronius makes but
one soliloquy, and immedately in comes Syphax, and then the
two politicians are at it immediately. They lay their heads
together, with their snuff-boxes in their hands, as Mr. Bayes
has it, and feague it away. But in the midst of· that wise
scene, Syphax seems to give a seasonable caution to Sempronius :

> '' ' *Syph.* But is it true, Sempronius, that your senate
> Is called together ? Gods ! thou must be cautious ;
> Cato has piercing eyes.'

'' There is a great deal of caution shown indeed, in meeting
in a governor's own hall to carry on their plot against him.
Whatever opinion they have of his eyes, I suppose they have
none of his ears, or they would never have talked at this foolish rate so near :

> '' ' Gods ! thou must be cautious.'

'' Oh ! yes, very cautious ; for if Cato should overhear you,
and turn you off for politicians, Cæsar would never take you ;
no, Cæsar would never take you.

'' When Cato, Act II., turns the senators out of the hall,
upon pretence of acquainting Juba with the result of their debates, he appears to me to do a thing which is neither reasonable nor civil. Juba might certainly have better been made
acquainted with the result of that debate in some private apartment of the place. But the poet was driven upon this absurd-

ity to make way for another ; and that is, to give Juba an opportunity to demand Marcia of her father.   But the quarrel
and rage of Juba and Syphax, in the same act ; the invectives
of Syphax against the Romans and Cato ; the advice that
he gives Juba, in her father's hall, to bear away Marcia by
force ; and his brutal and clamorous rage upon his refusal, and
at a time when Cato was scarcely out of sight, and perhaps not
out of hearing, at least some of his guards or domestics must
necessarily be supposed to be within hearing ; is a thing that is
so far from being probable that it is hardly possible.

" Sempronius, in the second act, comes back once more in
the same morning to the governor's hall, to carry on the conspiracy with Syphax against the governor, his country, and his
family ; which is so stupid that it is below the wisdom of the
O——'s, the Mac's, and the Teague's ; even Eustace Cummins
himself would never have gone to Justice Hall, to have conspired
against the government.   If officers at Portsmouth should lay
their heads together, in order to the carrying off J—— G——'s
niece or daughter, would they meet in J—— G——'s hall to
carry on that conspiracy ?   There would be no necessity for
their meeting there, at least till they came to the execution of
their plot, because there would be other places to meet in.
There would be no probability that they should meet there, because there would be places more private and more commodious.   Now there ought to be nothing in a tragical action but
what is necessary or probable.

" But treason is not the only thing that is carried on in this
hall ; that, and love, and philosophy take their turns in it,
without any manner of necessity or probability occasioned by
the action, as duly and as regularly, without interrupting one
another, as if there were a triple league between them, and a
mutual agreement that each should give place to and make
way for the other, in a due and orderly succession.

" We now come to the third act.   Sempronius, in this act,
comes into the governor's hall, with the leaders of the mutiny ;
but, as soon as Cato is gone, Sempronius, who but just before
had acted like an unparalleled knave, discovers himself, like an
egregious fool, to be an accomplice in the conspiracy.

> " ' *Semp*. Know, villains, when such paltry slaves presume
> To mix in treason, if the plot succeeds,
> They're thrown neglected by ; but, if it fails,
> They're sure to die like dogs, as you shall do.
> Here, take these factious monsters, drag them forth
> To sudden death.'

" It is true, indeed, the second leader says, there are none

there but friends ; but is that possible at such a juncture ?
Can a parcel of rogues attempt to assassinate the governor of a
town of war, in his own house, in mid-day ? and, after they are
discovered and defeated, can there be none near them but
friends ? Is it not plain from these words of Sempronius,

> ' 'Here, take these factious monsters, drag them forth
> To sudden death—'

and from the entrance of the guards upon the word of command, that those guards were within ear-shot ? Behold Sempronius then palpably discovered. How comes it to pass,
then, that instead of being hanged up with the rest, he remains
secure in the governor's hall and there carries on his conspiracy against the government, the third time in the same day,
with his old comrade Syphax, who enters at the same time that
the guards are carrying away the leaders, big with the news of
the defeat of Sempronius ; though where he had his intelligence so soon is difficult to imagine ? And now the reader
may expect a very extraordinary scene ; there is not abundance
of spirit indeed, nor a great deal of passion, but there is wisdom more than enough to supply all defects.

> " ' *Syph.* Our first design, my friend, has prov'd abortive,
> Still there remains an after-game to play :
> My troops are mounted, their Numidian steeds
> Snuff up the winds, and long to scour the desert.
> Let but Sempronius lead us in our flight,
> We'll force the gate, where Marcus keeps his guard,
> And hew down all that would oppose our passage :
> A day will bring us into Cæsar's camp.
> *Semp.* Confusion ! I have fail'd of half my purpose ;
> Marcia, the charming Marcia's left behind.'

" Well ! but though he tells us the half purpose he has failed
of, he does not tell us the half that he has carried. But what
does he mean by

> " ' Marcia, the charming Marcia's left behind ' ?

" He is now in her own house ! and we have neither seen
her nor heard of her, anywhere else since the play began.
But now let us hear Syphax :

> " ' What hinders then, but that you find her out,
> And hurry her away by manly force ? '

" But what does old Syphax mean by finding her out ? They
talk as if she were as hard to be found as a hare in a frosty
morning.

> " ' *Semp.* But how to gain admission ! '

" Oh ! she is found out then, it seems.

> " ' But how to gain admission ! for access
> Is given to none, but Juba and her brothers.'

"But, raillery apart, why access to Juba? For he was owned and received as a lover neither by the father nor by the daughter. Well ! but let that pass. Syphax puts Sempronius out of pain immediately ; and, being a Numidian, abounding in wiles, supplies him with a stratagem for admission that, I believe, is a non-pareille.

> " ' *Syph.* Thou shalt have Juba's dress, and Juba's guards.
> The doors will open when Numidia's prince
> Seems to appear before them.'

" Sempronius is, it seems, to pass for Juba in full day at Cato's house, where they were both so very well known, by having Juba's dress and his guards ; as if one of the marshals of France could pass for the Duke of Bavaria at noon-day, at Versailles, by having his dress and liveries. But How does Syphax pretend to help Sempronius to young Juba's dress? Does he serve him in a double capacity, as a general and master of his wardrobe ? But why Juba's guards? For the devil of any guards has Juba appeared with yet. Well ! though this is a mighty politic invention, yet, methinks, they might have done without it ; for, since the advice that Syphax gave to Sempronius was,

> " ' To hurry her away by manly force,'

in my opinion the shortest and likeliest way of coming at the lady was by demolishing, instead of putting on an impertinent disguise to circumvent two or three slaves. But Sempronius, it seems, is of another opinion. He extols to the skies the invention of old Syphax :

> " ' *Semp.* Heavens ! what a thought was there ! '

" Now I appeal to the reader if I have not been as good as my word. Did I not tell him that I would lay before him a very wise scene ?

" But now let us lay before the reader that part of the scenery of the fourth act which may show the absurdities which the author has run into through the indiscreet observance of the unity of place. I do not remember that Aristotle has said any thing expressly concerning the unity of place. It is true, implicitly he has said enough in the rules which he has laid down for the chorus. For, by making the chorus an essential part of tragedy, and by bringing it on the stage immediately after the opening of the scene, and retaining it till the very catastrophe, he has so determined and fixed the place of action that it was impossible for an author on the Grecian stage to break through that unity. I am of opinion that if a modern tragic poet can preserve the unity of place without destroying the probability of the incidents, it is always best for him to do it ; because, by the preserving of that unity, as we have taken notice above, he adds grace, and clearness, and comeliness to the representation. But since there are no express rules about it, and we are under no compulsion to keep it, since we have no chorus as the Grecian poet had, if it cannot be preserved without rendering the greater part of the incidents unreasonable and absurd, and perhaps sometimes monstrous, it is certainly better to break it.

" Now comes bully Sempronius, comically accoutred and equipped with his Numidian dress and his Numidian guards. Let the reader attend to him with all his ears ; for the words of the wise are precious :

" ' *Semp*. The deer is lodg'd, I've track'd her to her covert.'

" Now, I would fain know why this deer is said to be lodged, since we have heard not one word, since the play began, of her being at all out of harbor ; and if we consider the discourse with which she and Lucia begin the act, we have reason to believe that they had hardly been talking of such matters in the street. However, to pleasure Sempronius, let us suppose for once that the deer is lodged.

" ' The deer is lodg'd, I've track'd her to her covert.'

" If he had seen her in the open field, what occasion had he to track her, when he had so many Numidian dogs at his heels, which, with one halloo, he might have set upon her haunches ? If he did not see her in the open field, how could he possibly track her ? If he had seen her in the street, why did he not set upon her in the street, since through the street she must be carried at last ? Now here, instead of having his thoughts upon his business and upon the present danger ; instead of meditating and contriving how he shall pass with his mistress through the southern gate (where her brother Marcus is upon the guard, and where he would certainly prove an impediment to him), which is the Roman word for the baggage ; instead of doing this, Sempronius is entertaining himself with whimsies :

> " ' *Semp*. How will the young Numidian rave to see
> His mistress lost ! If aught could glad my soul,
> Beyond th' enjoyment of so bright a prize,
> 'Twould be to torture that young, gay barbarian.
> But, hark ! what noise ? Death to my hopes ! 'tis he,
> 'Tis Juba's self ! There is but one way left !
> He must be murder'd, and a passage cut
> Through those his guards.'

" Pray, what are ' those his guards ' ? I thought, at present, that Juba's guards had been Sempronius's tools, and had been dangling after his heels.

" But now let us sum up all these absurdities together. Sempronius goest at noon-day, in Juba's clothes and with Juba's guards, to Cato's palace, in order to pass for Juba, in a place where they were both so very well known ; he meets Juba there, and resolves to murder him with his own guards. Upon the guards appearing a little bashful, he threatens them :

> " ' Hah ! Dastards, do you tremble !
> Or act like men ; or, by yon azure heav'n—'

" But the guards still remaining restive, Sempronius himself attacks Juba, while each of the guards is representing Mr. Spectator's sign of the Gaper, awed, it seems, and terrified by Sempronius's threats. Juba kills Sempronius, and takes his own army prisoners, and carries them in triumph away to Cato. Now I would fain know if any part of Mr. Bayes's tragedy is so full of absurdity as this ?

" Upon hearing the clash of swords, Lucia and Marcia come in. The question is, why no men come in upon hearing the noise of swords in the governor's hall ? Where was the governor himself ? Where were his guards ? Where were his servants ? Such an attempt as this, so near the person of a governor of a place of war, was enough to alarm the whole garrison ; and yet, for almost half an hour after Sempronius was killed, we find none of those appear who were the likeliest in the world to be alarmed ; and the noise of swords is made to draw only two poor women thither, who were most certain to run away from it. Upon Lucia and Marcia's coming in, Lucia appears in all the symptoms of an hysterical gentlewoman :

> " ' *Luc*. Sure 'twas the clash of swords ! my troubled heart
> Is so cast down, and sunk amidst its sorrows,
> It throbs with fear, and aches at every sound !'

And immediately her old whimsy returns upon her :

> " ' O Marcia, should thy brothers, for my sake—
> I die away with horror at the thought.'

" She fancies that there can be no cutting of throats but it must be for her. If this is tragical, I would fain know what is comical. Well! upon this they spy the body of Sempronius ; and Marcia, deluded by the habit, it seems, takes him for Juba ; for, says she,

"'The face is muffled up within the garment.'

" Now, how a man could fight and fall, with his face muffled up in his garment, is, I think, a little hard to conceive ! Besides, Juba, before he killed him, knew him to be Sempronius. It was not by his garment that he knew this ; it was by his face then : his face therefore was not muffled. Upon seeing this man with his muffled face, Marcia falls a-raving ; and, owning her passion for the supposed defunct, begins to make his funeral oration. Upon which Juba enters listening, I suppose on tiptoe ; for I cannot imagine how any one can enter listening in any other posture. I would fain know how it comes to pass that during all this time he had sent nobody, no, not so much as a candle-snuffer, to take away the dead body of Sempronius. Well ! but let us regard him listening. Having left his apprehension behind him, he, at first, applies what Marcia says to Sempronius. But finding at last, with much ado, that he himself is the happy man, he quits his eavesdropping, and discovers himself just time enough to prevent his being cuckolded by a dead man, of whom the moment before he had appeared so jealous ; and greedily intercepts the bliss which was fondly designed for one who could not be the better for it. But here I must ask a question : how comes Juba to listen here, who had not listened before throughout the play ? Or how comes he to be the only person of this tragedy who listens, when love and treason were so often talked in so public a place as a hall ? I am afraid the author was driven upon all these absurdities only to introduce this miserable mistake of Marcia, which, after all, is much below the dignity of tragedy, as any thing is which is the effect or result of trick.
" But let us come to the scenery of the fifth act. Cato appears first upon the scene, sitting in a thoughtful posture ; in his hand Plato's treatise on the Immortality of the Soul, a drawn sword on the table by him. Now, let us consider the place in which this sight is presented to us. The place, forsooth, is a long hall. Let us suppose that any one should place himself in this posture in the midst of one of our halls in London ; that he should appear *solus* in a sullen posture, a drawn sword on the table by him ; in his hand Plato's treatise on the Immortality of the Soul, translated lately by Bernard

Lintot : I desire the reader to consider whether such a person
as this would pass with them who beheld him for a great
patriot, a great philosopher, or a general, or some whimsical
person who fancied himself all these ? and whether the people
who belonged to the family would think that such a person
had a design upon their midriffs or his own ?

" In short, that Cato should sit long enough in the aforesaid
posture, in the midst of this large hall, to read over Plato's
treatise on the Immortality of the Soul, which is a lecture of
two long hours ; that he should propose to himself to be .pri-
vate there upon that occasion ; that he should be angry with
his son for intruding there ; then, that he should leave this hall
upon the pretence of sleep, give himself the mortal wound in
his bedchamber, and then be brought back into that hall to
expire, purely to show his good breeding and save his friends
the trouble of coming up to his bedchamber ; all this appears
to me to be improbable, incredible, impossible."

Such is the censure of Dennis. There is, as Dryden
expresses it, perhaps " too much horse-play in his raillery ;"
but if his jests are coarse his arguments are strong. Yet, as
we love better to be pleased than be taught, " Cato" is read
and the critic is neglected.

Flushed with consciousness of these detections of absurdity
in the conduct, he afterwards attacked the sentiments of Cato ;
but he then amused himself with petty cavils and minute objections.

Of Addison's smaller poems no particular mention is
necessary ; they have little that can employ or require a critic.
The parallel of the princes and gods, in his verses to Kneller,
is often happy, but is too well known to be quoted.

His translations, so far as I have compared them, want the
exactness of a scholar. That he understood his authors cannot be doubted ; but his versions will not teach others to understand them, being too licentiously paraphrastical. They
are, however, for the most part, smooth and easy, and—what is
the first excellence of a translator—such as may be read with
pleasure by those who do not know the originals.

His poetry is polished and pure, the product of a mind too
judicious to commit faults, but not sufficiently vigorous to
attain excellence. He has sometimes a striking line or a shining paragraph ; but in the whole he is warm rather than fervid,
and shows more dexterity than strength. He was, however,
one of our earliest examples of correctness.

The versification which he had learned from Dryden he debased rather than refined. His rhymes are often dissonant ; in his "Georgic" he admits broken lines. He uses both trip- lets and Alexandrines, but triplets more frequently in his trans- lations than his other works. The mere structure of verses seems never to have engaged much of his care. But his lines are very smooth in " Rosamond," and too smooth in " Cato."

Addison is now to be considered as a critic ; a name which the present generation is scarcely willing to allow him. His criticism is condemned as tentative or experimental, rather than scientific ; and he is considered as deciding by taste rather than by principles.

It is not uncommon for those who have grown wise by the labor of others to add a little of their own and overlook their masters. Addison is now despised by some who perhaps would never have seen his defects but by the lights which he afforded them. That he always wrote as he would think it necessary to write now, cannot be affirmed : his instructions were such as the characters of his readers made proper. That general knowledge which now circulates in common talk was in his time rarely to be found. Men not professing learning were not ashamed of ignorance ; and, in the female world, any acquaintance with books was distinguished only to be cen- sured. His purpose was to infuse literary curiosity, by gentle and unsuspected conveyance, into the gay, the idle, and the wealthy ; he therefore presented knowledge in the most allur- ing form, not lofty and austere, but accessible and familiar. When he showed them their defects, he showed them likewise that they might be easily supplied. His attempt succeeded ; inquiry was awakened and comprehension expanded. An emulation of intellectual elegance was excited ; and from this time to our own life has been gradually exalted and conver- sation purified and enlarged.

Dryden had, not many years before, scattered criticism over his prefaces with very little parsimony ; but though he sometimes condescended to be somewhat familiar, his manner was in general too scholastic for those who had yet their rudi- ments to learn, and found it not easy to understand their mas- ter. His observations were framed rather for those that were learning to write than for those that read only to talk.

An instructor like Addison was now wanting, whose remarks, being superficial, might be easily understood, and being just, might prepare the mind for more attainments. Had he presented " Paradise Lost " to the public with all the pomp of system and severity of science, the criticism would perhaps have been admired and the poem still have been neglected ; but by the blandishments of gentleness and facility he has made Milton an universal favorite, with whom readers of every class think it necessary to be pleased.

He descended now and then to lower disquisitions ; and by a serious display of the beauties of " Chevy-Chase," exposed himself to the ridicule of Wagstaffe, who bestowed a like pompous character on " Tom Thumb ;" and to the contempt of Dennis, who, considering the fundamental position of his criticism, that " Chevy-Chase" pleases, and ought to please because it is natural, observes that " there is a way of deviating from nature, by bombast or tumor, which soars above nature and enlarges images beyond their real bulk ; by affectation, which forsakes nature in quest of something unsuitable ; and by imbecility, which degrades nature by faintness and diminution, by obscuring its appearances, and weakening its effects." In " Chevy-Chase" there is not much of either bombast or affectation ; but there is chill and lifeless imbecility. The story cannot possibly be told in a manner that shall make less impression on the mind.

Before the profound observers of the present race repose too securely on the consciousness of their superiority to Addison, let them consider his Remarks on Ovid, in which may be found specimens of criticism sufficiently subtle and refined ; let them peruse likewise his " Essays on Wit " and on the " Pleasures of Imagination," in which he founds art on the base of nature, and draws the principles of invention from dispositions inherent in the mind of man with skill and elegance, such as his contemners will not easily attain.

As a describer of life and manners he must be allowed to stand perhaps the first of the first rank. His humor, which, as Steele observes, is peculiar to himself, is so happily diffused as to give the grace of novelty to domestic scenes and daily occurrences. He never "outsteps the modesty of nature," nor raises merriment or wonder by the violation of truth. His figures neither divert by distortion nor amaze by aggravation. He copies life with so much fidelity that he can be hardly said to invent ; yet his exhibitions have an air so much original, that it is difficult to suppose them not merely the product of imagination.

As a teacher of wisdom he may be confidently followed. His religion has nothing in it enthusiastic or superstitious ; he appears neither weakly credulous nor wantonly sceptical ; his morality is neither dangerously lax nor impracticably rigid. All the enchantment of fancy and all the cogency of argument are employed to recommend to the reader his real interest, the care of pleasing the Author of his being. Truth is shown sometimes as the phantom of a vision ; sometimes appears half-veiled in an allegory ; sometimes attracts regard in the robes of fancy ; and sometimes steps forth in the confidence of reason. She wears a thousand dresses, and in all is pleasing.

" Mille habet ornatus, mille decenter habet."

His prose is the model of the middle style ; on grave subjects not formal, on light occasions not grovelling ; pure without scrupulosity, and exact without apparent elaboration ; always equable and always easy, without glowing words or pointed sentences. Addison never deviates from his track to snatch a grace ; he seeks no ambitious ornaments and tries no hazardous innovations. His page is always luminous, but never blazes in unexpected splendor.

It was apparently his principal endeavor to avoid all harshness and severity of diction ; he is therefore sometimes verbose in his transitions and connections, and sometimes descends too much to the language of conversation ; yet if his language had been less idiomatical it might have lost somewhat of its genuine Anglicism. What he attempted he performed ; he is never feeble, and he did not wish to be energetic ; he is never rapid, and he never stagnates. His sentences have neither studied amplitude nor affected brevity ; his periods, though not diligently rounded, are voluble and easy. Whoever wishes to attain an English style, familiar but not coarse, and elegant but not ostentatious, must give his days and nights to the volumes of Addison.

DR. SAMUEL JOHNSON ON POPE.

ALEXANDER POPE was born in London, May 2½, 1688, of parents whose rank or station was never ascertained : we are informed that they were of " gentle blood ;" that his father was of a family of which the Earl of Downe was the head ; and that his mother was the daughter of William Turner, Esquire, of York, who had likewise three sons, one of whom had the honor of being killed and the other of dying in the service of Charles the First ; the third was made a general officer in Spain, from whom the sister inherited what sequestrations· and forfeitures had left in the family.

This, and this only, is told by Pope, who is more willing, as I have heard observed, to show what his father was not than what he was. It is allowed that he grew rich by trade ; but whether in a shop or on the exchange was never discovered till Mr. Tyers told, on the authority of Mrs. Racket, that he was a linen-draper in the Strand. Both parents were papists.

Pope was from his birth of a constitution tender and delicate, but is said to have shown remarkable gentleness and sweetness of disposition. The weakness of his body continued through his life ; but the mildness of his mind perhaps ended with his childhood. His voice, when he was young, was so pleasing that he was called in fondness " The Little Nightingale."

Being not sent early to school, he was taught to read by an aunt ; and when he was seven or eight years old became a lover of books. He first learned to write by imitating printed books ; a species of penmanship in which he retained great excellence through his whole life, though his ordinary hand was not elegant.

When he was about eight he was placed in Hampshire, under Taverner, a Romish priest, who, by a method very rarely practised, taught him the Greek and Latin rudiments together. He was 'now first regularly initiated in poetry by the perusal of Ogilby's Homer and Sandys's Ovid. Ogilby's assistance he never repaid with any praise ; but of Sandys he declared, in his notes to the " Iliad," that English poetry owed much of its beauty to his translations. Sandys very rarely attempted original composition.

From the care of Taverner, under whom his proficiency

was considerable, he was removed to a school at Twyford, near Winchester, and again to another school, about Hyde Park Corner ; from which he used sometimes to stroll to the playhouse, and was so delighted with theatrical exhibitions that he formed a kind of play from Ogilby's " Iliad," with some verses of his own intermixed, which he persuaded his school-fellows to act, with the addition of his master's gardener, who personated Ajax.

At the two last schools he used to represent himself as having lost part of what Taverner had taught him ; and on his master at Twyford he had already exercised his poetry in a lampoon.   Yet under those masters he translated more than a fourth part of the " Metamorphoses."   If he kept the same proportion in his other exercises, it cannot be thought that his loss was great.

He tells of himself, in his poems, that " he lisped in numbers ;" and used to say that he could not remember the time when he began to make verses.   In the style of fiction it might have been said of him, as of Pindar, that when' he lay in his cradle " the bees swarmed about his mouth."

About the time of the Revolution his father, who was undoubtedly disappointed by the sudden blast of popish prosperity, quitted his trade and retired to Binfield, in Windsor Forest, with about twenty thousand pounds, for which, being conscientiously determined not to entrust it to the government, he found no better use than that of locking it up in a chest, and taking from it what his expenses required ; and his life was long enough to consume a great part of it before his son came to the inheritance.

To Binfield Pope was called by his father when he was about twelve years old ; and there he had, for a few months, the assistance of one Deane, another priest, of whom he learned only to construe a little of Tully's Offices.   How Mr. Deane could spend, with a boy who had translated so much of Ovid, some months over a small part of Tully's Offices, it is now vain to inquire.

Of a youth so successfully employed, and so conspicuously improved, a minute account must be naturally desired ; but curiosity must be contented with confused, imperfect, and sometimes improbable intelligence.   Pope, finding little advantage from external help, resolved thenceforward to direct himself, and at twelve formed a plan of study which he completed with little other incitement than the desire of excellence.

His primary and principal purpose was to be a poet, with which his father accidentally concurred by proposing subjects and obliging him to correct his performances by many revisals, after which the old gentleman, when he was satisfied, would say, " These are good rhymes."

In his perusal of the English poets he soon distinguished the versification of Dryden, which he considered as the model to be studied, and was impressed with such veneration for his instructor that he persuaded some friends to take him to the coffee-house which Dryden frequented, and pleased himself with having seen him.

Dryden died May 1, 1701, some days before Pope was twelve ; so early must he therefore have felt the power of harmony and the zeal of genius. Who does not wish that Dryden could have known the value of the homage that was paid him, and foreseen the greatness of his young admirer ?

The earliest of Pope's productions is his " Ode on Solitude," written before he was twelve, in which there is nothing more than other forward boys have attained, and which is not equal to Cowley's performances at the same age.

His time was now wholly spent in reading and writing. As he read the classics he amused himself with translating them ; and at fourteen made a version of the first book of " The Thebais," which, with some revision, he afterwards published. He must have been at this time, if he had no help, a considerable proficient in the Latin tongue.

By Dryden's Fables, which had then been not long published, and were much in the hands of poetical readers, he was tempted to try his own skill in giving Chaucer a more fashionable appearance, and put " January and May," and the " Prologue of the Wife of Bath," into modern English. He translated likewise the epistle of " Sappho to Phaon," from Ovid, to complete the version which was before imperfect, and wrote some other small pieces which he afterwards printed.

He sometimes imitated the English poets, and professed to have written at fourteen his poem upon " Silence" after Rochester's " Nothing." He had now formed his versification, and the smoothness of his numbers surpassed his original ; but this is a small part of his praise : he discovers such acquaintance both with human life and public affairs as is not easily conceived to have been attainable by a boy of fourteen in Windsor Forest.

Next year he was desirous of opening to himself new sources of knowledge, by making himself acquainted with modern languages, and removed for a time to London, that he might study French and Italian, which, as he desired nothing more

than to read them, were by diligent application soon despatched.   Of Italian learning he does not appear to have ever
made much use in his subsequent studies.

He then returned to Binfield, and delighted himself with his
own poetry.   He tried all styles and many subjects.   He wrote
a comedy, a tragedy, an epic poem, with panegyrics on all the
princes of Europe ; and, as he confesses, '' thought himself the
greatest genius that ever was.''   Self-confidence is the first
requisite to great undertakings.   He, indeed, who forms his
opinion of himself in solitude, without knowing the powers of
other men, is very liable to error ; but it was the felicity of
Pope to rate himself at his real value.

Most of his puerile productions were, by his maturer judgment, afterwards destroyed.   '' Alcander,'' the epic poem,
was burnt by the persuasion of Atterbury.   The tragedy was
founded on the legend of St. Genevieve.   Of the comedy there
is no account.

Concerning his studies it is related that he translated Tully
on Old Age ; and that besides his books of poetry and criticism he read Temple's Essays and Locke on the Human Understanding.''   His reading, though his favorite authors are
not known, appears to have been sufficiently extensive and
multifarious ; for his early pieces show with sufficient evidence
his knowledge of books.

He that is pleased with himself easily imagines that he shall
please others.   Sir William Trumbull, who had been ambassador at Constantinople, and secretary of state, when he retired
from business, fixed his residence in the neighborhood of Binfield.   Pope, not yet sixteen, was introduced to the statesman
of sixty, and so distinguished himself that their interviews
ended in friendship and correspondence.   Pope was, through
his whole life, ambitious of splendid acquaintance ; and he
seems to have wanted neither diligence nor success in attracting
the notice of the great ; for from his first entrance into the
world, and his entrance was very early, he was admitted to
familiarity with those whose rank or station made them most
conspicuous.

From the age of sixteen the life of Pope, as an author, may
be properly computed.   He now wrote his Pastorals, which
were shown to the poets and critics of that time ; as they well
deserved, they were read with admiration, and many praises
were bestowed upon them and upon the Preface, which is both
elegant and learned in a high degree ; they were, however, not
published till five years afterwards.

Cowley, Milton, and Pope are distinguished among the

English poets by the early exertion of their powers ; but the works of Cowley alone were published in his childhood, and therefore of him only can it be certain that his puerile perform- ances received no improvement from his maturer studies.

At this time began his acquaintance with Wycherley, a man who seems to have had among his contemporaries his full share of reputation, to have been esteemed without virtue, and ca- ressed without good-humor. Pope was proud of his notice ; Wycherley wrote verses in his praise, which he was charged by Dennis with writing to himself, and they agreed for awhile to flatter one another. It is pleasant to remark how soon Pope learned the cant of an author, and began to treat critics with contempt, though he had yet suffered nothing from them.

But the fondness of Wycherley was too violent to last. His esteem of Pope was such that he submitted some poems to his revision ; and when Pope, perhaps proud of such confi- dence, was sufficiently bold in his criticisms and liberal in his alterations, the old scribbler was angry to see his pages de- faced, and felt more pain from the detection than content from the amendment of his faults. They parted ; but Pope always considered him with kindness, and visited him a little time before he died.

Another of his early correspondents was Mr. Cromwell, of whom I have learned nothing particular but that he used to ride a hunting in a tie-wig. He was fond, and perhaps vain, of amusing himself with poetry and criticism ; and sometimes sent his performances to Pope, who did not forbear such re- marks as were now and then unwelcome. Pope, in his turn, put the juvenile version of " Statius" into his hands for cor- rection.

Their correspondence afforded the public its first knowl- edge of Pope's epistolary powers ; for his Letters were given by Cromwell to one Mrs. Thomas, and she, many years after- wards, sold them to Curll, who inserted them in a volume of his Miscellanies.

Walsh, a name yet preserved among the minor poets, was one of his first encouragers. His regard was gained by the Pastorals, and from him Pope received the counsel by which he seems to have regulated his studies. Walsh advised him to correctness, which, as he told him, the English poets had hitherto neglected, and which therefore was left to him as a basis of fame ; and, being delighted with rural poems, recom- mended to him to write a pastoral comedy, like those which are read so eagerly in Italy, a design which Pope probably did not approve, as he did not follow it,

Pope had now declared himself a poet ; and, thinking himself entitled to poetical conversation, began at seventeen to frequent Will's, a coffee-house on the north side of Russell Street,
in Covent Garden, where the wits of that time used to assemble, and where Dryden had, when he lived, been accustomed
to preside.

During this period of his life he was indefatigably diligent
and insatiably curious, wanting health for violent and money
for expensive pleasures ; and having excited in himself very
strong desires of intellectual eminence, he spent much of his
time over his books ; but he read only to store his mind with
facts and images, seizing all that his authors presented with undistinguishing voracity, and with an appetite for knowledge too
eager to be nice. In a mind like his, however, all the faculties
were at once involuntarily improving. Judgment is forced
upon us by experience. He that reads many books must
compare one opinion or one style with another, and when he
compares must necessarily distinguish, reject, and prefer.
But the account given by himself of his studies was, that from
fourteen to twenty he read only for amusement, from twenty
to twenty-seven for improvement and instruction ; that in the
first part of this time he desired only to know, and in the second he endeavored to judge.

The Pastorals, which had been for some time handed about
among poets and critics, were at last printed (1709) in Tonson's " Miscellany," in a volume which began with the Pastorals of Philips and ended with those of Pope.

The same year was written the "Essay on Criticism," a
work which displays such extent of comprehension, such nicety
of distinction, such acquaintance with mankind, and such
knowledge both of ancient and modern learning, as are not
often attained by the maturest age and longest experience. It
was published about two years afterwards ; and, being praised
by Addison in the " Spectator" with sufficient liberality, met
with so much favor as enraged Dennis, " who," he says,
" found himself attacked, without any manner of provocation on
his side, and attacked in his person, instead of his writings, by
one who was wholly a stranger to him, at a time when all the
world knew he was persecuted by fortune ; and not only saw
that this was attempted in a clandestine manner, with the
utmost falsehood and calumny, but found that all this was
done by a little affected hypocrite, who had nothing in his
mouth at the same time but truth, candor, friendship, good
nature, humanity, and magnanimity."

How the attack was clandestine is not easily perceived, nor

how his person is depreciated ; but he seems to have known something of Pope's character, in whom may be discovered an appetite to talk too frequently of his own virtues.

The pamphlet is such as rage might be expected to dictate. He supposes himself to be asked two questions ; whether the Essay will succeed, and who or what is the author.

Its success he admits to be secured by the false opinions then prevalent ; the author he concludes to be "young and raw."

" First, because he discovers a sufficiency beyond his little ability, and hath rashly undertaken a task infinitely above his force. Secondly, while this little author struts and affects the dictatorian air, he plainly shows that at the same time he is under the rod ; and while he pretends to give laws to others, is a pedantic slave to authority and opinion. Thirdly, he hath, like schoolboys, borrowed both from living and dead. Fourthly, he knows not his own mind, and frequently contradicts himself. Fifthly, he is almost perpetually in the wrong."

All these positions he attempts to prove by quotations and remarks ; but his desire to do mischief is greater than his power. He has, however, justly criticised some passages in these lines :

> " There are whom Heaven has bless'd with store of wit,
> Yet want as much again to manage it ;
> For Wit and Judgment ever are at strife."

It is apparent that wit has two meanings, and that what is wanted, though called wit, is truly judgment. So far Dennis is undoubtedly right ; but, not content with argument, he will have a little mirth, and triumphs over the first couplet in terms too elegant to be forgotten. " By the way, what rare numbers are here ! Would not one swear that this youngster had espoused some antiquated muse, who had sued out a divorce on account of impotence from some superannuated sinner ; and having been p—xed by her former spouse, has got the gout in her decrepit age, which makes her hobble so damnably ?" This was the man who would reform a nation sinking into barbarity.

In another place Pope himself allowed that Dennis had detected one of those blunders which are called "bulls." The first edition had this line :

> " What is this Wit—
> Where wanted, scorn'd ; and envied where acquir'd ?"

" How," says the critic, " can wit be scorned where it is

not ? Is not this a figure frequently employed in Hibernian
land ? The person that wants this wit may indeed be scorned,
but the scorn shows the honor which the contemner has for
wit." Of this remark Pope made the proper use by correcting
the passage.

I have preserved, I think, all that is reasonable in Dennis's
criticism ; it remains that justice be done to his delicacy.
" For his acquaintance (says Dennis) he names Mr. Walsh,
who had by no means the qualification which this author reck-
ons absolutely necessary to a critic, it being very certain that
he was, like this essayer, a very indifferent poet ; he loved to
be well dressed ; and I remember a little young gentleman
whom Mr. Walsh used to take into his company as a double
foil to his person and capacity. Inquire, between Sunninghill
and Oakingham, for a young, short, squab gentleman, the
very bow of the god of love, and tell me whether he be a
proper author to make personal reflections ? He may extol the
ancients, but he has reason to thank the gods that he was born
a modern ; for had he been born of Grecian parents, and his
father consequently had by law had the absolute disposal of
him, his life had been no longer than that of one of his poems,
the life of half a day. Let the person of a gentleman of his
parts be never so contemptible, his inward man is ten times
more ridiculous ; it being impossible that his outward form,
though it be that of downright monkey, should differ so much
from human shape as his unthinking immaterial part does from
human understanding." Thus began the hostility between
Pope and Dennis, which, though it was suspended for a short
time, never was appeased. Pope seems at first to have attacked him wantonly ; but, though he always professed to despise him, he discovers, by mentioning him very often, that he
felt his force or his venom.

Of this essay Pope declared that he did not expect the
sale to be quick, because " not one gentleman in sixty, even of
liberal education, could understand it." The gentlemen and
the education of that time seem to have been of a lower character than they are of this. He mentioned a thousand copies
as a numerous impression.

Dennis was not his only censurer ; the zealous papists
thought the monks treated with too much contempt and Erasmus too studiously praised ; but to these objections he had not
much regard.

The Essay has been translated into French by Hamilton,
author of the " Comte de Grammont," whose version was
never printed ; by Robotham, secretary to the king for Han-

over, and by Resnel ; and commented by Dr. Warburton, who has discovered in it such order and connection as was not perceived by Addison, nor, as is said, intended by the author.

Almost every poem consisting of precepts is so far arbitrary and immethodical that many of the paragraphs may change places with no apparent inconvenience ; for of two or more positions depending upon some remote and general principle there is seldom any cogent reason why one should precede the other. But for the order in which they stand, whatever it be, a little ingenuity may easily give a reason. " It is possible," says Hooker, " that by long circumduction from any one truth all truth may be inferred." Of all homogeneous truths, at least of all truths respecting the same general end, in whatever series they may be produced, a concatenation by intermediate ideas may be formed, such as, when it is once shown, shall appear natural ; but if this order be reversed, another mode of connection equally specious may be found or made. Aristotle is praised for naming Fortitude first of the cardinal virtues, as that without which no other virtue can steadily be practised ; but he might, with equal propriety, have placed Prudence and Justice before it, since without Prudence Fortitude is mad ; without Justice it is mischievous.

As the end of method is perspicuity, that series is sufficiently regular that avoids obscurity, and where there is no obscurity it will not be difficult to discover method.

In the " Spectator" was published the Messiah, which he first submitted to the perusal of Steele, and corrected in compliance with his criticisms.

It is reasonable to infer, from his Letters, that the " Verses on an Unfortunate Lady" were written about the time when his Essay was published. The lady's name and adventures I have sought with fruitless inquiry.

I can therefore tell no more than I have learned from Mr. Ruffhead, who writes with the confidence of one who could trust his information. She was a woman of eminent rank and large fortune, the ward of an uncle, who, having given her a proper education, expected, like other guardians, that she should make at least an equal match ; and such he proposed to her, but found it rejected in favor of a young gentleman of inferior condition.

Having discovered the correspondence between the two lovers, and finding the young lady determined to abide by her own choice, he supposed that separation might do what can rarely be done by arguments, and sent her into a foreign country, where she was obliged to converse only with those from whom her uncle had nothing to fear.

Her lover took care to repeat his vows ; but his letters were intercepted and carried to her guardian, who directed her to be watched with still greater vigilance, till of this restraint she grew so impatient that she bribed a woman servant to procure her a sword, which she directed to her heart.

From this account, given with evident intention to raise the lady's character, it does not appear that she had any claim to praise, nor much to compassion. She seems to have been impatient, violent, and ungovernable. Her uncle's power could not have lasted long ; the hour of liberty and choice would have come in time. But her desires were too hot for delay, and she liked self-murder better than suspense.

Nor is it discovered that the uncle, whoever he was, is with much justice delivered to posterity as " a false guardian ;" he seems to have done only that for which a guardian is appointed ; he endeavored to direct his niece till she should be able to direct herself. Poetry has not often been worse employed than in dignifying the amorous fury of a raving girl.

Not long after, he wrote " The Rape of the Lock," the most airy, the most ingenious, and the most delightful of all his compositions, occasioned by a frolic of gallantry, rather too familiar, in which Lord Petre cut off a lock of Mrs. Arabella Fermor's hair. This, whether stealth or violence, was so much resented that the commerce of the two families, before very friendly, was interrupted. Mr. Caryl, a gentleman who, being secretary to King James's queen, had followed his mistress into France, and who, being the author of " Sir Solomon Single," a comedy, and some translations, was entitled to the notice of a wit, solicited Pope to endeavor a reconciliation by a ludicrous poem, which might bring both the parties to a better temper. In compliance with Caryl's request, though his name was for a long time marked only by the first and last letters, C—l, a poem of two cantos was written (1711), as is said, in a fortnight, and sent to the offended lady, who liked it well enough to show it ; and, with the usual process of literary transactions, the author, dreading a surreptitious edition, was forced to publish it.

The event is said to have been such as was desired, the pacification and diversion of all to whom it related, except Sir George Brown, who complained with some bitterness that, in the character of Sir Plume, he was made to talk nonsense. Whether all this be true I have some doubt ; for at Paris, a few years ago, a niece of Mrs. Fermor, who presided in an

English convent, mentioned Pope's work with very little gratitude, rather as an insult than an honor ; and she may be supposed to have inherited the opinion of her family.

At its first appearance it was termed by Addison *merum sal.* Pope, however, saw that it was capable of improvement, and, having luckily contrived to borrow his machinery from the Rosicrucians, imparted the scheme with which his head was teeming to Addison, who told him that his work, as it stood, was '' a delicious little thing,'' and gave him no encouragement to retouch it.

This has been too hastily considered as an instance of Addison's jealousy ; for, as he could not guess the conduct of the new design, or the possibilities of pleasure comprised in a fiction of which there had been no examples, he might very reasonably and kindly persuade the author to acquiesce in his own prosperity, and forbear an attempt which he considered as an unnecessary hazard.

Addison's counsel was happily rejected. Pope foresaw the future efflorescence of imagery then budding in his mind, and resolved to spare no art or industry of cultivation. The soft luxuriance of his fancy was already shooting, and all the gay varieties of diction were ready at his hand to color and embellish it.

His attempt was justified by its success. '' The Rape of the Lock '' stands forward, in the classes of literature, as the most exquisite example of ludicrous poetry. Berkeley congratulated him upon the display of powers more truly poetical than he had shown before : with elegance of description and justness of precepts he had now exhibited boundless fertility of invention.

He always considered the intermixture of the machinery with the action as his most successful exertion of poetical art. He indeed could never afterwards produce any thing of such unexampled excellence. Those performances which strike with wonder are combinations of skilful genius with happy casualty ; and it is not likely that any felicity like the discovery of a new race of preternatural agents should happen twice to the same man.

Of this poem the author was, I think, allowed to enjoy the praise for a long time without disturbance. Many years afterwards, Dennis published some remarks upon it, with very little force, and with no effect ; for the opinion of the public was already settled, and it was no longer at the mercy of criticism.

About this time he published '' The Temple of Fame,'' which, as he tells Steele in their correspondence, he had writ-

ten two years before—that is, when he was only twenty-two
years old, an early time of life for so much learning and so
much observation as that work exhibits.

On this poem Dennis afterwards published some remarks,
of which the most reasonable is, that some of the lines represent Motion as exhibited by Sculpture.

Of the epistle from "Eloisa to Abelard," I do not know
the date. His first inclination to attempt a composition of that
tender kind arose, as Mr. Savage told me, from his perusal of
Prior's "Nut-brown Maid." How much he has surpassed
Prior's work it is not necessary to mention, when perhaps it
may be said with justice that he has excelled every composition of the same kind. The mixture of religious hope and
resignation gives an elevation and dignity to disappointed love
which images merely natural cannot bestow. The gloom of a
convent strikes the imagination with far greater force than the
solitude of a grove.

This piece was, however, not much his favorite in his latter
years, though I never heard upon what principle he slighted it.

In the next year (1713) he published "Windsor Forest;"
of which part was, as he relates, written at sixteen, about the
same time as his Pastorals, and the latter part was added afterwards : where the addition begins we are not told. The lines
relating to the peace confess their own date. It is dedicated
to Lord Lansdowne, who was then high in reputation and influence among the Tories ; and it is said that the conclusion of
the poem gave great pain to Addison, both as a poet and a
politician. Reports like this are always spread with boldness
very disproportionate to their evidence. Why should Addison
receive any particular disturbance from the last lines of
"Windsor Forest"? If contrariety of opinion could poison a
politician, he would not live a day ; and as a poet he must
have felt Pope's force of genius much more from many other
parts of his works.

The pain that Addison might feel it is not likely that he
would confess ; and it is certain that he so well suppressed
his discontent that Pope now thought himself his favorite ;
for, having been consulted in the revisal of "Cato," he introduced it by a Prologue ; and when Dennis published his Remarks, undertook, not indeed to vindicate, but to revenge his
friend, by a "Narrative of the Frenzy of John Dennis."

There is reason to believe that Addison gave no encouragement to this disingenuous hostility ; for, says Pope, in a
letter to him, "indeed your opinion, that it is entirely to be
neglected, would be my own in my own case ; but I felt more

warmth here than I did when I first saw his book against myself (though indeed in two minutes it made me heartily merry)."' Addison was not a man on whom such cant of sensibility could make much impression. He left the pamphlet to itself, having disowned it to Dennis, and perhaps did not think Pope to have deserved much by his officiousness.

This year was printed in the "Guardian" the ironical comparison between the Pastorals of Philips and Pope, a composition of artifice, criticism, and literature, to which nothing equal will easily be found. The superiority of Pope is so ingeniously dissembled, and the feeble lines of Philips so skilfully preferred, that Steele, being deceived, was unwilling to print the paper, lest Pope should be offended. Addison immediately saw the writer's design, and, as it seems, had malice enough to conceal his discovery, and to permit a publication which, by making his friend Philips ridiculous, made him forever an enemy to Pope.

It appears that about this time Pope had a strong inclination to unite the art of painting with that of poetry, and put himself under the tuition of Jervas. He was near-sighted, and therefore not formed by nature for a painter; he tried, however, how far he could advance, and sometimes persuaded his friends to sit. A picture of Betterton, supposed to be drawn by him, was in the possession of Lord Mansfield : if this was taken from the life, he must have begun to paint earlier, for Betterton was now dead. Pope's ambition of this new art produced some encomiastic verses to Jervas, which certainly show his power as a poet ; but I have been told that they betray his ignorance of painting.

He appears to have regarded Betterton with kindness and esteem ; and after his death published, under his name, a version into modern English of Chaucer's Prologues, and one of his Tales, which, as was related by Mr. Harte, were believed to have been the performance of Pope himself by Fenton, who made him a gay offer of five pounds if he would show them in the hand of Betterton.

The next year (1713) produced a bolder attempt, by which profit was sought as well as praise. The poems which he had hitherto written, however they might have diffused his name, had made very little addition to his fortune. The allowance which his father made him, though, proportioned to what he had, it might be liberal, could not be large ; his religion hindered him from the occupation of any civil employment ; and he complained that he wanted even money to buy books.

He therefore resolved to try how far the favor of the pub-lic extended, by soliciting a subscription to a version of the "Iliad," with large notes.

To print by subscription was, for some time, a practice peculiar to the English. The first considerable work. for which this expedient was employed is said to have been Dryden's "Virgil," and it had been tried again with success when the "Tatlers" were collected into volumes.

There was reason to believe that Pope's attempt would be successful. He was in the full bloom of reputation, and was personally known to almost all whom dignity of employment or splendor of reputation had made eminent; he conversed indifferently with both parties, and never disturbed the public with his political opinions; and it might be naturally expected, as each faction then boasted its literary zeal, that the great men, who on other occasions practised all the violence of opposition, would emulate each other in their encouragement of a poet who had delighted all and by whom none had been offended.

With those hopes he offered an English "Iliad" to subscribers, in six volumes in quarto, for six guineas; a sum, according to the value of money at that time, by no means inconsiderable, and greater than I believe to have been ever asked before. His proposal, however, was very favorably received, and the patrons of literature were busy to recommend his undertaking and promote his interest. Lord Oxford, indeed, lamented that such a genius should be wasted upon a work not original; but proposed no means by which he might live without it. Addison recommended caution and moderation, and advised him not to be content with the praise of half the nation when he might be universally favored.

The greatness of the design, the .popularity of the author, and the attention of the literary world, naturally raised such expectations of the future sale that the booksellers made their offers with great eagerness; but the highest bidder was Bernard Lintot, who became proprietor on condition of supplying at his own expense all the copies which were to be delivered to subscribers or presented to friends, and paying two hundred pounds for every volume.

Of the quartos it was, I believe, stipulated that none should be printed but for the author, that the subscription might not be depreciated; but Lintot impressed the same pages upon a small folio, and paper perhaps a little thinner, and sold exactly at half the price, for half a guinea each volume, books so little inferior to the quartos that, by a fraud of trade, those folios, being afterwards shortened by cutting away the top and bottom, were sold as copies printed for the subscribers.

Lintot printed two hundred and fifty on royal paper in folio, for two guineas a volume ; of the small folio, having printed seventeen hundred and fifty copies of the first volume, he reduced the number in the other volumes to a thousand.

It is unpleasant to relate that the bookseller, after all his hopes and all his liberality, was, by a very unjust and illegal action, defrauded of his profit. An edition of the English " Iliad " was printed in Holland, in duodecimo, and imported clandestinely for the gratification of those who were impatient to read what they could not yet afford to buy. This fraud could only be counteracted by an edition equally cheap and more commodious ; and Lintot was compelled to contract his folio at once into a duodecimo and lose the advantage of an intermediate gradation. The notes, which in the Dutch copies were placed at the end of each book, as they had been in the large volumes, were now subjoined to the text in the same page, and are therefore more easily consulted. Of this edition two thousand five hundred were first printed, and five thousand a few weeks afterwards ; but indeed great numbers were neces- sary to produce considerable profit.

Pope, having now emitted his proposals, and engaged not only his own reputation, but in some degree that of his friends who patronized his subscription, began to be frighted at his own undertaking ; and finding himself at first embarrassed with difficulties which retarded and oppressed him, he was for a time timorous and uneasy, had his nights disturbed by dreams of long journeys through unknown ways, and wished, as he said, " that somebody would hang him."

This misery, however, was not of long continuance ; he grew by degrees more acquainted with Homer's images and expressions, and practice increased his facility of versification. In a short time he represents himself as despatching regularly fifty verses a day, which would show him by an easy computa- tion the termination of his labor.

His own diffidence was not his only vexation. He that. asks a subscription soon finds that he has enemies. All who do not encourage him defame him. He that wants money will rather be thought angry than poor ; and he that wishes to save his money conceals his avarice by his malice. Addison had hinted his suspicion that Pope was too much a Tory ; and some of the Tories suspected his principles because he had con- tributed to the " Guardian," which was carried on by Steele.

To those who censured his politics were added enemies yet

more dangerous, who called in question his knowledge of
Greek and his qualifications for a translator of Homer.   To
these he made no public opposition ; but in one of his letters
escapes from them as well as he can.   At an age like his, for he
was not more than twenty-five, with an irregular education,
and a course of life of which much seems to have passed in conversation, it is not very likely that he overflowed with Greek.
But when he felt himself deficient he sought assistance ; and
what man of learning would refuse to help him ?   Minute inquiries into the force of words are less necessary in translating
Homer than other poets, because his positions are general
and his representations natural, with very little dependence on
local or temporary customs, on those changeable scenes of
artificial life which, by mingling originally with accidental
notions, and crowding the mind with images which time
effaces, produces ambiguity in diction and obscurity in books.
To this open display of unadulterated nature it must be
ascribed that Homer has fewer passages of doubtful meaning
than any other poet either in the learned or in modern languages.   I have read of a man who, being by his ignorance
of Greek compelled to gratify his curiosity with the ¦Latin
printed on the opposite page, declared that from the rude
simplicity of the lines literally rendered he formed nobler
ideas of the Homeric majesty than from the labored elegance
of polished versions.

Those literal translations were always at hand, and from them
he could easily obtain his author's sense with sufficient certainty ; and among the readers of Homer the number is very
small of those who find much in the Greek more than in the
Latin, except the music of the numbers.

If more help was wanting, he had the poetical translation
of Eobanus Hessus, an unwearied writer of Latin verses ; he
had the French Homers of La Valterie and Dacier, and the
ₗEnglish of Chapman, Hobbes, and Ogilby.   With Chapman,
whose work, though now totally neglected, seems to have been
popular almost to the end of the last century, he had very frequent consultations, and perhaps never translated any passage
till he had read his version, which indeed he has been sometimes suspected of using instead of the original.

Notes were likewise to be provided, for the six volumes
would have been very little more than six pamphlets without
them.   What the mere perusal of the text could suggest, Pope
wanted no assistance to collect or methodize ; but more was
necessary ; many pages were to be filled, and learning must
supply materials to wit and judgment.   Something might be

gathered from Dacier ; but no man loves to be indebted to his contemporaries, and Dacier was accessible to common readers. Eustathius was therefore necessarily consulted. To read Eustathius, of whose work there was then no Latin version, I suspect Pope, if he had been willing, not to have been able ; some other was therefore to be found who had leisure as well as abilities ; and he was doubtless most readily employed who would do much work for little money.

The history of the notes has never been traced. Broome, in his preface to his poems, declares himself the commentator " in part upon the Iliad ;" and it appears from Fenton's letter, preserved in the Museum, that Broome was at first engaged in consulting Eustathius, but that after a time, whatever was the reason, he desisted ; another man of Cambridge was then employed, who soon grew weary of the work ; and a third, that was recommended by Thirlby, is now discovered to have been Jortin, a man since well known to the learned world, who complained that Pope, having accepted and approved his performance, never testified any curiosity to see him, and who professed to have forgotten the terms on which he worked. The terms which Fenton uses are very mercantile : " I think at first sight that his performance is very commendable, and have sent word for him to finish the seventeenth book, and to send it with his demands for his trouble. I have here enclosed the specimen ; if the rest come before the return, I will keep them till I receive your order.''

Broome then offered his service a second time, which was probably accepted, as they had afterwards a closer correspondence. Parnell contributed the life of Homer, which Pope found so harsh that he took great pains in correcting it ; and by his own diligence, with such help as kindness or money could procure him, in somewhat more than five years he completed his version of the " Iliad,'' with the notes. He began it in 1712, his twenty-fifth year, and concluded it in 1718, his thirtieth year.

When we find him translating fifty lines a day, it is natural to suppose that he would have brought his work to a moie speedy conclusion. The " Iliad,'' containing less than sixteen thousand verses, might have been despatched in less than three hundred and twenty days by fifty verses in a day. The notes, compiled with the assistance of his mercenaries, could not be supposed to require more time than the text.

According to this calculation, the progress of Pope may seem to have been slow ; but the distance is commonly very great between actual performances and speculative possibility. It is natural to suppose that as much as has been done to-day may be done to-morrow ; but on the morrow some difficulty emerges, or some external impediment obstructs. Indolence, interruption, business, and pleasure, all take their turns of retardation ; and every long work is lengthened by a thousand causes that can, and ten thousand that cannot, be recounted. Perhaps no extensive and multifarious performance was ever effected within the term originally fixed in the undertaker's mind. He that runs against time has an antagonist not subject to casualties.

The encouragement given to this translation, though report seems to have overrated it, was such as the world has not often seen. The subscribers were five hundred and seventy-five. The copies for which subscriptions were given were six hundred and fifty-four, and only six hundred and sixty were printed. For these copies Pope had nothing to pay ; he therefore received, including the two hundred pounds a volume, five thousand three hundred and twenty pounds four shillings, without deduction, as the books were supplied by Lintot.

By the success of his subscription Pope was relieved from those pecuniary distresses with which, notwithstanding his popularity, he had hitherto struggled. Lord Oxford had often lamented his disqualification for public employment, but never proposed a pension. While the translation of Homer was in its progress, Mr. Craggs, then secretary of state, offered to procure him a pension, which, at least during his ministry, might be enjoyed with secrecy. This was not accepted by Pope, who told him, however, that if he should be pressed with want of money, he would send to him for occasional supplies. Craggs was not long in power, and was never solicited for money by Pope, who disdained to beg what he did not want.

With the product of this subscription, which he had too much discretion to squander, he secured his future life from want by considerable annuities. The estate of the Duke of Buckingham was found to have been charged with five hundred pounds a years, payable to Pope, which doubtless his translation enabled him to purchase.

It cannot be unwelcome to literary curiosity that I deduce thus minutely the history of the English " Iliad." It is certainly the noblest version of poetry which the world has ever seen ; and its publication must therefore be considered as one of the great events in the annals of learning.

To those who have skill to estimate the excellence and difficulty of this great work, it must be very desirable to know how

it was performed, and by what gradations it advanced to correctness. Of such an intellectual process the knowledge has
very rarely been attainable ; but happily there remains the
original copy of the " Iliad," which, being obtained by Bolingbroke as a curiosity, descended from him to Mallet, and
is now, by the solicitation of the late Dr. Maty, reposited in
the Museum.

Between this manuscript, which is written upon accidental
fragments of paper, and the printed edition, there must have
been an intermediate copy, that was perhaps destroyed as it returned from the press.

From the first copy I have procured a few transcripts, and
shall exhibit first the printed lines, distinguished by inverted
commas ; then those of the manuscripts, with all their variations. Those words which are given in *italics* are cancelled in
the copy, and the words placed under them adopted in their
stead.

The beginning of the first book stands thus :

> " The wrath of Peleus' son, the direful spring
> Of all the Grecian woes, O Goddess, sing,
> That wrath which hurl'd to Pluto's gloomy reign
> The souls of mighty chiefs untimely slain."

> The stern Pelides' *rage*, O Goddess, sing,
>   wrath
> Of all the woes *of Greece* the fatal spring,
>   Grecian
> That strew'd with *warriors* dead the Phrygian plain,
>   heroes
> And *peopled the dark hell with heroes* slain ;
> fill'd the shady hell with chiefs untimely

> " Whose limbs, unburied on the naked shore,
> Devouring dogs and hungry vultures tore,
> Since great Achilles and Atrides strove :
> Such was the sovereign doom, and such the will of Jove.'

> Whose limbs, unburied on the hostile shore,
> Devouring dogs and greedy vultures tore,
> Since first Atrides and Achilles strove :
> Such was the sovereign doom, and such the will of Jove.

> " Declare, O Muse, in what ill-fated hour
> Sprung the fierce strife, from what offended Power ?
> Latona's son a dire contagion spread,
> And heap'd the camp with mountains of the dead ;
> The King of men his reverend priest defied,
> And for the King's offence the people died."

Declare, O Goddess, what offended Power
Enflam'd their *rage*, in that *ill-omen'd* hour ;
        anger   fatal, hapless
Phœbus himself the *dire* debate procur'd,
        fierce
T' avenge the wrongs his injur'd priest endur'd ;
For this the God a dire infection spread,
And heap'd the camp with millions of the dead ;
The King of men the sacred Sire defied,
And for the King's offence the people died.

" For Chryses sought with costly gifts to gain
His captive daughter from the Victor's chain ;
Suppliant the venerable Father stands,
Apollo's awful ensigns grace his hands ;
By these he begs, and, lowly bending down,
Extends the sceptre and the laurel crown."

For Chryses sought by *presents to regain*
        costly gifts to gain
His captive daughter from the Victor's chain !
Suppliant the venerable Father stands,
Apollo's awful ensigns grac'd his hands.
By these he begs, and, lowly bending down
The golden sceptre and the laurel crown,
Presents the sceptre
For these as ensigns of his God he bare
The God that sends his golden shafts afar ,
Then, low on earth, the venerable man,
Suppliant, before the brother kings began.

" He sued to all, but chief implor'd for grace
The brother kings of Atreus' royal race : ·
Ye kings and warriors, may your vows be crown'd,
And Troy's proud walls lie level with the ground :
May Jove restore you, when your toils are o'er,
Safe to the pleasures of your native shore."

To all he sued, but chief implor'd for grace
The brother Kings of Atreus' royal race :
Ye *sons of Atreus*, may your vows be crown'd,
  kings and warriors
Your labors, by the Gods be all your labors crown'd,
So may the Gods your arms with conquest bless,
And Troy's proud walls *lie* level with the ground ;
Till   laid
And crown your labors with deserv'd success ;
May Jove restore you, when your toils are o'er,
Safe to the pleasures of your native shore.

" But, oh ! relieve a wretched parent's pain,
And give Chryseis to these arms again ;
If mercy fail, yet let my present move,
And dread avenging Phœbus, son of Jove."

But, oh ! relieve a hapless parent's pain,
And give my daughter to these arms again ;
Receive my gifts ; if mercy fails, yet let my present move,
And fear *the God that deals his darts around.*
      avenging Phœbus, son of Jove.

" The Greeks, in shouts, their joint assent declare
The priest to reverence and release the fair.
Not so Atrides ; he, with kingly pride,
Repuls'd the sacred Sire, and thus replied."

He said, the Greeks their joint assent declare,
The father said, the gen'rous Greeks relent,
T' accept the ransom, and release the fair ;
Revere the priest, and speak their joint assent ;
Not so *the tyrant,* he, with kingly pride,
      Atries
Repuls'd the sacred Sire, and thus replied.
    [Not so the tyrant. Dryden.]

Of these lines, and of the whole first book, I am told that
there was yet a former copy, more varied and more deformed
with interlineations.

The beginning of the second book varies very little from
the printed page, and is therefore set down without a parallel ;
the few differences do not require to be elaborately displayed.

    " Now pleasing sleep had seal'd each mortal eye ;
Stretch'd in their tents the Grecian leaders lie ;
Th' Immortals slumber'd on their thrones above,
All but the ever-watchful eye of Jove.
To honor Thetis' son he bends his care,
And plunge the Greeks in all the woes of war.
Then bids an empty phantom rise to sight,
And thus *commands* the vision of the night :
    directs
Fly hence, delusive dream, and, light as air,
To Agamemnon's royal tent repair ;
Bid him in arms draw forth th' embattled train,
March all his legions to the dusty plain.
Now tell the King 'tis giv'n him to destroy
Declare ev'n now
The lofty *walls* of wide-extended Troy ;
    tow'rs
For now no more the Gods with fate contend ;
At Juno's suit the heavenly factions end.
Destruction *hovers* o'er yon devoted wall,
    hangs
And nodding Ilium waits th' impending fall."

Invocation to the catalogue of ships.

" Say, Virgins, seated round the throne divine,
All-knowing Goddesses ! immortal Nine !
Since Earth's wide regions, Heav'n's unmeasur'd height,
And Hell's abyss, hide nothing from your sight
(We, wretched mortals ! lost in doubts below,
But guess by rumor, and but boast we know),
Oh ! say what heroes, fir'd by thirst of fame,
Or urg'd by wrongs, to Troy's destruction came !
To count them all demands a thousand tongues,
A throat of brass and adamantine lungs."

Now, Virgin Goddesses, immortal Nine !
That round Olympus' heavenly summit shine,
Who see through Heav'n and Earth, and Hell profound,
And all things know, and all things can resound !
Relate what armies sought the Trojan land,
What nations follow'd, and what chiefs command
(For doubtful fame distracts mankind below,
And nothing can we tell and nothing know) ;
Without your aid, to count th' unnumber'd train,
A thousand mouths, a thousand tongues, were vain.

Book v. *v.* I.

" But Pallas now Tydides' soul inspires,
Fills with her force, and warms with all her fires :
Above the Greeks his deathless fame to raise,
And crown her hero with distinguish'd praise,
High on his helm celestial lightnings play,
His beamy shield emits a living ray ;
Th' unwearied blaze incessant streams supplies,
Like the red star that fires th' autumnal skies."

But Pallas now Tydides' soul inspires,
Fills with her *rage*, and warms with all her fires ;
        force
O'er all the Greeks decrees his fame to raise,
Above the Greeks *her warrior's* fame to raise,
        his deathless
And crown her hero with *immortal* praise :
        distinguish'd
Bright from his beamy *crest* the lightnings play,
 High on   helm
From his broad buckler flash'd the living ray ;
High on his helm celestial lightnings play,
His beamy shield emits a living ray ;
The Goddess with her breath the flames supplies,
Bright as the star whose fires in Autumn rise ;
Her breath divine thick streaming flames supplies,
Bright as the star fires th' autumnal skies :
Th' unwearied blaze incessant streams supplies,
Like the red star that fires th' autumnal skies.

" When first he rears his radiant orb to sight,
And, bath'd in Ocean, shoots a keener light.

Such glories Pallas on the chief bestow'd,
Such from his arms the fierce effulgence flow'd ;
Onward she drives him, furious to engage,
Where the fight burns, and where the thickest rage."

When fresh he rears his radiant orb to sight
And gilds old Ocean with a blaze of light.
Bright as the star that fires th' autumnal skies,
Fresh from the deep, and gilds the seas and skies ;
Such glories Pallas on her chief bestow'd,
Such sparkling rays from his bright armor flow'd ;
Such from his arms the fierce effulgence flow'd ;
Onward she drives him *headlong* to engage,
          furious
Where the *war bleeds*, and where the *fiercest* rage.
   fight burns,   thickest

" The sons of Dares first the combat sought,
A wealthy priest, but rich without a fault ;
In Vulcan's fane the father's days were led,
The sons to toils of glorious battle bred."

There liv'd a Trojan—Dares was his name,
The priest of Vulcan, rich, yet void of blame ;
The sons of Dares first the combat sought,
A wealthy priest, but rich without a fault.

Conclusion of Book viii. *v.* 687.

" As when the moon, refulgent lamp of night,
O'er Heav'n's clear azure spreads her sacred light,
When not a breath disturbs the deep serene,
And not a cloud o'ercasts the solemn scene ;
Around her throne the vivid planets roll,
And stars unnumber'd gild the glowing pole ;
O'er the dark trees a yellower verdure shed,
And tip with silver every mountain's head ;
Then shine the vales, the rocks in prospect rise,
A flood of glory bursts from all the skies ;
The conscious swains, rejoicing in the sight,
Eye the blue vault, and bless the useful light.
So many flames before proud Ilion blaze,
And lighten glimmering Xanthus with their rays :
The long reflections of the distant fires
Gleam on the walls, and tremble on the spires.
A thousand piles the dusky horrors gild,
And shoot a shady lustre o'er the field.
Full fifty guards each flaming pile attend,
Whose umber'd arms by fits thick flashes send ;
Loud neigh the coursers o'er the heaps of corn,
And ardent warriors wait the rising morn."

As when in stillness of the silent night,
As when the moon in all her lustre bright ;
As when the moon, refulgent lamp of night,
O'er Heav'n's *clear* azure *sheds* her *silver* light ;
        pure   spreads   sacred

As still in air the trembling lustre stood,
And o'er its golden border shoots a flood ;
When *no loose gale* disturbs the deep serene,
  not a breath
And *no dim* cloud o'ercasts the solemn scene ;
  not a
Around her silver throne the planets glow,
And stars unnumber'd trembling beams bestow :
Around her throne the vivid planets roll
And stars unnumber'd gild the glowing pole ;
Clear gleams of light o'er the dark trees are seen,
    o'er the dark trees a yellow sheds,
O'er the dark trees a yellower *green* they shed
    gleam
    verdure
And tip with silver all the *mountain* heads,
    forest
And tip with silver every mountain's head,
The valleys open, and the forests rise,
The vales appear, the rocks in prospect rise,
Then shine the vales, the rocks in prospect rise,
All nature stands reveal'd before our eyes ;
A flood of glory bursts from all the skies.
The conscious shepherd, joyful at the sight,
Eyes the blue vault, and numbers every light.
The conscious *swains, rejoicing at the sight,*
    shepherds, gazing with delight
Eye the blue vault, and bless the *vivid* light,
    glorious
    useful
So many flames before *the navy* blaze,
    proud Ilion
And lighten glimmering Xanthus with their rays ;
Wide o'er the fields to Troy extend the gleams,
And tip the distant spires with fainter beams ;
The long reflections of the distant fires
Gild the high walls, and tremble on the spires ;
Gleam on the walls, and tremble on the spires ;
A thousand fires, at distant stations, bright,
Gild the dark prospect, and dispel the night.

Of these specimens every man who has cultivated poetry, or who delights to trace the mind from the rudeness of its first conceptions to the elegance of its last, will naturally desire a greater number ; but most other readers are already tired, and I am not writing only to poets and philosophers.

The " Iliad " was published volume by volume, as the translation proceeded : the four first books appeared in 1715. The expectation of this work was undoubtedly high, and every man who had connected his name with criticism or poetry was desirous of such intelligence as might enable him to talk upon the popular topic.   Halifax, who, by having been first a poet and then a patron of poetry, had acquired the right of being a judge, was willing to hear some books while they were yet unpublished. Of this rehearsal Pope afterwards gave the following account :

"The famous Lord Halifax was rather a pretender to taste than really possessed of it. When I had finished the two or three first books of my translation of the ' Iliad,' that lord desired to have the pleasure of hearing them read at his house— Addison, Congreve, and Garth were there at the reading. In four or five places Lord Halifax stopped me very civilly, and with a speech each time of much the same kind, ' I beg your pardon, Mr. Pope ; but there is something in that passage that does not quite please me. Be so good as to mark the place, and consider it a little at your leisure. I am sure you can give it a little turn.' I returned from Lord Halifax's with Dr. Garth, in his chariot ; and as we were going along was saying to the doctor that my lord had laid me under a great deal of difficulty by such loose and general observations ; that I had been thinking over the passages almost ever since, and could not guess at what it was that offended his lordship in either of them. Garth laughed heartily at my embarrassment ; said I had not been long enough acquainted with Lord Halifax to know his way yet ; that I need not puzzle myself about looking those places over and over when I got home. ' All you need do (says he) is to leave them just as they are ; call on Lord Halifax two or three months hence, thank him for his kind observations on those passages, and then read them to him as altered. I have known him much longer than you have, and will be answerable for the event.' I followed his advice, waited on Lord Halifax some time after, said I hoped he would find his objections to those passages removed, read them to him exactly as they were at first, and his lordship was extremely pleased with them, and cried out, ' Ay, now they are perfectly right ; nothing can be better.' "

It is seldom that the great or the wise suspect that they are despised or cheated. Halifax, thinking this a lucky opportunity of securing immortality, made some advances of favor and some overtures of advantage to Pope, which he seems to have received with sullen coldness. All our knowledge of this transaction is derived from a single letter (December 1, 1714), in which Pope says, "I am obliged to you, both for the favors you have done me and those you intend me. I distrust neither your will nor your memory, when it is to do good ; and if I ever become troublesome or solicitous, it must not be out of expectation, but out of gratitude. Your lordship may cause

me to live agreeably in the town, or contentedly in the country, which is really all the difference I set between an easy fortune and a small one.   It is indeed a high strain of generosity
in you to think of making me easy all my life, only because I
have been so happy as to divert you some few hours ; but, if I
may have leave to add, it is because you think me no enemy to
my native country, there will appear a better reason ; for I
must of consequence be very much (as I sincerely am) yours,
etc.''

These voluntary offers, and this faint acceptance, ended
without effect.   The patron was not accustomed to such frigid
gratitude, and the poet fed his own pride with the dignity of
independence.   They probably were suspicious of each other.
Pope would not dedicate till he saw at what rate his praise was
valued ; he would be '' troublesome out of gratitude, not expectation.''   Halifax thought himself entitled to confidence,
and would give nothing unless he knew what he should receive.
Their commerce had its beginning in hope of praise on one
side and of money on the other, and ended because Pope was
less eager of money than Halifax of praise.   It is not likely
that Halifax had any personal benevolence to Pope ; it is evident that Pope looked on Halifax with scorn and hatred.

The reputation of this great work failed of gaining him a
patron, but it deprived him of a friend.   Addison and he were
now at the head of poetry and criticism ; and both in such a
state of elevation, that, like the two rivals in the Roman state,
one could no longer bear an equal nor the other a superior.
Of the gradual abatement of kindness between friends, the beginning is often scarcely discernible to themselves, and the
process is continued by petty provocations and incivilities,
sometimes peevishly returned and sometimes contemptuously
neglected, which would escape all attention but that of pride,
and drop from any memory but that of resentment.   That the
quarrel of these two wits should be minutely deduced, is not to
be expected from a writer to whom, as Homer says, '' nothing
but rumor has reached, and who has no personal knowledge.''

Pope doubtless approached Addison, when the reputation
of their wit first brought them together, with the respect due to
a man whose abilities were acknowledged, and who, having
attained that eminence to which he was himself aspiring, had
in his hands the distribution of literary fame.   He paid court
with sufficient diligence by his prologue to '' Cato,'' by his
abuse of Dennis, and with praise yet more direct by his poem
on the '' Dialogues on Medals,'' of which the immediate publication was then intended.   In all this there was no hypocrisy ;

for he confessed that he found in Addison something more pleasing than in any other man.

It may be supposed, that as Pope saw himself favored by the world, and more frequently compared his own powers with those of others, his confidence increased and his submission lessened ; and that Addison felt no delight from the advances of a young wit who might soon contend with him for the highest place. Every great man, of whatever kind be his greatness, has among his friends those who officiously or insidiously quicken his attention to offences, heighten his disgust, and stimulate his resentment. Of such adherents Addison doubtless had many, and Pope was now too high to be without them.

From the emission and reception of the proposals for the " Iliad," the kindness of Addison seems to have abated. Jervas the painter once pleased himself (August 20, 1714) with imagining that he had re-established their friendship, and wrote to Pope that Addison once suspected him of too close a confederacy with Swift, but was now satisfied with his conduct. To this Pope answered, a week after, that his engagements to Swift were such as his services in regard to the subscription demanded, and that the Tories never put him under the necessity of asking leave to be grateful. " But," says he, " as Mr. Addison must be the judge in what regards himself, and seems to have no very just one in regard to me, so I must own to you I expect nothing but civility from him." In the same letter he mentions Philips as having been busy to kindle animosity between them ; but in a letter to Addison he expresses some consciousness of behavior inattentively deficient in respect.

Of Swift's industry in promoting the subscription there remains the testimony of Kennet, no friend to either him or Pope.

" November 2, 1713, Dr. Swift came into the coffee-house, and had a bow from everybody but me, who, I confess, could not but despise him. When I came to the ante-chamber to wait, before prayers, Dr. Swift was the principal man of talk and business, and acted as master of requests. Then he instructed a young nobleman that the *best poet in England* was Mr. Pope (a papist), who had begun a translation of Homer into English verse, for which *he must have them all subscribe ;* for, says he, the author *shall not* begin to print till *I have* a thousand guineas for him."

About this time it is likely that Steele, who was, with all his political fury, good-natured and officious, procured an interview between these angry rivals, which ended in aggravated malevolence. On this occasion, if the reports be true, Pope made his complaint with frankness and spirit, as a man undeservedly neglected or opposed, and Addison affected a contemptuous unconcern, and, in a calm, even voice, reproached Pope with his vanity, and telling him of the improvements which his early works had received from his own remarks and those of Steele, said that he, being now engaged in public business, had no longer any care for his poetical reputation, nor had any other desire, with regard to Pope, than that he should not by too much arrogance alienate the public.

To this Pope is said to have replied with great keenness and severity, upbraiding Addison with perpetual dependence, and with the abuse of those qualifications which he had obtained at the public cost, and charging him with mean endeavors to obstruct the progress of rising merit. The contest rose so high that they parted at last without any interchange of civility.

The first volume of Homer was (1715) in time published, and a rival version of the first "Iliad," for rivals the time of their appearance inevitably made them, was immediately printed, with the name of Tickell. It was soon perceived that among the followers of Addison, Tickell had the preference, and the critics and poets divided into factions. "I," says Pope, "have the town, that is, the mob, on my side ; but it is not uncommon for the smaller party to supply by industry what it wants in numbers. I appeal to the people as my rightful judges, and while they are not inclined to condemn me shall not fear the high-flyers at Button's." This opposition he immediately imputed to Addison, and complained of it in terms sufficiently resentful to Craggs, their common friend.

When Addison's opinion was asked, he declared the versions to be both good, but Tickell's the best that had ever been written ; and sometimes said that they were both good, but that Tickell had more of Homer.

Pope was now sufficiently irritated ; his reputation and his interest were at hazard. He once intended to print together the four versions of Dryden, Maynwaring, Pope, and Tickell, that they might be readily compared and fairly estimated. This design seems to have been defeated by the refusal of Tonson, who was the proprietor of the other three versions.

Pope intended, at another time, a rigorous criticism of Tickell's translation, and had marked a copy, which I have seen, in all places that appeared defective. But while he was thus meditating defence or revenge, his adversary sunk before him without a blow ; the voice of the public was not long divided, and the preference was universally given to Pope's performance.

He was convinced, by adding one circumstance to another, that the other translation was the work of Addison himself ; but if he knew it in Addison's lifetime, it does not appear that he told it. He left his illustrious antagonist to be punished by what has been considered as the most painful of all reflections, the remembrance of a crime perpetrated in vain.

The other circumstances of their quarrel were thus related by Pope :

" Philips seemed to have been encouraged to abuse me in coffee-houses and conversations ; and Gildon wrote a thing about Wycherley, in which he had abused both me and my relations very grossly. Lord Warwick himself told me one day that it was in vain for me to endeavor to be well with Mr. Addison ; that his jealous temper would never admit of a settled friendship between us ; and to convince me of what he had said, assured me that Addison had encouraged Gildon to publish those scandals, and had given him ten guineas after they were published. The next day, while I was heated with what I had heard, I wrote a letter to Mr. Addison, to let him know that I was not unacquainted with this behavior of his ; that, if I was to speak severely of him in return for it, it should be not in such a dirty way ; that I should rather tell him, himself, fairly of his faults, and allow his good qualities ; and that it should be something in the following manner ; I then adjoined the first sketch of what has since been called my satire on Addison. Mr. Addison used me very civilly ever after."

The verses on Addison, when they were sent to Atterbury, were considered by him as the most excellent of Pope's performances ; and the writer was advised, since he knew where his strength lay, not to suffer it to remain unemployed.

This year (1715) being by the subscription enabled to live more by choice, having persuaded his father to sell their estate at Binfield, he purchased, I think only for his life, that house at Twickenham, to which his residence afterwards procured so much celebration, and removed thither with his father and mother.

Here he planted the vines and the quincunx which his verses mention ; and being under the necessity of making a subterraneous passage to a garden on the other side of the road he adorned it with fossil bodies, and dignified it with the title of a grotto, a place of silence and retreat, from which he endeavored to persuade his friends and himself that cares and passions could be excluded.

A grotto is not often the wish or pleasure of an Englishman, who has more frequent need to solicit than exclude the sun ; but Pope's excavation was requisite as an entrance to his garden, and, as some men try to be proud of their defects, he extracted an ornament from an inconvenience, and vanity produced a grotto where necessity enforced a passage. It may be frequently remarked of the studious and speculative that they are proud of trifles, and that their amusements seem frivolous and childish ; whether it be that men conscious of great reputation think themselves above the reach of censure, and safe in the admission of negligent indulgences, or that mankind expect from elevated genius an uniformity of greatness, and watch its degradation with malicious wonder, like him who, having followed with his eye an eagle into the clouds, should lament that she ever descended to a perch.

While the volumes of his Homer were annually published, he collected his former works (1717) into one quarto volume, to which he prefixed a preface written with great sprightliness and elegance, which was afterwards reprinted, with some passages subjoined that he at first omitted ; other marginal additions of the same kind he made in the later editions of his poems. Waller remarks that poets lose half their praise because the reader knows not what they have blotted. Pope's voracity of fame taught him the art of obtaining the accumulated honor both of what he had published and of what he had suppressed.

In this year his father died suddenly, in his seventy-fifth year, having passed twenty-nine years in privacy. He is not known but by the character which his son has given him. If the money with which he retired was all gotten by himself, he had traded very successfully in times when sudden riches were rarely attainable.

The publication of the " Iliad" was at last completed in 1720. The splendor and success of this work raised Pope many enemies that endeavored to depreciate his abilities. Burnet, who was afterwards a judge of no mean reputation, censured him, in a piece called " Homerides," before it was published. Ducket likewise endeavored to make him ridiculous. Dennis was the perpetual persecutor of all his studies. But whoever his critics were, their writings are lost, and the names which are preserved are preserved in the " Dunciad."

In this disastrous year (1720) of national infatuation, when more riches than Peru can boast were expected from the South Sea, when the contagion of avarice tainted every mind, and even poets panted after wealth, Pope was seized with the universal passion and ventured some of his money. The stock rose in its price, and for awhile he thought himself the lord of thousands. But this dream of happiness did not last long, and he seems to have waked soon enough to get clear with the loss of what he once thought himself to have won, and perhaps not wholly of that.

Next year he published some select poems of his friend Dr. Parnell, with a very elegant dedication to the Earl of Oxford, who, after all his struggles and dangers, then lived in retirement, still under the frown of a victorious faction, who could take no pleasure in hearing his praise.

He gave, the same year (1721), an edition of Shakespeare. His name was now of so much authority that Tonson thought himself entitled, by annexing it, to demand a subscription of six guineas for Shakespeare's plays in six quarto volumes ; nor did his expectation much deceive him, for of seven hundred and fifty which he printed, he dispersed a great number at the price proposed. The reputation of that edition indeed sunk afterwards so low that one hundred and forty copies were sold at sixteen shillings each.

On this undertaking, to which Pope was induced by a reward of two hundred and seventeen pounds twelve shillings, he seems never to have reflected afterwards without vexation ; for Theobald, a man of heavy diligence, with very slender powers, first, in a book called " Shakespeare Restored," and then in a formal edition, detected his deficiencies with all the insolence of victory ; and as he was now high enough to be feared and hated, Theobald had from others all the help that could be supplied by the desire of humbling a haughty character.

From this time Pope became an enemy to editors, collators, commentators, and verbal critics, and hoped to persuade the world that he miscarried in this undertaking only by having a mind too great for such minute employment.

Pope in his edition undoubtedly did many things wrong, and left many things undone ; but let him not be defrauded of his due praise. He was the first that knew, at least the first that told, by what helps the text might be improved. If he inspected the early editions negligently, he taught others to be more accurate. In his preface he expanded with great skill and elegance the character which had been given of Shakespeare by Dryden, and he drew the public attention upon his works, which, though often mentioned, had been little read.

Soon after the appearance of the " Iliad," resolving not to let the general kindness cool, he published proposals for a

translation of the " Odyssey," in five volumes, for five guineas.
He was willing, however, now to have associates in his labor,
being either weary with toiling upon another's thoughts, or
having heard, as Ruffhead relates, that Fenton and Broome had
already begun the work, and liking better to have them con-
federates than rivals.

In the patent, instead of saying that he had " translated"
the " Odyssey," as he had said of the " Iliad," he says that he
had " undertaken" a translation ; and in the proposals the
subscription is said to be not solely for his own use, but for
that of " two of his friends who have assisted him in this
work."

In 1723, while he was engaged in this new version, he appeared before the Lords at the memorable trial of Bishop Atterbury, with whom he had lived in great familiarity and frequent
correspondence.   Atterbury had honestly recommended to him
the study of the popish controversy, in hope of his conversion,
to which Pope answered in a manner that cannot much recommend his principles or his judgment.   In questions and projects of learning they agreed better.   He was called at the trial
to give an account of Atterbury's domestic life and private employment, that it might appear how little time he had left for
plots.   Pope had but few words to utter, and in those few he
made several blunders.

His letters to Atterbury express the utmost esteem, tenderness, and gratitude ; " perhaps," says he, " it is not only in
this world that I may have cause to remember the Bishop of
Rochester."   At their last interview in the tower Atterbury
presented him with a Bible.

Of the " Odyssey" Pope translated only twelve books, the
rest were the work of Broome and Fenton ; the notes were
written wholly by Broome, who was not over-liberally rewarded.   The public was carefully kept ignorant of the several
shares, and an account was subjoined at the conclusion which
is now known not to be true.

The first copy of Pope's books, with those of Fenton, are
to be seen in the Museum.   The parts of Pope are less inter-
lined than the " Iliad," and the latter books of the " Iliad"
less than the former.   He grew dexterous by practice, and
every sheet enabled him to write the next with more facility.
The books of Fenton have very few alterations by the hand of
Pope.   Those of Broome have not been found ; but Pope
complained, as it is reported, that he had much trouble in correcting them.

His contract with Lintot was the same as for the " Iliad,"

except that only one hundred pounds were to be paid him for each volume. The number of subscribers were five hundred and seventy-four, and of copies eight hundred and nineteen ; so that his profit, when he had paid his assistants, was still very considerable. The work was finished in 1725, and from that time he resolved to make no more translations.

The sale did not answer Lintot's expectation ; and he then pretended to discover something of fraud in Pope, and commenced or threatened a suit in Chancery.

On the English " Odyssey" a criticism was published by Spence, at that time prelector of poetry at Oxford, a man whose learning was not very great, and whose mind was not very powerful. His criticism, however, was commonly just. What he thought he thought rightly, and his remarks were recommended by his coolness and candor. In him Pope had the first experience of a critic without malevolence, who thought it as much his duty to display beauties as expose faults ; who censured with respect and praised with alacrity.

With this criticism Pope was so little offended that he sought the acquaintance of the writer, who lived with him from that time in great familiarity, attended him in his last hours, and compiled memorials of his conversation. The regard of Pope recommended him to the great and powerful, and he obtained very valuable preferments in the church.

Not long after, Pope was returning home from a visit in a friend's coach, which, in passing a bridge, was overturned into the water ; the windows were closed, and being unable to force them open, he was in danger of immediate death, when the postilion snatched him out by breaking the glass, of which the fragments cut two of his fingers in such a manner that he lost their use.

Voltaire, who was then in England, sent him a letter of consolation. He had been entertained by Pope at his table, where he talked with so much grossness that Mrs. Pope was driven from the room. Pope discovered, by a trick, that he was a spy for the court, and never considered him as a man worthy of confidence.

He soon afterwards (1727) joined with Swift, who was then in England, to publish three volumes of " Miscellanies," in which among other things he inserted the " Memoirs of a Parish Clerk," in ridicule of Burnet's importance in his own History, and a " Debate upon Black and White Horses," written in all the formalities of a legal process, by the assistance, as is said, of Mr. Fortescue, afterwards master of the rolls. Before these " Miscellanies" is a preface signed by Swift and

Pope, but apparently written by Pope, in which he makes a ridiculous and romantic complaint of the robberies committed upon authors by the clandestine seizure and sale of their papers. He tells in tragic strains how " the cabinets of the sick and the closets of the dead have been broken open and ransacked ;" as if those violences were often committed for papers of uncertain and accidental value which are rarely provoked by real treasures ; as if epigrams and essays were in danger where gold and diamonds are safe. A cat hunted for his musk is, according to Pope's account, but the emblem of a wit winded by booksellers.

His complaint, however, received some attestation ; for the same year the " Letters" written by him to Mr. Cromwell in his youth were sold by Mrs. Thomas to Curll, who printed them.

In these " Miscellanies" was first published the " Art of Sinking in Poetry," which, by such a train of consequences as usually passes in literary quarrels, gave in a short time, according to Pope's account, occasion to the " Dunciad."

In the following year (1728) he began to put Atterbury's advice in practice, and showed his satirical powers by publishing the " Dunciad," one of his greatest and most elaborate performances, in which he endeavored to sink into contempt all the writers by whom he had been attacked, and some others whom he thought unable to defend themselves.

At the head of the dunces he placed poor Theobald, whom he accused of ingratitude, but whose real crime was supposed to be that of having revised " Shakespeare" more happily than himself. This satire had the effect which he intended, by blasting the characters which it touched. Ralph, who unnecessarily interposing in the quarrel, got a place in a subsequent edition, complained that for a time he was in danger of starving, as the booksellers had no longer any confidence in his capacity.

The prevalence of this poem was gradual and slow : the plan, if not wholly new, was little understood by common readers. Many of the allusions required illustration ; the names were often expressed only by the initial and final letters, and, if they had been printed at length, were such as few had known or recollected. The subject itself had nothing generally interesting, for whom did it concern to know that one or another scribbler was a dunce ? If, therefore, it had been possible for those who were attacked to conceal their pain and their resentment, the " Dunciad" might have made its way very slowly in the world.

This, however, was not to be expected : every man is of

importance to himself, and therefore, in his own opinion, to others, and, supposing the world already acquainted with all his pleasures and his pains, is perhaps the first to publish injuries or misfortunes which had never been known unless related by himself, and at which those that hear them will only laugh ; for no man sympathizes with the sorrows of vanity.

The history of the " Dunciad " is very minutely related by Pope himself in a dedication which he wrote to Lord Middlesex in the name of Savage.

" I will relate the war of the ' Dunces ' (for so it has been commonly called), which began in the year 1727 and ended in 1730.

" When Dr. Swift and Mr. Pope thought it proper, for reasons specified in the preface to their Miscellanies, to publish such little pieces of theirs as had casually got abroad, there was added to them the ' Treatise of the Bathos,' or the ' Art of Sinking in Poetry.' It happened that in one chapter of this piece the several species of bad poets were ranged in classes, to which were prefixed almost all the letters of the alphabet (the greatest part of them at random) ; but such was the number of poets eminent in that art that some one or other took every letter to himself ; all fell into so violent a fury that for half a year or more the common newspapers (in most of which they had some property, as being hired writers) were filled with the most abusive falsehoods and scurrilities they could possibly devise ; a liberty noways to be wondered at in those people and in those papers that for many years during the uncontrolled license of the press had aspersed almost all the great characters of the age, and this with impunity, their own persons and names being utterly secret and obscure.

" This gave Mr. Pope the thought that he had now some opportunity of doing good by detecting and dragging into light these common enemies of mankind ; since, to invalidate this universal slander, it sufficed to show what contemptible men were the authors of it. He was not without hopes that by manifesting the dulness of those who had only malice to recommend them, either the booksellers would not find their account in employing them, or the men themselves, when discovered, want courage to proceed in so unlawful an occupation. This it was that gave birth to the ' Dunciad ;' and he thought it a happiness that by the late flood of slander on himself he had acquired such a peculiar right over their names as was necessary to this design.

" On the 12th of March, 1729, at St. James's, that poem was presented to the king and queen (who had before been pleased to read it) by the right honorable Sir Robert Walpole ; and, some days after, the whole impression was taken and dispersed by several noblemen and persons of the first distinction.

" It is certainly a true observation that no people are so impatient of censure as those who are the greatest slanderers, which was wonderfully exemplified on the occasion. On the day the book was first vended, a crowd of authors besieged the shop ; entreaties, advices, threats of law and battery, nay, cries of treason, were all employed to hinder the coming out of the ' Dunciad ; ' on the other side, the booksellers and hawkers made as great efforts to procure it. What could a few poor authors do against so great majority as the public ? There was no stopping a current with a finger ; so out it came.

" Many ludicrous circumstances attended it. The ' Dunces ' (for by this name they were called) held weekly clubs to consult of hostilities against the author : one wrote a letter to a great minister, assuring him Mr. Pope was the greatest enemy the government had ; and another bought his image in clay, to execute him in effigy, with which sad sort of satisfaction the gentlemen were a little comforted.

" Some false editions of the book having an owl in their frontispiece, the true one, to distinguish it, fixed in his stead an ass laden with authors. Then another surreptitious one being printed, with the same ass, the new edition in octavo returned for distinction to the owl again. Hence arose a great contest of booksellers against booksellers, and advertisements against advertisements, some recommending the edition of the owl and others the edition of the ass, by which names they came to be distinguished, to the great honor also of the gentlemen of the ' Dunciad.' "

Pope appears by this narrative to have contemplated his victory over the " Dunces" with great exultation ; and such was his delight in the tumult which he had raised, that for a while his natural sensibility was suspended, and he read reproaches and invectives without emotion, considering them only as the necessary effects of that pain which he rejoiced in having given.

It cannot, however, be concealed that by his own confession he was the aggressor ; for nobody believes that the letters in the " Bathos" were placed at random ; and it may be discovered that when he thinks himself concealed he indulges the common vanity of common men, and triumphs in those distinctions which he had affected to despise. He is proud that his book was presented to the king and queen by the right honorable Sir Robert Walpole ; he is proud that they had read it before ; he is proud that the edition was taken off by the nobility and persons of the first distinction.

The edition of which he speaks was, I believe, that which, by telling in the text the names, and in the notes the characters, of those whom he had satirized, was made intelligible and diverting. The critics had now declared their approbation of the plan, and the common reader began to like it without fear ; those who were strangers to petty literature, and therefore unable to decipher initials and blanks, had now names and persons brought within their view, and delighted in the visible effect of those shafts of malice which they had hitherto contemplated as shot into the air.

Dennis, upon the fresh provocation now given him, renewed the enmity which had for a time been appeased by mutual civilities, and published remarks, which he had till then suppressed, upon "The Rape of the Lock." Many more grumbled in secret, or vented their resentment in the newspapers by epigrams or invectives.

Ducket, indeed, being mentioned as loving Burnet with "pious passion," pretended that his moral character was injured, and for some time declared his resolution to take vengeance with a cudgel. But Pope appeased him by changing "pious passion" to "cordial friendship," and by a note, in which he vehemently disclaims the malignity of meaning imputed to the first expression.

Aaron Hill, who was represented as diving for the prize, expostulated with Pope in a manner so much superior to all mean solicitation, that Pope was reduced to sneak and shuffle, sometimes to deny, and sometimes to apologize : he first endeavors to wound, and is then afraid to own that he meant a blow.

The "Dunciad," in the complete edition, is addressed to Dr. Swift : of the notes, part were written by Dr. Arbuthnot ; and an apologetical letter was prefixed signed by Cleland, but supposed to have been written by Pope.

After this general war upon dulness he seems to have indulged himself awhile in tranquillity ; but his subsequent productions prove that he was not idle. He published (1731) a poem on "Taste," in which he very particularly and severely criticises the house, the furniture, the gardens, and the entertainments of Timon, a man of great wealth and little taste. By Timon he was universally supposed, and by the Earl of Burlington, to whom the poem is addressed, was privately said, to mean the Duke of Chandos ; a man perhaps too much delighted with pomp and show, but of a temper kind and beneficent, and who had consequently the voice of the public in his favor.

A violent outcry was therefore raised against the ingratitude and treachery of Pope, who was said to have been indebted to the patronage of Chandos for a present of a thousand pounds, and who gained the opportunity of insulting him by the kindness of his invitation.

The receipt of the thousand pounds Pope publicly denied ; but from the reproach which the attack on a character so amiable brought upon him he tried all means of escaping. The name of Cleland was again employed in an apology, by which no man was satisfied, and he was at last reduced to shelter his temerity behind dissimulation, and endeavor to make that disbelieved which he never had confidence openly to deny. He wrote an exculpatory letter to the duke, which was answered with great magnanimity, as by a man who accepted his excuse without believing his professions. He said that to have ridiculed his taste or his buildings had been an indifferent action in another man ; but that in Pope, after the reciprocal kindness that had been exchanged between them, it had been less easily excused.

Pope, in one of his letters, complaining of the treatment which his poem had found, " owns that such critics can intimidate him, nay, almost persuade him to write no more, which is a compliment this age deserves." The man who threatens the world is always ridiculous ; for the world can easily go on without him, and in a short time will cease to miss him. I have heard of an idiot who used to revenge his vexations by lying all night upon the bridge. " There is nothing," says Juvenal, " that a man will not believe in his own favor." Pope had been flattered till he thought himself one of the moving powers in the system of life. When he talked of laying down his pen those who sat round him entreated and implored, and self-love did not suffer him to suspect that they went away and laughed.

The following year deprived him of Gay, a man whom he had known early, and whom he seemed to love with more tenderness than any other of his literary friends. Pope was now forty-four years old ; an age at which the mind begins less easily to admit new confidence, and the will to grow less flexible ; and when, therefore, the departure of an old friend is very acutely felt.

In the next year he lost his mother, not by an unexpected death, for she lasted to the age of ninety-three ; but she did not die unlamented. The filial piety of Pope was in the highest degree amiable and exemplary; his parents had the happiness of living till he was at the summit of poetical reputation, till he was at ease in his fortune, and without a rival in his fame, and found no diminution of his respect or tenderness. Whatever was his pride, to them he was obedient; and whatever was his irritability, to them he was gentle. Life has among its soothing and quiet comforts few things better to give than such a son.

One of the passages of Pope's life which seems to deserve some inquiry was a publication of letters between him and many of his friends, which falling into the hands of Curll, a rapacious bookseller of no good fame, were by him printed and sold. This volume containing some letters from noblemen, Pope incited a prosecution against him in the House of Lords for breach of privilege, and attended himself to stimulate the resentment of his friends. Curll appeared at the bar, and, knowing himself in no great danger, spoke of Pope with very little reverence. " He has," said Curll, " a knack at versifying, but in prose I think myself a match for him." When the orders of the House were examined, none of them appeared to be infringed; Curll went away triumphant, and Pope was left to seek some other remedy.

Curll's account was, that one evening a man in a clergyman's gown, but with a lawyer's band, brought and offered to sale a number of printed volumes, which he found to be Pope's epistolary correspondence; that he asked no name, and was told none, but gave the price demanded, and thought himself authorized to use his purchase to his own advantage.

That Curll gave a true account of the transaction it is reasonable to believe, because no falsehood was ever detected; and when, some years afterwards, I mentioned it to Lintot, the son of Bernard, he declared his opinion to be that Pope knew better than anybody else how Curll obtained the copies, because another was at the same time sent to himself, for which no price had ever been demanded, as he made known his resolution not to pay a porter, and consequently not to deal with a nameless agent.

Such care had been taken to make them public that they were sent at once to two booksellers; to Curll, who was likely to seize them as prey, and to Lintot, who might be expected to give Pope information of the seeming injury. Lintot, I believe, did nothing; and Curll did what was expected. That to make them public was the only purpose may be reasonably supposed, because the numbers offered for sale by the

private messengers showed that hope of gain could not have
been the motive of the impression.

It seems that Pope, being desirous of printing his Letters, and not knowing how to do so without imputation of vanity, what has in this country been done very rarely, contrived
an appearance of compulsion, that when he could complain
that his letters were surreptitiously published, he might decently and defensively publish them himself.

Pope's private correspondence, thus promulgated, filled the
nation with praises of his candor, tenderness, and benevolence,
the purity of his purposes, and the fidelity of his friendship.
There were some letters which a very good or a very wise man
would wish suppressed; but as they had been already exposed it was impracticable now to retract them.

From the perusal of those Letters, Mr. Allen first conceived the desire of knowing him; and with so much zeal did
he cultivate the friendship which he had newly formed, that
when Pope told his purpose of vindicating his own property by
a genuine edition he offered to pay the cost.

This, however, Pope did not accept; but in time solicited
a subscription for a quarto volume, which appeared (1737), I
believe, with sufficient profit. In the preface he tells that his
Letters were reposited in a friend's library, said to be the
Earl of Oxford's, and that the copy thence stolen was sent to
the press. The story was doubtless received with different degrees of credit. It may be suspected that the preface to the
Miscellanies was written to prepare the public for such an
incident; and to strengthen this opinion James Worsdale, a
painter, who was employed in clandestine negotiations, but
whose veracity was very doubtful, declared that he was the
messenger who carried, by Pope's direction, the books to
Curll.

When they were thus published and avowed, as they had
relation to recent facts and persons either then living or not
yet forgotten, they may be supposed to have found readers;
but as the facts were minute, and the characters, being either
private or literary, were little known or little regarded, they
awakened no popular kindness or resentment : the book never
became much the subject of conversation; some read it as a
contemporary history, and some perhaps as a model of epistolary language; but those who read it did not talk of it. Not
much therefore was added by it to fame or envy, nor do I
remember that it produced either public praise or public censure.

It had however, in some degree, the recommendation of

novelty ; our language had few letters, except those of statesmen. Howel, indeed, about a century ago, published his Letters, which are commended by Morhoff, and which alone, of
his hundred volumes, continue his memory. Loveday's Letters
were printed only once ; those of Herbert and Suckling
are hardly known. Mrs. Phillips's [Orinda's] are equally
neglected. And those of Walsh seem written as exercises,
and were never sent to any living mistress or friend. Pope's
epistolary excellence had an open field ; he had no English
rival living or dead.

Pope is seen in this collection as connected with the other
contemporary wits, and certainly suffers no disgrace in the
comparison ; but it must be remembered that he had the
power of favoring himself ; he might have originally had publication in his mind, and have written with care, or have afterwards selected those which he had most happily conceived or
most diligently labored ; and I know not whether there does
not appear something more studied and artificial in his productions than the rest, except one long letter by Bolingbroke, composed with the skill and industry of a professed author. It is
indeed not easy to distinguish affectation from habit ; he that
has once studiously formed a style rarely writes afterwards
with complete ease. Pope may be said to write always with
his reputation in his head ; Swift, perhaps, like a man who
remembered he was writing to Pope ; but Arbuthnot, like one
who lets thoughts drop from his pen as they rise into his mind.

Before these Letters appeared, he published the first
part of what he persuaded himself to think a system of ethics,
under the title of " An Essay on Man ;" which, if his letter to
Swift (of September 14, 1725) be rightly explained by the commentator, had been eight years under his consideration, and of
which he seems to have desired the success with great solicitude. He had now many open and doubtless many secret enemies. The " Dunces" were yet smarting with the war ; and
the superiority which he publicly arrogated disposed the world
to wish his humiliation.

All this he knew, and against all this he provided. His
own name, and that of his friend to whom the work is inscribed, were in the first editions carefully suppressed ; and the
poem, being of a new kind, was ascribed to one or another, as
favor determined or conjecture wandered : it was given, says
Warburton, to every man, except him only who could write it.
Those who like only when they like the author, and who are
under the dominion of a name, condemned it ; and those admired it who are willing to scatter praise at random, which,

while it is unappropriated, excites no envy. Those friends of Pope that were trusted with the secret went about lavishing honors on the new-born poet, and hinting that Pope was never so much in danger from any former rival.

To those authors whom he had personally offended, and to those whose opinion the world considered as decisive, and whom he suspected of envy or malevolence, he sent his essay as a present before publication, that they might defeat their own enmity by praises which they could not afterwards decently retract.

With these precautions (1733) was published the first part of the "Essay on Man." There had been for some time a report that Pope was busy on a system of morality ; but this design was not discovered in the new poem, which had a form and a title with which its readers were unacquainted. Its reception was not uniform ; some thought it a very imperfect piece, though not without good lines. When the author was unknown, some, as will always happen, favored him as an adventurer, and some censured him as an intruder ; but all thought him above neglect ; the sale increased and editions were multiplied.

The subsequent editions of the first epistle exhibited two memorable corrections. At first the poet and his friend

> " Expatiate freely o'er the scene of man,
> A mighty maze *of walks without a plan :*"

for which he wrote afterwards,

> " A mighty maze, *but not without a plan ;*"

for if there were no plan it were in vain to describe or to trace the maze.

The other alteration was of these lines :

> " And spite of pride, *and in thy reason's spite,*
> One truth is clear, whatever is, is right ;"

but having afterwards discovered, or been shown, that the "truth" which subsisted "in spite of reason" could not be very "clear," he substituted

> " And spite of pride, *in erring reason's spite.*"

To such oversights will the most vigorous mind be liable when it is employed at once upon argument and poetry.

The second and third epistles were published, and Pope was, I believe, more and more suspected of writing them ; at last, in 1734, he avowed the fourth, and claimed the honor of a moral poet.

In the conclusion it is sufficiently acknowledged that the doctrine of the "Essay on Man" was received from Bolingbroke, who is said to have ridiculed Pope, among those who enjoyed his confidence, as having adopted and advanced principles of which he did not perceive the consequence, and as blindly propagating opinions contrary to his own. That those communications had been consolidated into a scheme regularly drawn, and delivered to Pope, from whom it returned only transformed from prose to verse, has been reported, but can hardly be true. The Essay plainly appears the fabric of a poet ; what Bolingbroke supplied could be only the first principles ; the order, illustration, and embellishments must all be Pope's.

These principles it is not my business to clear from obscurity, dogmatism, or falsehood ; but they were not immediately examined ; philosophy and poetry have not often the same readers ; and the Essay abounded in splendid amplifications and sparkling sentences, which were read and admired with no great attention to their ultimate purpose ; its flowers caught the eye, which did not see what the gay foliage concealed, and for a time flourished in the sunshine of universal approbation. So little was any evil tendency discovered, that, as innocence is unsuspicious, many read it for a manual of piety.

Its reputation soon invited a translator. It was first turned into French prose, and afterwards by Resnel into verse. Both translations fell into the hands of Crousaz, who first, when he had the version in prose, wrote a general censure, and afterwards reprinted Resnel's version, with particular remarks upon every paragraph.

Crousaz was a professor of Switzerland, eminent for his treatise of Logic and his "Examen de Pyrrhonisme ;" and, however little known or regarded here, was no mean antagonist. His mind was one of those in which philosophy and piety are happily united. He was accustomed to argument and disquisition, and perhaps was grown too desirous of detecting faults ; but his intentions were always right, his opinions were solid, and his religion pure.

His incessant vigilance for the promotion of piety disposed him to look with distrust upon all metaphysical systems of theology, and all schemes of virtue and happiness purely rational ; and therefore it was not long before he was persuaded that the positions of Pope, as they terminated for the most part in natural religion, were intended to draw mankind away from revelation, and to represent the whole course of things as a necessary concatenation of indissoluble fatality ; and it is undeniable that

in many passages a religious eye may easily discover expressions not very favorable to morals or to liberty.

About this time Warburton began to make his appearance
in the first ranks of learning. He was a man of vigorous faculties, a mind fervid and vehement, supplied by incessant and
unlimited inquiry, with wonderful extent and variety of knowledge, which yet had not oppressed his imagination nor clouded his perspicacity. To every work he brought a memory full
fraught, together with a fancy fertile of original combinations,
and at once exerted the powers of the scholar, the reasoner, and
the wit. But his knowledge was too multifarious to be always
exact, and his pursuits too eager to be always cautious. His
abilities gave him an haughty confidence, which he disdained
to conceal or mollify ; and his impatience of opposition disposed him to treat his adversaries with such contemptuous superiority as made his readers commonly his enemies, and excited against the advocate the wishes of some who favored the
cause. He seems to have adopted the Roman emperor's determination, *oderint dum metuant ;* he used no allurements of
gentle language, but wished to compel rather than persuade.

His style is copious without selection, and forcible without
neatness ; he took the words that presented themselves ; his
diction is coarse and impure, and his sentences are unmeas-
ured.

He had in the early part of his life pleased himself with
the notice of inferior wits, and corresponded with the enemies
of Pope. A letter was produced, when he had perhaps himself forgotten it, in which he tells Concanen, " Dryden, I observe, borrows for want of leisure, and Pope for want of genius ; Milton out of pride, and Addison out of modesty." And
when Theobald published " Shakespeare," in opposition to
Pope, the best notes were supplied by Warburton.

But the time was now come when Warburton was to change
his opinion, and Pope was to find a defender in him who had
contributed so much to the exaltation of his rival.

The arrogance of Warburton excited against him every artifice of offence, and therefore it may be supposed that his
union with Pope was censured as hypocritical inconstancy ; but
surely to think differently, at different times, of poetical merit,
may be easily allowed. Such opinions are often admitted, and
dismissed, without nice examination. Who is there that has not
found reason for changing his mind about questions of greater
importance ?

Warburton, whatever was his motive, undertook, without
solicitation, to rescue Pope from the talons of Crousaz, by freeing

him from the imputation of favoring fatality, or rejecting revelation, and from month to month continued a vindication of
the " Essay on Man" in the literary journal of that time, called " The Republic of Letters."

Pope, who probably began to doubt the tendency of his
own work, was glad that the positions, of which he perceived
himself not to know the full meaning, could by any mode of
interpretation be made to mean well. How much he was
pleased with his gratuitous defender, the following letter evidently shows :

" April 11, 1732.
" SIR,

" I have just received from Mr. R. two more of your letters. It is in the greatest hurry imaginable that I write this ;
but I cannot help thanking you in particular for your third letter, which is so extremely clear, short, and full, that I think
Mr. Crousaz ought never to have another answer, and deserved
not so good an one. I can only say, you do him too much
honor, and me too much right, so odd as the expression
seems ; for you have made my system as clear as I ought to
have done, and could not. It is indeed the same system as
mine, but illustrated with a ray of your own, as they say our
natural body is the same still when it is glorified. I am sure I
like it better than I did before, and so will every man else. I
know I meant just what you explain ; but I did not explain my
own meaning so well as you. You understand me as well as I
do myself ; but you express me better than I could express
myself. Pray accept the sincerest acknowledgments. I cannot but wish these letters were put together in one book, and
intend (with your leave) to procure a translation of part at
least, or of all of them, into French ; but I shall not proceed a
step without your consent and opinion," etc.

By this fond and eager acceptance of an exculpatory comment, Pope testified that, whatever might be the seeming or
real import of the principles which he had received from Bolingbroke, he had not intentionally attacked religion ; and Bolingbroke, if he meant to make him, without his own consent,
an instrument of mischief, found him now engaged, with his
eyes open, on the side of truth.

It is known that Bolingbroke concealed from Pope his real
opinions. He once discovered them to Mr. Hooke, who related them again to Pope, and was told by him that he must
have mistaken the meaning of what he heard ; and Bolingbroke, when Pope's uneasiness incited him to desire an explanation, declared that Hooke had misunderstood him.

Bolingbroke hated Warburton, who had drawn his pupil from him ; and a little before Pope's death they had a dispute, from which they parted with mutual aversion.

From this time Pope lived in the closest intimacy with his commentator, and amply rewarded his kindness and his zeal, for he introduced him to Mr. Murray, by whose interest he became preacher at Lincoln's-Inn ; and to Mr. Allen, who gave him his niece and his estate, and by consequence a bishopric.   When he died he left him the property of his works, a legacy which may be reasonably estimated at four thousand pounds.

Pope's fondness for the " Essay on Man" appeared by his desire of its propagation.   Dobson, who had gained reputation by his version of Prior's " Solomon," was employed by him to translate it into Latin verse, and was for that purpose some time at Twickenham ; but he left his work, whatever was the reason, unfinished, and, by Benson's invitation, undertook the longer task of " Paradise Lost."   Pope then desired his friend to find a scholar who should turn his Essay into Latin prose ; but no such performance has ever appeared.

Pope lived at this time *among the great*, with that reception and respect to which his works entitled him, and which he had not impaired by any private misconduct or factious partiality. Though Bolingbroke was his friend, Walpole was not his enemy ; but treated him with so much consideration, as, at his request, to solicit and obtain from the French minister an abbey for Mr. Southcot, whom he considered himself as obliged to reward, by this exertion of his interest, for the benefit which he had received from his attendance in a long illness.

It was said that when the court was at Richmond, Queen Caroline had declared her intention to visit him.   This may have been only a careless effusion, thought on no more : the report of such notice, however, was soon in many mouths ; and, if I do not forget or misapprehend Savage's account, Pope, pretending to decline what was not yet offered, left his house for a time, not, I suppose, for any other reason than lest he should be thought to stay at home in expectation of an honor which would not be conferred.   He was therefore angry at Swift, who represents him as " refusing the visits of a queen," because he knew that what had never been offered had never been refused.

Besides the general system of morality supposed to be contained in the " Essay on Man," it was his intention to write distinct poems upon the different duties or conditions of life ; one of which is the epistle to Lord Bathurst (1733) " On the Use of Riches," a piece on which he declared great labor to have been bestowed.

Into this poem some hints are historically thrown, and some known characters are introduced, with others of which it is difficult to say how far they are real or fictitious ; but the, praise of Kyrl, the Man of Ross, deserves particular examination, who, after a long and pompous enumeration of his public works and private charities, is said to have diffused all those blessings from *five hundred a year*. Wonders are willingly told and willingly heard. The truth is, that Kyrl was a man of known integrity and active benevolence, by whose solicitation the wealthy were persuaded to pay contributions to his charitable schemes ; this influence he obtained by an example of liberality exerted to the utmost extent of his power, and was thus enabled to give more than he had. This account Mr. Victor received from the minister of the place ; and I have preserved it that the praise of a good man, being made more credible, may be more solid. Narrations of romantic and impracticable virtue will be read with wonder, but that which is unattainable is recommended in vain ; that good may be endeavored, it must be shown to be possible.

This is the only piece in which the author has given a hint of his religion, by ridiculing the ceremony of burning the pope, and by mentioning with some indignation the inscription on the Monument.

When this poem was first published, the dialogue, having no letters of direction, was perplexed and obscure. Pope seems to have written with no very distinct idea ; for he calls that an " Epistle to Bathurst" in which Bathurst is introduced as speaking.

He afterwards (1734) inscribed to Lord Cobham his " Characters of Men," written with close attention to the operations of the mind and modifications of life. In this poem he has endeavored to establish and exemplify his favorite theory of the *ruling passion*, by which he means an original direction of desire to some particular object ; an innate affection, which gives all action a determinate and invariable tendency, and operates upon the whole system of life, either openly or more secretly by the intervention of some accidental or subordinate propension.

Of any passion thus innate and irresistible the existence may reasonably be doubted. Human characters are by no means constant ; men change by change of place, of fortune, of acquaintance ; he who is at one time a lover of pleasure is at another a lover of money. Those indeed who attain any excellence commonly spend life in one pursuit ; for excellence is not often gained upon easier terms. But to the particular species of excellence men are directed not by an ascendant planet or predominating humor, but by the first book which they read, some early conversation which they heard, or some accident which excited ardor and emulation.

It must at least be allowed that this *ruling passion*, antecedent to reason and observation, must have an object independent of human contrivance ; for there can be no natural desire of artificial good. No man therefore can be born, in the strict acceptation, a lover of money ; for he may be born where money does not exist : nor can he be born, in a moral sense, a lover of his country ; for society, politically regulated, is a state contradistinguished from a state of nature ; and any attention to that coalition of interests which makes the happiness of a country is possible only to those whom inquiry and reflection have enabled to comprehend it.

This doctrine is in itself pernicious as well as false ; its tendency is to produce the belief of a kind of moral predestination or overruling principle which cannot be resisted ; he that admits it is prepared to comply with every desire that caprice or opportunity shall excite, and to flatter himself that he submits only to the lawful dominion of Nature in obeying the resistless authority of his *ruling passion*.

Pope has formed his theory with so little skill, that in the examples by which he illustrates and confirms it he has confounded passions, appetites, and habits.

To the " Characters of Men," he added soon after, in an epistle supposed to have been addressed to Martha Blount, but which the last edition has taken from her, the " Characters of Women." This poem, which was labored with great diligence, and in the author's opinion with great success, was neglected at its first publication, as the commentator supposes, because the public was informed by an advertisement that it contained *no character drawn from the life;* an assertion which Pope probably did not expect, nor wish to have been believed, and which he soon gave his readers sufficient reason to distrust by telling them in a note that the work was imperfect, because part of his subject was *vice too high* to be yet exposed.

The time, however, soon came in which it was safe to display the Duchess of Marlborough under the name of Atossa ; and her character was inserted with no great honor to the writer's gratitude.

He published from time to time (between 1730 and 1740) imitations of different poems of Horace, generally with his name, and once, as was suspected, without it. What he was upon moral principles ashamed to own, he ought to have suppressed. Of these pieces it is useless to settle the dates, as they had seldom much relation to the times, and perhaps had been long in his hands. /

This mode of imitation, in which the ancients are familiarized by adapting their sentiments to modern topics, by making Horace say of Shakespeare what he originally said of Ennius, and accommodating his satires on Pantolabus and Nomentanus to the flatterers and prodigals of our own time, was first practised in the reign of Charles the Second by Oldham and Rochester ; at least I remember no instances more ancient. It is a kind of middle composition between translation and original design, which pleases when the thoughts are unexpectedly applicable and the parallels lucky. It seems to have been Pope's favorite amusement, for he has carried it further than any former poet.

He published likewise a revival, in smoother numbers, of Dr. Donne's " Satires," which was recommeded to him by the Duke of Shrewsbury and the Earl of Oxford. They made no great impression on the public. Pope seems to have known their imbecility, and therefore suppressed them while he was yet contending to rise in reputation, but ventured them when he thought their deficiencies more likely to be imputed to Donne than to himself.

The epistle to Dr. Arbuthnot, which seems to be derived in its first design from Boileau's " Address á son Esprit," was published in January, 1735, about a month before the death of him to whom it is inscribed. It is to be regretted that either honor or pleasure should have been missed by Arbuthnot, a man estimable for his learning, amiable for his life, and venerable for his piety.

Arbuthnot was a man of great comprehension, skilful in his profession, versed in the sciences, acquainted with ancient literature, and able to animate his mass of knowledge by a bright and active imagination ; a scholar with great brilliance of wit ; a wit who, in the crowd of life, retained and discovered a noble ardor of religious zeal.

In this poem Pope seems to reckon with the public. He vindicates himself from censures, and with dignity rather than arrogance enforces his own claims to kindness and respect.

Into this poem are interwoven several paragraphs which had been before printed as a fragment, and among them the satirical lines upon Addison, of which the last couplet has been twice corrected. It was at first,

" Who would not smile if such a man there be ?
Who would not laugh if Addison were he ?"

Then,

" Who would not grieve if such a man there be ?
Who would not laugh if Addison were he ?"

At last it is,

" Who but must laugh if such a man there be ?
Who would not weep if Atticus were he ?"

He was at this time at open war with Lord Hervey, who had distinguished himself as a steady adherent to the ministry ; and, being offended with a contemptuous answer to one of his pamphlets, had summoned Pulteney to a duel. Whether he or Pope made the first attack, perhaps cannot now be easily known : he had written an invective against Pope, whom he calls " Hard as thy heart, and as thy birth obscure," and hints that his father was a *hatter*. To this Pope wrote a reply in verse and prose ; the verses are in this poem, and the prose, though it was never sent, is printed among his letters, but to a cool reader of the present time exhibits nothing but tedious malignity.

His last satires of the general kind were two dialogues, named, from the year in which they were published, " Seventeen Hundred and Thirty-eight." In these poems many are praised and many reproached. Pope was then entangled in the opposition, a follower of the Prince of Wales, who dined at his house, and the friend of many who obstructed and censured the conduct of the ministers. His political partiality was too plainly shown ; he forgot the prudence with which he passed, in his earlier years, uninjured and unoffending, through much more violent conflicts of faction.

In the first dialogue, having an opportunity of praising Allen of Bath, he asked his leave to mention him as a man not illustrious by any merit of his ancestors, and called him in his verses " low-born Allen." Men are seldom satisfied with praise introduced or followed by any mention or defect. Allen seems not to have taken any pleasure in his epithet, which was afterwards softened into " humble Allen."

In the second dialogue he took some liberty with one of the Foxes, among others, which Fox, in a reply to Lyttleton, took an opportunity of repaying by reproaching him with the friendship of a lampooner, who scattered his ink without fear or decency, and against whom he hoped the resentment of the legislature would quickly be discharged.

About this time Paul Whitehead, a small poet, was summoned before the Lords for a poem called " Manners," together with Dodsley his publisher. Whitehead, who hung loose upon society, skulked and escaped ; but Dodsley's shop and family made his appearance necessary. He was, however, soon dismissed, and the whole process was probably intended rather to intimidate Pope than to punish Whitehead.

Pope never afterwards attempted to join the patriot with the poet, nor drew his pen upon statesmen. That he desisted from his attempts of reformation is imputed by his commentator to his despair of prevailing over the corruption of the time. He was not likely to have been ever of opinion that the dread of his satire would countervail the love of power or of money ; he pleased himself with being important and formidable, and gratified sometimes his pride, and sometimes his resentment, till at last he began to think he should be more safe if he were less busy.

The '' Memoirs of Scriblerus,'' published about this time, extend only to the first book of a work projected in concert by Pope, Swift, and Arbuthnot, who used to meet in the time of Queen Anne, and denominated themselves the '' Scriblerus Club.'' Their purpose was to censure the abuses of learning by a fictitious life of an infatuated scholar. They were dispersed, the design was never completed, and Warburton laments its miscarriage as an event very disastrous to polite letters.

If the whole may be estimated by this specimen, which seems to be the production of Arbuthnot, with a few touches perhaps by Pope, the want of more will not be much lamented ; for the follies which the writer ridicules are so little practised that they are not known ; nor can the satire be understood but by the learned : he raises phantoms of absurdity and then drives them away. He cures diseases that were never felt.

For this reason this joint production of three great writers has never obtained any notice from mankind ; it has been little read, or when read has been forgotten, as no man could be wiser, better, or merrier by remembering it.

The design cannot boast of much originality ; for besides its general resemblance to '' Don Quixote,'' there will be found in it particular imitations of the '' History of Mr. Ouffle.''

Swift carried so much of it into Ireland as supplied him with hints for his '' Travels,'' and with those the world might have been contented though the rest had been suppressed.

Pope had sought for images and sentiments in a region not known to have been explored by many other of the English writers ; he had consulted the modern writers of Latin poetry, a class of authors whom Boileau endeavored to bring into contempt, and who are too generally neglected. Pope, how-

ever, was not ashamed of their acquaintance, nor ungrateful
for the advantages which he might have derived from it.   A
small selection from the Italians who wrote in Latin had been
published at London, about the latter end of the last century,
by a man who concealed his name, but whom his preface shows
to have been well qualified for his undertaking.   This collection
Pope amplified by more than half, and (1740) published it in
two volumes, but injuriously omitted his predecessor's preface.
To these books, which had nothing but the mere text, no regard was paid ; the authors were still neglected, and the editor
was neither praised nor censured.

He did not sink into idleness ; he had planned a work,
which he considered as subsequent to his " Essay on Man," of
which he has given this account to Dr. Swift :

" March 25, 1736.

" If ever I write any more epistles in verse, one of them
shall be addressed to you.   I have long concerted it, and begun it ; but I would make what bears your name as finished as
my last work ought to be, that is to say, more finished than
any of the rest.   The subject is large, and will divide into four
epistles, which naturally follow the ' Essay on Man,' viz., 1. Of
the Extent and Limits of Human Reason and Science.   2. A
View of the useful and therefore attainable, and of the un-
useful and therefore unattainable, Arts.   3. Of the Nature,
Ends, Application, and Use of different Capacities.   4. Of the
Use of Learning, of the Science of the World, and of Wit.   It
will conclude with a satire against the misapplication of all
these, exemplified by pictures, characters, and examples."

This work, in its full extent, being now afflicted with an
asthma, and finding the powers of life gradually declining, he
had no longer courage to undertake ; but from the materials
which he had provided, he added, at Warburton's request, another book to the " Dunciad," of which the design is to ridicule such studies as are either hopeless or useless, as either
pursue what is unattainable, or what, if it be attained, is of no
use.

When this book was printed (1742) the laurel had been for
some time upon the head of Cibber, a man whom it cannot
be supposed that Pope could regard with much kindness or
esteem, though in one of the imitations of Horace he has liberally enough praised the " Careless Husband."   In the " Dunciad," among other worthless scribblers, he had mentioned
Cibber, who, in his " Apology," complains of the great poet's

unkindness as more injurious "because," says he, "I never have offended him."

It might have been expected that Pope should have been, in some degree, mollified by this submissive gentleness, but no such consequence appeared. Though he condescended to commend Cibber once, he mentioned him afterwards contemptuously in one of his satires, and again in his epistle to Arbuthnot ; and in the fourth book of the "Dunciad" attacked him with acrimony, to which the provocation is not easily discoverable. Perhaps he imagined that in ridiculing the laureate, he satirized those by whom the laurel had been given, and gratified that ambitious petulance with which he affected to insult the great.

The severity of this satire left Cibber no longer any patience. He had confidence enough in his own powers to believe that he could disturb the quiet of his adversary, and doubtless did not want instigators, who, without any care about the victory, desired to amuse themselves by looking on the contest. He therefore gave the town a pamphlet, in which he declares his resolution from that time never to bear another blow without returning it, and to tire out his adversary by perseverance, if he cannot conquer him by strength.

The incessant and unappeasable malignity of Pope he imputes to a very distant cause. After the "Three Hours after Marriage" had been driven off the stage, by the offence which the mummy and crocodile gave the audience, while the exploded scene was yet fresh in memory, it happened that Cibber played Bayes in the "Rehearsal ;" and as it had been usual to enliven the part by the mention of any recent theatrical transactions, he said that he once thought to have introduced his lovers disguised in a mummy and a crocodile. "This," says he, "was received with loud claps, which indicated contempt of the play." Pope, who was behind the scenes, meeting him as he left the stage, "attacked him," as he says, "with all the virulence of a wit out of his senses ;" to which he replied, "That he would take no other notice of what was said by so particular a man, than to declare that as often as he played that part he would repeat the same provocation."

He shows his opinion to be that Pope was one of the authors of the play which he so zealously defended ; and adds an idle story of Pope's behavior at a tavern.

The pamphlet was written with little power of thought or language, and if suffered to remain without notice would have been very soon forgotten. Pope had now been enough acquainted with human life to know, if his passion had not been too powerful for his understanding, that, from a contention like his with Cibber, the world seeks nothing but diversion, which is given at the expense of the higher character. When Cibber lampooned Pope, curiosity was excited ; what Pope could say of Cibber nobody inquired, but in hope that Pope's asperity might betray his pain and lessen his dignity.

He should therefore have suffered the pamphlet to flutter and die, without confessing that it stung him. The dishonor of being shown as Cibber's antagonist could never be compensated by the victory. Cibber had nothing to lose ; when Pope had exhausted all his malignity upon him, he would rise in the esteem both of his friends and his enemies. Silence only could have made him despicable ; the blow which did not appear to be felt would have been struck in vain.

But Pope's irascibility prevailed, and he resolved to tell the whole English world that he was at war with Cibber ; and to show that he thought him no common adversary, he prepared no common vengeance ; he published a new edition of the " Dunciad," in which he degraded Theobald from his painful pre-eminence and enthroned Cibber in his stead. Unhappily the two heroes were of opposite characters, and Pope was unwilling to lose what he had already written ; he has therefore depraved his poem by giving to Cibber the old books, the old pedantry, and the sluggish pertinacity of Theobald.

Pope was ignorant enough of his own interest to make another change, and introduced Osborne contending for the prize among the booksellers. Osborne was a man entirely destitute of shame, without sense of any disgrace but that of poverty. He told me, when he was doing that which raised Pope's resentment, that he should be put into the " Dunciad ;" but he had the fate of ⸜ Cassandra. ⸝ I gave no credit to his prediction till in time I saw it accomplished. The shafts of satire were directed equally in vain against Cibber and Osborne, being repelled by the impenetrable impudence of one, and deadened by the impassive dulness of the other. Pope confessed his own pain by his anger ; but he gave no pain to those who had provoked him. He was able to hurt none but himself ; by transferring the same ridicule from one to another, he reduced himself to the insignificance of his own magpie, who from his cage calls cuckold at a venture.

Cibber, according to his engagement, repaid the " Dunciad " with another pamphlet, which Pope said " would be as good as a dose of hartshorn to him ;" but his tongue and his heart were at variance. I have heard Mr. Richardson relate that he attended his father, the painter, on a visit when one of

Cibber's pamphlets came into the hands of Pope, who said, "These things are my diversion." They sat by him while he perused it, and saw his features writhing with anguish ; and young Richardson said to his father, when they returned, that he hoped to be preserved from such diversion as had been that day the lot of Pope.

From this time, finding his diseases more oppressive, and his vital powers gradually declining, he no longer strained his faculties with any original composition, nor proposed any other employment for his remaining life than the revisal and correction of his former works, in which he received advice and assistance from Warburton, whom he appears to have trusted and honored in the highest degree.

He laid aside his epic poem, perhaps without much loss to mankind ; for his hero was Brutus the Trojan, who, according to a ridiculous fiction, established a colony in Britain. The subject therefore was of the fabulous age ; the actors were a race upon whom imagination has been exhausted and attention wearied, and to whom the mind will not easily be recalled when it is invited in blank verse, which Pope had adopted with great imprudence, and, I think, without due consideration of the nature of our language. The sketch is, at least in part, preserved by Ruffhead, by which it appears that Pope was thoughtless enough to model the names of his heroes with terminations not consistent with the time or country in which he places them.

He lingered through the next year, but perceived himself, as he expresses it, "going down the hill." He had for at least five years been afflicted with an asthma and other disorders which his physicians were unable to relieve. Towards the end of his life he consulted Dr. Thomson, a man who had, by large promises and free censures of the common practice of physic, forced himself up into sudden reputation. Thomson declared his distemper to be a dropsy, and evacuated part of the water by tincture of jalap, but confessed that his belly did not subside. Thomson had many enemies, and Pope was persuaded to dismiss him.

While he was yet capable of amusement and conversation, as he was one day sitting in the air with Lord Bolingbroke and Lord Marchmont, he saw his favorite, Martha Blount, at the bottom of the terrace, and asked Lord Bolingbroke to go and hand her up. Bolingbroke, not liking his errand, crossed his legs and sat still ; but Lord Marchmont, who was younger and less captious, waited on the lady, who, when he came to her, asked, "What, is he not dead yet ?" She is said to have neglected him with shameful unkindness in the latter time of his decay ; yet of the little which he had to leave she had a very great part. Their acquaintance began early ; the life of each was pictured on the other's mind ; their conversation therefore was endearing, for when they met there was an immediate coalition of congenial notions. Perhaps he considered her unwillingness to approach the chamber of sickness as female weakness or human frailty ; perhaps he was conscious to himself of peevishness and impatience, or, though he was offended by her inattention, might yet consider her merit as overbalancing her fault ; and if he had suffered his heart to be alienated from her, he could have found nothing that might fill her place ; he could have only shrunk within himself ; it was too late to transfer his confidence or fondness.

In May, 1744, his death was approaching ; on the 6th he was all day delirious, which he mentioned four days afterwards as a sufficient humiliation of the vanity of man ; he afterwards complained of seeing things as through a curtain and in false colors, and one day, in the presence of Dodsley, asked what arm it was that came out from the wall. He said that his greatest inconvenience was inability to think.

Bolingbroke sometimes wept over him in this state of helpless decay ; and being told by Spence that Pope, at the intermission of his deliriousness, was always saying something kind either of his present or absent friends, and that his humanity seemed to have survived his understanding, answered, " It has so ;" and added, " I never in my life knew a man that had so tender a heart for his particular friends, or more general friendship for mankind." At another time he said, " I have known Pope these thirty years, and value myself more in his friendship than—" His grief then suppressed his voice.

Pope expressed undoubting confidence of a future state. Being asked by his friend Mr. Hooke, a papist, whether he would not die like his father and mother, and whether a priest should not be called, he answered, " I do not think it is essential, but it will be very right, and I thank you for putting me in mind of it."

In the morning after the priest had given him the last sacraments, he said, " There is nothing that is meritorious but virtue and friendship, and indeed friendship itself is only a part of virtue."

He died in the evening of the 30th day of May, 1744, so placidly that the attendants did not discern the exact time of his expiration. He was buried at Twickenham, near his father and mother, where a monument has been erected to him by his commentator the Bishop of Gloucester.

He left the care of his papers to his executors ; first to Lord Bolingbroke, and, if he should not be living, to the Earl of Marchmont, undoubtedly expecting them to be proud of the trust and eager to extend his fame. But let no man dream of influence beyond his life. After a decent time, Dodsley the bookseller went to solicit preference as the publisher, and was told that the parcel had not been yet inspected ; and, whatever was the reason, the world has been disappointed of what was '' reserved for the next age.''

He lost, indeed, the favor of Bolingbroke by a kind of posthumous offence. The political pamphlet called '' The Patriot King'' had been put into his hands that he might pro-cure the impression of a very few copies, to be distributed, ac-cording to the author's direction, among his friends, and Pope assured him that no more had been printed than were allowed ; but, soon after his death, the printer brought and resigned a complete edition of fifteen hundred copies, which Pope had ordered him to print and retain in secret. He kept, as was observed, his engagement to Pope, better than Pope had kept it to his friend ; and nothing was known of the transaction till, upon the death of his employer, he thought himself obliged to deliver the books to the right owner, who, with great indig-nation, made a fire in his yard and delivered the whole impres-sion to the flames.

Hitherto nothing had been done which was not naturally dictated by resentment of violated faith ; resentment more acrimonious as the violator had been more loved or more trusted. But here the anger might have stopped ; the injury was private, and there was little danger from the example.

Bolingbroke, however, was not yet satisfied ; his thirst of vengeance incited him to blast the memory of the man over whom he had wept in his last struggles ; and he employed Mal-let, another friend of Pope, to tell the tale to the public with all its aggravations. Warburton, whose heart was warm with his legacy, and tender by the recent separation, thought it proper for him to interpose ; and undertook, not indeed to vindicate the action, for breach of trust has always something criminal, but to extenuate it by an apology. Having advanced what cannot be denied, that moral obliquity is made more or less excusable by the motives that produce it, he inquires what evil purpose could have induced Pope to break his promise. He could not delight his vanity by usurping the work, which, though not sold in shops, had been shown to a number more

than sufficent to preserve the author's claim ; he could not
gratify his avarice, for he could not sell his plunder till Bolingbroke was dead ; and even then, if the copy was left to another
his fraud would be defeated, and if left to himself, would be
useless.

Warburton therefore supposes, with great appearance of
reason, that the irregularity of his conduct proceeded wholly
from his zeal for Bolingbroke, who might perhaps have destroyed the pamphlet which Pope thought it his duty to pre-
seive, even without its author's approbation.   To this apology
an answer was written in "A Letter to the most impudent Man
Living."

He brought some reproach upon his own memory by the
petulant and contemptuous mention made in his will of Mr.
Allen, and an affected repayment of his benefactions.   Mrs.
Blount, as the known friend and favorite of Pope, had been
invited to the house of Allen, where she comported herself with
such indecent arrogance that she parted from Mrs. Allen in a
state of irreconcilable dislike, and the door was forever barred
against her.   This exclusion she resented with so much bitterness as to refuse any legacy from Pope, unless he left the world
with a disavowal of obligation to Allen.   Having been long
under her dominion, now tottering in the decline of life, and
unable to resist the violence of her temper, or, perhaps, with
the prejudice of a lover, persuaded that she had suffered improper treatment, he complied with her demand, and polluted
his will with female resentment.   Allen accepted the legacy,
which he gave to the hospital at Bath, observing that Pope
was always a bad accountant, and that if to 150*l.* he had put a
cipher more, he had come nearer to the truth.

The person of Pope is well known not to have been formed
by the nicest model.   He has, in his account of the " Little
Club," compared himself to a spider, and by another is described as protuberant behind and before.   He is said to have
been beautiful in his infancy ; but he was of a constitution
originally feeble and weak ; and as bodies of a tender frame
are easily distorted, his deformity was probably in part the
effect of his application.   His stature was so low that, to bring
him to a level with common tables, it was necessary to raise his
seat.   But his face was not displeasing, and his eyes were animated and vivid.

By natural deformity or accidental distortion his vital
functions were so much disordered that his life was a " long
disease."   His most frequent assailment was the headache,

which he used to relieve by inhaling the steam of coffee, which he very frequently required.

Most of what can be told concerning his petty peculiarities was communicated by a female domestic of the Earl of Oxford, who knew him perhaps after the middle of life. He was then so weak as to stand in perpetual need of female attendance ; extremely sensible of cold, so that he wore a kind of fur doublet under a shirt of a very coarse warm linen with fine sleeves. When he rose, he was invested in bodices made of stiff canvas, being scarcely able to hold himself erect till they were laced, and he then put on a flannel waistcoat. One side was contracted. His legs were so slender that he enlarged their bulk with three pair of stockings, which were drawn on and off by the maid ; for he was not able to dress or undress himself, and neither went to bed nor rose without help. His weakness made it very difficult for him to be clean.

His hair had fallen almost all away ; and he used to dine sometimes with Lord Oxford, privately, in a velvet cap. His dress of ceremony was black, with a tie-wig and a little sword.

The indulgence and accommodation which his sickness required had taught him all the unpleasing and unsocial qualities of a valetudinary man. He expected that every thing should give way to his ease or humor, as a child, whose parents will not hear her cry, has an unresisted dominion in the nursery.

> " *C'est que l'enfant toujours est homme,*
> *C'est que l'homme est toujours enfant.*"

When he wanted to sleep, he " nodded in company ;" and once slumbered at his own table while the Prince of Wales was talking of poetry.

The reputation which his friendship gave procured him many invitations ; but he was a very troublesome inmate. He brought no servant, and had so many wants that a numerous attendance was scarcely able to supply them. Wherever he was, he left no room for another, because he exacted the attention and employed the activity of the whole family. His errands were so frequent and frivolous, that the footmen in time avoided and neglected him ; and the Earl of Oxford discharged some of the servants for their resolute refusal of his messages. The maids, when they had neglected their business, alleged that they had been employed by Mr. Pope. One of his constant demands was for coffee in the night, and to the woman that waited on him in his chamber he was very burdensome ; but he was careful to recompense her want of sleep ; and

Lord Oxford's servant declared that in the house where her business was to answer his call she would not ask for wages.

He had another fault, easily incident to those who, suffering much pain, think themselves entitled to whatever pleasures they can snatch. He was too indulgent to his appetite : he loved meat highly seasoned and of strong taste ; and at the intervals of the table amused himself with biscuits and dry conserves. If he sat down to a variety of dishes, he would oppress his stomach with repletion ; and though he seemed angry when a dram was offered him, did not forbear to drink it. His friends, who knew the avenues to his heart, pampered him with presents of luxury, which he did not suffer to stand neglected. The death of great men is not always proportioned to the lustre of their lives. Hannibal, says Juvenal, did not perish by the javelin or the sword ; the slaughters of Cannæ were revenged by a ring. The death of Pope was imputed by some of his friends to a silver saucepan, in which it was his delight to heat potted lampreys.

That he loved too well to eat is certain ; but that his sensuality shortened his life will not be hastily concluded, when it is remembered that a conformation so irregular lasted six-and-fifty years, notwithstanding such pertinacious diligence of study and meditation.

In all his intercourse with mankind he had great delight in artifice, and endeavored to attain all his purposes by indirect and unsuspected methods. " He hardly drank tea without a stratagem." If at the house of his friends he wanted any accommodation, he was not willing to ask for it in plain terms ; but would mention it remotely as something convenient ; though, when it was procured, he soon made it appear for whose sake it had been recommended. Thus he teased Lord Orrery till he obtained a screen. He practised his arts on such small occasions that Lady Bolingbroke used to say, in a French phrase, that " he played the politician about cabbages and turnips." His unjustifiable impression of " The Patriot King," as it can be imputed to no particular motive, must have proceeded from his general habit of secrecy and cunning : he caught an opportunity of a sly trick, and pleased himself with the thought of outwitting Bolingbroke.

In familiar or convivial conversation it does not appear that he excelled. He may be said to have resembled Dryden, as being not one that was distinguished by vivacity in company. It is remarkable that so near his time so much should be known of what he has written, and so little of what he has said : traditional memory retains no sallies of raillery nor sentences of observation ; nothing either pointed or solid, either wise or merry. One apothegm only stands upon record. When an objection, raised against his inscription for Shakespeare, was defended by the authority of *Patrick,* he replied —" horresco referens"—that "he would allow the publisher of a dictionary to know the meaning of a single word, but not of two words put together."

He was fretful and easily displeased, and allowed himself to be capriciously resentful. He would sometimes leave Lord Oxford silently, no one could tell why, and was to be courted back by more letters and messages than the footmen were willing to carry. The table was indeed infested by Lady Mary Wortley, who was the friend of Lady Oxford, and who, knowing his peevishness, could by no entreaties be restrained from contradicting him, till their disputes were sharpened to such asperity that one or the other quitted the house.

He sometimes condescended to be jocular with servants or inferiors ; but by no merriment, either of others or his own, was he ever seen excited to laughter.

Of his domestic character frugality was a part eminently remarkable. Having determined not to be dependent, he determined not to be in want, and therefore wisely and magnanimously rejected all temptations to expense unsuitable to his fortune. This general care must be universally approved ; but it sometimes appeared in petty artifices of parsimony, such as the practice of writing his compositions on the back of letters, as may be seen in the remaining copy of the " Iliad," by which perhaps in five years five shillings were saved ; or in a niggardly reception of his friends and scantiness of entertainment, as, when he had two guests in his house, he would set at supper a single pint upon the table, and having himself taken two small glasses, would retire and say, " Gentlemen, I leave you to your wine." Yet he tells his friends that " he has a heart for all, a house for all, and, whatever they may think, a fortune for all."

He sometimes, however, made a splendid dinner, and is said to have wanted no part of the skill or elegance which such performances require. That this magnificence should be often displayed, that obstinate prudence with which he conducted his affairs would not permit, for his revenue, certain and casual, amounted only to about eight hundred pounds a year, of which, however, he declares himself able to assign one hundred to charity.

Of this fortune, which, as it arose from public approbation, was very honorably obtained, his imagination seems to have

been too full ; it would be hard to find a man so well entitled
to notice by his wit that ever delighted so much in talking of his
money. In his letters and his poems, his garden and his
grotto, his quincunx and his vines, or some hints of his opulence, are always to be found. The great topic of his ridicule
is poverty ; the crimes with which he reproaches his antagonists
are their debts, their habitation in the Mint, and their want of
a dinner. He seems to be of an opinion, not very uncommon
in the world, that to want money is to want every thing.

Next to the pleasure of contemplating his possessions
seems to be that of enumerating the men of high rank with
whom he was acquainted, and whose notice he loudly proclaims not to have been obtained by any practices of meanness
or servility ; a boast which was never denied to be true, and to
which very few poets have ever aspired. Pope never set his
genius to sale, he never flattered those whom he did not love,
or praised those whom he did not esteem. Savage, however,
remarked that he began a little to relax his dignity when he
wrote a distich for his " Highness's Dog."

His admiration of the great seems to have increased in the
advance of life. He passed over peers and statesmen to in-
scribe his " Iliad " to Congreve, with a magnanimity of which
the praise had been complete had his friend's virtue been
equal to his wit. Why he was chosen for so great an honor it
is not now possible to know ; there is no trace in literary history of any particular intimacy between them. The name of
Congreve appears in the letters among those of his other
friends, but without any observable distinction or consequence.

To his latter works, however, he took care to annex names
dignified with titles, but was not very happy in his choice ; for
except Lord Bathurst none of his noble friends were such as
that a good man would wish to have his intimacy with them
known to posterity ; he can derive little honor from the notice
of Cobham, Burlington, or Bolingbroke.

Of his social qualities, if an estimate be made from his letters, an opinion too favorable cannot easily be formed ; they
exhibit a perpetual and unclouded effulgence of general benevolence and particular fondness. There is nothing but liberality, gratitude, constancy, and tenderness. It has been so long
said as to be commonly believed that the true characters of
men may be found in their letters, and that he who writes to
his friend lays his heart open before him. But the truth is,
that such were the simple friendships of the Golden Age, and
are now the friendships only of children. Very few can boast
of hearts which they dare lay open to themselves, and of

which, by whatever accident exposed, they do not shun a distinct and continued view ; and certainly what we hide from ourselves we do not show to our friends. There is, indeed, no transaction which offers stronger temptations to fallacy and sophistication than epistolary intercourse. In the eagerness of conversation the first emotions of the mind often burst out before they are considered ; in the tumult of business, interest and passion have their genuine effect ; but a friendly letter is a calm and deliberate performance in the cool of leisure, in the stillness of solitude, and surely no man sits down to depreciate by design his own character.

Friendship has no tendency to secure veracity ; for by whom can a man so much wish to be thought better than he is as by him whose kindness he desires to gain or keep ! Even in writing to the world there is less constraint ; the author is not confronted with his reader, and takes his chance of approbation among the different dispositions of mankind ; but a letter is addressed to a single mind, of which the prejudices and partialities are known, and must therefore please, if not by favoring them, by forbearing to oppose them.

To charge those favorable representations which men give of their own minds with the guilt of hypocritical falsehood would show more severity than knowledge. The writer commonly believes himself. Almost every man's thoughts, while they are general, are right ; and most hearts are pure while temptation is away. It is easy to awaken generous sentiments in privacy ; to despise death when there is no danger ; to glow with benevolence when there is nothing to be given. While such ideas are formed they are felt ; and self-love does not suspect the gleam of virtue to be the meteor of fancy.

If the letters of Pope are considered merely as compositions, they seem to be premeditated and artificial. It is one thing to write, because there is something which the mind wishes to discharge ; and another to solicit the imagination, because ceremony or vanity requires something to be written. Pope confesses his early letters to be vitiated with *affectation and ambition ;* to know whether he disentangled himself from these perverters of epistolary integrity, his book and his life must be set in comparison.

(One of his favorite topics is contempt of his own poetry. For this, if it had been real, he would deserve no commendation ; and in this he was certainly not sincere, for his high value of himself was sufficiently observed ; and of what could he be proud but of his poetry ? He writes, he says, when " he has just nothing else to do ;" yet Swift complains that he was never at leisure for conversation, because he had "always some poetical scheme in his head." It was punctually required that his writing-box should be set upon his bed before he rose ; and Lord Oxford's domestic related that in the dreadful winter of forty she was called from her bed by him four times in one night, to supply him with paper, lest he should lose a thought.

He pretends insensibility to censure and criticism, though it was observed by all who knew him that every pamphlet disturbed his quiet, and that his extreme irritability laid him open to perpetual vexation ; but he wished to despise his critics, and therefore hoped that he did despise them.

As he happened to live in two reigns when the court paid little attention to poetry, he nursed in his mind a foolish disesteem of kings, and proclaims that "he never sees courts." Yet a little regard shown him by the Prince of Wales melted his obduracy ; and he had not much to say when he was asked by his Royal Highness, "how he could love a prince while he disliked kings ?"

He very frequently professes contempt of the world, and represents himself as looking on mankind sometimes with gay indifference, as on emmets of a hillock, below his serious attention, and sometimes with gloomy indignation, as on monsters more worthy of hatred than of pity. These were dispositions apparently counterfeited. How could he despise those whom he lived by pleasing, and on whose approbation his esteem of himself was superstructed ? Why should he hate those to whose favor he owed his honor and his ease ? Of things that terminate in human life the world is the proper judge ; to despise its sentence, if it were possible, is not just ; and if it were just, is not possible. Pope was far enough from this unreasonable temper : he was sufficiently *a fool to fame,* and his fault was that he pretended to neglect it. His levity and his sullenness were only in his letters ; he passed through common life sometimes vexed and sometimes pleased with the natural emotions of common men.

His scorn of the great is too often repeated to be real ; no man thinks much of that which he despises ; and as falsehood is always in danger of inconsistency, he makes it his boast at another time that he lives among them.

It is evident that his own importance swells often in his mind. He is afraid of writing, lest the clerks at the post-office should know his secrets ; he has many enemies ; he considers himself as surrounded by universal jealousy ; "after many deaths and many dispersions, two or three of us," says he, "may still be brought together, not to plot, but to divert ourselves, and the world too if it pleases;" and they can live together and "show what friends wits may be, in spite of all the fools in the world." All this while it was likely that the clerks did not know his hand; he certainly had no more enemies than a public character like his inevitably excites; and with what degree of friendship the wits might live, very few were so much fools as ever to inquire.

Some part of this pretended discontent he learned from Swift, and expresses it, I think, most frequently in his correspondence with him. Swift's resentment was unreasonable, but it was sincere; Pope's was the mimicry of his friend, a fictitious part which he began to play before it became him. When he was only twenty-five years old, he related that "a glut of study and retirement had thrown him on the world," and that there was danger lest "a glut of the world should throw him back upon study and retirement." To this Swift answered with great propriety that Pope had not yet acted or suffered enough in the world to have become weary of it. And indeed it must have been some very powerful reason that can drive back to solitude him who has once enjoyed the pleasures of society.

In the letters both of Swift and Pope there appears such narrowness of mind as makes them insensible of any excellence that has not some affinity with their own, and confines their esteem and approbation to so small a number, that whoever should form his opinion of the age from their representation would suppose them to have lived amidst ignorance and barbarity, unable to find among their contemporaries either virtue or intelligence, and persecuted by those that could not understand them.

When Pope murmurs at the world, when he professes contempt of fame, when he speaks of riches and poverty, of success and disappointment, with negligent indifference, he certainly does not express his habitual and settled sentiments, but either wilfully disguises his own character, or, what is more likely, invests himself with temporary qualities, and sallies out in the colors of the present moment. His hopes and fears, his joys and sorrows, acted strongly upon his mind; and if he differed from others it was not by carelessness; he was irritable and resentful. His malignity to Philips, whom he had first made ridiculous, and then hated for being angry, continued too long. Of his vain desire to make Bentley contemptible, I never heard any adequate reason. He was sometimes wanton in his attacks; and before Chandos, Lady Wortley, and Hill was mean in his retreat.

The virtues which seem to have had most of his affection were liberality and fidelity of friendship, in which it does not appear that he was other than he describes himself. His fortune did not suffer his charity to be splendid and conspicuous ; but he assisted Dodsley with a hundred pounds that he might open a shop, and of the subscription of forty pounds a year that he raised for Savage, twenty were paid by himself. He was accused of loving money ; but his love was eagerness to gain, not solicitude to keep it.

In the duties of friendship he was zealous and constant ; his early maturity of mind commonly united him with men older than himself, and therefore, without attaining any considerable length of life, he saw many companions of his youth sink into the grave ; but it does not appear that he lost a single friend by coldness or by injury ; those who loved him once continued their kindness. His ungrateful mention of Allen in his will was the effect of his adherence to one whom he had known much longer, and whom he naturally loved with greater fondness. His violation of the trust reposed in him by Bolingbroke could have no motive inconsistent with the warmest affection ; he either thought the action so near to indifferent that he forgot it, or so laudable that he expected his friend to approve it.

It was reported with such confidence as almost to enforce belief, that in the papers intrusted to his executors was found a defamatory life of Swift, which he had prepared as an instrument of vengeance, to be used if any provocation should be ever given. About this I inquired of the Earl of Marchmont, who assured me that no such piece was among his remains.

The religion in which he lived and died was that of the Church of Rome, to which, in his correspondence with Racine, he professes himself a sincere adherent. That he was not scrupulously pious in some part of his life is known by many idle and indecent applications of sentences taken from the Scriptures, a mode of merriment which a good man dreads for its profaneness, and a witty man disdains for its easiness and vulgarity. But to whatever levities he has been betrayed, it does not appear that his principles were ever corrupted, or that he ever lost his belief of revelation. The positions which he transmitted from Bolingbroke he seems not to have understood, and was pleased with an interpretation that made them orthodox.

A man of such exalted superiority and so little moderation would naturally have all his delinquencies observed and aggravated ; those who could not deny that he was excellent would rejoice to find that he was not perfect.

Perhaps it may be imputed to the unwillingness with which the same man is allowed to possess many advantages that his learning has been depreciated. He certainly was, in his early life, a man of great literary curiosity ; and when he wrote his "Essay on Criticism" had, for his age, a very wide acquaintance with books. When he entered into the living world it seems to have happened to him, as to many others, that he was less attentive to dead masters ; he studied in the academy of Paracelsus, and made the universe his favorite volume. He gathered his notions fresh from reality, not from the copies of authors, but the originals of nature. Yet there is no reason to believe that literature ever lost his esteem ; he always professed to love reading ; and Dobson, who spent some time at his house translating his "Essay on Man," when I asked him what learning he found him to possess, answered, " More than I expected." His frequent references to history, his allusions to various kinds of knowledge, and his images selected from art and nature, with his observations on the operations of the mind and the modes of life, show an intelligence perpetually on the wing, excursive, vigorous, and diligent, eager to pursue knowledge and attentive to retain it.

From this curiosity arose the desire of travelling, to which he alludes in his verses to Jervas, and which, though he never found an opportunity to gratify it, did not leave him till his life declined.

Of his intellectual character the constituent and fundamental principle was good sense, a prompt and intuitive perception of consonance and propriety. He saw immediately, of his own conceptions, what was to be chosen and what to be rejected, and in the works of others what was to be shunned and what was to be copied.

But good sense alone is a sedate and quiescent quality, which manages its possessions well, but does not increase them ; it collects few materials for its own operations, and preserves safety, but never gains supremacy. Pope had likewise genius ; a mind active, ambitious, and adventurous, always investigating, always aspiring ; in its widest searches still longing to go forward, in its highest flights still wishing to be higher ; always imagining something greater than it knows, always endeavoring more than it can do.

To assist these powers he is said to have had great strength and exactness of memory. That which he had heard or read was not easily lost ; and he had before him not only what his own meditation suggested, but what he had found in other writers that might be accommodated to his present purpose.

These benefits of nature he improved by incessant and unwearied diligence ; he had recourse to every source of intelligence, and lost no opportunity of information ; he consulted the living as well as the dead ; he read his compositions to his friends, and was never contented with mediocrity when excellence could be attained.   He considered poetry as the business of his life ; and however he might seem to lament his occupation, he followed it with constancy ; to make verses was his first labor, and to mend them was his last.

From his attention to poetry he was never diverted.   If conversation offered any thing that could be improved, he committed it to paper ; if a thought, or perhaps an expression more happy than was common, rose to his mind, he was careful to write it ; an independent distich was preserved for an opportunity of insertion ; and some little fragments have been found containing lines, or parts of lines, to be wrought upon at some other time.

He was one of those few whose labor is their pleasure : he was never elevated to negligence nor wearied to impatience ; he never passed a fault unamended by indifference, nor quitted it by despair.   He labored his works, first to gain reputation, and afterwards to keep it.

Of composition there are different methods.   Some employ at once memory and invention, and, with little intermediate use of the pen, form and polish large masses by continued meditation, and write their productions only when, in their own opinion, they have completed them.   It is related of Virgil that his custom was to pour out a great number of verses in the morning, and pass the day in retrenching exuberances and correcting inaccuracies.   The method of Pope, as may be collected from his translation, was to write his first thoughts in his first words, and gradually to amplify, decorate, rectify, and refine them.

With such faculties and such dispositions he excelled every other writer in poetical prudence : he wrote in such a manner as might expose him to few hazards.   He used almost always the same fabric of verse ; and indeed by those few essays which he made of any other he did not enlarge his reputation. Of this uniformity the certain consequence was readiness and dexterity.   By perpetual practice language had, in his mind, a systematical arrangement ; having always the same use for words, he had words so selected and combined as to be ready at his call. This increase of facility he confessed himself to have perceived in the progress of his translation.

But what was yet of more importance, his effusions were always voluntary, and his subjects chosen by himself. His independence secured him from drudging at a task and laboring upon a barren topic ; he never exchanged praise for money, nor opened a shop of condolence or congratulation. His poems, therefore, were scarcely ever temporary. He suffered coronations and royal marriages to pass without a song ; and derived no opportunities from recent events, or any popularity from the accidental disposition of his readers. He was never reduced to the necessity of soliciting the sun to shine upon a birthday, of calling the Graces and Virtues to a wedding, or of saying what multitudes have said before him. When he could produce nothing new he was at liberty to be silent.

His publications were, for the same reason, never hasty. He is said to have sent nothing to the press till it had lain two years under his inspection ; it is at least certain that he ventured nothing without nice examination. He suffered the tumult of imagination to subside, and the novelties of invention to grow familiar. He knew that the mind is always enamoured of its own productions, and did not trust his first fondness. He consulted his friends, and listened with great willingness to criticism ; and, what was of more importance, he consulted himself, and let nothing pass against his own judgment.

He professed to have learned his poetry from Dryden, whom, whenever an opportunity was presented, he praised through his whole life with unvaried liberality ; and perhaps his character may receive some illustration if he be compared with his master.

Integrity of understanding and nicety of discernment were not allotted in a less proportion to Dryden than to Pope. The rectitude of Dryden's mind was sufficiently shown by the dismission of his poetical prejudices, and the rejection of unnatural thoughts and rugged numbers. But Dryden never desired to apply all the judgment that he had. He wrote, and professed to write, merely for the people ; and when he pleased others he contented himself. He spent no time in struggles to rouse latent powers ; he never attempted to make that better which was already good, nor often to mend what he must have known to be faulty. He wrote, as he tells us, with very little consideration ; when occasion or necessity called upon him he poured out what the present moment happened to supply, and when once it had passed the press ejected it from his mind ; for when he had no pecuniary interest he had no further solicitude.

Pope was not content to satisfy, he desired to excel ; and therefore always endeavored to do his best ; he did not court the candor. but dared the judgment of his reader, and expecting no indulgence from others, he showed none to himself. He examined lines and words with minute and punctilious observation, and retouched every part with indefatigable diligence till he had left nothing to be forgiven.

For this reason he kept his pieces very long in his hands while he considered and reconsidered them. The only poems which can be supposed to have been written with such regard to the times as might hasten their publication were the two satires of " Thirty-eight ;" of which Dodsley told me that they were brought to him by the author that they might be fairly copied. " Almost every line," he said, " was then written twice over ; I gave him a clean transcript, which he sent some time afterwards to me for the press with almost every line written twice over a second time."

His declaration that his care for his works ceased at their publication was not strictly true. His parental attention never abandoned them ; what he found amiss in the first edition he silently corrected in those that followed. He appears to have revised the " Iliad," and freed it from some of its imperfections ; and the " Essay on Criticism" received many improvements after its first appearance. It will seldom be found that he altered without adding clearness, elegance, or vigor. Pope had perhaps the judgment of Dryden ; but Dryden certainly wanted the diligence of Pope.

In acquired knowledge the superiority must be allowed to Dryden, whose education was more scholastic, and who, before he became an author, had been allowed more time for study, with better means of information. His mind has a larger range, and he collects his images and illustrations from a more extensive circumference of science. Dryden knew more of man in his general nature, and Pope in his local manners. The notions of Dryden were formed by comprehensive speculation, and those of Pope by minute attention. There is more dignity in the knowledge of Dryden, and more certainty in that of Pope.

Poetry was not the sole praise of either ; for both excelled likewise in prose ; but Pope did not borrow his prose from his predecessor. The style of Dryden is capricious and varied ; that of Pope is cautious and uniform. Dryden observes the motions of his own mind ; Pope constrains his mind to his own rules of composition. Dryden is sometimes vehement and rapid ; Pope is always smooth, uniform, and gentle. Dryden's page is a natural field, rising into inequalities, and diversified by the varied exuberance of abundant vegetation ; Pope's is a velvet lawn, shaven by the scythe and levelled by the roller.

Of genius, that power which constitutes a poet ; that quality without which judgment is cold and knowledge is inert ; that energy which collects, combines, amplifies, and animates, the superiority must, with some hesitation, be allowed to Dryden. It is not to be inferred that of this poetical vigor Pope had only a little because Dryden had more ; for every other writer since Milton must give place to Pope ; and even of Dryden it must be said that, if he has brighter paragraphs, he has not better poems. Dryden's performances were always hasty, either excited by some external occasion or extorted by domestic necessity ; he composed without consideration, and published without correction. What his mind could supply at call, or gather in one excursion, was all that he sought and all that he gave. The dilatory caution of Pope enabled him to condense his sentiments, to multiply his images, and to accumulate all that study might produce or chance might supply. If the flights of Dryden therefore are higher, Pope continues longer on the wing. If of Dryden's fire the blaze is brighter, of Pope's the heat is more regular and constant. Dryden often surpasses expectation, and Pope never falls below it. Dryden is read with frequent astonishment, and Pope with perpetual delight.

This parallel will, I hope, when it is well considered, be found just ; and if the reader should suspect me, as I suspect myself, of some partial fondness for the memory of Dryden, let him not too hastily condemn me ; for meditation and inquiry may perhaps show him the reasonableness of my determination.

The works of Pope are now to be distinctly examined, not so much with attention to slight faults or petty beauties, as to the general character and effect of each performance.

It seems natural for a young poet to initiate himself by pastorals, which, not professing to imitate real life, require no experience ; and, exhibiting only the simple operation of unmingled passions, admit no subtle reasoning or deep inquiry. Pope's Pastorals are not, however, composed but with close thought ; they have reference to the times of the day, the seasons of the year, and the periods of human life. The last, that which turns the attention upon age and death, was the author's favorite. To tell of disappointment and misery, to thicken the darkness of futurity, and perplex the labyrinth of uncertainty has been always a delicious employment of the poets. His preference was probably just. I wish, however, that his fondness had not overlooked a line in which the *Zephyrs* are made *to lament in silence.*

To charge these Pastorals with want of invention is to require what was never intended. The imitations are so ambitiously frequent that the writer evidently means rather to show his literature than his wit. It is surely sufficient for an author of sixteen not only to be able to copy the poems of antiquity with judicious selection, but to have obtained sufficient power of language and skill in metre to exhibit a series of versification which had in English poetry no precedent, nor has since had an imitation.

The design of "Windsor Forest" is evidently derived from "Cooper's Hill," with some attention to Waller's poem on "The Park;" but Pope cannot be denied to excel his masters in variety and elegance, and the art of interchanging description, narrative, and morality. The objection made by Dennis is the want of plan, of a regular subordination of parts terminating in the principal and original design. There is this want in most descriptive poems, because as the scenes which they must exhibit successively are all subsisting at the same time, the order in which they are shown must by necessity be arbitrary, and more is not to be expected from the last part than from the first. The attention, therefore, which cannot be detained by suspense must be excited by diversity, such as his poem offers to its reader.

But the desire of diversity may be too much indulged ; the parts of "Windsor Forest" which deserve least praise are those which were added to enliven the stillness of the scene, the appearance of Father Thames and the transformation of Lodona. Addison had, in his "Campaign," derided the rivers that "rise from their oozy beds" to tell stories of heroes ; and it is therefore strange that Pope should adopt a fiction not only unnatural but lately censured. The story of Lodona is told with sweetness ; but a new metamorphosis is a ready and puerile expedient ; nothing is easier than to tell how a flower was once a blooming virgin, or a rock an obdurate tyrant.

The "Temple of Fame" has, as Steele warmly declared, "a thousand beauties." Every part is splendid ; there is great luxuriance of ornaments ; the original vision of Chaucer was never denied to be much improved ; the allegory is very skilfully continued, the imagery is properly selected and learn-edly displayed ; yet with all this comprehension of excellence, as its scene is laid in remote ages, and its sentiments, if the concluding paragraph be excepted, have little relation to gen-eral manners or common life, it never obtained much notice, but is turned silently over and seldom quoted or mentioned with either praise or blame.

That "The Messiah" excels the "Polio" is no great praise, if it be considered from what original the improve-ments are derived.

The "Verses on an Unfortunate Lady" have drawn much attention by the illaudable singularity of treating suicide with respect ; and they must be allowed to be written in some parts with vigorous animation, and in others with gentle tenderness ; nor has Pope produced any poem in which the sense predomi-nates more over the diction. But the tale is not skilfully told ; it is not easy to discover the character of either the Lady or her Guardian. History relates that she was about to disparage herself by a marriage with an inferior ; Pope praises her for the dignity of ambition, and yet condemns the uncle to detestation for his pride ; the ambitious love of a niece may be opposed by the interest, malice, or envy of an uncle, but never by his pride. On such an occasion a poet may be allowed to be ob-scure, but inconsistency never can be right.

The "Ode for St. Cecilia's Day" was undertaken at the desire of Steele. In this the author is generally confessed to have miscarried ; yet he has miscarried only as compared with Dryden, for he has far outgone other competitors. Dryden's plan is better chosen ; history will always take stronger hold of the attention than fable : the passions excited by Dryden are the pleasures and pains of real life ; the scene of Pope is laid in imaginary existence ; Pope is read with calm acquiescence, Dryden with turbulent delight ; Pope hangs upon the ear, and Dryden finds the passes of the mind.

Both the odes want the essential constitutent of metrical compositions, the stated recurrence of settled numbers. It may be alleged that Pindar is said by Horace to have written *numeris lege solutis ;* but as no such lax performances have been transmitted to us, the meaning of that expression cannot be fixed ; and perhaps the like return might properly be made to a modern Pindarist, as Mr. Cobb received from Bentley, who, when he found his criticisms upon a Greek Exercise, which Cobb had presented, refuted one after another by Pin-dar's authority, cried out at last, "Pindar was a bold fellow, but thou art an impudent one."

If Pope's ode be particularly inspected, it will be found that the first stanza consists of sounds, well chosen indeed, but only sounds.

The second consists of hyperbolical commonplaces, easily to be found, and perhaps without much difficulty to be as well expressed.

In the third, however, there are numbers, images, harmony, and vigor not unworthy the antagonist of Dryden. Had all been like this—but every part cannot be the best.

The next stanzas place and detain us in the dark and dismal regions of mythology, where neither hope nor fear, neither joy nor sorrow can be found : the poet, however, faithfully attends us : we have all that can be performed by elegance of diction or sweetness of versification ; but what can form avail without better matter ?

The last stanza recurs again to commonplaces. The conclusion is too evidently modelled by that of Dryden ; and it may be remarked that both end with the same fault ; the comparison of each is literal on one side and metaphorical on the other.

Poets do not always express their own thoughts ; Pope, with all this labor in the praise of Music, was ignorant of its principles and insensible of its effects.

One of his greatest, though of his earliest works, is the "Essay on Criticism ;" which, if he had written nothing else, would have placed him among the first critics and the first poets, as it exhibits every mode of excellence that can embellish or dignify didactic composition: selection of matter, novelty of arrangement, justness of precept, splendor of illustration, and propriety of digression. I know not whether it be pleasing to consider that he produced this piece at twenty, and never afterwards excelled it : he that delights himself with observing that such powers may be soon attained cannot but grieve to think that life was ever at a stand.

To mention the particular beauties of the Essay would be unprofitably tedious ; but I cannot forbear to observe that the comparison of a student's progress in the sciences with the journey of a traveller in the Alps, is perhaps the best that English poetry can show. A simile, to be perfect, must both illustrate and ennoble the subject ; must show it to the understanding in a clearer view, and display it to the fancy with greater dignity, but either of these qualities may be sufficient to recommend it. In didactic poetry, of which the great purpose is instruction, a simile may be praised which illustrates, though it does not ennoble ; in heroics, that may be admitted which ennobles, though it does not illustrate. That it may be complete it is required to exhibit, independently of its references, a pleasing image ; for a simile is said to be a short episode. To this antiquity was so attentive that circumstances were sometimes added, which, having no parallels, served only to fill the imagination and produced what Perrault ludicrously called " comparisons with a long tail." In their similes the greatest writers have sometimes failed ; the ship-race, compared with the chariot-race, is neither illustrated not aggrandized ; land and water make all the difference : when Apollo, running after Daphne, is likened to a greyhound chasing a hare, there is nothing gained ; the ideas of pursuit and flight are too plain to be made plainer ; and a god, and the daughter of a god, are not represented much to their advantage by a hare and dog. The simile of the Alps has no useless parts, yet affords a striking picture by itself ; it makes the foregoing position better understood, and enables it to take faster hold on the attention ; it assists the apprehension and elevates the fancy.

Let me likewise dwell a little on the celebrated paragraph in which it is directed that " the sound should seem an echo to the sense ;" a precept which Pope is allowed to have observed beyond any other English poet.

This notion of representative metre, and the desire of discovering frequent adaptations of the sound to the sense, have produced, in my opinion, many wild conceits and imaginary beauties. All that can furnish this representation are the sounds of the words considered singly, and the time in which they are pronounced. Every language has some words framed to exhibit the noises which they express, as *thump*, *rattle*, *growl*, *hiss*. These, however, are but few, and the poet cannot make them more, nor can they be of any use but when sound is to be mentioned. The time of pronunciation was in the dactylic measures of the learned languages capable of considerable variety ; but that variety could be accommodated only to motion or duration, and different degrees of motion were perhaps expressed by verses rapid or slow, without much attention of the writer, when the image had full possession of his fancy ; but our language having little flexibility, our verses can differ very little in their cadence. The fancied resemblances, I fear, arise sometimes merely from the ambiguity of words ; there is supposed to be some relation between a *soft* line and a *soft* couch, or between *hard* syllables and *hard* fortune.

Motion, however, may be in some sort exemplified ; and yet it may be suspected that in such resemblances the mind often governs the ear, and the sounds are estimated by their mean-

ing.   One of their most successful attempts has been to describe
the labor of Sisyphus :

> " With many a weary step, and many a groan,
> Up a high hill he heaves a huge round stone ;
> The huge round stone, resulting with a bound,
> Thunders impetuous down, and smokes along the ground."

Who does not perceive the stone to move slowly upward, and
roll violently back ?   But set the same numbers to another
sense :

> " While many a merry tale, and many a song,
> Cheer'd the rough road, we wished the rough road long.
> The rougu road then, returning in a round,
> Mock'd our impatient steps, for all was fairy ground."

We have now surely lost much of the delay and much of the
rapidity.

But to show how little the greatest master of numbers can
fix the principles of representative harmony, it will be sufficient to remark that the poet who tells us that

> " When Ajax strives some rock's vast weight to throw,
> The line too labors, and the words move slow :
> Not so when swift Camilla scours the plain,
> Flies o'er the unbending corn, and skims along the main—"

when he had enjoyed for about thirty years the praise of Ca-
milla's lightness of foot, he tried another experiment upon
sound and *time*, and produced this memorable triplet :

> " Waller was smooth ; but Dryden taught to join
> The varying verse, the full resounding line,
> The long majestic march, and energy divine."

Here are the swiftness of the rapid race, and the march of
slow-paced majesty, exhibited by the same poet in the same
sequence of syllables, except that the exact prosodist will find
the line of *swiftness* by one time longer than that of *tardiness*.

Beauties of this kind are commonly fancied ; and when
real are technical and nugatory, not to be rejected and not to
be solicited.

To the praises which have been accumulated on " The
Rape of the Lock," by readers of every class, from the critic to
the waiting-maid, it is difficult to make any addition.   Of that
which is universally allowed to be the most attractive of all ludicrous compositions, let it rather be now inquired from what
sources the power of pleasing is derived.

Dr. Warburton, who excelled in critical perspicacity, has
remarked that the preternatural agents are very happily adapt-

ed to the purposes of the poem. The heathen deities can no longer gain attention ; we should have turned away from a contest between Venus and Diana. The employment of allegorical persons always excites conviction of its own absurdity ; they may produce effects, but cannot conduct actions : when the phantom is put in motion, it dissolves : thus Discord may raise a mutiny ; but Discord cannot conduct a march nor besiege a town. Pope brought into view a new race of beings, with powers and passions proportionate to their operation. The Sylphs and Gnomes act at the toilet and the tea-table, what more terrific and more powerful phantoms perform on the stormy ocean or the field of battle ; they give their proper help and do their proper mischief.

Pope is said, by an objector, not to have been the inventor of this petty notion ; a charge which might with more justice have been brought against the author of the " Iliad," who doubtless adopted the religious system of his country ; for what is there but the names of his agents which Pope has not invented ? Has he not assigned them characters and operations never heard of before ? Has he not, at least, given them their first poetical existence ? If this is not sufficient to denominate his work original, nothing original ever can be written.

In this work are exhibited, in a very high degree, the two most engaging powers of an author. New things are made familiar, and familiar things are made new. A race of aërial people, never heard of before, is presented to us in a manner so clear and easy that the reader seeks for no further information, but immediately mingles with his new acquaintance, adopts their interests, and attends their pursuits ; loves a Sylph and detests a Gnome.

That familiar things are made new, every paragraph will prove. The subject of the poem is an event below the common incidents of common life ; nothing real is introduced that is not seen so often as to be no longer regarded ; yet the whole detail of a female day is here brought before us, invested with so much art of decoration that, though nothing is disguised, every thing is striking, and we feel all the appetite of curiosity for that from which we have a thousand times turned fastidiously away.

The purpose of the poet is, as he tells us, to laugh at " the little unguarded follies of the female sex." It is therefore without justice that Dennis charges " The Rape of the Lock " with the want of a moral, and for that reason sets it below the " Lutrin," which exposes the pride and discord of the clergy. Perhaps neither Pope nor Boileau has made the world much better than he found it ; but if they had both succeeded, it were easy to tell who would have deserved most from public gratitude. The freaks and humors, and spleen and vanity of women, as they embroil families in discord, and fill houses with disquiet, do more to obstruct the happiness of life in a year than the ambition of the clergy in many centuries. It has been well observed that the misery of man proceeds not from any single crush of overwhelming evil, but from small vexations continually repeated.

It is remarked by Dennis, likewise, that the machinery is superfluous ; that by all the bustle of preternatural operation the main event is neither hastened nor retarded. To this charge an efficacious answer is not easily made. The Sylphs cannot be said to help or to oppose ; and it must be allowed to imply some want of art that their power has not been sufficiently intermingled with the action. Other parts may likewise be charged with want of connection : the game at *ombre* might be spared ; but if the lady had lost her hair while she was intent upon her cards, it might have been inferred that those who are too fond of play will be in danger of neglecting more important interests. Those perhaps are faults ; but what are such faults to so much excellence !

The Epistle of " Eloisa to Abelard " is one of the most happy productions of human wit : the subject is so judiciously chosen that it would be difficult, in turning over the annals of the world, to find another which so many circumstances concur to recommend. We regularly interest ourselves most in the fortune of those who most deserve our notice. Abelard and Eloise were conspicuous in their days for eminence of merit. The heart naturally loves truth. The adventures and misfortunes of this illustrious pair are known from undisputed history. Their fate does not leave the mind in hopeless dejection ; for they both found quiet and consolation in retirement and piety. So new and so affecting is their story that it supersedes invention ; and imagination ranges at full liberty without straggling into scenes of fable.

The story, thus skilfully adopted, has been diligently improved. Pope has left nothing behind him which seems more the effect of studious perseverance and laborious revisal. Here is particularly observable the *curiosa felicitas*, a fruitful soil and careful cultivation. Here is no crudeness of sense nor asperity of language.

The sources from which sentiments which have so much vigor and efficacy have been drawn are shown to be the mystic writers by the learned author of the " Essay on the Life and

Writings of Pope," a book which teaches how the brow of Criticism may be smoothed, and how she may be enabled, with all her severity, to attract and to delight.

The train of my disquisition has now conducted me to that poetical wonder, the translation of the " Iliad," a performance which no age or nation can pretend to equal. To the Greeks translation was almost unknown ; it was totally unknown to the inhabitants of Greece. They had no recourse to the barbarians for poetical beauties, but sought for every thing in Homer, where, indeed, there is but little which they might not find.

The Italians have been very diligent translators ; but I can hear of no version, unless perhaps Anguilara's Ovid may be excepted, which is read with eagerness. The " Iliad " of Salvini every reader may discover to be punctiliously exact ; but it seems to be the work of a linguist skilfully pedantic ; and his countrymen, the proper judges of its power to please, reject it with disgust.

Their predecessors, the Romans, have left some specimens of translations behind them, and that employment must have had some credit in which Tully and Germanicus engaged ; but unless we suppose, what is perhaps true, that the plays of Terence were versions of Menander, nothing translated seems ever to have risen to high reputation. The French, in the meridian hour of their learning, were very laudably industrious to enrich their own language with the wisdom of the ancients ; but found themselves reduced, by whatever necessity, to turn the Greek and Roman poetry into prose. Whoever could read an author could translate him. From such rivals little can be feared.

The chief help of Pope in this arduous undertaking was drawn from the versions of Dryden. Virgil had borrowed much of his imagery from Homer, and part of the debt was now paid by his translator. Pope searched the pages of Dryden for happy combinations of heroic diction ; but it will not be denied that he added much to what he found. He cultivated our language with so much diligence and art that he has left in his Homer a treasure of poetical elegances to posterity. His version may be said to have tuned the English tongue ; for since its appearance no writer, however deficient in other powers, has wanted melody. Such a series of lines, so elaborately corrected and so sweetly modulated, took possession of the public ear ; the vulgar was enamoured of the poem, and the learned wondered at the translation.

But in the most general applause discordant voices will always be heard. It has been objected by some, who wish to be numbered among the sons of learning, that Pope's version of

Homer is not Homerical ; that it exhibits no resemblance of
the original and characteristic manner of the Father of Poetry,
as it wants his awful simplicity, his artless grandeur, his unaffected majesty.   This cannot be totally denied ; but it must
be remembered that *necessitas quod cogit defendit*, that may be
lawfully done which cannot be forborne.   Time and place will
always enforce regard.   In estimating this translation consideration must be had of the nature of our language, the form of
our language, the form of our metre, and, above all, of the
change which two thousand years have made in the modes of
life and the habits of thought.   Virgil wrote in a language of
the same general fabric with that of Homer, in verses of the
same measure, and in an age nearer to Homer's time by eighteen hundred years ; yet he found, even then, the state of the
world so much altered, and the demand for elegance so increased, that mere nature would be endured no longer ; and
perhaps in the multitude of borrowed passages very few can
be shown which he has not embellished.

There is a time when nations, emerging from barbarity, and
falling into regular subordination, gain leisure to grow wise,
and feel the shame of ignorance and the craving pain of unsatisfied curiosity.   To this hunger of the mind plain sense is
grateful ; that which fills the void removes uneasiness, and to
be free from pain for a while is pleasure ; but repletion generates fastidiousness ; a saturated intellect soon becomes luxurious, and knowledge finds no willing reception till it is recommended by artificial diction.   Thus it will be found in the
progress of learning that in all nations the first writers are
simple, and that every age improves in elegance.   One refinement always makes way for another, and what was expedient
to Virgil was necessary to Pope.

I suppose many readers of the English " Iliad," when they
have been touched with some unexpected beauty of the lighter
kind, have tried to enjoy it in the original, where, alas ! it was
not to be found.   Homer doubtless owes to his translator
many Ovidian graces not exactly suitable to his character ; but
to have added can be no great crime, if nothing be taken away.
Elegance is surely to be desired, if it be not gained at the expense of dignity.   A hero would wish to be loved as well as
to be reverenced.

To a thousand cavils one answer is sufficient ; the purpose
of a writer is to be read, and the criticism which would destroy
the power of pleasing must be blown aside.   Pope wrote for
his own age and his own nation : he knew that it was necessary
to color the images and point the sentiments of his author ;

he therefore made him graceful, but lost him some of his sublimity.

The copious notes with which the version is accompanied,
and by which it is recommended to many readers, though they
were undoubtedly written to swell the volumes, ought not to
pass without praise ; commentaries which attract the reader by
the pleasure of perusal have not often appeared ; the notes of
others are read to clear difficulties, those of Pope to vary entertainment.

It has, however, been objected with sufficient reason that
there is in the commentary too much of unseasonable levity
and affected gayety ; that too many appeals are made to the
ladies, and the ease which is so carefully preserved is sometimes the ease of a trifler. Every art has its terms, and every
kind of instruction its proper style ; the gravity of common
critics may be tedious, but is less despicable than childish
merriment.

Of the '' Odyssey '' nothing remains to be observed ;
the same general phrase may be given to both translations, and
a particular examination of either would require a large volume. The notes were written by Broome, who endeavored,
not unsuccessfully, to imitate his master.

Of the '' Dunciad '' the hint is confessedly taken from Dryden's '' Mac Flecknoe ;'' but the plan is so enlarged and diversified as justly to claim the praise of an original. and affords,
the best specimen that has yet appeared of personal satire ludicrously pompous.

That the design was moral, whatever the author might tell
either his readers or himself, I am not convinced. The first motive was the desire of revenging the contempt with which Theobald had treated his Shakespeare, and regaining the honor
which he had lost, by crushing his opponent. Theobald was not
of bulk enough to fill a poem, and therefore it was necessary
to find other enemies with other names at whose expense he
might divert the public.

In this design there was petulance and malignity enough ;
but I cannot think it very criminal. An author places himself
uncalled before the tribunal of criticism, and solicits fame at
the hazard of disgrace. Dulness or deformity are not culpable
in themselves, but may be very justly reproached when they
pretend to the honor of wit or the influence of beauty. If
bad writers were to pass without reprehension, what should restrain them ? *impune diem consumpscrit ingens Telephus ;* and
upon bad writers only will censure have much effect. The sa-

tire which brought Theobald and Moore into contempt dropped impotent from Bentley like the javelin of Priam.

All truth is valuable, and satirical criticism may be considered as useful when it rectifies error and improves judgment : he that refines the public taste is a public benefactor.

The beauties of this poem are well known ; its chief fault is the grossness of its images. Pope and Swift had an unnatural delight in ideas physically impure, such as every other tongue utters with unwillingness, and of which every ear shrinks from the mention.

But even this fault, offensive as it is, may be forgiven for the excellence of other passages ; such as the formation and dissolution of Moore, the account of the traveller, the misfortune of the florist, and the crowded thoughts and stately numbers which dignify the concluding paragraph.

The alterations which have been made in the " Dunciad," not always for the better, require that it should be published with all its variations.

The " Essay on Man " was a work of great labor and long consideration, but certainly not the happiest of Pope's performances. The subject is perhaps not very proper for poetry, and the poet was not sufficiently master of his subject ; metaphysical morality was to him a new study : he was proud of his acquisitions, and, supposing himself master of great secrets, was in haste to teach what he had not learned. Thus he tells us, in the first epistle, that from the nature of the Supreme Being may be deduced an order of beings such as mankind, because infinite excellence can do only what is best. He finds out that these beings must be "somewhere ;" and that " all the question is, whether man be in a wrong place." Surely if, according to the poet's Leibnitian reasoning, we may infer that man ought to be, only because he is, we may allow that his place is the right place, because he has it. Supreme Wisdom is not less infallible in disposing than in creating. But what is meant by *somewhere* and *place*, and *wrong place*, it had been vain to ask Pope, who probably had never asked himself.

Having exalted himself into the chair of wisdom, he tells us much that every man knows, and much that he does not know himself ; that we see but little, and that the order of the universe is beyond our comprehesion ; an opinion not very uncommon ; and that there is a chain of subordinate beings " from infinite to nothing," of which himself and his readers are equally ignorant. But he gives us one comfort, which without his help he supposes unattainable, in the position " that though we are fools yet God is wise."

This Essay affords an egregious instance of the predominance of genius, the dazzling splendor of imagery, and the seductive powers of eloquence. Never were penury of knowledge and vulgarity of sentiment so happily disguised. The reader feels his mind full, though he learns nothing ; and, when he meets it in its new array, no longer knows the talk of his mother and his nurse. When these wonder-working sounds sink into sense, and the doctrine of the Essay, disrobed of its ornaments, is left to the powers of its naked excellence, what shall we discover? That we are, in comparison with our Creator, very weak and ignorant ; that we do not uphold the chain of existence ; and that we could not make one another with more skill than we are made. We may learn yet more ; that the arts of human life were copied from the instinctive operations of other animals ; that, if the world be made for man, it may be said that man was made for geese. To these profound principles of natural knowledge are added some moral instructions equally new ; that self-interest well understood will produce social concord ; that men are mutual gainers by mutual benefits ; that evil is sometimes balanced by good ; that human advantages are unstable and fallacious, of uncertain duration and doubtful effect ; that our true honor is, not to have a great part, but to act it well ; that virtue only is our own ; and that hapiness is always in our power.

Surely a man of no very comprehensive search may venture to say that he has heard all this before ; but it was never till now recommended by such a blaze of embellishments or such sweetness of melody. The vigorous contraction of some thoughts, the luxuriant amplification of others, the incidental illustrations, and sometimes the dignity, sometimes the softness of the verses, enchain philosophy, suspend criticism, and oppress judgment by overpowering pleasure.

This is true of many paragraphs ; yet, if I had undertaken to exemplify Pope's felicity of composition before a rigid critic, I should not select the "Essay on Man," for it contains more lines unsuccessfully labored, more harshness of diction, more thoughts imperfectly expressed, more levity without elegance, and more heaviness without strength than will easily be found in all his other works.

The *Characters of Men and Women* are the product of diligent speculation upon human life ; much labor has been bestowed upon them, and Pope very seldom labored in vain. That his excellence may be properly estimated I recommend a comparison of his *Characters of Women* with Boileau's satire ; it will then be seen with how much more perspicacity female nature is investigated and female excellence selected ; and he surely is no mean writer to whom Boileau should be found inferior.   The *Characters of Men*, however, are written with more, if not with deeper, thought, and exhibit many passages exquisitely beautiful.   The " Gem and the Flower " will not easily be equalled.   In the women's part are some defects ; the character of Atossa is not so neatly finished as that of Clodio ; and some of the female characters may be found perhaps more frequently among men ; what is said of Philomede was true of Prior.

In the Epistles to Lord Bathurst and Lord Burlington, Dr. Warburton has endeavored to find a train of thought which was never in the writer's head, and to support his hypothesis has printed that first which was published last.   In one, the most valuable passage is perhaps the Elegy on " Good Sense ;" and the other the " End of the Duke of Buckingham."

The epistle to Arbuthnot, now arbitrarily called " The Prologue to the Satires," is a performance consisting, as it seems, of many fragments wrought into one design, which by this union of scattered beauties contains more striking paragraphs than could probably have been brought together into an occasional work. As there is no stronger motive to exertion than self-defence, no part has more elegance, spirit, or dignity than the poet's vindication of his own character.   The meanest passage is the satire upon Sporus.

Of the two poems which derived their names from the year, and which are called " The Epilogue to the Satires," it was very justly remarked by Savage that the second was in the whole more strongly conceived and more equally supported, but that it had no single passage equal to the contention in the first for the dignity of vice and the celebration of the triumph of corruption.

The imitations of Horace seem to have been written as relaxations of his genius.   This employment became his favorite by its facility ; the plan was ready to his hand, and nothing was required but to accommodate as he could the sentiments of an old author to recent facts or familiar images ; but what is easy is seldom excellent ; such imitations cannot give pleasure to common readers : the man of learning may be sometimes surprised and delighted by an unexpected parallel ; but the comparison requires knowledge of the original, which will likewise often detect strained applications.   Between Roman images and English manners there will be an irreconcilable dissimilitude, and the work will be generally uncouth and party-colored, neither original nor translated, neither ancient nor modern.

Pope had, in proportions very nicely adjusted to each other, all the qualities that constitute genius. He had *inven-tion*, by which new trains of events are formed and new scenes of imagery displayed, as in the " Rape of the Lock ;" and by which extrinsic and adventitious embellishments and illustrations are connected with a known subject, as in the " Essay on Criticism." He had *imagination,* which strongly impresses on the writer's mind and enables him to convey to the reader the various forms of nature, incidents of life, and energies of passion, as in his " Eloisa, " " Windsor Forest," and the " Ethic Epistles." He had *judgment*, which selects from life or nature what the present purpose requires, and, by separating the essence of things from its concomitants, often makes the representation more powerful than the reality ; and he had colors of language always before him, ready to decorate his matter with every grace of elegant expression, as when he accommodates his diction to the wonderful multiplicity of Homer's sentiments and descriptions.

Poetical expression includes sound as well as meaning : " Music," says Dryden, " is inarticulate poetry ;" among the excellences of Pope, therefore, must be mentioned the melody of his metre. By perusing the works of Dryden he discovered the most perfect fabric of English verse, and habituated himself to that only which he found the best ; in consequence of which restraint his poetry has been censured as too uniformly musical, and as glutting the ear with unvaried sweetness. I suspect this objection to be the cant of those who judge by principles rather than perception ; and who would even themselves have less pleasure in his works if he had tried to relieve attention by studied discords, or affected to break his lines and vary his pauses.

But though he was thus careful of his versification, he did not oppress his powers with superfluous rigor. He seems to have thought with Boileau. that the practice of writing might be refined till the difficulty should overbalance the advantage. The construction of his language is not always strictly grammatical : with those rhymes which prescription had conjoined he contented himself, without regard to Swift's remonstrances, though there was no striking consonance ; nor was he very careful to vary his terminations, or to refuse admission, at a small distance, to the same rhymes.

To Swift's edict for the exclusion of Alexandrines and triplets he paid little regard : he admitted them, but, in the opinion of Fenton, too rarely ; he uses them more liberally in the translations than his poems.

He has a few double rhymes, and always, I think, unsuc-cessfully, except once in the " Rape of the Lock."

Expletives he very early ejected from his verses ; but he now and then admits an epithet rather commodious than im-portant. Each of the six first lines of " Iliad " might lose two syllables with very little diminution of the meaning ; and sometimes, after all his art and labor, one verse seems to be made for the sake of another. In his latter productions the dic-tion is sometimes vitiated by French idioms, with which Boling-broke had perhaps infected him.

I have been told that the couplet by which he declared his own ear to be most gratified was this :

> " Lo, where Mæotis sleeps, and hardly flows
> The freezing Tanais through a waste of snows."

But the reason of this preference I cannot discover.

It is remarked by Watts that there is scarcely a happy com-bination of words, or a phrase poetically elegant in the English language, which Pope has not inserted into his version of Ho-mer. How he obtained possession of so many beauties of speech it were desirable to know. That he gleaned from au-thors, obscure as well as eminent, what he thought brilliant or useful, and preserved it all in a regular collection, is not un-likely. When, in his last years, Hall's Satires were shown him, he wished that he had seen them sooner. New senti-ments and new images others may produce ; but to attempt any further improvement of versification will be dangerous. Art and diligence have now done their best, and what shall be added will be the effort of tedious toil and needless curiosity.

After all this, it is surely superfluous to answer the question that has once been asked, Whether Pope was a poet ? other-wise than by asking, in return, If Pope be not a poet, where is poetry to be found ? To circumscribe poetry by a definition will only show the narrowness of the definer, though a defini-tion which shall exclude Pope will not easily be made. Let us look round upon the present time, and back upon the past ; let us inquire to whom the voice of mankind has decreed the wreath of poetry ; let their productions be examined and their claims stated, and the pretensions of Pope will be no more dis-puted. Had he given the world only his version, the name of poet must have been allowed him ; if the writer of the " Iliad " were to class his successors, he would assign a very high place to his translator, without requiring any other evidence of genius.

The following letter, of which the original is in the hands

of Lord Hardwicke, was communicated to me by the kindness of Mr. Jodrell :

" To Mr. BRIDGES, at the Bishop of London's, at Fulham.
" SIR,
    " The favor of your letter, with your remark, can never be enough acknowledged ; and the speed with which you dis-charged so troublesome a task doubles the obligation.
    " I must own you have pleased me very much by com-mendation so ill bestowed upon me ; but, I assure you, much more by the frankness of your censure, which I ought to take the more kindly of the two, as it is more advantageous to a scribbler to be improved in his judgment than to be soothed in his vanity.   The greater part of those deviations from the Greek which you have observed, I was led into by Chapman and Hobbes ; who are, it seems, as much celebrated for their knowledge of the original as they are decried for the badness of their translations.   Chapman pretends to have restored the genuine sense of the author, from the mistakes of all former explainers, in several hundred places ; and the Cambridge edi-tors of the large Homer, in Greek and Latin, attributed so much to Hobbes that they confess they have corrected the old Latin interpretation very often by his version.   For my part, I generally took the author's meaning to be as you have ex-plained it ; yet their authority, joined to the knowledge of my own imperfectness in the language, overruled me.   However, sir, you may be confident I think you in the right, because you happen to be of my opinion ; for men (let them say what they will) never approve any other's sense but as it squares with their own.   But you have made me much more proud of and positive in my judgment, since it is strengthened by yours.   I think your criticisms which regard the expression very just, and shall make my profit of them ; to give you some proof that I am in earnest, I will alter three verses on your bare objec-tion, though I have Mr. Dryden's example for each of them. And this, I hope, you will account no small piece of obedience from one who values the authority of one true poet above that of twenty critics or commentators.   But, though I speak thus of commentators, I will continue to read carefully all I can procure, to make up, that way, for my own want of critical un-derstanding in the original beauties of Homer.   Though the greatest of them are certainly those of invention and design, which are not at all confined to the language ; for the distin-guishing excellences of Homer are (by the consent of the best critics of all nations) first in the manners (which include all the

speeches, as being no other than the representations of each person's manners by his words), and then in that rapture and fire which carries you away with him, with that wonderful force that no man who has a true poetical spirit is master of himself while he reads him. Homer makes you interested and concerned before you are aware, all at once, whereas Virgil does it by soft degrees. This, I believe, is what a translator of Homer ought principally to imitate ; and it is very hard for any translator to come up to it, because the chief reason why all translations fall short of their originals is that the very constraint they are obliged to renders them heavy and dispirited.

" The great beauty of Homer's language, as I take it, consists in that noble simplicity which runs through all his works (and yet his diction, contrary to what one would imagine consistent with simplicity, is at the same time very copious). I don't know how I have run into this pedantry in a letter, but I find I have said too much, as well as spoken too inconsiderately : what further thoughts I have upon this subject I shall be glad to communicate to you (for my own improvement) when we meet, which is a happiness I very earnestly desire, as I do likewise some opportunity of proving how much I think myself obliged to your friendship, and how truly I am, sir,

" Your most faithful, humble servant,

" A. POPE."

The criticism upon Pope's Epitaphs, which was printed in " The Universal Visitor," is placed here, being too minute and particular to be inserted in the Life :

Every art is best taught by example. Nothing contributes more to the cultivation of propriety than remarks on the works of those who have most excelled. I shall therefore endeavor, at this *visit*, to entertain the young students in poetry with an examination of Pope's Epitaphs.

To define an epitaph is useless ; every one knows that it is an inscription on a tomb. An epitaph, therefore, implies no particular character of writing, but may be composed in verse or prose. It is indeed commonly panegyrical ; because we are seldom distinguished with a stone but by our friends ; but it has no rule to restrain or modify it, except this, that it ought not to be longer than common beholders may be expected to have leisure and patience to peruse.

I.

On CHARLES *Earl of* DORSET, *in the Church of Wythyham in Su. sex.*

> Dorset, the grace of courts, the muse's pride,
> Patron of arts, and judge of nature, died—
> The scourge of pride, though sanctified or great ;
> Of fops in learning, and of knaves in state ;
> Yet soft in nature, though severe his lay,
> His anger moral, and his wisdom gay.
> Blest satirist ! who touch'd the means so true,
> As show'd Vice had his hate and pity too.
> Blest courtier ! who could king and country please,
> Yet sacred kept his friendships and his ease.
> Blest peer ! his great forefather's every grace
> Reflecting, and reflected on his race ;
> Where other Buckhursts, other Dorsets shine,
> And patriots still, or poets, deck the line.

The first distich of this epitaph contains a kind of information which few would want, that the man for whom the tomb
was erected died. There are indeed some qualities worthy of
praise ascribed to the dead, but none that were likely to exempt him from the lot of man, or incline us much to wonder
that he should die. What is meant by ''judge of nature'' is
not easy to say. Nature is not the object of human judgment ;
for it is vain to judge where we cannot alter. If by nature is
meant what is commonly called *nature* by the critics, a just representation of things really existing and actions really performed, nature cannot be properly opposed to *art;* nature
being, in this sense, only the best effect of *art.*

> The scourge of pride—

Of this couplet the second line is not what is intended, a n
illustration of the former. *Pride* in the *great* is indeed well
enough connected with knaves in state, though *knaves* is a word
rather too ludicrous and light ; but the mention of *sanctifiea*
pride will not lead the thoughts to *fops in learning*, but rather to
some species of tyranny or oppression, something more gloomy
and more formidable than foppery.

> Yet soft his nature—

This is a high compliment, but was not first bestowed on
Dorset by Pope. The next verse is extremely beautiful.

> Blest satirist !—

In this distich is another line of which Pope was not the
author. I do not mean to blame these imitations with much
harshness ; in long performances they are scarcely to be

avoided, and in shorter they may be indulged, because the train of the composition may naturally involve them, or the scantiness of the subject allow little choice.   However, what is borrowed is not to be enjoyed as our own ; and it is the business of critical justice to give every bird of the muses his proper feather.

Blest courtier !—

Whether a courtier can properly be commended for keeping his *ease sacred* may perhaps be disputable.   To please king and country, without sacrificing friendship to any change of times, was a very uncommon instance of prudence or felicity, and deserved to be kept separate from so poor a commendation as care of his ease.   I wish our poets would attend a little more accurately to the use of the word *sacred*, which surely should never be applied in a serious composition.but where some reference may be made to a higher Being, or where some duty is exacted or implied.   A man may keep his friendship sacred, because promises of friendship are very awful ties ; but methinks he cannot, but in a burlesque sense, be said to keep his ease *sacred*.

Blest peer !—

The blessing ascribed to the *peer* has no connection with his peerage ; they might happen to any other man whose ancestors were remembered, or whose posterity are likely to be regarded.

I know not whether this epitaph be worthy either of the writer or the man entombed.

II.

On Sir WILLIAM TRUMBULL, *one of the principal Secretaries of State to King* WILLIAM III., *who, having resigned his place, died in his retirement at Easthamstead in Berkshire,* 1716.

> A pleasing form ; a firm, yet cautious mind ;
> Sincere, though prudent, constant, yet resign'd ;
> Honor unchang'd, a principle profest,
> Fix'd to one side, but moderate to the rest ;
> An honest courtier, yet a patriot too ;
> Just to his prince, and to his country true ;
> Fill'd with the sense of age, the fire of youth,
> A scorn of wrangling, yet a zeal for truth ;
> A generous faith, from superstition free ;
> A love to peace, and hate of tyranny ;
> Such this man was ; who, now from earth remov'd,
> At length enjoys that liberty he lov'd.

In this epitaph, as in many others, there appears, at the first view, a fault which I think scarcely any beauty can compensate. The name is omitted. The end of an epitaph is to convey some account of the dead ; and to what purpose is any thing told of him whose name is concealed ? An epitaph and a history of a nameless hero are equally absurd, since the virtues and qualities so recounted in either are scattered at the mercy of fortune to be appropriated by guess. The name, it is true, may be read upon the stone ; but what obligation has it to the poet, whose verses wander over the earth and leave their subject behind them, and who is forced, like an unskilful painter, to make his purpose known by adventitious help ?

This epitaph is wholly without elevation, and contains nothing striking or particular ; but the poet is not to be blamed for the defects of his subject. He said, perhaps, the best that could be said. There are, however, some defects which were not made necessary by the character in which he was employed. There is no opposition between an *honest courtier* and a *patriot ;* for an *honest courtier* cannot but be a *patriot.*

It was unsuitable to the nicety required in short compositions to close his verse with the word *too :* every rhyme should be a word of emphasis ; nor can this rule be safely neglected, except where the length of the poem makes slight inaccuracies excusable, or allows room for beauties sufficient to overpower the effects of petty faults.

At the beginning of the seventh line the word *filled* is weak and prosaic, having no particular adaptation to any of the words that follow it.

The thought in the last line is impertinent, having no connection with the foregoing character, nor with the condition of the man described. Had the epitaph been written on the poor conspirator[1] who died lately in prison, after a confinement of more than forty years, without any crime proved against him, the sentiment had been just and pathetical ; but why should Trumbull be congratulated upon his liberty, who had never known restraint ?

III.

On the Hon. SIMON HARCOURT, *only son of the Lord Chancellor* HARCOURT, *at the Church of Stanton-Harcourt in Oxfordshire,* 1720.

> To this sad shrine, whoe'er thou art, draw near ;
> Here lies the friend most lov'd, the son most dear,
> Who ne'er knew joy, but friendship might divide,
> Or gave his father grief but when he died.
> How vain is reason ! eloquence how weak !
> If Pope must tell what Harcourt cannot speak.
> Oh ! let thy once-lov'd friend inscribe thy stone,
> And with a father's sorrows mix his own !

[1] Bernadi.

This epitaph is principally remarkable for the artful introduction of the name, which is inserted with a peculiar felicity, to which chance must concur with genius, which no man can hope to attain twice, and which cannot be copied but with servile imitation.

I cannot but wish that of this inscription the two last lines had been omitted, as they take away from the energy what they do not add to the sense.

IV.

On JAMES CRAGGS, *Esq.*

In Westminster-Abbey.

JACOBVS CRAGGS,

REGI MAGNÆ BRITANNIÆ A SECRETIS

ET CONSILIIS SANCTIORIBVS,

PRINCIPIS PARITER AC POPVLI AMOR ET DELICIÆ.

VIXIT TITVLIS ET INVIDIA MAJOR

ANNOS HEV PAVCOS, XXXV.

OB. FEB. XVI. MDCCXX.

Statesman, yet friend to truth ! of soul sincere,
In action faithful, and in honor clear !
Who broke no promise, serv'd no private end,
Who gain'd no title, and who lost no friend !
Ennobled by himself, by all approv'd,
Prais'd, wept, and honor'd, by the Muse he lov'd !

The lines on Craggs were not originally intended for an epitaph ; and therefore some faults are to be imputed to the violence with which they are torn from the poem that first contained them. We may, however, observe some defects. There is a redundancy of words in the first couplet : it is superfluous to tell of him who was *sincere, true,* and *faithful,* that he was *in honor clear.*

There seems to be an opposition intended in the fourth line, which is not very obvious ; where is the relation between the two positions, that he *gained no title,* and *lost no friend?*

It may be proper here to remark the absurdity of joining in the same inscription Latin and English, or verse and prose. If either language be preferable to the other, let that only be used ; for no reason can be given why part of the information should be given in one tongue and part in another, on a tomb more than in any other place or any other occasion ; and to tell all that can be conveniently told in verse, and then to call in the help of prose, has always the appearance of a very artless expedient. or of an attempt unaccomplished. Such an epitaph resembles the conversation of a foreigner, who tells part of his meaning by words, and conveys part by signs.

V.

Intended for Mr. ROWE.
In Westminster-Abbey.

Thy relics, Rowe, to this fair urn we trust,
And, sacred, place by Dryden's awful dust ;
Beneath a rude and nameless stone he lies,
To which thy tomb shall guide inquiring eyes.
Peace to thy gentle shade, and endless rest !
Blest in thy genius, in thy love too blest !
One grateful woman to thy fame supplies
What a whole thankless land to his denies.

Of this inscription the chief fault is, that it belongs less to Rowe, for whom it is written, than to Dryden, who was buried near him ; and indeed gives very little information concerning either.

To wish *Peace to thy shade* is too mythological to be admitted into a Christian temple : the ancient worship has infected almost all our other compositions, and might therefore be contented to spare our epitaphs. Let fiction at least cease with life, and let us be serious over the grave.

VI.

On Mrs. CORBET,
Who died of a Cancer in her Breast.

Here rests a woman, good without pretence,
Blest with plain reason and with sober sense ;
No conquest she, but o'er herself, desir'd :
No arts essay'd, but not to be admir'd.
Passion and pride were to her soul unknown,
Convinc'd that virtue only is our own.
So unaffected, so compos'd a mind,
So firm, yet soft, so strong, yet so refin'd,
Heaven, as its purest gold, by tortures tried ;
The saint sustain'd it, but the woman died.

I have always considered this as the most valuable of all Pope's epitaphs ; the subject of it is a character not discriminated by any shining or eminent peculiarities ; yet that which really makes, though not the splendor, the felicity of life, and that which every wise man will choose for his final and lasting companion in the languor of age, in the quiet of privacy, when he departs weary and disgusted from the ostentatious, the volatile, and the vain. Of such a character, which the dull overlook and the gay despise, it was fit that the value should be made known and the dignity established. Domestic virtue, as it is exerted without great occasions, or conspicuous consequences, in an even unnoted tenor, required the genius of Pope to display it in such a manner as might attract regard and enforce reverence. Who can forbear to lament that this amiable woman has no name in the verses ?

If the particular lines of this inscription be examined, it will appear less faulty than the rest. There is scarcely one line taken from commonplaces, unless it be that in which *only virtue* is said to be *our own*. I once heard a lady of great beauty and elegance object to the fourth line, that it contained an unnatural and incredible panegyric. Of this let the ladies judge.

VII.

On the Monument of the Hon. ROBERT DIGBY, *and of his Sister* MARY, *erected by their Father, the Lord* DIGBY, *in the Church of Sherborne in Dorsetshire,* 1727.

> Go ! fair example of untainted youth,
> Of modest wisdom and pacific truth :
> Compos'd in sufferings, and in joy sedate,
> Good without noise, without pretension great :
> Just of thy word, in every thought sincere,
> Who knew no wish but what the world might hear :
> Of softest manners, unaffected mind,
> Lover of peace, and friend of human kind :
> Go, live ! for heaven's eternal year is thine,
> Go, and exalt thy moral to divine.
>   And thou, blest maid ! attendant on his doom,
> Pensive has follow'd to the silent tomb ;
> Steer'd the same course to the same quiet shore,
> Not parted long, and now to part no more !
> Go, then, where only bliss sincere is known !
> Go, where to love and to enjoy are one !
>   Yet take these tears, Mortality's relief,
> And, till we share your joys, forgive our grief :
> These little rites, a stone, a verse receive,
> 'Tis all a father, all a friend can give !

This epitaph contains of the brother only a general indiscriminate character, and of the sister tells nothing but that she died. The difficulty in writing epitaphs is to give a particular and appropriate praise. This, however, is not always to be performed, whatever be the diligence or ability of the writer ; for the greater part of mankind *have no character at all*, have little that distinguishes them from others equally good or bad, and therefore nothing can be said of them which may not be applied with equal propriety to a thousand more. It is indeed no great panegyric that there is inclosed in this tomb one who was born in one year and died in another ; yet many useful and amiable lives have been spent which yet leave little materials for any other memorial. These are, however, not the proper subjects of poetry ; and whenever friendship or any other motive obliges a poet to write on such subjects, he must be forgiven if he sometimes wanders in generalities and utters the same praises over different tombs.

The scantiness of human praises can scarcely be made more apparent than by remarking how often Pope has, in the few epitaphs which he composed, found it necessary to borrow from himself. The fourteen epitaphs which he has written comprise about a hundred and forty lines, in which there are more repetitions than will easily be found in all the rest of his works. In the eight lines which make the character of Digby there is scarce any thought or word which may not be found in the other epitaphs.

The ninth line, which is far the strongest and most elegant, is borrowed from Dryden. The conclusion is the same with that on Harcourt, but is here more elegant and better connected.

VIII.

On Sir GODFREY KNELLER.

In Westminster-Abbey, 1723.

> Kneller, by Heaven, and not a master taught,
> Whose art was nature and whose pictures thought,
> Now for two ages, having snatch'd from fate
> Whate'er was beauteous or whate'er was great,
> Lies crown'd with prince's honors, poet's lays,
> Due to his merit and brave thirst of praise.
>   Living, great Nature fear'd he might outvie
> Her works ; and dying, fears herself may die.

Of this epitaph the first couplet is good, the second not bad, the third is deformed with a broken metaphor, the word *crowned* not being applicable to the *honors* or the *lays ;* and the fourth is not only borrowed from the epitaph on Raphael, but of a very harsh construction.

IX.

On General HENRY WITHERS.

In Westminster-Abbey, 1729.

> Here, Withers, rest ! thou bravest, gentlest mind !
> Thy country's friend, but more of human kind.
> .O ! born to arms ! O ! worth in youth approv'd !
> O ! soft humanity in age belov'd !

> For thee the hardy veteran drops a tear,
> And the gay courtier feels the sigh sincere.
>   Withers, adieu ! yet not with thee remove
> Thy martial spirit or thy social love !
> Amidst corruption, luxury, and rage,
> Still leave some ancient virtues to our age ;
> Nor let us say (those English glories gone)
> The last true Briton lies beneath this stone.

The epitaph on Withers affords another instance of commonplaces, though somewhat diversified by mingled qualities and his peculiarity of a profession.

The second couplet is abrupt, general, and unpleasing ; exclamation seldom succeeds in our language ; and, I think, it may be observed that the particle O ! used at the beginning of the sentence always offends.

The third couplet is more happy ; the value expressed for him by different sorts of men raises him to esteem : there is yet something of the common cant of superficial satirists who suppose that the insincerity of a courtier destroys all his sensations, and that he is equally a dissembler to the living and the dead.

At the third couplet I should wish the epitaph to close, but that I should be unwilling to lose the two next lines, which yet are dearly bought if they cannot be retained without the four that follow them.

X.

On Mr. ELIJAH FENTON.

At Easthamstead in Berkshire, 1730.

> This modest stone, what few vain marbles can,
> May truly say, Here lies an honest man :
> A poet, blest beyond the poet's fate,
> Whom Heaven kept sacred from the proud and great :
> Foe to loud praise, and friend to learned ease,
> Content with science in the vale of peace.
> Calmly he look'd on either life, and here
> Saw nothing to regret, or there to fear ;
> From Nature's temperate feast rose satisfied,
> Thank'd Heaven that he liv'd, and that he died.

The first couplet of this epitaph is borrowed from Crashaw. The four next lines contain a species of praise peculiar, original, and just. Here, therefore, the inscription should have ended, the latter part containing nothing but what is common to every man who is wise and good. The character of Fenton was so amiable that I cannot forbear to wish for some poet or biographer to display it more fully for the advantage of posterity. If he did not stand in the first rank of genius he may claim a place in the second ; and whatever criticism may object to his writings, censure could find very little to blame in his life.

XI.

On Mr. GAY.
In Westminster-Abbey, 1732.

Of manners gentle, of affections mild ;
In wit, a man ; simplicity, a child ;
With native humor tempering virtuous rage,
Form'd to delight at once and lash the age :
Above temptation in a low estate,
And uncorrupted, ev'n among the great ;
A safe companion and an easy friend,
Unblam'd through life, lamented in thy end,
These are thy honors ! not that here thy bust
Is mix'd with heroes, or with kings thy dust ;
But that the worthy and the good shall say,
Striking their pensive bosoms—Here lies GAY !

As Gay was the favorite of our author this epitaph was probably written with an uncommon degree of attention ; yet it is not more successfully executed than the rest, for it will not always happen that the success of a poet is proportionate to his labor. The same observation may be extended to all works of imagination, which are often influenced by causes wholly out of the performer's power, by hints of which he perceives not the origin, by sudden elevations of mind which he cannot produce in himself, and which sometimes rise when he expects them least.

The two parts of the first line are only echoes of each other ; *gentle manners* and *mild affections*, if they mean any thing, must mean the same.

That Gay was a *man in wit* is a very frigid commendation ; to have the wit of a man is not much for a poet. The *wit of man* and the *simplicity of a child* make a poor and vulgar contrast, and raise no ideas of excellence either intellectual or moral.

In the next couplet *rage* is less properly introduced after the mention of *mildness* and *gentleness*, which are made the constitutents of his character ; for a man so *mild* and *gentle* to *temper* his *rage* was not difficult.

The next line is inharmonious in its sound and mean in its conception ; the opposition is obvious, and the word *lash*, used absolutely, and without any modification, is gross and improper.

To be *above temptation* in poverty, and *free from corruption among the great*, is indeed such a peculiarity as deserved notice. But to be a *safe companion* is a praise merely negative, arising not from possession of virtue, but the absence of vice, and that one of the most odious.

As little can be added to his character by asserting that he was *lamented in his end.* Every man that dies is, at least by the writer of his epitaph, supposed to be lamented, and therefore this general lamentation does no honor to Gay.

The first eight lines have no grammar; the adjectives are without any substantive, and the epithets without a subject.

The thought in the last line, that Gay is buried in the bosoms of the *worthy* and the *good*, who are distinguished only to lengthen the line, is so dark that few understand it, and so harsh when it is explained that still fewer approve.

XII.

Intended for Sir ISAAC NEWTON.
In Westminster-Abbey.

ISAACUS NEWTONIUS:
Quem Immortalem
Testantur, *Tempus, Natura, Cælum :*
Mortalem
Hoc marmor fatetur.

Nature and Nature's laws lay hid in night,
God said, *Let Newton be !* And all was light.

Of this epitaph, short as it is, the faults seem not to be very few. Why part should be Latin and part English, it is not easy to discover. In the Latin the opposition of *Immortalis* and *Mortalis* is a mere sound or a mere quibble ; he is not *immortal* in any sense contrary to that in which he is *mortal*.

In the verses the thought is obvious, and the words *night* and *light* are too nearly allied.

XIII.

On EDMUND *Duke of* BUCKINGHAM, *who died in the* 19th *Year of his Age,*
1735.

If modest youth, with cool reflection crown'd,
And every opening virtue blooming round,
Could save a parent's justest pride from fate,
Or add one patriot to a sinking state ;
This weeping marble had not ask'd thy tear,
Or sadly told how many hopes lie here !
The living virtue now had shone approv'd,
The senate heard him, and his country lov'd.
Yet softer honors, and less noisy fame,
Attend the shade of gentle Buckingham ;

In whom a race, for courage fam'd and art,
Ends in the milder merit of the heart :
And, chiefs or sages long to Britain given,
Pays the last tribute of a saint to Heaven.

This epitaph Mr. Warburton prefers to the rest ; but I know not for what reason. To *crown* with *reflection* is surely a mode of speech approaching to nonsense. *Opening virtues blooming round* is something like tautology : the six following lines are poor and prosaic. *Art* is in another couplet used for *arts*, that a rhyme may be had to *heart*. The last six lines are the best, but not excellent.

The rest of his sepulchral performances hardly deserve the notice of criticism. The contemptible " Dialogue" between HE and SHE should have been suppressed for the author's sake.

In his last epitaph on himself, in which he attempts to be jocular upon one of the few things that make wise men serious, he confounds the living man with the dead :

Under this stone, or under this sill,
Or under this turf, etc.

When a man is once buried, the question under what he is buried is easily decided. He forgot that though he wrote the epitaph in a state of uncertainty, yet it could not be laid over him till his grave was made. Such is the folly of wit when it is ill employed.

The world has but little new ; even this wretchedness seems to have been borrowed from the following tuneless lines :

Ludovici Areosti humantur ossa
Sub hoc marmore, vel sub hac humo, seu
Sub quicquid voluit benignus hæres
Sive hærede benignior comes, seu
Opportunius incidens Viator :
Nam scire haud potuit futura, sed nec
Tanti erat vacuum sibi cadaver
Ut urnam cuperet parare vivens,
Vivens ista tamen sibi paravit.
Quæ inscribi voluit suo sepulchro
Olim siquod haberet is sepulchrum.

Surely Ariosto did not venture to expect that his trifle would have ever had such an illustrious imitator.

DR. SAMUEL JOHNSON ON GRAY.

THOMAS GRAY, the son of Mr. Philip Gray, a scrivener of London, was born in Cornhill, November 26, 1716. His grammatical education he received at Eton, under the care of Mr. Antrobus, his mother's brother, then assistant to Dr. George, and when he left school, in 1734, entered a pensioner at Peterhouse in Cambridge.

The transition from the school to the college is, to most young scholars, the time from which they date their years of manhood, liberty, and happiness ; but Gray seems to have been very little delighted with academical qualifications ; he liked at Cambridge neither the mode of life nor the fashion of study, and lived sullenly on to the time when his attendance on lectures was no longer required. As he intended to profess the common law he took no degree.

When he had been at Cambridge about five years, Mr. Horace Walpole, whose friendship he had gained at Eton, invited him to travel with him as his companion. They wandered through France into Italy ; and Gray's " Letters" contain a very pleasing account of many parts of their journey. But unequal friendships are easily dissolved : at Florence they quarrelled and parted ; and Mr. Walpole is now content to have it told that it was by his fault. If we look, however, without prejudice on the world, we shall find that men whose consciousness of their own merit sets them above the compliances of servility are apt enough in their association with superiors to watch their own dignity with troublesome and punctilious jealousy, and in the fervor of independence to exact that attention which they refuse to pay. Part they did, whatever was the quarrel ; and the rest of their travels was doubtless more unpleasant to them both. Gray continued his journey in a manner suitable to his own little fortune, with only an occasional servant.

He returned to England in September, 1741, and in about two months afterwards buried his father, who had, by an injudicious waste of money upon a new house, so much lessened his fortune that Gray thought himself too poor to study the law. He therefore retired to Cambridge, where he soon after became bachelor of civil law, and where, without liking the place or its inhabitants, or professing to like them, he passed, except a short residence at London, the rest of his life.

About this time he was deprived of Mr. West, the son of a chancellor of Ireland, a friend on whom he appears to have set a high value, and who deserved his esteem by the powers which he shows in his letters, and in the " Ode to May," which Mr. Mason has preserved, as well as by the sincerity with which, when Gray sent him part of " Agrippina," a tragedy that he had just begun, he gave an opinion which probably intercepted the progress of the work, and which the judgment of every reader will confirm. It was certainly no loss to the English stage that " Agrippina" was never finished.

In this year (1742) Gray seems to have applied himself seriously to poetry ; for in this year were produced the " Ode to Spring," his " Prospect of Eton," and his " Ode to Adversity." He began likewise a Latin poem, " De Principiis Cogitandi."

It may be collected from the narrative of Mr. Mason that his first ambition was to have excelled in Latin poetry : perhaps it were reasonable to wish that he had prosecuted his design ; for, though there is at present some embarrassment in his phrase, and some harshness in his lyric numbers, his copiousness of language is such as very few possess ; and his lines, even when imperfect, discover a writer whom practice would have made skilful.

He now lived on at Peterhouse, very little solicitous what others did or thought, and cultivated his mind and enlarged his views without any other purpose than of improving and amusing himself ; when Mr. Mason, being elected fellow of Pembroke Hall, brought him a companion who was afterwards to be his editor, and whose fondness and fidelity has kindled in him a zeal of admiration which cannot be reasonably expected from the neutrality of a stranger and the coldness of a critic.

In his retirement he wrote (1747) an ode on the " Death of Mr. Walpole's Cat ;" and the year afterwards attempted a poem of more importance, on " Government and Education," of which the fragments which remain have many excellent lines.

His next production (1750) was his far-famed " Elegy in a Country Churchyard," which, finding its way into a magazine, first, I believe, made him known to the public.

An invitation from Lady Cobham about this time gave occasion to an odd composition called " A Long Story," which adds little to Gray's character.

Several of his pieces were published (1753) with designs by Mr. Bentley : and that they might in some form or other make a book, only one side of each leaf was printed. I believe the poems and the plates recommended each other so well that the whole impression was soon bought. This year he lost his mother.

Some time afterwards (1756) some young men of the college, whose chambers were near his, diverted themselves with disturbing him by frequent and troublesome noises, and, as is said, by pranks yet more offensive and contemptuous. This insolence, having endured it awhile, he represented to the governors of the society, among whom perhaps he had no friends ; and finding his complaint little regarded removed himself to Pembroke Hall.

In 1757 he published "The Progress of Poetry," and "The Bard," two compositions at which the readers of poetry were at first content to gaze in mute amazement. Some that tried them confessed their inability to understand them, though Warburton said that they were understood as well as the works of Milton and Shakespeare, which it is the fashion to admire. Garrick wrote a few lines in their praise. Some hardy champions undertook to rescue them from neglect ; and in a short time many were content to be shown beauties which they could not see.

Gray's reputation was now so high that, after the death of Cibber, he had the honor of refusing the laurel, which was then bestowed on Mr. Whitehead.

His curiosity, not long after, drew him away from Cambridge to a lodging near the Museum, where he resided near three years, reading and transcribing ; and, so far as can be discovered, very little affected by two odes on "Oblivion" and "Obscurity," in which his lyric performances were ridiculed with much contempt and much ingenuity.

When the professor of modern history at Cambridge died, he was, as he says, "cockered and spirited up," till he asked it of Lord Bute, who sent him a civil refusal ; and the place was given to Mr. Brocket, the tutor of Sir James Lowther.

His constitution was weak, and believing that his health was promoted by exercise and change of place, he undertook (1765) a journey into Scotland, of which his account, so far as it extends, is very curious and elegant ; for, as his comprehension was ample, his curiosity extended to all the works of art, all the appearances of nature, and all the monuments of past events. He naturally contracted a friendship with Dr. Beattie, whom he found a poet, a philosopher, and a good man. The Mareschal College at Aberdeen offered him the degree of

doctor of laws, which, having omitted to take it at Cambridge, he thought it decent to refuse.

What he had formerly solicited in vain was at last given
him without solicitation. The professorship of history became
again vacant, and he received (1768) an offer of it from the
Duke of Grafton. He accepted and retained it to his death,
always designing lectures, but never appearing reading them,
uneasy at his neglect of duty, and appeasing his uneasiness
with designs of reformation, and with a resolution which he believed himself to have made of resigning the office if he found
himself unable to discharge it.

Ill health made another journey necessary, and he visited
(1769) Westmoreland and Cumberland. He that reads his
epistolary narration wishes that to travel, and to tell his
travels, had been more of his employment ; but it is by studying at home that we must obtain the ability of travelling with
intelligence and improvement.

His travels and his studies were now near their end. The
gout, of which he had sustained many weak attacks, fell upon
his stomach, and, yielding to no medicines, produced strong
convulsions, which (July 30, 1771) terminated in death.

His character I am willing to adopt, as Mr. Mason has
done, from a letter written to my friend Mr. Boswell by the
Rev. Mr. Temple, rector of St. Gluvias in Cornwall, and am
as willing as his warmest well-wisher to believe it true.

" Perhaps he was the most learned man in Europe. He
was equally acquainted with the elegant and profound parts of
science, and that not superficially, but thoroughly. He knew
every branch of history, both natural and civil ; had read all
the original historians of England, France, and Italy, and
was a great antiquarian. Criticism, metaphysics, morals, politics, made a principal part of his study ; voyages and travels of
all sorts were his favorite amusements ; and he had a fine
taste in painting, prints, architecture, and gardening. With such
a fund of knowledge his conversation must have been equally
instructing and entertaining ; but he was also a good man, a
man of virtue and humanity. There is no character without
some speck, some imperfection ; and I think the greatest defect in his was an affectation in delicacy, or rather effeminacy,
and a visible fastidiousness, or contempt and disdain of his inferiors in science. He also had, in some degree, that weakness
which disgusted Voltaire so much in Mr. Congreve : though he
seemed to value others chiefly according to the progress that
they had made in knowledge, yet he could not bear to be considered merely as a man of letters ; and though without birth,

or fortune, or station, his desire was to be looked upon as a private independent gentleman who read for his amusement. Perhaps it may be said, What signifies so much knowledge when it produced so little ? Is it worth taking so much pains to leave no memorials but a few poems ? But let it be considered that Mr. Gray was to others at least innocently employed ; to himself certainly beneficially. His time passed agreeably : he was every day making some new acquisition in science ; his mind was enlarged, his heart softened, his virtue strengthened ; the world and mankind were shown to him without a mask ; and he was taught to consider every thing as trifling, and unworthy of the attention of a wise man, except the pursuit of knowledge and practice of virtue in that state wherein God hath placed us.''

To this character Mr. Mason has added a more particular account of Gray's skill in zoology. He has remarked that Gray's effeminacy was affected most '' before those whom he did not wish to please ;'' and that he is unjustly charged with making knowledge his sole reason of preference, as he paid his esteem to none whom he did not likewise believe to be good.

What has occurred to me, from the slight inspection of his Letters in which my undertaking has engaged me is, that his mind had a large grasp, that his curiosity was unlimited, and his judgment cultivated ; that he was a man likely to love much where he loved at all ; but that he was fastidious and hard to please. His contempt, however, is often employed where I hope it will be approved, upon scepticism and infidelity. His short account of Shaftesbury I will insert.

'' You say you cannot conceive how Lord Shaftesbury came to be a philosopher in vogue ; I will tell you : first, he was a lord ; secondly, he was as vain as any of his readers ; thirdly, men are very prone to believe what they do not understand ; fourthly, they will believe any thing at all, provided they are under no obligation to believe it ; fifthly, they love to take a new road, even when that road leads nowhere ; sixthly, he was reckoned a fine writer, and seems always to mean more than he said. Would you have any more reasons ? An interval of above forty years has pretty well destroyed the charm. A dead lord ranks with commoners ; vanity is no longer interested in the matter ; for a new road has become an old one.''

Mr. Mason has added, from his own knowledge, that though Gray was poor he was not eager of money ; and that out of the little that he had he was very willing to help the necessitous.

As a writer he had this peculiarity, that he did not write his pieces first rudely, and then correct them, but labored every line as it arose in the train of composition ; and he had a notion, not very peculiar, that he could not write but at certain times or at happy moments ; a fantastic foppery, to which my kindness for a man of learning and virtue wishes him to have been superior.

Gray's poetry is now to be considered ; and I hope not to be looked on as an enemy to his name if I confess that I contemplate it with less pleasure than his life.

His ode " On Spring " has something poetical both in the language and the thought ; but the language is too luxuriant and the thoughts have nothing new.   There has of late arisen a practice of giving to adjectives derived from substantives the termination of participles ; such as the *cultured* plain, the *daisied* bank ; but I was sorry to see, in the lines of a scholar like Gray, the *honied* Spring.   The morality is natural, but too stale ; the conclusion is pretty.

The poem " On the Cat " was doubtless by its author considered as a trifle ; but it is not a happy trifle.   In the first stanza, " the azure flowers *that* blow" show resolutely a rhyme is sometimes made when it cannot easily be found.   Selima, the Cat, is called a nymph, with some violence both to language and sense ; but there is no good use made of it when it is done ; for of the two lines,

> " What female heart can gold despise ?
> What cat's averse to fish ?"

the first relates merely to the nymph, and the second only to the cat.   The sixth stanza contains a melancholy truth, that " a favorite has no friend ;" but the last ends in a pointed sentence of no relation to the purpose ; if *what glistered* had been *gold*, the cat would not have gone into the water ; and if she had, would not less have been drowned.

The " Prospect of Eton College" suggests nothing to Gray which every beholder does not equally think and feel.   His supplication to Father Thames, to tell him who drives the hoop or tosses the ball, is useless and puerile.   Father Thames has no better means of knowing than himself.   His epithet " buxom health" is not elegant ; he seems not to understand the word. Gray thought his language more poetical as it was more remote from common use ; finding in Dryden " honey redolent of Spring," an expression that reaches the utmost limits of our language, Gray drove it a little more beyond common apprehension by making " gales " to be " redolent of joy and youth."

Of the " Ode on Adversity" the hint was at first taken from " O Diva, gratum quæ regis Antium :" but Gray has excelled his original by the variety of his sentiments and by their moral application. Of this piece, at once poetical and rational, I will not by slight objections violate the dignity.

My process has now brought me to the *wonderful* " Wonder of Wonders," the two Sister Odes, by which, though either vulgar ignorance or common-sense at first universally rejected them, many have been since persuaded to think themselves delighted. I am one of those that are willing to be pleased, and therefore would gladly find the meaning of the first stanza of " The Progress of Poetry."

Gray seems in his rapture to confound the images of " spreading sound and running water." A " stream of music " may be allowed ; but where does " music," however " smooth and strong," after having visited the " verdant vales, roll down the steep amain," so as that " rocks and nodding groves rebellow to the roar " ? If this be said of music, it is nonsense ; if it be said of water, it is nothing to the purpose.

The second stanza, exhibiting Mars's car and Jove's eagle, is unworthy of further notice. Criticism disdains to chase a school-boy to his commonplaces.

To the third it may likewise be objected that it is drawn from mythology, though such as may be more easily assimilated to real life. Idalia's " velvet green" has something of cant. An epithet or metaphor drawn from nature ennobles art ; an epithet or metaphor drawn from art degrades nature. Gray is too fond of words arbitrarily compounded. " Many-twinkling " was formerly censured as not analogical ; we may say " many spotted," but scarcely " many spotting." This stanza, however, has something pleasing.

Of the second ternary of stanzas, the first endeavors to tell something, and would have told it, had it not been crossed by Hyperion : the second describes well enough the universal prevalence of poetry ; but I am afraid that the conclusion will not arise from the premises. The caverns of the North and the plains of Chili are not the residences of " Glory and generous Shame." But that Poetry and Virtue go always together is an opinion so pleasing that I can forgive him who resolves to think it true.

The third stanza sounds big with " Delphi," and " Ægean," and " Ilissus," and " Meander," and " hallowed fountains," and " solemn sounds ;" but in all Gray's odes there is a kind of cumbrous splendor which we wish away. His position is at last false : in the time of Dante and Petrarch, from whom we derive our first school of poetry, Italy was overrun by "tyrant power," and "coward vice;" nor was our state much better when we first borrowed the Italian arts. Of the third ternary, the first gives us a mythological birth of Shakespeare. What is said of that mighty genius is true ; but it is not said happily : the real effects of this poetical power are put out of sight by the pomp of machinery. Where truth is sufficient to fill the mind, fiction is worse than useless ; the counterfeit debases the genuine.

His account of Milton's blindness, if we suppose it caused by study in the formation of his poem, a supposition surely allowable, is poetically true and happily imagined. But the *car* of Dryden, with his *two coursers*, has nothing in it peculiar ; it is a car in which any other rider may be placed.

"The Bard" appears, at the first view, to be, as Algarotti and others have remarked, an imitation of the prophecy of Nereus. Algarotti thinks it superior to its original ; and if preference depends only on the imagery and animation of the two poems his judgment is right. There is in "The Bard" more force, more thought, and more variety. But to copy is less than to invent, and the copy has been unhappily produced at a wrong time. The fiction of Horace was to the Romans credible ; but its revival disgusts us with apparent and unconquerable falsehood. *Incredulus odi.*

To select a singular event, and swell it to a giant's bulk by fabulous appendages of spectres and predictions, has little difficulty ; for he that forsakes the probable may always find the marvellous. And it has little use ; we are affected only as we believe ; we are improved only as we find something to be imitated or declined. I do not see that "The Bard" promotes any truth, moral or political.

His stanzas are too long, especially his epodes ; the ode is finished before the ear has learned its measures, and consequently before it can receive pleasure from their consonance and recurrence.

Of the first stanza the abrupt beginning has been celebrated ; but technical beauties can give praise only to the inventor. It is in the power of any man to rush abruptly upon his subject that has read the ballad "Johnny Armstrong,"

"Is there ever a man in all Scotland—"

The initial resemblances, or alliterations, "ruin, ruthless, helm or hauberk," are below the grandeur of a poem that endeavors at sublimity.

In the second stanza the Bard is well described ; but in the third we have the puerilities of obsolete mythology. When we are told that " Cadwallo hush'd the stormy main," and that " Modred made huge Plinlimmon bow his cloud-topp'd head," attention recoils from the repetition of a tale that, even when it was first heard, was heard with scorn.

The *weaving* of the *winding sheet* he borrowed, as he owns, from the Northern Bards : but their texture, however, was very properly the work of female powers, as the act of spinning the thread of life is another mythology. Theft is always dangerous. Gray has made weavers of slaughtered bards by a fiction outrageous and incongruous. They are then called upon to " weave the warp and weave the woof," perhaps with no great propriety ; for it is by crossing the *woof* with the *warp* that men weave the *web* or piece ; and the first line was dearly bought by the admission of its wretched correspondent, " Give ample room and verge enough." He has, however, no other line as bad.

The third stanza of the second ternary is commended, I think, beyond its merit. The personification is indistinct. *Thirst* and *Hunger* are not alike ; and their features, to make the imagery perfect, should have been discriminated. We are told in the same stanza how " towers are fed." But I will no longer look for particular faults ; yet let it be observed that the ode might have been concluded with an action of better example ; but suicide is always to be had without expense of thought.

These odes are marked by glittering accumulations of ungraceful ornaments ; they strike rather than please ; the images are magnified by affectation ; the language is labored into harshness. The mind of the writer seems to work with unnatural violence. " Double, double, toil and trouble." He has a kind of strutting dignity, and is tall by walking on tiptoe. His art and his struggle are too visible, and there is too little appearance of ease and nature.

To say that he had no beauties would be unjust ; a man like him, of great learning and great industry, could not but produce something valuable. When he pleases least, it can only be said that a good design was ill directed.

His translations of Northern and Welsh Poetry deserve praise ; the imagery is preserved, perhaps often improved ; but the language is unlike the language of other poets.

In the character of his Elegy I rejoice to concur with the common reader ; for by the common-sense of readers, uncorrupted with literary prejudices, after all the refinements of subtilty and the dogmatism of learning, must be finally decided all claim to poetical honors. The "Churchyard" abounds with images which find a mirror in every mind, and with sentiments to which every bosom returns an echo. The four stanzas beginning, "Yet even these bones," are to me original : I have never seen the notions in any other place ; yet he that reads them here persuades himself that he has always felt them. Had Gray written often thus, it had been vain to blame and useless to praise him.

APPENDIX.

ESSAYS

ON

BOSWELL'S LIFE OF JOHNSON.

BY

MACAULAY AND CARLYLE.

MACAULAY ON BOSWELL'S LIFE OF JOHNSON.

This work has greatly disappointed us.[1] Whatever faults we may have been prepared to find in it, we fully expected that it would be a valuable addition to English literature ; that it would contain many curious facts and many judicious re-marks ; that the style of the notes would be neat, clear,.and pre-cise ; and that the typographical execution would be, as in new editions of classical works it ought to be, almost faultless. (We are sorry to be obliged to say that the merits of Mr. Croker's performance are on a par with those of a certain leg of mutton on which Dr. Johnson dined, while travelling from London to Oxford, and which he, with characteristic energy, pronounced to be " as bad as bad could be ; ill fed, ill killed, ill kept, and ill dressed.") This edition is ill compiled, ill arranged, ill writ-ten, and ill printed.

Nothing in the work has astonished us so much as the igno-rance or carelessness of Mr. Croker with respect to facts and dates. Many of his blunders are such as we should be sur-prised to hear any well-educated gentleman commit, even in conversation. The notes absolutely swarm with misstatements into which the editor never would have fallen, if he had taken the slightest pains to investigate the truth of his assertions, or if he had even been well acquainted with the book on which he undertook to comment. We will give a few instances.

Mr. Croker tells us in a note that Derrick, who was master of the ceremonies at Bath, died very poor in 1760.[2] We read on ; and, a few pages later, we find Dr. Johnson and Boswell talking of this same Derrick as still living and reigning, as hav-ing retrieved his character, as possessing so much power over his subjects at Bath that his opposition might be fatal to Sheri-dan's lectures on oratory.[3] And all this is in 1763. The fact is, that Derrick died in 1769.

In one note we read that Sir Herbert Croft, the author of that pompous and foolish account of Young which appears among the " Lives of the Poets," died in 1805.[4] Another

[1] " The Life of Samuel Johnson, LL.D. Including a Journal of a Tour to the Hebrides, by James Boswell, Esq." A new edition, with numer-ous Additions and Notes. By John Wilson Croker, LL.D., F.R.S. Five volumes, 8vo. London, 1831.
[2] I. 394.   [3] I. 404.   [4] IV. 321.

note in the same volume states that this same Sir Herbert Croft died at Paris, after residing abroad for fifteen years, on the 27th of April, 1816.[1]

Mr. Croker informs us that Sir William Forbes, of Pitsligo, the author of the "Life of Beattie," died in 1816.[2] A Sir William Forbes undoubtedly died in that year, but not the Sir William Forbes in question, whose death took place in 1806. It is notorious, indeed, that the biographer of Beattie lived just long enough to complete the history of his friend. Eight or nine years before the date which Mr. Croker has assigned for Sir William's death, Sir Walter Scott lamented that event in the introduction to the fourth canto of "Marmion." Every school-girl knows the lines :

> " Scarce had lamented Forbes paid
> The tribute to his Minstrel's shade ;
> The tale of friendship scarce was told,
> Ere the narrator's heart was cold :
> Far may we search before we find
> A heart so manly and so kind !"

In one place we are told that Allan Ramsay, the painter, was born in 1709, and died in 1784 ;[3] in another, that he died in 1784, in the seventy-first year of his age.[4]

In one place, Mr. Croker says that at the commencement of the intimacy between Dr. Johnson and Mrs. Thrale, in 1765, the lady was twenty-five years old.[5] In other places he says that Mrs. Thrales thirty-fifth year coincided with Johnson's seventieth.[6] Johnson was born in 1709. If, therefore, Mrs. Thrale's thirty-fifth year coincided with Johnson's seventieth, she could have been only twenty-one years old in 1765. This is not all. Mr. Croker, in another place, assigns the year 1777 as the date of the complimentary lines which Johnson made on Mrs. Thrale's thirty-fifth birthday.[7] If this date be correct, Mrs. Thrale must have been born in 1742, and could have been only twenty-three when her acquaintance with Johnson commenced. Mr. Croker therefore gives us three different statements as to her age. Two of the three must be incorrect. We will not decide between them ; we will only say that the reasons which Mr. Croker gives for thinking that Mrs. Thrale was exactly thirty-five years old when Johnson was seventy, appear to us utterly frivolous.

Again, Mr. Croker informs his readers that " Lord Mans-

[1] IV. 428.   [2] II. 262.   [3] IV. 105.   [4] V. 281.
[5] I. 510.   [6] IV. 271, 322.   [7] III. 463.

field survived Johnson full ten years." [1] Lord Mansfield survived Dr. Johnson just eight years and a quarter.

Johnson found in the library of a French lady, whom he
visited during his short visit to Paris, some works which he regarded with great disdain. "I looked," says he, "into the
books in the lady's closet, and, in contempt, showed them to
Mr. Thrale. 'Prince Titi,' 'Bibliothèque des Fées,' and other
books." [2] "'The History of Prince Titi,'" observes Mr. Croker, "was said to be the autobiography of Frederick Prince of
Wales, but was probably written by Ralph his secretary." A
more absurd note never was penned. The "History of Prince
Titi," to which Mr. Croker refers, whether written by Prince
Frederick or by Ralph, was certainly never published. If Mr.
Croker had taken the trouble to read with attention that very
passage in "Park's Royal and Noble Authors" which he cites
as his authority, he would have seen that the manuscript was
given up to the government. Even if this memoir had been
printed, it is not very likely to find its way into a French lady's
bookcase. And would any man in his senses speak contemptuously of a French lady for having in her possession an English work, so curious and interesting as a "Life of Prince Frederick," whether written by himself or by a confidential secretary, must have been? The history at which Johnson laughed
was a very proper companion to the "Bibliothèque des Fées,"
a fairy tale about good Prince Titi and naughty Prince Violent.
Mr. Croker may find it in the "Magasin des Enfans," the first
French book which the little girls of England read to their gov-
ernesses.

Mr. Croker states that Mr. Henry Bate, who afterwards assumed the name of Dudley, was proprietor of the *Morning
Herald*, and fought a duel with George Robinson Stoney, in
consequence of some attacks on Lady Strathmore which appeared in that paper. [3] Now, Mr. Bate was then connected, not
with the *Morning Herald*, but with the *Morning Post ;* and the
dispute took place before the *Morning Herald* was in existence.
The duel was fought in January, 1777. The Chronicle of the
"Annual Register" for that year contains an account of the
transaction, and distinctly states that Mr. Bate was editor of the
Morning Post. The *Morning Herald*, as any person may see
by looking at any number of it, was not established till some
years after this affair. For this blunder there is, we must acknowledge, some excuse ; for it certainly seems almost incredible to a person living in our time that any human being should
ever have stooped to fight with a writer in the *Morning Post.*

[1] II. 151.   [2] III. 271.   [3] V. 196.

" James de Duglas," says Mr. Croker, " was requested by
King Robert Bruce, in his last hours, to repair with his heart to
Jerusalem, and humbly to deposit it at the sepulchre of our
Lord, which he did in 1329."[1]   Now, it is well known that he
did no such thing, and for a very sufficient reason, because he
was killed by the way.   Nor was it in 1329 that he set out.
Robert Bruce died in 1329, and the expedition of Douglas
took place in the following year, " Quand le printems vint et la
saison," says Froissart, in June 1330, says Lord Hailes, whom
Mr. Croker cites as the authority for his statement.

Mr. Croker tells us that the great Marquis of Montrose was
beheaded at Edinburgh in 1650.[2]   There is not a forward boy
at any school in England who does not know that the marquis
was hanged.   The account of the execution is one of the finest
passages in Lord Clarendon's History.   We can scarcely
suppose that Mr. Croker has never read that passage ; and yet
we can scarcely suppose that any person who has ever perused
so noble and pathetic a story can have utterly forgotten all its
most striking circumstances.

" Lord Townshend," says Mr. Croker, " was not secretary
of state till 1720."[3]   Can Mr. Croker possibly be ignorant
that Lord Townshend was made secretary of state at the accession of George I. in 1714, that he continued to be secretary of
state till he was displaced by the intrigues of Sunderland and
Stanhope at the close of 1716, and that he returned to the office
of secretary of state, not in 1720, but in 1721 ?

Mr. Croker, indeed, is generally unfortunate in his statements respecting the Townshend family.   He tells us that
Charles Townshend, the chancellor of the exchequer, was
" nephew of the prime minister, and son of a peer who was
secretary of state, and leader of the House of Lords."[4]
Charles Townshend was not nephew, but grandnephew, of
the Duke of Newcastle, not son, but grandson, of the Lord
Townshend who was secretary of state, and leader of the House
of Lords.

" General Burgoyne surrendered at Saratoga," says Mr.
Croker, " in March, 1778."[5]   General Burgoyne surrendered
on the 17th of October, 1777.

" Nothing," says Mr. Croker, " can be more unfounded
than the assertion that Byng fell a martyr *to political party.*
By a strange coincidence of circumstances, it happened that
there was a total change of administration between his condemnation and his death ; so that one party presided at his

---

[1] IV. 29.   [2] II. 526.   [3] III. 52.
[4] III. 368.   [5] IV. 222.

trial and another at his execution : there can be no stronger
proof that he was *not* a political martyr."[1] Now, what will
our readers think of this writer when we assure them that this
statement, so confidently made respecting events so notorious,
is absolutely untrue ? One and the same administration was in
office when the court-martial on Byng commenced its sittings,
through the whole trial, at the condemnation and at the execution. In the month of November, 1756, the Duke of Newcastle
and Lord Hardwicke resigned ; the Duke of Devonshire became first lord of the treasury, and Mr. Pitt secretary of state.
This administration lasted till the month of April, 1757.
Byng's court-martial began to sit on the 28th of December,
1756. He was shot on the 14th of March, 1757. There is
something at once diverting and provoking in the cool and authoritative manner in which Mr. Croker makes these random
assertions. We do not suspect him of intentionally falsifying
history. But of this high literary misdemeanor we do without
hesitation accuse him, that he has no adequate sense of the
obligation which a writer, who professes to relate facts, owes to
the public. We accuse him of a negligence and an ignorance
analogous to that *crassa negligentia* and that *crassa ignorantia*,
on which the law animadverts in magistrates and surgeons, even
when malice and corruption are not imputed. We accuse him
of having undertaken a work which, if not performed with
strict accuracy, must be very much worse than useless, and of
having performed it as if the difference between an accurate
and an inaccurate statement was not worth the trouble of looking into the most common book of reference.

But we must proceed. These volumes contain mistakes
more gross, if possible, than any that we have yet mentioned.
Boswell has recorded some observations made by Johnson on the
changes which had taken place in Gibbon's religious opinions.
That Gibbon when a lad at Oxford turned Catholic is well
known. " It is said," cried Johnson, laughing, " that he has
been a Mohammedan." " This sarcasm," says the editor,
" probably alludes to the tenderness with which Gibbon's malevolence to Christianity induced him to treat Mohammedanism
in his history." Now, the sarcasm was uttered in 1776 ; and
that part of the " History of the Decline and Fall of the Roman
Empire" which relates to Mohammedanism was not published
till 1788, twelve years after the date of this conversation, and
near four years after the death of Johnson.[2]

[1] I. 298.
[2] A defence of this blunder was attempted. That the celebrated chapters in which Gibbon has traced the progress of Mohammedanism were

"It was in the year 1761," says Mr. Croker, "that Goldsmith published his 'Vicar of Wakefield.' This leads the editor to observe a more serious inaccuracy of Mrs. Piozzi than Mr. Boswell notices, when he says Johnson left her table to go and sell the 'Vicar of Wakefield' for Goldsmith. Now, Dr. Johnson was not acquainted with the Thrales till 1765, four years after the book had been published." [1] Mr. Croker, in reprehending the fancied inaccuracy of Mrs. Thrale, has himself shown a degree of inaccuracy, or, to speak more properly, a degree of ignorance, hardly credible. In the first place, Johnson became acquainted with the Thrales, not in 1765, but in 1764, and during the last weeks of 1764 dined with them every Thursday, as is written in Mrs. Piozzi's anecdotes. In the second place, Goldsmith published the "Vicar of Wakefield," not in 1761, but in 1766. Mrs. Thrale does not pretend to remember the precise date of the summons which called Johnson from her table to the help of his friend. She says only that it was near the beginning of her acquaintance with Johnson, and certainly not later than 1766. Her accuracy is therefore completely vindicated. It was probably after one of her Thursday dinners in 1764 that the celebrated scene of the landlady, the sheriff's officer, and the bottle of Madeira, took place. [2]

The very page which contains this monstrous blunder contains another blunder, if possible, more monstrous still. Sir Joseph Mawbey, a foolish member of Parliament, at whose speeches and whose pigstyes the wits of Brookes's were, fifty

not written in 1776 could not be denied. But it was confidently asserted that his partiality to Mohammedanism appeared in his first volume. This assertion is untrue. No passage which can by any art be construed into the faintest indication of the faintest partiality for Mohammedanism has ever been quoted or ever will be quoted from the first volume of the 'History of the Decline and Fall of the Roman Empire."

To what, then, it has been asked, could Johnson allude? Possibly to some anecdote or some conversation of which all trace is lost. One conjecture may be offered, though with diffidence. Gibbon tells us in his "Memoirs," that at Oxford he took a fancy for studying Arabic, and was prevented from doing so by the remonstrances of his tutor. Soon after this the young man fell in with Bossuet's controversial writings, and was speedily converted by them to the Roman Catholic faith. The apostasy of a gentleman commoner would of course be for a time the chief subject of conversation in the common room of Magdalene. His whim about Arabic learning would naturally be mentioned, and would give occasion to some jokes about the probability of his turning Mussulman. If such jokes were made, Johnson, who frequently visited Oxford, was very likely to hear of them.

[1] V. 409.

[2] This paragraph has been altered; and a slight inaccuracy, immaterial to the argument, has been removed.

years ago, in the habit of laughing most unmercifully, stated, on the authority of Garrick, that Johnson, while sitting in a coffee-house at Oxford, about the time of his Doctor's degree, used some contemptuous expressions respecting Home's play and Macpherson's "Ossian." "Many men," he said, "many women, and many children, might have written Douglas." Mr. Croker conceives that he has detected an inaccuracy, and glories over poor Sir Joseph in a most characteristic manner. "I have quoted this anecdote solely with the view of showing to how little credit hearsay anecdotes are in general entitled. Here is a story published by Sir Joseph Mawbey, a member of the House of Commons, and a person every way worthy of credit, who says he had it from Garrick. Now mark : Johnson's visit to Oxford, about the time of his Doctor's degree, was in 1754, the first time he had been there since he left the uni-· versity. But "Douglas" was not acted till 1756, and "Ossian" not published till 1760. All, therefore, that is new in Sir Joseph Mawbey's story is false." [1] Assuredly we need not go far to find ample proof that a member of the House of Commons may commit a very gross error. Now mark, say we, in the language of Mr. Croker. The fact is, that Johnson took his Master's degree in 1754,[2] and his Doctor's degree in 1775.[3] In the spring of 1776[4] he paid a visit to Oxford, and at this visit a conversation respecting the works of Home and Macpherson might have taken place, and, in all probability, did take place. The only real objection to the story Mr. Croker has' missed. Boswell states, apparently on the best authority, that as early at least as the year 1763, Johnson, in conversation with Blair, used the same expressions respecting "Ossian" which Sir Joseph represents him as having used respecting "Douglas."[5] Sir Joseph or Garrick confounded, we suspect, the two stories. But their error is venial, compared with that of Mr. Croker.

We will not multiply instances of this scandalous inaccuracy. It is clear that a writer who, even when warned by the text on which he is commenting, falls into such mistakes as these, is entitled to no confidence whatever. Mr. Croker has committed an error of five years with respect to the publication of Goldsmith's novel, an error of twelve years with respect to the publication of part of Gibbon's History, an error of twenty-one years with respect to an event in Johnson's life so important as the taking of the doctoral degree. Two of these three errors he has committed, while ostentatiously displaying his own accuracy, and correcting what he represents as the loose

[1] V. 409. [2] I. 262. [3] III. 205.
[4] III. 326 [5] I. 405.

assertions of others. How can his readers take on trust his statements concerning the births, marriages, divorces, and deaths of a crowd of people whose names are scarcely known to this generation? It is not likely that a person who is ignorant of what almost every body knows can know that of which almost every body is ignorant. We did not open this book with any wish to find blemishes in it. We have made no curious researches. The work itself and a very common knowledge of literary and political history have enabled us to detect the mistakes which we have pointed out, and many other mistakes of the same kind. We must say, and we say it with regret, that we do not consider the authority of Mr. Croker, unsupported by other evidence, as sufficient to justify any writer who may follow him in relating a single anecdote or in assigning a date to a single event.

Mr. Croker shows almost as much ignorance and heedlessness in his criticisms as in his statements concerning facts. Dr. Johnson said, very reasonably as it appears to us, that some of the satires of Juvenal are too gross for imitation. Mr. Croker, who, by the way, is angry with Johnson for defending Prior's tales against the charge of indecency, resents this aspersion on Juvenal, and indeed refuses to believe that the doctor can have said any thing so absurd. " He probably said—some *passages* of them—for there are none of Juvenal's satires to which the same objection may be made as to one of Horace's, that it is *altogether* gross and licentious." [1] Surely Mr. Croker can never have read the second and ninth satires of Juvenal.

Indeed, the decisions of this editor on points of classical learning, though pronounced in a very authoritative tone, are generally such that, if a schoolboy under our care were to utter them, our soul assuredly should not spare for his crying. It is no disgrace to a gentleman who has been engaged during near thirty years in political life that he has forgotten his Greek and Latin. But he becomes justly ridiculous if, when no longer able to construe a plain sentence, he affects to sit in judgment on the most delicate questions of style and metre. From one blunder, a blunder which no good scholar would have made, Mr. Croker was saved, as he informs us, by Sir Robert Peel, who quoted a passage exactly in point from Horace. We heartily wish that Sir Robert, whose classical attainments are well known, had been more frequently consulted. Unhappily he was not always at his friend's elbow ; and we have therefore a rich abundance of the strangest errors. Boswell has preserved a poor epigram by Johnson, inscribed " Ad Lauram paritu-

[1] I. 167.

ram." Mr. Croker censures the poet for applying the word puella to a lady in Laura's situation, and for talking of the beauty of Lucina. "Lucina," he says, "was never famed for her beauty."[1] If Sir Robert Peel had seen this note, he probably would have again refuted Mr. Croker's criticisms by an appeal to Horace. In the secular ode, Lucina is used as one of the names of Diana, and the beauty of Diana is extolled by all the most orthodox doctors of the ancient mythology, from Homer in his "Odyssey" to Claudian in his "Rape of Proserpine." In another ode, Horace describes Diana as the goddess who assists the "laborantes utero puellas." But we are ashamed to detain our readers with this fourth-form learning.

Boswell found, in his tour to the Hebrides, an inscription written by a Scotch minister. It runs thus : "Joannes Macleod, &c., gentis suæ Philarchus, &c., Floræ Macdonald matrimoniali vinculo conjugatus turrem hanc Beganodunensem proævorum habitaculum longe vetustissimum, diu penitus labefactatam, anno æræ vulgaris MDCLXXXVI. instauravit."— "The minister," says Mr. Croker, "seems to have been no contemptible Latinist. Is not Philarchus a very happy term to express the paternal and kindly authority of the head of a clan?"[2] The composition of this eminent Latinist, short as it is, contains several words that are just as much Coptic as Latin, to say nothing of the incorrect structure of the sentence. The word Philarchus, even if it were a happy term expressing a paternal and kindly authority, would prove nothing for the minister's Latin, whatever it might prove for his Greek. But it is clear that the word Philarchus means, not a man who rules by love, but a man who loves rule. The Attic writers of the best age use the word φίλαρχος in the sense which we assign to it. Would Mr. Croker translate φιλοσοφος, a man who acquires wisdom by means of love, or φιλοκερδής, a man who makes money by means of love? In fact, it requires no Bentley or Casaubon to perceive that Philarchus is merely a false spelling for Phylarchus, the chief of a tribe.

Mr. Croker has favored us with some Greek of his own. "At the altar," says Dr. Johnson, "I recommended my Ϩ φ." "These letters," says the editor "(which Dr. Strahan seems not to have understood), probably mean Ϩνητοι φιλοι, *departed friends.*"[3] Johnson was not a first-rate Greek

---

[1] I. 133.   [2] II. 458.
[3] IV. 251. An attempt was made to vindicate this blunder by quoting a grossly corrupt passage from the Ἱκέτιδες of Euripides :

βᾶθι καὶ ἀντίασον γονάτων, ἔπι χεῖρα βαλοῦσα,
τέκνων τε θνατῶν κομίσαι δέμας.

scholar ; but he knew more Greek than most boys when they leave school ; and no schoolboy could venture to use the word Ϟνητοι in the sense which Mr. Croker ascribes to it without imminent danger of a flogging.

Mr. Croker has also given us a specimen of his skill in translating Latin. Johnson wrote a note in which he consulted his friend, Dr. Lawrence, on the propriety of losing some blood. The note contains these words : " Si per te licet, imperatur nuncio Holderum ad me deducere." Johnson should rather have written " imperatum est." But the meaning of the words is perfectly clear. " If you say yes, the messenger has orders to bring Holder to me." Mr. Croker translates the words as follows : " If you consent, pray tell the messenger to bring Holder to me." ¹ If Mr. Croker is resolved to write on points of classical learning, we would advise him to begin by giving an hour every morning to our old friend Corderius.

Indeed, we cannot open any volume of this work in any place, and turn it over for two minutes in any direction, without lighting on a blunder. Johnson, in his Life of Tickell, stated that a poem entitled the Royal Progress, which appears in the last volume of the " Spectator," was written on the accession of George I. The word " arrival" was afterwards substituted for " accession." " The reader will observe," says Mr. Croker, " that the Whig term *accession*, which might imply legality, was altered into a statement of the simple fact of King George's *arrival*." ² Now, Johnson, though a bigoted Tory, was not quite such a fool as Mr. Croker here represents him to be. In the Life of Granville, Lord Lansdowne, which stands a very few pages from the Life of Tickell, mention is made of the accession of Anne, and of the accession of George I. The word arrival was used in the Life of Tickell for the simplest of all reasons. It was used because the subject of the poem called the Royal Progress was the arrival of the king, and not his accession, which took place near two months before his arrival.

The editor's want of perspicacity is indeed very amusing. He is perpetually telling us that he cannot understand something in the text which is as plain as language can make it. " Mattaire," said Dr. Johnson, " wrote Latin verses from time to time, and published a set in his old age, which he

---

The true reading, as every scholar knows, is, τέκνων τεκνεώτων κομίσαι δέμας. Indeed, without this emendation it would not be easy to construe the words, even if ϑνατῶν could bear the meaning which Mr. Croker assigns to it.
¹ V. 17.   ² IV. 425.

called *Senilia*, in which he shows so little learning or taste in
writing as to make Carteret a dactyl."[1] Hereupon we have
this note : "The editor does not understand this objection,
nor the following observation." The following observation,
which Mr. Croker cannot understand, is simply this : "In
matters of genealogy," says Johnson, "it is necessary to give
the bare names as they are. But in poetry and in prose of any
elegance in the writing, they require to have inflection given to
them." If Mr. Croker had told Johnson that this was unintelligible, the doctor would probably have replied, as he replied
on another occasion, "I have found you a reason, sir ; I am
not bound to find you an understanding." Every body who
knows any thing of Latinity knows that, in genealogical tables,
Joannes Baro de Carteret, or Vicecomes de Carteret, may be
tolerated, but that in compositions which pretend to elegance,
Carteretus, or some other form which admits of inflection,
ought to be used.

All our readers have doubtless seen the two distichs of Sir
William Jones, respecting the division of the time of a lawyer.
One of the distichs is translated from some old Latin lines ;
the other is original. The former runs thus :

> " Six hours to sleep, to law's grave study six,
> Four spend in prayer, the rest on nature fix."

"Rather," says Sir William Jones,

> " Six hours to law, to soothing slumbers seven,
> Ten to the world allot, and all to heaven."

The second couplet puzzles Mr. Croker strangely. "Sir
William," says he, "has shortened his day to twenty-three
hours, and the general advice of 'all to heaven' destroys the
peculiar appropriation of a certain period to religious exercises."[2] Now, we did not think that it was in human dulness
to miss the meaning of the lines so completely. Sir William
distributes twenty-three hours among various employments.
One hour is thus left for devotion. The reader expects that the
verse will end with "and one to heaven." The whole point
of the lines consists in the unexpected substitution of "all"
for "one." The conceit is wretched enough ; but it is perfectly intelligible, and never, we will venture to say, perplexed
man, woman, or child before.

Poor Tom Davies, after failing in business, tried to live by
his pen. Johnson called him "an author generated by the
corruption of a bookseller." This is a very obvious and even

[1] IV. 335. [2] V. 233.

a commonplace allusion to the famous dogma of the old physi-
ologists. Dryden made a similar allusion to that dogma before
Johnson was born. Mr. Croker, however, is unable to understand what the doctor meant. "The expression," he says,
"seems not quite clear." And he proceeds to talk about the
generation of insects, about bursting into gaudier life, and
Heaven knows what.[1]

There is a still stranger instance of the editor's talent for
finding out difficulty in what is perfectly plain. "No man,"
said Johnson, "can now be made a bishop for his learning and
piety." "From this too just observation," says Boswell,
"there are some eminent exceptions." Mr. Croker is puzzled
by Boswell's very natural and simple language. "That a general observation should be pronounced *too just*, by the very person who admits that it is not universally just, is not a little
odd."[2]

A very large proportion of the two thousand five hundred
notes which the editor boasts of having added to those of Boswell and Malone consists of the flattest and poorest reflections,
reflections such as the least intelligent reader is quite competent to make for himself, and such as no intelligent reader
would think it worth while to utter aloud. They remind us of
nothing so much as of those profound and interesting annota-
tions which are pencilled by sempstresses and apothecaries'
boys on the dog-eared margins of novels borrowed from circulating libraries : "How beautiful !" "Cursed prosy !" "I
don't like Sir Reginald Malcolm at all." "I think Pelham is
a sad dandy." Mr. Croker is perpetually stopping us in our
progress through the most delightful narrative in the language,
to observe that really Dr. Johnson was very rude, that he
talked more for victory than for truth, that his taste for port
wine with capillaire in it was very odd, that Boswell was impertinent, that it was foolish in Mrs. Thrale to marry the music-
master ; and so forth.

We cannot speak more favorably of the manner in which
the notes are written than of the matter of which they consist.
We find in every page words used in wrong senses, and con-
structions which violate the plainest rules of grammar. We
have the vulgarism of "mutual friend" for "common friend."
We have "fallacy" used as synonymous with "falsehood."
We have many such inextricable labyrinths of pronouns as that
which follows : "Lord Erskine was fond of this anecdote ; he
told it to the editor the first time that he had the honor of

---

[1] IV. 323.   [2] III. 228.

being in his company." Lastly, we have a plentiful supply of sentences resembling those which we subjoin. " Markland, *who*, with Jortin and Thirlby, Johnson calls three contemporaries of great eminence." [1] "Warburton himself did not feel, as Mr. Boswell was disposed to think he did, kindly or gratefully *of* Johnson." [2] "It was *him* that Horace Walpole called a man who never made a bad figure but as an author." [3] One or two of these solecisms should perhaps be attributed to the printer, who has certainly done his best to fill both the text and the notes with all sorts of blunders. In truth, he and the editor have between them made the book so bad that we do not well see how it could have been worse.

When we turn from the commentary of Mr. Croker to the work of our old friend Boswell, we find it not only worse printed than in any other edition with which we are acquainted, but mangled in the most wanton manner. Much that Boswell inserted in his narrative is, without the shadow of a reason, degraded to the appendix. The editor has also taken upon himself to alter or omit passages which he considers as indecorous. This prudery is quite unintelligible to us. There is nothing immoral in Boswell's book, nothing which tends to inflame the passions. He sometimes uses plain words. But if this be a taint which requires expurgation, it would be desirable to begin by expurgating the morning and evening lessons. The delicate office which Mr. Croker has undertaken he has performed in the most capricious manner. One strong, old-fashioned English word, familiar to all who read their Bibles, is changed for a softer synonyme in some passages, and suffered to stand unaltered in others. In one place a faint allusion made by Johnson to an indelicate subject, an allusion so faint that, till Mr. Croker's note pointed it out to us, we had never noticed it, and of which we are quite sure that the meaning would never be discovered by any of those for whose sake books are expurgated, is altogether omitted. In another place, a coarse and stupid jest of Dr. Taylor on the same subject, expressed in the broadest language, almost the only passage, as far as we remember, in all Boswell's book, which we should have been inclined to leave out, is suffered to remain.

We complain, however, much more of the additions than of the omissions. We have half of Mrs. Thrale's book, scraps of Mr. Tyers, scraps of Mr. Murphy, scraps of Mr. Cradock, long prosings of Sir John Hawkins, and connecting observations by Mr Croker himself, inserted into the midst of Boswell's text.

[1] IV. 377.   [2] IV. 415.   [3] II. 461.

To this practice we most decidedly object.   An editor might as well publish Thucydides with extracts from Diodorus interspersed, or incorporate the Lives of Suetonius with the History and Annals of Tacitus.   Mr. Croker tells us, indeed, that he has done only what Boswell wished to do, and was prevented from doing by the law of copyright.   We doubt this greatly. Boswell has studiously abstained from availing himself of the information given by his rivals, on many occasions on which he might have cited them without subjecting himself to the charge of piracy.   Mr. Croker has himself, on one occasion, remarked very justly that Boswell was unwilling to owe any obligation to Hawkins.   But, be this as it may, if Boswell had quoted from Sir John and from Mrs. Thrale, he would have been guided by his own taste and judgment in selecting his quotations.   On what Boswell quoted he would have commented with perfect freedom ; and the borrowed passages, so selected, and accompanied by such comments, would have become original.   They would have dovetailed into the work. No hitch, no crease, would have been discernible.   The whole would appear one and indivisible,

> " Ut per læve severos
> Effundat junctura ungues."

This is not the case with Mr. Croker's insertions.   They are not chosen as Boswell would have chosen them.   They are not introduced as Boswell would have introduced them.   They differ from the quotations scattered through the original " Life of Johnson," as a withered bough stuck in the ground differs from a tree skilfully transplanted with all its life about it.

Not only do these anecdotes disfigure Boswell's book ; they are themselves disfigured by being inserted in his book.   The charm of Mrs. Thrale's little volume is utterly destroyed.   The feminine quickness of observation, the feminine softness of heart, the colloquial incorrectness and vivacity of style, the little amusing airs of a half-learned lady, the delightful garrulity, the " dear Doctor Johnson," the " it was so comical," all disappear in Mr. Croker's quotations.   The lady ceases to speak in the first person ; and her anecdotes, in the process of transfusion, become as flat as champagne in decanters, or Herodotus in Beloe's version.   Sir John Hawkins, it is true, loses nothing ; and for the best of reasons : Sir John had nothing to lose.

The course which Mr. Croker ought to have taken is quite clear.   He should have reprinted Boswell's narrative precisely as Boswell wrote it ; and in the notes or the appendix he should have placed any anecdotes which he might have thought it advisable to quote from other writers. This would have been a much more convenient course for the reader, who has now constantly to keep his eye on the margin in order to see whether he is perusing Boswell, Mrs. Thrale, Murphy, Hawkins, Tyers, Cradock, or Mr. Croker. We greatly doubt whether even the "Tour to the Hebrides" ought to have been inserted in the midst of the Life. There is one marked distinction between the two works. Most of the Tour was seen by Johnson in manuscript. It does not appear that he ever saw any part of the Life.

We love, we own, to read the great productions of the human mind as they were written. We have this feeling even about scientific treatises ; though we know that the sciences are always in a state of progression, and that the alterations made by a modern editor in an old book on any branch of natural or political philosophy are likely to be improvements. Some errors have been detected by writers of this generation in the speculations of Adam Smith. A short cut has been made to much knowledge at which Sir Isaac Newton arrived through arduous and circuitous paths. Yet we still look with peculiar veneration on the "Wealth of Nations" and on the "Principia," and should regret to see either of those great works garbled even by the ablest hands. But in works which owe much of their interest to the character and situation of the writers the case is infinitely stronger. What man of taste and feeling can endure *rifacimenti*, harmonies, abridgments, expurgated editions ? Who ever reads a stage copy of a play when he can procure the original ? Who ever cut open Mrs. Siddons's Milton ? Who ever got through ten pages of Mr. Gilpin's translation of John Bunyan's Pilgrim into modern English ? Who would lose, in the confusion of a Diatessaron, the peculiar charm which belongs to the narrative of the disciple whom Jesus loved ? The feeling of a reader who has become intimate with any great original work is that which Adam expressed towards his bride :

> " Should God create another Eve, and I
> Another rib afford, yet loss of thee
> Would never from my heart."

No substitute, however exquisitely formed, will fill the void left by the original. The second beauty may be equal or superior to the first ; but still it is not she.

The reasons which Mr. Croker has given for incorporating passages from Sir John Hawkins and Mrs. Thrale with the narrative of Boswell would vindicate the adulteration of half the classical works in the language. If Pepys's Diary and Mrs.

Hutchinson's Memoirs had been published a hundred years ago, no human being can doubt that Mr. Hume would have made great use of those books in his "History of England." But would it, on that account, be judicious in a writer of our own times to publish an edition of Hume's "History of England," in which large extracts from Pepys and Mrs. Hutchinson should be incorporated with the original text? Surely not. Hume's history, be its faults what they may, is now one great entire work, the production of one vigorous mind, working on such materials as were within its reach. Additions made by another hand may supply a particular deficiency, but would grievously injure the general effect. With Boswell's book the case is stronger. There is scarcely, in the whole compass of literature, a book which bears interpolation so ill. We know no production of the human mind which has so much of what may be called the race, so much of the peculiar flavor of the soil from which it sprang. The work could never have been written if the writer had not been precisely what he was. His character is displayed in every page, and this display of character gives a delightful interest to many passages which have no other interest.

The "Life of Johnson" is assuredly a great, a very great work. Homer is not more decidedly the first of heroic poets, Shakespeare is not more decidedly the first of dramatists, Demosthenes is not more decidedly the first of orators, than Boswell is the first of biographers. He has no second. He has distanced all his competitors so decidedly that it is not worth while to place them. Eclipse is first, and the rest nowhere.

We are not sure that there is in the whole history of the human intellect so strange a phenomenon as this book. Many of the greatest men that ever lived have written biography. Boswell was one of the smallest men that ever lived, and he has beaten them all. He was, if we are to give any credit to his own account or to the united testimony of all who knew him, a man of the meanest and feeblest intellect. Johnson described him as a fellow who had missed his only chance of immortality by not having been alive when the "Dunciad" was written. Beauclerk used his name as a proverbial expression for a bore. He was the laughing-stock of the whole of that brilliant society which has owed to him the greater part of its fame. He was always laying himself at the feet of some eminent man, and begging to be spit upon and trampled upon. He was always earning some ridiculous nickname, and then "binding it as a crown unto him," not merely in metaphor, but literally. He exhibited himself, at the Shakespeare Jubilee, to all the

crowd which filled Stratford-on-Avon, with a placard round his
hat bearing the inscription of Corsica Boswell. In his Tour,
he proclaimed to all the world that at Edinburgh he was known
by the appellation of Paoli Boswell. Servile and impertinent,
shallow and pedantic, a bigot and a sot, bloated with family
pride, and eternally blustering about the dignity of a born gentleman, yet stooping to be a talebearer, an eavesdropper, a
common butt in the taverns of London, so curious to know
every body who was talked about, that, Tory and High Churchman as he was, he manœuvred, we have been told, for an introduction to Tom Paine, so vain of the most childish distinctions, that when he had been to court, he drove to the office
where his book was printing without changing his clothes, and
summoned all the printer's devils to admire his new ruffles and
sword ; such was this man, and such he was content and proud
to be. Every thing which another man would have hidden,
every thing the publication of which would have made another
man hang himself, was matter of gay and clamorous exultation
to his weak and diseased mind. What silly things he said,
what bitter retorts he provoked, how at one place he was troubled with evil presentiments which came to nothing, how at
another place, on waking from a drunken doze, he read the
prayer-book and took a hair of the dog that had bitten him,
how he went to see men hanged and came away maudlin, how
he added five hundred pounds to the fortune of one of his
babies because she was not scared at Johnson's ugly face, how
he was frightened out of his wits at sea, and how the sailors
quieted him as they would have quieted a child, how tipsy he
was at Lady Cork's one evening and how much his merriment
annoyed the ladies, how impertinent he was to the Duchess of
Argyle and with what stately contempt she put down his impertinence, how Colonel Macleod sneered to his face at his
impudent obtrusiveness, how his father and the very wife of his
bosom laughed and fretted at his fooleries—all these things he
proclaimed to all the world, as if they had been subjects for
pride and ostentatious rejoicing. All caprices of his temper,
all the illusions of his vanity, all his hypochondriac whimsies,
all his castles in the air, he displayed with a cool self-compla-
cency, a perfect unconsciousness that he was making a fool of
himself, to which it is impossible to find a parallel in the whole
history of mankind. He has used many people ill ; but
assuredly he has used nobody so ill as himself.

That such a man should have written one of the best books
in the world is strange enough. But this is not all. Many
persons who have conducted themselves foolishly in active life,

and whose conversation has indicated no superior powers of
mind, have left us valuable works. Goldsmith was very justly
described by one of his contemporaries as an inspired idiot,
and by another as a being,

"Who wrote like an angel, and talked like poor Poll."

La Fontaine was in society a mere simpleton. His blunders
would not come in amiss among the stories of Hierocles.
But these men attained literary eminence in spite of their weaknesses. Boswell attained it by reason of his weaknesses. If
he had not been a great fool, he would never have been a great
writer. Without all the qualities which made him the jest and
the torment of those among whom he lived, without the officiousness, the inquisitiveness, the effrontery, the toad-eating,
the insensibility to all reproof, he never could have produced
so excellent a book. He was a slave proud of his servitude, a
Paul Pry, convinced that his own curiosity and garrulity were
virtues, an unsafe companion who never scrupled to repay the
most liberal hospitality by the basest violation of confidence, a
man without delicacy, without shame, without sense enough to
know when he was hurting the feelings of others or when he
was exposing himself to derision ; and because he was all this,
he has, in an important department of literature, immeasurably
surpassed such writers as Tacitus, Clarendon, Alfieri, and his
own idol Johnson.
    Of the talents which ordinarily raise men to eminence as
writers, Boswell had absolutely none. There is not in all his
books a single remark of his own on literature, politics, religion, or society, which is not either commonplace or absurd.
His dissertations on hereditary gentility, on the slave-trade,
and on the entailing of landed estates, may serve as examples.
To say that these passages are sophistical would be to pay
them an extravagant compliment. They have no pretence to
argument, or even to meaning. He has reported innumerable
observations made by himself in the course of conversation.
Of those observations we do not remember one which is above
the intellectual capacity of a boy of fifteen. He has printed
many of his own letters, and in these letters he is always rant-
ing or twaddling. Logic, eloquence, wit, taste, all those
things which are generally considered as making a book valuable, were utterly wanting to him. He had, indeed, a quick
observation and a retentive memory. These qualities, if he
had been a man of sense and virtue, would scarcely of themselves have sufficed to make him conspicuous ; but because he

was a dunce, a parasite, and a coxcomb, they have made him immortal.

Those parts of his book which, considered abstractedly, are most utterly worthless, are delightful when we read them as illustrations of the character of the writer. Bad in themselves, they are good dramatically, like the nonsense of Justice Shallow, the clipped English of Dr. Caius, or the misplaced consonants of Fluellen. Of all confessors, Boswell is the most candid. Other men who have pretended to lay open their own hearts, Rousseau, for example, and Lord Byron, have evidently written with a constant view to effect, and are to be then most distrusted when they seem to be most sincere. There is scarcely any man who would not rather accuse himself of great crimes and of dark and tempestuous passions than proclaim all his little vanities and wild fancies. It would be easier to find a person who would avow actions like those of Cæsar Borgia or Danton, than one who would publish a day-dream like those of Alnaschar and Malvolio. Those weaknesses which most men keep covered up in the most secret places of the mind, not to be disclosed to the eye of friendship or of love, were precisely the weaknesses which Boswell paraded before all the world. He was perfectly frank, because the weakness of his understanding and the tumult of his spirits prevented him from knowing when he made himself ridiculous. His book resembles nothing so much as the conversation of the inmates of the Palace of Truth.

His fame is great ; and it will, we have no doubt, be lasting ; but it is fame of a peculiar kind, and indeed marvellously resembles infamy. We remember no other case in which the world has made so great a distinction between a book and its author. In general, the book and the author are considered as one. To admire the book is to admire the author. The case of Boswell is an exception, we think the only exception, to this rule. His work is universally allowed to be interesting, instructive, eminently original ; yet it has brought him nothing but contempt. All the world reads it ; all the world delights in it ; yet we do not remember ever to have read or ever to have heard any expression of respect and admiration for the man to whom we owe so much instruction and amusement. While edition after edition of his book was coming forth, his son, as Mr. Croker tells us, was ashamed of it, and hated to hear it mentioned. This feeling was natural and reasonable. Sir Alexander saw that, in proportion to the celebrity of the work, was the degradation of the author. The very editors of this unfortunate gentleman's books have forgotten their allegiance, and, like those Puritan casuists who took arms by the authority of the king against his person, have attacked the writer while doing homage to the writings. Mr. Croker, for example, has published two thousand five hundred notes on the life of Johnson, and yet scarcely ever mentions the biographer whose performance he has taken such pains to illustrate without some expression of contempt.

An ill-natured man Boswell certainly was not; yet the malignity of the most malignant satirist could scarcely cut deeper than his thoughtless loquacity. Having himself no sensibility to derision and contempt, he took it for granted that all others were equally callous. He was not ashamed to exhibit himself to the whole world as a common spy, a common tattler, a humble companion without the excuse of poverty, and to tell a hundred stories of his own pertness and folly, and of the insults which his pertness and folly brought upon him. It was natural that he should show little discretion in cases in which the feelings or the honor of others might be concerned. No man, surely, ever published such stories respecting persons whom he professed to love and revere. He would infallibly have made his hero as contemptible as he has made himself, had not his hero really possessed some moral and intellectual qualities of a very high order. The best proof that Johnson was really an extraordinary man is that his character, instead of being degraded, has, on the whole, been decidedly raised by a work in which all his vices and weaknesses are exposed more unsparingly than they ever were exposed by Churchill or by Kenrick.

Johnson grown old, Johnson in the fulness of his fame and in the enjoyment of a competent fortune, is better known to us than any other man in history. Every thing about him, his coat, his wig, his figure, his face, his scrofula, his St. Vitus's dance, his rolling walk, his blinking eye, the outward signs which too clearly marked his approbation of his dinner, his insatiable appetite for fish-sauce and veal-pie with plums, his inextinguishable thirst for tea, his trick of touching the posts as he walked, his mysterious practice of treasuring up scraps of orange-peel, his morning slumbers, his midnight disputations, his contortions, his mutterings, his gruntings, his puffings, his vigorous, acute, and ready eloquence, his sarcastic wit, his vehemence, his insolence, his fits of tempestuous rage, his queer inmates, old Mr. Levett and blind Mrs. Williams, the cat Hodge and the negro Frank, all are as familiar to us as the objects by which we have been surrounded from childhood. But we have no minute information respecting those years of

Johnson's life during which his character and his manners became immutably fixed. We know him, not as he was known to the men of his own generation, but as he was known to men whose father he might have been. That celebrated club of which he was the most distinguished member contained few persons who could remember a time when his fame was not fully established and his habits completely formed. He had made himself a name in literature while Reynolds and the Wartons were still boys. He was about twenty years older than Burke, Goldsmith, and Gerard Hamilton, about thirty years older than Gibbon, Beauclerk, and Langton, and about forty years older than Lord Stowell, Sir William Jones, and Windham. Boswell and Mrs. Thrale, the two writers from whom we derive most of our knowledge respecting him, never saw him till long after he was fifty years old, till most of his great works had become classical, and till the pension bestowed on him by the Crown had placed him above poverty. Of those eminent men who were his most intimate associates towards the close of his life, the only one, as far as we remember, who knew him during the first ten or twelve years of his residence in the capital, was David Garrick; and it does not appear that, during those years, David Garrick saw much of his fellow-townsman.

Johnson came up to London precisely at the time when the condition of a man of letters was most miserable and degraded. It was a dark night between two sunny days. The age of patronage had passed away. The age of general curiosity and intelligence had not arrived. The number of readers is at present so great that a popular author may subsist in comfort and opulence on the profits of his works. In the reigns of William the Third, of Anne, and of George the First, even such men as Congreve and Addison would scarcely have been able to live like gentlemen by the mere sale of their writings. But the deficiency of the natural demand for literature was, at the close of the seventeenth and at the beginning of the eighteenth century, more than made up by artificial encouragement, by a vast system of bounties and premiums. There was, perhaps, never a time at which the rewards of literary merit were so splendid, at which men who could write well found such easy admittance into the most distinguished society, and to the highest honors of the state. The chiefs of both the great parties into which the kingdom was divided patronized literature with emulous munificence. Congreve, when he had scarcely attained his majority, was rewarded for his first comedy with places which made him independent for life. Smith,

though his "Hippolytus" and "Phædra" failed, would have
been consoled with three hundred a year but for his own folly.
Rowe was not only poet-laureate, but also land-surveyor of
the customs in the port of London, clerk of the council to the
Prince of Wales, and secretary of the Presentations to the Lord
Chancellor. Hughes was secretary to the Commissions of the
Peace. Ambrose Philips was judge of the Prerogative Court
in Ireland. Locke was commissioner of appeals and of the
Board of Trade. Newton was master of the Mint. Stepney
and Prior were employed in embassies of high dignity and importance. Gay, who commenced life as apprentice to a silk
mercer, became a secretary of legation at five-and-twenty. It
was to a poem on the Death of Charles the Second, and to the
City and Country Mouse, that Montague owed his introduction
into public life, his earldom, his garter, and his auditorship of
the exchequer. Swift, but for the unconquerable prejudice of
the queen, would have been a bishop. Oxford, with his white
staff in his hand, passed through the crowd of his suitors to
welcome Parnell, when that ingenious writer deserted the
Whigs. Steele was a commissioner of stamps and a member of
Parliament. Arthur Mainwaring was a commissioner of the
customs, and auditor of the imprest. Tickell was secretary to
the Lords Justices of Ireland. Addison was secretary of state.

This liberal patronage was brought into fashion, as it seems,
by the magnificent Dorset, almost the only noble versifier in the
court of Charles the Second who possessed talents for composition which were independent of the aid of a coronet. Montague owed his elevation to the favor of Dorset, and imitated
through the whole course of his life the liberality to which he
was himself so greatly indebted. The Tory leaders, Harley
and Bolingbroke in particular, vied with the chiefs of the Whig
party in zeal for the encouragement of letters. But soon after
the accession of the house of Hanover a change took place.
The supreme power passed to a man who cared little for poetry
or eloquence. The importance of the House of Commons was
constantly on the increase. The government was under the
necessity of bartering for parliamentary support much of that
patronage which had been employed in fostering literary merit ;
and Walpole was by no means inclined to divert any part of
the fund of corruption to purposes which he considered as idle.
He had eminent talents for government and for debate. But
he had paid little attention to books, and felt little respect for
authors. One of the coarse jokes of his friend, Sir Charles
Hanbury Williams, was far more pleasing to him than Thomson's "Seasons" or Richardson's "Pamela." He had ob-

served that some of the distinguished writers whom the favor of
Halifax had turned into statesmen had been mere encumbrances to their party, dawdlers in office, and mutes in Parliament.
During the whole course of his administration, therefore, he
scarcely befriended a single man of genius. The best writers
of the age gave all their support to the opposition, and contributed to excite that discontent which, after plunging the
nation into a foolish and unjust war, overthrew the minister to
make room for men less able and equally immoral. The opposition could reward its eulogists with little more than promises and caresses. St. James's would give nothing : Leicester
house had nothing to give.

Thus, at the time when Johnson commenced his literary
career, a writer had little to hope from the patronage of powerful individuals. The patronage of the public did not yet furnish the means of comfortable subsistence. The prices paid
by booksellers to authors were so low that a man of considerable talents and unremitting industry could do little more than
provide for the day which was passing over him. The lean
kine had eaten up the fat kine. The thin and withered ears had
devoured the good ears. The season of rich harvests was over,
and the period of famine had begun. All that is squalid and
miserable might now be summed up in the word Poet. That
word denoted a creature dressed like a scarecrow, familiar
with compters and sponging-houses, and perfectly qualified to
decide on the comparative merits of the Common Side in the
King's Bench prison and of Mount Scoundrel in the Fleet.
Even the poorest pitied him ; and they well might pity him.
For if their condition was equally abject, their aspirings were
not equally high, nor their sense of insult equally acute. To
lodge in a garret up four pair of stairs, to dine in a cellar
among footmen out of place, to translate ten hours a day for
the wages of a ditcher, to be hunted by bailiffs from one haunt
of beggary and pestilence to another, from Grub Street to St.
George's Fields, and from St. George's Fields to the alleys
behind St. Martin's church, to sleep on a bulk in June and
amidst the ashes of a glass-house in December, to die in an
hospital and to be buried in a parish vault, was the fate of
more than one writer who, if he had lived thirty years earlier,
would have been admitted to the sittings of the Kitcat or the
Scriblerus Club, would have sat in Parliament, and would have
been intrusted with embassies to the High Allies ; who, if he
had lived in our time, would have found encouragement
scarcely less munificent in Albemarle Street or in Paternoster
Row.

As every climate has its peculiar diseases, so every walk of life has its peculiar temptations. The literary character, assuredly, has always had its share of faults: vanity, jealousy, morbid sensibility. To these faults were now superadded the faults which are commonly found in men whose livelihood is precarious, and whose principles are exposed to the trial of severe distress. All the vices of the gambler and of the beggar were blended with those of the author. The prizes in the wretched lottery of book-making were scarcely less ruinous than the blanks. If good fortune came, it came in such a manner that it was almost certain to be abused. After months of starvation and despair, a full third night or a well-received dedication filled the pocket of the lean, ragged, unwashed poet with guineas. He hastened to enjoy those luxuries with the images of which his mind had been haunted while he was sleeping amidst the cinders and eating potatoes at the Irish ordinary in Shoe Lane. A week of taverns soon qualified him for another year of night-cellars. Such was the life of Savage, of Boyse, and of a crowd of others. Sometimes blazing in gold-laced hats and waistcoats ; sometimes lying in bed because their coats had gone to pieces, or wearing paper cravats because their linen was in pawn ; sometimes drinking Champagne and Tokay with Betty Careless ; sometimes standing at the window of an eating-house in Porridge Island, to snuff up the scent of what they could not afford to taste : they knew luxury ; they knew beggary ; but they never knew comfort. These men were irreclaimable. They looked on a regular and frugal life with the same aversion which an old gypsy or a Mohawk hunter feels for a stationary abode and for the restraints and securities of civilized communities. They were as untamable, as much wedded to their desolate freedom, as the wild ass. They could no more be broken in to the offices of social man than the unicorn could be trained to serve and abide by the crib. It was well if they did not, like beasts of a still fiercer race, tear the hands which ministered to their necessities. To assist them was impossible ; and the most benevolent of mankind at length became weary of giving relief which was dissipated with the wildest profusion as soon as it had been received. If a sum was bestowed on the wretched adventurer, such as, properly husbanded, might have supplied him for six months, it was instantly spent in strange freaks of sensuality, and, before forty-eight hours had elapsed, the poet was again pestering all his acquaintance for twopence to get a plate of shin of beef at a subterraneous cook-shop. If his friends gave him an asylum in their houses, those houses were

forthwith turned into bagnios and taverns. All order was destroyed ; all business was suspended. The most good-natured
host began to repent of his eagerness to serve a man of genius
in distress when he heard his guest roaring for fresh punch at
five o'clock in the morning.

A few eminent writers were more fortunate. Pope had
been raised above poverty by the active patronage which, in his
youth, both the great political parties had extended to his
Homer. Young had received the only pension ever bestowed,
to the best of our recollection, by Sir Robert Walpole, as the
reward of mere literary merit. One or two of the many poets
who attached themselves to the opposition, Thomson in particular and Mallet, obtained, after much severe suffering, the
means of subsistence from their political friends. Richardson,
like a man of sense, kept his shop ; and his shop kept him,
which his novels, admirable as they are, would scarcely have
done. But nothing could be more deplorable than the state
even of the ablest men, who at that time depended for subsistence on their writings. Johnson, Collins, Fielding, and
Thomson were certainly four of the most distinguished persons that England produced during the eighteenth century. It
is well known that they were all four arrested for debt.

Into calamities and difficulties such as these Johnson
plunged in his twenty-eighth year. From that time till he was
three or four and fifty, we have little information respecting
him—little, we mean, compared with the full and accurate information which we possess respecting his proceedings and
habits towards the close of his life. He emerged at length
from cocklofts and sixpenny ordinaries into the society of the
polished and the opulent. His fame was established. A pension sufficient for his wants had been conferred on him ; and
he came forth to astonish a generation with which he had
almost as little in common as with Frenchmen or Spaniards.

In his early years he had occasionally seen the great ; but
he had seen them as a beggar. He now came among them as
a companion. The demand for amusement and instruction
had, during the course of twenty years, been gradually increasing. The price of literary labor had risen ; and those rising
men of letters with whom Johnson was henceforth to associate
were for the most part persons widely different from those who
had walked about with him all night in the streets for want of a
lodging. Burke, Robertson, the Wartons, Gray, Mason, Gibbon, Adam Smith, Beattie, Sir William Jones, Goldsmith, and
Churchill, were the most distinguished writers of what may be
called the second generation of the Johnsonian age. Of these

men Churchill was the only one in whom we can trace the stronger lineaments of that character which, when Johnson first came up to London, was common among authors. Of the rest, scarcely any had felt the pressure of severe poverty. Almost all had been early admitted into the most respectable society on an equal footing. They were men of quite a different species from the dependents of Curll and Osborne.

Johnson came among them the solitary specimen of a past age, the last survivor of the genuine race of Grub-street hacks ; the last of that generation of authors whose abject misery and whose dissolute manners had furnished inexhaustible matter to the satirical genius of Pope. From nature he had received an uncouth figure, a diseased constitution, and an irritable temper. The manner in which the earlier years of his manhood had been passed had given to his demeanor, and even to his moral character, some peculiarities appalling to the civilized beings who were the companions of his old age. The perverse irregularity of his hours, the slovenliness of his person, his fits of strenuous exertion, interrupted by long intervals of sluggishness, his strange abstinence, and his equally strange voracity, his active benevolence, contrasted with the constant rudeness and the occasional ferocity of his manners in society, made him, in the opinion of those with whom he lived during the last twenty years of his life, a complete original. An original he was, undoubtedly, in some respects. But if we possessed full information concerning those who shared his early hardships, we should probably find that what we call his singularities of manner were, for the most part, failings which he had in common with the class to which he belonged. He ate at Streatham Park as he had been used to eat behind the screen at St. John's Gate, when he was ashamed to show his ragged clothes. He ate as it was natural that a man should eat, who, during a great part of his life, had passed the morning in doubt whether he should have food for the afternoon. The habits of his early life had accustomed him to bear privation with fortitude, but not to taste pleasure with moderation. He could fast ; but when he did not fast, he tore his dinner like a famished wolf, with the veins swelling on his forehead, and the perspiration running down his cheeks. He scarcely ever took wine ; but when he drank it he drank it greedily and in large tumblers. These were, in fact, mitigated symptoms of that same moral disease which raged with such deadly malignity in his friends Savage and Boyse. The roughness and violence which he showed in society were to be expected from a man whose temper, not naturally gentle, had been long tried by the bitterest calamities, by the want of meat, of fire, and of clothes, by the importunity of creditors, by the insolence of booksellers, by the derision of fools, by the insincerity of patrons, by that bread which is the bitterest of all food, by those stairs which are the most toilsome of all paths, by that deferred hope which makes the heart sick.   Through all these things the ill-dressed, coarse, ungainly pedant had struggled manfully up to eminence and command.   It was natural that, in the exercise of his power, he should be ''eo immitior, quia toleraverat,'' that, though his heart was undoubtedly generous and humane, his demeanor in society should be harsh and despotic.   For severe distress he had sympathy, and not only sympathy, but munificent relief.   But for the suffering which a harsh world inflicts upon a delicate mind he had no pity ; for it was a kind of suffering which he could scarcely conceive.   He would carry home on his shoulders a sick and starving girl from the streets.   He turned his house into a place of refuge for a crowd of wretched old creatures who could find no other asylum ; nor could all their peevishness and ingratitude weary out his benevolence.   But the pangs of wounded vanity seemed to him ridiculous ; and he scarcely felt sufficient compassion even for the pangs of wounded affection.   He had seen and felt so much of sharp misery, that he was not affected by paltry vexations ; and he seemed to think that every body ought to be as much hardened to those vexations as himself. He was angry with Boswell for complaining of a headache, with Mrs. Thrale for grumbling about the dust on the road or the smell of the kitchen.   These were, in his phrase, ''foppish lamentations,'' which people ought to be ashamed to utter in a world so full of sin and sorrow.   Goldsmith crying because the ''Good-natured Man'' had failed inspired him with no pity. Though his own health was not good, he detested and despised valetudinarians.   Pecuniary losses, unless they reduced the loser absolutely to beggary, moved him very little   People whose hearts had been softened by prosperity might weep, he said, for such events ; but all that could be expected of a plain man was not to laugh.   He was not much moved even by the spectacle of Lady Tavistock dying of a broken heart for the loss of her lord.   Such grief he considered as a luxury reserved for the idle and the wealthy.   A washerwoman, left a widow with nine small children, would not have sobbed herself to death.

   A person who troubled himself so little about small or sentimental grievances was not likely to be very attentive to the feelings of others in the ordinary intercourse of society.   He could not understand how a sarcasm or a reprimand could make any man really unhappy. "My dear doctor," said he to Goldsmith, "what harm does it do to a man to call him Holofernes?" "Pooh, ma'am," he exclaimed to Mrs. Carter, "who is the worse for being talked of uncharitably?" Politeness has been well defined as benevolence in small things. Johnson was impolite, not because he wanted benevolence, but because small things appeared smaller to him than to people who had never known what it was to live for fourpence halfpenny a day.

The characteristic peculiarity of his intellect was the union of great powers with low prejudices. If we judged of him by the best parts of his mind, we should place him almost as high as he was placed by the idolatry of Boswell; if by the worst parts of his mind, we should place him even below Boswell himself. Where he was not under the influence of some strange scruple or some domineering passion, which prevented him from boldly and fairly investigating a subject, he was a wary and acute reasoner, a little too much inclined to scepticism, and a little too fond of paradox. No man was less likely to be imposed upon by fallacies in argument or by exaggerated statements of fact. But if, while he was beating down sophisms and exposing false testimony, some childish prejudices, such as would excite laughter in a well-managed nursery, came across him, he was smitten as if by enchantment. His mind dwindled away under the spell from gigantic elevation to dwarfish littleness. Those who had lately been admiring its amplitude and its force were now as much astonished at its strange narrowness and feebleness as the fisherman in the Arabian tale, when he saw the Genie, whose stature had overshadowed the whole sea-coast, and whose might seemed equal to a contest with armies, contract himself to the dimensions of his small prison, and lie there the helpless slave of the charm of Solomon.

Johnson was in the habit of sifting with extreme severity the evidence for all stories which were merely odd. But when they were not only odd but miraculous, his severity relaxed. He began to be credulous precisely at the point where the most credulous people begin to be sceptical. It is curious to observe, both in his writings and in his conversation, the contrast between the disdainful manner in which he rejects unauthenticated anecdotes, even when they are consistent with the general laws of nature, and the respectful manner in which he mentions the wildest stories relating to the invisible world. A man who told him of a water-spout or a meteoric stone gen-

erally had the lie direct given him for his pains. A man who
told him of a prediction or a dream wonderfully accomplished
was sure of a courteous hearing. "Johnson," observed
Hogarth, "like King David, says in his haste that all men
are liars." "His incredulity," says Mrs. Thrale, "amounted
almost to disease." She tells us how he browbeat a gentleman who gave him an account of a hurricane in the West Indies, and a poor Quaker who related some strange circumstance
about the red-hot balls fired at the siege of Gibraltar. "It is
not so ; it cannot be true. Don't tell that story again. You
cannot think how poor a figure you make in telling it." He
once said, half jestingly we suppose, that for six months he
refused to credit the fact of the earthquake at Lisbon, and that
he still believed the extent of the calamity to be greatly exaggerated. Yet he related with a grave face how old Mr. Cave
of St. John's Gate saw a ghost, and how this ghost was something of a shadowy being. He went himself on a ghost-hunt to
Cock Lane, and was angry with John Wesley for not following
up another scent of the same kind with proper spirit and perseverance. He rejects the Celtic genealogies and poems without
the least hesitation ; yet he declares himself willing to believe
the stories of the second sight. If he had examined the claims
of the Highland seers with half the severity with which he sifted
the evidence for the genuineness of "Fingal," he would, we
suspect, have come away from Scotland with a mind fully made
up. In his "Lives of the Poets," we find that he is unwilling
to give credit to the accounts of Lord Roscommon's early
proficiency in his studies ; but he tells with great solemnity an
absurd romance about some intelligence preternaturally impressed on the mind of that nobleman. He avows himself to
be in great doubt about the truth of the story, and ends by
warning his readers not wholly to slight such impressions.

Many of his sentiments on religious subjects are worthy of
a liberal and enlarged mind. He could discern clearly enough
the folly and meanness of all bigotry except his own. When
he spoke of the scruples of the Puritans, he spoke like a person
who had really obtained an insight into the divine philosophy
of the New Testament, and who considered Christianity as a
noble scheme of government, tending to promote the happiness
and to elevate the moral nature of man. The horror which the
sectaries felt for cards, Christmas ale, plum-porridge, mince-
pies, and dancing bears excited his contempt. To the arguments urged by some very worthy people against showy dress
he replied with admirable sense and spirit, "Let us not be
found, when our Master calls us, stripping the lace off our

waistcoats, but the spirit of contention from our souls and tongues. Alas! sir, a man who cannot get to heaven in a green coat will not find his way thither the sooner in a gray one." Yet he was himself under the tyranny of scruples as unreasonable as those of Hudibras or Ralpho, and carried his zeal for ceremonies and for ecclesiastical dignities to lengths altogether inconsistent with reason or with Christian charity. He has gravely noted down in his diary that he once committed the sin of drinking coffee on Good Friday. In Scotland he thought it his duty to pass several months without joining in public worship solely because the ministers of the kirk had not been ordained by bishops. His mode of estimating the piety of his neighbors was somewhat singular. " Campbell," said he, " is a good man, a pious man. I am afraid he has not been in the inside of a church for many years ; but he never passes a church without pulling off his hat : this shows he has good principles." Spain and Sicily must surely contain many pious robbers and well-principled assassins. Johnson could easily see that a Roundhead who named all his children after Solomon's singers, and talked in the House of Commons about seeking the Lord, might be an unprincipled villain, whose religious mummeries only aggravated his guilt. But a man who took off his hat when he passed a church episcopally consecrated must be a good man, a pious man, a man of good principles. Johnson could easily see that those persons who looked on a dance or a laced waistcoat as sinful, deemed most ignobly of the attributes of God and of the ends of revelation. But with what a storm of invective he would have overwhelmed any man who had blamed him for celebrating the redemption of mankind with sugarless tea and butterless buns !

Nobody spoke more contemptuously of the cant of patriotism. Nobody saw more clearly the error of those who regarded liberty not as a means but as an end, and who proposed to themselves, as the object of their pursuit, the prosperity of the state as distinct from the prosperity of the individuals who compose the state. His calm and settled opinion seems to have been that forms of government have little or no influence on the happiness of society. This opinion, erroneous as it is, ought at least to have preserved him from all intemperance on political questions. It did not, however, preserve him from the lowest, fiercest, and most absurd extravagances of party spirit, from rants which, in every thing but the diction, resembled those of Squire Western. He was, as a politician, half ice and half fire. On the side of his intellect he was a mere Pococurante, far too apathetic about public affairs, far too sceptical as to the good or evil tendency of any form of polity. His passions, on the contrary, were violent even to slaying against all who leaned to Whiggish principles. The well-known lines which he inserted in Goldsmith's "Traveller" express what seems to have been his deliberate judgment:

> "How small, of all that human hearts endure,
> That part which kings or laws can cause or cure!"

He had previously put expressions very similar into the mouth of Rasselas. It is amusing to contrast these passages with the torrents of raving abuse which he poured forth against the Long Parliament and the American Congress. In one of the conversations reported by Boswell this inconsistency displays itself in the most ludicrous manner.

"Sir Adam Ferguson," says Boswell, "suggested that luxury corrupts a people and destroys the spirit of liberty." JOHNSON: "Sir, that is all visionary. I would not give half a guinea to live under one form of government rather than another. It is of no moment to the happiness of an individual. Sir, the danger of the abuse of power is nothing to a private man. What Frenchman is prevented passing his life as he pleases?" SIR ADAM: "But, sir, in the British constitution it is surely of importance to keep up a spirit in the people, so as to preserve a balance against the crown." JOHNSON: "Sir, I perceive you are a vile Whig. Why all this childish jealousy of the power of the crown? The crown has not power enough."

One of the old philosophers, Lord Bacon tells us, used to say that life and death were just the same to him. "Why then," said an objector, "do you not kill yourself?" The philosopher answered, "Because it is just the same." If the difference between two forms of government be not worth half a guinea, it is not easy to see how Whiggism can be viler than Toryism, or how the crown can have too little power. If the happiness of individuals is not affected by political abuses, zeal for liberty is doubtless ridiculous. But zeal for monarchy must be equally so. No person could have been more quick-sighted than Johnson to such a contradiction as this in the logic of an antagonist.

The judgments which Johnson passed on books were, in his own time, regarded with superstitious veneration, and in our time are generally treated with indiscriminate contempt. They are the judgments of a strong but enslaved understanding. The mind of the critic was hedged round by an uninterrupted fence of prejudices and superstitions. Within his narrow limits he displayed a vigor and an activity which ought to have enabled him to clear the barrier that confined him.

How it chanced that a man who reasoned on his premises so ably should assume his premises so foolishly, is one of the great mysteries of human nature. The same inconsistency may be observed in the schoolmen of the middle ages. Those writers show so much acuteness and force of mind in arguing on their wretched data, that a modern reader is perpetually at a loss to comprehend how such mind came by such data. Not a flaw in the superstructure of the theory which they are rearing escapes their vigilance. Yet they are blind to the obvious unsoundness of the foundation. It is the same with some eminent lawyers. Their legal arguments are intellectual prodigies, abounding with the happiest analogies and the most refined distinctions. The principles of their arbitrary science being once admitted, the statute-book and the reports being once assumed as the foundations of reasoning, these men must be allowed to be perfect masters of logic. But if a question arises as to the postulates on which their whole system rests, if they are called upon to vindicate the fundamental maxims of that system which they have passed their lives in studying, these very men often talk the language of savages or of children. Those who have listened to a man of this class in his own court, and who have witnessed the skill with which he analyzes and digests a vast mass of evidence, or reconciles a crowd of precedents which at first sight seem contradictory, scarcely know him again when, a few hours later, they hear him speaking on the other side of Westminster Hall in his capacity of legislator. They can scarcely believe that the paltry quirks which are faintly heard through a storm of coughing, and which do not impose on the plainest country gentleman, can proceed from the same sharp and vigorous intellect which had excited their admiration under the same roof and on the same day.

Johnson decided literary questions like a lawyer, not like a legislator. He never examined foundations where a point was already ruled. His whole code of criticism rested on pure assumption, for which he sometimes quoted a precedent or an authority, but rarely troubled himself to give a reason drawn from the nature of things. He took it for granted that the kind of poetry which flourished in his own time, which he had been accustomed to hear praised from his childhood, and which he had himself written with success, was the best kind of poetry. In his biographical work he has repeatedly laid it down as an undeniable proposition that during the latter part of the seventeenth century, and the earlier part of the eighteenth, English poetry had been in a constant progress of im-provement. Waller, Denham, Dryden, and Pope had been, according to him, the great reformers. He judged of all works of the imagination by the standard established among his own contemporaries. Though he allowed Homer to have been a greater man than Virgil, he seems to have thought the "Æneid" a greater poem than the "Iliad." Indeed he well might have thought so ; for he preferred Pope's "Iliad" to Homer's. He pronounced that, after Hoole's translation of Tasso, Fairfax's would hardly be reprinted. He could see no merit in our fine old English ballads, and always spoke with the most provoking contempt of Percy's fondness for them. Of the great original works of imagination which appeared during his time, Richard-son's novels alone excited his admiration. He could see little or no merit in "Tom Jones," in "Gulliver's Travels," or in "Tristram Shandy." To Thomson's "Castle of Indolence" he vouchsafed only a line of cold commendation, of com-mendation much colder than what he has bestowed on the "Creation" of that portentous bore, Sir Richard Blackmore. Gray was, in his dialect, a barren rascal. Churchill was a block-head. The contempt which he felt for the trash of Macpher-son was indeed just ; but it was, we suspect, just by chance. He despised the "Fingal" for the very reason which led many men of genius to admire it. He despised it, not because it was essentially commonplace, but because it had a superficial air of originality.

He was undoubtedly an excellent judge of compositions fashioned on his own principles. But when a deeper philos-ophy was required, when he undertook to pronounce judg-ment on the works of those great minds which "yield homage only to eternal laws," his failure was ignominious. He criti-cised Pope's "Epitaphs" excellently. But his observations on Shakespeare's plays and Milton's poems seem to us for the most part as wretched as if they had been written by Rymer himself, whom we take to have been the worst critic that ever lived.

Some of Johnson's whims on literary subjects can be com-pared only to that strange nervous feeling which made him uneasy if he had not touched every post between the Mitre tavern and his own lodgings. His preference of Latin epitaphs to English epitaphs is an instance. An English epitaph, he said, would disgrace Smollett. He declared that he would not pollute the walls of Westminster Abbey with an English ep-itaph on Goldsmith. What reason there can be for celebrating a British writer in Latin, which there was not for covering the

Roman arches of triumph with Greek inscriptions, or for com·
memorating the deeds of the heroes of Thermopylæ in Egyptian
hieroglyphics, we ·are utterly unable to imagine.

On men and manners, at least on the men and manners of
a particular place and a particular age, Johnson had certainly
looked with a most observant and discriminating eye. His remarks on the education of children, on marriage, on the economy of families, on the rules of society, are always striking, and
generally sound. In his writings, indeed, the knowledge of life
which he possessed in an eminent degree is very imperfectly exhibited. Like those unfortunate chiefs of the middle ages who
were suffocated by their own chain-mail and cloth of gold, his
maxims perish under that load of words which was designed for
their defence and their ornament. But it is clear, from the remains of his conversation, that he had more of that homely wisdom which nothing but experience and observation can give
than any writer since the time of Swift. If he had been content to write as he talked, he might have left books on the
practical art of living superior to the " Directions to Servants."

Yet even his remarks on society, like his remarks on literature, indicate a mind at least as remarkable for narrowness as
for strength. He was no master of the great science of human
nature. He had studied, not the genus man, but the species
Londoner. Nobody was ever so thoroughly conversant with
all the forms of life and all the shades of moral and intellectual
character which were to be seen from Islington to the Thames,
and from Hyde-Park corner to Mile-End green. But his philosophy stopped at the first turnpike-gate. Of the rural life of
England he knew nothing ; and he took it for granted that
every body who lived in the country was either stupid or miserable. " Country gentlemen," said he, " must be unhappy ;
for they have not enough to keep their lives in motion ;" as if
all those peculiar habits and associations which made Fleet
Street and Charing Cross the finest views in the world to himself had been essential parts of human nature. Of remote
countries and past times he talked with wild and ignorant presumption. " The Athenians of the age of Demosthenes," he
said to Mrs. Thrale, " were a people of brutes, a barbarous
people." In conversation with Sir Adam Ferguson he used
similar language. " The boasted Athenians," he said, " were
barbarians. The mass of every people must be barbarous
where there is no printing." The fact was this : he saw that
a Londoner who could not read was a very stupid and brutal
fellow ; he saw that great refinement of taste and activity of intellect were rarely found in a Londoner who had not read

much ; and, because it was by means of books that people acquired almost all their knowledge in the society with which he was acquainted, he concluded, in defiance of the strongest and clearest evidence, that the human mind can be cultivated by means of books alone. An Athenian citizen might possess very few volumes ; and the largest library to which he had access might be much less valuable than Johnson's bookcase in Bolt Court. But the Athenian might pass every morning in conversation with Socrates, and might hear Pericles speak four or five times every month. He saw the plays of Sophocles and Aristophanes ; he walked amidst the friezes of Phidias and the paintings of Xeuxis ; he knew by heart the choruses of Æschylus ; he heard the rhapsodist at the corner of the street reciting the Shield of Achilles or the Death of Argus ; he was a legislator, conversant with high questions of alliance, revenue, and war ; he was a soldier, trained under a liberal and generous discipline ; he was a judge, compelled every day to weigh the effect of opposite arguments. These things were in themselves an education, an education eminently fitted, not, indeed, to form exact or profound thinkers, but to give quickness to the perceptions, delicacy to the taste, fluency to the expression, and politeness to the manners. All this was overlooked. An Athenian who did not improve his mind by reading was, in Johnson's opinion, much such a person as a Cockney who made his mark, much such a person as black Frank before he went to school, and far inferior to a parish clerk or a printer's devil.

Johnson's friends have allowed that he carried to a ridiculous extreme his unjust contempt for foreigners. He pronounced the French to be a very silly people, much behind us, stupid, ignorant creatures. And this judgment he formed after having been at Paris about a month, during which he would not talk French, for fear of giving the natives an advantage over him in conversation. He pronounced them, also, to be an indelicate people, because a French footman touched the sugar with his fingers. That ingenious and amusing traveller, M. Simond, has defended his countrymen very successfully against Johnson's accusation, and has pointed out some English practices which, to an impartial spectator, would seem at least as inconsistent with physical cleanliness and social decorum as those which Johnson so bitterly reprehended. To the sage, as Boswell loves to call him, it never occurred to doubt that there must be something eternally and immutably good in the usages to which he had been accustomed. In fact, Johnson's remarks on society beyond the bills of mortality are generally

of much the same kind with those of honest Tom Dawson, the
English footman in Dr. Moore's "Zeluco." "Suppose the
King of France has no sons, but only a daughter, then, when
the king dies, this here daughter, according to that there law,
cannot be made queen, but the next near relative, provided he is
a man, is made king, and not the last king's daughter, which,
to be sure, is very unjust. The French foot-guards are dressed
in blue, and all the marching regiments in white, which has a
very foolish appearance for soldiers ; and as for blue regimen-
tals, it is only fit for the blue horse or the artillery."

Johnson's visit to the Hebrides introduced him to a state
of society completely new to him ; and a salutary suspicion of
his own deficiencies seems on that occasion to have crossed his
mind for the first time. He confessed, in the last paragraph of
his Journey, that his thoughts on national manners were the
thoughts of one who had seen but little, of one who had passed
his time almost wholly in cities. This feeling, however, soon
passed away. It is remarkable that to the last he entertained
a fixed contempt for all those modes of life and those studies
which tend to emancipate the mind from the prejudices of a
particular age or a particular nation. Of foreign travel and
of history he spoke with the fierce and boisterous contempt
of ignorance. "What does a man learn by travelling ? Is
Beauclerk the better for travelling ? What did Lord Charle-
mont learn in his travels, except that there was a snake in one
of the pyramids of Egypt ?" History was, in his opinion, to
use the fine expression of Lord Plunkett, an old almanac ;
historians could, as he conceived, claim no higher dignity than
that of almanac-makers ; and his favorite historians were
those who, like Lord Hailes, aspired to no higher dignity. He
always spoke with contempt of Robertson. Hume he would
not even read. He affronted one of his friends for talking to
him about Catiline's conspiracy, and declared that he never
desired to hear of the Punic war again as long as he lived.

Assuredly one fact which does not directly affect our own
interests, considered in itself, is no better worth knowing than
another fact. The fact that there is a snake in a pyramid, or
the fact that Hannibal crossed the Alps, are in themselves as
unprofitable to us as the fact that there is a green blind in a
particular house in Threadneedle Street, or the fact that a Mr.
Smith comes into the city every morning on the top of one of
the Blackwall stages. But it is certain that those who will not
crack the shell of history will never get at the kernel. Johnson, with hasty arrogance, pronounced the kernel worthless,
because he saw no value in the shell. The real use of travel-

ling to distant countries and of studying the annals of past times is to preserve men from the contraction of mind which those can hardly escape whose whole communion is with one generation and one neighborhood, who arrive at conclusions by means of an induction not sufficiently copious, and who therefore constantly confound exceptions with rules, and accidents with essential properties. In short, the real use of travelling and of studying history is to keep men from being what Tom Dawson was in fiction and Samuel Johnson in reality.

Johnson, as Mr. Burke most justly observed, appears far greater in Boswell's books than in his own. His conversation appears to have been quite equal to his writings in matter, and far superior to them in manner. When he talked, he clothed his wit and his sense in forcible and natural expressions. As soon as he took his pen in his hand to write for the public, his style became systematically vicious. All his books are written in a learned language, in a language which nobody hears from his mother or his nurse, in a language in which nobody ever quarrels, or drives bargains, or makes love, in a language in which nobody ever thinks. It is clear that Johnson himself did not think in the dialect in which he wrote. The expressions which came first to his tongue were simple, energetic, and picturesque. When he wrote for publication, he did his sentences out of English into Johnsonese. His letters from the Hebrides to Mrs. Thrale are the original of that work of which the "Journey to the Hebrides" is the translation ; and it is amusing to compare the two versions. "When we were taken upstairs," says he in one of his letters, " a dirty fellow bounced out of the bed on which one of us was to lie." This incident is recorded in the Journey as follows : "Out of one of the beds on which we were to repose started up, at our entrance, a man black as a Cyclops from the forge." Sometimes Johnson translated aloud. " ' The Rehearsal,' " he said, very unjustly, " has not wit enough to keep it sweet ;" then, after a pause, " it has not vitality enough to preserve it from putrefaction."

Mannerism is pardonable, and is sometimes even agreeable, when the manner, though vicious, is natural. Few readers, for example, would be willing to part with the mannerism of Milton or of Burke. But a mannerism which does not sit easy on the mannerist, which has been adopted on principle, and which can be sustained only by constant effort, is always offensive. And such is the mannerism of Johnson.

The characteristic faults of his style are so familiar to all

our readers, and have been so often burlesqued, that it is almost superfluous to point them out.   It is well known that he
made less use than any other eminent writer of those strong
plain words, Anglo-Saxon or Norman-French, of which the
roots lie in the inmost depths of our language ; and that he felt
a vicious partiality for terms which, long after our own speech
had been fixed, were borrowed from the Greek and Latin, and
which, therefore, even when lawfully naturalized, must be considered as born aliens, not entitled to rank with the king's English.   His constant practice of padding out a sentence with useless epithets, till it became as stiff as the bust of an exquisite,
his antithetical forms of expression, constantly employed even
where there is no opposition in the ideas expressed, his big
words wasted on little things, his harsh inversions, so widely
different from those graceful and easy inversions which give
variety, spirit, and sweetness to the expression of our great old
writers—all these peculiarities have been imitated by his admirers and parodied by his assailants, till the public has become sick of the subject.

    Goldsmith said to him, very wittily and very justly, " If you
were to write a fable about little fishes, doctor, you would make
the little fishes talk like whales."   No man surely ever had so
little talent for personation as Johnson.   Whether he wrote in
the character of a disappointed legacy-hunter or an empty town
fop, of a crazy virtuoso or a flippant coquette, he wrote in the
same pompous and unbending style.   His speech, like Sir
Piercy Shafton's euphuistic eloquence, bewrayed him under
every disguise.   Euphelia and Rhodoclea talk as finely as Imlac the poet, or Seged, Emperor of Ethiopia.   The gay Corne-
lia describes her reception at the country-house of her relations
in such terms as these : " I was surprised, after the civilities
of my first reception, to find, instead of the leisure and tranquillity which a rural life always promises, and, if well conducted, might always afford, a confused wildness of care, and a
tumultuous hurry of diligence, by which every face was clouded and every motion agitated."   The gentle Tranquilla informs us that she " had not passed the earlier part of life
without the flattery of courtship and the joys of triumph ; but
had danced the round of gayety amidst the murmurs of envy
and the gratulations of applause, had been attended from pleasure to pleasure by the great, the sprightly, and the vain, and
had seen her regard solicited by the obsequiousness of gallantry, the gayety of wit, and the timidity of love."   Surely Sir
John Falstaff himself did not wear his petticoats with a worse
grace.   The reader may well cry out, with honest Sir Hugh

Evans, " I like not when a 'oman has a great peard : I spy a great peard under her muffler." [1]

We had something more to say. But our article is already too long ; and we must close it. We would fain part in good humor from the hero, from the biographer, and even from the editor, who, ill as he has preformed his task, has at least this claim to our gratitude, that he has induced us to read Boswell's book again. As we close it the club-room is before us, and the table on which stands the omelet for Nugent and the lemons for Johnson. There are assembled those heads which live forever on the canvas of Reynolds. There are the spectacles of Burke and the tall thin form of Langton, the courtly sneer of Beauclerk and the beaming smile of Garrick, Gibbon tapping his snuff-box and Sir Joshua with his trumpet in his ear. In the foreground is that strange figure which is as familiar to us as the figures of those among whom we have been brought up, the gigantic body, the huge massy face, seamed with the scars of disease, the brown coat, the black worsted stockings, the gray wig with the scorched foretop, the dirty hands, the nails bitten and pared to the quick. We see the eyes and mouth moving with convulsive twitches ; we see the heavy form rolling ; we hear it puffing ; and then comes the " Why, sir !" and the " What then, sir ?" and the " No, sir !" and the " You don't see your way through the question, sir !"

What a singular destiny has been that of this remarkable man ! To be regarded in his own age as a classic, and in ours as a companion ! To receive from his contemporaries that full homage which men of genius have in general received only -from posterity ! To be more intimately known to posterity than other men are known to their contemporaries ! That kind of fame which is commonly the most transient is, in his case, the most durable. The reputation of those writings, which he probably expected to be immortal, is every day fading ; while those peculiarities of manner and that careless table-talk, the memory of which he probably thought would die with him, are likely to be remembered as long as the English language is spoken in any quarter of the globe.

[1] It is proper to observe that this passage bears a very close resemblance to a passage in the " Rambler" (No. 20). The resemblance may possibly be the effect of unconscious plagiarism.

CARLYLE ON BOSWELL'S LIFE OF JOHNSON.[1]

[1832.]

ÆSOP'S fly, sitting on the axle of the chariot, has been
much laughed at for exclaiming : What a dust I do raise ! Yet
which of us, in his way, has not sometimes been guilty of the
like ? Nay, so foolish are men, they often, standing at ease
and as spectators on the highway, will volunteer to exclaim of
the fly (not being tempted to it, as *he* was) exactly to the same
purport : What a dust *thou* dost raise ! Smallest of mortals,
when mounted aloft by circumstances, come to seem great ;
smallest of phenomena connected with them are treated as important, and must be sedulously scanned, and commented upon
with loud emphasis.

That Mr. Croker should undertake to edit " Boswell's Life
of Johnson" was a praiseworthy but no miraculous procedure ;
neither could the accomplishment of such undertaking be, in
an epoch like ours, anywise regarded as an event in universal
history ; the right or the wrong accomplishment thereof was,
in very truth, one of the most insignificant of things. However,
it sat in a great environment, on the axle of a high, fast-rolling,
parliamentary chariot ; and all the world has exclaimed over
it, and the author of it : What a dust thou dost raise ! List to
the reviews and " organs of public opinion," from the *National Omnibus* upwards : criticisms, vituperative and laudatory,
stream from their thousand throats of brass and of leather ;
here chanting *Io-pæans ;* there grating harsh thunder or vehement shrewmouse squeaklets ; till the general ear is filled and
nigh deafened. Boswell's book had a noiseless birth compared
with this edition of Boswell's book. On the other hand, consider with what degree of tumult " Paradise Lost" and the
" Iliad " were ushered in !

To swell such clamor, or prolong it beyond the time, seems
nowise our vocation here. At most, perhaps, we are bound to
inform simple readers, with all possible brevity, what manner
of performance and edition this is ; especially, whether, in our
poor judgment, it is worth laying out three pounds sterling

---

[1] *Fraser's Magazine*, No. 28.—" The Life of Samuel Johnson, LL.D. ;
including a Tour to the Hebrides." By James Boswell, Esq. A New
Edition, with numerous Additions and Notes, by John Wilson Croker,
LL.D., F.R.S. 5 vols. London, 1831.

upon, yea or not.   The whole business belongs distinctly to
the lower ranks of the trivial class.

Let us admit, then, with great readiness, that as Johnson
once said, and the editor repeats, " All works which describe
manners require notes in sixty or seventy years, or less ;" that,
accordingly, a new edition of Boswell was desirable ; and that
Mr. Croker has given one.   For this task he had various qualifications : his own voluntary resolution to do it ; his high place
in society, unlocking all manner of archives to him ; not less,
perhaps, a certain anecdotico-biographic turn of mind, natural
or acquired ; we mean a love for the *minuter* events of history, and talent for investigating these.   Let us admit, too, that
he has been very diligent ; seems to have made inquiries per-
severingly far and near ; as well as drawn freely from his own
ample stores ; and so tells us, to appearance quite accurately,
much that he has not found lying on the highways, but has had
to seek and dig for.   Numerous persons, chiefly of quality,
rise to view in these notes ; when and also where they came
into this world, received office or promotion, died and were
buried (only what they *did*, except digest, remaining often too
mysterious), is faithfully enough set down.   Whereby all that
their various and doubtless widely-scattered tombstones could
have taught us, is here presented, at once, in a bound book.
Thus is an indubitable conquest, though a small one, gained over
our great enemy, the all-destroyer Time, and as such shall
have welcome.

Nay, let us say that the spirit of diligence exhibited in this
department seems to attend the editor honestly throughout ;
he keeps everywhere a watchful outlook on his text ; reconciling the distant with the present, or at least indicating and re-
gretting their irreconcilability ; elucidating, smoothing down ;
in all ways exercising, according to ability, a strict editorial
superintendence.   Any little Latin or even Greek phrase is rendered into English, in general with perfect accuracy ; citations
are verified, or else corrected.   On all hands, moreover, there
is a certain spirit of decency maintained and insisted on : if
not good morals, yet good manners are rigidly inculcated ; if
not religion, and a devout Christian heart, yet orthodoxy, and
a cleanly shovel-hatted look, which, as compared with flat
nothing, is something very considerable.   Grant, too, as no
contemptible triumph of this latter spirit, that though the editor is known as a decided politician and party-man, he has
carefully subdued all temptations to trangress in that way : except by quite involuntary indications, and rather as it were the
pervading temper of the whole, you could not discover on

which side of the political warfare he is enlisted and fights. This, as we said, is a great triumph of the decency-principle : for this, and for these other graces and performances, let the editor have all praise.

Herewith, however, must the praise unfortunately terminate. Diligence, fidelity, decency, are good and indispensable ; yet, without faculty, without light, they will not do the work. Along with that tombstone-information, perhaps even without much of it, we could have liked to gain some answer, in one way or other, to this wide question : What and how was *English life* in Johnson's time ; wherein has ours grown to differ therefrom ? In other words : What things have we to forget, what to fancy and remember, before we, from such distance, can put ourselves in Johnson's *place ;* and so, in the full sense of the term, *understand* him, his sayings and his doings ? This was indeed specially the problem which a commentator and editor had to solve : a complete solution of it should have lain in him, his whole mind should have been filled and prepared with perfect insight into it ; then, whether in the way of express dissertation, of incidental exposition and indication, opportunities enough would have occurred of bringing out the same : what was dark in the figure of the past had thereby been enlightened ; Boswell had, not in show and word only, but in very fact, been made *new* again, readable to us who are divided from him, even as he was to those close at hand. Of all which very little has been attempted here ; accomplished, we should say, next to nothing, or altogether nothing.

Excuse, no doubt, is in readiness for such omission ; and, indeed, for innumerable other failings—as where, for example, the editor will punctually explain what is already sun-clear ; and then anon, not without frankness, declare frequently enough that " the editor does not understand," that " the editor cannot guess"—while, for most part, the reader cannot help both guessing and seeing. Thus, if Johnson say, in one sentence, that " English names should not be used in Latin verses;" and then, in the next sentence, speak blamingly of " Carteret being used as a dactyl," will the generality of mortals detect any puzzle there ? Or again, where poor Boswell writes, " I always remember a remark made to me by a Turkish lady, educated in France : ' *Ma foi, monsieur, notre bonheur dépend de la façon que notre sang circule* ' "—though the Turkish lady here speaks English-French, where is the call for a note like this : " Mr. Boswell no doubt fancied these words had some meaning, or he would hardly have quoted them ; but what that meaning is the editor cannot guess " ? The editor is clearly no witch at a riddle. For these and all kindred deficiencies the excuse, as we said, is at hand ; but the fact of their existence is not the less certain and regrettable.

Indeed it, from a very early stage of the business, becomes afflictively apparent how much the editor, so well furnished with all external appliances and means, is from within unfurnished with means for forming to himself any just notion of Johnson or of Johnson's Life ; and therefore of speaking on that subject with much hope of edifying. Too lightly is it from the first taken for granted that *hunger*, the great basis of our life, is also its apex and ultimate perfection ; that as "neediness and greediness and vainglory" are the chief qualities of most men, so no man, not even a Johnson, acts or can think of acting on any other principle. Whatsoever, therefore, cannot be referred to the two former categories (deed and greed) is without scruple ranged under the latter. It is here properly that our editor becomes burdensome, and, to the weaker sort, even a nuisance. "What good is it," will such cry, "when we had still some faint shadow of belief that man was better than a selfish digesting-machine, what good is it to poke in, at every turn, and explain how this and that, which we thought noble in old Samuel, was vulgar, base ; that for him, too, there was no reality but in the stomach ; and except pudding, and the finer species of pudding which is named praise, life had no pabulum ? Why, for instance, when we know that Johnson *loved* his good wife, and says expressly that their marriage was 'a love-match on both sides,' should two closed lips open to tell us only this : 'Is it not possible that the obvious advantage of having a woman of experience to superintend an establishment of this kind (the Edial school) may have contributed to a match so disproportionate in point of age ?—Ed.'? Or again when, in the text, the honest cynic speaks freely of his former poverty, and it is known that he once lived on fourpence-halfpenny a day, need a commentator advance and comment thus : 'When we find Dr. Johnson tell unpleasant truths to, or of, other men, let us recollect that he does not appear to have spared himself, on occasions in which he might be forgiven for doing so'? Why, in short," continues the exasperated reader, "should notes of this species stand affronting me, when there might have been no note at all ?" Gentle Reader, we answer, be not wroth. What other could an honest commentator do than give thee the best he had ? Such was the picture and theorem he had fashioned for himself of the world and of man's doings therein : take it, and draw wise inferences from it. If there did exist a leader of public opinion, and champion of orthodoxy in the Church of Jesus of Nazareth, who reckoned that man's glory consisted in not being poor ; and that a sage, and prophet of his time, must needs blush because the world had paid him at that easy rate of fourpence-halfpenny *per diem*—was not the fact of such existence worth knowing, worth considering?

Of a much milder hue, yet to us practically of an all-defacing, and for the present enterprise quite ruinous character, is another grand fundamental failing ; the last we shall feel ourselves obliged to take the pain of specifying here. It is, that our editor has fatally, and almost surprisingly, mistaken the limits of an editor's function ; and so, instead of working on the margin with his pen, to elucidate as best might be, strikes boldly into the body of the page with his scissors, and there clips at discretion ! Four books Mr. C. had by him, wherefrom to gather light for the fifth, which was Boswell's. What does he do but now, in the placidest manner, slit the whole five into slips, and sew these together into a *sextum quid*, exactly at his own convenience, giving Boswell the credit of the whole ! By what art-magic, our readers ask, has he united them ? By the simplest of all : by brackets. Never before was the full virtue of the bracket made manifest. You begin a sentence under Boswell's guidance, thinking to be carried happily through it by the same : but no ; in the middle, perhaps after your semicolon, and some consequent " for," starts up one of these bracket-ligatures, and stitches you in from half a page to twenty or thirty pages of a Hawkins, Tyers, Murphy, Piozzi ; so that often one must make the old sad reflection, Where we are, we know ; whither we are going, no man knoweth ! It is truly said also, There is much between the cup and the lip ; but here the case is still sadder : for not till after consideration can you ascertain, now when the cup is *at* the lip, what liquor it is you are imbibing ; whether Boswell's French wine which you began with, or some of Piozzi's gingerbeer, or Hawkins's entire, or perhaps some other great brewer's penny-swipes or even alegar, which has been surreptitiously substituted instead thereof. A situation almost original ; not to be tried a second time ! But, in fine, what ideas Mr. Croker entertains of a literary *whole* and the thing called *book*, and how the very printer's devils did not rise in mutiny against such a conglomeration as this, and refuse to print it, may remain a problem.

And now happily our say is said. All faults, the moralists tell us, are properly *shortcomings ;* crimes themselves are nothing other than a *not doing enough ;* a *fighting*, but with defective vigor.   How much more a mere insufficiency, and this after good efforts, in handicraft practice !   Mr. Croker says, " The worst that can happen is that all the present editor has contributed may, if the reader so pleases, be rejected as *surplusage*."   It is our pleasant duty to take with hearty welcome what he has given ; and render thanks even for what he meant to give.   Next, and finally, it is our painful duty to declare, aloud if that be necessary, that his gift, as weighed against the hard money which the booksellers demand for giving it you, is (in our judgment) very greatly the lighter.   No portion, accordingly, of our small floating capital has been embarked in the business, or shall ever be ; indeed, were we in the market for such a thing, there is simply *no* edition of *Boswell* to which this last would seem preferable.   And now enough, and more than enough !

We have next a word to say of James Boswell.   Boswell has already been much commented upon ; but rather in the way of censure and vituperation than of true recognition.   He was a man that brought himself much before the world ; confessed that he eagerly coveted fame, or if that were not possible, notoriety ; of which latter as he gained far more than seemed his due, the public were incited, not only by their natural love of scandal, but by a special ground of envy, to say whatever ill of him could be said.   Out of the fifteen millions that then lived, and had bed and board, in the British islands, this man has provided us a greater *pleasure* than any other individual, at whose cost we now enjoy ourselves ; perhaps has done us a greater *service* than can be specially attributed to more than two or three : yet, ungrateful that we are, no written or spoken eulogy of James Boswell anywhere exists ; his recompense in solid pudding (so far as copyright went) was not excessive ; and as for the empty praise, it has altogether been denied him. Men are unwiser than children ; they do *not* know the hand that feeds them.

Boswell was a person whose mean or bad qualities lay open to the general eye ; visible, palpable to the dullest.   His good qualities, again, belonged not to the time he lived in ; were far from common then ; indeed, in such a degree, were almost unexampled ; not recognizable therefore by every one ; nay, apt even (so strange had they grown) to be confounded with the very vices they lay contiguous to and had sprung out of. That he was a wine-bibber and gross liver ; gluttonously fond of whatever would yield him a little solacement, were it only of a stomachic character, is undeniable enough.   That he was

vain, heedless, a babbler ; had much of the sycophant, alternat-
ing with the braggadocio, curiously spiced too with an all-per-
vading dash of the coxcomb ; that he gloried much when the
tailor, by a court-suit, had made a new man of him ; that he
appeared at the Shakespeare Jubilee with a ribbon, imprinted
" Corsica Boswell," round his hat ; and in short, if you will,
lived no day of his life without doing and saying more than one
pretentious ineptitude : all this unhappily is evident as the sun
at noon. The very look of Boswell seems to have signified so
much. In that cocked nose, cocked partly in triumph over his
weaker fellow-creatures, partly to snuff-up the smell of coming
pleasure, and scent it from afar ; in those bag-cheeks, hanging
like half-filled wine-skins, still able to contain more ; in that
coarsely-protruded shelf-mouth, that fat dewlapped chin : in all
this, who sees not sensuality, pretension, boisterous imbecility
enough ; much that could not have been ornamental in the
temper of a great man's overfed great man (what the Scotch
name *flunky*), though it had been more natural there ? The
under part of Boswell's face is of a low, almost brutish character.

Unfortunately, on the other hand, what great and genuine
good lay in him was nowise so self-evident. That Boswell was
a hunter after spiritual notabilities, that he loved such, and
longed, and even crept and crawled to be near them ; that he
first (in old Touchwood Auchinleck's phraseology) '' took on
with Paoli ;'' and then being off with '' the Corsican land-
louper,'' took on with a schoolmaster, '' ane that keeped a
schule, and ca'd it an academy :'' that he did all this, and
could not help doing it, we account a very singular merit. The
man, once for all, had an '' open sense,'' an open loving heart,
which so few have : where excellence existed, he was compelled to acknowledge it ; was drawn towards it, and (let the
old sulphur-brand of a laird say what he liked) *could not but*
walk with it—if not as superior, if not as equal, then as inferior
and lackey, better so than not at all. If we reflect now that
this love of excellence had not only such an evil *nature* to
triumph over ; but also what an *education* and social position
withstood it and weighed it down, its innate strength, victorious over all these things, may astonish us. Consider what an
inward impulse there must have been, how many mountains of
impediment hurled aside, before the Scottish laird could, as
humble servant, embrace the knees (the bosom was not permitted him) of the English dominie ! Your Scottish laird,
says an English naturalist of these days, may be defined as the
hungriest and vainest of all bipeds yet known. Boswell too

was a Tory ; of quite peculiarly feudal, genealogical, pragmati-
cal temper ; had been nurtured in an atmosphere of heraldry, at
the feet of a very Gamaliel in that kind ; within bare walls,
adorned only with pedigrees, amid serving-men in threadbare
livery ; all things teaching him, from birth upwards, to remember that a laird was a laird.   Perhaps there was a special
vanity in his very blood : old Auchinleck had, if not the gay,
tail-spreading, peacock vanity of his son, no little of the slow-
stalking, contentious, hissing vanity of the gander ; a still more
fatal species.   Scottish advocates will yet tell you how the ancient man, having chanced to be the first sheriff appointed (after the abolition of '' hereditary jurisdictions'') by royal authority, was wont, in dull-snuffling pompous tone, to preface many
a deliverance from the bench with these words : '' I, the first
king's sheriff in Scotland.''

And now behold the worthy Bozzy, so prepossessed and
held back by nature and by art, fly nevertheless like iron to its
magnet, whither his better genius called !   You may surround
the iron and the magnet with what enclosures and encumbrances you please—with wood, with rubbish, with brass : it
matters not, the two feel each other, they struggle restlessly
towards each other, they *will* be together.   The iron may be
a Scottish squirelet, full of gulosity and '' gigmanity ;'' [1] the
magnet an English plebeian, and moving rag-and-dust mountain, coarse, proud, irascible, imperious : nevertheless, behold
how they embrace, and inseparably cleave to one another !   It
is one of the strangest phenomena of the past century, that at
a time when the old reverent feeling of discipleship (such as
brought men from far countries, with rich gifts, and prostrate
soul, to the feet of the prophets) had passed utterly away from
men's practical experience, and was no longer surmised to
exist (as it does), perennial, indestructible, in man's inmost
heart—James Boswell should have been the individual, of all
others, predestined to recall it, in such singular guise, to the
wondering .and, for a long while, laughing and unrecognizing
world.   It has been commonly said, The man's vulgar vanity
was all that attached him to Johnson ; he delighted to be seen
near him, to be thought connected with him.   Now let it be at
once granted that no consideration springing out of vulgar
vanity could well be absent from the mind of James Boswell,
in this his intercourse with Johnson, or in any considerable

---

[1] '' *Q.* What do you mean by 'respectable' ?—*A.* He always kept a
gig.'' (*Thurtell's Trial.*)—'' Thus,'' it has been said, '' does society naturally divide itself into four classes : Noblemen, Gentlemen, Gigmen, and
Men.''

transaction of his life. At the same time, ask yourself :
Whether such vanity, and nothing else, actuated him therein ;
whether this was the true essence and moving principle of the
phenomenon, or not rather its outward vesture, and the accidental environment (and defacement) in which it came to light ?
The man was, by nature and habit, vain ; a sycophant-cox-
comb, be it granted : but had there been nothing more than
vanity in him, was Samuel Johnson the man of men to whom
he must attach himself ? At the date when Johnson was a poor
rusty-coated '' scholar,'' dwelling in Temple-lane, and indeed
throughout their whole intercourse afterwards, were there not
chancellors and prime ministers enough ; graceful gentlemen,
the glass of fashion ; honor-giving noblemen ; dinner-giving
rich men ; renowned fire-eaters, swordsmen, gownsmen ;
quacks and realities of all hues—any one of whom bulked
much larger in the world's eye than Johnson ever did ? To
any one of whom, by half that submissiveness and assiduity,
our Bozzy might have recommended himself ; and sat there,
the envy of surrounding lickspittles ; pocketing now solid
emolument, swallowing now well-cooked viands and wines of
rich vintage ; in each case, also, shone-on by some glittering
reflex of renown or notoriety, so as to be the observed of innumerable observers. To no one of whom, however, though
otherwise a most diligent solicitor and purveyor, did he so attach himself : such vulgar courtierships were his paid drudgery,
or leisure amusement ; the worship of Johnson was his grand,
ideal, voluntary business. Does not the frothy-hearted, yet enthusiastic man, doffing his advocate's-wig, regularly take post,
and hurry up to London, for the sake of his sage chiefly ; as to
a feast of tabernacles, the Sabbath of his whole year ? The
plate-licker and wine-bibber dives into Bolt Court, to sip muddy coffee with a cynical old man and a sour-tempered blind
old woman (feeling the cups, whether they are full, with her
finger) ; and patiently endures contradictions without end ; too
happy so he may but be allowed to listen and live. Nay, it
does not appear that vulgar vanity could ever have been much
flattered by Boswell's relation to Johnson. Mr. Croker says,
Johnson was, to the last, little regarded by the great world ;
from which, for a vulgar vanity, all honor, as from its fountain,
descends. Bozzy, even among Johnson's friends and special
admirers, seems rather to have been laughed at than envied :
his officious, whisking, consequential ways, the daily reproofs
and rebuffs he underwent, could gain from the world no
golden but only leaden opinions. His devout discipleship
seemed nothing more than a mean spanielship, in the general

eye. His mighty "constellation," or sun, round whom he, as
satellite, observantly gyrated, was, for the mass of men, but a
huge ill-snuffed tallow-light, and he a weak night-moth, cir-
cling foolishly, dangerously about it, not knowing what he
wanted. If he enjoyed Highland dinners and toasts, as hench-
man to a new sort of chieftain, Henry Erskine, in the domestic
" Outer-House," could hand him a shilling " for the sight of his
bear." Doubtless the man was laughed at, and often heard
himself laughed at for his Johnsonism. To be envied is the
grand and sole aim of vulgar vanity ; to be filled with good
things is that of sensuality : for Johnson perhaps no man living
envied poor Bozzy ; and of good things (except himself paid
for them) there was no vestige in that acquaintanceship. Had
nothing other or better than vanity and sensuality been there,
Johnson and Boswell had never come together, or had soon
and finally separated again.

In fact, the so copious terrestrial dross that welters chaoti-
cally, as the outer sphere of this man's character, does but render for us more remarkable, more touching, the celestial spark
of goodness, of light, and reverence for wisdom which dwelt
in the interior, and could struggle through such encumbrances,
and in some degree illuminate and beautify them. There is
much lying yet undeveloped in the love of Boswell for Johnson.
A cheering proof, in a time which else utterly wanted and still
wants such, that living wisdom is quite *infinitely* precious to
man, is the symbol of the godlike to him, which even weak
eyes may discern ; that loyalty, discipleship, all that was ever
meant by *hero-worship*, lives perennially in the human bosom,
and waits, even in these dead days, only for occasions to unfold it, and inspire all men with it, and again make the world
alive ! James Boswell we can regard as a practical witness, or
real *martyr*, to this high everlasting truth. A wonderful martyr, if you will ; and in a time which made such martyrdom
doubly wonderful : yet the time and its martyr perhaps suited
each other. For a decrepit, death-sick era, when CANT had
first decisively opened her poison-breathing lips to proclaim
that God-worship and Mammon-worship were one and the same,
that life was a *lie*, and the earth Beelzebub's, which the *Supreme Quack* should inherit ; and so all things were fallen into
the yellow leaf, and fast hastening to noisome corruption : for
such an era, perhaps no better prophet than a parti-colored
zany-prophet, concealing, from himself and others, his prophetic significance in such unexpected vestures, was deserved,
or would have been in place. A precious medicine lay hidden
in floods of coarsest, most composite treacle ; the world swal-

lowed the treacle, for it suited the world's palate ; and now, after half a century, may the medicine also begin to show itself ! James Boswell belonged, in his corruptible part, to the lowest classes of mankind ; a foolish, inflated creature, swimming in an element of self-conceit : but in his corruptible there dwelt an incorruptible, all the more impressive and indubitable for the strange lodging it had taken.

Consider, too, with what force, diligence, and vivacity he has rendered back all this which, in Johnson's neighborhood, his " open sense" had so eagerly and freely taken in. That loose-flowing, careless-looking work of his is as a picture by one of nature's own artists ; the best possible resemblance of a reality ; like the very image thereof in a clear mirror. Which indeed it was : let but the mirror be *clear*, this is the great point ; the picture must and will be genuine. How the babbling Bozzy, inspired only by love, and the recognition and vision which love can lend, epitomizes nightly the words of wisdom, the deeds and aspects of wisdom, and so, by little and little, unconsciously works together for us a whole *Johnsoniad ;* a more free, perfect, sunlit and spirit-speaking likeness than for many centuries had been drawn by man of man !. Scarcely since the days of Homer has the feat been equalled ; indeed, in many senses, this also is a kind of heroic poem. The fit " Odyssey" of our unheroic age was to be written, not sung ; of a thinker, not of a fighter ; and (for want of a Homer) by the first open soul that might offer—looked such even through the organs of a Boswell. We do the man's intellectual endowment great wrong, if we measure it by its mere logical outcome ; though here, too, there is not wanting a light ingenuity, a figurativeness and fanciful sport, with glimpses of insight far deeper than the common. But Boswell's grand intellectual talent was, as such ever is, an *unconscious* one, of far higher reach and significance than logic ; and showed itself in the whole, not in parts. Here again we have that old saying verified, " The heart sees farther than the head."

Thus does poor Bozzy stand out to us as an ill-assorted, glaring mixture of the highest and the lowest. What, indeed, is man's life generally but a kind of beast-godhood ; the god in us triumphing more and more over the beast ; striving more and more to subdue it under his feet ? Did not the ancients, in their wise, perennially-significant way, figure nature itself, their sacred ALL, or PAN, as a portentous commingling of these two discords ; as musical, humane, oracular in its upper part, yet ending below in the cloven hairy feet of a goat ? The union of melodious, celestial free-will and reason with foul

irrationality and lust ; in which, nevertheless, dwelt a mysterious unspeakable fear and half-mad *panic* awe ; as for mortals there well might !   And is not man a microcosm, or epito-
mized mirror of that same universe ; or rather, is not that
universe even himself, the reflex of his own fearful and wonderful being, " the waste fantasy of his own dream " ?   No wonder that man, that each man, and James Boswell like the
others, should resemble it !   The peculiarity in his case was
the unusual defect of amalgamation and subordination : the
highest lay side by side with the lowest ; not morally combined
with it and spiritually transfiguring it, but tumbling in half-me-
chanical juxtaposition with it, and from time to time, as the
mad alternation chanced, irradiating it, or eclipsed by it.

The world, as we said, has been but unjust to him ;
discerning only the outer terrestrial and often sordid mass ;
without eye, as it generally is, for his inner divine secret ; and
thus figuring him nowise as a god Pan, but simply of the bestial species, like the cattle on a thousand hills.   Nay, sometimes a strange enough hypothesis has been started of him ; as
if it were in virtue even of these same bad qualities that he did
his good work ; as if it were the very fact of his being among
the worst men in this world that had enabled him to write one
of the best books therein !   Falser hypothesis, we may venture
to say, never rose in human soul.   *Bad* is by its nature negative, and can do *nothing ;* whatsoever enables us to *do* any thing
is by its very nature *good.*   Alas, that there should be teachers
in Israel, or even learners, to whom this world-ancient fact is
still problematical, or even deniable !   Boswell wrote a good
book because he had a heart and an eye to discern wisdom,
and an utterance to render it forth ; because of his free insight,
his lively talent—above all, of his love and childlike open-
mindedness.   His sneaking sycophancies, his greediness and
forwardness, whatever was bestial and earthy in him, are so
many blemishes in his book, which still disturb us in its clearness ; wholly hindrances, not helps.   Towards Johnson, however, his feeling was not sycophancy, which is the lowest, but
reverence, which is the highest of human feelings.   None but
a *reverent* man (which so unspeakably few are) could have
found his way from Boswell's environment to Johnson's : if
such worship for real God-made superiors showed itself also as
worship for apparent tailor-made superiors, even as hollow interested mouth-worship for such—the case, in this composite
human nature of ours, was not miraculous, the more was the
pity !   But for ourselves, let every one of us cling to this last
article of faith, and know it as the beginning of all knowledge

worth the name : That neither James Boswell's good book, nor any other good thing, in any time or in any place, was, is, or can be performed by any man in virtue of his *badness*, but always and solely in spite thereof.

As for the book itself, questionless the universal favor entertained for it is well merited. In worth as a book we have rated it beyond any other product of the eighteenth century : all Johnson's own writings, laborious and in their kind genuine above most, stand on a quite inferior level to it ; already, indeed, they are becoming obsolete for this generation ; and for some future generation may be valuable chiefly as prolegomena and expository scholia to this *Johnsoniad* of Boswell. Which of us but remembers, as one of the sunny spots in his existence, the day when he opened these airy volumes, fascinating him by a true natural magic ! It was as if the curtains of the past were drawn aside, and we looked mysteriously into a kindred country, where dwelt our fathers ; inexpressibly dear to us, but which had seemed forever hidden from our eyes. For the dead night had engulfed it ; all was gone, vanished as if it had not been. Nevertheless, wondrously given back to us, there once more it lay ; all bright, lucid, blooming ; a little island of creation amid the circumambient void. There it still lies ; like a thing stationary, imperishable, over which changeful time were now accumulating itself in vain, and could not, any longer, harm it or hide it.

If we examine by what charm it is that men are still held to this " Life of Johnson," now, when so much else has been forgotten, the main part of the answer will perhaps be found in that speculation " on the import of *Reality*," communicated to the world, last month, in this magazine. The *Johnsoniad* of Boswell turns on objects that in very deed existed ; it is all *true*. So far other in melodiousness of tone, it vies with the " Odyssey," or surpasses it, in this one point : to us these read pages, as those chanted hexameters were to the first Greek hearers, are, in the fullest, deepest sense, wholly *credible*. All the wit and wisdom lying embalmed in Boswell's book, plenteous as these are, could not have saved it. Far more scientific *instruction* (mere excitement and enlightenment of the *thinking power*) can be found in twenty other works of that time, which make but a quite secondary impression on us. The other works of that time, however, fall under one of two classes : either they are professedly didactic ; and, in that way, mere abstractions, philosophic diagrams, incapable of interesting us much otherwise than as Euclid's Elements may do ; or else, with all their vivacity and pictorial richness of color, *they are fictions and not realities.* Deep truly, as Herr Sauerteig urges, is the force of this consideration : the thing he restated is a fact ; those figures, that local habitation, are not shadow but substance. In virtue of such advantages, see how a very Boswell may become poetical !

Critics insist much on the poet that he should communicate an "infinitude" to his delineation ; that by intensity of conception, by that gift of "transcendental thought," which is fitly named *genius* and inspiration, he should *inform* the finite with a certain infinitude of significance ; or, as they sometimes say, ennoble the actual into idealness. They are right in their precept ; they mean rightly. But in cases like this of the *Johnsoniad*, such is the dark grandeur of that "time element," wherein man's soul here below lives imprisoned, the poet's task is, as it were, done to his hand : time itself, which is the outer veil of eternity, invests, of its own accord, with an authentic, felt "infinitude" whatsoever it has once embraced in its mysterious folds. Consider all that lies in that one word *Past !* What a pathetic, sacred, in every sense *poetic*, meaning is implied in it ; a meaning growing ever the clearer, the farther we recede in time—the *more* of that same past we have to look through ! On which ground indeed must Sauerteig have built, and not without plausibility, in that strange thesis of his : "That history, after all, is the true poetry ; that reality, if rightly interpreted, is grander than fiction ; nay that even in the right interpretation of reality and history does genuine poetry consist."

Thus for Boswell's "Life of Johnson" has time done, is time still doing, what no ornament of art or artifice could have done for it. Rough Samuel and sleek wheedling James *were*, and *are not*. Their life and whole personal environment has melted into air. The Mitre Tavern still stands in Fleet Street ; but where now is its scot-and-lot paying, beef-and-ale loving, cocked-hatted, pot-bellied landlord ; its rosy-faced assiduous landlady, with all her shining brass-pans, waxed tables, well-filled larder-shelves ; her cooks, and bootjacks, and errand-boys, and watery-mouthed hangers-on ? Gone ! gone ! The becking waiter who, with wreathed smiles, was wont to spread for Samuel and Bozzy their supper of the gods, has long since pocketed his last sixpence ; and vanished, sixpences and all, like a ghost at cock-crowing. The bottles they drank out of are all broken, the chairs they sat on all rotted and burnt ; the very knives and forks they ate with have rusted to the heart, and become brown oxide of iron, and mingled with the indiscriminate clay. All, all has vanished ; in very deed and truth, like that baseless fabric of Prospero's air-vision. Of the Mitre Tavern nothing but the bare walls remain there : of London, of England, of the world, nothing but the bare walls remain ; and these also decaying (were they of adamant), only slower. The mysterious river of existence rushes on : a new billow thereof has arrived, and lashes wildly as ever round the old embankments ; but the former billow, with *its* loud, mad eddyings, where is it ? Where ! Now this book of Boswell's, this is precisely a revocation of the edict of Destiny ; so that time shall not utterly, not so soon by several centuries, have dominion over us. A little row of naphtha-lamps, with its line of naphtha-light, burns clear and holy through the dead night of the past : they who are gone are still here ; though hidden they are revealed, though dead they yet speak. There it shines, that little miraculously lamplit. pathway ; shedding its feebler and feebler twilight into the boundless dark oblivion—for all that our Johnson *touched* has become illuminated for us : on which miraculous little pathway we can still travel, and see wonders.

It is not speaking with exaggeration, but with strict measured sobriety, to say that this book of Boswell's will give us more real insight into the *history of England* during those days than twenty other books, falsely entitled " Histories," which take to themselves that special aim. What good is it to me though innumerable Smolletts and Belshams keep dinning in my ears that a man named George the Third was born and bred up, and a man named George the Second died ; that Walpole, and the Pelhams, and Chatham, and Rockingham, and Shelburne, and North, with their Coalition or their Separation Ministries, all ousted one another ; and vehemently scrambled for " the thing they called the rudder of government, but which was in reality the spigot of taxation " ? That debates were held, and infinite jarring and jargoning took place ; and road-bills, and enclosure-bills, and game-bills, and India-bills, and laws which no man can number, which happily few men needed to trouble their heads with beyond the passing moment, were enacted, and printed by the king's stationer ? That he who sat in Chancery, and rayed-out speculation from the Woolsack, was now a man that squinted, now a man that did not squint ? To the hungry and thirsty mind all this avails next to nothing. These men and these things, we indeed know, did swim, by strength or by specific levity, as apples or as horse-dung, on the top of the current ; but is it by painfully noting the courses, eddyings, and bobbings hither and thither of such drift-articles that you will unfold to me the nature of the current itself ; of that mighty-rolling, loud-roaring life-current, bottomless as the foundations of the universe, mysterious as its Author ? The thing I want to see is not Redbook Lists, and Court Calendars, and Parliamentary Registers, but the LIFE OF MAN in England : what men did, thought, suffered, enjoyed ; the form, especially the spirit, of their terrestrial existence, its outward environment, its inward principle ; *how* and *what* it was ; whence it proceeded, whither it was tending.

Mournful, in truth, is it to behold what the business called " History," in these so enlightened and illuminated times, still continues to be. Can you gather from it, read till your eyes go out, any dimmest shadow of an answer to that great question : How men lived and had their being ; were it but economically, as, what wages they got, and what they bought with these ? Unhappily you cannot. History will throw no light on any such matter. At the point where living memory fails, it is all darkness ; Mr. Senior and Mr. Sadler must still debate this simplest of all elements in the condition of the past : Whether men were better off, in their mere larders and pantries, or were worse off than now ! History, as it stands all bound up in gilt volumes, is but a shade more instructive than the wooden volumes of a backgammon-board. How my prime minister was appointed is of less moment to me than how my house servant was hired. In these days, ten ordinary histories of kings and courtiers were well exchanged against the tenth part of one good history of booksellers.

For example, I would fain know the history of Scotland : who can tell it me ? " Robertson," say innumerable voices ; " Robertson against the world." I open Robertson ; and find there, through long ages too confused for narrative, and fit only to be presented in the way of epitome and distilled essence, a cunning answer and hypothesis, not to this question : By whom, and by what means, when and how, was this fair broad Scotland, with its arts and manufactures, temples, schools, institutions, poetry, spirit, national character, created, and made arable, verdant, peculiar, great, here as I can see some fair section of it lying, kind and strong (like some Bacchus-tamed lion), from the Castle-hill of Edinburgh ?—but to this other question : How did the king keep himself alive in those old days ; and restrain so many butcher-barons and ravenous henchmen from utterly extirpating one another, so that killing went on in some sort of moderation ? In the one little Letter of Æneas Sylvius, from old Scotland, there is more of history than in all this. At length, however, we come to a luminous age, interesting enough : to the age of the Reformation. All Scotland is awakened to a second higher life ; the Spirit of the Highest stirs in every bosom, agitates every bosom ; Scotland is convulsed, fermenting, struggling to body itself forth anew. To the herdsman, among his cattle in remote woods ; to the craftsman, in his rude, heath-thatched workshop, among his rude guild-brethren ; to the great and to the little, a new light has arisen : in town and hamlet groups are gathered, with eloquent looks, and governed or ungovernable tongues ; the great and the little go forth together to do battle for the Lord against the mighty. We ask, with breathless eagerness : How was it ; how went it on ? Let us understand it, let us see it, and know it ! In reply, is handed us a really graceful and most dainty little Scandalous Chronicle (as for some Journal of Fashion) of two persons : Mary Stuart, a beauty, but over light-headed ; and Henry Darnley, a booby who had fine legs. How these first courted, billed, and cooed, according to nature ; then pouted, fretted, grew utterly enraged, and blew one another up with gunpowder : this, and not the history of Scotland, is what we good-naturedly read. Nay, by other hands, something like a horse-load of other books have been written to prove that it was the beauty who blew up the booby, and that it was not she. Who or what it was, the thing once for all *being* so effectually done, concerns us little. To know Scotland, at that great epoch, were a valuable increase of knowledge : to know poor Darnley, and see him with burning candle, from centre to skin, were no increase of knowledge at all. Thus is history written.

Hence, indeed, comes it that history, which should be " the essence of innumerable biographies," will tell us, question it as we like, less than one genuine biography may do, pleasantly and of its own accord ! The time is approaching when history will be attempted on quite other principles ; when the court, the senate, and the battle-field, receding more and more into the background, the temple, the workshop, and social hearth will advance more and more into the foreground ; and history will not content itself with shaping some answer to that question : How were men *taxed* and *kept quiet* then ? but will seek to answer this other infinitely wider and higher question : How and what *were men* then ? Not our Government only, or the " *house* wherein our life was led," but the *life* itself we led there, will be inquired into. Of which latter it may be found that government, in any modern sense of the word, is, after all, but a secondary condition : in the mere sense of *taxation* and *keeping quiet*, a small, almost a pitiful one. Meanwhile let us welcome such Boswells, each in his degree, as bring us any genuine contribution, were it never so inadequate, so inconsiderable.

An exception was early taken against this " Life of Johnson," and all similar enterprises, which we here recommend ; and has been transmitted from critic to critic, and repeated in their several dialects, uninterruptedly, ever since : That such jottings-down of careless conversation are an infringement of social privacy ; a crime against our highest freedom, the freedom of man's intercourse with man. To this accusation, which we have read and heard oftener than enough, might it not be well for once to offer the flattest contradiction, and plea of *Not at all guilty?* Not that conversation is noted down, but that conversation should not deserve noting down, is the evil. Doubtless, if conversation be falsely recorded, then is it simply a lie, and worthy of being swept, with all despatch, to the father of lies. But if, on the other hand, conversation can be authentically recorded, and any one is ready for the task, let him by all means proceed with it ; let conversation be kept in remembrance to the latest date possible. Nay, should the consciousness that a man may be among us " taking notes " tend, in any measure, to restrict those floods of idle, insincere *speech*, with which the *thought* of mankind is well-nigh drowned, were it other than the most indubitable benefit ? He who speaks ·honestly cares not, needs not care, though his words be preserved to remotest time : for him who speaks *dis*honestly, the fittest of all punishments seems to be this same, which the nature of the case provides. The dishonest speaker, not he only who purposely utters falsehoods, but he who does not purposely, and with sincere heart, utter truth, and truth alone ; who babbles he knows not what, and has clapped no bridle on his tongue, but lets it run racket, ejecting chatter and futility— is among the most indisputable malefactors omitted, or inserted, in the Criminal Calendar. To him that will well consider it, idle speaking is precisely the beginning of all hollowness, halfness, *infidelity* (want of faithfulness) ; the genial atmosphere in which rank weeds of every kind attain the mastery over noble fruits in man's life, and utterly choke them out : one of the most crying maladies of these days, and to be testified against, and in all ways to the uttermost withstood. Wise, of a wisdom far beyond our shallow depth, was that old precept : *Watch thy tongue ;* out of it are the issues of life ! " Man is properly an *incarnated word :* " the *word* that he speaks is the *man* himself. Were eyes put into our head, that we might *see ;* or only that we might fancy, and plausibly pretend, we had *seen ?* Was the tongue suspended there, that it might tell truly what we had seen, and make man the soul's-brother of man ; or only that it might utter vain sounds, jar-gon, soul-confusing, and so *divide* man, as by enchanted walls of darkness, from union with man ? Thou who wearest that cunning, heaven-made organ, a tongue, think well of this. Speak not, I passionately entreat thee, till thy thought hath silently matured itself, till thou have other than mad and mad-making noises to emit : *hold thy tongue* (thou hast it a-holding) till *some* meaning lie behind to set it wagging. Consider the significance of SILENCE ; it is boundless, never by meditating to be exhausted ; unspeakably profitable to thee ! Cease that chaotic hubbub, wherein thy own soul runs to waste, to con-fused suicidal dislocation and stupor : out of silence comes thy strength. "Speech is silvern, silence is golden ; speech is human, silence is divine." Fool ! thinkest thou that because no Boswell is there with ass-skin and blacklead to note thy jar-gon, it therefore dies and is harmless ? Nothing dies, nothing can die. No idlest word thou speakest but is a seed cast into time, and grows through all eternity ! The recording angel, consider it well, is no fable, but the truest of truths : the paper tablets thou canst burn ; of the " iron leaf " there is no burning. Truly, if we can permit God Almighty to note down our con-versation, thinking it good enough for him, any poor Boswell need not scruple to work his will of it.

Leaving now this our English " Odyssey," with its singer and scholiast, let us come to the *Ulysses ;* that great Samuel John-son himself, the far-experienced, " much-enduring man," whose labors and pilgrimage are here sung. A full-length image of his existence has been preserved for us : and he, perhaps, of all living Englishmen, was the one who best deserved that hon-or. For if it is true, and now almost proverbial, that " the life of the lowest mortal, if faithfully recorded, would be in-teresting to the highest ;" how much more when the mortal in question was already distinguished in fortune and natural qual-ity, so that his thinkings and doings were not significant of himself only, but of large masses of mankind ! " There is not a man whom I meet on the streets," says one, " but I could like, were it otherwise convenient, to know his biography :" nevertheless, could an enlightened curiosity be so far gratified, it must be owned the biography of most ought to be, in an extreme degree, *summary*. In this world there is so wonder-fully little self-subsistence among men ; next to no originality (though never absolutely *none*) : one life is too servilely the copy of another ; and so in whole thousands of them you find little that is properly new ; nothing but the old song sung by a new voice, with better or worse execution, here and there an ornamental quaver, and false notes enough : but the fundamental tune is ever the same ; and for the *words*, these, all that they meant stands written generally on the churchyard stone : *Natus sum ; esuriebam, quœrebam ; nunc repletus requiesco.* Mankind sail their life-voyage in huge fleets, following some single whale-fishing or herring-fishing commodore : the log-book of each differs not, in essential purport, from that of any other : nay the most have no legible log-book (reflection, observation not being among their talents) ; keep no reckoning, only *keep in sight* of the flagship—and fish. Read the commodore's papers (know *his* life) ; and even your lover of that street biography will have learned the most of what he sought after.

Or, the servile *imitancy*, and yet also a nobler relationship and mysterious union to one another which lies in such imitancy, of mankind might be illustrated under the different figure, itself nowise *original*, of a flock of sheep. Sheep go in flocks for three reasons : first, because they are of a gregarious temper, and *love* to be together ; secondly, because of their cowardice—they are afraid to be left alone ; thirdly, because the common run of them are dull of sight, to a proverb, and can have no choice in roads ; sheep can in fact *see* nothing ; in a celestial luminary, and a scoured pewter tankard, would discern only that both dazzled them, and were of unspeakable glory. How like their fellow-creatures of the human species ! Men, too, as was from the first maintained here, are gregarious ; then surely faint-hearted enough, trembling to be left by themselves ; above all, dull-sighted, down to the verge of utter blindness. Thus are we seen ever running in torrents, and mobs, if we run at all ; and after what foolish scoured tankards, mistaking them for suns ! Foolish turnip-lanterns likewise, to all appearance supernatural, keep whole nations quaking, their hair on end. Neither know we, except by blind habit, where the good pastures lie : solely when the sweet grass is between our teeth, we know it, and chew it ; also when grass is bitter and scant, we know it—and bleat and butt : these last two facts we know of a truth and in very deed. Thus do men and sheep play their parts on this nether earth ; wandering restlessly in large masses, they know not whither ; for most part each following his neighbor, and his own nose.

Nevertheless, not always ; look better, you shall find certain that do, in some small degree, *know whither.* Sheep have their bell-wether ; some ram of the folds, endued with more valor, with clearer vision than other sheep ; he leads them through the wolds, by height and hollow, to the woods and water-courses, for covert or for pleasant provender ; courageously marching, and if need be leaping, and with hoof and horn doing battle, in the van : him they courageously and with assured heart follow. Touching it is, as every herdsman will inform you, with what chivalrous devotedness these woolly hosts adhere to their wether ; and rush after him, through good report and through bad report, were it into safe shelters and green thymy nooks, or into asphaltic lakes and the jaws of devouring lions. Ever also must we recall that fact which we owe Jean Paul's quick eye : " If you hold a stick before the wether, so that he, by necessity, leaps in passing you, and then withdraw your stick, the flock will nevertheless all leap as he did ; and the thousandth sheep shall be found impetuously vaulting over air, as the first did over an otherwise impassable barrier." Reader, wouldst thou understand society, ponder well those ovine proceedings ; thou wilt find them all curiously significant.

Now if sheep always, how much more must men always, have their chief, their guide ! Man too is by nature quite thoroughly *gregarious :* nay ever he struggles to be something more, to be *social ;* not even when society has become impossible does that deep-seated tendency and effort forsake him. Man, as if by miraculous magic, imparts his thoughts, his mood of mind to man ; an unspeakable communion binds all past, present, and future men into one indissoluble whole, almost into one living individual. Of which high, mysterious truth, this disposition to *imitate,* to lead and be led, this impossibility *not* to imitate, is the most constant, and one of the simplest manifestations. To imitate ! which of us all can measure the significance that lies in that one word ? By virtue of which the infant man, born at Woolsthorpe, grows up not to be a hairy savage, and chewer of acorns, but an Isaac Newton and discoverer of solar systems ! Thus, both in a celestial and terrestrial sense, are we a *flock*, such as there is no other : nay, looking away from the base and ludicrous to the sublime and sacred side of the matter (since in every matter there are two sides), have not we also a SHEPHERD, " if we will but hear his voice " ? Of those stupid multitudes there is no one but has an immortal soul within him ; a reflex and living image of God's whole universe : strangely, from its dim environment, the light of the Highest looks through him ; for which reason, indeed, it is that we claim a brotherhood with him, and so love to know his history, and come into clearer and clearer union with all that he feels, and says, and does.

However, the chief thing to be noted was this : Amid those dull millions, who, as a dull flock, roll hither and thither, whithersoever they are led ; and seem all sightless and slavish, accomplishing, attempting little save what the animal instinct in its somewhat higher kind might teach, to keep themselves and their young ones alive, are scattered here and there superior natures, whose eye is not destitute of free vision, nor their heart of free volition. These latter, therefore, examine and determine, not what others do, but what it is right to do ; towards which, and which only, will they, with such force as is given them, resolutely endeavor : for if the machine, living or inanimate, is merely *fed*, or desires to be fed, and so *works*, the person can *will*, and so *do*. These are properly our men, our great men ; the guides of the dull host, which follows them as by an irrevocable decree. They are the chosen of the world ; they had this rare faculty not only of " supposing" and " inclining to think," but of *knowing* and *believing ;* the nature of their being was, that they lived not by hearsay, but by clear vision ; while others hovered and swam along, in the grand Vanity-fair of the world, blinded by the mere shows of things, these saw into the things themselves, and could walk as men having an eternal loadstar, and with their feet on sure paths. Thus was there a *reality* in their existence ; something of a perennial character ; in virtue of which indeed it is that the memory of them is perennial. Whoso belongs only to his own age, and reverences only *its* gilt Popinjays or soot-smeared Mumbojumbos, must needs die with it : though he have been crowned seven times in the Capitol, or seventy-and-seven times, and Rumor have blown his praises to all the four winds, deafening every ear therewith, it avails not ; there was nothing universal, nothing eternal in him ; he must fade away, even as the Popinjay-gildings and scarecrow-apparel, which he could not see through. The great man does, in good truth, belong to his own age ; nay more so than any other man ; being properly the synopsis and epitome of such age with its interests and influences : but belongs likewise to all ages, otherwise he is not great. What was transitory in him passes away ; and an immortal part remains, the significance of which is in strict speech inexhaustible—as that of every *real* object is. Aloft, conspicuous, on his enduring basis, he stands there, serene, unaltering ; silently addresses to every new generation a new lesson and monition. Well is his life worth writing, worth interpreting ; and ever, in the new dialect of new times, of rewriting and reinterpreting.

Of such chosen men was Samuel Johnson : not ranking

among the highest, or even the high, yet distinctly admitted
into that sacred band ; whose existence was no idle dream,
but a reality which he transacted *awake ;* nowise a clothes-
horse and patent digester, but a genuine man. By nature he
was gifted for the noblest of earthly tasks, that of priesthood,
and guidance of mankind ; by destiny, moreover, he was appointed to this task, and did actually, according to strength,
fulfil the same : so that always the question, *How ; in what
spirit ; under what shape ?* remains for us to be asked and
answered concerning him. For as the highest gospel was a
biography, so is the life of every good man still an indubitable gospel, and preaches to the eye and heart and whole man,
so that devils even must believe and tremble, these gladdest
tidings : ' ' Man is heaven-born ; not the thrall of circumstances, of necessity, but the victorious subduer thereof : behold how he can become the ' announcer of himself and of his
freedom ; ' and is ever what the thinker has named him, ' the
Messias of Nature.' '' Yes, reader, all this that thou hast so
often heard about '' force of circumstances,'' '' the creature of
the time,'' '' balancing of motives,'' and who knows what melancholy stuff to the like purport, wherein thou, as in a nightmare
dream, sittest paralyzed, and hast no force left, was in very
truth, if Johnson and waking men are to be credited, little
other than a hag-ridden vision of death-sleep ; some *half*-fact,
more fatal at times than a whole falsehood. Shake it off ;
awake ; up and be doing, even as it is given thee !
  The contradiction which yawns wide enough in every life,
which it is the meaning and task of life to reconcile, was in
Johnson's wider than in most. Seldom, for any man, has the
contrast between the ethereal heavenward side of things and
the dark sordid earthward been more glaring : whether we·
look at Nature's work with him or Fortune's, from first to last,
heterogeneity, as of sunbeams and miry clay, is on all hands
manifest. Whereby indeed, only this was declared, That *much
life* had been given him ; many things to triumph over, a great
work to *do.* Happily also he did it ; better than the most.
  Nature had given him a high, keen-visioned, almost poetic
soul ; yet withal imprisoned it in an inert, unsightly body : he
that could never rest had not limbs that would move with him,
but only roll and waddle : the inward eye, all-penetrating, all-
embracing, must look through bodily windows that were dim,
half-blinded ; he so loved men, and '' never once *saw* the
human face divine'' ! Not less did he prize the love of men ;
he was eminently social ; the approbation of his fellows was
dear to him, '' valuable,'' as he owned, '' if from the meanest of

human beings ;" yet the first impression he produced on every man was to be one of aversion, almost of disgust. By nature it was further ordered that the imperious Johnson should be born poor : the ruler-soul, strong in its native royalty, generous, uncontrollable, like the lion of the woods, was to be housed, then, in such a dwelling-place : of disfigurement, disease, and, lastly, of a poverty which itself made him the servant of servants. Thus was the born king likewise a born slave : the divine spirit of music must awake imprisoned amid dull-croaking universal discords ; the Ariel finds himself encased in the coarse hulls of a Caliban. So is it more or less, we know (and thou, O reader, knowest and feelest even now), with all men : yet with the fewest men in any such degree as with Johnson.

Fortune, moreover, which had so managed his first appearance in the world, lets not her hand lie idle, or turn the other way, but works unweariedly in the same spirit, while he is journeying through the world. What such a mind, stamped of nature's noblest metal, though in so ungainly a die, was specially and best of all fitted for, might still be a question. To none of the world's few incorporated guilds could he have adjusted himself without difficulty, without distortion ; in none been a guild-brother well at ease. Perhaps, if we look to the strictly practical nature of his faculty, to the strength, decision, method that manifests itself in him, we may say that his calling was rather towards active than speculative life ; that as statesman (in the higher, now obsolete sense), lawgiver, ruler, in short as doer of the work, he had shone even more than as speaker of the word. His honesty of heart, his courageous temper, the value he set on things outward and material, might have made him a king among kings. Had the golden age of those new French prophets, when it shall be *à chacun selon sa capacité, à chaque capacité selon ses œuvres*, but arrived ! Indeed, even in our brazen and Birmingham-lacquer age, he himself regretted that he had not become a lawyer, and risen to be Chancellor, which he might well have done. However, it was otherwise appointed. To no man does Fortune throw open all the kingdoms of this world, and say : It is thine ; choose where thou wilt dwell ! To the most she opens hardly the smallest cranny or doghutch, and says, not without asperity : There, that is thine while thou canst keep it ; nestle thyself there, and bless Heaven ! Alas, men must fit themselves into many things : some forty years ago, for instance, the noblest and ablest man in all the British lands might be seen not swaying the royal sceptre, or the pontiff's censer, on the pinnacle of the world, but gauging ale-tubs in the little burgh of Dumfries ! Johnson came a little nearer the mark than Burns : but with him too "strength was mournfully denied its arena ;" he too had to fight Fortune at strange odds all his life long.

Johnson's disposition for *royalty* (had the Fates so ordered it) is well seen in early boyhood. " His favorites," says Boswell, " used to receive very liberal assistance from him ; and such was the submission and deference with which he was treated, that three of the boys, of whom Mr. Hector was sometimes one, used to come in the morning as his humble attendants, and carry him to school. One in the middle stooped, while he sat upon his back, and one on each side supported him ; and thus was he borne triumphant." The purfly, sandblind lubber and blubber, with his open mouth, and face of bruised honeycomb ; yet already dominant, imperial, irresistible ! Not in the " king's-chair" (of human arms), as we see, do his three satellites carry him along : rather on the *tyrant's-saddle*, the back of his fellow-creature, must he ride prosperous ! The child is father of the man. He who had seen fifty years into coming time would have felt that little spectacle of mischievous schoolboys to be a great one. For us, who look back on it, and what followed it, now from afar, there arise questions enough : How looked these urchins ? What jackets and galligaskins had they ; felt headgear, or of dogskin leather ? What was old Lichfield doing then ; what thinking ? —and soon, through the whole series of Corporal Trim's " auxiliary verbs." A picture of it all fashions itself together— only unhappily we have no brush and no fingers.

Boyhood is now past ; the ferula of pedagogue waves harmless in the distance : Samuel has struggled up to uncouth bulk and youthhood, wrestling with disease and poverty, all the way ; which two continue still his companions. At college we see little of him ; yet thus much, that things went not well. A rugged wild man of the desert, awakened to the feeling of himself ; proud as the proudest, poor as the poorest ; stoically shut up, silently enduring the incurable : what a world of blackest gloom, with sun-gleams and pale tearful moon-gleams, and flickerings of a celestial and an infernal splendor, was this that now opened for him ! But the weather is wintry ; and the toes of the man are looking through his shoes. His muddy features grow of a purple and sea-green color ; a flood of black indignation mantling beneath. A truculent, raw-boned figure ! Meat he has probably little ; hope he has less : his feet, as we said, have come into brotherhood with the cold mire.

"Shall I be particular," inquires Sir John Hawkins, "and relate a circumstance of his distress, that cannot be imputed to him as an effect of his own extravagance or irregularity, and consequently reflects no disgrace on his memory? He had scarce any change of raiment, and, in a short time after Corbet left him, but one pair of shoes, and those so old that his feet were seen through them : a gentleman of his college, the father of an eminent clergyman now living, directed a servitor one morning to place a new pair at the door of Johnson's chamber ; who seeing them upon his first going out, so far forgot himself and the spirit which must have actuated his unknown benefactor, that, with all the indignation of an insulted man, he threw them away."

How exceedingly surprising ! The Rev. Dr. Hall remarks : "As far as we can judge from a cursory view of the weekly account in the buttery-books, Johnson appears to have lived as well as other commoners and scholars." Alas ! such "cursory view of the buttery-books," now from the safe distance of a century, in the safe chair of a College Mastership, is one thing ; the continual view of the empty or locked buttery itself was quite a different thing. But hear our knight, how he further discourses. "Johnson," quoth Sir John, could "not at this early period of his life divest himself of an idea that poverty was disgraceful ; and was very severe in his censures of that economy in both our universities, which exacted at meals the attendance of poor scholars, under the several denominations of servitors in the one, and sizars in the other : he thought that the scholar's, like the Christian life, levelled all distinctions of rank and worldly pre-eminence ; but in this he was *mistaken :* civil polity," etc., etc. Too true ! It is man's lot to err.

However, destiny, in all ways, means to prove the mistaken Samuel, and see what stuff is in him. He must leave these butteries of Oxford, Want, like an armed man, compelling him ; retreat into his father's mean home ; and there abandon himself for a season to inaction, disappointment, shame, and nervous melancholy nigh run mad : he is probably the wretchedest man in wide England. In all ways he too must " become perfect through *suffering*." High thoughts have visited him ; his college exercises have been praised beyond the walls of college ; Pope himself has seen that *Translation*, and approved of it : Samuel had whispered to himself : I too am " one and somewhat." False thoughts ; that leave only misery behind ! The fever-fire of ambition is too painfully extinguished (but not cured) in the frost-bath of poverty. Johnson has knocked at the gate, as one having a right ; but there was no opening : the world lies all encircled as with brass ; nowhere can he find or force the smallest entrance. An ushership at Market Bosworth, and "a disagreement between him and Sir Wolstan Dixie, the patron of the school," yields him bread of affliction and water of affliction ; but so bitter, that unassisted human nature cannot swallow them. Young Samson will grind no more in the Philistine mill of Bosworth ; quits hold of Sir Wolstan, and the " domestic chaplaincy, so far at least as to say grace at table," and also to be " treated with what he represented as intolerable harshness ;" and so, after " some months of such complicated misery," feeling doubtless that there are worse things in the world than quick death by famine, " relinquishes a situation, which all his life afterwards he recollected with the strongest aversion, and even horror." Men like Johnson are properly called the forlorn hope of the world : judge whether his hope was forlorn or not, by this letter to a dull oily printer who called himself *Sylvanus Urban :*

" Sir : As you appear no less sensible than your readers of the defect of your poetical article, you will not be displeased if (in order to the improvement of it) I communicate to you the sentiments of a person who will undertake, on reasonable terms, sometimes to fill a column.

" His opinion is, that the public would," etc. etc.

" If such a correspondence will be agreeable to you, be pleased to inform me in two posts what the conditions are on which you shall expect it. Your late offer (for a Prize Poem) gives me no reason to distrust your generosity. If you engage in any literary projects besides this paper, I have other designs to impart."

Reader, the generous person, to whom this letter goes addressed, is " Mr. Edmund Cave, at St. John's Gate, London ;" the addresser of it is Samuel Johnson, in Birmingham, Warwickshire.

Nevertheless, life rallies in the man ; reasserts its right to be *lived,* even to be enjoyed. " Better a small bush," say the Scotch, " than no shelter ;" Johnson learns to be contented with humble human things ; and is there not already an actual realized human existence, all stirring and living on every hand of him ? Go thou and do likewise ! In Birmingham itself, with his own purchased goose-quill, he can earn " five guineas ;" nay, finally, the choicest terrestrial good : a friend, who will be wife to him ! Johnson's marriage with the good Widow Porter has been treated with ridicule by many mortals, who apparently had no understanding thereof. That the purblind, seamy-faced wild man, stalking lonely, woe-stricken, like some Irish gallowglass with peeled club, whose speech no man knew, whose look all men both laughed at and shuddered at, should find any brave female heart to acknowledge, at first sight and hearing of him, " This is the most sensible man I ever met with ;" and then, with generous courage, to take him to itself, and say, Be thou mine ; be thou warmed here, and thawed to life !—in all this, in the kind widow's love and pity for him, in Johnson's love and gratitude, there is actually no matter for ridicule. Their wedded life, as is the common lot, was made up of drizzle and dry weather ; but innocence and worth dwelt in it ; and when death had ended it, a certain sacredness : Johnson's deathless affection for his Tetty was always venerable and noble.

However, be all this as it might, Johnson is now minded to wed ; and will live by the trade of pedagogy, for by this also may life be kept in. Let the world therefore take notice : " *At Edial near Lichfield, in Staffordshire, young gentlemen are boarded, and taught the Latin and Greek languages, by*—Samuel Johnson." Had this Edial enterprise prospered, how different might the issue have been ! Johnson had lived a life of unnoticed nobleness, or swoln into some amorphous Dr. Parr, of no avail to us ; Bozzy would have dwindled into official insignificance, or risen by some other elevation ; old Auchinleck had never been afflicted with " ane that keeped a schule," or obliged to violate hospitality by a " Cromwell do ? God, sir, he gart kings ken that there was a *lith* in their neck !" But the Edial enterprise did not prosper ; destiny had other work appointed for Samuel Johnson ; and young gentlemen got board where they could elsewhere find it. This man was to become a teacher of grown gentlemen, in the most surprising way ; a man of letters, and ruler of the British nation for some time—not of their bodies merely but of their minds, not *over* them but *in* them.

The career of literature could not, in Johnson's day, any more than now, be said to lie along the shores of a Pactolus : whatever else might be gathered there, gold-dust was nowise the chief produce. The world, from the times of Socrates, St. Paul, and far earlier, has always had its teachers ; and always treated them in a peculiar way. A shrewd town-clerk (not of Ephesus), once, in founding a burgh-seminary, when the question came, How the schoolmasters should be maintained ? delivered this brief counsel : " D—n them, keep them *poor !*" Considerable wisdom may lie in this aphorism. At all events, we see, the world has acted on it long, and indeed improved on it, putting many a schoolmaster of its great burgh-seminary to a death which even *cost* it something. The world, it is true, had for some time been too busy to go out of its way, and *put* any author to death ; however, the old sentence pronounced against them was found to be pretty sufficient. The first writers, being monks, were sworn to a vow of poverty ; the modern authors had no need to swear to it. This was the epoch when an Otway could still die of hunger ; not to speak of your innumerable Scrogginses, whom "the Muse found stretched beneath a rug," with "rusty grate unconscious of a fire," stocking-nightcap, sanded-floor, and all the other escutcheous of the craft, time out of mind the heirlooms of authorship. Scroggins, however, seems to have been but an idler ; not at all so diligent as worthy Mr. Boyce, whom we might have seen *sitting up* in bed, with his wearing-apparel of blanket about him, and a hole slit in the same, that his hand might be at liberty to work in its vocation. The worst was, that too frequently a blackguard recklessness of temper ensued, incapable of turning to account what good the gods even here had provided : your Boyces acted on some stoico-epicurean principle of *carpe diem*, as men do in bombarded towns, and seasons of raging pestilence ; and so had lost not only their life and presence of mind, but their status as persons of respectability. The trade of author was at about one of its lowest ebbs when Johnson embarked on it.

Accordingly we find no mention of illuminations in the city of London when this same ruler of the British nation arrived in it : no cannon-salvos are fired ; no flourish of drums and trumpets greets his appearance on the scene. He enters quite quietly, with some copper halfpence in his pocket ; creeps into lodgings in Exeter Street, Strand ; and has a coronation pontiff also, of not less peculiar equipment, whom, with all submissiveness, he must wait upon, in his Vatican of St. John's Gate. This is the dull oily printer alluded to above.

"Cave's temper," says our Knight Hawkins, "was phlegmatic : though he assumed, as the publisher of the Magazine, the name of Sylvanus Urban, he had few of those qualities that constitute urbanity. Judge of his want of them by this question, which he once put to an author : ' Mr. ——, I hear you have just published a pamphlet, and am told there is a very good paragraph in it upon the subject of music : did you write that yourself ? ' His discernment was also slow ; and as he had already at his command some writers of prose and verse, who, in the language of booksellers, are called good hands, he was the backwarder in making advances, or courting an intimacy with Johnson. Upon the first approach of a stranger, his practice was to continue sitting ; a posture in which he was ever to be found, and for a few minutes to continue silent : if at any time he was inclined to begin the discourse, it was generally by putting a leaf of the Magazine, then in the press, into the hand of his visitor, and asking his opinion of it.

"He was so incompetent a judge of Johnson's abilities, that meaning at one time to dazzle him with the splendor of some of those luminaries in literature who favored him with their correspondence, he told him that if he would, in the evening, be at a certain alehouse in the neighborhood of Clerkenwell, he might have a chance of seeing Mr. Browne and another or two of those illustrious contributors : Johnson accepted the invitation ; and being introduced by Cave, dressed in a loose horseman's coat, and such a great bushy wig as he constantly wore, to the sight of Mr. Browne, whom he found sitting at the upper end of a long table, in a cloud of tobacco-smoke, had his curiosity gratified." [1]

In fact, if we look seriously into the condition of authorship at that period, we shall find that Johnson had undertaken one of the ruggedest of all possible enterprises ; that here as elsewhere fortune had given him unspeakable contradictions to reconcile. For a man of Johnson's stamp, the problem was twofold : *First*, not only as the humble but indispensable condition of all else, to keep himself, if so might be, *alive ;* but, *secondly*, to keep himself alive by speaking forth the *truth* that was in him, and speaking it *truly*, that is, in the clearest and fittest utterance the heavens had enabled him to give it, let the earth say to this what she liked. Of which twofold problem if it be hard to solve either member separately, how incalculably more so to solve it, when both are conjoined, and work with endless complication into one another ! He that finds himself already *kept alive* can sometimes (unhappily not always) speak a little truth ; he that finds himself able and willing, to all lengths, to *speak lies*, may, by watching how the wind sits, scrape together a livelihood, sometimes of great splendor : he, again, who finds himself provided with *neither* endowment, has but a ticklish game to play, and shall have praises if he win it. Let us look a little at both faces of the matter ; and see what front they then offered our adventurer, what front he offered them.

At the time of Johnson's appearance on the field, literature, in many senses, was in a transitional state ; chiefly in this sense, as respects the pecuniary subsistence of its cultivators. It was in the very act of passing from the protection of patrons into that of the public ; no longer to supply its necessities by laudatory dedications to the great, but by judicious bargains with the booksellers. This happy change has been much sung and celebrated ; many a " lord of the lion heart and eagle eye" looking back with scorn enough on the bygone system of dependency : so that now it were perhaps well to consider, for a moment, what good might also be in it, what gratitude we owe it. That a good was in it, admits not of doubt. Whatsoever has existed has had its value : without some truth and worth lying in it, the thing could not have hung together, and been the organ and sustenance and method of action for men that reasoned and were alive. Translate a falsehood which is wholly false into practice, the result comes out *zero ;* there is

[1] Hawkins, pp. 46–50.

no fruit or issue to be derived from it. That in an age, when a nobleman was still noble, still with his wealth the protector of worthy and humane things, and still venerated as such, a poor man of genius, his brother in nobleness, should, with unfeigned reverence, address him and say, "I have found wisdom here, and would fain proclaim it abroad ; wilt thou, of thy abundance, afford me the means?"—in all this there was no baseness ; it was wholly an honest proposal, which a free man might make, and a free man listen to. So might a Tasso, with a *Gerusalemme* in his hand or in his head, speak to a Duke of Ferrara ; so might a Shakespeare to his Southampton ; and continental artists generally to their rich protectors, in some countries, down almost to these days. It was only when the reverence became *feigned*, that baseness entered into the transaction on both sides ; and, indeed, flourished there with rapid luxuriance, till that became disgraceful for a Dryden which a Shakespeare could once practise without offence.

Neither, it is very true, was the new way of bookseller Mæcenasship worthless ; which opened itself at this juncture, for the most important of all transport-trades, now when the old way had become too miry and impassable. Remark, moreover, how this second sort of Mæcenasship, after carrying us through nearly a century of literary time, appears now to have well-nigh discharged *its* function also ; and to be working pretty rapidly towards some *third* method, the exact conditions of which are yet nowise visible. Thus all things have their end ; and we should part with them all, not in anger, but in peace. The bookseller-system, during its peculiar century, the whole of the eighteenth, did carry us handsomely along ; and many good works it has left us, and many good men it maintained : if it is now expiring by PUFFERY, as the patronage-system did by FLATTERY (for *lying* is ever the forerunner of death, nay is itself death), let us not forget its benefits ; how it nursed literature through boyhood and school-years, as patronage had wrapped it in soft swaddling-bands ; till now we see it about to put on the *toga virilis*, could it but *find* any such !

There is tolerable travelling on the beaten road, run how it may ; only on the new road not yet levelled and paved, and on the old road all broken into ruts and quagmires, is the travelling bad or impracticable. The difficulty lies always in the *transition* from one method to another. In which state it was that Johnson now found literature ; and out of which, let us also say, he manfully carried it. What remarkable mortal *first paid copyright* in England we have not ascertained ; perhaps, for almost a century before, some scarce visible or ponderable pittance of wages had occasionally been yielded by the seller of books to the writer of them : the original covenant, stipulating to produce " Paradise Lost" on the one hand, and " five pounds sterling" on the other, still lies (we have been told) in black-on-white, for inspection and purchase by the curious, at a bookshop in Chancery Lane.   Thus had the matter gone on, in a mixed confused way, for some threescore years ; as ever, in such things, the old system *overlaps* the new, by some generation or two, and only dies quite out when the new has got a complete organization and weather-worthy surface of its own.   Among the first authors, the very first of any significance, who lived by the day's wages of his craft, and composedly faced the world on that basis, was Samuel Johnson.

At the time of Johnson's appearance there were still two ways on which an author might attempt proceeding : there were the Mæcenases proper in the West End of London ; and the Mæcenases virtual of St. John's Gate and Paternoster Row.   To a considerate man it might seem uncertain which method were preferable : neither had very high attractions ; the patron's aid was now well-nigh *necessarily* polluted by sycophancy, before it could come to hand : the bookseller's was deformed with greedy stupidity, not to say entire woodenheadedness and disgust (so that an Osborne even required to be knocked down by an author of spirit), and could barely keep the thread of life together.   The one was the wages of suffering and poverty ; the other, unless you gave strict heed to it, the wages of sin.   In time, Johnson had opportunity of looking into both methods, and ascertaining what they were ; but found, at first trial, that the former would in nowise do for him.   Listen, once again, to that far-famed blast of doom, proclaiming into the ear of Lord Chesterfield, and, through him, of the listening world, that patronage should be no more !

" Seven years, my Lord, have now past, since I waited in your outward rooms, or was repulsed from your door ; during which time I have been pushing on my work [1] through difficulties, of which it is useless to complain, and have brought it at last to the verge of publication, without one act of assistance, [2] one word of encouragement, or one smile of favor.

[1] The English Dictionary.
[2] Were time and printer's space of no value, it were easy to wash away certain foolish soot-stains dropped here as " notes :" especially two: the one on this word and on Boswell's note to it ; the other on the paragraph which follows.   Let " ED." look a second time ; he will find that Johnson's sacred regard for *truth* is the only thing to be " noted " in the former case ; also, in the latter, that this of " Love' being a native of the rocks" actually *has* a " meaning."

" The Shepherd in Virgil grew at last acquainted with Love and found him a native of the rocks.

" Is not a patron, my Lord, one who looks with unconcern on a man struggling for life in the water, and when he has reached ground encumbers him with help ? The notice which you have been pleased to take of my labors, had it been early, had been kind ; but it has been delayed till I am indifferent and cannot enjoy it ; till I am solitary and cannot impart it ; till I am known and do not want it. I hope it is no very cynical asperity not to confess obligations where no benefit has been received ; or to be unwilling that the public should consider me as owing that to a patron which Providence has enabled me to do for myself.

" Having carried on my work thus far with so little obligation to any favorer of learning, I shall not be disappointed though I should conclude it, if less be possible, with less ; for I have long been awakened from that dream of hope in which I once boasted myself with so much exaltation,

" My Lord, your Lordship's most humble, most obedient servant,
" SAM. JOHNSON."

And thus must the rebellious " Sam. Johnson" turn him to the bookselling guild, and the wondrous chaos of " author by trade ;" and, though ushered into it only by that dull oily printer, " with loose horseman's coat and such a great bushy wig as he constantly wore," and only as subaltern to some commanding officer " Browne, sitting amid tobacco-smoke at the head of a long table in the alehouse at Clerkenwell "—gird himself together for the warfare ; having no alternative !

Little less contradictory was that other branch of the twofold problem now set before Johnson : the speaking forth ot *truth*. Nay, taken by itself, it had in those days become so complex as to puzzle strongest heads, with nothing else imposed on them for solution ; and even to turn high heads of that sort into mere hollow *vizards*, speaking neither truth nor falsehood, nor any thing but what the prompter and player (ὑποκριτῆς) put into them. Alas ! for poor Johnson, contradiction abounded ; in spirituals and in temporals, within and without. Born with the strongest unconquerable love of just insight, he must begin to live and learn in a scene where prejudice flourishes with rank luxuriance. England was all confused enough, sightless and yet restless, take it where you would ; but figure the best intellect in England nursed up to manhood in the idol-cavern of a poor tradesman's house, in the cathedral city of Lichfield ! What is truth ? said jesting Pilate. What is truth ? might earnest Johnson much more emphatically say. Truth, no longer, like the phœnix, in rainbow plumage, poured, from her glittering beak, such tones of sweetest melody as took captive every ear : the phœnix (waxing old) had well-nigh ceased her singing, and empty wearisome cuckoos, and doleful monotonous owls, innumerable jays also, and twittering sparrows on the housetop, pretended they were repeating her.

It was wholly a divided age, that of Johnson ; unity existed nowhere, in its heaven or in its earth. Society, through every fibre, was rent asunder ; all things, it was then becoming visible, but could not then be understood, were moving onwards, with an impulse received ages before, yet now first with a decisive rapidity, towards that great chaotic gulf, where, whether in the shape of French Revolutions, Reform Bills, or what shape soever, bloody or bloodless, the descent and engulfment assume, we now see them weltering and boiling. Already Cant, as once before hinted, had begun to play its wonderful part, for the hour was come : two ghastly apparitions, unreal *simulacra* both, HYPOCRISY and ATHEISM are already, in silence, parting the world. Opinion and action, which should live together as wedded pair, " one flesh," more properly as soul and body, have commenced their open quarrel, and are suing for a separate maintenance, as if they could exist separately. To the earnest mind, in any position, firm footing and a life of truth was becoming daily more difficult : in Johnson's position it was more difficult than in almost any other.

If, as for a devout nature was inevitable and indispensable, he looked up to religion, as to the polestar of his voyage, already there was no *fixed* polestar any longer visible ; but two stars, a whole constellation of stars, each proclaiming itself as the true. There was the red portentous comet-star of infidelity ; the dim fixed-star, burning ever dimmer, uncertain now whether not an atmospheric *meteor*, of orthodoxy : which of these to choose ? The keener intellects of Europe had, almost without exception, ranged themselves under the former : for some half century, it had been the general effort of European speculation to proclaim that destruction of falsehood was the only truth ; daily had denial waxed stronger and stronger, belief sunk more and more into decay. From our Bolingbrokes and Tolands the sceptical fever had passed into France, into Scotland ; and already it smouldered, far and wide, secretly eating out the heart of England. Bayle had played his part ; Voltaire, on a wider theatre, was playing his—Johnson's senior by some fifteen years : Hume and Johnson were children almost of the same year.[1] To this keener order of intellects did Johnson's indisputably belong ; was he to join them ; was he to oppose them ? A complicated question ; for, alas ! the Church itself is no longer, even to him, wholly of true adamant, but of adamant and baked mud conjoined : the zeal-

[1] Johnson, September 1709 ; Hume, April 1711.

ously devout has to find his Church tottering; and pause
amazed to see, instead of inspired priest, many a swine-feeding
Trulliber ministering at her altar. It is not the least curious
of the incoherences which Johnson had to reconcile, that,
though by nature contemptuous and incredulous, he was, at
that time of day, to find his safety and glory in defending, with
his whole might, the traditions of the elders.

Not less perplexingly intricate, and on both sides hollow or
questionable, was the aspect of politics. Whigs struggling
blindly forward, Tories holding blindly back; each with some
forecast of a half truth; neither with any forecast of the
whole! Admire here this other contradiction in the life of
Johnson; that, though the most ungovernable, and in practice
the most independent of men, he must be a Jacobite, and wor-
shipper of the divine right. In politics also there are
Irreconcilables enough for him. As, indeed how could it be
otherwise? For when religion is torn asunder, and the very
heart of man's existence set against itself, then in all subordinate departments there must needs be hollowness, incoherence.
The English nation had rebelled against a tyrant; and, by
the hands of religious tyrannicides, exacted stern vengeance of
him: Democracy had risen iron-sinewed, and, "like an infant
Hercules, strangled serpents in its cradle." But as yet none
knew the meaning or extent of the phenomenon: Europe was
not ripe for it; not to be ripened for it but by the culture and
various experience of another century and a half. And now,
when the king-killers were all swept away, and a milder *second*
picture was painted over the canvas of the *first*, and betitled
"Glorious Revolution," who doubted but the catastrophe was
over, the whole business finished, and Democracy gone to its
long sleep? Yet was it like a business finished and not finished; a lingering uneasiness dwelt in all minds: the deep-
lying, resistless tendency, which had still to be *obeyed*, could no
longer be *recognized*; thus was there halfness, insincerity, uncertainty in men's ways; instead of heroic Puritans and heroic
Cavaliers, came now a dawdling set of argumentative Whigs,
and a dawdling set of deaf-eared Tories; each half-foolish,
each half-false. The Whigs were false and without basis;
inasmuch as their whole object was resistance, criticism,
demolition—they knew not why, or towards what issue. In
Whiggism, ever since a Charles and his Jeffries had ceased to
meddle with it, and to have any Russel or Sydney to meddle
with, there could be no divineness of character; not till, in
these latter days, it took the figure of a thorough-going, all-
defying Radicalism, was there any solid footing for it to stand

on. Of the like uncertain, half-hollow nature had Toryism
become in Johnson's time ; preaching forth indeed an everlasting truth, the duty of loyalty ; yet now, ever since the final
expulsion of the Stuarts, having no *person*, but only an *office*
to be loyal to ; no living *soul* to worship, but only a dead vel-
vet-cushioned *chair*. Its attitude, therefore, was stiff-necked
refusal to move ; as that of Whiggism was clamorous command
to move—let rhyme and reason, on both hands, say to it what
they might. The consequence was, immeasurable floods of
contentious jargon, tending nowhither ; false conviction ; false
resistance to conviction ; decay (ultimately to become decease)
of whatsoever was once understood by the words *principle* or
honesty of heart ; the louder and louder triumph of *half*ness
and plausibility over *whole*ness and truth ; at last, this all-
overshadowing efflorescence of QUACKERY, which we now see,
with all its deadening and killing fruits, in all its innumerable
branches, down to the lowest. How, between these jarring
extremes, wherein the rotten lay so inextricably intermingled
with the sound, and as yet no eye could see through the ulte-
rior meaning of the matter, was a faithful and true man to
adjust himself ?

That Johnson, in spite of all drawbacks, adopted the Conservative side ; stationed himself as the unyielding opponent of
innovation, resolute to hold fast the form of sound words,
could not but increase, in no small measure, the difficulties he
had to strive with. We mean the *moral* difficulties ; for in
economical respects, it might be pretty equally balanced ; the
Tory servant of the public had perhaps about the same chance
of promotion as the Whig : and all the promotion Johnson
aimed at was the privilege *to live*. But, for what, though
unavowed, was no less indispensable, for his peace of conscience, and the clear ascertainment and feeling of his duty as
an inhabitant of God's world, the case was hereby rendered
much more complex. To resist innovation is easy enough on
one condition : that you resist inquiry. This is, and was, the
common expedient of your common Conservatives ; but it
would not do for Johnson : he was a zealous recommender and
practiser of inquiry ; once for all, could not and would not
believe, much less speak and act, a falsehood : the *form* of
sound words, which he held fast, must have a *meaning* in it.
Here lay the difficulty : to behold a portentous mixture of
true and false, and feel that he must dwell and fight there ;
yet to love and defend only the true. How worship, when
you cannot and will not be an idolater ; yet cannot help discerning that the symbol of your divinity has half become idol-

atrous ?   This was the question, which Johnson, the man both
of clear eye and devout believing heart, must answer—at peril
of his life.   The Whig or sceptic, on the other hand, had a
much simpler part to play.   To him only the idolatrous side of
things, nowise the divine one, lay visible : not *worship*, therefore, nay in the strict sense not heart-honesty, only at most lip-
and hand-honesty, is required of him.   What spiritual force is
his, he can conscientiously employ in the work of cavilling, of
pulling-down what is false.   For the rest, that there is or can
be any truth of a higher than sensual nature, has not occurred
to him.   The utmost, therefore, that he as man has to aim at,
is RESPECTABILITY, the suffrages of his fellow-men.   Such
suffrages   he   may   weigh   as   well   as   count,   or   count   only,
according   as   he   is   a   Burke   or   a   Wilkes.   But   beyond   these
there   lies   nothing   divine   for   him ;   these   attained,   all   is
attained.   Thus is his whole world distinct and rounded-in ; a
clear goal is set before him ; a firm path, rougher or smoother ;
at worst a firm region wherein to seek a path : let him gird up
his loins, and travel on without misgivings !   For the honest
Conservative, again, nothing is distinct, nothing rounded-in :
RESPECTABILITY can nowise be his highest Godhead ; not one
aim, but two conflicting aims to be continually reconciled by
him, has he to strive after.   A difficult position, as we said ;
which accordingly the most did, even in those days, but half
defend : by the surrender, namely, of their own too cumbersome *honesty*, or even *understanding ;* after which the com-
pletest defence was worth little.   Into this difficult position
Johnson, nevertheless, threw himself : found it indeed full of
difficulties ; yet held it out manfully, as an honest-hearted,
open-sighted man, while life was in him.

Such was that same " twofold problem" set before Samuel
Johnson.   Consider all these moral difficulties ; and add to
them the fearful aggravation, which lay in that other circumstance, that he needed a continual appeal to the public, must
continually produce a certain impression and conviction on the
public ; that if he did not, he ceased to have " provision for
the day that was passing over him," he could not any longer
live !   How a vulgar character, once launched into this wild
element ; driven onwards by fear and famine ; without other
aim than to clutch what provender (of enjoyment in any kind)
he could get, always if possible keeping *quite* clear of the gallows and pillory—that is to say, minding heedfully both " person" and " character"—would have floated hither and thither
in it ; and contrived to eat some three repasts daily, and wear
some three suits yearly, and then to depart and disappear, having

consumed his last ration : all this might be worth knowing, but were in itself a trivial knowledge.   How a noble man, resolute for the truth, to whom shams and lies were once for all an abomination, was to act in it : *here* lay the mystery.   By what methods, by what gifts of eye and hand, does a heroic Samuel Johnson, now when cast forth into that waste chaos of author- ship, maddest of things, a mingled Phlegethon and Fleet-ditch, with its floating lumber, and sea-krakens, and mud-spectres, shape himself a voyage ; of the *transient* driftwood, and the *enduring* iron, build him a seaworthy life-boat, and sail therein, undrowned, unpolluted, through the roaring '' mother of dead dogs,'' onwards to an eternal landmark, and city that haih foundations ?   This high question is even the one an- swered in Boswell's book ; which book we therefore, not so falsely, have named a '' heroic poem ;'' for in it there lies the whole argument of such.   Glory to our brave Samuel !   He accomplished this wonderful problem ; and now through long generations we point to him, and say : Here also was a man ; let the world once more have assurance of a man !

   Had there been in Johnson, now when afloat on that con- fusion worse confounded of grandeur and squalor, no light but an earthly outward one, he too must have made shipwreck. With his diseased body, and vehement voracious heart, how easy for him to become a *carpe-diem* philosopher, like the rest, and live and die as miserably as any Boyce of that brother- hood !   But happily there was a higher light for him ; shining as a lamp to his path ; which, in all paths, would teach him to act and walk not as a fool, but as wise, and in those evil days too '' redeeming the time.''   Under dimmer or clearer manifes- tations, a truth had been revealed to him : I also am a man ; even in this unutterable element of authorship, I may live as beseems a man !   That wrong is not only different from right, but that it is in strict scientific terms *infinitely* different ; even as the gaining of the whole world set against the losing of one's own soul, or (as Johnson had it) a Heaven set against a Hell ; that in all situations out of the pit of Tophet, wherein a living man has stood or can stand, there is actually a prize of quite *infinite* value placed within his reach—namely, a *duty* for him to do : this highest gospel, which forms the basis and worth of all other gospels whatsoever, had been revealed to Samuel Johnson ; and the man had believed it, and laid it faithfully to heart.   Such knowledge of the *transcendental*, im- measurable character of duty we call the basis of all gospels, the essence of all religion : he who with his whole soul knows not this as yet knows nothing, as yet *is* properly nothing.

This, happily for him, Johnson was one of those that knew; under a certain authentic symbol it stood forever present to his eyes : a symbol, indeed, waxing old as doth a garment ; yet which had guided forward, as their banner and celestial pillar of fire, innumerable saints and witnesses, the fathers of our modern world ; and for him also had still a sacred significance. It does not appear that at any time Johnson was what we call irreligious : but in his sorrows and isolation, when hope died away, and only a long vista of suffering and toil lay before him to the end, then first did religion shine forth in its meek, everlasting clearness ; even as the stars do in black night, which in the daytime and dusk were hidden by inferior lights. How a true man, in the midst of errors and uncertainties, shall work out for himself a sure life-truth ; and adjusting the transient to the eternal, amid the fragments of ruined temples build up, with toil and pain, a little altar for himself, and worship there ; how Samuel Johnson, in the era of Voltaire, can purify and fortify his soul, and hold real communion with the Highest, " in the Church of St. Clement Danes :" this too stands all unfolded in his biography, and is among the most touching and memorable things there ; a thing to be looked at with pity, admiration, awe. Johnson's religion was as the light of life to him ; without it his heart was all sick, dark, and had no guidance left.

He is now enlisted, or impressed, into that unspeakable shoeblack-seraph army of authors ; but can feel hereby that he fights under a celestial flag, and will quit him like a man. The first grand requisite, an assured heart, he therefore has : what his outward equipments and accoutrements are, is the next question ; an important, though inferior one. His intellectual stock, intrinsically viewed, is perhaps inconsiderable : the furnishings of an English school and English university ; good knowledge of the Latin tongue, a more uncertain one of Greek : this is a rather slender stock of education wherewith to front the world. But then it is to be remembered that his world was England ; that such was the culture England commonly supplied and expected. Besides, Johnson has been a voracious reader, though a desultory one, and oftenest in strange scholastic, too obsolete libraries ; he has also rubbed shoulders with the press of actual life for some thirty years now : views or hallucinations of innumerable things are weltering to and fro in him. Above all, be his weapons what they may, he has an arm that can wield them. Nature has given him her choicest gift—an open eye and heart. He will look on the world, wheresoever he can catch a glimpse of it, with eager curiosity : to the last, we find this a striking character-istic of him ; for all human interests he has a sense ; the meanest handicraftsman could interest him, even in extreme age, by speaking of his craft : the ways of men are all interest-ing to him ; any human thing that he did not know he wished to know. Reflection, moreover, meditation, was what he practised incessantly, with or without his will : for the mind of the man was earnest, deep as well as humane. Thus would the world, such fragments of it as he could survey, form itself, or continually tend to form itself, into a coherent whole ; on any and on all phases of which his vote and voice must be well worth listening to. As a speaker of the word, he will speak real words ; no idle jargon or hollow triviality will issue from him. His aim, too, is clear, attainable ; that of *working for his wages ;* let him *do* this honestly, and all else will follow of its own accord.

With such omens, into such a warfare, did Johnson go forth. A rugged hungry kerne or gallowglass, as we called him : yet indomitable ; in whom lay the true spirit of a sol-dier. With giant's force he toils, since such is his appoint-ment, were it but at hewing of wood and drawing of water for old sedentary bushy-wigged Cave ; distinguishes himself by mere quantity, if there is to be no other distinction. He can write all things ; frosty Latin verses, if these are the salable commodity ; book-prefaces, political philippics, review arti-cles, parliamentary debates : all things he does rapidly ; still more surprising, all things he does thoroughly and well. How he sits there, in his rough-hewn, amorphous bulk, in that upper-room at St. John's Gate, and trundles off sheet after sheet of those Senate-of-Lilliput Debates, to the clamorous printer's devils waiting for them with insatiable throat, down-stairs ; himself perhaps *impransus* all the while ! Admire also the greatness of literature ; how a grain of mustard-seed cast into its Nile-waters, shall settle in the teeming mould, and be found, one day, as a tree, in whose branches all the fowls of heaven may lodge. Was it not so with these Lilliput Debates ? In that small project and act began the stupendous FOURTH ESTATE ; whose wide world-embracing influences what eye can take in ; in whose boughs are there not already fowls of strange feather lodged ? Such things, and far stranger, were done in that wondrous old portal, even in latter times. And then figure Samuel dining " behind the screen," from a trencher covertly handed in to him, at a preconcerted nod from the " great bushy wig ;" Samuel too ragged to show face, yet " made a happy man of " by hearing his praise spoken. If to Johnson himself, then much more to us, may that St. John's Gate be a place we can " never pass without veneration." [1] Poverty, distress, and as yet obscurity, are his companions ; so poor is he that his wife must leave him, and seek shelter among other relations ; Johnson's household has accommodation for one inmate only. To all his ever-varying, ever-recurring troubles, moreover, must be added this continual one of ill-health, and its concomitant depressiveness : a galling load, which would have crushed most common mortals into desperation, is his appointed ballast and life-burden ; he " could not remember the day he had passed free from pain." Nevertheless, life, as we said before, is always life : a healthy soul, imprison it as you will, in squalid garrets, shabby coat,

---

[1] All Johnson's places of resort and abode are venerable, and now indeed to the many as well as to the few ; for his name has become great ; and, as we must often with a kind of sad admiration recognize, there is, even to the rudest man, no greatness so venerable as intellectual, as spiritual greatness ; nay, properly there is no other venerable at all. For example, what soul-subduing magic, for the very clown or craftsman of our England, lies in the word " scholar" ! " He is a scholar :" he is a man *wiser* than we ; of a wisdom to us *boundless*, infinite : who shall speak his worth ! Such things, we say, fill us with a certain pathetic admiration of defaced and obstructed yet glorious man ; archangel though in ruins, or, rather, though in *rubbish* of encumbrances and mud-incrustations, which also are not to be perpetual.

Nevertheless, in this mad-whirling, all-forgetting London, the haunts of the mighty that were can seldom without a strange difficulty be discovered. Will any man, for instance, tell us which *bricks* it was in Lincoln's Inn Buildings that Ben Jonson's hand and trowel laid ? No man, it is to be feared—and also grumbled at. With Samuel Johnson may it prove otherwise ! A gentleman of the British Museum is said to have made drawings of all *his* residences : the blessing of Old Mortality be upon him ! We ourselves, not without labor and risk, lately discovered GOUGH SQUARE, between Fleet Street and Holborn (adjoining both to BOLT COURT and to JOHNSON'S COURT) ; and on the second day of search, the very house there, wherein the *English Dictionary* was composed. It is the first or corner house on the right hand, as you enter through the arched way from the North-west. The actual occupant, an elderly, well-washed, decent-looking man, invited us to enter ; and courteously undertook to be *cicerone ;* though in his memory lay nothing but the foolishest jumble and hallucination. It is a stout, old-fashioned, oak-balustraded house : " I have spent many a pound and penny on it since then," said the worthy landlord : " here, you see, this bedroom was the Doctor's study ; that was the garden" (a plot of delved ground somewhat larger than a bed-quilt), " where he walked for exercise ; these three garret bedrooms" (where his three copyists sat and wrote) " were the place he kept his—*pupils* in" ! *Tempus edax rerum !* Yet *ferax* also : for our friend now added, with a wistful look, which strove to seem merely historical : " I let it all in lodgings, to respectable gentlemen ; by the quarter or the month ; it's all one to me."—" To me also," whispered the ghost of Samuel, as we went pensively our ways.

bodily sickness, or whatever else, will assert its heaven-granted indefeasible freedom, its right to conquer difficulties, to do work, even to feel gladness. Johnson does not whine over his existence, but manfully makes the most and best of it. " He said, a man might live in a garret at eighteenpence a week : few people would inquire where he lodged ; and if they did, it was easy to say, ' Sir, I am to be found at such a place.' By spending threepence in a coffee-house, he might be for some hours every day in very good company ; he might dine for six-pence, breakfast on bread-and-milk for a penny, and do with-out supper. On *clean-shirt day* he went abroad and paid visits.'' Think by whom and of whom this was uttered, and ask then, Whether there is more pathos in it than in a whole cir-culating-library of Giaours and Harolds, or less pathos ? On another occasion, '' when Dr. Johnson, one day, read his own Satire, in which the life of a scholar is painted, with the various obstructions thrown in his way to fortune and to fame, he burst into a passion of tears : Mr. Thrale's family and Mr. Scott only were present, who, in a jocose way, clapped him on the back, and said, ' What's all this, my dear sir ? Why, you and I and Hercules, you know, were all troubled with *melan-choly.'* He was a very large man, and made-out the triumvi-rate with Johnson and Hercules comically enough.'' These were sweet tears ; the sweet victorious remembrance lay in them of toils indeed frightful, yet never flinched from, and now tri-umphed over. " One day it shall delight you also to remember labor done !'' Neither, though Johnson is obscure and poor, need the highest enjoyment of existence, that of heart freely communing with heart, be denied him. Savage and he wan-der homeless through the streets ; without bed, yet not without friendly converse ; such another conversation not, it is like, producible in the proudest drawing-room of London. Nor, under the void night, upon the hard pavement, are their own woes the only topic : nowise ; they '' will stand by their coun-try,'' they there, the two '' Backwoodsmen'' of the Brick Desert !

Of all outward evils obscurity is perhaps in itself the least. To Johnson, as to a healthy-minded man, the fantastic article, sold or given under the title of *Fame*, had little or no value but its intrinsic one. He prized it as the means of getting him employment and good wages ; scarcely as any thing more. His light and guidance came from a loftier source ; of which, in honest aversion to all hypocrisy or pretentious talk, he spoke not to men ; nay perhaps, being of a *healthy* mind, had never spoken to himself. We reckon it a striking fact in Johnson's history, this carelessness of his to fame. Most authors speak of their "fame" as if it were a quite priceless matter; the grand ultimatum, and heavenly Constantine's-banner they had to follow, and conquer under. Thy "fame"! Unhappy mortal, where will it and thou both be in some fifty years? Shakespeare himself has lasted but two hundred; Homer (partly by accident) three thousand : and does not already an ETERNITY encircle every *Me* and every *Thee?* Cease, then, to sit feverishly hatching on that "fame" of thine ; and flapping and shrieking with fierce hisses, like brood-goose on her last egg, if man shall or dare approach it ! Quarrel not with me, hate me not, my brother : make what thou canst of thy egg, and welcome : God knows, I will not steal it ; I believe it to be *addle.* Johnson, for his part, was no man to be killed by a review ; concerning which matter, it was said by a benevolent person : If any author *can* be reviewed to death, let it be, with all convenient despatch, *done.* Johnson thankfully receives any word spoken in his favor ; is nowise disobliged by a lampoon, but will look at it, if pointed out to him, and show how it might have been done better : the lampoon itself is indeed *nothing*, a soap-bubble that next moment will become a drop of sour suds ; but in the meanwhile, if it do any thing, it keeps him more in the world's eye, and the next *bargain* will be all the richer : "Sir, if they should cease to talk of me, I must starve." Sound heart and understanding head : these fail no man, not even a man of letters !

Obscurity, however, was, in Johnson's case, whether a light or heavy evil, likely to be no lasting one. He is animated by the spirit of a true *workman*, resolute to do his work well ; and he *does* his work well ; all his work, that of writing, that of living. A man of this stamp is unhappily not so common in the literary or in any other department of the world, that he can continue always unnoticed. By slow degrees, Johnson emerges ; looming, at first, huge and dim in the eye of an observant few ; at last disclosed, in his real proportions, to the eye of the whole world, and encircled with a "light-nimbus" of glory, so that whoso is not blind must and shall behold him. By slow degrees, we said ; for this also is notable ; slow but sure : as his fame waxes not by exaggerated clamor of what he *seems* to be, but by better and better insight of what he *is*, so it will last and stand wearing, being genuine. Thus indeed is it always, or nearly always, with true fame. The heavenly luminary rises amid vapors ; star-gazers enough must scan it with critical telescopes ; it makes no blazing, the world can either look at it, or forbear looking at it ; not till after a time

and times does its celestial eternal nature become indubitable. Pleasant, on the other hand, is the blazing of a tar-bar-
rel ; the crowd dance merrily round it, with loud huzzaing,
universal three-times-three, and, like Homer's peasants, " bless
the useful light :" but unhappily it so soon ends in darkness,
foul choking smoke ; and is kicked into the gutters, a nameless
imbroglio of charred staves, pitch-cinders, and *vomissement du
diable !*
     But indeed, from of old, Johnson has enjoyed all, or nearly
all, that fame can yield any man : the respect, the obedience
of those that are about him and inferior to him ; of those
whose opinion alone can have any forcible impression on him.
A little circle gathers round the wise man ; which gradually
enlarges as the report thereof spreads, and more can come to
see and to believe ; for wisdom is precious, and of irresistible
attraction to all.   "An inspired-idiot," Goldsmith, hangs
strangely about him ; though, as Hawkins says, " he loved not
Johnson, but rather envied him for his parts ; and once entreated a friend to desist from praising him, ' for in doing so,'
said he, ' you harrow up my very soul ! ' '' Yet, on the whole,
there is no evil in the " gooseberry-fool ;" but rather much
good ; of a finer, if of a weaker, sort than Johnson's ; and all
the more genuine that he himself could never become *conscious*
of it, though unhappily never cease *attempting* to become so :
the author of the genuine " Vicar of Wakefield," nill he, will he,
must needs fly towards such a mass of genuine manhood ; and
Dr. Minor keep gyrating round Dr. Major, alternately attracted and repelled.   Then there is the chivalrous Topham
Beauclerk, with his sharp wit, and gallant courtly ways : there
is Bennet Langton, an orthodox gentleman, and worthy ;
though Johnson once laughed, louder almost than mortal, at
his last will and testament ; and " could not stop his merriment,
but continued it all the way till he got without the Temple-
gate ; then burst into such a fit of laughter that he appeared to
be almost in a convulsion ; and, in order to support himself,
laid hold of one of the posts at the side of the foot-pavement,
and sent forth peals so loud that, in the silence of the night,
his voice seemed to resound from Temple-bar to Fleet-ditch !"
Lastly comes his solid-thinking, solid-feeding Thrale, the well-
beloved man ; with *Thralia*, a bright papilionaceous creature,
whom the elephant loved to play with, and wave to and fro
upon his trunk.   Not to speak of a reverent Bozzy, for what
need is there farther ?   Or of the spiritual luminaries, with
tongue or pen, who made that age remarkable ; or of Highland
lairds drinking, in fierce usquebaugh, " Your health, Toctor

Shonson !'' Still less of many such as that poor " Mr. F.
Lewis,'' older in date, of whose birth, death, and whole terrestrial *res gestæ*, this only, and strange enough this actually, sur-
vives : " Sir, he lived in London, and hung loose upon soci·
ety !'' *Stat* PARVI *nominis umbra.*

In his fifty-third year he is beneficed, by the royal bounty,
with a pension of three-hundred pounds. Loud clamor is
always more or less insane : but probably the insanest of all
loud clamors in the eighteenth century was this that was
raised about Johnson's pension. Men seem to be led by the
noses : but, in reality, it is by the ears, as some ancient slaves
were, who had their ears bored ; or as some modern quadru-
peds may be, whose ears are long. Very falsely was it said,
" Names do not change things.'' Names do change things ;
nay, for most part they are the only substance which mankind
can discern in things. The whole sum that Johnson, during
the remaining twenty-two years of his life, drew from the public funds of England, would have supported some supreme
priest for about half as many weeks ; it amounts very nearly to
the revenue of our poorest Church-overseer for one twelve-
month. Of secular administrators of provinces, and horse-
subduers, and game-destroyers, we shall not so much as speak :
but who were the Primates of England, and the Primates of
all England, during Johnson's days ? No man has remembered. Again, is the Primate of all England something, or is he
nothing ? If something, then what but the man who, in the
supreme degree, teaches and spiritually edifies, and leads towards Heaven by guiding wisely through the earth, the living
souls that inhabit England ? We touch here upon deep matters ;
which but remotely concern us, and might lead us into still
deeper : clear, in the mean while, it is that the true Spiritual
Edifier and Soul's Father of all England was, and till very
lately continued to be, the man named Samuel Johnson—
whom this scot-and-lot-paying world cackled reproachfully to see
remunerated like a supervisor of excise !

If Destiny had beaten hard on poor Samuel, and did
never cease to visit him too roughly, yet the last section of his
life might be pronounced victorious, and on the whole happy.
He was not idle ; but now no longer goaded-on by want ; the
light which had shone irradiating the dark haunts of poverty
now illuminates the circles of wealth, of a certain culture and
elegant intelligence ; he who had once been admitted to speak
with Edmund Cave and Tobacco Browne, now admits a Reynolds and a Burke to speak with him. Loving friends are
there ; listeners, even answerers : the fruit of his long labors

lies round him in fair legible writings, of philosophy, eloquence, morality, philology ; some excellent, all worthy and
genuine works ; for which, too, a deep, earnest murmur of
thanks reaches him from all ends of his Fatherland.   Nay, there
are works of goodness, of undying mercy, which even he has
possessed the power to do : " What I gave I have ; what I spent
I had !"   Early friends had long sunk into the grave ; yet in his
soul they ever lived, fresh and clear, with soft pious breathings
towards them, not without a still hope of one day meeting them
again in purer union.   Such was Johnson's life : the victorious
battle of a free, true man.   Finally he died the death of the
free and true : a dark cloud of death, solemn and not untinged
with haloes of immortal Hope, " took him away," and our eyes
could no longer behold him ; but can still behold the trace
and impress of his courageous honest spirit, deep-legible in the
world's business, wheresoever he walked and was.

To estimate the quantity of work that Johnson performed,
how much poorer the world were had it wanted him, can, as
in all such cases, never be accurately done ; cannot, till after
some longer space, be approximately done.   All work is as
seed sown ; it grows and spreads, and sows itself anew, and
so, in endless palingenesia, lives and works.   To Johnson's
writings, good and solid, and still profitable as they are, we
have already rated his life and conversation as superior.   By
the one and by the other, who shall compute what effects have
been produced, and are still, and into deep Time, producing ?
So much, however, we can already see : It is now some three
quarters of a century that Johnson has been the prophet of the
English ; the man by whose light the English people, in public and in private, more than by any other man's, have guided
their existence.   Higher light than that immediately *practical*
one ; higher virtue than an honest PRUDENCE, he could not
then communicate ; nor perhaps could they have received :
such light, such virtue, however, he did communicate.   How
to thread this labyrinthic Time, the fallen and falling ruin of
Times ; to silence vain scruples, hold firm to the last the fragments of old belief, and with earnest eye still discern some
glimpses of a true path, and go forward thereon, " in a world
where there is much to be done, and little to be known :" this
is what Samuel Johnson, by act and word, taught his nation ;
what his nation received and learned of him, more than of any
other.   We can view him as the preserver and transmitter of
whatsoever was genuine in the spirit of Toryism ; which genuine spirit, it is now becoming manifest, must again embody

itself in all new forms of society, be what they may, that are to exist, and have continuance—elsewhere than on paper. The *last* in many things, Johnson was the last genuine Tory ; the last of Englishmen who, with strong voice and wholly-believing heart, preached the doctrine of standing-still ; who, without selfishness or slavishness, reverenced the existing powers, and could assert the privileges of rank, though himself poor, neglected, and plebeian ; who had heart-devoutness with heart-hatred of cant, was orthodox-religious with his eyes open ; and in all things and everywhere spoke out in plain English, from a soul wherein Jesuitism could find no harbor, and with the front and tone not of a diplomatist but of a man.

The last of the Tories was Johnson : not Burke, as is often said ; Burke was essentially a Whig, and only, on reaching the verge of the chasm towards which Whiggism from the first was inevitably leading, recoiled ; and, like a man vehement rather than earnest, a resplendent far-sighted rhetorician rather than a deep, sure thinker, recoiled with no measure, convulsively, and damaging what he drove back with him.

In a world which exists by the balance of antagonisms the respective merit of the conservator and the innovator must ever remain debatable. Great, in the meanwhile, and undoubted for both sides, is the merit of him who, in a day of change, walks wisely, honestly. Johnson's aim was in itself an impossible one : this of stemming the eternal flood of Time ; of clutching all things and anchoring them down, and saying, Move not !—how could it or should it ever have success ? The strongest man can but retard the current partially and for a short hour. Yet even in such shortest retardation may not an inestimable value lie ? If England has escaped the blood-bath of a French Revolution ; and may yet, in virtue of this delay and of the experience it has given, work out her deliverance calmly into a new era, let Samuel Johnson, beyond all contemporary or succeeding men, have the praise for it. We said above that he was appointed to be ruler of the British nation for a season : whoso will look beyond the surface, into the heart of the world's movements, may find that all Pitt administrations, and continental subsidies, and Waterloo victories rested on the possibility of making England, yet a little while, *Toryish*, loyal to the old ; and this again on the anterior reality, that the wise had found such loyalty still practicable, and recommendable. England had its Hume, as France had its Voltaires and Diderots ; but the Johnson was peculiar to us.

If we ask now, by what endowment it mainly was that

Johnson realized such a life for himself and others ; what quality of character the main phenomena of his life may be most
naturally deduced from, and his other qualities most naturally
subordinated to in our conception of him, perhaps the answer
were : The quality of Courage, of Valor ; that Johnson was a
brave man. The courage that can go forth, once and away,
to Chalk-Farm, and have itself shot, and snuffed out, with
decency, is nowise wholly what we mean here. Such courage
we indeed esteem an exceeding small matter ; capable of coex-
isting with a life full of falsehood, feebleness, poltroonery, and
despicability. Nay oftener it is cowardice rather that produces the result : for consider, Is the Chalk-Farm pistoleer
inspired with any reasonable belief and determination ; or is
he hounded on by haggard indefinable fear—how he will be *cut*
at public places, and " plucked geese of the neighborhood " will
wag their tongues at him a plucked goose ? If he go then, and
be shot without shrieking or audible uproar, it is well for him :
nevertheless there is nothing amazing in it. Courage to manage all this has not perhaps been denied to any man, or to any
woman. Thus, do not recruiting sergeants drum through the
streets of manufacturing towns, and collect ragged losels
enough ; every one of whom, if once dressed in red, and
trained a little, will receive fire cheerfully for the small sum of
one shilling *per diem*, and have the soul blown out of him at
last, with perfect propriety. The courage that dares only *die*
is on the whole no sublime affair ; necessary indeed, yet universal ; pitiful when it begins to parade itself. On this globe of
ours there are some thirty-six persons that manifest it, seldom
with the smallest failure, during every second of time. Nay,
look at Newgate : do not the offscourings of creation, when
condemned to the gallows, as if they were not men but vermin,
walk thither with decency, and even to the scowls and hootings
of the whole universe, give their stern good-night in silence ?
What is to be undergone only once, we may undergo ; what
must be, comes almost of its own accord. Considered as
duellist, what a poor figure does the fiercest Irish Whiskerando
make in comparison with any English game-cock, such as you
may buy for fifteenpence !

The courage we desire and prize is not the courage to die
decently, but to live manfully. This, when by God's grace it
has been given, lies deep in the soul ; like genial heat, fosters
all other virtues and gifts ; without it they could not live. In
spite of our innumerable Waterloos and Peterloos, and such
campaigning as there has been, this courage we allude to and
call the only true one, is perhaps rarer in these last ages than it

has been in any other since the Saxon Invasion under Hengist. Altogether extinct it can never be among men ; otherwise the species Man were no longer for this world : here and there, in all times, under various guises, men are sent hither not only to demonstrate but exhibit it, and testify, as from heart to heart, that it is still possible, still practicable.

Johnson, in the eighteenth century, and as man of letters, was one of such ; and, in good truth, "the bravest of the brave." What mortal could have more to war with ? Yet, as we saw, he yielded not, faltered not ; he fought, and even, such was his blessedness, prevailed. Whoso will understand what it is to have a man's heart may find that, since the time of John Milton, no braver heart had beat in any English bosom than Samuel Johnson now bore. Observe, too, that he never called himself brave, never felt himself to be so ; the more completely *was* so. No Giant Despair, no Golgotha Death-dance or Sorcerer's-Sabbath of " Literary Life in London," appals this pilgrim ; he works resolutely for deliverance ; in still defiance steps stoutly along. The thing that is given him to do, he can make himself do ; what is to be endured, he can endure in silence.

How the great soul of old Samuel, consuming daily his own bitter unalleviable allotment of misery and toil, shows beside the poor flimsy little soul of young Boswell ; one day flaunting in the ring of vanity, tarrying by the wine-cup and crying, Aha, the wine is red ; the next day deploring his downpressed, night-shaded, quite poor estate, and thinking it unkind that the whole movement of the universe should go on, while *his* digestive-apparatus had stopped ! We reckon Johnson's "talent of silence" to be among his great and too rare gifts. Where there is nothing farther to be done, there shall nothing farther be said : like his own poor blind Welshwoman, he accomplished somewhat, and also "endured fifty years of wretchedness with unshaken fortitude." How grim was life to him ; a sick prison-house and Doubting-castle ! " His great business," he would profess, " was to escape from himself." Yet towards all this he has taken his position and resolution ; can dismiss it all " with frigid indifference, having little to hope or to fear." Friends are stupid, and pusillanimous, and parsimonious ; " wearied of his stay, yet offended at his departure :" it is the manner of the world. " By popular delusion," remarks he with a gigantic calmness, " illiterate writers will rise into renown :" it is portion of the history of English literature ; a perennial thing, this same popular delusion ; and will—alter the character of the language.

Closely connected with this quality of valor, partly as springing from it, partly as protected by it, are the more recognizable qualities of truthfulness in word and thought, and honesty in action. There is a reciprocity of influence here : for as the realizing of truthfulness and honesty is the life-light and great aim of valor, so without valor they cannot, in anywise, be realized. Now, in spite of all practical shortcomings, no one that sees into the significance of Johnson will say that his prime object was not truth. In conversation, doubtless, you may observe him, on occasion, fighting as if for victory ; and must pardon these ebulliences of a careless hour, which were not without temptation and provocation. Remark likewise two things : that such prize-arguings were ever on merely superficial debatable questions ; and then that they were argued generally by the fair laws of battle and logic-fence, by one cunning in that same. If their purpose was excusable, their effect was harmless, perhaps beneficial : that of taming noisy mediocrity, and showing it another side of a debatable matter ; to see *both* sides of which was, for the first time, to see the truth of it. In his writings themselves are errors enough, crabbed prepossessions enough ; yet these also of a quite extráneous and accidental nature, nowhere a wilful shutting of the eyes to the truth. Nay, is there not everywhere a heartfelt discernment, singular, almost admirable, if we consider through what confused conflicting lights and hallucinations it had to be attained, of the highest everlasting truth, and beginning of all truths : this namely, that man is ever, and even in the age of Wilkes and Whitefield, a revelation of God to man ; and lives, moves, and has his being in truth only ; is either true, or, in strict speech, *is* not at all ?

Quite spotless, on the other hand, is Johnson's love of truth, if we look at it as expressed in practice, as what we have named honesty of action. '' Clear your mind of cant ;'' *clear* it, throw cant utterly away : such was his emphatic, repeated precept ; and did not he himself faithfully conform to it ? The life of this man has been, as it were, turned inside out, and examined with microscopes by friend and foe ; yet was there no lie found in him. His doings and writings are not *shows* but *performances :* you may weigh them in the balance, and they will stand weight. Not a line, not a sentence is dishonestly done, is other than it pretends to be. Alas ! and he wrote not out of inward inspiration, but to earn his wages : and with that grand perennial tide of '' popular delusion'' flowing by ; in whose waters he nevertheless refused to fish, to whose rich oyster-beds the dive was too muddy for him. Observe, again, with what innate hatred of cant, he takes for himself, and offers to others, the lowest possible view of his business, which he followed with such nobleness. Motive for writing he had none, as he often said, but money ; and yet he wrote *so*. Into the region of Poetic Art he indeed never rose ; there was no *ideal* without him avowing itself in his work : the nobler was that unavowed *ideal* which lay within him, and commanded saying, Work out thy artisanship in the spirit of an artist ! They who talk loudest about the dignity of art, and fancy that they too are artistic guild-brethren, and of the celestials, let them consider well what manner of man this was, who felt himself to be only a hired day-laborer. A laborer that was worthy of his hire ; that has labored not as an eye-servant, but as one found faithful ! Neither was Johnson in those days perhaps wholly a unique. Time was when, for money, you might have ware : and needed not, in all departments, in that of the epic poem, in that of the blacking-bottle, to rest content with the mere *persuasion* that you had ware. It was a happier time. But as yet the seventh Apocalyptic Bladder (of PUFFERY) had not been rent open, to whirl and grind, as in a West-Indian tornado, all earthly trades and things into wreck, and dust, and consummation—and regeneration. Be it quickly, since it must be !

That mercy can dwell only with valor, is an old sentiment or proposition ; which in Johnson again receives confirmation. Few men on record have had a more merciful, tenderly affectionate nature than old Samuel. He was called the Bear ; and did indeed too often look, and roar, like one ; being forced to it in his own defence : yet within that shaggy exterior of his there beat a heart warm as a mother's, soft as a little child's. Nay generally, his very roaring was but the anger of affection : the rage of a bear, if you will ; but of a bear bereaved of her whelps. Touch his religion, glance at the Church of England, or the divine right ; and he was upon you ! These things were his symbols of all that was good and precious for men ; his very Ark of the Covenant : whoso laid hand on them tore asunder his heart of hearts. Not out of hatred to the opponent, but of love to the thing opposed, did Johnson grow cruel, fiercely contradictory : this is an important distinction ; never to be forgotten in our censure of his conversational outrages. But observe also with what humanity, what openness of love, he can attach himself to all things : to a blind old woman, to a Doctor Levett, to a cat " Hodge." " His thoughts in the latter part of his life were frequently employed on his deceased friends ; he often muttered these or suchlike sentences : ' Poor man ! and then he died.' " How he patiently converts his poor home into a Lazaretto; endures, for long years, the contradiction of the miserable and unreasonable; with him unconnected, save that they had no other to yield them refuge! Generous old man! Worldly possession he has little; yet of this he gives freely; from his own hard-earned shilling, the halfpence for the poor, that "waited his coming out," are not withheld: the poor "waited the coming out" of one not quite so poor! A Sterne can write sentimentalities on dead asses: Johnson has a rough voice; but he finds the wretched daughter of vice fallen down in the streets, carries her home on his own shoulders, and like a good Samaritan gives help to the help-needing, worthy or unworthy. Ought not Charity, even in that sense, to cover a multitude of sins? No Penny-a-week Committee-lady, no manager of soup-kitchens, dancer at charity-balls, was this rugged, stern-visaged man; but where, in all England, could there have been found another soul so full of pity, a hand so heavenlike bounteous as his? The widow's mite, we know, was greater than all the other gifts.

Perhaps it is this divine feeling of affection, throughout manifested, that principally attracts us towards Johnson. A true brother of men is he; and filial lover of the earth; who, with little bright spots of attachment, "where lives and works some loved one," has beautified "this rough solitary earth into a peopled garden." Lichfield, with its mostly dull and limited inhabitants, is to the last one of the sunny islets for him: *Salve magna parens!* Or read those letters on his mother's death: what a genuine solemn grief and pity lies recorded there; a looking back into the Past, unspeakably mournful, unspeakably tender. And yet calm, sublime; for he must now act, not look: his venerated mother has been taken from him; but he must now write a "Rasselas" to defray her funeral! Again in this little incident, recorded in his Book of Devotion, are not the tones of sacred sorrow and greatness deeper than in many a blank-verse tragedy; as, indeed, "the fifth act of a tragedy," though unrhymed, does "lie in every death-bed, were it a peasant's, and of straw:"

"Sunday, October 18, 1767. Yesterday, at about ten in the morning, I took my leave forever of my dear old friend, Catherine Chambers, who came to live with my mother about 1724, and has been but little parted from us since. She buried my father, my brother, and my mother. She is now fifty-eight years old.

"I desired all to withdraw; then told her that we were to part forever; that as Christians, we should part with prayer; and that I would, if she was willing, say a short prayer beside her. She expressed great desire to hear me; and held up her poor hands as she lay in bed, with great fervor, while I prayed kneeling by her. . . . .

" I then kissed her. She told me that to part was the greatest pain she had ever felt, and that she hoped we should meet again in a better place. I expressed, with swelled eyes and great emotion of tenderness, the same hopes. We kissed and parted ; I humbly hope, to meet again, and to part no more."

Tears trickling down the granite rock : a soft well of pity springs within ! Still more tragical is this other scene : " Johnson mentioned that he could not in general accuse himself of having been an undutiful son. ' Once, indeed,' said he, ' I was disobedient : I refused to attend my father to Uttoxeter market. Pride was the source of that refusal, and the remembrance of it was painful. A few years ago I desired to atone for this fault.' " But by what method ? What method was now possible ? Hear it ; the words are again given as his own, though here evidently by a less capable reporter :

" Madam, I beg your pardon for the abruptness of my departure in the morning, but I was compelled to it by conscience. Fifty years ago, madam, on this day, I committed a breach of filial piety. My father had been in the habit of attending Uttoxeter market, and opening a stall there for the sale of his books. Confined by indisposition, he desired me, that day, to go and attend the stall in his place. My pride prevented me ; I gave my father a refusal. And now to-day I have been at Uttoxeter ; I went into the market at the time of business, uncovered my head, and stood with it bare, for an hour, on the spot where my father's stall used to stand. In contrition I stood, and I hope the penance was expiatory."

Who does not figure to himself this spectacle, amid the " rainy weather, and the sneers," or wonder, " of the bystanders" ? The memory of old Michael Johnson, rising from the far distance ; sad-beckoning in the " moonlight of memory :" how he had toiled faithfully hither and thither ; patiently among the lowest of the low ; been buffeted and beaten down, yet ever risen again, ever tried it anew—And oh, when the wearied old man, as bookseller, or hawker, or tinker, or whatsoever it was that Fate had reduced him to, begged help of *thee* for one day, how savage, diabolic, was that mean vanity, which answered, No ! He sleeps now ; after life's fitful fever, he sleeps well : but thou, O Merciless, how now wilt thou still the sting of that remembrance ? The picture of Samuel Johnson standing bareheaded in the market there, is one of the grandest and saddest we can paint. Repentance ! repentance ! he proclaims, as with passionate sobs : but only to the ear of Heaven, if Heaven will give him audience : the earthly ear and heart, that should have heard it, are now closed, unresponsive forever.

That this so keen-loving, soft-trembling affectionateness, the inmost essence of his being, must have looked forth, in one form or another, through Johnson's whole character, practical and intellectual, modifying both, is not to be doubted. Yet through what singular distortions and superstitions, moping melancholies, blind habits, whims about "entering with the right foot," and "touching every post as he walked along:" and all the other mad chaotic lumber of a brain that, with sun-clear intellect, hovered forever on the verge of insanity, must that same inmost essence have looked forth; unrecognizable to all but the most observant! Accordingly it was not recog-nized; Johnson passed not for a fine nature, but for a dull, al-most brutal one. Might not, for example, the first-fruit of such a lovingness, coupled with his quick insight, have been expected to be a peculiarly courteous demeanor as man among men? In Johnson's "Politeness," which he often, to the wonder of some, asserted to be great, there was indeed some-what that needed explanation. Nevertheless, if he insisted al-ways on handing lady-visitors to their carriage; though with the certainty of collecting a mob of gazers in Fleet Street, as might well be, the beau having on, by way of court-dress, "his rusty brown morning suit, a pair of old shoes for slippers, a little shrivelled wig sticking on the top of his head, and the sleeves of his shirt and the knees of his breeches hanging loose:" in all this we can see the spirit of true politeness, only shining through a strange medium. Thus again, in his apartments, at one time, there were unfortunately no chairs. "A gentleman who frequently visited him whilst writing his 'Idlers,' constantly found him at his desk, sitting on one with three legs; and on rising from it, he remarked that Johnson never forgot its defect; but would either hold it in his hand, or place it with great composure against some support; taking no notice of its imperfection to his visitor," who meanwhile, we suppose, sat upon folios, or in the sartorial fashion. "It was remarkable in Johnson," continues Miss Reynolds (*Renny dear*), "that no external circumstances ever prompted him to make any apology, or to seem even sensible of their existence. Whether this was the effect of philosophic pride, or of some partial notion of his respecting high-breeding, is doubtful." That it *was*, for one thing, the effect of genuine politeness, is nowise doubtful. Not of the Pharisaical Brummellean politeness, which would suffer crucifixion rather than ask twice for soup: but the noble universal politeness of a man that knows the dignity of men, and feels his own; such as may be seen in the patriarchal bearing of an Indian sachem; such as Johnson himself exhibited, when a sudden chance brought him into dia-logue with his king. To us, with our view of the man, it no-wise appears "strange" that he should have boasted himself cunning in the laws of politeness ; nor "stranger still," habit-ually attentive to practise them.

More legibly is this influence of the loving heart to be traced in his intellectual character. What, indeed, is the be-ginning of intellect, the first inducement to the exercise there-of, but attraction towards somewhat, *affection* for it ? Thus, too, who ever saw, or will see, any true talent, not to speak of genius, the foundation of which is not goodness, love ? From Johnson's strength of affection we deduce many of his intel-lectual peculiarities ; especially that threatening array of per-versions, known under the name of "Johnson's Prejudices." Looking well into the root from which these sprang, we have long ceased to view them with hostility, can pardon and rever-ently pity them. Consider with what force early-imbibed opinions must have clung to a soul of this affection. Those evil-famed prejudices of his, that Jacobitism, Church-of-Eng-landism, hatred of the Scotch, belief in witches, and suchlike, what were they but the ordinary beliefs of well-doing, well-meaning provincial Englishmen in that day ? First gathered by his father's hearth ; round the kind "country fires," of na-tive Staffordshire ; they grew with his growth and strengthened with his strength : they were hallowed by fondest sacred recol-lections ; to part with them was parting with his heart's blood. If the man who has no strength of affection, strength of be-lief, have no strength of prejudice, let him thank Heaven for it, but to himself take small thanks.

Melancholy it was, indeed, that the noble Johnson could not work himself loose from these adhesions ; that he could only purify them, and wear them with some nobleness. Yet let us understand how they grew out from the very centre of his being : nay, moreover, how they came to cohere in him with what formed the business and worth of his life, the sum of his whole spiritual endeavor. For it is on the same ground that he became throughout an edifier and repairer, not, as the others of his make were, a puller-down ; that in an age of universal scepticism, England was still to produce its believer. Mark, too, his candor even here ; while a Dr. Adams, with placid surprise, asks, "Have we not evidence enough of the soul's immortality ?" Johnson answers, "I wish for more."

But the truth is, in prejudice, as in all things, Johnson was the product of England ; one of those *good* yeomen whose limbs were made in England : alas, the last of *such* Invincibles, their day being now done ! His culture is wholly English ; that not of a thinker but of a "scholar :" his interests are wholly English ; he sees and knows nothing but England ; he is the John Bull of spiritual Europe : let him live, love him,

as he was and could not but be ! Pitiable it is, no doubt, that
a Samuel Johnson must confute Hume's irreligious philosophy
by some " story from a Clergyman of the Bishoprick of Dur-
ham ;" should see nothing in the great Frederick but " Voltaire's lackey ;" in Voltaire himself but a man *acerrimi in-
genii, paucarum literarum ;* in Rousseau but one worthy to be
hanged ; and in the universal, long-prepared, inevitable tendency of European thought but a green-sick milkmaid's crotch-
et of, for variety's sake, " milking the bull ". Our good,
dear John ! Observe, too, what it is that he sees in the city of
Paris : no feeblest glimpse of those D'Alemberts and Diderots,
or of the strange questionable work they did ; solely some Bene-
dictine priests, to talk kitchen-latin with them about *Editiones
Principes.* "*Monsheer Nongtongpaw !*" Our dear, foolish
John : yet is there a lion's heart within him ! Pitiable all these
things were, we say ; yet nowise inexcusable ; nay, as basis or
as foil to much else that was in Johnson, almost venerable.
Ought we not, indeed, to honor England, and English institutions and way of life, that they could still equip such a man ;
could furnish him in heart and head to be a Samuel Johnson,
and yet to love them, and unyieldingly fight for them ? What
truth and living vigor must such institutions once have had,
when, in the middle of the eighteenth century, there was still
enough left in them for this !

It is worthy of note that, in our little British isle, the two
grand antagonisms of Europe should have stood embodied,
under their very highest concentration, in two men produced
simultaneously among ourselves. Samuel Johnson and David
Hume, as was observed, were children nearly of the same year :
through life they were spectators of the same life-movement ;
often inhabitants of the same city. Greater contrast, in all
things, between two great men, could not be. Hume, well-
born, competently provided for, whole in body and mind, of
his own determination forces a way into literature : Johnson,
poor, moonstruck, diseased, forlorn, is forced into it " with
the bayonet of necessity at his back." And what a part did
they severally play there ! As Johnson became the father of all
succeeding Tories ; so was Hume the father of all succeeding
Whigs, for his own Jacobitism was but an accident, as worthy to
be named prejudice as any of Johnson's. Again, if Johnson's
culture was exclusively English ; Hume's, in Scotland, became
European ; for which reason, too, we find his influence spread
deeply over all quarters of Europe, traceable deeply in all speculation, French, German, as well as domestic ; while Johnson's
name, out of England, is hardly anywhere to be met with. In
spiritual stature they are almost equal ; both great, among the

greatest ; yet how unlike in likeness ! Hume has the widest, methodizing, comprehensive eye ; Johnson the keenest for perspicacity and minute detail : so had, perhaps chiefly, their education ordered it. Neither of the two rose into poetry ; yet both to some approximation thereof : Hume to something of an epic clearness and method, as in his delineation of the Commonwealth Wars ; Johnson to many a deep lyric tone of plaintiveness and impetuous graceful power, scattered over his fugitive compositions. Both, rather to the general surprise, had a certain rugged humor shining through their earnestness : the indication, indeed, that they *were* earnest men, and had *subdued* their wild world into a kind of temporary home and safe dwelling. Both were, by principle and habit, Stoics : yet Johnson with the greater merit, for he alone had very much to triumph over ; farther, he alone ennobled his Stoicism into devotion. To Johnson life was as a prison, to be endured with heroic faith ; to Hume it was little more than a foolish Bartholomew-Fair show-booth, with the foolish crowdings and elbowings of which it was not worth while to quarrel ; the whole would break up, and be at liberty, so *soon.* Both realized the highest task of manhood, that of living like men ; each died not unfitly, in his way : Hume as one, with factitious, half-false gayety, taking leave of what was itself wholly but a lie : Johnson as one, with awe-struck, yet resolute and piously expectant heart, taking leave of a reality, to enter a reality still higher. Johnson had the harder problem of it, from first to last : whether, with some hesitation, we can admit that he was intrinsically the better-gifted, may remain undecided.

These two men now rest ; the one in Westminster Abbey here ; the other in the Calton-Hill Churchyard of Edinburgh. Through life they did not meet : as contrasts, " like in unlike," love each other ; so might they two have loved, and communed kindly, had not the terrestrial dross and darkness that was in them withstood ! One day, their spirits, what truth was in each, will be found working, living in harmony and free union, even here below. They were the two half-men of their time : whoso should combine the intrepid candor and decisive scientific clearness of Hume, with the reverence, the love, and devout humility of Johnson, were the whole man of a new time. Till such whole man arrive for us, and the distracted time admit of such, might the Heavens but bless poor England with half-men worthy to tie the shoe-latchets of these, resembling these even from afar ! Be both attentively regarded, let the true effort of both prosper ; and for the present, both take our affectionate farewell !

NOTES.

JOHNSON.

Page xvii. *Politian.*—Politian (1454-1494), the friend of Lorenzo de' Medici and tutor to his children, was one of the leaders of the Italian Renascence. His Latin poems were famous, and have been repeatedly printed.

Page xxxii. *Ben.*—The dramatist and poet, Ben Jonson (1574-1637).

Page xli. *Malone.*—Edmund Malone (1741-1812), a celebrated critic, and among the best of the commentators on Shakespeare.

Page xliii. *Windham.*—William Windham (1750-1810), Secretary for War in Lord Grenville's ministry of " The Talents."

Ib. Frances Burney.—The authoress of *Evelina* and *Cecilia*. She was born in 1752, married in 1793 M. d'Arblay, a French emigrant, and died in 1840.

MILTON.

Page 3. *Mr. Fenton's elegant Abridgement.*—Elijah Fenton (1683-1730), who assisted Pope in translating Homer's *Odyssey*, " undertook," says Johnson in his Life of Fenton, " to revise the punctuation of Milton's poems, which, as the author neither wrote the original copy nor corrected the press, was supposed capable of amendment. To this edition he prefixed a short and elegant account of Milton's life, written at once with tenderness and integrity."

Page 4. *Alabaster's Roxana.*—William Alabaster, an English scholar and divine, brought out the Latin tragedy of " Roxana" in 1632. It was acted in the hall of Trinity College, Cambridge. Alabaster died in 1640.

Page 7. *" A quo."*—These lines are from the Roman poet Propertius, and mean that Homer is a perpetual source of inspiration to all poets.

Ib. Sir Henry Wotton.—Wotton (1568-1639), a scholar, diplomatist, and poet, died Provost of Eton. His life was written by Izaak Walton.

Ib. Grotius.—Hugo Grotius (1583-1645), a scholar, theologian, and diplomatist; one of the most celebrated men whom Holland has produced.

Page 13. *Hell grows darker.*—
" So frown'd the mighty combatants, that Hell
Grew darker at their frown."—*Paradise Lost*, ii. 719.

Page 14. *Two Sonnets.*—The tenth and eleventh of Milton's Sonnets.

Page 16. *A treatise.*—This treatise, entitled *The Tenure of Kings and Magistrates*, was first published in the month following the King's execution, and was afterwards enlarged.

Ib. Icon Basilike.—This famous literary forgery, *The Picture of a King*, was published by Dr. Gauden, afterwards Bishop of Exeter, from a manuscript said to have been entrusted to him by Charles I. himself, and became very popular. Milton answered it by his *Iconoclastes.*

Page 17. *Which he performed.*—By writing his *Defensio pro Populo Anglicano.*

Page 21. *Arthur was reserved.*—Fenton here refers to Blackmore's heroic poem of *Prince Arthur*, published in 1695;—a poem once famous, but now forgotten.

Page 24. *Seemly arts and affairs.*—See page 12.

Ib. Bated no jot, etc.—These words are from Milton's twenty-second Sonnet.

Ib. Harrington.—James Harrington (1611–1677), a writer on government and author of *Oceana*, was for a time groom of the bed-chamber to Charles I., and attended him on the scaffold.

Page 25. *Goodwin.*—Thomas Goodwin (1600–1679), a leading Independent minister and theologian, was made President of Magdalen College, Oxford, by Cromwell, and attended him on his death-bed.

Ib. Betterton—Davenant.—Thomas Betterton (1635–1710), a celebrated actor when the stage regained popularity after the Restoration; Sir William Davenant (1605–1668), Ben Jonson's successor in the poet-laureateship, author of the heroic poem of *Gondebert*, and also a popular writer for the stage, and theatre-manager.

Page 29. *Hellibore.*—The ancients thought hellibore a cure for madness and mental delusion.

Page 30. *An age too late.*—The reference is to what Milton says in his Tract, *The Reason of Church Government urged against Prelaty* (1642).

Ib. Climate.—The reference is to the same Tract. Milton's words are: " If that there be nothing adverse in our climate, or the fate of this age." In the same Tract he declares his hope that he "might perhaps leave something so written to after times, as they should not willingly let die."

Page 41. *Queen Caroline.*—Caroline of Anspach, wife of George II.

Ib. Tonson.—A celebrated publisher of the last century, whose great-uncle and predecessor in business, Jacob Tonson, "the prince of booksellers," and the first of the great English publishers, is mentioned in the Life of Dryden. This Jacob died in 1736; his great-nephew in 1767.

Page 47. *Bossu.*—A French critic of the seventeenth century, whose dissertation on the laws of epic poetry was famous in its day, and was translated into English.

Page 52. *The Cyanean Rocks.*—These rocks, more commonly called the Symplegades, were islands of rock in the Euxine Sea, fabled to close upon ships passing between them.

Page 59. *Butler.*—The author of *Hudibras*. He died in 1680.

DRYDEN.

Page 77. *Lee.*—Nathaniel Lee (1657–1692), a dramatic poet, of whose thirteen tragedies *Alexander the Great* is the best known.

Page 81. *Lopez de Vega.*—A very famous Spanish poet (1562–1635), who wrote, he tells us himself, more than 1,500 dramas, one hundred of . which were composed in as many days.

Page 85. *Lord Shaftesbury's escape.*—Anthony Ashley Cooper (1621–1683), Lord Chancellor in 1672, was zealous for the exclusion of the Duke of York, afterwards James II., from the succession to the throne. The Court party had him tried for high treason in 1681, but he was acquitted.

Page 88. *Little Bayes.*—For the play of *The Rehearsal* and Bayes, see *ante*, page 82.

Page 106. *Statius.*—A Latin poet of the first century after Christ. His *Thebais* is his chief work.

Ib. Gorbuduc.—The earliest known tragedy in English, by Sackville, afterwards Lord Buckhurst. It was brought out in 1562.

Page 110. *Horace.*—Ben Jonson (see note to p. xxxii) translated the *Ars Poetica* of Horace, and one or two of the Odes. Jonson's contemporary, Owen Feltham, was the author of a book very popular in its day, and which still has readers : *Resolves, Divine, Political, and Moral.*

Ib. Sandys.—George Sandys (1577–1643), son of Archbishop Sandys, translated Ovid's *Metamorphoses.*

Ib. Holyday.—Barten Holyday (1593–1661), Archdeacon of Oxford, translated Juvenal and Persius.

Page 114. *Malherbe.*—François de Malherbe (1555–1628), a famous French poet, the first man, says the great critic Boileau, who in France wrote verse with correctness.

Page 116.—*The poem on the Civil War of Rome.*—The *Pharsalia* of Lucan, a Latin poet of the first century after Christ.

Page 128. *The Pollio.*—Virgil's Fourth Eclogue.

Page 132. *Trapp.*—Joseph Trapp (1679–1747), the first professor of poetry at Oxford.

Page 138. *The Alexandrine.*—By this in English poetry is meant merely a twelve-syllable line. By the Alexandrine metre is meant a poem in couplets of such lines, rhyming together. If is the celebrated metre of French tragedy, and takes its name from the *Alexandreis*, a popular romance poem in French on Alexander the Great, published in 1184.

Page 140. *Davis.*—Sir John Davies (1570–1626), Attorney-general in Ireland, and afterwards Chief-Justice in England, wrote a powerful philosophical poem, entitled *Nosce Teipsum.* ·

Page 142. *Rymer.*—Thomas Rymer (1638–1714) is best known as a historical antiquary, but was also a poet and critic.

Ib. Rapin.—René Rapin (1621–1687), a French Jesuit, author of a good Latin poem on gardens, and of works of literary criticism famous in their day, is to be distinguished from Paul de Rapin, Sieur de Theyras, the Protestant and historian, who was protected by William III.

Page 145. *He meant.*—Rymer meant, not what Dryden says, but what is true—that Sophocles improved the tragic drama by " bringing a third interlocutor to the two who before alone appeared on the scene at once."

SWIFT.

Page 151. *Hawkesworth.*—John Hawkesworth brought out in 1752 *The Adventurer*, and afterwards edited Swift's works, with a life prefixed. He died in 1773.

Page 155. *In France.*—Charles Perrault brought out, between 1688 and 1696, his *Parallèle des Anciens et des Modernes*, in which he assigns the superiority to the moderns. He was answered by Boileau.

Page 156. *Mr. Harley.*—The Tory prime minister under Queen Anne, afterwards Earl of Oxford. He died in 1724.

Page 165. *The Duchess of Munster.*—The German mistress of George I.

Page 172. *At last.*—Johnson here refers to the measures for the removal of restrictions on Irish trade and for the partial relief of Irish Catholics, which were carried between 1778 and 1782.

ADDISON.

Page 179. *The Chartreux.*—Charterhouse School.

Page 181. *Montague.*—Charles Montague (1661-1715), afterwards Lord Halifax.

Page 183. *Lord Godolphin.*—Prime minister from the accession of Queen Anne until August, 1710.

Ib. Birmingham's Tower.—The Birmingham Tower is within the precincts of Dublin Castle. It was once a state prison, but is now, as in Addison's time it had already become, a Record Office.

Page 185. *Casa and Castiglione.*—Giovanni della Casa (1503-1556), an Italian, author of *Galateo*, or, Art of Living in the World, a book which was translated into most of the European languages; Baldassare Castiglione (1478-1529), also an Italian, author of *Cortegiano* (*the Courtier*), a book called by his countrymen The Book of Gold.

Ib. La Bruyère's Manners of the Age.—The work meant is the Characters of Jean de la Bruyère (1644-1696), a celebrated French writer, and still, like Addison himself, a classic.

Page 187. *"Para mi,"* etc.—"For me only was Don Quixote born and I for him."

Page 189. *Dennis.*—John Dennis (1657-1734), a play-writer and critic, whose criticism made much noise in its day.

Ib. The Distrest Mother.—By Ambrose Philips, Addison's friend.

Page 191. *Strada's Prolusions.*—Famiano Strada (1572-1649), a critic and historian, was professor of rhetoric in the Gregorian College at Rome.

Page 196. *Little Dicky.*—Macaulay has conclusively shown that Johnson was wrong in supposing that by "little Dicky" Addison meant Steele. In an article in the Edinburgh Review (July, 1843), on Miss Aikin's *Life and Writings of Addison*, Macaulay says:—" It is asserted in the Biographia Britannica that Addison designated Steele as 'little Dicky.' This assertion was repeated by Johnson, who had never seen The Old Whig, and was therefore excusable. It is true that the words 'little Dicky' occur in The Old Whig, and that Steele's name was Richard. It is equally true that the words 'little Isaac' occur in The Duenna, and that Newton's name was Isaac. But we confidently affirm that Addison's 'little Dicky' had no more to do with Steele than Sheridan's 'little Isaac' with Newton. If we apply the words 'little Dicky' to Steele, we deprive a very lively and ingenious passage not only of all its wit but of all its meaning. 'Little Dicky' was evidently the nickname of some comic actor who played the usurer Gomez, then a most popular part, in Dryden's Spanish Friar."

Shortly afterwards, in a letter to Mr. Napier, the editor of the Edinburgh Review, Macaulay writes as follows :—" I am much pleased with one thing. You may remember how confidently I asserted that 'little Dicky,' in The Old Whig, was the nickname of some comic actor. Several people thought that I risked too much in assuming this so strongly on mere internal evidence. I have now, by an odd accident, found out who the actor was. An old prompter of Drury Lane theatre, named Chetwood, published, in 1749, a small volume containing an account of all the famous performers he remembered, arranged in alphabetical order. This little volume I picked up yesterday, for sixpence, at a bookstall in Holborn; and the first name on which I opened was that of Henry Norris, a favourite comedian, who was nicknamed ' Dicky ' because he first obtained celebrity by acting the part of Dicky in the Trip to the Jubilee. It is added that his figure was very diminutive. He was, it seems, in the height of his popularity at the very time when The Old Whig was written. You will, I think, agree with me that this is decisive. I am a little vain of my sagacity, which I really think would have dubbed me a *vir clarissimus*, if it had been shewn on a point of Greek or Latin learning; but I am still more pleased that the vindication of Addison from an unjust charge, which has been universally believed since the publication of the Lives of the Poets, should thus be complete. Should you have any objection to inserting a short note at the end of the next Number ?"

Page 201. *Mandeville.*—Author of the Fable of the Bees. He died in 1733.

Page 202. *A great writer.*—Bishop Warburton.

Page 206. *The late collection.*—Of English Poets.

POPE.

Page 221. *Ogylby's Homer and Sandys's Ovid.*—John Ogylby (1600–1676) was patronised by Lord Strafford, and after Strafford's death translated both Virgil and Homer. For Sandys, see note to page 110.

Page 223. *The Thebais.*—See note to page 106.

Page 228. *Hamilton.*—Anthony Hamilton (1646–1720) wrote the Memoirs of Count Grammont, in which the Court of Charles II. is described.

Page 232. *Lord Lansdowne.*—George Granville, Lord Lansdowne (1643–1735), a verse-writer whose life is in Johnson's Lives of the Poets.

Page 236. *La Valterie and Dacier.*—La Valterie, a French abbé in the latter half of the seventeenth century, translated Homer, Juvenal and Persius; the more celebrated Madame Dacier (1645–1720) translated both the Iliad and the Odyssey into French prose.

Ib. Chapman, Hobbes, and Ogylby.—The translation of Homer by George Chapman, who died in 1604, is still read. Thomas Hobbes, of Malmesbury (1588–1679) translated Homer and Thucydides, but his fame is due to his philosophical work, *Leviathan*. For Ogylby, see note to page 221.

Page 237. *Eustathius.*—Archbishop of Thessalonica in the 12th century, and famous as a commentator on Homer.

Ib. Jortin.—John Jortin (1698–1770), known by his Life of Erasmus.

Page 252. *Trial of Bishop Atterbury.*—Francis Atterbury, Bishop of Rochester, was tried for correspondence with the Pretender, and died in exile at Paris, 1731.

Page 254. *Ralph.*—James Ralph, a poet and journalist, attacked Pope in a piece called *Sawney.* Pope alludes to him and to a poem of his on Night in two famous lines of the Dunciad :—

" Silence, ye wolves, while Ralph to Cynthia howls,
    And makes night hideous—Answer him, ye owls !"

Page 264. *Warburton.*—William Warburton (1698–1779), Bishop of Gloucester, a celebrated critic and controversialist. See p. 202, and note.

Page 266. *Mr. Murray.*—Afterwards Lord Mansfield, the well-known Chief-Justice. He died in 1783.

Ib. Benson.—William Benson, Surveyor of Buildings to George I., "endeavoured," says a note to the Dunciad, "to raise himself to fame by erecting monuments, striking coins, setting up heads, and procuring translations of Milton."

Page 267. *The inscription on the Monument.*—This inscription attributes the Fire of London to the Catholics; and therefore Pope says that the Monument,

" Like some tall bully, lifts its head and lies."

Page 270. *The verses.*—The famous lines on Sporus, beginning :— " Let Sporus tremble."

Page 271. *History of Mr. Ouffle.*—" A History of the Ridiculous Extravagancies of Monsieur Oufle," London, 1711. This was a translation from a French work, of which the author, the Abbé Bordelon, sought to do for witchcraft what Cervantes had done for knight-errantry.

Page 272. *Cibber.*—Colley Cibber (1671–1757), actor, dramatist, and poet-laureate, wrote an Apology for his own life.

Page 277. *The Patriot King.*—This and the Letter to Sir William Windham are the most famous of Bolingbroke's political writings. He died in 1751.

Page 287. *Paracelsus.*—An empiric and alchemist, born in Switzerland in 1493. He died in 1541.

Page 292. *Cooper's Hill.*—The poem to which Sir John Denham (1615–1668) owes his reputation.

Page 295. *Perrault.*—See note to page 155.

Page 298. *The learned author, etc.*—Joseph Warton (1722–1800). His brother, the Rev. Thomas Warton, was professor of poetry at Oxford and author of the History of English Poetry.

Page 302. *The javelin of Priam.*—See Virgil's Æneid, ii. 544.

Page 308. *The Visitor.*—" The Universal Visiter and Monthly Memorialist," 1756. This was a magazine which lived for one year only, but to which Johnson contributed.

Page 309. *Charles, Earl of Dorset.*—A wit and poet, author of the well-known song beginning, " To all you ladies now on land." He died in 1706.

Page 311. *Bernadi.*—Major Bernardi, who was arrested in 1696 as a partisan of James II., and confined in Newgate until his death in 1736. See *Gentleman's Magazine*, Vol. 50, p. 125.

Page 313. *Mr. Rowe.*—Nicholas Rowe (1673–1718), poet-laureate, author of The Fair Penitent, Jane Shore, and a translation of Lucan's Pharsalia.

Page 317. *The wit of man, etc.*—Pope had probably in his mind

I Corinthians, xiv., 20 : " In malice be ye children, but in understanding be men." But Dryden, also, had said of Mrs. Killigrew: " Her wit was more than man, her innocence a child."

Page 319. *Areosti.*—Ludovico Ariosto (1474–1533), one of the most famous of Italian poets, author of Orlando Furioso. The sense of the Latin lines in the text is as follows :—

"The bones of Ludovico Ariosto lie buried under this stone, or under this sod, or under whatsoever his kind heir chose, or a comrade kinder than his heir, or a traveller lighting by good hap on his remains. For what would befall him he could not tell, but neither did he esteem his empty carcase enough to desire to provide for it an urn in his lifetime: how-beit in his lifetime he provided this inscription for his sepulchre, if any sepulchre he was hereafter to have."

GRAY.

Page 322. *Mr. Mason.*—William Mason (1725–1797), author of the tragedy of *Caractacus*, published a Life of Gray and some of his Letters.

Page 326. *Buxom health.*—Buxom means originally " easily bended," thence nimble and brisk; it is often erroneously used as if it meant stout and florid.

Ib. " *O Diva,*" *etc.*—The Ode to Fortune, the thirty-fifth in the First Book of Horace's Odes.

Page 328. *The prophecy of Nereus.*—In the fifteenth Ode of the First Book of Horace's Odes.

Page 329. *Heard with scorn.*—Johnson is seen at his worst in his criticism of " the two Sister Odes ;" but it is instructive to read him on Gray, and to weigh for oneself the value of what he says. Gray's Pro-gress of Poesy gives, with admirable skill, a poetical history of Poetry; his Bard gives, with like skill, a poetical history of England.

INDEX.